IS REALITY MEANINGFUL?

IS REALITY

MEANINGFUL?

Static Contradictions and Dynamic
Resolutions between Facts and Value

by

KELVIN VAN NUYS

Wilmington College

PHILOSOPHICAL LIBRARY

New York

To my wife

RENA

TABLE OF CONTENTS

THE FRAMEWORK OF DISCUSSION

All chapters from Chapter V on are constructed according to the following framework, more fully explained in Chapter IV. The basic thought is that in order to understand a philosophy's conclusion as to whether Reality is Meaningful or not, its conception of Meaningfulness, and what this implies *ought* to exist, must be compared with its conception of Reality, i.e., what *does* exist.

The key abbreviations are as follows:

SM: the Static Idea of Meaningfulness, based on the Static Idea of Good.

DM: the Dynamic Idea of Meaningfulness, based on the Dynamic Idea of Good.

SIR: the Static Idealistic Theory of Reality, based on static essences, and including monistic and dualistic methods of "making" the facts of reality fit the implications of SM.

SMR: the Static Mechanistic Theory of Reality, based on material atomism with no theory of wholes.

DR: the Dynamic, Organismic Theory of Reality, based on Field Theory and Evolution, and whole-part relationship.

The Types of Philosophy, then, are as follows: with the arrangement of material under each one as it will be found in each chapter.

SM with SIR:
    The implications of SM to the topic in question.
    The adjustments that SIR makes in its theory of facts to achieve congruence with SM on the topic.

SM with SMR:
    The findings of SMR concerning the facts in the topic.
    The contradictions between SMR and SM-SIR.
    Recourses that have been used to escape from these contradictions, returning to SM-SIR.

SM with DR:
    The findings of DR concerning the facts in the topic.
    Comparison of DR with SM, noting remaining contradictions.

DM with DR:
    The implications of DM to the topic in question.
    Correspondence of DR with DM.

The conclusions of each combination as to Meaningfulness are:

SM with SIR: Theistic. Most orthodox Christian theology falls here.

SM with SMR: Deistic at first; later atheistic. Materialism.

SM with DR: Humanistic and agnostic; or limited Theism. Includes most currently popular philosophies; Pragmatism, Existentialism, Realism, Positivism, etc.

DM with DR: Can be theistic (Cosmic Purpose for Good) without logical contradiction.

ACKNOWLEDGEMENTS

The author wishes to express appreciation to the following for permission to reprint from their publications:

George Allen & Unwin, Ltd.; "Some Reflections on Moral Sense Theories" by C. D. Broad in *Contemporary British Philosophy; Philosophical Essays* by Bertrand Russell; *Mysticism and Logic* by Bertrand Russell.

American Association for the Advancement of Science: "Mysterium Iniquitatis of Sinful Man Aspiring unto the Place of God" by Warren S. McCulloch in *Scientific Monthly,* January, 1955.

American Book Company: *Living Issues in Philosophy* by Harold Titus.

Appleton-Century-Crofts: *The Field of Philosophy* by J. A. Leighton, 4th edition, copyright 1930; *Readings in Ethical Theory* selected and edited by Wilfrid Sellars and John Hospers, copyright 1962.

J. W. Arrowsmith, Ltd., and the University of Bristol: *Studies in Philosophy* by G. C. Field.

Barnes & Noble, Inc.: *Philosophy, an Introduction* by Randall and Buchler.

Curtis Brown, Ltd.: *God and Evil* by C. E. M. Joad.

Cambridge University Press: *A History of Science* by W. C. Dampier; *Principia Ethica* by G. E. Moore; *Physics and Philosophy* by Sir James Jeans.

J. M. Dent & Sons, Ltd.: *Winds of Doctrine* by George Santayana.

E. P. Dutton & Company, Inc.: *The Writer in America* by Van Wyck Brooks.

Victor Gollancz, Ltd.: *Language, Truth and Logic* by Alfred J. Ayer.

Harcourt, Brace & World, Inc.: *In the Name of Sanity* by Lewis Mumford; *The Modern Temper* by Joseph Wood Krutch.

Harper & Row, Publishers: *Four Philosophies and Their Prac-*

tice in Education and Religion by J. Donald Butler; *Human Values* by DeWitt H. Parker; *Physics and Philosophy* by Werner Heisenberg.

Harvard University Press: *Realms of Value* by R. B. Perry.

Holt, Rinehart and Winston, Inc.: *Reconstruction in Philosophy* by John Dewey; *Ethics* by J. L. Mothershead.

Houghton Mifflin Company: *Introduction to Philosophy* by G. T. W. Patrick; *The Making of the Modern Mind* by J. H. Randall; *The Ascent from Below* by W. L. Reese.

Humanities Press: *Five Types of Ethical Theory* by C. D. Broad: *The Metaphysical Foundations of Modern Science* by E. A. Burtt.

Journal of Philosophy: "Evaluation and Obligation: Two Functions of Judgment in the Language of Conduct" by H. D. Aiken, Vol. 47, 1950.

Liveright Publishing Corp.: *Gestalt Psychology* by Wolfgang Kohler.

The Macmillan Company: *Reason in the Art of Living* by J. B. Pratt; *Preface to Philosophy* by William E. Hocking *et al.; The Logic of the Sciences and Humanities* and *Science and First Principles* by F. S. C. Northrop; *Adventures of Ideas, Modes of Thought, Religion in the Making, Process and Reality* and *Science and the Modern World* by A. N. Whitehead.

McGraw-Hill Book Company: *The Nature of Physical Reality* by Henry Margenau.

Methuen and Company, Ltd.: *Plato, the Man and His Work* by A. E. Taylor; G. C. Field, *Moral Theory.*

Dr. Otto Nathan, the Estate of Albert Einstein: *The Evolution of Physics* by Einstein and Infeld.

Thomas Nelson & Sons, Ltd.: "Moral and Non-moral Values" by C. A. Campbell in *Mind,* Vol. 44, 1935; "Subjectivism and Naturalism in Ethics" by A. C. Ewing in *Mind,* Vol. 53, 1944; "Does Moral Philosophy Rest on a Mistake?" by H. A. Prichard in *Mind,* Vol. 21, 1912.

The Odyssey Press: *The Way of Philosophy* by Philip Wheelwright.

Open Court Publishing Company: *Experience and Nature* by John Dewey; *The Logic of Perfection* by Charles Hartshorne; *The Philosophy of Alfred North Whitehead* edited by Paul Schilpp.

Oxford University Press: *Ethics* by G. E. Moore; *The Idea of*

God in the Light of Present Philosophy by Seth Pringle-Pattison; *The Right and the Good* by Sir David Ross; *Religion and Science* by Bertrand Russell.

Philosophical Library, Inc.: *Theism and Cosmology* by John Laird; *Twentieth Century Philosophy* by Dagobert D. Runes.

Porter Sargent: *The Integration of Human Knowledge* by Oliver L. Reiser.

Princeton University Press: *Philosophy of Mathematics and Natural Science* by Hermann Weyl.

Principia Press of Trinity University, San Antonio, Texas: *Philosophy and Modern Science* by Harold T. Davis.

G. P. Putnam & Sons: *The Quest for Certainty* by John Dewey.

Paul R. Reynolds, Inc., and Longmans, Green & Company: *Some Problems of Philosophy* by William James.

The Rockefeller Institute: *The Mechanistic Conception of Life* by Jacques Loeb.

The Ronald Press: *Personality — Development and Assessment* by Charles Harsh and H. G. Schrickel, copyright 1950.

Routledge & Kegan Paul, Ltd.: *Philosophy and Logical Syntax* by Rudolf Carnap.

University of Chicago Press: "Theory of Valuation" by John Dewey in *International Encyclopedia of Unified Sciences,* Vol 2; *Essays in Experimental Logic* by John Dewey; *The Thinking Machine* by C. Judson Herrick.

The Westminster Press: *Man in Revolt* by Emil Brunner, translated by Olive Wyon, copyright 1947 by W. L. Jenkins.

John Wiley and Sons, Inc.: *Philosophy, an Introduction* by Archie Bahm.

Yale University Press: *A Common Faith* by John Dewey.

PART I

BASIC PROBLEMS AND KINDS
OF APPROACH TO SOLUTIONS

CHAPTER I

THE FAILURE OF EVERY EXISTING 'ISM THROUGH A COMMON ERROR; THE MAIN CONTRADICTIONS

The Consequences of Meaninglessness. The much-deplored meaninglessness of modern life needs no amplification here; yet a vivid sense of it is required to make us feel the urgency of our title question. Most thinkers who understand the nature of this meaninglessness, this profane secularism, this prosaic materialism — whatever it be called — suspect that it is the root source of modern destruction and decay. If so, the question "Is Reality Meaningful?" becomes the most practically, as well as emotionally urgent of questions.

The destructive violence of our times has been traced to meaninglessness in various ways. Some, suffocated by the ennui of pointlessness, plunge into delinquency or "the gratuitous act" hoping to convince themselves that they are still alive. Others — both as individuals and states — simply relapse into disintegrated violence because meaninglessness had left them uninspired to strive for any more adequate level of living. Then there are those modern majorities, living only for material pleasure, who, ultimately discovering such a life leaves them feeling still empty, know of nothing to do to escape the great flatness, but to try more of the same, only now in more violent and corrosive forms.

Certainly the degradation of modern art and literature can be traced to meaninglessness. The practitioners of a writing reduced largely to a pornography of futile sex and terror, and of an art reduced to trivial abstraction, will usually admit being motivated by what has most lately been named "that nothing feeling." This must mean the loss of conviction that there is anything of importance, much less of sacred significance, to express, defend or aspire unto. It means, more particularly, that the artists have noted the failure of modern experience and of modern science's picture of reality to fulfill traditional standards of purpose and

3

meaning, and they refuse, honestly enough, to go on parroting old piosities. But, unfortunately, none of them are genuinely creative enough even to suspect the possibility of a new standard of meaning, let alone to contribute any concrete suggestions how it might be expressed. Instead, although they proudly claim to a brave facing up to hard facts and dropping old meanings, they have not really stopped demanding, unconsciously perhaps, that the old meanings *ought* to have been true. Their real attitude, then, is, rather than a constructive search for new meaning, only an immovable sulk over losing the old.

The peripheral status of most current forms of organized religion can also be traced to this failure to find conceptions of meaning and purpose which genuinely encompass modern experience and science. The ancient Mediterranean modes of religious expression, still too exclusively relied on by the churches — whether crack-pot cult or respectable suburban — inexorably lose more and more of their ability to mediate significance to scientific civilization. In the absence of a valid meaningfulness and sanctity, then, atavistic forms of worship — the pagan rites at Nuremberg, mummy-worship on the Red Square, playing at Zen — revive, blindly hungering for some depth, mystery, color. The philosophers of history suggest that there will be no escape from all these retrogressive developments nor a genuine recovery of cultural health until men can find intellectually valid grounds for reverencing the universe and respecting themselves — in short, grounds for religious seriousness in living in the very presence of modern evils and modern evolutionary knowledge.

Our claim is that this meaninglessness and pervasive disorder in both the philosophico-religious world and the practical world are the issue of a contradiction between the facts of reality and experience as they must be accepted from a science more adequate than any previous source of knowledge; and expectations or demands based upon a certain traditional assumption about the nature of meaning, purpose and value which has never yet been rightly criticized and changed. All present views that frankly admit and accept meaninglessness surreptitiously make this assumption as to how things *ought* to be in order to be meaningful, and then vociferously complain that things are not that way. And all present attempts to recover meaning and purpose also make this assumption, then adopt devices to camouflage the conflicting facts,

4

only to render themselves temporary and futile rear-guard defenses that end by dropping their ancient traditions back into the meaninglessness, under more disrepute than ever.

But I believe that even now, after almost a century of ever deepening despair and ever greater derision of man and life, there is still one more step, one more untried approach, which will succeed in illumining the meaning of our chaotic world as nothing yet suggested has done. This book attempts a not too technical presentation of this idea and its relations to science and values.

But now let us approach an understanding of the nature of meaningfulness by a little more illustration of the portentous consequences of its lack. We will also feel more vividly the seriousness of this claim, that no existing philosophy or religion succeeds in any large extrication of present civilization from this abyss.

Perhaps the most threatening consequence of meaninglessness is the indifference to the human soul and body, now left without meaning, that makes not only communists and fascists, but many within our own tradition of reverence for the dignity of the individual, quite careless in treating men as automatons, invading their brains with chemicals, purging out masses of them like beef cattle. Are we not already almost exceeding "them" in our complacent acceptance of robot-like "organization men"? An active loathing of man is dangerously pervasive in our literature and entertainment, because thinkers can find no meaningful reason why man should be either as imperfect as they are rediscovering him to be, or constructed as modern biological science has discovered he is. The latter has forced into greater consciousness some of man's apparently repulsive mechanisms of blood, sweat and faeces, which never have been too comfortably at home with accustomed ideas of meaningfulness. Darwinism is supposed to prove that man is essentially (or at least starts out as) a ruthless, competitive brute, which again is not at all what meaningfulness is assumed to imply. Psychology with Freud is taken to indicate that a dehumanized life of more or less perverse forms of sex is the only "real" state for man, with most of what were formerly considered more meaningful occupations entirely unfounded in the nature of things. Our current literature is almost unanimous in evaluating man as a meaninglessly violent jumping-jack, hopelessly inclined toward degeneracy, beyond any believable salvation, whose most characteristic parts are not his soul but his eliminative organs. The belief in the original goodness and rationality of human nature has been universally dropped by writers approved by the critics, without, however, dropping the demand these characteristics *ought* to have been original if our life were to be meaningful. Still worse, however, convinced of the meaninglessness of transformation, they then drop any faith that the weak and imperfect human nature they espouse either can or should be improved by any sort of effort, with or without divine aid. Christianity had once accepted the corruption of human nature, but had managed to fit this fact into a meaningful world view that included salvation. But now theories abound, from which our writers find no escape, enfeebling their resolve to labor for improvement by implying man's pointless fatedness to depravity and destruction.

If these are our true beliefs, what have we got to defend against a totalitarian, materialistic enemy? Why should men have freedom if they are really only animal mechanisms? Why shouldn't cruelty be visited upon individuals if our philosophy concedes that they are essentially corrupt and not worthy of loving assistance toward rescue or cure? If we do not bother to seek a solid refutation of these profane and impersonal views of man, of the compassionless callousness of modern attitudes — our own as well as the Nazis' or Communists' —it will be our own skins that will be made into lamp shades sooner or later.

Another consequence of meaninglessness will surely be what the philosophers of history unanimously agree is a real threat, already sufficiently under way — our whole culture's following Rome down the road to decline and fall. Marx himself was one of the first to declare western civilization self-destroyed by commercializing all values unto meaninglessness. Our literary and intellectual leaders, not forgetting the degenerate behavior and softening of standards during and following the wars as soon as the rest of us forget it, insist unendingly on the futility and doom these things portend. They reject the faith in automatic progress upon which the lazy and thoughtless had based the meaning of life ever since the seventeenth century and incline more to the conclusion that when enough men discover that God and meaning are dead, their weakness, as above described, will produce the collapse of rational democratic life.

And now perhaps an uneasiness about our culture has at last spread to the masses and the business men, who have clung to their optimism through two world wars, several depressions and recessions, and on into the beginnings of atomic destruction. Popular literature is becoming cynical now, with the magazine stands full of the same derision of man, the same loss of interest in making any effort to preserve any values. The habit of capitulating to, of *accepting* crime, delinquency, sexual perversion is becoming pervasive enough so that our resemblance to Rome's decay is apparent even to the man on the street. If we cannot regain meaningful grounds for resisting corruption, then we are obviously not going to last very long or stand for very much in history.

The Nature of Meaningfulness. Such weaknesses, we are saying, have as their most fundamental source the loss of meaningfulness. Now meaningfulness, we shall be arguing, in its fullest sense, requires not only the belief and feeling of a reason and purpose for one's individual life, but the ability to believe in reason and purpose behind reality itself. We must believe that existence as such expresses or embodies divine intention and design, that it is *required* by some intelligible meaning. Only such belief will produce profound enough conviction of the importance of things to inspire persons to their highest efforts.

How many of our intelligentsia, however, will smile at such supposedly romantic specifications! We have changed our pledge to the flag to include reference to God; yet how far almost everyone is from having answers to the great contradictories of God's existence — the problems of knowledge, mechanism, and evil — that will touch the skeptics in the least. A great sector of our intellectuals is just as certain as the Communists that a mechanical, materialistic nature rules out the possibility of a cosmic mind.

But, to counter complacency about this relinquishment of divine meaning, we must remind ourselves vividly of that enhancement and vivifying of life, that inspiration and stamina, that accompany a vital enough conviction of the purposiveness, or as I shall like to speak of it, the *requiredness,* of reality as a whole. This reminder should at least waken a receptive interest in searching for a recovery of belief. Even those who feel obliged by modern science or by the evils of life to give up such belief would probably agree that to live feeling that life and the world do have profound, holy meaning and sacred importance (supposing this were believable) would be more exhilarating than to live feeling everything to be quite trivial, existing by mere blind, pointless

7

chance. The most convinced atheist or cynic must recognize that it would be desirable, if it were possible, to spend his time in joy and enthusiasm for an existence felt to be of wondrous import rather than in prosy disillusionment, or flat derisiveness. The untrammeled "freedom" to enjoy what one pleases is sometimes given as an advantage of the skeptic state—but what if the enjoyments are felt to be trivial? Even the humanist, who honors *human* purposes, must see that an aura of sublimity, a depth of reverence, would be added to life if we could believe that it reflected *cosmic* purpose also. To give our life the deepest quality and most intensive flavor, that sense of holy importance is requisite which comes only from sensing that reality as such expresses some grand intelligible meaning, some divine design.

What a glory the early Christians felt in life, with their conviction that they partook in a sacramental drama, and that the very universe mystically cooperated in their awesome ceremonies! Whether they were deluded or not, there was more vividness and intensity in their lives than in the earth-bound callousness of their satiated Roman persecutors, and of many a modern sophisticate. Rudolf Otto, who best elucidates this most unutterable and supreme quality of life—the idea of the holy—makes us feel the

> . . . greatness and marvel absolute . . . "the mysterious" itself in its dual character as awe-compelling yet all-attracting, glimmering in an atmosphere of genuine "religious awe." As such, it sheds a color, a mood, a tone, upon whatever stands in relation to it. . . . All is made into a mystery—all, that is, becomes numinous.[1]

This loss of conviction of holy importance for life and man is the great loss of modern secularized life. The trouble with humanism and atheism is not so much that they are "bad" beliefs as that they are prosaic, flat ones. No one will deny that all other values diminish if we lose a basic reverence for reality itself as embodying important meaning. Art, for instance, if it cannot celebrate and symbolize mystical meanings, grows empty and busies itself with the ridiculous, fragmentary and bestial. Nations that stop the worship of God have not been able to keep from worshipping exceptionally unworthy men instead, making the rest into either cattle or the sport of sadistic torturers. When man is not thought to be significant in the designs of a cosmic creator, he loses his nobility and his inviolability as a child of God. No matter how much we cry that individuals can now be the admirably intelligent masters of their own fates, we seem rather to end up despoiling those individuals, for we have lost a basic reverence for them as holders of a divine destiny. Thus in the absence of the conviction of cosmic meaning, human attitudes seem fated to slip down into triviality, profanity, degradation.

The hunger for holy meaning is evident everywhere. Distress with humdrum civilization and the meaninglessness of atomic war have given rise to a much-vaunted "revival of religion." Suffocation in earthbound futilities produces a frenzied search for more mystic glamour and color in life. Weird cults proliferate, promising strange but vivid salvation from pointlessness. But all these efforts fail and will fail in the absence of genuine rapprochement between our science and our conception of meaning.

Two Inadequate Solutions. Many great minds in science and religion have been speaking in recent years as though the conflict between the two was an outmoded issue. These tidings may have something to do with the above religious revival, if they have reduced some people's fear of religious obscurantism. But it is questionable whether there is really widespread understanding among the re-joiners of existing churches just how the issues between science and religion may be resolved. More significantly, it is doubtful whether any large part of these people have gained a unified world view that makes their *present* experience and knowledge meaningful.

Much of this new religiosity seems only the old compartmentalization of the mind over again: a willful going back to believing on Sundays in comfortable old stories about another time when meaning once apparently existed; and on weekdays in a matter-of-fact world that has nothing to do with meaning. The burgeoning sects resolve the conflict only by excising one side of it — the scientific — and not at all by genuine synthesis. They revive wholesale primitive anthropomorphic superstitions from which the Enlightenment had supposedly freed men and which are quite irrelevant to the kind of world that surrounds them today. More intellectually conscientious religious organizations do what they can to maintain informed belief, but continue so enmeshed in archaic terminology that they do not interest the most

9

alive and creative minds, nor do they really succeed in sanctifying modern experience. Some of the supposedly more responsible religionists seem to end as devoted to a block of irrelevant prescientific, predynamic, mythological concepts as the cultists.

On the other hand, the second group — the humanists and agnostics — equally failing in any genuine synthesis, excise the other side of the conflict, the religious belief in cosmic purpose. Throwing out the bath of primitive myth and symbol, they also throw out the baby of holy meaningfulness. They argue that such belief is not only impossible, but even undesirable; they say it leads to unnecessary guilt complexes and tempts us into unrealistic escape and soft sentimentality. They like to declare that they have actually gained something in losing belief in any cosmic intelligibility. They at least have got rid of superstition; they have won freedom from prissy inhibitions supposedly intrinsic to religion. They are proud of having faced up to the hard facts in all their meaninglessness. The humanists keep themselves from slipping on into cynicism by stubbornly insisting on the greatness of man. He can, they claim, lift himself up to a high level of life even within the cold, empty universe said to be indicated by science. It is good for him to rely on himself, they say, and to stop worrying about "being saved."

Neither of these two groups however provides us with much strength against moral listlessness and the apathy of meaninglessness. The traditionalists, with their textproofs from a scripture whose absolute authenticity is itself never safely placed beyond endless dispute, are too irrelevant to the fundamental intellectual problems to generate an effective enthusiasm and a sacrificial devotion to high, unified and beautiful culture for modern times. Anyone who has followed the repetitive oscillations of Christology, for instance, sees that the paucity of evidence will forever prevent those entrapped in the futile discussion from ever extricating themselves from the power-dissipating jungle of anomalies, tenuous distinctions and unverifiable interpretations.

But neither is there much hope that humanism will galvanize many people into regenerative effort. For the discovery of the perfidy of human nature, upon whose essential goodness humanists had based their whole case, has always exposed them to the enemy's own terminal nihilism. Our humanistic literature has never been able to keep itself on a high level of inspiration and reverence for man. It has made, occasionally, a little effort to

10

affirm greatness of life without divine meaning. Of the first Lost Generation, Dos Passos for instance, turned from despising our mercenary national character to a temporary hope in the New Deal; Hemingway from disgust with bestial soldiers to admiration for fatalistically resolute protagonists in Spain. Wolfe and Steinbeck of the depression years worshipped a mystique of the American soul. The new writers of the second lost generation can make a man buck army regimentation, or walk into death in heroic exasperation. Dos Passos however, went on to discover corruption still all-pervasive in reform social systems; and Hemingway's heroes, more dedicated though they might be, continue to die meaninglessly and hopelessly, and he himself has now done the same in suicide. In the face of carnage and injustice, of ever more myopic preoccupation with the physical mechanics of rapine and murder, most writers obviously despise as mere sissy sentimentality the humanist hope for human nobility. They prefer to confine themselves to characters who drink and fornicate themselves into meaningless violence and futility as the only believable types. They seek no further deepening meaning in mature contemplation after the sensations of sex and drink have become stale and youthful chemistry has burnt out. Our literature is entering the fourth or fifth generation of bitter, salacious books, exploring on an ever lower level the loathsomeness of man, always taking it as a proof that there can be no meaning in reality, no saving purpose behind existence. Rather than pay serious attention to any kind of regeneration or salvation of this evil creature, current literature merely accepts the status-seeking of modern life alternating with the subhuman excitants of alcohol and perverted sex. The wry smile and the bitter wisecrack are its prevalent responses to the decay of civilization and the slaughter of men.

Humanists and atheists, then, lost something more precious than they realized when they lost belief in cosmic purpose. However, we are not trying to drive them into the arms of traditional religionists, for these can no longer supply the kind of meaningfulness and holiness we need. Even an intimation of what the feeling of real meaningfulness within current living experience would be like, should drive the traditionalists as much as the humanists to a more determined effort to think out a real synthesis between modern knowledge and religious affirmations.

Real Resources at Hand: Now the extraordinary fact is that

11

fundamental science and the latest developments in the understanding of nature promise strong support for the longed-for kinds of beliefs. A basis for a real meaningfulness and a reverence for man *is* available, though it is as unrealized by the humanists as by the traditionalists. Intellectual barriers to a genuinely meaningful world view have been falling. To come to rest nowadays in any conviction that science explains away, once and for all, belief in cosmic purpose implies a highly premature giving up of the search. It is true that a formidable mass of old superstitions clutter the religious field, contradicting one another as well as science. And men fail to discern the significant whole in the plethora of fragments of new science and fall instead into all manner of fanatic one-sided gospels or ill-digested cynicisms. But the truth is that the humanists and materialists have simply not won their spurs in the quest for meaning. An intelligibility lies near at hand, awaiting more intensive work in putting in order what we already know, arranging meaningfully the miscellaneous facts which science has been pouring out for four centuries.

The movement toward meaningless materialism has run its course. The melancholy transition of the last three or four centuries is about over — the transition from the great Christian view of the world as a hierarchy of purposes to science's supposed world of purposeless causal connections between neutral facts. From rapt meditation on the Why of life to drowning in an infinity of knowledge about the meaningless How of things; from working out one's salvation to pointless busyness; from concern with sacred human souls to tinkering with bodily mechanisms; from profound values to wearisome trivialities: the end of these trends is in sight. For our science is coming to see that ours is not a world of mechanism but *organism;* that so far from a world of dead matter, we have a world that is through and through living energy; that isolated, blind atoms are not the basic principle of causation, but patterned wholes or fields of energy; that the world is not essentially neutral fact, but the embodiment of importance and value-feeling. There is more recognition that putting knowledge together into understandable patterns of meaning is as legitimate a mental operation as scientific analysis and taking apart. The medieval desire to know the meaning of things by knowing where they fit an overall design is again permissible. Indeed the basic science, physics, can seem sometimes more spiritual with its unsolid atoms and structured space, than

12

older religion with its solid gold heavens and white-bearded God. There has indeed been a revolution in science to a form distinctly more hospitable to value and meaning than was the old Newtonian form.

And yet the implications of these changed ideas are so unfamiliar to our materialists and cynics that they are ready to grant the Communists their baseless claim that nature itself supports a ruthless materialism. The rest of us Americans, in our famous anti-intellectualism, don't bother to learn these new resources, and keep parroting the old fine phrases or piously quoting Bible passages which not only the Communists but our own creative thinkers had long since undercut. For instance, when we recite the preamble of our Declaration of Independence as though no one could possibly challenge it, we expose it to their debunking if we still admit that it is to be defended in terms of static 17th century rationalism, or a romantic view of human nature. We allow them then to triumphantly proclaim themselves the "wave of the future" in basing their doctrine on more modern evolutionary theory. But if we took the trouble to understand what a truly dynamic world-view is, we could then defend our way not by going back to the old theories, but by showing how it is more genuinely dynamic, more honestly evolutionary than "their" outmoded materialism and static sociology. And we could claim that the new physics supports a purposive cosmos rather than their impersonal materialism, whatever their skepticism about Biblical "proofs" may be.

Failure of All Existing Philosophies to Take Advantage of These Resources. But most of our philosophical and religious thinking today continues a frustrated grubbing about in the ruins to which modern science has reduced Greek and medieval categories. Now and then a movement appears proclaiming some escape from the unholy secularism which is the issue of science's contradiction of traditional expectations. "Neo-orthodoxy" believes that religious enthusiasm will return if we drop the efforts of natural theology and frankly go back to accepting scriptural revelation in a certain mythological sense not particularly concerned with how it fits the scientific world view. But after two decades of this, we are now observing a spate of confessions in recent religious writing that what had seemed quite predictable back in the thirties has indeed come to pass: the neo-orthodox unconcern with the older liberal efforts to harmonize science and religion has left the church more isolated and irrelevant than ever. The increased membership of the fifties now shows signs of concluding that the offered bread, so predominantly concerned with ancient Greek and Jewish thought modes, has turned out to be a stone. Once again the church may embarrassedly retreat, as Whitehead notes it has been doing ever since scientific method began producing its evidence four centuries ago.

Or take the atheistic brand of Existentialism, putting itself out as a fundamental revolution from static categories of Being, a genuine acceptance of dynamic Existence as fundamental. But it clearly assumes, as much as Plato ever did, that value itself must be a static essence, for which this world of problem and striving is not really logically necessary; and so this latter kind of world becomes "absurd" and "nauseous." The literature that results, in the Beats and "New Wave", is creative only in finding new extremes of silliness to top, or rather bottom, the preceding four generations of "realistic" disillusionment.

Pragmatic and process philosophies are more enthusiastic about reality, but rarely envisage more than a limited God battling evils which they agree He would never have knowingly created. But the cynics like to smile at their romanticism, while the orthodox will have none of their eternity of change, which so jeopardizes the hope of heavenly rest, and convicts God of being an incompetent tinkerer who can never get his creation into adequate shape.

These and other movements, however "non-Aristotelian" they may proclaim themselves, can be shown to continue to think in terms of static essences — at least in the case of the *concept of value*. Most claim to have come to terms with evolutionary theory in their metaphysics; but however dynamically they conceive the facts of nature and human nature, they have not budged in their nostalgic demand for *goodness* itself to be a fixed and final state, substance or essence. It is the static idea of good that drives the orthodox, in the effort to absolve omnipotent God of error, to their lugubrious blaming of man for all evil and struggle, little though this tack avoids the anomalous picture of perfect, omnipotent God being at pains to correct his creation that somehow went bad. It is also the static idea of good that convinces the atheistic existentialists and the humanistic pragmatists that no cosmic God could ever have purposively created such a dynamic existence

14

as we find, full of struggle against unsatisfying conditions. Both still equate the existence of any God with the pre-existence of perfect essences.

Most of the remainder of professional philosophy (insofar as the Positivists, or Logical Empiricists, have captured it) counsels giving up the question of meaningfulness entirely, obvious though it should be that this question can never cease being philosophy's true center, and turns to logical and grammatical tinkerings on the doorstep of knowledge.

I claim then that there is a new root concept and another sequence or order of categories which are more correct for demonstrating what meaning reality has than anything that has been presented heretofore. Most or all of the ideas involved have been in familiar use for some time (even the new dynamic idea of value has been adumbrated here and there, though not moved to the center as it is in my order); but the "winning combination," the revealing pattern of these ideas, has not heretofore been hit upon. I believe that the present rearrangement resolves age-old dilemmas and present contradictions so successfully as to form the basis from which all future philosophical and religious advance must begin.

This book presents the schema in its main essentials without too much detailed application, for fear of losing the comprehension of the forest among the trees. It is my hope that others may work out further detail in future applications.

The Requirements of Meaningfulness. I will argue in more detail later my possibly banal though much-denied thesis: that the fullest sense of meaningfulness, which produces an accompanying sense of holy importance in the experiences of life, requires the conviction that reality is intelligently designed, as opposed to believing it blind, pointless, accidental. This has ordinarily meant the belief that all that exists is required to be as it is by some intelligible purpose of a cosmic mind, or God. There must be a reason that demands the sort of embodiment that we find in the world and life.

But, I now suggest, this requirement amounts in the final analysis to this: that we must be able to see that the *facts* of reality are required to be as we find them by the nature of *value*. We must be able logically to deduce from some conception of value all that we *empirically* find. If there is a "good" God behind phenomena, then He must have arranged those phenomena in the manner that *good* requires.

These statements may seem, if not laughably obvious, then such a large and patently impossible order, that any book to follow is already guaranteed to be pipedreaming. All the ages have hoped or tried to show this, and it is just the vastness of the negative results that will make any skeptical reader quite certain that it was not reserved for our dying age, and the present insignificant author to stumble at this late date upon the true resolution of the great impasse. And yet, if he hasn't, what does the wonderfully neat way in which so many details fall into our pattern signify? We hope readers will stay with us long enough to see what placing a new idea of value at the center of the structure can do.

Now we assume that it is scientific method that is to tell us what the *facts* are, what the nature of reality is. All through the book, then, the statements of empirical science will be kept clearly in one place. But to know what these facts *mean*, we shall consistently maintain, it is not enough simply to do more scientific research and get more facts about how things actually operate. Rather, it will always be necessary to show *logical requirement* from value. In another part of our framework, extending through each chapter, we will be carrying on a train of deductive implications, or statements of requirement, originating from the definition of value. Scientific method, then, with its objective observation, inductive hypothesizing and verification, gives us the facts. For their meaning, we must deduce those same facts from the idea of value, that is, show that *good requires* them.

Now the great problem of Western thought is that the facts of its science cannot be deduced from the idea of value that is universally assumed by every existing type of philosophy. The received idea of value has not been clarified, remaining an assumption so implicit that no one has become aware of its most significant feature. This is, of course, the static aspect of the traditional idea of value, which we have hinted at above, and must make much clearer below. Our main claim is that a dynamic idea of value with very good credentials is available, from which so many facts as they are beginning to be understood in the "new" (post-Newtonian) science can be deduced, that we feel grounds for hope that all further facts will prove consonant too in the future.

Perhaps, then, one of the most important of all possible steps in the history of philosophy is before us here: to remove philosophy more truly than has ever been done yet from the old static Platonic foundations over to the foundations of dynamic value — a move which I claim neither pragmatism, existentialism, positivism or any other popular philosophy today has done. And with this move, a new theodicy then becomes logically possible (though I hardly claim that it becomes absolutely demonstrated), and that is something that the leaders of thought have long despaired of.

The Causes of the Loss of Meaningfulness. Now we might remind ourselves of the basic reasons given by modern disillusioned atheists and cynics for being convinced that there can be no meaning, purpose, value or God behind the universe, or behind reality itself. These are the obstacles to belief that we have to surmount if we are to show correspondence between expectations about meaning and facts. We will also hint very briefly now at the nature of the answers to those obstacles that are to be worked out in the book.

Much of the "hatred of God," of course, is not necessarily deeply thought out — for thought itself is under suspicion by this generation for whom the static ideals of the past have failed and only the moment of frantic experience seems real. The second "lost generation," or the "beat generation" and "angry young men", differs from the first only in not having had many ideals to be disillusioned about. They scarcely aspire to understand the trouble, nor to risk any hope. Thus they may not see what all our talk about mechanistic science indicating a purposeless universe has to do with their disgust with life, nor why an understanding of the reductive fallacy in such science is a basic step in escaping from their nihilism. Also, few of the recognized spokesmen of the war and depression generations would see how the restoration of cosmic religion could matter. They assume so implicitly that religion is necessarily the stodgy or fearful superstition that they find in many of its organizations, that they seldom even stoop to revile it. They just ignore it entirely, so foregone a conclusion is it that religious belief can be only the pious concern of half-men and half-women unable to "take" the pace of gay, tough and real living. The idea of religion as a potential enhancement of life never occurs to them, so certain are they that it is mere dullness. Many agree with the Communists that for man to wonder about his relation to the cosmos as a whole is merely to seek an opiate for the material sufferings of life.

Meanwhile small help in clarifying and refuting these confusions is forthcoming from the centers of learning. The ablest minds habitually devote themselves either to scientific grubbing for facts to add to the welter of inchoate information, or to the not very meaningful life of business aggrandisement. Some of this activity may be practical, and undoubtedly useful for the military. But from a longer term view it may not be so practical either, if the failure to direct a sufficient portion of time and energy to clarifying the bases for meaningful and inspired behavior results finally in self-annihilation. If such conviction *is* necessary for adequate coping with the demands of life, the ambition of men of ability certainly must turn in much larger measure toward spiritual search rather than upholding, or at any rate but weakly deploring, the exclusive focus of life upon the making and having of things.

The real reasons for the nihilism of both serious and popular thinking today are, then, we claim, as follows, however unclear the thinkers and writers may be about them. These reasons lie behind those relatively insignificant contradictions *in detail* between scientific facts and the tales and myths of various "inspired" scriptures at which many skeptics like to boggle. Actually, religious belief does not stand or fall according to whether God actually did or did not create the world as told in Genesis. Whether God appeared in Jesus Christ or in Krishna is not as basic a question as those stated below, nor does the truth of religious belief really depend on whether or not miracles have taken place. The fundamental questions are whether there is any cosmic purposiveness at all — let alone whether God actually performed this or that particular purposive act.

All basic difficulties in the way of belief therefore group into a simple enough classification which divides first into two main sorts.

A. *Problems of Knowledge.* The first is the obvious possibility that man may not have enough knowledge, experience, or personal development to be able to pronounce on the question. We may distinguish two aspects of this problem.

1. *Specialization and Fragmentation.* Human knowledge and experience may fall into such a state of multiplicity, confusion and

fragmentation that any meaning that might exist just could not be discerned amidst the random scatter of facts. This point does not relate to definite, logical proofs that there can be no meaning or God. It merely implies that human minds may be crippled, kept from that condition of sufficiently unified awareness which may be required to grasp or sense the meaning that may exist. Or it may imply a state of not having lived and searched enough yet to have found the meaning there is to *be* found. The reason that many modern men do not believe is not that they have any clear idea of a logical contradiction to meaning in life, but that their experience has been too specialized or chaotic; they have confined their attention too narrowly in some laboratory, or on some assembly line, or to momentary "kicks," ever to feel the full force of life as a complex integration or to grasp a grandeur in things that might change their feeling. The modern scientific expert is particularly dogged by this lack of experience, for he must confine his attention so narrowly in order to remain an expert. Science has ramified so hugely that within the smallest division there are still enough facts and figures to monopolize a man's lifetime. Everyone knows the modern bromide: man learns more and more about less and less. And awareness of God may require a far greater variety of experience. It may be that knowledge of meaningfulness is not entirely a matter of propositions proved, required facts ascertained; but may be, as Job learned, more in the nature of a total appreciation and wonder at the greatness and intricacy of the whole. Our first type of difficulty then, is the obstruction of sufficiently whole awareness.

2. *Epistemological theories.* There is also under this head the vexed question of certain theories of the knowing process that purport to prove that knowledge of God is impossible no matter how enriched a man's experience may be. Positivistic theories claim to be able to prove that *knowledge* of values and purposes and of the ultimate nature of things is impossible. Some atomistic sensationalisms, for that matter, imply that man cannot know purposes within himself, let alone know it in the universe.

This brings us to the second class of blocks to belief.

B. *Contrary Arguments.* We are here dealing with the stumbling block that definite arguments, based on definite supposed facts, appear to prove there can be no meaning or no God in the commonly assumed senses. And all such arguments will be found to group into two main kinds: the problem of mechanism and the problem of evil.

1. *Mechanism and Materialism.* Under the first comes everything in science that has seemed to indicate that nothing exists in reality but matter, and that it operates mechanically. The implication is that the universe and all its creatures are the outcome of blind, insensate forces, or mindless material particles, operating possibly according to necessary laws of motion, but definitely not toward envisioned goals or value-purposes. One great body of arguments consists of this idea applied in every branch of science. It is claimed that all effects are the automatic outcome of analyzable atomic causes which did not "choose" those effects in the light of values, but forced them by automatic concatenation. In physiology, for instance, man's behavior has been said to be the necessary outcome of the workings of his glands, senses, nerves and muscles, all connected up and operating as mechanically as any telephone exchange. Psychology has filled out the picture with the conception of man as a collection of reflexes that have become joined into sequences by localized conditioning. Marxism declares that no human behavior is genuinely motivated by ideals or religious convictions, but that such apparent ideas can only be rationalizations for action motivated exclusively by economic forces based ultimately on the blind hungers and greeds of our material bodies. These ways of thinking have permeated deeply into our own society, and many people can fluently debunk all ideals by this uncovering of underlying mechanisms, brute urges, blind chemistries supposedly enforcing every act. If Marxism is infected by this way of thinking, which most believe it is to some extent, then insofar as we find arguments against reductive materialism, we would find valid opposition to Marxism.

2. *Evil.* But it is the problem of evil which is the source of the larger part of the unbelief of the times, and the remaining objections to belief in God are of this type. We have just seen how the imponderable horrors of war experiences, the frustrations of dehumanized society, the mass dishonesty and injustice, the decadence and perversion, have soured the cynics (though we can well wonder which causes which — the evils the cynicism, or the cynicism the corrupt behavior that proliferates the evils). At any rate, the presence of any evil at all, much or little, constitutes the main proof for these persons that value-purpose cannot be overruling.

The cynics are also easily convinced that preying of life on life is the final law of the universe — that the "fit" survive only by violent elimination of the weak — and they are certain that no deeper consideration can modify these facts or change their import. They are positive that the only conceivable idea of God would require a universe with none of these "tougher" aspects. As for the methods used by traditional thinking to obviate the problem — the dualisms or the "Appearance-vs.-Reality" monisms that strove to relegate evil to a realm of relative unreality — they have been largely (and rightly, we shall admit) rejected by modern minds who rather despise these devices as sentimental avoidance of "facing reality." Science itself is on the side of our admitting as real the pains and destructions that empirically present themselves.

But believers as much as cynics admit that Good, as they assume its meaning, certainly does not require such evil. Thus the Problem of Evil remains as much the main threat for the first as the main basis for the second.

These then, are the obstacles to belief in cosmic meaningfulness.

Prior Hints as to Solutions: First, on the problem of knowledge, we will concede in this book that even if the definite arguments under B above were to be met, the problem of positively knowing or proving the existence of universal purpose or God would remain. And in the end, we will find it still dubious whether there is any absolutely clinching proof, empirical or rational, on this matter. But we will find new grounds for asking whether conviction on this matter should ever have been expected to be a matter of mere intellectual "proof." A new understanding in the area of psychology will lead us to wonder whether "knowledge of God" should not be expected to be a much more "holistic" matter than that. "Gestalt" or "Organismic" psychology does offer a new ground for believing that the mind can grasp, understand, and feel patterned wholes of thought which may undergird religious experience in another than a merely logical way. The mind is no longer confined to mechanical atoms of sensation, to blind enforced trains of association as the older theory implied. A whole area is opened up and given scientific status in which something like mystical experience may again find a place. This problem is dealt with in detail in Part II of the book on Theories of Knowledge.

As for the fragmentation of knowledge, men are undoubtedly sooner or later going to have to do much more sustained work on the ordering and integrating of knowledge than they have cared to devote to it so far. Some starts have been made and there are many calls for more. The medieval wish to know the meaning of things through knowing how they fit into an overall design is again permissible, in a sense, in the light of the new science's finding reality for the whole realm of organization. Our careful attention to the order and sequence of material, already mentioned, bears on this problem.

To meet, secondly, the problem of mechanism versus purposiveness, the above mentioned revolution in science toward dynamic and organismic concepts almost solves the problem for us, as explained in more detail in Part III, Theories of Reality.

Thirdly, in answering the problem of evil, the new dynamic concept of value not only serves our basic purpose of deducing all facts from value, but provides the best leverage available on this most difficult of problems. Just as science has completed its transition from static theories of reality to dynamic evolutionary ones, it remains to transform our idea of value to a genuinely dynamic one. When that is done the dynamic world of science, *including* its evil and imperfection, becomes derivable from the idea of Good. Part IV of the book is especially concerned with this problem. A Cosmic Purpose for Good then becomes conceivable as the source of science's reality, as summarized in Part V.

With these resources, we have a basis not merely for believing in a God in one part of our minds confining itself to a group of old tales and arbitrary declarations by previous ages. But we can aspire to understanding throughout our *whole* mind why divinity created *this* sort of reality; and to feeling, in the most real, immediate sense, holy importance in the facts as we know them today — especially in the concrete, individual things and creatures that science explains for us. The question is, can we feel sanctity in this earth of a billion years of fiery growth and ups and downs of evolution (rather than of an instant creation in 4004 B.C.)? Can we revere man with all of the biological structure and processes as we now know him to consist of? Can we feel something else than cold desolation in the universe with its infinite spaces and bodies whirling through endless time?

Yes, mystic wonder and holy reverence can be returned to us as we increasingly succeed in dynamizing our concepts. We shall not want to waste our lives in derision and triviality when it is no longer necessary.

In summary:

This book brings two main new resources to the task of adumbrating this meaning: it finds a new idea of value (or at least it adheres more unwaveringly to an idea of value that has been only occasionally touched on by philosophers) from which the dynamic reality of modern science, and the evils of life, can be deduced; and it provides a rearrangement of subject matter which makes explicit what has been obscured in many recent approaches to a dynamic world view: the right sequence between dynamic facts and dynamic value. This structure of discussion, carried through every chapter (from Part II on) makes it possible, first, to reveal more clearly than heretofore the conflicts of assumptions and findings that prompt modern doubt and disbelief. Then, shifting not only to the dynamic concepts of the new science, but, what has never been clearly and systematically done, also shifting to the dynamic idea of value and to the whole new set of demands or expectations derived therefrom, the framework clarifies the fundamental lines of thought required for any reaffirmation of the priority of human and divine values today.

The framework of ideas is explained in general in Part I, and applied to the main problems of philosophy in the remainder of the book. The sequence of topics itself is part of the rearrangement that serves to bring out explicitly the meaning of the facts.

The framework is presented to enable us to understand why a cosmic intelligence, or God, if there is one, would have created facts or realities such as dynamic science finds them to be in each particular area of knowledge. This means that we find a way to defend the statement: "Value requires the facts to be as science finds them." In other words, the author believes that we can now dare again to undertake the task that the Middle Ages undertook prematurely: to seek and at least begin to find the *meaning* of the facts. We can pass from mere chaotic amassing of blank facts, characteristic of the last several centuries, to seeing how all that man knows may fit into a value cosmos, conceivably intended by a divine good intention. There is a great difference however from the medieval picture: we accept that God must create a dynamic, unfinished universe and life, rather than a static, perfect one; a freer, more adventurous world, rather than the neat, preplanned one of the earlier theodicy; and that it is goodness itself in its proper meaning that requires Him to do this.

CHAPTER II

THE MEANING OF THINGS: FORMAL REQUIREMENTS FOR DEALING WITH THE QUESTION

"Life Is Meaningless!" We have just argued that the prevalence of this belief is the ultimate problem of our times; or at least the root source of all disinclination and failure to deal with any other problems. The most momentous and all-inclusive question of philosophy, most people would agree, is "What Is the Meaning of Life?"

Philosophers might object to the phrasing: this form of the question may unduly narrow us to human life on this planet, prejudging that we are not concerned with the meaning of the whole universe as well. Professional philosophers may prefer this phrasing: "What is the nature of reality?" where "reality" is meant to be absolutely all-inclusive: of all facts, ideas, values — everything that exists in any sense. Also this form of the question does not pre-commit us to any prior assumptions about reality and whether it has any meaning at all. On the other hand, it does tend to start us off as though we had nothing to do but investigate what factually exists. It has lost, perhaps not technically, but at least atmospherically, the urgency of the popular form of the question, "What is the meaning of things?" It does not directly remind us that, after all, the thing we really do care about is whether reality has any significance, and what we ought to *do* about it.

The following phrasing seems to ask this most urgent question, yet remains sufficiently inclusive and non-committed; and it also, I think, directs us most adequately into the proper lines of investigation and reveals the right relationship between the different sides of the answer. Most briefly, we may ask: *"Is reality meaningful?"* More fully, and perhaps more satisfactorily: "What is the nature of reality and what, if any, is its meaning?" This indicates that philosophy, unlike religion, starts its task with the question of the purpose and meaning of existence left open for the possibility of either a negative or a positive answer. This phrasing also immediately indicates that the question of the meaning of reality requires two sorts of investigation to answer it.

A. We must study reality itself, to find the facts; to find out what actually exists in the universe and how it actually works.

B. We must think out what we mean by "meaningful." Obviously, we must know what our criterion is according to which we decide if those facts do or do not exemplify meaningfulness.

Now it is quite possible that the sort of thought and method that leads to knowledge about facts may not necessarily also settle the question of whether there is any meaning in them. Too many moderns reject belief in God or any other meaning without being at all clear that they are judging reality to be meaningless in the light of some personal criterion; and that they did not get this criterion from science; and that their criterion may be neither consistent nor necessary. There is a tendency to suppose that we can settle the question of the meaning of things by merely keeping on observing and analyzing external reality by the methods of science, until we eventually turn "meaning" up under the microscope as a definite object to see and touch. When we do not find it there, we announce a negative conclusion; actually we have dismissed meaning according to some unconsciously assumed criterion — in this case, that meaning must exist as a visible, tangible object. More usually the criterion is based on some notion of the scriptures absorbed in Sunday school. But we will find the meaning of meaningfulness is adjustable in the light of closer thinking.

Of course, we customarily feel that "meaningfulness" requires that there be a reason or purpose behind reality itself — a God. Many people however would be ready to reinterpret meaningfulness as being present in life even if the universe is not divinely planned. We shall be studying very carefully just what makes some thinkers relinquish that "maximum" meaningfulness, and whether it is necessary to do so or not. Now, however, I only want to make the point that anyone who believes there is no God, purpose or meaning in life and the universe, believes so because there is a conflict between his idea of the facts of reality, and some conception in his mind of meaningfulness and God and what they imply *ought* to be the case. Theoretically, then, he might be able to return to belief either by getting a new idea about the facts which fits his old ideas of meaning (or God); or a new idea of meaning which fits his old facts; or he might have revisions of both sides of his ideas so that they came to correspond with each other. The plan of this book purports to show that the general thought of western science about the facts has been revised in recent decades in such a way as to make belief in a divinely meaningful world easier than formerly; but it also shows that a certain revision on the side of meaning is required to complete the correspondence. But how we decide what the essential meaning of meaningfulness is remains to be brought out.

The Basic Question and the Methods of Philosophy.

A. *Knowledge of Reality: Philosophy and Science.* In studying the reality side of the central question, man has developed as his most fruitful means the scientific method. We will explain what this is in Part II. For the present we will point out that it originates in sensations and feelings taken only as cues to the presence or absence of measurable or countable phenomena; it then brings to bear rational processes of thought upon the data thus experienced, and terminates with a further test by the senses and feelings as above qualified. Man's senses and feelings are not considered by science in terms of their absolute value; nor is the reasoning allowed simply to follow the scientists' wishes. It must always be checked by sense experience in the sense just stated. For this reason, scientific method is also called "empirical" method. It produces knowledge of whatever relations in reality are repetitive or stable in some degree.

Philosophy helps science in its study of reality in two ways. In its *analytical* function it clarifies the concepts science uses in interpreting the sense experience. And in its *synthetic* function it gathers up and arranges all the findings of the various branches of science. But this synthetic work is actually a continuation of theoretical interpretations which the sciences have already brought up to a certain level of synthesis. There is no sharp line here between the sciences and philosophy.[1] In fact, physicists today habitually deal with such wide concepts. summarizing such vast bodies of detailed sensory experience in their field, that it is difficult to distinguish them from philosophers. They even seem to verge on statements about the meaning or "why" of things, though

26

not in the ultimate sense that I am attempting in this book, and which I do reserve for philosophy. Up to a certain point, then, the synthetic work of philosophy is the systematization of all that man has learned through sensory experience of *how* the world actually functions. It is the culmination of the scientific study of the nature of reality. But somewhere within this work, we begin to see the meaning of reality.

B. *Knowledge of Meaning: Philosophy and Religion.* There are two questions involved at this point: the sources and methods of thought for *defining the requirements* of meaningfulness; and those for determining whether reality actually has such meaningfulness as has been specified. At this juncture we are thinking primarily of the first problem, though the following points bear on the second to some extent. The full answer to the second question constitutes the remainder of the book.

We can distinguish four factors that go into building our conception of the requirements of meaningfulness.

1. Traditional Expectations.

Man starts off with a mass of habitual notions of what reality is and why it is that way. The two sides of thought are much entangled with each other: beliefs about what nature *is* are apt to conform with expectations about what nature ought to be; and beliefs about what nature ought to be are often derived from former beliefs about what nature is. If formerly men thought it reasonable to expect their God to inflict punishment on their enemies, then they believed that earthquakes were factually caused by their God to punish their enemies. A later generation then insists that nature *ought* to be what their fathers thought it *was*: a place where natural phenomena occur only in very definite relationship to human deserts.

In the beginning, men's feelings, desires and dreams affected their ideas of reality very largely, because in the absence of an adequate method of studying reality, they tended to assume that whatever their own imaginations wished for as meaningful actually existed. If they wanted a power who would strike their foe down if they stuck a pin into his image, they proceeded to believe in it as factual. Thus human ideas about the meaning and reality of life were as wishful and imprecise as might be expected when there was no leisure to invent modes of precision, no time to accumulate knowledge, and no method of recording it if it were accumulated.

But the earliest minds had one advantage: they could look out upon the world freshly and, unburdened by a profusion of ideas, they could get a relatively pristine impression of the nature of reality. Their minds could operate as wholes, unaffected by distortions from too narrow specialism or by bias from some established dogma. It is possible that some aspects of the early reactions to reality might be trusted to reveal a sort of truth about things as well or better than later more complex ideas. The universal conviction that there was some point in life, some guiding force or forces, however partially conceived, is significant.

However, this early general impression becomes tied up with local experience and with very particular, concrete images, practices, and habitual reasons for them. The savage is content to go through his elaborate rituals simply because his tribe has always done so. He does not ask why his gods designated just those rituals as the essence of meaningfulness. The Eskimo assumes that reality is by necessity composed of snow, ocean and fish, and that "good" is in essence anything that tends to increase the fish supply. The meaning of life is to obey the communal code and cooperate in the hunt, as his environment has forced him to do from time immemorial.

But experience increases and thinking goes on. Different tribes come to have more intercourse with one another, and they discover that a variety of ideas of meaning and reality are in existence. More generalized formulations begin to develop. Reality and its significance are conceived more broadly, including added experience, less tied to arbitrary concrete practices. Contradictions are eliminated, practices which lead to poor results are discarded. Ideas of reality and of meaning interact on each other; discoveries about reality sometimes chasten men's expectations, while men's inner desires still affect their beliefs about facts.

Each generation inherits formulations of the meaning of things which are crystallizations of the experiences and desires of a small or large portion of the preceding generations. The ideas of meaning which we inherit today are the result of an age-long winnowing. They root back into the primeval religious fiber of man, yet they also represent the work of great thinkers, philosophers and religious geniuses from more sophisticated periods of human history. These ideas are probably better than most of those we could create by ourselves, though they undoubtedly are susceptible to still further refining. They have given us, for instance, the great concept of a cosmic God, a divine Creator.

So we inevitably begin our own efforts to synthesize facts and meanings already outfitted with a body of interpretations which we have absorbed unconsciously from our milieu. Most men have accepted the inherited formulations taught them by the preceding generation without question, any contradictions between these and their own experiences of reality apparently prompting little or no doubt. Society gives them a pattern of activities, and they scarcely distinguish any clear concept of meaningfulness from the total gestalt of habits, beliefs and practices.

. . . every society . . . provides its members with a set of habitual or customary ways of performing these activities. . . . Thus activities and goals or values do not come isolated and piecemeal, but as integral parts of this complex habitual way of doing things. . . . Philosophic reflection thus does not have to create an organization of experience; experience always comes organized in the institutions of a culture. Philosophy does not have to provide all "meaning" for life; life normally follows some meaningful pattern. . . .

Our western society, like most others, used to provide the young with the accepted answer to the question, "What is the chief end of man?" through its institutions of organized religion. Most men were content to go through life satisfied with what they were taught about the controlling power in the universe and its relation to their destiny. The pattern of their daily living was provided by the various activities in which they normally took part without much question — their family obligations, their way of making a living, their intercourse with their neighbors, their recreations and diversions. . . . It is all so clear as to require no debate. The things to be done are meaningful and significant, they all fit together into a familiar and well-rounded pattern; they need no reason why.[2]

On the other hand, some men become conscious of a split between their factual knowledge and their habitual notions of what is meaningful. Perhaps this condition has never been so largely the case as in current western civilization. The theory of reality

29

has diverged so noticeably from traditional expectations, that the problem of meaningfulness as such is forced out into the open. The thought that "life is meaningless" is able to be born, as men stop taking for granted the customary ways and reasons. Some men remain permanently caught in this conclusion. Others set to work with critical reflection to inquire into the essentials of meaningfulness and to see whether some of the old claims are as intrinsic to it as they were taught to believe.

. The great source of ideas of meaning is of course religion, which by definition stands for the affirmation that reality *is* meaningful. We must begin our investigation of the meaning of things with this body of given customs and beliefs. Now the particular religions have always added elaborately detailed ideas as to the specific content of meaning, derived from the early sources which we have just studied. Men tend to assume that the very specific assertions about the purposes of God which religions make are identifiable with the very essence of the idea of meaningfulness itself. Yet it is usually these claims of religion at a relatively specific level that are most in conflict with science, and with the claims of other religions. But people fear that if they relinquish any part of their religion's assertions, they have jeopardized it *in toto.*

However, in our study of meaning and in our defense of a place for the religious attitude in modern culture, we cannot admit that meaningfulness or religious significance is definable by some of the clusters of quaint beliefs, superstitions, arbitrary practices and definite perversions which have been deposited upon the current scene by the religious vicissitudes of the past. We find that we must work over these detailed claims to distinguish what is more essential, what is more subordinate and what is false and irrelevant. In carrying on a process of reinterpretation of the meaning of things, which is only continuing what mankind has been doing through all the ages, we are forced to seek a more essential formulation of the meaning of meaning, a clarification of what has been handed to us. We must proceed to revise and clarify the living stream of thought. But how is this to be done? We now come to the second factor in formulating the idea of meaningfulness.

2. Analytic Philosophy.
This is, once more, the analytical function of philosophy which

30

also came in under the study of reality. Before we condemn as meaningless the world science describes, we must critically examine the criterion of meaning which we are using in so condemning it. We must endeavor to think whether the traditional expectations are really necessary or intrinsic to the idea. We must define and distinguish levels of thought, trying to disentangle the significant from accidental adherences. We hope to discover some essential definition of meaning that underlies the profusion of religious claims. We seek some more general formulation that will indicate the necessary core in what men have meant when they asserted that life was meaningful.

3. Synthetic Philosophy.

We have pointed out that within the synthesizing and systematizing of knowledge about reality, where science and philosophy converge, meaning begins to appear. One of the intrinsic aspects of meaningfulness is awareness of design and thence grasping where, in the ordered pattern, a particular thing "belongs." As man begins to discern great principles that explain vast bodies of phenomena, he begins to be able to say, in some degree, *why* things are as they are, for he perceives that they are called for or "required" to be so by the nature of the total pattern.

However, the synthesis of science's external facts answers the question *why* only in a limited sense, for it presupposes the existence of things as such. We can see why, for instance, the human body must breathe and consume food, insofar as we can see that the general laws of combustion require that any process (at least in this corner of the universe) must conform to them. We see "why" there is a bisexual reproductive system with Mendelian inheritance: because it fits into, or can be seen to serve, the larger scheme of evolution and adaptation of organisms.

But men have, or at least seek, ideas of meaning in a larger sense than this: answers to why life should exist at all, as a process of combustion and adaptation or as anything else; or why there should be a world in the first place. The *ultimate* why takes us at last to the problem of *value*: if there is any final why, it must be that *Good* somehow requires all the phenomena to be as science has found them to be. We thus come back to our opening thesis.

4. The Analysis of Feeling and Value.

The fourth factor in, or source of, the idea of meaning is the concept of value itself, including the realm of qualitative feeling considered directly for itself, in just that respect that science does *not* consider it (p. 26). We mean by this that component of enjoyment or non-enjoyment, or of "good" and "bad" feeling that is associated with almost every, if not absolutely every, experience, sensation or thought that we have. Since this factor is crucially involved in the theory of value and good itself which, we have said, must be shown to require the facts to be as they are, if they are to be meaningful, then whatever methods are necessary to work out a theory of feeling will be relevant to the meaning side of our study.

In Part II, these methods are analyzed in more detail, and in Part IV the findings on the nature of feeling and value are stated. For the present we will state summarily that a properly dynamic theory of feeling is the outcome of factual observation; in fact, it is perhaps the ultimate theory of empirical science. When we now take that as the very essence of value or good itself, we have the supreme generalization we need, from which, first, all observations and theories of science can be deduced — the source, we have said, of the most ultimate reason "Why" things are as they are. We also have, second, a principle upon which we may base *standards of evaluation.* The first of these points is illustrated in the final division of every chapter of the book (from Part II onwards) where, under the topic being considered, the deduction of the facts from the dynamic idea of value is always worked out. The second point is taken up in Part IV, in the special chapters on axiology.

The Requirements of Meaningfulness.

Now, if we can get such an ultimate why, I believe we will become aware of that sense of holy importance, that reverence toward things felt as integral in a profoundly sacred whole, for the desirability of which we argued in the first chapter. This sense of holiness, so difficult to define, but man's greatest experience, is the sure sign of meaningfulness. One must not, of course, think of holiness as mere moral goodness, but as including elements of mystery, wonder, awe. It is opposite from feeling nature and life to be trivial, insignificant.

"Inspiration" — which comes from the sense of holiness — is the term to cover religion's most essential task. Devotion to an idea of religious meaning has always been man's source of courage, his source of the inclination to strive for higher values, greater brotherhood, less despair in the face of death. The respect in which religion is best differentiated from philosophy and science is as motivational, inspirational power. Undoubtedly the best thing philosophy could do for man would be to show a way to belief which can provide this sense of wonder and praise, this strengthening enthusiasm which enables men to surpass themselves, as they must if they are to replace destruction with construction. Adequate religion is not a dour, repressive force, as many suppose; but rather life at its fullest and most creative. It can replace dull profaneness and prosy stuffiness of living with the conviction that life is for meaning and glory. Even in times of decay and calamity like ours, exaltation may be available.

Does the contemplation of this sense of holiness give us any hint as to the sort of belief which is essential to produce it? We now proceed to our preliminary specification of the requirements of meaningfulness.

Holy meaningfulness, in the higher religions, has always implied the belief in some intelligible principle, which usually means some great Mind, which has caused reality to be as it is because of its purpose for value or good. Ordinarily, to say that life or reality is "meaningful" (in post-primitive thought) has meant that we affirm that valuing mind or purpose is basic to or "behind" reality as a whole. The most adequate formula, I think, is that we must believe reality results from "Cosmic Purpose for Good." These three terms when defined, state the essence of the "maximum" idea of meaning, and of high religion. They are also, evidently, a reasonably good definition of "God." Such belief, we hold, is necessary for a sense of holiness. This is the essence of religious meaning, stated at a sufficiently general level to be worth philosophy's defense.

Each of the three terms will be discussed more fully below. Here let us point out their connection with the three basic objections to meaningfulness (Chapter I). "Cosmic" refers to the whole of things, to the entirety of the universe, to reality as such. The first problem — of the incompleteness and fragmentation of our knowledge — obviously raises doubt that we can ever know enough to make any statements about the cosmic whole

33

— or any lesser whole, for that matter. The second problem — mechanistic theories of reality — is the contradiction of Purposiveness. And the third problem — Evil — contradicts expectations about Good.

I. Cosmic.

The developed monotheistic religions have stood for the belief that God, the Purposer of Good, was the author of *all* reality. The traditional Christian sense of "meaningfulness" has meant that all things were created by this Cosmic Mind, and take a necessary place in His design. Christianity, like other great religions, would not be satisfied with even Plato's near-monotheism, which held that though there was one cosmic mind, it had not created matter itself, but had to struggle with it as something that was just "given," or already present. For this view has already lost the pearl of great price — the ability to feel that reality as such has been intended, is required for an intelligible purpose.

Of course, religion in its early history does not seem to have stood for cosmic purpose. It believed in local gods and spirits, who inhabited a world not of their own making, just as man did. But perhaps we can say that men conceived of gods in as cosmic a way as their mental development allowed in each period. When men know of nothing beyond their own forest, a god of the forest is cosmic for them. Or if the Greeks had a polytheism where no God was the actual creator of reality, we may remark that the greatest Greek minds were pushing on to a sufficiently cosmic concept of Zeus, when Christianity appeared to supplement Greek thought with Jewish monotheism.

Religion can degenerate and fall back onto more partial gods, from time to time. There are always the less cultivated minds with their worship of anthropomorphic God-ideas; and the unconcerned — with their various idolatries of money, sex, communism, and all the other partial ends. Nevertheless, religion at its best, has stood for belief in *cosmic* purpose.

However, in modern times the three basic problems in one form or another have caused men to call this "cosmic" dimension in question. Besides the fragmentation of the mind which prevents any mystic awareness of cosmic meaning that might have validity, the problem of evil is the strongest force driving men to non-cosmic views. Many who seek to retain belief in God at all have therefore felt it necessary to satisfy themselves with a "limited" God, one whose power is definitely greater than man's, but not equal to omnipotence. For they are convinced that an omnipotent, good God would not permit the evil to exist, being able to prevent it.

Others give up trying to convince themselves of the existence of any kind of God, and satisfy themselves with such limited purpose as exists in men. All views for which human purposes, operating within a purposeless universe, are considered the ultimate, highest meaning available to men — come under the name "Humanism." Social democracy, the Communist system, art for art's sake, etc., are some of the goals which are taken as supreme by different types of humanists.

And then of course there are those who give up finding purpose or meaning at any level, and are frankly cynical. If such people find it worthwhile to live at all, they may take some interest, such as making money, as their reason for living. Sometimes the word "religion" is understood in a very broad sense so as to include all these views. It is said that *any* kind of belief that is actually held anywhere by anyone as his highest loyalty, is his "religion." Communism is said to be a religion because it is the ultimate loyalty of some men who explicitly deny the existence of a cosmic purpose over and beyond human purposes. "Business" is a religion for those who live for it alone.

Humanists often argue that they have a nobler belief than have many believers in a cosmic God. They point to humanists who live more creative lives than do many religious believers. They explain that the release from the confining demands supposedly intrinsic to religion is invigorating and that life becomes more colorful and interesting when one is freed from the fear of God.

But it is in the face of these claims that we need to think again about the experience of religious holiness. No one who has an adequate grasp upon what this experience is will deny that it is the supreme value of life. It is the highest and deepest sense of greatness, majesty, glory, wondrousness. Now, I am suggesting that this feeling about reality cannot exist in full degree except in conjunction with belief in meaningfulness in the "maximum" sense; the belief that *all* reality expresses divine meaning. When the humanists and communists point out some earthly goal or system for us to work for, they are not really giving us "meaning" for life in the sense that men have always

35

understood meaning. The vision of humanity scurrying about on the surface of this planet occupied in solving its practical and social problems one after another, while a blind and mechanical universe grinds on oblivious of any purpose human or otherwise — such a vision fails to suffuse our life with that deepest dimension of mystery and holy importance that comes from genuine religious belief. Of course, such views offer "purposes" of a sort for life. But this is not what we ordinarily mean by a "meaning" in life. The exclusive focus of attention upon systems of guaranteeing food and happiness for all seems to leave our world in a relatively prosy, grubbing frame of mind, that often sinks to a kind of hankering bitterness. Certainly moods of prayerful exaltation, of enthusiastic and renewing wonder, which seem the whole point of religion, are not engendered by these earthbound purviews.

When we say, then, that philosophy's basic question is whether reality is meaningful or not, we normally mean that it is to show us whether we may assert the full statement of religion or not, and if so, in what specific manner. The term "cosmic," then, excludes all forms of humanism and limited-God views as real answers to the meaning of "meaningful."

At least for the purposes of this book, the term "religion" will be used only for views which do maintain that all reality as such emanates from or exemplifies *cosmic* purpose for good. And the basic question of the book becomes: Does scientific philosophy permit belief in meaning in this maximum sense? Can the picture of the world which science gives us be seen to be what a Cosmic God would have designed? Can we therefore feel holy importance in the concrete life about us?

II. Purpose.

In this section we must try to confine ourselves to the abstract meaning of the term "purpose," without getting confused with specific content — that is, with particular, concrete purposes. The word is used in several different ways. We use it in regard to things, when we say, "the purpose of an automobile is to transport people," or "the purpose of the piston is to convey the power of the expanding steam to the wheel." But of course we do not mean that the automobile itself purposes to transport the people, nor that the piston itself intends to perform its service.

It is implied that these things were arranged by some purposing *mind* to perform functions *it* desires. Sometimes the term "external purpose" is used to refer to this kind of use or function which a thing may have in the designs of some purposing being who uses it. Objects with such external purpose may also be called means or instruments to the ends conceived by the purposing creature.

In the case of the purposing creature, then, purpose can mean the *end* or goal itself, conceived beforehand as an idea in the mind that raises a desire to purpose it. The reference here is to the state of things which is being aimed at. The purpose is the future condition that is envisioned. Things which may be made and used in the process of getting to that goal have external purpose with reference to that goal. But the purpose itself exists in a mind as an idea or vision of a final state.

But purpose can also refer not to the goal-concept alone, but to the mode of operation by which a mind is supposed to have the power to conceive such a goal, then somehow set in motion activities, including the selection or contrivance of means, to bring that end or idea into reality. This is "to purpose" as a verb. Purposiveness would be the *mode of functioning* which creatures traditionally have been supposed to possess, and which we desire to find they do possess, by which a concept or an ideal in their minds should be able to control or direct actions in the parts of their bodies so as to bring the concept or ideal into existence. This sense of the term "purpose" is sometimes distinguished as "internal purpose."

Purpose, in the second sense of goal-concept, can refer either to more immediate and partial goals or to larger, final goals. One speaks of his immediate purposes, desires or plans; but also of "the purpose of life" as a whole. By this is often meant some final, perfect condition that is demanded, before one will concede that life had any purpose or meaning. This outcome may be located either in this life or a future life. In a still larger sense, the "purpose of life" can be taken to mean some ultimate social adjustment for the whole human race, a Utopia, and nothing short of this will be accepted as indicating that life is meaningful. However, such tendencies to base the question of purposefulness of life on how it finally turns out already involve the static idea of meaning and value to be clarified below.

We shall find that, for the dynamic idea of meaning and value, we neither can nor need to base our case on knowing final outcomes, which we can never know anyway. It is on the third conception of "internal purpose" as a kind of functioning where the whole creature is able to control its parts toward envisioned, not necessarily final, but partial goals, that we may base our arguments for meaningfulness. Purposive functioning in this sense must exist if intelligible ideals, reasons, values are to have effective reality in the operations of the universe. If we find such reality *within* the universe, we can then inquire whether anything absolutely contradicts the possibility of purpose in the same sense behind the universe as a whole.

But what can purpose mean when modified by the term "cosmic"? Formally at least, we can see analogous meanings at this level to those we have just distinguished at the human level. It could mean (1) that things and creatures of the world — the created universe, and nature itself have "external" purpose from the point of view of a cosmic mind. That is, they are designed and used by God as means in the execution of His purposes, just as man designs and uses automobiles in the execution of his. In this sense, we would very much like to be able to believe that the world as we find it *is* "required," to use a significant term, to be as it is by the purpose or intention of a cosmic purposer.

Or (2) it could refer to the goal-ideas of the cosmic mind. It could mean that there is a concept of a final state of things, or an ideal vision existing in a cosmic mind, and this is the goal of all reality. "Cosmic purpose" would refer to some perfect condition to which all the working of the cosmic mind's creations were directed, requiring us to wait until that state was achieved before we could be sure of cosmic purposiveness. But again, this notion already assumes the static idea of value and is not therefore an intrinsically necessary idea.

Finally (3) cosmic purpose could refer to the mode of operation of a cosmic mind; it could require only that the universe be created so that partial purposes or ends may exist within it. We would have the notion of a cosmic purpose continually purposing and creating at each moment. We would not have to wait for a final outcome before we pronounced on cosmic purposiveness. It would be rather a question of whether the nature of processes here and now was purposive.

When is a process purposive? One thing that seems clear, in the case of finite creatures at least, is that a purposive creature must be able, as a whole, to control or direct its parts in some sense and in some degree. It will not do to suppose that the creature's parts, or external forces, in some blind, automatic way, enforce its final behavior regardless of any ideas or intentions of the whole creature. Purpose in creatures means a directive control that emanates from that creature in its total selfhood and is able to govern its parts and select external means so as to accomplish an organized result. The part must appear and behave for the sake of the whole; the whole must be the reason why the part is as it is and does as it does.

What does this idea mean for cosmic purpose? The existence of all the concrete phenomena of reality must be because of some intelligible reason. They are not to have appeared blindly as the result of arbitrary tossings about of meaningless parts; they must be required to be as they are by value.

It is in whether or not science contradicts purposiveness in this sense, then, that we are most interested: both for individual creatures and for the nature of things as a whole. As we shall see, it was in just this sense that science has seemed to contradict purposiveness during the last few centuries. But there has been a hopeful change in recent scientific development.

In this section the discussion has been confined to the form, as it were, of the idea of purpose. The *content* of purpose, what is purposed, takes us to the third element in the definition of meaningfulness.

III. Good (Value)

The idea of Good, of course, is the crucial idea which provides the actual content or criterion by which we decide whether things in the universe are meaningful. We might find the form of processes to be purposeful in the above sense, yet producing evil rather than good. We must know a criterion by which to determine if they have the right content. At this point, then, we need to give enough definition to get started on, but we do not want to go into all the specific detail about the nature of values, for there are innumerable kinds of value, negative and positive (the latter being the "goods"), which will fit into later divisions of the book. But there is one general aspect of all kinds of goods of which an understanding will be an "open Sesame" to understanding what men in the past have thought "meaningfulness" required, and what we might ourselves feel it requires. This is the distinction between the Static and Dynamic conceptions of Value.

CHAPTER III

THE STATIC AND DYNAMIC IDEAS OF VALUE

I. The Static Idea of Value and Good.

Our distinction between static and dynamic applies to the whole realm of value, bad as well as good, but the following discussion applies it primarily to positive value, or Good.

The inquiry into the essential nature of value must begin in human experience; it can be asked afterwards whether value has any meaning at other levels of reality, sub-human or super-human. Human experience reveals a vast variety of different kinds of experience which are evaluated as good or bad: a whole group of sensuous experiences, ranging from simple taste, color, etc., to muscular and sexual gratifications; the related aesthetic experiences of art and beauty; the values of logic and truth; and the moral or ethical experiences. The term "good" is sometimes used in special connection with these last, and sometimes to cover all types.

Static Value as Objective. The way of thinking of values that seems most prevalent in early thought is to suppose they are definite, objective qualities outside of us and in the things we are considering to be pleasant, beautiful, true or good. The good taste is a substance of some kind adhering to the food. The beauty is a definite external entity that exists there in the woman or in the picture, and thence affects us. Truth itself may be thought of as a property that exists in itself, attached, as it were, to ideas. And moral goodness, too, may be a quality that is permanently what it is, somehow existing in good people and in their acts, known by us through apprehending its presence there. "Essence" is the technical term philosophy uses to cover all these qualities.

"Good" itself then, the general class that includes all these

40

varieties of good, is also thought of as an objective quality or essence, almost as a substance of some kind, which things must contain if they are to be good. Plato in some of his discussions gives classic examples of this way of conceiving good. Specific values were substantial qualities which existed in their own right, to begin with; they did not even have to be "in" objects. They existed in some mystic realm by themselves, in a "metaphysical showcase in heaven," made out of a sort of thin "mental substance." All of the material things of this world were formed on the model of these value ideas. "Squareness" for instance was a substantial thing or idea in itself which on occasion could become embodied in square objects in the world, such as tables. Or he could speak of the objects as "copying" the model ideas. Goodness itself, then, was thought of as a model idea, a quality in which all "good" things partook. And Plato considered the "Idea of the Good" as the supreme reality which all things strove to conform to as well as they could. This perfect good was never more than imperfectly embodied in the material world. In fact, the main reason why objects in the world changed at all, was that they were trying to come closer to the model. It was a main purpose of Plato's theory to explain how things and creatures could know of their own imperfection and what direction to aim for. He assumed that a perfect, fixed model was needed to explain how you could evaluate the comparative goodness of things.

This, at least, is the popular understanding of Plato's Idea of Good — a perfect pattern or state of things abiding fixedly, which can be known or experienced through passive contemplation alone.

. . . the being who possesses good always, everywhere and in all things has the most perfect sufficiency, and is never in need of anything else.[1]

. . . it is a note of *the* good that it is something "finished" or "complete," and consequently that it is "sufficient" and finally, therefore, that it is the one thing and the whole of the thing at which any creature which apprehends it ever aims, the whole and complete fulfillment of desire.[2]

There is, however, another aspect of Plato's Idea of Good. He sometimes discusses it as relating to proper discharge of function. At the end of the first book of the Republic (353 ff.), and in other passages, examples of agents or organs accomplishing their proper services are given: e.g., eye, ear and soul here. The eye has an end, or function to serve: seeing. It also has an excellence, which is the power of serving its function well. For the soul, living is the end, and justice is the excellence that produces the end at its best: i.e., good or happy living. This sounds dynamic — as though good existed within a certain kind of process — but it is a process that permanently abides by some proper measure or standard.

In the Republic, also, Plato has the idea of a whole or unity which is made of a number of functioning parts: man, for instance, has spiritual, mental and bodily parts. Good is present when they all function according to a measure or limit, which he calls "justice," deriving from the pattern or organization of the whole. Thus he assumes that such a thing as "perfection" or "perfect functioning" is both meaningful and supremely desirable; that it would be best if the parts fell into some right, harmonious routine of operation and continued smoothly in it forever with no interruption or "change" in the sense of transformation or development.

But Plato knows that such a perfect pattern of functioning is never actually attained in this world. This brings him back to the first idea of good as a final perfect end or ideal which can never be fully realized. The Good in itself would be this final, finished pattern of parts which man never fully experiences. The only reason he doesn't is that a realm of matter is accidentally present, arbitrarily interfering. But no reason for the existence of this producer of imperfection can be derived from the concept of good itself. Reality might just as well have been total harmony.

In either sense — good as a motionless perfect form, or as embodied in a perfect, undeviating functioning — the concept may be considered static. In either case, good is something that could exist complete and full-fledged in the first instant of creation, and in a reality which does not need to change or develop out of imperfection. It is something that can be known through passive contemplation without striving and transformation. Taylor says, discussing the *Phaedo*:

> The ultimate aim of the "philosopher" is not to *do* things, but to enjoy the vision of a reality to which he grows like as he looks upon it. . . .[3]

The way for men to be good, then, is simply to look upon, know, or fit themselves to a given pattern — whether of fixed motionless forms, or of fixed, routine functioning. Most of western thought since Plato has continued to think of value in this manner — as an unchanging, objective quality inhering in things which we recognize externally.

Static Value as Subjective. To-day there is a larger recognition of the subjective aspect of values. Some theories go so far as to locate the essence of value or good exclusively in the inner feelings of human beings rather than in any outer object or process that causes those feelings. Since the same object often causes one person to report a good feeling, another to report a bad one, it is concluded that goodness must be entirely relative to individuals' feelings rather than to objects. Since you love jazz music and I hate it, its value must not be in the music itself, but in something about you and me — our peculiar ways of feeling pleasure or happiness.

The only aspect of this theory to be taken up at this point is its static interpretation: that good exists as an internal feeling which could conceivably exist permanently without the feeler having to be in any kind of process or growth. Pleasure or happiness might as well be permanent states. Of course they never are, but this is assumed to be only because of the cussedness of things, not because of any intrinsic principle that could be understood.

Plato, as usual, was already in the field with speculations about the subjective, or pleasure, aspect of good. In this connection he confessed some doubt whether it could exist in a perfect, routine functioning after all, even if man *could* attain such a state. In the Republic, Plato discusses the connection that obtains in some cases between release from pain, and pleasure. For a moment he implies that pleasure and pain exist only within processes of transition to their opposites.

> . . . nothing is pleasanter than health. But then they never knew this to be the greatest of pleasures until they were ill. . . . there are many other cases of suffering in which the mere rest and cessation of pain, and not any positive enjoyment, is extolled by them as the greatest pleasure. . . . And both pleasure and pain are motions of the soul, are they not?[4]

But he quickly distinguishes between such feelings as relate to change of state, or to a let-up of pain, and what he calls "true pleasure" or "positive enjoyment," which is again identified with a static state of full, changeless being, having nothing to do with preceding contrasting conditions.

> Look at the other class of pleasures which have no antecedent pains and you will no longer suppose, as you perhaps may at present, that pleasure is only the cessation of pain, or pain of pleasure . . . the pleasures of smell . . . have no antecedent pains. . . .[5]

However, in the *Philebus* (53 ff) Plato considers the doctrine of certain "ingenious philosophers" or "wits" who deny that pleasure exists *in* the state of harmonious functioning and insist that it exists only in the *approaching* to such a state. Taylor expresses the point with crystal clarity:

> [The wits] say that pleasure is always a "process of becoming": that it has *no* stable and determinate *being*. That is, the theory is that pleasure is an accompaniment of transitions, incompleted developments. It is felt while the development is going on, but falls away when the definite and permanent goal of the "evolution" is reached. . . . The thought arises by a natural, though illegitimate, extension of the depletion-repletion formula to cover all cases of pleasures. On this theory, the good, healthy, or normal state is, of course, that of balance or equilibrium; pain and pleasure are both felt only when there is a departure from this ideal condition. . . . The natural end or goal of this "repletion" is the establishment of an equilibrium, and the best that could befall a man is that the equilibrium, once restored, should be permanent. But, on this theory, pleasure is only felt during the "filling-up." . . . Pleasure attends our progress to the good, but not our fruition of it; that will be the "neutral condition," painless but not pleasurable.[6]

Here again, the *Good* is unquestioningly associated with balance, equilibrium, i.e. with perfect, routine, "natural" functioning. The only question is whether *pleasure* would be present under those circumstances; or does it require the process of approaching that state? Now Plato bends every effort toward refuting this suggestion that value means, intrinsically, feeling that occurs only within processes of transformation — not only for the Idea of Good itself but even for the psychology of pleasure. One tack he pursues is to distinguish between bodily pleasures which do relate to processes of depletion and repletion, and mental pleasures which seem to exist without accompanying organic processes.[7] For instance, the anticipation by a thirsty man of a drink is pleasant before any drink has caused any processes in his body.

The modern physiologist, however, has discovered neural processes underlying the mental feelings unknown to Plato. Besides, the mental pleasure of anticipation is relatively tenuous compared with that which accompanies actual drinking — possibly just about proportional to the amount of energy transaction involved in mere neural processes as compared with that involved in massive tissue changes in mouth, throat and alimentary canal.

Plato also argues that these superior mental pleasures — such as the enjoyment of perfect geometrical figures and colors — are independent of process out of pain because he thinks of such a process as meaning that pleasure must be partly neutralized by the pain. He begins by granting that a proportionality seems to exist between intensity of pleasurable feeling and the amount of contrast with pain.

> . . . the most vehement and violent pleasures . . . are found in their most exciting degree not in health, but in disease. The delight of refreshing thirst with a cool draught, for example, is much more intense when one is suffering the heat of a raging fever . . . because the preceding want or craving is so much more violent.[8]

But against such a significant connection between pain or want, and pleasure, Plato argues that when thus "mixed," they will average out to a zero point. That is, he thinks of their "mixture" quasi-statically as ingredients neutralized in a compound, and not dynamically as a sequential, *felt* transformation. It behooves us, then, Plato says, to search for "pure pleasures" which are not mixed with and thus reduced by pain.

> . . . with the maintainers of the opinion that all pleasures are a cessation of pain, I do not agree. . . . True pleasures

are those which are given by beauty of colour and form, and most of those which arise from smells; . . . and in general those of which the want is painless and unconscious, and of which the fruition is palpable to sense and pleasant and unalloyed with pain.[9]

Plato is aware that he is running a risk of implying that the purest pleasure, in having the least contrast to pain and the least transition toward order, would have the least feeling.

> . . . let us now ask what will be the condition of animated beings who are neither in process of restoration nor of dissolution. . . . If a man chooses the life of wisdom, there is no reason why he should not live in this neutral state . . . no degree of pleasure . . . was thought to be necessary to him who chose the life of thought and wisdom. . . . Then he will live without pleasure; and who knows whether this may not be the most divine of all lives?[10]

The implication is obviously that if there is no change, there is no pleasure. In the end, Plato decides that for men, at least, if not for gods, something of pleasure — the "pure" pleasures — must be allowed as part of the good.[11] And pure pleasure, he admits at last, has an intrinsic connection to generation, though the painful state out of which it is generated must be so minimal as to be unconscious.

And so we come to the question: how does pleasure, with this small factor of process, bear on *Good?* Plato now[12] discusses the claim of some anti-hedonists that pleasure can be proved *not* to be the good precisely because it *is* connected to generation or becoming. The good is said to be the essence or the end of process; therefore it cannot be *of* the process as pleasure is. But Plato does not entirely accept this separation of pleasure from good. The *Philebus* ends by admitting the "pure" pleasures to the status of ingredients in the nature of good. Though "wisdom" and "measure" and "symmetry" are more important elements in good, they would be relatively worthless unless *felt* as pleasurable.

Here, then, there seems to be a dilemma. Whether Plato felt it or not is unclear; but Taylor points out that it was a real enough dilemma to cause Aristotle to make an effort to clarify it. We have seen that Plato accepts the idea that good relates to the end of processes, to the fulfillment, to completed Being. But pleasure, which he admits as an element in the good, cannot be divorced entirely from process; even "pure pleasure" involves process out of unconscious want. Taylor, I think, touches the crux of the problem when he points out the distinction of terminology that Aristotle invented in this connection.

> . . . what gives rise to the feeling of pleasure which accompanies return to the "normal-state" after disturbance, is not the process of return itself, but the successful reassertion of the activities of the organism which were not affected by the disturbance. The "filling-up" only gives rise to the pleasure *accidentally* because it is attended with the removal of an inhibition. The thought is that the feeling-tone of normal organic life is itself pleasant. . . . Hence we need to correct the proposed definition of pleasure as "sensible transition to a natural state" into "unimpeded exercise of a natural activity." The pleasure-giving process is not a "coming-to-be" . . . but the discharge in act . . . of an already developed function. The insistence on the difference between the two kinds of process, "coming-to-be" and "activity," is a correction of first-rate importance in the Academic terminology."[13]

Good, then, and that kind of pleasure which can be admitted as part of it, once again turn out, even for Aristotle, to be related to smoothly running, repetitive "activity" rather than "coming-to-be" process; to a functioning that abides undeviatingly by some established unchangeable plan. Good could exist, then, in a perfect machine, such as a watch, that simply repeats its routine perfectly forever. Always, the idea is that, though there may be development, it is the final right measure and arrangement of function which is the good itself.

The Static Idea of Good, then, implies that value, whether objective, subjective, external or internal, could exist either in a permanent stasis, or in a permanent routine functioning which *lacks real development that resolves painful disorder.*

Static Value and Cosmic Purpose. All philosophy and religion until recent times has based its expectations as to what the universe *ought* to be like, in order to be meaningful, upon value ideas of this nature. A cosmic, omnipotent God, if He is to create

47

a world good in the static sense, must place perfect, permanent goodness into his creation from the first moment. "Perfection" is assumed to have an understandable meaning — the complete fullness of this goodness. There is no reason in the nature of static good for there to be any pain, evil or any "coming-to-be" growth.

Thus, the distinction which Aristotle made, and Taylor seems to approve, was bought at a great price: *it sacrifices all hope of ever being able to deduce an imperfect, growing world from the idea of value. As the book proceeds, we will work out the implications of this idea of good in each special realm in more detail, and then show how science invariably fails to confirm them.*

II.   The Dynamic Idea of Value and Good.

The opposing concept is the dynamic idea of value, and the use made of this concept is a special and central feature of this text. For it seems to the author that this is the most powerful concept there is for clearing up some of the contradictions in philosophy. It is introduced here with some of its basic implications; and it will appear in each topic to follow, more and more meaning being added to it as we see its further implications.

We have already said (p. 32) that this conception of value comes out of an empirical study of the experience of value and feeling, the findings of which are then applied to the definition of value. In chapter XIV the empirical source of the dynamic idea of value will be explained in detail. This definition of value, then, is taken as an ultimate principle from which all reality may be deduced, or shown as required.

Thus we are doing nothing less than accepting the idea of the "wits" in the *Philebus* concerning *pleasure,* and with sufficient qualification, applying the thought to the idea of *good* itself. We shall hold, first, that all feeling, including pleasurable and painful, exists only when some kind of transformation or energy change is "coming-to-be"; and that *pleasurable* feeling occurs when the transformation is in the very act of simultaneously relaxing tension, escaping from pain, working out of disorder *and* achieving equilibrium, healing disturbance, increasing inclusive order. At least, pleasure requires present living awareness of contrast between the earlier less satisfactory state and the present improved state — which would be lacking in Aristotle's smooth "activity" where all moments are alike.

48

Secondly, this first principle holds that these characteristics belong to the very essence of Good itself; that Good itself can have no meaning or existence except as a feeling of contrast inhering in processes constructive in some sense, that "take up" former occasions into themselves, so that the organizing can be felt as it happens. It cannot be completely defined in terms of the properties of end states alone: the nature of final order or perfect harmony. The process of advancing toward that end state from some earlier, lesser degree of order, inclusiveness and harmony must be included in the definition.

I would defend this idea of good as being exemplified in all psychological experience of good.[14] From physical pleasures through the "higher values" of spiritual experience, good inheres in *creative* or restoring processes, not in repetitive, homogeneous ones. In terms of fact, the weight of opinion holds that all organic activity is prompted by some "depletion," or tension, or disorder; and that activity, or even thought, continues only as long as need in some sense is felt. The dynamic idea of good defines good as a feeling which *requires* such activity. Good exists only within the actual process of passing from disorder to order, from vagueness toward definiteness, from tension toward equilibrium, from miscellaneity toward design, from pain toward relief of pain. Aristotle's "harmonious organic activity" probably consists of innumerable small *developments* at cellular and molecular levels. His *summum bonum* of contemplation cannot be enjoyed except as it contrasts to preceding turmoil. I am convinced that the same holds of Buddhism's Nirvana, however much its metaphysics would like to deny it. We have no experience of good except as the very sensation of the untwisting of a disorder, as the very feeling of design coming into being.

This definition holds not only in such relatively banal instances as these: that we enjoy food only while hunger is being relieved; that the thrill in music comes from the resolving of the discord, not just from the harmonious chord; that the thinker's pleasure in his flash of insight depends upon its resolving a preceding strain or puzzling disorder of thoughts. The thesis can also be maintained in cases seemingly more illustrative of static contemplation of formal good, such as visual art, at first sight an illustration of Plato's "unmixed" static good. The painting, once finished, seems unchanging, and somehow to contain timelessly permanent beauty of line and proportion. But actually it

49

is called "good" only as a shorthand to cover the fact that it is capable of giving rise to a *felt* process in the eye, optic nerve and optic tract of a brain, that brings muscle and sensory cells that were first in some miscellaneous, random relationship into some more highly organized relationship. As long as we are actively appreciating the picture, we can be sure that eye-muscles are following patterned lines, and retinal cells are transmitting varying frequencies and brain is *feeling the process* of building dynamic order out of these ingredients. Also, fully to appreciate the painting's greatness, we must think our way back to the problems the artist faced at first in organizing his design, and, as it were, solve them again with him.

The bodily appetites and passions, such as hunger and sex show the same phases of tension or depletion, process and satisfaction-felt-in-resolution. All muscular activities which are enjoyed reveal prior conditions of some kind of felt disorder, vagueness or strain. It can be in the muscle-nerve tissues already (the untrained child's hand); or freshly caused in them by sensed external objects to be dealt with (unassembled building materials, the incalculables of the ball game). In each case, some variety of *felt* resolving process is given rise to.

As for ethical good, it has point and importance only as a solution of some painfulness or threat of destruction. The "good" man is so judged because in some sense we see that his modes of behavior are efficacious for transforming destructive possibilities toward creativity. Ethical standards themselves may seem unchanging (although we know that they have developed too). Yet value itself will exist only in the felt processes that standards may instigate. The term "good" is applied to them in exactly the same sense as to the picture: as a shorthand to cover the fact that, when followed, they may guide felt action along a constructive route, increasing the chances that good feeling will be had. But we must first have felt the pains of unethical, or unsuccessful behavior in our own experience, or at least in some substitute process of reading or observation of others, before we can grasp the importance of the standard. And that pain or frustration to which the standard is applied is as essential in producing the process of behavior as the standard itself is.

Finally, scientific and philosophical thinking is a process that utilizes large portions of the organism's various processes, endeavoring to work out in the focussing area of the brain, highly inclusive patterns of organization. The enjoyment still depends upon these processes not having been organized at first.

As for Plato's argument about "pure" pleasures, I would question whether the antecedent condition of pain — or at least discomfort or vagueness — is as irrelevant or "unconscious" as he claims. He says there is no conscious pain prior to enjoying a beautiful color; and that not to possess geometrical knowledge, prior to attaining it, is not painful. But the fact is that we do not enjoy a color in staring at it for hours. We enjoy it when it comes as a change from looking at a gray, littered street. The nerves of the retina move from some random arrangement to a vivid simplicity that refreshes. And the geometrician does not begin to enjoy geometry until he has plunged himself into the difficulties of the subject and then passed from confusion of thoughts to the elegance of his proofs.

I would also see more significance in the proportionality of pleasure to the magnitude of transition from pain than Plato does. He dismisses all pleasures associated with greater process from pain as liable to being destructive, wanton or diseased. They lack "measure." He is left with "pure pleasures" which are admittedly relatively mild, not to say pallid, experiences. But there are certain more exciting pleasures that do not necessarily fall into his class of discreditable pleasures that lack measure. Those saved from deeper despairs, or succeeding in more desperate struggles, have experienced ecstasies that did not prevent them from being considered saints. The real difficulty with the acute pleasures that are accompanied by destruction is not the amount of contrast between the pain and pleasure involved, but the narrowness and non-inclusiveness of factors involved. Scratching that yields bliss but also bleeding sores; sexual excess that leads to personal decay; drinking that leads to hangovers and dementia: all share in (1) stimulating sharply localized parts of the organism so acutely as to destroy tissue and (2) simultaneously preventing more inclusive processes of vocational, personal and social integration which could be foundational to wider and deeper satisfactions. But the dynamic idea of good implies that good feeling will be proportional to the amount of transition from painful disorder *provided that* the inclusiveness of factors is also increased in the pattern that is being organized. The acute, "vicious" pleasures certainly have sharp contrasts between tension and relief, so sharp as to lead sometimes to burning or disin-

51

tegration and final pain rather than pleasure. But their fault is in lack of order and integration, rather than in the degree of pain overcome.

Dynamic Value as Relational. Under the static idea of value we found the purely objective and the purely subjective theories. In the dynamic view it becomes immediately apparent that values exist only as processes of *interaction* take place between objects and subjective feelers of those objects. The value is certainly not merely an external quality in objects, nor is it a permanently abiding feeling in the subject independent of objects. It exists only when a process is prompted in the subject by an object. The object must have optimum specifications in order to cause a process of increasing vividness and order in *that* subject. How this point resolves subjectivist and relativistic problems in value theory will be studied in Part IV.

Our dynamic idea of good may not seem very different from familiar relational and functional theories of value. But even some of the more recent treatments that place action or a process of satisfy*ing* desire at the center of value's meaning may lose hold, at times, of the dynamic conception, at least in temporary lapses of terminology. They can fall again into associating it only with the outcomes of processes, to terminal moments of high satisfaction feeling. They lose sight of value as the feeling *of* the dynamic relationships between entities or energies *while they are passing* from a condition strained or awkward in some sense and *resolving toward* a condition less strained and more organized in some sense. Insofar as value is identified with the ends of processes, or is dualized against the striving, the transforming, the resolving, we have lost the fully dynamic conception. We then lose our advantage, and the dynamic reality to which modern science testifies — the process — becomes an independent given underivable from the idea of value itself.

As for the question of the qualities, essences, forms that traditional logic found necessary for thought, knowledge and truth, further discussion will be found later in the book, though I haven't space for a complete presentation. The only point I shall make here is that whatever else may fall entirely into the category of essences, value or good itself does not. Value may involve the recurrent qualities, but it also includes the feeling of creating

52

them, of reaching them from contrasting conditions, organizing some plurality of components or parts into those final qualities.

III. Basic Implications of the Dynamic Idea of Value.

Let us now briefly introduce some of the most general and prior implications of the dynamic idea of value. In the remainder of the book, each chapter will terminate with further discussion of these and of further implications or deductions from these, as we pursue our project of showing how the findings of science in every realm of reality correspond to what the dynamic idea of meaningfulness and value logically implies.

Let us take, as a starting point, the brief formula, "Satisfying Feeling of Organizing Process,"[15] as a definition of dynamic value. The "ing" in each phrase is to be taken as active, operative, to indicate that the feeling exists only while the unsatisfied is becoming satisfied, the unorganized is becoming organized. The concepts are numbered for purposes of reference.

1.0. Satisfying feeling.[15]

2.0. Organizing Process.

The following concepts, then, are implicit in 1.0 and 2.0:

1.1. A center or centers of feeling, "feelers," or subjects are required or implied by 1.0 the notion of feeling. These must be wholes which can feel parts (whose derivation is considered below) moving in the organizing process and coming into ordered togetherness.

2.1. The idea of *process,* transition, change, is of course implied by the basic definition. This step in thought is the subject of Chapter VII.

2.2. *Parts* are implied by 2.1, the notion of process. As has been understood since the beginning of philosophy, there could be no motion or change without parts which can move and change their positions or relations with respect to one another. (This point will be the subject of Chapter VIII.) Yet these parts must be of such a nature as to be able to be felt in togetherness, as specified in 1.1.

2.21. There must be the parts that constitute the feeler.

2.22. There must be additional parts outside of the feeler, usually called the objects. These are the materials or supplementary energies to be used both in raising problems, strains, disorders (the —.—1 items below) at the start of value-process, and for completing or fulfilling processes thus instigated.

2.3. *Differentiating,* then is implied as a source of parts. It would be one aspect or kind of process — the process of analyzing or bringing more and more definite parts out of vague undifferentiated wholeness, both external and internal. Satisfying feeling could come from this aspect of process itself, as well as from the later phase of ordering the parts that have been differentiated (2.4, 2.5).

    2.31. Conditions of vague indefiniteness, then, are required priorly, if the process of differentiating is to exist.

    2.32. Conditions of relatively greater definiteness and distinctness must be possible latterly if satisfaction is to be felt (though it is to be felt only as such conditions are in the process of emerging, according to the basic thesis).

The question whether satisfaction should also be felt in a process that moves in the opposite direction in this respect (from excessive definiteness, sharpness, etc., toward vaguer, smoother, more synthetic wholeness) is involved in 2.42.

2.4. *Ordering* is practically the same notion as organizing itself, our basic assumption, but emphasizes the synthesizing phase of organizing more than the preceding item. This covers the arranging of the parts, which have been differentiated or analyzed, into patterns.

    2.41. Conditions of disorder then are required priorly, if the process of ordering is to exist. These, of course, must be associated with unsatisfying feeling.

    2.42. Conditions of order, pattern, design must be possible latterly to undergird satisfying feeling (which again is to be felt only as such conditions are in the act of emerging).

The question whether satisfaction can also be felt in destruction of order — if it becomes too rigid or repetitive for instance — will be considered elsewhere and is also involved in item 2.7 below.

2.5. *Resolving* is a term I have chosen to point more especially to the dynamic and felt aspects of the above "ordering" which itself points more to the objective, structural aspect. The organizing process would arise not out of a group of static material parts lying about in a merely objective state of disorder, but out of a distorted field of energy, where "strains" or "tensions" can be felt "in between" the parts, so to speak. The arranging, or ordering of the parts would then also be felt as a change of tensions, or a resolution of strains.

2.51. Tension within the disordered field, felt as unsatisfying or painful, is required priorly if the feeling of resolv*ing* is to exist.

2.52. Equilibrium, balance, etc., in energy fields, felt as satisfying must be possible latterly as the very substance of satisfaction (always to be felt only as it is in the act of emerging).

2.6. *Increasing* or including is implied by the notion of organizing and resolving, if these are to continue indefinitely as long as good is to exist. There must be ever new ingredients to provide new disorders and tensions, which are necessary for *real* organizing. For, if we assume that real organizing requires genuine problems and creativity rather than merely repetition of old processes, then an increase, or a greater complexity would be necessary.

2.61. Conditions of lack are required priorly, as one source of tension. This can apply to factors both inside and outside of the feeler.

2.62. The existence of additional ingredients and their successful appropriating and adding to the order must of course be possible. This is only item 2.22 considered again from the present viewpoint.

2.63. Proportionality of the amount of value-feeling to the amount of inclusion seems to follow from the present item, though this point must be discussed more carefully in Part IV. The amount of good feeling might be expected to relate to the number of factors or elements successfully being ordered or harmonized in the process. This notion of inclusiveness will turn out to be fundamental to the problem of evaluation, as we shall see.

2.7. *Contrast* or Novelty is an aspect of processes, whose necessity might be derived from 2.3, Differentiating or 2.6, Increasing. Contrast would be necessary both to tell one part from another; and to give meaning to the idea of inclusion of "new" ingredients. Also 2.5, Resolving, if it connotes solving a genuine puzzle, real creating, implies the necessity of fresh, contrasting elements.

2.71. Conditions of excessive sameness, of tiresome repetitiveness, would be required priorly if the experience of refreshing contrast or newness is to exist.

2.72. Conditions of refreshing contrast must be possible latterly if such satisfaction is to be felt (only in the emerging, as usual).

Satisfaction can apparently also be felt in a process that moves from excessive contrast or violent chaos back toward sameness. There will be many kinds of contrast — spatial, temporal, etc.

2.6 and 2.7 together thus imply that processes must either advance to new levels of inclusiveness and complexity in the given area of experience, or else move into new areas of experience at the same or lower levels of complexity. If we have grown bored with painting pictures we must in order to remain interested either advance and improve our skill so that we can paint more complex and difficult pictures; or if we are not capable of handling further complexity in painting, we must turn to carpentry or some other hobby where we can develop an equivalent level of skill but on novel materials.

This requirement of contrast and novelty opposes Plato's and Aristotle's favoring of routine "normal" activity over "coming-to-be" process as the locus of value. It associates good feeling more especially with processes that resolve real strains and create new order. Of course, a good deal of experience seems to be repetitive and mildly enjoyable at the same time. But surely, the more absolutely repetitive it is, the more mild the enjoyment unto total boredom. But it has often been argued that Nature never absolutely repeats, and that there are always small variations at least to undergird some modicum of interest. We might also argue that the supposed "normal" activity really consists of subepisodes, however minute, of "coming-to-be" processes, that is, of *creative* resolutions of tensions at some level of cell or molecule. The mildly pleasant feeling tone of "normal activity" might be the precipitate of constant little *creative* resolutions going on in the parts of the organism. It may be hard to believe that each depletion-repletion of a cell is genuinely a fresh, novel solution of a problem; but at least it is a transition from a real lack or tension to a real resolution of it. The greater pleasures and values, at any rate, would require greater inclusion and novelty. Aristotle's notion of "discharge of an already developed function," which does not solve anything or create something new, would be a prescription for a feelingless and meaningless clockwork.

2.8. *Intensity.* That value feeling should come in differing de-

56

grees of intensity is, if not a direct implication of the dynamic idea of good as such, at least to be expected in the light of these other kinds of variation and their degrees. The intensity of feeling would vary with all the above variables, perhaps as some kind of product of all taken together.

2.81. Unsatisfying degrees of intensity (insufficient or excessive) would need to exist priorly so that a process of changing intensity might be felt and enjoyed.

2.82. Satisfying degrees of intensity should be possible in subsequent phases of process.

We shall see that the present factor has to be balanced with 2.6, Inclusiveness, in many cases.

2.9. Proportionality of good feeling or value to the *advance*, that is the "distance" moved by the value-process. The dynamic idea of value implies, finally, that the amount of value will not be measured by a single figure applying to just one given state. Rather, it would be expected to be measured as most factors are measured in dynamic science: by the difference between two figures, taken at two points in the process. This also implies that it is not necessary to have a fixed, perfect and final standard in order to avoid a relativistic denial of the possibility of evaluation, by comparing any given state to such a standard. For it will always be possible to tell whether a value-process has advanced by comparing any later phase of it with any earlier; or to compare two processes as to their amount of advance. Plato denied the relevance of this quantity to evaluation (p. 45). That is, he denied that the amount of contrast or gradient between the prior disorder with its pain and discomfort and the later resolution had anything essential to do with the amount of good. But a realistic and fair evaluation of goodness requires as much attention to be paid to where one starts from as to where he arrives. We need grounds for commending a man who has risen from the lower dregs to a medium level of achievement as much as or more than the man born to a higher level than the first ever reaches, who however advances only a little or not at all from his starting point. This final measure or value, then, is roughly the difference between the amount of inclusiveness, harmony and other criteria at the beginning of a segment of process and that at the end.

The dynamic idea of value means, as noted under several of the above items, that value cannot exist when a final state has been achieved in any of these respects. But this does not expose us to the Schopenhauerean complaint that nothing can ever be achieved or any desire satisfied. A degree of consummation may be possessed, and although the feeling of it will not continue if the emerging process is stilled, man is not doomed to be forever starting from scratch, or cheated of attainment. He may retain the achievement as a foundation for subsequent value-experience — as, in fact, the very enablement of new processes which will not have to merely re-do the old one. True, he cannot continue to enjoy the old process, but preservation of its accomplishment enables him to enjoy the new one to which he must go next, if he is to experience good again.

The intensity of the good feeling may vary from moment to moment in the process, and may be liable to rise to a crescendo toward the end of the episode, with the more rapid crystallization that is apt to occur then. This would be the source of men's age-old supposition that good exists only as the terminal result of striving. But it should be clear, once attention is directed to it, that this good feeling at the climax could have no existence, no meaning, no importance, except as the resolving of a struggle, the solving of a problem. An after phase of dwindling activity is a usual part of experience, with milder good feeling associated with it; but if all reverberations of process are finally quieted, feeling must vanish, and good will no longer be actual.

If it be urged that there is more permanence in good feeling than this allows for, that the good can at least be remembered and known, we can still maintain that resolving process must be present. When we remember a good experience, and appreciate its value again, some part of our nervous system, some group of nerve cells is surely running through an organizing process analogous to the first one, and this undergirds our feeling again, in some less vivid manner, a similar good here and now.

On our definition, then, the dynamic *felt* contrast of changing tensions — not merely logical or conceptual contrast — is necessary to the existence of value; and the inveterate association of good with end stases, universal in the history of philosophy, becomes the most basic mistake of human thought.

IV. Summary of the Requirements of Meaningfulness.

We have now made certain prescriptions for what we will

accept as meaningful, in the maximum sense. We are saying that it is necessary to be able to believe that the facts of reality are what they have to be in order to exemplify Cosmic Purpose for Good, that is, divine purposiveness. We then suggest that only such belief can bring that deepest sense of holiness, those most regenerative feelings of enthusiasm, reverence and awe which are requisite to inspire men to their highest levels of adequate living.

This formulation of the necessities of religious meaning has remained on as purely formal and abstract a level as possible. It has left more specific characteristics of God unsettled — whether he is impersonal or personal, immanent or transcendent, supernatural or natural, etc. We will get to some of these questions only in the last chapters.

We have, however, descended from the formal level far enough to characterize a certain basic distinction in the definition of value. For our whole project of finding whether the facts of science "fit" what we would expect a divine designer to create reduces largely to finding whether the facts are what could be logically deduced from some idea of good. And we have found two basic ways of conceiving good, which lead to quite different sets of expectations or requirements. We have worked out some of the preliminary implications of the dynamic idea of good, and in the remainder of the book will work out others, as needed, from those given here. In each chapter to follow the implications of the static idea of good will also be worked out, and their contradiction by various theories of reality will be made explicit. In general, we shall find that modern science has changed its basic theory from one which flatly contradicts any view of Cosmic Purpose for Good whatever, to one that "fits" the requirements in innumerable ways, *if* those requirements are adjusted in the way that has been here introduced.

CHAPTER IV

THE TYPES OF PHILOSOPHY

After 2500 years of philosophizing, men have become conscious that there are a number — apparently not very large — of kinds of general conclusions, or ubiquitous attitudes that turn up again and again in all times and places of human history. Each of these types of philosophical attitude prompts its own distinguishable sort of answer to all the questions or topics of thought. A prevalent fourfold classification made up of "Idealism," "Realism," "Naturalism," and "Pragmatism" appears in more than one current text. "Materialism," "Existentialism," "Organicism," "Logical Positivism" are other terms that sometimes get onto the master list. "Humanism," "Personalism," "Neo-Thomism," "Phenomenalism" are types that are more usually subsumed under one of the above types as only a variation of the more general classes. There is some tendency to pare the categories down to two essential ones: "Idealism" and "Realism."

When we come to studying these classifications, we find so much overlapping and such diverse principles of division that we can well wonder why the suggestion is made that there are any distinct types of philosophy at all. "Materialism" and "Pragmatism" both turn out to be types of "Naturalism"; all three of these can at the same time be realistic, but Pragmatism can also be idealistic. Realism and Idealism themselves seem to overlap in something called "Objective Idealism," etc., etc.

However, on the basis of our distinction between Ideas of Meaning and Ideas of Reality, we may be able to make some of these philosophical types take their places in a more intelligible sequence which helps explain why they turn up as they do. Of course our present treatment will be forced to oversimplify — we haven't space to exhaust all the philosophical views in history. Many hybrid types or transitional forms that have appeared in

60

different eras will have to be neglected. But the presumption is that the following classification in terms of the possible combinations between two main ideas of Meaningfulness, and three main ideas of Reality, which have appeared in human thought, does bring out highly significant core types of philosophy.

In this chapter, we are only introducing the types — barely mentioning some of their main features. The remaining chapters of the book will be built upon the sequence outlined here, so that more meaning will be continually added to each of these types of philosophy, as we see what each type has to say for every topic.

One further qualification is that this classification is primarily a classification of types of *metaphysics* or ontology. Some of the familiar "isms" are *epistemological* types: "Empiricism," "Rationalism," "Positivism," "Phenomenalism" etc., arising out of different theories of the relationship between man's knowing process and what sort of thing it is he finally can know. However epistemological and metaphysical considerations are not mutually exclusive, and the former often have bearing upon our classification.

We have just spoken of the two basic conceptions of (maximum) Meaningfulness: they are the two introduced in the preceding chapter, distinguished according to whether they are based on a static or dynamic idea of value. Let us label these Static Idea of Meaning (SM) and Dynamic Idea of Meaning (DM). We also spoke of three basic ideas of reality. These are also distinguished in static versus dynamic terms; and also according to their treatment of *wholes* and *parts*. There is the static-whole theory, the static-part theory, and the dynamic part-whole theory.

The *first* idea of reality is fundamentally characterized by the attempt to explain things by unchanging wholes, or unanalyzed, static essences or ideas. I will label it the Static Idealistic Theory of Reality, abbreviated throughout the book as SIR. Under it come most of the prevalent conceptions of reality from the early Greeks up through the Middle Ages until the rise of early modern science made the second theory more preponderant. (Not included, of theories worked out during the period mentioned, are earlier forms of the second and third views which Greek thinkers had already produced.) Whatever its variations may be, they all unite in seeking to understand reality as conforming somehow to the implications of SM. SIR has to begin by granting that Reality *appears* at least to consist of material substance, imperfect in-

61

dividual things, and motion or change. But, as we shall see, these phenomena do not exactly conform to the purest logical implications of SM, which, strictly, implies only mental substance, a single divine mind, and changelessness. SIR, then, has a large task in trying to get rid of this conflict; it falls back on two main devices. Either it subordinates material substance, imperfection, individual parts and change to a primary world of unchanging, perfect thought, a realm of holistic "mental substance," in a *dualistic* theory. Or it eliminates those unwanted phenomena by considering them illusions or appearances in a *monistic* theory. By thus denying full reality to them, it returns as closely as possible to SM's purely mental realm. SIR then must include both kinds of theory of reality: the matter-under-mind type, and the mind-only types.

The second view of Reality is mechanistic materialism, fundamentally characterized by explanations in terms of *parts* that do not synthesize into wholes. I definitely exclude from this class, for this book's purposes, any form of theory that construes "matter" or "material" as energy in the modern sense. Many scientists continue to call themselves "materialists" as long as they believe that all things can be "explained in terms of physical or chemical laws," even if energy rather than "matter" has become the subject of those laws. This usage obscures a crucial difference between my second and third theories of reality, based on their treatment of the whole-part relationship. So my second theory is confined to views like Democritus's and Epicurus's in ancient times, and Newton's in early modern times, which specify that all things are made of *material* atoms of such a nature that they cannot operate *holistically*. My classification also implies, contrary to many presentations which consider mechanistic materialism only as a minor, and rather insignificant, sub-type under "Naturalism," that it is actually a most basic type of philosophy, one of the fundamental poles of thought, in fact. For it is the philosophy that carries the emphasis on unsynthesized *parts* to the ultimate extreme, just as SIR does for unanalyzed wholes. This theory of reality is labeled SMR (Static Mechanistic Theory of Reality).

The third view of reality is what has resulted from the great revolution in science which everyone agrees has taken place within the last century, with Darwin's and Einstein's names looming prominently in its history. (As usual, the Greeks had already suggested features of it, with Heraclitus and Aristotle.) There is general agreement that this revolution has made the notion of dynamic process central to its ontology, so I label it DR, the Dynamic Theory of Reality. It includes modern field-energy theories which, we shall find, explain all things neither in terms of mystic essences (wholes) without parts, nor in terms of material parts without wholes, but in terms of wholes-with-parts, or parts organizing into wholes.

We now have our two ideas of meaningfulness and three ideas of reality, based primarily on the distinction between Static and Dynamic concepts, and the kind of theory of wholes and parts. The essential types of philosophy arise from the possible combinations of these ideas. To understand any complete philosophy, we must know (1) what Idea of Meaningfulness it assumes; (2) what implications it draws from this as to what the facts of Reality *ought* to be; (3) what it believes the facts of Reality actually are (or appear to be); (4) whether (2) and (3) agree with or contradict each other. *If* they clearly agree, of course, the philosophy rests in satisfaction that reality is meaningful; if they disagree it may rest in a negative conclusion. But there may be a fifth part of the philosophy to understand in case of *disagreement, if* the philosophy does not rest in a negative conclusion: (5) what devices for changing (3) it resorts to, in the effort to *make* (3) agree with (2).

We are now ready for our actual types. Since historically men have seemed to adopt static categories first, and have always accepted dynamic ones only under protest — not fully grasping the dynamic theory of reality until the current century — the following classification is not only a typological one but a rough historical one also. Not that more or less dynamic theories had not previously turned up, as we have said, with the early Greeks; but on the whole the static types held sway more extensively earlier in history, and the dynamic ones have been diffused more recently.

Type I. SM with SIR: Traditional Static Idealism.

The first main type of philosophy results from the combination of SM with SIR. The Static Idea of Good, implying as we have seen, that Good can exist as a fixed state, quality, idea or thought, implies in turn, that a Reality that is going to contain Good need not be other than some changeless, perfect state of things, without motion or even necessarily, material substance. If good can exist as pure thought or as a fixed system of concepts, then reality to contain it need not be more than a realm of thought and idea.

But SIR, as we have seen, starts off by noticing a *seeming* reality at least, of material substance and change, albeit under the control (perhaps only partial) of mind, thought or value ideas. To get complete congruence, some thinkers have resorted to denying the reality of material substance and change, in the face of all experience. It is difficult to find simon-pure examples of such a belief in static, motionless reality, since it so obviously conflicts with immediate experience. Perhaps the predecessor of Plato in Greek philosophy, Parmenides, is the closest to it, for he boldly went ahead and declared that all the apparent motion in the world was utterly illusory and did not exist. He worked out a logical proof of this besides, in addition to our above approach from the requirements of static value. Some forms of Hinduism also come close with their fondness for dismissing changing experience as "Maya" or "Illusion." Our own Christian Science has something of this feature. This form of the first type of philosophy can be called static monistic idealism, for it believes only one reality exists, a realm of unchanging ideas.

A more preponderant form of Type I, however, cannot bear such flouting of apparent experience, and ends by granting actuality to material substance, motion and evil. Plato for example conceded that Matter existed, uncalled-for though it was by his idea of value. For him matter had to be simply a brute existent that was there for no reason at all, neither planned, created nor desired by a cosmic value creator. But once granting its existence, he found it very useful for explaining his other two unrequired realities, motion and evil. These occurred in spite of cosmic intentions, simply because mischievous matter was there, arbitrarily forcing them into existence. Plato ends up with a dualistic idealism, since a second kind of substance besides the required Idea-world also is admitted.

Most or all of the many forms of Idealism that cropped up from Plato onward through the Roman and Medieval periods can be seen as essentially one or the other of these two basic types: monistic or dualistic. They get rid of contradictory aspects of reality either by calling them "illusion" and "appearance"; or else by foisting them off on some second realm that is just arbitrarily there. Orthodox Christian theology by and large starts in the same way accepting the implications of SM but also accepting certain theories about the nature of reality that do not exactly correspond: for instance, that there is a created, changing, substantial world; that it includes creatures who are evil or sinful. Christianity then resorts to further ideas to explain why a statically perfect God should have produced such things: "Love" is introduced as a new category, apparently requiring creatures to love and be loved; "Creation from Nothing" comes next, to get Plato's uncreated matter safely under God's plan; "The Fall of Man" is appealed to as explaining evil, etc.

It is necessary to be clear here that SIR, though it may grant a realm of Matter, never conceives that realm mechanistically — for this would take us into SMR. In SIR matter is always amenable — partially at least — to control by *holistic* ideas, forms, purposes, values. It is a thing of potentiality and tendency toward goals, for instance, in Aristotle.

However, when the concept of matter does become mechanistic, in SMR, we shall find that these two idealistic devices are still used as escapes from the contradictions. This means that Idealism is a perennial type of philosophy and can find a way to make its claims whatever the theory of reality may be. And yet men have never been fully satisfied with idealism's ways of arguing that "the facts are not what they seem." They have continued to wish for a philosophy that could accept what experience seems to be and yet show how *it* fits the requirements of value.

Type II. SM with SMR: *Mechanistic Materialism; Escapes from It.*

The next basic type of philosophy results from the combination of SM with SMR. It happens that the mechanistic theory of reality (SMR) in its pure form, extended to all phenomena, mental and physical, flatly contradicts the implications of SM in every respect. We shall see exactly how and why (due fundamentally to the whole-part error) in later chapters. Therefore this philosophy normally concludes that reality is meaningless or purposeless. But it does not follow that this philosophy has no conception of meaningfulness at all, just because it concludes there is no meaning. For such a conclusion could only result if the philosophy *did* have a theory of meaning which it believes to be contradicted by

65

the facts. And the theory of meaning that mechanistic materialism had was simply the old traditional theory with its implications that we have just presented.

This second type of philosophy must, as we have said, be restricted to the purer form of materialism based on the older, non-energistic concept of matter. It held that reality consists of solid, inert material atoms which cause all effects automatically while following fixed laws of motion. These atoms do not operate purposively, therefore the idea of *purpose* in SM is contradicted. This philosophy also refuses to dismiss the evil in existence by any of the idealistic devices ("Appearance" etc.); that is, it is "realistic" about evil, and this contradicts the implications of the Static Idea of *Good* in SM. Nor can this philosophy find any way for our knowing anything at a *cosmic* level, so it must finally reach an atheistic or at least an agnostic conclusion.

"Logical Positivism" is a modern philosophy that accepts these conclusions, with special stress on this last point. It finds additional proofs, based on epistemological and semantic considerations, that we can know nothing of meanings, purposes, values, or over-all metaphysical conclusions about the nature of reality or cosmos as a whole.

As already mentioned, many types of Idealism in the 17th, 18th, and 19th, centuries would be classified at this point as kinds of "squirming," so to speak, to escape from the intolerable conclusions that result from SM and SMR being combined in their pure forms. I think I am safe in saying, however, that all these types preserve SM, the static interpretation of meaning and value, and try to find some way of showing that the facts fit its implications. Descartes' dualism, for instance, was a sort of revival of Plato's: the mechanical, material substance is kept under the partial control of mental substance. Berkeley's subjective idealism, and Kant's phenomenalism were closer to the appearance-vs.-reality kind of escape, trying to turn the tables on SMR and show that it is only an illusion, a mere construct of man's mind. Spinoza worked out a unique way of accepting mechanical reality as one aspect of a single substance which did duty as God for him. His philosophy is sometimes called Neutral Monism.

Type III. SM with DR: Dynamic Naturalisms.

The majority of currently popular philosophies belong to this third type, all of them working with the combination of SM and DR, the dynamic idea of reality. DR is characterized by its readmitting of qualities, wholes, feelings, etc., into reality. Most important, this view of reality is not at all so clearly non-purposive as SMR, and in fact is widely understood to permit that holistic, purposive beings may exist. So the contradiction with the requirement of *purpose*, in SM, is greatly eased. However, this view continues to be realistic about the existence of evil and of course holds that change and process is the essence of reality. But neither of these is implied or required by SM. Therefore all the current varieties of Naturalism (and this includes Pragmatism, Existentialism and others), characteristically refrain from asserting that reality is meaningful in our maximum sense. They cannot maintain that all existence is purposefully designed by a cosmic good purpose, for, interpreted statically, this would require a reality of fixed perfection rather than DR's reality of imperfection and change.

What these philosophies commonly do hold is that, since we find many purposive processes in reality which sometimes succeed in achieving some good, we may conclude that there might be some divine purposiveness back of it all; but it is clear that it cannot be a fully cosmic, or *omnipotent* good purpose, because processes do not always succeed, and there is always much evil and imperfection. So, some of the Pragmatists, Existentialists, Organicists, Naturalists, etc., will defend the existence of a "limited God."

Others out of each of these groups will not go even that far — for positivistic or other reasons — and it is here that one of our more familiar isms thus falls: Humanism. DR permits humanists to believe that *human beings* can be purposive, and that they can create goods through aspirational effort. Since this is all that humanists can be sure of, they refrain from making any claims about cosmic purpose though they are usually not atheistic, but only agnostic. That is, they see no more grounds for a negative than for a positive proof concerning cosmic purpose. Their great claim is that man can create the good life without divine aid, without faith that the universe is teleological.

And of course, there are those, working with SM and DR, who will go ahead and defend a definite atheism: the most prominent example being the dialectical materialists, or Marxists. However, whether their philosophy deserves to be classified with dynamic naturalism, in spite of its use of the term "materialism" is not absolutely clear. True, it has put into its term "matter" so much of the idea of process, evolution, energy, that it clearly escapes the pure implications of mechanism. On the other hand it remains highly averse to the notion that ideas or purposes can ever control or cause material processes. In fact, one of the most important advantages of the sequence of philosophies which we are here outlining and will proceed to develop in the remainder of the book, is that, in clarifying what was inadequate about mechanistic materialism and in supplying a valid answer to it, we shall be providing some ammunition against our Communist adversaries — perhaps far more effective than atomic missiles will ever be.

Each of the "ism" words used in this section, then, point to various aspects of this modern naturalistic belief that reality is *process,* conceivably including aim, purpose, feeling, creativity, but also destruction and failure. "Naturalism" in its *modern* use points to the emphasis on "nature" as including all processual reality, with no additional, separated realm of the "supernatural," that is, no reality outside of natural law. If Naturalism has a God concept at all, it will be a God who is in nature; or, vice versa, nature will be in God, that is, nature and its laws themselves will be thought of as God's working. Naturalism has had other meanings in earlier thought: for instance SMR was a naturalism, for it too believed that nothing existed but nature, conceived in the Newtonian manner, and excluding any power operating outside the laws of Physics. Present day naturalism, however, is usually emphatic about its including under "nature" far more of the qualitative and purposive experience of man than did SMR. Rousseau's theory that man should always conform to Nature, or go back to primitive, savage "naturalness" is another use of the word.

"Pragmatism" (from a Greek word meaning "practical") emphasizes man's ability to understand the natural processes by his own thought processes (which are themselves continuous with all other natural processes), and to cooperate with them in solving his practical problems. It generalizes the scientific method of learning about nature through creative hypothesizing and experimental verification by results (see chapter VI) into an answer to man's general problem of deciding his goals and achieving them. As created by Charles Pierce and William James, Pragmatism is called America's most typical contribution to philosophy, making

68

our national "practical" attitude into a general solution of the nature of truth itself. For, in a sense, pragmatists say, truth is determined by the consequences of action undertaken to solve practical problems. John Dewey, as the most famous of current American philosophers, was also a pragmatist, under his own labels of "Instrumentalism", or "Experimentalism." A still more recent version of Pragmatism is "Operationalism", suggesting that all statements of truth must come down in the end to a description of certain operations, or processes, that investigators must go through in experimenting with nature. Dewey and James definitely defend "limited God" ideas, and the author is satisfied that this is precisely because they continued to work with SM and DR.[1]

"Meliorism" is an aspect of pragmatism, making explicit that, since goods are *not* already given (as SM implies they should be) man had better get busy and create them for himself, i.e., he should ameliorate the difficulties and problems that are always present around him (unrequired as they are by SM).

"Pluralism" is also associated with Pragmatism and other forms of Naturalism, signifying the giving up of the attempt to trace all reality back to either one principle (Monism) or two (Dualism). It resigns itself to many kinds of reality not in any necessary consistency or unity with one another at all.

"Organismic Philosophy" or "Organicism" are terms that are being used for the especially thorough attempts to work out a complete metaphysics on the basis of the idea of process, with special emphasis on the fact that process operates "organically" and creatively, rather than mechanistically, and this means holistically rather than atomistically. In the greatest of these philosophers, Alfred North Whitehead, the question whether he still assumes SM becomes very difficult to decide, but the author is satisfied that he is not as clear about DM as he could be.[1] "Emergent Evolutionism" is a closely related term.

"Existentialism", in its modern agnostic form, so popular in Europe since World War II, finds it necessary simply to accept Reality as consisting of "Existence" as man discovers it moment by moment — a risky, struggling existence that calls upon us to be constantly making decisions in the midst of crises. It is impossible to know beforehand of any absolute rules or divine indications what we ought to do — that is, we have no knowledge of absolute "essences" prior to immediate existence. "Existence precedes Essence." The atheistic form of existentialism explicitly denies any possibility of deriving such a kind of reality from any understanding of an intelligible meaning behind the cosmos. The resulting picture is one of creatures that accidentally appear within reality, and must gropingly create themselves, so to speak, through their decisions concerning the emergencies and materials that "Existence" arbitrarily thrusts at them. Also, there is no hope of any final success in their strivings, and they must be prepared to lose all attainment at any time, to start over again, and finally to die without any sort of "Essential" immortality. It seems apparent that these thinkers still conceive of "Essence" after the manner of SM, and are honest enough to admit that an Existence of dynamic creativity does not fit its implications.

The term "Realism" remains unallotted in our classification, though we have made a good deal of use of its opposite "Idealism." Actually "Realism" (in its modern use) seems more confined to epistemological matters than Idealism is. Its essential affirmation is that there are objects and processes of nature that are "Real" in their own right: that is, that they exist whether any mind, cosmic or human, is observing them or thinking about or desiring them or not. Realism sets itself against the "Appearance" or "Illusion" device that Idealism is always so tempted to use in escaping the apparent hard facts. One who proudly insists that he is "realistic" usually means to indicate that he resists believing that anything is true or real just because he would enjoy believing it. He means that he is one who "faces facts" however unpleasant, and refuses any kind of wishful dreaming to soften those facts or eliminate them. He is highly impressed with the fact that there is a world of things outside of himself that does not bow to him and his wishes; that stubbornly pursues its way regardless of his own awareness of it or wishes for it. He especially insists that there are evils that cannot be explained away.

Any one of the above forms of Naturalism can also uphold Realism. But apparently a realist can also believe in God — that is, in the thesis that reality as a whole is the work of a cosmic mind. In this case his realism is only insisting that there are realities independent of *human* minds, or his *own* mind, not of a cosmic mind.

We finally come back again to the use of the term "Idealism" in Type III philosophy. As we have been using the term in the first two sections, it means any philosophy that tries to find a way of believing that the facts of reality fit the requirements of meaning and value, so that one may conclude that reality exemplifies, or is under the direction of, or has been created by, Ideas, values, or mind. Now ordinarily, as we have said, these naturalistic philosophies do not go so far as to make this statement in the maximum, cosmic sense. They would usually call themselves realist for this reason, maintaining that there are real things that exist independently of any kind of mental knowing or intending, human *or* cosmic. However, the distinction gets blurred, and Organismic philosophy, for instance, is presented by some as a synthesis of Realism and Idealism.

Now, in case a would-be idealist feels that dynamic theory of reality is definitely not what a cosmic mind aiming at SM would have created, he might still resort to the same kind of methods his earlier prototypes used to erase any conflict: either to insist once more that DR belongs to the realm of illusion; or else that it is a second realm, a stubborn "Given", that is there for no reason except brute fact. Examples of this attitude can be found in some Personalists, and possibly in Whitehead, who defend a fully personal idea of God but frankly admit that He cannot be omnipotent, for the process of reality, with its occasional failures and evils, could not be entirely imputed to His creative intention and design. Brightman, for instance, grants that there must be a Given beyond God's intentional control that forces the creation to be imperfect, when it should be perfect if he were omnipotent — that is, according to SM.

Type IV. DM with DR: Dynamic Naturalistic Idealism.

Our own approach on the basis of the dynamic idea of value will be presented under this heading as a fourth type of philosophy, which provides a basis for making a higher claim in regard to cosmic purpose than Types II or III, without having to distort or dismiss facts as Type I must do.

This philosophy, of course, results from combining DR with DM, which means that instead of trying to change modern, dynamic science's notion of the facts, or to rob them of reality (as so many kinds of idealism and organized religion have always done) we make a fundamental change, at last, on the *Meaning* side of the equation. This change to a dynamic idea of value has already been outlined, and will be filled out more and more throughout the remainder of the book. It enables us to defend the thesis that the dynamic world, including its imperfection and evil, which current science reveals to us, is precisely what the dynamic idea of meaning and value *requires;* thus precisely what could be expected of a cosmic purpose, an omnipotent, good, creator God.

This completes the basic varieties of philosophy. The remaining possible combinations of ideas of Meaning and Reality (DM with SIR, DM with SMR) do not need to be taken up, obviously, since there has been no occasion for them to become living philosophies.

In the remaining chapters, the preceding structure of discussion will be applied to each problem of philosophy. This structure of discussion is, briefly:

SM with SIR:
  The implications of SM to the topic in question.
  The adjustments that SIR makes in its theory of phenomena to achieve congruence with SM on the topic.

SM with SMR:
  The theory of SMR concerning the facts in the topic.
  The contradictions between SMR and SM-SIR. Recourses that have been used to escape them.

SM with DR:
  The theory of DR concerning the facts in the topic.
  Comparison of DR with SM.

DM with DR:
  The implications of DM to the topic in question and their correspondence with DR.

Since the implications of DM are always very close to what DR finds in fact, it is usually not necessary to present much new material under DM with DR, beyond pointing out its harmony with the details presented at length under SM with DR.

The general problems of philosophy are divided into the three familiar categories of Epistemology, Ontology or Metaphysics, and Axiology. In Part II on Epistemology, the theories of how man attains knowledge of what is real are taken up. This material has a special relationship to the "Cosmic" term in our basic formula for meaningfulness. Part III on Ontology deals with the resulting conclusions on the fundamental nature of reality — its substance, units and causal relationships. These questions relate especially to the "Purpose" term in the basic formula. In Part IV, on axiology, we come back to a more detailed consideration of value and evaluation, concluding with a consideration of the problem of evil. In Part V, Philosophy of Religion, the final conclusions about our knowledge of Cosmic Purpose are dealt with. Having considered how man can know truth in finite matters within his own experience in Part II, we thus finally consider what man can know about the cosmic extent of such truth.

PART II

EPISTEMOLOGY: THEORIES OF KNOWLEDGE
(THE PROBLEM OF KNOWLEDGE)

CHAPTER V

THE SOURCES AND CONSTRUCTION OF KNOWLEDGE

The method of acquiring knowledge, how to ascertain the truth about reality, is a prior topic. Although it is difficult to decide whether epistemology or ontology presupposes concepts from the other more, we will start with the former. Also, there is a certain affinity between the problem of knowledge and our first term ("Cosmic") in the basic formula for meaningfulness — that is, the problem of knowledge grows especially acute on the question whether man can know anything of the nature of the universe as a whole. On that additional hint, then, we will adopt the present sequence.

This chapter will give some of the essential contrasts between the types of philosophy just outlined on (1) the sources, and (2) the method of constructing or developing knowledge.

SM with SIR.

Implications of SM: 1. Sources. Our first step is to understand what sort of thing the static idea of meaning and value implies that knowledge and its source *should* be. The static idea of good, we saw, implies that value might exist in a state of changeless perfection, as an essence or quality. As we shall explain in Chapter VII, there is a connection between this assumption and the notion that reality, if it is to exemplify value, need be no more than a realm of thought or ideas; also that this realm might as well consist of already perfect thoughts or ideas which need not necessarily undergo any growth or change. Plato conceived "reality" to be just such a mental realm of perfect forms or ideas, perhaps contained in the mind of God, but not necessarily embodied in any material. The world of moving and changing material things was less real, or even (for more extreme idealists) nothing but appearance or illusion.

77

What should the source of man's knowledge of this fixed truth be, then? In strictest static logic, he should not need to "start" a process of knowing it at all, but should know it fully at once. The basic notion is that the mind should not have to create solutions to problems, but that it need only reflect or mirror pre-existent perfect truth; it need only passively "know" what is already there. Knowledge should be already deposited with no process of building it up required at all. Why would not a perfect God outfit His creatures with final knowledge to start with, if development of thought is not necessary for Good?

The term "a priori" is often used for this knowledge already in the mind prior to dynamic experience, search and solution. One of the many senses of "intuition" also refers to a direct insight into truth without having to reason it out or construct it in any way.

SM might also imply divine revelation as a source of knowledge, if that means that God dictates all truth in a prior announcement for men to know fully and immediately. Early thinkers seem always to assume that their customs and beliefs were commanded by God or gods who knew from the first moment how things are and should be for all time.

2. Construction. It is already clear that strictly speaking, there is no implication from the static idea of value that the value of Truth would need to be constructed in any sense. Only an unchanging mind contemplating fixed, ready-made truth is implied. It is not even implied that such a mind should have to go to the trouble of deducing consequences from given premises.

Adjustments of SIR: 1. Sources. Now men discovered, of course, that intuitions were not always perfectly correct; and that various scriptures claiming divine finality contradicted one another, or even were internally self-contradictory. What was to be done now? Traditional thinking accepts the sources implied by SM as much as it can, but it perforce must recognize that there is a certain amount of effort and modification involved in using them, however un-called-for by SM.

First SIR has to make greater use of *authoritarianism*. In the absence of intuited certainty or unambiguous revelation for each individual immediately, men fall back upon the opinions of certain special men who, it is hoped, have some better contact with truth than the general run. Assuming that certain superior men in the past received perfect truth, perhaps directly from God's original dictation, it becomes important to hand this truth down with unchanged accuracy, from authority to authority. If truth never changes, and if early geniuses had found it, then later mankind had nothing more to do than to receive and pass on the fixed truth forever. The extremes to which this attitude was carried — with medieval doctors preferring to believe Aristotle's erroneous count of horse's teeth to what their own senses reported — have been a laughing matter to us ever since.

Faith is sometimes listed as one of the traditional sources of truth — about the nature of reality as well as about its meaning. However, faith does not seem as much a source of information as an attitude toward sources. At least in one of its traditional meanings it has meant a kind of stubborn insistence on believing in the utterances of custom or of authority, either in the absence of personal experience and evidence, or in spite of them. In this sense, of course, it would seem difficult to defend it as source of knowledge. In another sense, faith may have a part to play in any complete theory of knowledge: since it is impossible for each of us in one short life-time to go through all the personal experiments that might demonstrate truth in every area of thought, we are forced to take much of our belief from faith and authority. But we expect the authority to have had the requisite experience, and to place upon public record, as modern scientific authorities do, the evidence and methods by which he arrived at his conclusions, permitting one to follow it through for himself, if he wishes to. Actually, then, authority can never be more than a practical aid to which we are forced to turn for many matters of knowledge. And when authorities or faiths conflict with one another, men are driven on to seek more genuine sources of truth.

Intuition: We saw that intuition was implied in a purely static sense by SM. The conception of intuition can be modified for SIR's purposes, as by Plato, to allow for the effort which is discovered to be necessary to become clear about *a priori* knowledge. Thinking especially of mathematical knowledge, Plato suggested that we are born with a complete complement of knowledge already in our minds. But something has made us forget it; therefore it remains only to clear away the cobwebs and become conscious of, or "remember", what is already established in our minds. For instance, we seem to understand immediately — that is with only a little reflection not dependent on the sense-organs — the axioms of Euclid's geometry. We "know" that parallel lines will never meet, without having to go out and measure actual lines and angles. We know that "if equals be added to equals, the sums are equal," without having to try it out with apples, or sticks, or money.

In early modern times, Descartes revived this same emphasis on intuition as the source of knowledge:

> By intuition I understand, not the fluctuating testimony of the senses, nor the misleading judgment that proceeds from the blundering constructions of imagination, but the conception which an unclouded and attentive mind gives us so readily and distinctly that we are wholly freed from doubt about that which we understand. Or, what comes to the same thing, *intuition* . . . springs from the light of reason alone; it is more certain than deduction itself, in that it is simpler. . . . Thus each individual can mentally have intuition of the fact that he exists, and that he thinks; that the triangle is bounded by three lines only, the sphere by a single superficies, and so on.[1]

This quotation also shows the connection between intuitional theory of the sources of knowledge and rationalistic theory of the method of knowledge (see #2). Perhaps we might speak in passing of "reason" as a source here, distinguished from reason as a method of constructing knowledge. But when considered as a source, the meaning seems identical with what we have just said above under intuition. The term "self-evident" is also often used in this connection: the source of knowledge is in "self-evident" principles, immediately grasped by reason. Self-evidence, however, might better be argued to belong in the next chapter on methods of testing truth.

Mysticism: Mystical experience as a source of knowledge is closely related to the above concept of intuition. When we ask, where did the great authority get *his* knowledge, the answer often is that he got it while in a special state of mind that highly enhanced his ability to grasp truth in all its perfection.

> The Mystics believe that certain kinds of knowledge, particularly knowledge of God, come not through the labored efforts of reflective thinking, but through direct insight and intui-

tion. The powers of reason may sometimes be transcended and we may have a direct approach to God, or an immediate union with reality, so that truth is felt, apprehended, or grasped in a single pulse of the soul life.[2]

Mysticism can be thought of in two ways. It may mean either (1) that this wonderful state of mind increased the seer's intuitional powers so that he could understand more clearly what was already present somewhere in his mind; or (2) that his mind was so prepared and purified that he was able to receive a direct communication of truth from some supernatural power. In either case, mysticism connotes a certain marvelous state of consciousness. In the past it has been habitually associated with such mental phenomena as dreams, voices, and trances, which the modern mind is rather inclined to class as abnormal. On the other hand, when we understand such methods of attaining mystical insight as meditation or Yoga, it does not seem to be entirely without acceptable rationale. For what the seer is apparently trying to do is to train his entire organic and mental processes up to a height of efficiency, purity and unity. Therefore why should we not expect him to reach some superior grasp on the meaning of things if he has so athleticized his organism, especially his nervous system and brain? In this sense, we shall find a permanent place for mystical consciousness in a modern theory of knowledge.

Sensory Experience: SIR is naturally reluctant to admit that knowledge should depend in any way on the fragmentary and changeable phenomena of sensory experience; or that it should have to be laboriously constructed from these blank, non-self-explanatory sources. Besides, the sense organs have a habit of failing to confirm, in any simple way, what the above sources of knowledge often claim. Therefore, SIR tends to discount what our sense organs report, and to emphasize how prone to error they are. Plato gave the sense organs no other function than to confirm, in their weak, inaccurate way, that reality did conform sufficiently to the knowledge gotten from inside the mind. Aristotle gave the senses somewhat more emphasis than this, but was in more hurry to pass to rational theories after only a small amount of sense observation than are either SMR or DR. We have just referred to Descartes' suspicion of knowledge based on sense experience, though he was a pioneer in modern science. However, as a mathematician, he did not realize how much science was going to turn to the empirical approach of his earlier contemporary, Francis Bacon.

2. Construction. SIR is forced to concede to the notion of thought *development* only the minimal necessity of deducing details of truth from the given, intuited or revealed, premises. Such rationalism still finds no essential place for sensory experience. Plato admits that the mind has fallen at the outset, for some unknown reason, into a vague and muddy state, forgetting some of its pre-endowment of knowledge. But it has the ability to expand from a few basic truths which intuition or revelation have reminded it of to further detailed knowledge, by a process of reasoning, using formal methods of mathematics and deductive logic. The power of knowing correct logical and mathematical implications is built into men's mind in the same intuitional manner that the original principles themselves were. Descartes restated the same method in early modern philosophy. Following his statement about intuition (p. 80), he goes on to one about deductive reasoning:

> . . . We are in a position to raise the question as to why we have, besides intuition, given this supplementary method of knowing, viz., knowing by *deduction,* by which we understand all necessary inference from other facts that are known with certainty. This, however, we could not avoid, because many things are known with certainty, though not by themselves evident, but only deduced from true and known principles by the continuous and uninterrupted action of a mind that has a clear vision (intuition) of each step in the process . . . the first principles themselves are given by intuition alone, while, on the contrary, the remote conclusions are furnished only by deduction.
>
> These two methods are the most certain routes to knowledge, and the mind should admit no others. All the rest should be rejected as suspect of error and dangerous.[3]

This statement also illustrates the rationalist's demand for *certainty* of knowledge, and this has an obvious relationship to the static presumptions of SM. For man could not have final certainty unless truth never changed. Strangely enough, this method with its claim of certainty, was never able to achieve universal agreement among men, whereas DR's method, as we shall see, not claiming certainty, attains a much larger measure of agreement.

For the intuitional and rationalistic method was more and more found to fail to guarantee absolute knowledge which could compel all men to agree to it. Experience and observation kept failing to confirm its deductions and kept producing new findings never suspected by SM-SIR.

SM with SMR.

Findings of SMR: 1. Sources. Early modern science, then, began in skepticism of the supposedly divinely revealed, intuited or self-evident principles. Bacon, Hobbes, Descartes and the other pioneers of the new empirical method ridiculed the endless conflict among authorities, the lack of any check upon biases (Bacon's "Idols"), the indisputable errors of "self-evidence," the failure to bring forth much practical knowledge of how to control nature, the triviality and uselessness of much of the formal deductive conclusions, etc. Very few of the "truths" formerly claimed as self-evident have not been either doubted or actually disproved. The claims of mystics have never convinced large percentages of the human race; and too many beliefs which their holders saw with perfect clarity have turned out to be unfounded in nature. For instance, it was *not* self-evident or even true that heavy bodies would fall faster than light ones; it is *not* logically necessary that there be a First Mover. As for miraculous mystical visions, Hume pointed out that they are too prone to take place only in ignorant and uneducated sections of the world.

Empiricism: Thus the early founders of SMR concluded that, fallible though SIR had proven the senses to be, there still was nothing else to base knowledge on: men would have to make the best of sensory experience. "Empiricism" is the theory of the source of knowledge accepted by early modern science, and still strongly emphasized by late modern science, though perhaps not so exclusively as it was. Locke in the eighteenth century made the most famous statement of the empirical starting point when, in rejecting the belief in self-evident principles built into the mind, he memorably likened the mind to a blank tablet quite empty of any ideas until the senses began feeding some into it. Earlier, Francis Bacon had been so anxious to break with the medieval emphasis on intuition and deduction, that he tried to do with a purely empirical method of knowledge that involved nothing but sensory experience and induction. However, as we shall see in #2, science soon had to readmit something of rationalism into its method.

At this point, we find the early empiricists employing the term "intuition" again, but in quite a new sense. They granted that the mind knew something immediately — but it was not the *a priori,* self-evident truths of SM; it was merely the simplest direct consciousness of sense impressions themselves. The incontrovertible fact that one is at this moment hearing a tone of sound, or feeling a pain, or seeing a patch of yellow color would be all that the earlier empiricist would allow to "intuition."

Now in conceiving its experiential starting point, earlier science fell into certain errors almost as crippling for truth as the preceding dogmatism based on supposed self-evidence.

I. Static Errors. (A) Knowledge as Passive Reflection.

To begin with, the whole earlier conception of science was vitiated by its carrying over SM's underlying notion of knowledge as static mirroring, except that now it was reflecting an external material world rather than a system of ideas. The mind was thought of as passively receiving into itself by way of the senses, a picture of the things, the reality, that existed outside of it. The knower was conceived as inertly regarding the outer world. He was not essentially acting in that world, desiring, needing, selecting, creating solutions to specific problems; he was just disinterestedly "soaking up" whatever happened to lie before him.

(B) Ignoring Dynamic Aspects of Sensation and Feeling.

Therefore, the senses were regarded only in their aspects as transmitters of factual data about external objects; they were only passive doorways through which streamed neutral signs indicating that something existed out there. Early science (which was all in the area of Physical science) confined itself to sensory experience taken only as cues to the existence and to the quantitative, measurable aspects of external objects. The qualitative and feeling aspects of sensory and other experiences — the fact that they give us enjoyment or pain — was ignored, except insofar as qualitative differences need to be distinguished in order to determine external existences. For instance, one must be able to distinguish the quality red from blue in observing litmus paper in order to know whether acid or base exists before one; but one does not regard the colors for the enjoyment of their quality as such.

This disregard of qualitative feeling is of course justified from a certain point of view in physical science. Human enjoyment, desire, preference must be kept out of scientific research, insofar as they might bias the findings. Scientific obectivity still requires that the scientist never accept anything as true simply because it would be pleasant to believe it. He emphasizes those sensory experiences that seem most dependent upon objective events, least influenced by subjective desires. However, it seems that the physical scientist's ignoring for his special purposes this factor of qualitative enjoyment as such, has led to a pervasive tendency today to suppose that science proves that feeling and enjoyment of qualities are somehow not as real and as significant a part of reality as are the quantitative aspects of what appears to the senses; and when limited as we have just indicated, the senses seem to testify that pieces of unconscious, feelingless matter are the most real things. The notion of blind, dead matter following purposeless but inexorable laws of motion (see Part III) was the main product of the early physical scientist's peculiar way of regarding his senses (especially vision) as essentially passive transmitters of neutral cues.

(C) Taking Macroscopic Impressions at Face Value.

Another aspect of the earlier empirical approach that led to this unattractive outcome was that it quite naturally paid attention primarily to those of our senses that are most definite and conscious, which happen also to be the ones most adapted to receiving or "mirroring" data from the external world. These are touch and vision. These senses were directed at first, naturally, to the more available and obvious objects in the environment — the larger or "macroscopic" things that give those senses such a strong impression of being made of "solid matter." Nowadays we are aware of the fact that there is apparently a good deal more in "matter" than what these particular sense organs are capable of registering; but in earlier science, the reports of touch and vision were taken at face value, thus giving rise to the mechanistic concept of matter which we will study in a later chapter.

A recognition of the inadequacy of this static conception of sensory experience provides one way out from the purposeless, meaningless world of the earlier physics.

II. Atomistic Errors.

The tendency to explain everything too atomistically will be understood more fully later as the result of the conception of solid material atoms; applied to sensory experience it led to the theory that all knowledge arises from individual, disconnected atomistic sensations. It implied that in vision, for instance, the first thing we are aware of is a vast number of individual rays, or specks of light. Each individual cell of the retina of the eye is separately stimulated by its own ray of light. In hearing, each separate cell of the ear is stimulated by its own separate tone of sound. Afterward somehow, all these individual sensations are "associated" so that we finally realize that we are seeing the image of a single plaid shirt perhaps, made up of innumerable different-colored rays of light received by innumerable retinal cells. And yet, it was never completely explained just *what* it was that was seeing this unified object. If nothing exists but the individual cells and light rays, how do we ever pass over from the experience of a collection of separate flashes of colored lights to the experience of a unified object or pattern which we (as somehow a unity in ourselves) sense as one thing? How is it that we do not hear only a collection of separate tones, but that we also have a unique impression of harmony as such? No adequate explanation has ever been given how, if you assume that objects and sense organs are essentially to be identified with their ultimate parts, or atoms, experiences and ideas of wholes and relationships can possibly exist.

We must quote again the much quoted passage from Hume that denies that there is any unified entity, such as the self, or any unified comprehensions of wholes for such a self to have.

There are some philosophers who imagine we are every moment intimately conscious of what we call our *self*, that we feel its existence and its continuance in existence. . . . For my part, when I enter most intimately into what I call *my-self*, I always stumble upon some particular perception or other, of heat or cold, light or shade, love or hatred, pain or pleasure. I never can catch *myself* at any time without a perception, and never can observe anything but the perception. . . . [The mind or self is] nothing but a bundle or collection of different perceptions, which succeed each other with an inconceivable rapidity and are in a perpetual flux and movement. . . .[4]

This question of the atomicity of sensations is important; because such ideas as Meaning, Purpose, Value will be found to involve essentially the reality of wholes, patterns, relationships — i.e. of parts that are together in wholes. The older empiricism made it impossible to explain what knowledge of wholes could be; and thus ultimately contributed to the still popular notion that science proves there is no meaning, purpose or value in reality.

2. Construction. We will now outline the empirical or scientific method with special reference to the earlier limitations in men's understanding of it. Conceived even this narrowly, scientific method still created more agreement and more useful results than man had ever before known.

I. The first step for earlier theory was *observation* by the senses. That is, what was discussed above under #1 as SMR's empirical origin takes its place here as the first step of scientific method. We remember the basic analogy of the mirror passively reflecting whatever data lie before it. Discussions during the 16th to 19th centuries did not bring out the "awareness of a problem" explicitly, as we shall find it under DR. Bacon's illustration of his pure inductive method suggested that we make long lists of "instances" each of which contained some common feature, such as heat, which we might be studying. We simply collect, exhaustively, and at random, a vast number of observations.

He held that, by recording all available facts, making all possible observations, performing all feasible experiments, and by collecting and tabulating the results by rules which he only very imperfectly formulated, the connections between the phenomena would become manifest and general laws describing their relations would emerge almost automatically.[5]

As we shall see under DR, this approach fails to acknowledge the *selective* or *directed* approach of the scientist and thereby misses an essential feature of the knowledge process. Of course, Bacon actually was selective in his observation, being guided by his problem "What is heat?" But he made nothing of this selection as such.

To Galileo goes the credit of adding to Bacon's theory of observation, that precise measurement should be used wherever possible. Descartes included among his rules too, the necessity of "dividing" or analyzing the matter into its parts. This analytical feature of earlier method, emphasized at the expense of any understanding of the equal place of "synthesis" led to some of its worst errors as we shall see.

If we take Galileo's classic work on discovering the law of acceleration as illustration of this earlier understanding of scientific method, we would begin with his observing objects — pieces of wood, rocks, feathers — falling. Then we would suppose that these sensations, passively received into his mind, somehow enforce the appearance of an explanatory idea in a kind of inevitable, mechanical way. But this is already the second step of the method.

II. The Induction or tentative explanation. Induction refers to the mode of thought by which the mind passes from observation of particulars, or individual sensory data, to generalizations or universals, the concepts or principles that the particular data seem to exemplify. This generalization is called the hypothesis, at this stage, since it is as yet a tentative guess until it is verified (which step belongs in the next chapter). In SMR's earlier interpretation, however, the hypothesis would have been thought of more as a necessary, automatic product of the data. Bacon suggests that the mind, in reviewing the data, arranged in tables of instances positive and negative, is compelled by the data itself to conceive a generalization that relates the data intelligibly.

The British empiricists from Bacon and Locke to Hume, assuming the atomistic notion of sensations and mental activity, tried to work out an "associationist" theory of mental induction to explain the mind's power of putting specific sensations together into general ideas. The theory was never entirely satisfactory however, as Hume saw, both because it did not really explain how a collection of particular sensations got transformed into a single idea which itself was not a sensation, nor how we could know the general idea was universally true, when we could never experience or sense more than a finite number of instances of it. This is the problem of induction which will be discussed further in the next chapter.

III. The Deduction. Bacon had wanted to exclude deduction from his method, while Descartes saw no essential place for induction. It was Galileo who first incorporated both into scientific method, seeing that one needed to go on and deduce logical consequences from his hypothesis to be further tested in experience. Neither the induction from observation nor the deduction from hypotheses could be trusted to produce certain truth; further verification was always needed. What Bacon had really done was to find a better way than either authority or intuition to provide premises for deductions.

In Galileo's particular work in gravitation, he reasoned, "If my hypothesis is true, what else should be true — especially what other *measurable* thing would be true?" He then went through a rather complex series of deductions that finally issued in his believing that balls rolling down an inclined plane would follow the same law as freely falling bodies; but their velocity would be easier to measure. And definite measurement would show whether his hypothesis about their rate of acceleration was confirmed or not.

This is as far as our present topic of "construction" goes. The last step of scientific method, verification, belongs in the next chapter.

Contradictions between SM and SMR; Recourses: To understand fully why SMR's method of knowledge left many unsatisfied, so that they wished they could get back to something of SIR's kind of knowledge, we would need to jump ahead to the next chapter to see how many former beliefs had become unprovable by this method. Every traditional faith or intuition that could not be traced to definite atomized sensations lost its standing as knowledge. However definite, precise and useful for the control of nature SMR's knowledge may have been, its method seems to eliminate the kind of knowledge this book is concerned with — knowledge of the meaning of things, of "why" they exist. It also seems to have no place for the broad, though vague, wisdom, very useful for the survival of individual and race, that had got built up in SIR, however erroneous its knowledge method often proved to be.

For SMR addresses itself exclusively to the questions "what exists", and "how does it operate." Galileo was aware that he had departed from the scholastic concern with explaining why things were as they were, the answer having been always in terms of a complete rationalistic system of ideas that seemed to call for or require each partial thing, and to relate it to an ultimate purpose that produced the whole system. Galileo admitted that he did not know why objects fell with a speed proportional to the square of the time; he had satisfied himself with measuring *how* they fell, and he knew that bit of knowledge more certainly than anyone had ever known anything, though he knew no reason why for it. He did not even allow himself to assert that any force made objects fall, let alone that any God did. No force could be seen any more than a God could be seen.

As a matter of fact, Galileo's one bit of new knowledge happened to contradict traditional beliefs (SIR) in such a manner as to result in the total destruction of Aristotelian and medieval Physics. Where they had assumed the necessity of a constant force (God) to keep things moving, it was implied in Galileo's experimenting that things would move forever *without* any force; force (if such an invisible thing is to be mentioned at all) would be required only when the *rate* of motion was to be changed (accelerated or slowed) in any way.

In Galileo we also see that *analytical* attitude that was to characterize SMR for the next few centuries: breaking up the field of study into smaller, more manageable units of experiment, and contentment with isolated bits of knowledge; the relinquishing (temporarily supposedly, but permanently for many individuals of the age) of the scholastic hope of understanding the whole scheme of things.

> The old assumption of a complete and rationalized scheme of knowledge . . . has been given up. Facts are no longer deduced from and obliged to conform with, an authoritative and rational synthesis. . . . Each fact acquired by observation or experiment is accepted as it stands, with its immediate and inevitable consequences, irrespective of the human desire to make the whole of nature at once amenable to reason. Concordances between the isolated facts appear but slowly, and the little spheres of knowledge surrounding each fact come into touch here and there, and perhaps coalesce into larger spheres. The welding of knowledge, scientific or philosophical, into a higher and all-embracing unity, if not seen to be forever impossible, is relegated to the distant future.[6]

In short, SMR's method leads into the problem of specialization and fragmentation of knowledge which was mentioned (p.18) as the first block to knowledge of meaningfulness. It also illustrates the disconnectedness typical of the second stage of process in general (see p. 96 below). Thus men were no sooner elated over SMR's superiority over SIR's knowledge method in making contact with reality, than they were desperate to escape from its frigid findings about reality.

Kant strove for a compromise which would keep thought empirically in touch with the facts of Nature, as he saw the purely rationalist and intuitionist sources did not necessarily do; but would also achieve some understanding and certainty about relations and causal connections between the facts as Humean sensationalism failed to do. His solution was to admit that the mind was dependent on sensations for its contact with real fact, but that it itself contributed the forms and connections that made the sensations add up to knowledge of necessary relations.

We must credit Kant with making an important correction of the atomistic error above in his theory of "transcendental unity of apperception." He knew we must have some explanation of "putting together" sensations into concepts of understanding, and he directed attention to the reciprocal whole-part relationships in organisms and minds. The mind as a unity begins by asking its own questions of nature. It then directs its attention to those sensations that seem relevant, imposing its own forms or categories — such as quantitative, mathematical concepts, qualitative classes, spatial, temporal and causal connections, etc. — upon the data. By selecting and putting sensations together in these ways, the mind arrives at intelligible theories of regular relationships.

Kant, however, continued to conceive the mind, its sensing, its logic and its object (Nature) too statically, without enough emphasis on both mind and nature as comparable dynamisms, where the mind's interested and creative feelings find a counterpart in nature. Kant, then, thought his approach could achieve certain knowledge of some rational routines in nature, but it had to pay a terrible price for this certainty: the inability to know whether nature itself — "things in themselves" —had any likeness to the mind's picture of them, or not. His compromise thus gave us certainty about "phenomena", the mental experiences that result from the interaction of the mind with sensations caused by real objects, without letting us know much about the objects themselves. And what we can know of phenomena in any case seems rather idle, i.e. of little concern to the hopes and fears that really concern us.

Of course, Kant did go on to make a place for that kind of

91

knowledge men care more about, i.e., knowledge of values and religious realities. This was the domain of "practical reason", and our hopes and feelings had some scope here. But they were not as central as they became for later idealists and post-evolutionary philosophers. These tried many ways of assuring that the mental contribution to knowledge was more truly revelatory of nature-in-itself than Kant would allow. In so doing they moved closer and closer to DR.

Fichte was one of the first to suggest that "things-in-themselves" were more mind-like than Kant thought; and since for Fichte the mind itself was like will and feeling more than reason, then nature-in-itself must be too. Hegel returned toward Kant's rationality, only he began to correct the static error (p. 84) by trying to formulate a dynamic logic. Mind was a process of discriminating, then synthesizing opposites. He was also confident that all reality was the same sort of thing, so that in fully understanding our own mental process, we would have an adequate understanding of Nature-in-itself. Reflection on our own mental dialectic, then, was Hegel's source of knowledge of Nature's dialectic. Sensations were, for him, merely an early and undeveloped level of this mental understanding, a step on the way to full self-consciousness and comprehension. Schopenhauer returned to Fichte's emphasis on will, desire and feeling as the nature of both mind and Nature, with sensation and rationality only secondary and dependent. Bergson's source was the mind's instinctive experience of "duration", of real temporal process, from which definite sensations and intellection then evolved as supplementary but never completely adequate powers.

But these views have already taken us within the boundaries of DR, adumbrating its dynamic and holistic corrections upon SMR's approach.

In summary, the methods of SIR and SMR oscillated between producing meaningful systems without sure contact with fact; and factual knowledge without sure contact with values and meanings. The predominant opinion today is that these attempts to defend meaning and purpose by building speculative systems, while conceding that empirical method by itself was bound always to support SMR's mechanistic world picture, were not convincing. It continued to be SMR's science that discovered new things never suspected by the idealists nor deduced from their systems, while the idealists could only react and try to adjust themselves to each new discovery. Today, interest has turned to criticism of SMR's method itself, and to seeking legitimate ways to broaden it and to incorporate into it whatever is justified of the more systematic emphasis of rationalism.

SM with DR.

Findings of DR: 1. Sources. For Americans it is the pragmatists — Peirce, James, Dewey — who have given us our most familiar presentation of the dynamic, felt experience in which knowledge begins. James' great *Psychology* first apprised us of the new views of the mind as a continuous, dynamic, active process. The knower does not start out idly aware of precise, discrete sensations showering upon him, but is already engaged in directed processes, paying selective attention to such phenomena as he desires or needs. As Dewey puts it:

> We are only just now commencing to appreciate how completely exploded is the psychology that dominated philosophy throughout the eighteenth and nineteenth centuries. According to this theory, mental life originated in sensations which are separately and passively received, and which are formed, through laws of retention and association, into a mosaic of images, perceptions, and conceptions. The senses were regarded as gateways or avenues of knowledge. Except in combining atomic sensations, the mind was wholly passive and acquiescent in knowing. Volition, action, emotion, and desire follow in the wake of sensations and images. The intellectual and cognitive factor comes first and emotional and volitional life is only a consequent conjunction of ideas with sensations of pleasure and pain.
> The effect of the development of biology has been to reverse the picture. Wherever there is life, there is behavior, activity . . . adaptive adjustment . . . not wholly passive. . . .
> Note what a change this point of view entails in the traditional notions of experience. Experience becomes an affair primarily of doing. The organism does not stand about, Micawberlike, waiting for something to turn up. . . . The organism and environment, resulting in some adaptation which complex, upon its surroundings . . . the interaction of organism and environment, resulting in some adaptation which

secures utilization of the latter, is the primary fact, the basic category. Knowledge is relegated to a derived position, secondary in origin, even if its importance, when once it is established, is overshadowing. . . . The senses lose their place as gateways of knowing to take their rightful place as stimuli to action. To an animal an affection of the eye or ear is not an idle piece of information about something indifferently going on in the world. It is an invitation and inducement to act in a needed way. . . . The whole controversy between empiricism and rationalism as to the intellectual worth of sensations is rendered strangely obsolete.[7]

This statement includes correctives of most of the errors listed under SMR (p. 86 f.) Taking them in the same order:

I. Corrections of Static Errors.

(A) Knowledge as dynamic search rather than passive mirroring.

Instead of the static, mirror analogy for knowledge, we have the idea of a striving, creative, purposive process going on, with knowledge arising as a tool or instrument to enhance this process. The source of knowledge is within directed activity. This is sometimes also called the "Genetic" approach to knowledge with emphasis on the genesis of knowledge within the growing, self-maintaining activities of organisms.

(B) Dynamic and Qualitative Aspects of Sensation and Feeling.

The earlier conception of the source of knowledge in sensations considered as mere neutral cues to objective events is now viewed as too externalized and unselective. The whole project of seeking objective, scientific knowledge is now seen to take place within a purposive framework. Interest, feeling, evaluative selection are present from the beginning, directing the knower in the selection of what he will pay attention to. His mind is propelled by a sense of tension, a felt dissatisfaction in the puzzlement of the problem before him. A need or desire for a resolution of the tension motivates the search and effort to build a solution. And the solution, when it comes, is *enjoyed,* no matter how much the scientist meanwhile in honoring the ideal of objectivity has resisted subjective wishes. Though he uses his sensations, for scientific purposes, as much as possible only as objective tests of his solutions, he cannot deny that they are more fundamentally qualitative feelings themselves, and are in the service of more complex feelings of accomplishment.

(C) Macroscopic impressions qualified.

The new science, then, is not so inclined as earlier science to give the more static and externalized senses (touch and vision), as applied to large scale objects, special privileges in characterizing reality. When those senses seem to present us a picture of a feelingless, purposeless world of lumps of dead matter, we now realize that it is because they do not happen to be adapted to revealing more inner, dynamic and qualitative aspects of reality which we know, via other sources, truly exist. In pursuing the implications of what those senses themselves reported, considered as exclusively in their quantitative aspect as you please, science discovered that it could not take their impression of solid, inert matter at face value anyway. For the implication was to a world of whirling energy instead.

In general, the new empiricism broadens the meaning of "experience" to include, besides the older passive sensing, the entire dynamic process of living, including its aspects of aiming, searching, selecting, creating and enjoying. The feeling and qualitative aspects are as real and honorable as the quantitative and analytic.

II. Corrections of the atomistic error: Field, gestalt theory.

It is now widely accepted that experience and knowledge do not begin with precise, discrete sensations, but with vague awareness of whole objects and situations. Modern field or gestalt psychology has supported with experimental evidence Kant's speculative theories of the mind's ability to grasp patterned unities. It suggests in fact that a vague awareness of totality precedes and surrounds all analytic discrimination. This awareness includes the sense of significance, direction, interest mentioned above, as well as an immediate grasp of spread out spatial volumes and temporal extents. It is only afterwards that we focus attention on more precise sensations, through effortful discrimination of details, selected according to already existing purposes. Whitehead has made some of the best statements of this starting point.

> During many generations there has been an attempt to explain our ultimate insights as merely interpretative of sense-impressions. . . . I suggest to you that this basis for philosophic understanding is analogous to an endeavour to elucidate the sociology of modern civilization as wholly derivate from the traffic-signals on the main roads. The motions of the cars are

conditioned by these signals. But the signals are not the reasons for the traffic. . . .

It is this direct insight, vague as to detail and yet the basis of all rationality, that has been denied by the prevalent epistemology of the preceding century. Interest and importance are the primary reasons for the effort after exact discrimination of sense-data.[8]

Our primary experience is, rather than "high grade sensa of details," something so taken for granted that language hardly exists for it.

Our enjoyment of actuality is a realization of worth, good or bad. It is a value-experience. Its basic expression is — Have a care, here is something that matters! . . .

This experience provokes attention, dim and all but subconscious.[9]

This starting point would relieve us of SMR's hopeless task of explaining how awareness of wholes can ever come out of a collection of isolated, discrete sensations. Scientific analysis, the presumption now is, always takes place *within* a whole awareness that is already there. The knower always knows, vaguely, how the part that he is studying fits into its surroundings.

Within this total, living awareness, then, the knowledge process selects and refines, focussing attention on smaller wholes and more refined parts of wholes. If through exclusion and selection, SMR ends describing a neutral world of inert, well-defined objects and impersonal facts, this is because it has laboriously narrowed its attention to only those aspects. It is very important for modern thinking to deny that this narrowed, though more precise, knowledge is necessarily any closer to the "real" than the original more inclusive, though more vague, knowledge.

A threefold division of the knowledge process (and in fact, we shall find, of many if not all other processes) immediately suggests itself. The first phase would be this prior vague, undifferentiated condition. The middle phase would include the many steps of discrimination, moving toward ever more definite analysis of parts and details. The likelihood of confusion, tension and maladjustment among these parts would be present, as attention

96

focusses somewhat haphazardly within the original whole. A task of organizing and arranging the details thus arises, and is carried through an indefinite number of operations until we approach the third phase. This would be the return to the comprehension of the whole, except that now it is known as a definite pattern of definitely discriminated parts. A perfect design of the details within the whole would presumably remain an ideal, never finally attained. Thus we move from whole-without-parts through parts-without-whole, to whole-with-parts, or parts-in-design.

The first phase, and the beginnings of the second phase would fall under the present topic of "sources" of knowledge. And it would be within the transition to the second stage that we could find a place for many of the "sources" mentioned in the preceding divisions. Authority, for instance, would become essentially an aid in selecting where to focus attention. Every scientist as he starts his research refers to the authority of preceding researchers to hasten his own analysis by taking advantage of the precisions they have attained. Of course, the modern use of such authority requires that the authority stand ready to have his methods and reasoning critically reviewed or repeated whenever anyone else feels like taking the trouble. Thus the authoritativeness as such is not considered an ultimate source as SIR might have done. It is only a practical aid, referring back of itself to more ultimate sources.

There is a special strength that authority can conceivably possess, however, at least for the more complex beliefs in the realms of personal and social wisdom, ethics and religion. If we think of ancient authorities as representing the first of our three stages (in an application of them to the whole human race's growth in knowledge), they might demonstrate the special advantage that the first stage can often reveal: a certain freshness of grasp upon the main outlines of a truth. The first phase of vague, whole awareness is not necessarily erroneous; it may be merely hazy. The second phase, though more definite, has its own weakness — its tendency to lose itself among its details, forgetting the important base-lines of the problem, unable to see the forest for the trees. The ancient wise men, then, can serve to remind later analysts of significant cores.

The modern world is only too caught in "second phase" confusion — in fact, our "specialization and fragmentation," the first great block to belief in meaningfulness (Ch. I) is identical with it.

It is not only philosophers who have to reread their Plato and Aristotle to get their bearings, not only theologians who have to reread their Bible to recover the heights and the balance, however obscurely expressed, of earlier seers; but the scientists too, who must go back to Heraclitus or Democritus for hints about unnoticed assumptions that may have sent their work askew into years of barren research.[10] Men still have need of such early unspecialized authorities to keep them from the catastrophes brought on by such fragmentary gospels as "scientific Marxism" or "realistic Fascism."

Intuition and mystical experience, of the older "sources" can also find a place in the present theory of the origins of knowledge. In one sense they would simply be other names for this original vague awareness of wholeness. Intuition has other shades of meaning which we will find relate more to the creation of synthetic hypotheses under the next topic of method of construction of knowledge; and to the final return to holistic grasp discussed in Chapter VI. But it also has the present meaning, called by Wheelwright "pre-ratiocinative intuition", in contrast to that final type which he calls "post-ratiocinative" intuition.[11] We might include under this prior type that phenomenon which many have attributed to children: the ability to conceive and ask the profoundest questions, though they have not enough definite mental contents to either give or receive an answer.

Lastly, of the older sources, reason and sensory experience can now be seen as working more in the second phase of discrimination of detail, and thus will be better placed in # 2.

2. Construction. DR conceives scientific method as a more creative process than SMR's passive, mechanical one. Beginning in the above undifferentiated awareness, it proceeds to discriminate (or analyze) more partial and definite aspects of the situation. But DR then pays attention to a second and equally important phase: the synthesizing of the discriminated parts back into their places within a pattern or design of the whole. SMR thinks of knowledge too much as a collection of accurate pictures of isolated items. But the dynamic approach thinks of both reality and the mind's knowledge of it as processes of building organized patterns of energies and feelings that resolve tensions. Some sort of parts are always to be arranged both spatially and temporally in an ongoing creative process. Whitehead calls this basic characteristic of mind and nature "Composition."[12]

It is important to realize that as the knowledge process proceeds, the "composition" becomes constantly more inclusive, complex and interrelated. As the centuries of experience with scientific method passed, men became more conscious of the cumulation of knowledge. As the steps of the method were repeated in cycles, the hypotheses became ever more complex and whole in themselves. We saw in the earlier phases of any science, such as in Galileo's work, the problem and data men started with were more limited, simple, isolated, and disconnected from other knowledge; and the hypotheses and theories one comes to are less inclusive and less interconnected with others. These earlier, limited theories in turn become data, along with new evidence, for the next cycle of these steps of scientific method — producing more complex, inclusive and "explanatory" hypotheses within which the earlier theories take their place as sub-cases, and so on. In the next chapter we will find that this systematizing makes SMR's reconciling itself to never knowing the "why" of anything an apparently temporary emergency for mankind.

Some recent treatments (cf. Northrop, Titus) speak of "many scientific methods," listing Trial and Error, Experimentation, Sampling, Reflective Thinking, the Method of Hypothesis, the Method of Deductive Formulation, etc. Different types of problems are said to call for different methods of solution. However, this author prefers to stay with Dewey or Thomson, in considering the sequence of steps already introduced in SMR, and added to below, to be standard for all thinking. We shall consider some of those "methods" as either identical with one of the steps or as research techniques that may or may not be used within a certain step of the method. Different types of problems then may call for different emphases on one or the other of these techniques and steps.

In the following outline we discuss one new step added to SMR's method. For the other steps, we will discuss only the dynamic and holistic corrections to the steps already seen in SMR.

I. The Initiation of Inquiry. A. Awareness of Problem.

In older treatments (see p. 87 #I), the first step was thought to be a sort of idle awareness of precise, discrete sensations. We now add, as a new beginning step, this one, to contain what we have already said about the new conception of the origin of knowledge (p. 94f.). As scientific research begins in a vague grasp of a problematical situation, there are already hints as to the direction to search, as to what needs analysis, as to where the whole problem fits within the larger picture.

B. The Analysis of the Problem. Here scientific method attempts to advance from the vagueness of the starting point. It tries to locate the problem more exactly, formulate precisely what the contradiction is. It analyzes out some of the parts. We are still not ready actually, to begin "collecting data," the first step for Francis Bacon. There are too many facts in the world just to start collecting them at random. Of course, we already have some indeterminate data in step I A — the data that is giving rise to our sense of problem. This already restricts our field, indicates roughly what area to investigate for further facts. But in analyzing the problem more carefully we can probably narrow down our field even more, and in some types of problems get such an exact idea of what data we need that the data collecting can be done very rapidly. Other kinds of problems may never be able to reduce the collecting to a small task. Darwin collected material on species for years and years before he was ready to pass on to later steps. Yet analysis of his problem had already produced some hints of the evolutionary hypothesis, which helped him select data even at that early stage.

In some cases however, the problem is the other way around; we start off with some bias that leads us to restrict our data hunting too much, and then we cannot seem to get onto any fertile hypothesis. The only thing to do then is to broaden our search, begin paying attention to all kinds of possibly related facts. Whitehead insists on the importance of "assemblage" before too much analysis or systematization is done, avoiding in that way undue narrowness and specialism. Especially must *philosophy* "exclude nothing. Thus it should never start from systematization. Its primary stage can be termed assemblage."[13]

Looking again at Galileo's discovery of the law of falling bodies we would now surmise that he had already done a good deal of thinking before he began watching objects fall.[14] He became aware of a problem when he realized that Aristotle's explanation of motion of bodies did not adequately explain the motion of projectiles. For Aristotle, motion only took place while force was being applied. But projectiles kept moving after the force (the explosion) was over. Proceeding to analyze the problem, Galileo clarified the difficulty as being a matter of Aristotle's definition of force as related to *velocity* (rather than to *change* of velocity). This suggested just what kind of data he needed to observe — not so much projectiles as *any* body moving under a constant force — falling bodies under the influence of gravitation being simplest.

Northrop points out that this preliminary analysis of the problem is the point where scientific genius is most apparent. The great scientists show an ability to get at the heart of a problem, to reduce its vague complexity to some beautiful clarity. This analysis also indicates a great deal as to what methods of observation (in step II) would be best, and what emphasis each of the remaining steps will get. Copi calls this step that of "Preliminary Hypotheses."[15] Obviously a good deal of "rationalistic" method is called upon right here at the beginning of research.

II. Observation. A. Collecting Additional Data.

We have now arrived at the traditional starting point of science: the "empirical" or sensory-experience part. Of course in Step I above, we imply that the awareness of the problem arises partly from indefinite sensory experiences. But it is only now that the scientist begins to stress precise, measured sensations. It is now that the scientist needs his training in expert observation, where he must be superior to the ordinary man in clarity, precision, impartiality, caution. He must avoid selecting facts to suit his fancy, he must work out accurate methods of recording observations, must resist being satisfied with first impressions.

B. Arrangement, Classification of Facts.

In some research, the relevant data is so limited and simple that this step is accomplished almost simultaneously with the observation. Continuing with our example of Galileo's research on motion of bodies, his analysis of the projectile situation had indicated that the place to look for relevant phenomena was in the motion of freely falling bodies, acted on only by gravitation, since this was a simpler and more easily studied situation than that of projectiles. The fact gathering step, then, consisted of no more than watching falling bodies in hopes that something would be suggested to him. It was immediately apparent that three factors were present: the weight of the bodies, the distance they moved, the time. He probably tried to see as well as he could to which of these the velocity was related in any manner. Already he had three possible hypotheses each requiring that he figure out more accurate methods of observation in order to test them. But in Step II proper he had very little to do beyond the preliminary, rough watching of falling objects.

In other experiments dealing with more complex data, especially in biology or social science, this first tabulating, enumerating, graphing of data may take a longer time. In earlier phases of biological science there was a vast amount of collecting of specimens to be done followed by attempts to group or classify them according to various criteria. The evidence is analyzed, broken down to simpler terms, correlated. Not until then can hypotheses explaining their relationships begin to occur to men. This second step, in such cases, is sometimes called the "Natural History" stage of research, and it is understood that some branches of science, like biology or sociology, have scarcely got beyond this step at all. They consist largely of classifications of material, and lack many precise *explanatory* theories to explain what caused the phenomena to turn out in such groups.

Margenau calls science that has gone no further than step II B "correlational." It is possible to bring this step to a high degree of mathematical precision; correlations between different data may be measured as anything from zero correlation, indicating no relationship, to a correlation of nearly 1, indicating close cause-effect relationship. And yet science at this stage may remain quite without any *explanatory* theory as to why those data affect one another so. We may know that lightning is always accompanied by thunder and that the intensity of the lightning flashes is highly proportional to the loudness of the thunder; we conclude to a causal relationship, and yet we do not understand exactly how it is that lightning produces thunder. We have only correlational, and not explanatory science. "Historical evidence indicates that all sciences start upon the correlational level and evolve progressively toward the theoretic stage."[16]

Another and perhaps more correct understanding of this correlational stage would be that it consists of a whole sub-cycle of scientific method in itself, from problem awareness right through hypothesis to verification. The scheme for classifying or the conjecture as to what is correlated to what else, would itself be a hypothesis that gets a kind of rough verification before we go on.[17]

III. Induction.

Step III takes place within the mind of the scientist. He is no longer manipulating the environment and noting phenomena, but is thinking about what he has observed. The mind reveals a mysterious power of making possible connections among the data. DR is more conscious than SMR of the fact that these connections as such are not observed by the sense organs; they are "concepts," somehow created by the synthesizing power of the mind. But as "hypothesis," DR realizes that they are, as yet, only *trial* concepts, guesses, *possible* explanations. This implies that SMR is wrong in supposing that the data somehow mechanically *compel* one particular hypothesis to appear in the mind.

Recent treatments have devoted much attention to these mental concepts. Northrop calls them "concepts by postulation"; Margenau uses the term "constructs." The emphasis in both cases is on their artificial character, their nature as free creations of the mind. They are not "facts" in the sense of indubitably observed realities. In fact, in the more advanced stages of scientific theory, more and more use is made of constructs that can never be factually observed. "Electrons" for instance are mental constructs. They have never been seen and never will be seen. Certain effects of them can be seen, such as tracks in a cloud chamber, but cloud tracks are not electrons. Similarly with all the other sub-atomic particles of modern physics. Quantum theory especially has forced physical scientists to recognize that they advance their explanatory theory by the use of mentally imagined concepts of which no direct sensory observation can ever be made.

The power by which the mind is able to create these concepts is a third meaning to which the term "intuition" has been applied, in addition to SM's notion of intuition as direct insight into truth, and SMR's as the immediate awareness of sense data. Here it refers to this creative aspect of thought — to this insight which the scientists gets after he has collected his facts and brooded upon them.

These intuited hypotheses, as we have said, become more and more complex in the later cycles of scientific method. A high level construct can consist of a whole *system* of concepts, pulling together many preceding facts and theories. It can require for its statement pages of mathematical formulas. But it will still imply — that is, there can be deduced from it — certain specific, definite and perhaps rather simple consequences, the testing of which will confirm or unconfirm the whole system of thought. The very meaning of "electron" for instance is what Northrop calls a "deductively formulated system" of assumptions and concepts which science has been welding together for over a century.

The "higher" a hypothesis is — that is, the more it is a complex system of ideas with logical interconnections "requiring" the components to be as they are — the more "explanatory" it is — or rather, the more explanatory it *will be* when and if it is confirmed to become a theory. This point will be further discussed in Chapter VI.

The characteristics of a "good" hypothesis are often listed. Margenau gives: logical fertility, multiple connections, permanence and stability, extensibility, causality, and simplicity or "elegance." This last one is the famous "principle of parsimony": that the simplest hypothesis that adequately covers the facts should be preferred. Incidentally, none of these criteria are "factual" in the popular sense that supposes that science deals with nothing but "proven" facts. They are all assumptional, rationalistic and evaluational.[18] (They are further discussed on p. 450).

IV. Deduction.

In III, the thinker has imagined one or more concepts or constructs on the basis of his observations up to that time. Science well knows that a group of data may suggest a number of hypotheses. It remains to test the latter and find which one is "true." This requires deducing some consequence of each hypothesis that will call for some new data *other than* the original evidence we started with.

> . . . The theory connects the facts we already know, predicts facts we did not know, and in general, interprets a collection of scattered observations which previously had little meaning for us. That a hypothesis must enable us to deduce from it not merely facts we knew beforehand but facts we do not as yet know, needs great emphasis. This is essential for the process of testing it. . . . Thus by systematically deducing the consequences of a number of possible hypotheses and checking them experimentally we progressively eliminate the hypotheses that are false.[19]

The fifth step of the revised method (verification of any systematization) will be left for the next chapter.

Comparison of DR with SM: It remains to point out how

DR's method differs from what SM implies. Far from being merely an uncovering of ready-made knowledge that is already somehow in the mind, man seems rather to have to create effortfully, in a mind that is originally vague and unformed, whatever he is to know of the nature of things. The hypothesis now appears as a creative act of the mind, not mechanically compelled by the data, and not automatically correct. An unending process of testing and refining hypotheses is indicated. Apparently man will be able to experience *discovery* forever, for if knowledge was meant ever to be completed, why has it not been before this? It becomes doubtful that passive contemplation of given truth is ever to be the nature of human knowledge. Even if science should attain some finished theories, new generations of individuals could not attain comprehension of them except by dynamic mental processes of their own.

This is not a captivating prospect for the static idea of meaning. For it cannot see why God would not have everything already laid out as He wants it. Why should any God who knew His business want His creature to be eternally discovering and changing his knowledge? And why should He not reveal it all in final perfect completeness?

DM with DR.

Implications of DM, and Correspondence to DR: It will always be necessary to change SM to DM before we can get a perfect fit. For obviously the dynamic idea of meaning and good implies that knowledge, like all other features of reality, should be a matter of creative accomplishment, originating in some unsatisfactory condition. DM is not surprised to find that every human mind starts off nebulously, quite lacking in SM's "clear and distinct" ideas; or that the urge to know does not arise until a problematical situation prompts it, as the pragmatists have insisted. Nor is it consternated to find out that our sense organs always begin with fuzzy and inaccurate impressions that have to be refined and sharpened by all kinds of effort before we can escape error. Finally DM is not discouraged to learn that our fathers handed down to us many mistaken notions, that science forever changes its ideas, and that apparently men will never have "perfect" sources of knowledge. They would be deprived of the good experience of learning, if they did. The dynamic idea of Good of course precisely calls for such a knowledge situation. If value of any kind can exist only as a feeling of organizing process, then man can know and feel the value of knowledge only in the act of producing it out of ignorance and puzzlement. So an omnipotent God would purposively have arranged for His creature to be able to know only in the process of resolving vagueness and puzzlement.

CHAPTER VI

THE VERIFICATION AND NATURE OF KNOWLEDGE: WHAT CAN BE KNOWN

Traditional theories characteristically stressed the sources of knowledge and the deductions from them, and were oblivious of the need of any further testing. It is the supreme distinction of scientific method that it terminates in a new kind of verifying step which the older theories did not take. Thus a separate chapter on the topic of verification, and finally on what sort of content can be verified, seems justified. Can there be verified knowledge of values and meanings as well as of facts and existences?

SM with SIR.

Implications of SM: For the theory of knowledge implied by SM, no separate problem of verification would arise; and the connection between this fact, and the meaning of "static" is revealing. For, in not placing significance upon the actuality of process, in not implying knowledge as a development, SM naturally sees no reason for looking beyond the original source of ideas for truth. The origin should be self-validating, and no reference to ends or results should be necessary. Intuition should be "self-evident," revelation should be divinely authenticated, authority should be absolutely trustworthy: the sources of knowledge should be their own warrant of truth.

The static idea of meaning and value, thus, is behind the age-old and still widespread concern about the nature of the ancient beginnings of beliefs. The preoccupation with miracles, for example, derives from the supposition that something about the earliest appearance of an idea — some strange marvelousness — should be what tells whether it is true or not. Upon further reflection, we might think that the smoke and fire of Mt. Sinai were rather irrelevant criteria for deciding on the truth of such propositions as the Ten Commandments; but early thinkers found this a natural way to decide what to believe—at least in regard to beliefs remote from immediate practical problems, in which one would not be directly injured if he failed to test a belief empirically and logically.

What kind of things should we expect to be able to know from such sources, then? There is no implication why the mind should not have universal, certain and final truth from them—about both facts and values. Knowledge should be about perfections, unchanging essences, eternal logical relationships between them, and about ideas and systems of ideas deducible from these. The essences, ideas or forms are sometimes expected, as by Plato, to be objective, or external to the individual creature's mind. Or they may be internal to man's and to the divine mind. This kind of knowledge is to answer the question "why" existence is as it is, by demonstrating reasons or purposes for it. Plato argued that all lower essences somehow were derived from, or culminated in the Idea of the Good, and this was to explain why all things are as they are.

Such a mixed application of SM as orthodox Christian theology still claims that we can know that things are as they are because of God's purposes. It has not always claimed that men could understand all of the essences and implications in God's mind; but has been satisfied to accept all on faith as the decrees of God. One believes that God himself has some reason for everything He does, whether man can know what it is or not.

Adjustments of SIR: Men were forced to recognize that the sources of truth SM suggested as infallible do fall into error somehow, and that it is frequently necessary to check on intuition, authority and even supposed divine revelations, to find if they are from God or devil.

Some of the checks on authority first resorted to, and still considered basic by many, are: universality of acceptance, antiquity, prestige, etc. Concerning the first, there has always been the tendency to assume that if "everybody"—especially all authorities —thinks so, then it must be right. But, as Patrick says,

The *vox populi,* if it is the voice of God, is often the voice of a false God, as a most cursory observation of history

108

readily reveals. At almost every turn of the tide in history there are evident the tragic errors into which majority opinion can fall. The fact that it was universally accepted in ancient times that the earth is flat is a simple illustration of the worthlessness of this criterion.[1]

Concerning antiquity, SIR's tendency to seek the most ancient authority as the most reliable follows logically from the static assumption that the original deposition of knowledge should be perfect and final for all time. Therefore those closest to the earliest times when the nature of things was laid down would be in the best position to know the right and the true. Thus the great anxiety of institutions to demonstrate their age, their connections to the earliest revelations. The scriptures are trustworthy simply because they are *old;* the custom is right purely because "it has always been done."

This rule seems at first sight ridiculous to a progressive modern mind. The antiquity of a belief would seem to him presumptive of its primitive status, inadequacy, superstitiousness; and so it can very well be. There is nothing more ridiculous than those stubborn believers who preserve hoary nonsense, simply because of its aura of age. On the other hand this yardstick turns up unexpectedly, as a supplement to the pragmatic test in DR (see below). Provided a belief has passed the *other tests,* its long duration *might* be testimony to its success in having passed the pragmatic criterion generation after generation and survived. Especially for some of the more complex matters of morality, where you cannot perform your pragmatic test quickly but require vast amounts of experience, long-lastingness may signify the belief's "fitness to survive" a lot of winnowing.

But, of course, none of these supplementary criteria of authority and intuition remove them from their status of not being real tests of truth in the first place. A vivid criticism of SM-SIR's attitude toward truth and authority is John Dewey's:

> In just the degree in which existence is divided into two realms, a higher one of perfect being and a lower one of seeming, phenomenal, deficient reality, truth and falsity are thought of as fixed, ready-made static properties of things themselves. . . . Beliefs are false not because they mislead

us; they are not mistaken ways of thinking. They are false because they admit and adhere to false existences or subsistences. . . .

The older conception worked out practically to identify truth with authoritative dogma. A society that chiefly esteems order, that finds growth painful and change disturbing, inevitably seeks for a fixed body of superior truths upon which it may depend. It looks backward, to something already in existence, for the source and sanction of truth. It falls back upon what is antecedent, prior, original, a priori for assurance. The thought of looking ahead, toward the eventual, toward consequences creates uneasiness and fear. It disturbs the sense of rest that is attached to the ideas of fixed Truth already in existence.[2]

Coherence theory: Recognizing this fundamental inadequacy, and experiencing the errors, of "self-evident" principles and "ancient authorities," SIR turns to formal, logical criteria as its main test of truth. Of course the empirical test was always used by everybody for ordinary life experiences. But when it came to working out a philosophical theory for more elaborate beliefs not so easily tested by direct experience, the most usual type for classical and medieval times was what is now known as the "coherence" theory of truth. This supplements the appeal to the self-evidence of a belief by considering whether it is *consistent* with many or all of our other opinions. If it logically fits into a system of ideas that encompasses a large chunk of our knowledge, this constitutes further grounds for its truth. Of course the means by which we can know or recognize consistency is still the "intuitional" inbuilt power by which the mind grasps rational relationships.

But even this test, men more and more realized, did not exclude error. They could work out perfectly consistent systems of ideas that did not correctly lead to obvious facts. Deductive rationalism can be no stronger than the premises it starts with, and if our authority has been mistaken in those, then conclusions can be ever so correctly deduced from them, and ever so logically consistent with one another, and still be mistaken.

As for what kinds of things can be known, SIR never doubted that perfections and eternally fixed value essences could be, but it was forced to deal somehow with knowledge of the apparently changing world, though SM does not imply any place for such knowledge. Aristotle recognized that the essences do not exist except in concrete embodiments and that men cannot know them except by starting with observation of such embodiments, which synthesize matter and form into a unity. But he was confident that after not too much study of the individual objects, it would not be difficult to arrive at an understanding of the essences, universals, or "reasons why" the individual objects are as they are. His whole "science" was concerned with explaining why things moved, changed, and grew as they did, rather than with describing exactly how they did it.

The late Middle Ages got into an interminable argument about whether the essences or universals were real in their own right, as Plato believed, or whether Aristotle's insistence that they existed only in the individual embodiments necessarily meant that they had no reality at all, and were merely abstractions in human minds to which we applied words or "names." Nominalism, thus labeled, went to this extreme and considered the general ideas as having no reality except as names in human minds. This implied that individual things were more real than the relations or classes to which they belonged.

However, the prevailing feeling of SIR about the world is memorable: the medieval sense of sacramental meaning suffusing all objects, based on the confidence that they all played required roles in a divine drama called forth by an intelligible purpose or value. This is the attitude toward existence that was extolled at the beginning of this text, one there praised as a pearl of great price — worth seeking to recover. It was based on the belief that the meaning of things could be known by man to a degree at least; and the faith that where man could not understand the meaning, yet was there one known to God, fully objective and fully real.

And yet SIR's method failed to yield much useful knowledge or much practical help in easing the evils and pains of life. Men finally became so unsatisfied with its lack of contact with experience, that they turned to another way of verifying which did produce practical help, though it also seemed to demand the price of losing all the meaningfulness SM-SIR had provided.

SM with SMR.

Findings of SMR: The most characteristic difference between SMR's (and also DR's) method and SIR's is the addition of a final *empirical* step, following the deduction and coherence testing which kept leaving SIR out of contact with observation. This inadequacy of pure coherence theory was bitterly criticized by the founders of SMR in the Renaissance and Age of Reason. They demanded that the ideas in the mind, however coherently they fit other ideas must first of all fit facts, i.e. observed data. The "Correspondence theory" of truth results: that truth is a matter of mental concepts corresponding with realities outside of the mind. There must be agreement between ideas and objects, beliefs and facts, thoughts and reality.

The fourth step of SMR's scientific method, then, the "Verification," apparently exemplifies the correspondence theory of truth. After the scientist has made his original observations, generalized from them to a hypothesis (which should already thus stand a better chance of corresponding to observed facts), he then deduces some possible consequences from the hypothesis, and he returns to observation to determine still further whether reality "corresponds" to the ideas in his mind or not. Galileo actually performs the experiment whose specifications he had deduced from his supposition that falling or rolling bodies will cover distances proportional to either the weight or to time. Being now able to observe and measure the distance they go per unit of time, he is able to distinguish which hypothesis fits the facts: the distances are proportional not to the weights but to the square of the time.

> The true method of discovery is like the flight of an aeroplane. It starts from the ground of particular observation; it makes a flight in the thin air of imaginative generalization; and it again lands for renewed observation rendered acute by rational interpretation.
> . . . Thus the first requisite is to proceed by the method of generalization so that certainly there is some application; and the test of some success is application beyond the immediate origin.[3]

If anything that is deduced from the hypothesis is contradicted by the test experiment, then of course that hypothesis must be rejected. We then return to step II (p. 88) and start over again with another hypothesis. Also, if the one test confirms our hypothesis, it will usually be well to deduce as many other consequences as we can from the hypothesis and test them all. The more consequences that can be confirmed the stronger the probability of the hypothesis is felt to be.

What kind of things, then, can be verified by this method? Correspondence theory may seem so much what one means by "testing truth," that he may wonder what could be wrong with it. But, when interpreted with the older static and atomistic notion of sensory experience in mind, the theory led SMR to some very destructive results in regard to knowledge of meaning and religious belief. For thus qualified, it implied that nothing can be true or real except what can be directly observed by means of such sensations, and it is doubtful that many of the things we care most about knowing can be known this way.

The conception of verification that confines it thus to "positively" known sense experience has been called "Positivism" since Comte (1798-1857) coined the word for his anti-metaphysical philosophy. Many of this school have continued to deny the possibility of ethical, metaphysical or religious knowledge. They confine philosophy to its analytical side alone (p. 26), making it a sub-department of logic which, like logic and mathematics, does not make assertions about actual existence at all. Actual knowledge, they say, must be empirical, and as such belongs to science. Philosophy becomes merely the logical analysis of the language of such science. The traditional contents of philosophy —assertions about the ultimate nature of reality, whether mental or material, or purposive, etc.,—are classed as empty verbalization, because they cannot be put to this empirical test. Ethical propositions, too, are rejected because they concern what ought to be, which is not yet existent and is therefore unobservable.

The main reasons for these negations will be itemized for comparison with a parallel itemization under DR:

1. First we must remember SMR's static conception of sensation, as a passive mirroring of external realities, not essentially involved with feeling or creative activity. There is simply an endless series of sensations supposedly prompted by an endless series of external objects. On this basis, knowledge must depend first upon the sensations being really like the objects; and secondly upon the objects (and thence the reflected sensations) being con-

113

nected with one another in regular ways, ordinarily known as causal connections. This latter point was once phrased as knowing that the same cause will enforce the same effect at all times, until Hume showed that on a basis of static, atomistic sensationalism, we can not know of causal forces, only of sequences of specific sensations. But this in turn implies that positivistic knowledge must be confined to merely describing fixedly repetitive phenomena to the exclusion of creative or novel phenomena, which purposive experience may essentially be. In short, after a phenomenon has been observed, confirming a hypothesis, the continued truth of that theory depends upon nature repeating itself on all other verificatory occasions in the same manner. If there are any aspects of experience that are unique or non-repetitive, they could not be "known" in this sense. Only such statements as "That object has such and such properties"; or "These circumstances are always followed by those phenomena" can be known. The possibility of knowing *why* they exist or happen, or of knowing what use of them man ought to make, seems ruled out, since these questions do not seem to be merely questions of repeatedly observed sequences.

In this connection, however, a famous problem comes up which seems to cast doubt on the possibility of even the positivistic knowledge; the problem of induction is the question how we can legitimately make a universal conclusion about nature's sequences on the basis of a number of observations that must forever be finite. The mere fact that a law has been upheld in every case so far known provides no certain proof that it will be upheld forever. In other words we cannot prove that nature will remain uniform.

2. Next is SMR's exclusively quantitative approach to sensations, considering them only insofar as they can be discriminated from one another for purposes of precise measurement. At this point the problem is that the senses, even vision, are found to be incapable of absolute accuracy, so that perfect quantitative measurement is impossible. Science has to work out a theory of errors, and give up by so much the hope of "certain knowledge."

3. Closely related to the above is SMR's excessive discount upon the qualitative aspect of sensations and of dynamic experience. The emphasis upon sensations only as cues for quantitative measurement led to a suspicion of the factor of enjoy-

ment or non-enjoyment in all experience, including sensory, and a minimization of research on qualitative preference. A tendency to deny reality, or at least importance, to the whole area followed. And since qualitative feeling is essentially involved in the reality of value and meaningfulness, a denial of its reality tended to issue in a denial of theirs.

4. Now we come to some consequences of SMR's atomistic error (p. 86). This leads ultimately to the inability to consider any unseen, or otherwise unobserved, relations between sensations or objects sensed as real. SMR has no adequate theory of holistic relations in the sensory realm itself, let alone in any supposed objective world beyond those sensations. Positivists have objected to attributing any reality even to such unseen, relational concepts as science often uses (e.g., light wave or chemical bond) to say nothing of the older invisibilities of metaphysics and theology. None of these ideas appear before our senses as distinct separate objects. Some positivists objected, for instance, to such a concept as "electron," which relates many observations, but is not itself able to be observed by any sense organ. They might have permitted the idea if scientists could have been expected eventually to be able to see electrons through some future super-microscope. But when it became clear that what was understood by the term "electron" was intrinsically non-observable for all time, they wanted to deny its reality. How much more then were they averse to such a concept as "God" about which men did not even agree on sufficient definition to determine what indirect observations might confirm it, let alone have any particular, measurable sensory experience of it. As for such things as "beauty" or "good," how could they be verified by sensations taken separately? What reality would you compare them with to see if they corresponded?

Thus positivism has dismissed these kinds of ideas into a class of "emotive" sentences, which never "assert" propositions of the knowable kind, having "truth"; they only express personal feelings and correspond to nothing stable and repetitive outside at all.

SMR, then, in stressing the analysis of things into parts, ultimately into atoms, leaves the impression that all reality must be the unpurposed, unevaluable outcome of blind elements. These may operate in a lawful (i.e. repetitive) fashion, to be sure, but certainly not by intention or under the guidance of ideals, feelings or meanings. This is the subject of the next few chapters.

Combining SMR's static and atomistic inadequacies, then, we begin to understand its lack of any theory of how we can know and feel the building or creating of patterns, unified designs, out of the many part-causes; and on what basis we might conclude that such creative organizing goes on elsewhere besides in ourselves. That is, it has no basis for understanding purposive creation or planning, whereby we, and possibly other agents in nature, might assemble various knowledges of partial repetitive sequences into aimed-at activity with estimations of possible creative and novel outcomes.

5. Finally, SMR runs into another strange problem, hinted at above: subjectivism. This is the difficulty of proving that scientific knowledge is about anything outside of our own minds in the first place. Scientists have always taken it for granted that they were gaining objective knowledge about an external world, which world was in no way the product of their own minds. They have always wished to trust their sense organs, when sufficiently guarded, to be reporting an objective reality. Of course, they were forced away from "naive realism," the view that trusts the senses all the way, by experiencing the inaccuracies and hallucinations of the senses. But otherwise, science has favored realism, the belief in a world that would exist whether any mind was regarding it or not.

But Idealism, reviving in Berkeley, found a more basic criticism of correspondence theory than any of the above. The dualism which the theory assumes between the knowing mind and the reality that it is trying to know results in an unbridgeable split between them. Berkeley took advantage of this to turn the tables on SMR's negation of value and religious knowledge. The mind, in short, apparently can never know anything but its own sense data and resulting ideas. The belief that objects beyond those sensations and ideas "caused" them can never be tested. If, for instance, one suspects that his sense organs may have distorted whatever it is they observe (and the experience of hallucinations, dreams, illusions does show that the senses sometimes create their own impressions, not strictly correspondent to any outer reality at all), how is one ever going to find out just how much they have distorted it? You can never get outside your sensory experience to check with reality itself. This seems to dispose of correspondence theory for good.

Hume finished off this line of thinking by showing, as already mentioned above, that even for such a notion as cause — the very foundation of science — there is no direct sense impression anyway. For we never see or feel any causal force as such operating in the external world. We sense only sequences of impressions, which carry with them no knowledge of necessary cause-effect relations.

Contradiction between SM and SMR; Recourses: SM expected to have knowledge of universal and certain truth, but SMR's method blocks it both by the problem of induction and the inaccuracy of the senses. SM expected to have knowledge of value, purpose and meaning, but SMR blocks it by its denial of qualitative and relational knowledge. SM expected to have knowledge that a universe existed beyond one's individual awareness, which was value-oriented, but SMR's ego-centric predicament blocks that too. For SMR, if no purpose can be found in the separate sensations or atoms studied in isolation, then there can be none in any whole made up of such parts. If Physics, looking at reality from its special angle, ignoring many aspects as irrelevant to its task, seems to find no God, then no God can be found in a more complex grasp on the pattern of all things. If astronomy can spot no God as a distinct individual object in the Heavens with its telescope, then there is no God. But should God or value be expected to be one definite item among others within the world?

Upon the collapse of SMR's correspondence theory, Idealists felt privileged to try to polish up their intuitional and rational methods as more satisfactory ways of verification. The great idealist systems of the eighteenth and nineteenth centuries resulted, relying largely on the coherence test of truth, and making values and purpose fundamental to reality. The subjective escape from SMR's mechanical conclusions was also utilized in many ways to prove that reality was essentially mind-like, or will-like. If the only thing man could really be sure of was his own awareness, and if that included purposive thought, then science could be defied to prove that any material, mechanical reality exists outside of mental reality at all, let alone that it is more real. If this mentality oddly enough conjured up SMR's theory of purposeless material, the fact remained that it was a purposive mentality that had conjured up such a notion.

But this way of escaping from SMR has a serious weakness of its own, called the "ego-centric predicament," or "solipsism." How can the individual thinker prove that anything whatever exists outside of his own awareness? If I cannot prove that a material reality exists outside of my mental experience, neither can I prove that anything whatever exists outside of it. If my own mind creates its own dreams, hallucinations and delusions, how can I know that it does not create every other part of the panorama of sensory experience and ideas too?

In this emergency, Berkeley himself argued that he had not meant to say that everything outside of our minds is not real; only that it is not material. The whole external world, with its lawful order existed outside of us just as it seems to, but it is God's experience and thought, rather than the blind motion of matter. He answers the question, "Why, if all I know is the product of my own mentality, cannot I will my experience to be whatever I wish — why is my mind so helpless as to what experiences come to it?" by saying that our experience does come so largely from a world not ourselves — the world of God's thought.

Kant also believed in an external world as the original prompter of our sensations. But it acted only as a sort of cue to set in motion the mind's thought processes. The mind proceeded to organize these sensations by means of its own subjective categories or forms of understanding, such as Space, Time, quantity, quality, unity, plurality, etc. The product of this work, however, was largely a subjective thing, and not knowledge of the world as it really is. The latter, the "thing-in-itself" or "noumena" could never be known to the human mind, only its effects on our consciousness, the phenomena. Kant thus gained the point that no one could prove that the thing-in-itself was necessarily like the mechanical world our minds seemed to "know." It was only the mind's peculiar weaknesses, blindness, selectivities that kept it from being able to know through reason the God, Immortality and Moral Law that actually existed in the noumenal realm.

The idealists that followed Kant built up their purposive and value-centered systems with confidence, since it now appeared that the mind was so nearly all-powerful in the creation of knowledge. They soon came to the conclusion that the "thing-in-itself" must be very similar to one's mental experience anyway, and Hegel practically identified the two.

But although the subjectivist route seemed to let God, meaning and value back into knowledge, it also readmitted old weaknesses

118

of the rationalistic method: the failure to make contact with empirical observation, and to produce much new and useful knowledge of an objective world. The idealistic systems tended to leave us with great concepts and speculation which however were capable of neither proof nor disproof.

How are we to give empirical meaning to concepts like "monad," "Absolute," and so on? In what sense is the whole of reality reducible to the "activity of perception" or to the "self-consciousness of Spirit?"[4]

This excessive emphasis upon the autonomy of our reason and will also produced much failure to adjust to the realities of life on the part of many dreamy idealists, with consequent disappointment. Also, much idealism failed really to sanctify the concrete world about us, tending to reject the intricately structured realities science tells us of in favor of a world of grandiloquent ideas. The solipsist dilemma too still dogs this subjectivist escape. Berkeley was in an especially bad position when he held that only what is perceived exists. But we do not perceive God or other spirits as such, and they are his main appeal to escape from solipsism.

With both coherence and correspondence theories unsatisfactory, then, men could well wonder whether there was any way to test truth and to know anything at all. Modern science had started with skepticism of the older authoritarian knowledge, but only to clear the way for a new way to attain real knowledge. But now, with Hume, man was faced with a more hopeless skepticism, which some men might take as justification for believing or not believing whatever pleased them, scientifically, morally *and* religiously. Philosophy has been trying to deal with this more destructive skepticism ever since Hume, but corrosive denial is still very much with us, perhaps more than ever in our modern positivisms and existentialisms.

Can DR and DM save us from such skepticism in any really valid and convincing way? In this emergency that SMR presents to us, the majority of men fall back on faith and authority. The religions have by and large continued in their age-old appeal to revelation and the stubborn insistence upon belief in spite of evidence. But there is a large uneasiness today that is not laid to rest by these methods. It is not a strong situation to have the intellectual leaders of a society estranged from the traditional foundations of value and religion. There is a more and more ubiquitous awareness that the old beliefs are getting only lip-service. The empirical attitude forces itself on the people so that their ostensible faith-beliefs have less reality for them whether they admit it or not. It has been said that some more intellectually conscientious ministers do not dare let their congregations know how necessary they find it to reinterpret traditional terms and dogmas for their own personal intellectual consistency; and that, on the other hand, the congregations do not dare to let their ministers know how irrelevant they find much of the official dogma for their modern world of man-made satellites, museums of evolutionary history, and soul-cure by tranquillizers or psychiatry. Between the absurd beliefs of the sects that refuse to reinterpret a single jot or tittle of scripture, and the cocky sneers of cynics and secularists who can destroy beliefs but cannot construct them, a seeker finds little to choose.

Is there any more solid foundation for meaningfulness and value in observation and reason themselves? Can DR and DM between them find a way to verify other sorts of knowledge than mere blank statements of sensory fact? We want to keep from falling back into SMR's meaninglessness; yet avoid SIR's cheap escape through subjectivisms and dualisms that arbitrarily enunciate desirable beliefs independent of any empirical tests. To resort to a distinction between appearance and reality, so as to provide a realm for value and purpose that can be neither verified nor refuted by evidence, is widely suspected today as betraying some inadequacy of assumption and method. Something essential must have been omitted at the starting point of the philosophy which then has to be lugged in afterwards in an artificial dualism.

DR's revisions of SMR's method of verification and conclusions about what can be known are based on its understanding of the dynamic whole-part relationship. The basic discussion of this comes in Part III where we learn why science itself has come to uphold the reality of holistic relations. In the remainder of this chapter we will indicate some respects in which this attribution of reality to relationship and pattern provides a basis for knowledge of value and purpose. But further aspects of the problem remain for Part IV on Value itself.

Findings of DR: Pragmatic Theory as Dynamic Correspondence Theory. The American philosophy of pragmatism has contributed a good deal to a theory of verification for a dynamic theory of knowledge. Pragmatism's test is popularly supposed to be usefulness, satisfactory results, practical success. Incidentally, let us notice immediately how dynamic thinking transfers the emphasis here in the knowledge problem, as in other problems, from the origins of the idea or belief, as in SM and SIR, to the ends, or outcomes. Truth is not a kind of static property or quality that an idea has attached to it from its origination; it is something that the idea acquires within a process. In some sense, truth is a matter of how the idea "works," what it issues in, produces or creates. This sort of thing can be known about, even if Hume and the subjectivist idealists are right that we cannot know whether reality itself is like our sensations, ideas, or causal theories.

However, some confusion arises as to just what about "results" or "practical working" constitutes truth. First "working" was narrowed by many to mean any kind of practical success, no matter how shortsighted, or how productive of longer term calamity. Many philosophical critics, who should know better, have criticized pragmatism as though it officially stood for this perversion by the irresponsible. Secondly, "satisfactory working" was also left open by William James to a dangerous interpretation as a mere matter of human "will to believe" whatever gives emotional satisfaction.

The founder of pragmatism, Charles Peirce, had begun by pointing out that the meaning of descriptive and interpretive terms must be determined, for public communication, by indicating objective and verifiable operations they refer to. "Gravity," for example, really means what one would observe and measure if one dropped an object or rolled balls down inclined planes as Galileo did. "Hardness" means that, if one were to try to scratch a "hard" object, he would not be able to. That is, there must be (1) an implied process or operation; and (2) the results of this operation must be empirically observable as conforming to the specifications of the definition.

John Dewey applied this notion not only to the *meanings* of words or individual terms, but to the *truth of propositions*. Propositions are considered as practical instruments for solving problems, and they "acquire" truth only when they succeed in doing so. They are not true by having attached to them a mysterious, static property called "truth," as SIR might have supposed. Dewey extended this approach both to propositions involved in scientific research and to those involved in everyday experience.

William James, then, carried this pragmatic test still further to the verifying of knowledge in the areas interdicted by SMR: social, ethical and religious questions. If the test of ideas, hypotheses or propositions in the case of factual knowledge about natural events or practical technology was whether they "worked," in the sense of bringing predicted and desired results, then why not also in the other areas? However, it seems that he has let the meaning of "worked" change from "fulfilling predictions" or "empirically confirming expectations" to "giving emotional satisfaction." The predicted consequences in ordinary science might be incidentally desired emotionally by the scientist; but the satisfaction of his desire is not as such the criterion of truth, only the satisfaction of his prediction by observation. But James seems to allow the former kind of satisfaction as a test, when he says, for instance, that the ability to produce peace of mind and joy is testimony to the truth of a belief in God. James also could speak of the tendency of a belief to motivate "good" human behavior, in the sense of advantageous, or life-enhancing, or society-preserving behavior, as testimony to its truth. If it could be shown that belief in the non-existence of God led regularly to emotional breakdown, destructive behavior and loss of survival-fitness in a man or in a society committed to such belief, this would be pragmatic proof of the falsity of that belief.

When put this way there may seem to be something in James' idea, but it also seems to threaten us with all the old dangers of believing whatever we wish, putting us back to the original short-comings of knowledge method that started the search for better method. We know of too many beliefs that were held for long periods of time, "working satisfactorily" as far as their proponents' feelings were concerned, which finally were rejected as conflicting too much with verifying observation in the ordinary sense.

However, we may find a place for this sort of test, in a sense, in our complete dynamic theory, to which we now turn. We will outline this theory of verification, the fifth step of revised scientific method, following the same sequence as under SMR (cf. p. 113 ff.). Practically all of the test we have mentioned under SIR and SMR will find a place, either as basic or auxiliary.

1. Correction of the static error: Dynamic Correspondence [Pragmatic] Theory. First, let us incorporate DR's key feature: it no longer uses the mirror analogy for human knowing, thinking of knowledge as a passively reflected mosaic of sensations. Rather, it is a matter of building a dynamic process in our minds *parallel in form* to processes either elsewhere in the "external world" or (if the existence of such is held to be not yet substantiated) then at least elsewhere in our experience. We are trying to make the mental process "isomorphic" enough with any other process so that a conclusion or deduction in our mental process will be matched or "verified" by an outcome in the other process.

This then is pragmatic theory as "dynamic correspondence theory," as our primary test of truth. It is not a question of present agreement here and now between ideas and some current "mirrored" reality. It is rather a question of agreement with a future stage of a process.

> The agreement, correspondence, is between a purpose, plan, and its own execution, fullfillment; between a map and a course constructed for the sake or guiding behavior and the result attained in acting upon the indications of the map.[5]

How does this point bear upon SMR's restriction of knowledge to only what is repeated according to Natural Law? Well, it is difficult to see how we can have real knowledge after only one case where our prediction corresponded to observation. It does seem that nature must repeat itself according to uniform law if we are to take the result of one experiment with us as usable knowledge for future occasions of the same type. Any proposition, to be known as true, would seem to have to be repeatedly verifiable every time it is put to the test.

This faith in the uniformity of nature, however, would remain unverifiable itself, for the problem of induction would still interfere, for DR as for SMR, keeping us from any absolute knowledge since we are confined to only a finite number of instances. Therefore it must be a postulate, and science cannot claim to be what it is popularly supposed to be: "proven" truth, or "fact."

Causality is sometimes stated as a separate unproved assumption of science, but if we follow Hume's argument that we cannot have directly observed knowledge of causal forces necessarily producing their effects, only of regular sequences of sensations, then we are back to the postulate of uniformity of natural sequences.

If science then, even in DR, is still restricted to the repetitive aspects of nature, can it not deal with unique events, or with experience of novel creativity, which value experience may largely be? Well, unique events may include some components that are repeated in other contexts. For instance, although every human being as a whole is a unique combination or pattern of millions of elements, processes, characteristics, etc., still many of his parts considered separately are duplicated in other people; and many of his part-processes repeat themselves according to discoverable laws. These could become a subject of science then. But it is not clear that there could be a science of a particular whole person, or of unique complexes of factors pointing to unprecedented kinds of resolutions.

2. The Place of Quantitative Measurement. Only precise measurement can show whether the process has resulted as predicted; or whether different observers are objectively observing the same phenomena on repetition of the test. And so DR is as quantitative as SMR, more so in fact, since its advances have depended upon ever more refined measurement. And yet DR must still resign itself to the ultimate inaccuracy of the sense organs and thence of measurement which SMR had discovered as keeping science from final certainty.

Another reason for lack of certainty comes up too in that the techniques of observation and measurement have made contact with phenomena in nature so delicate that they cannot be observed without being affected by the observation itself. Passing beyond SMR's solid, massive objects that seemed so impervious to human desires or point of view, DR comes to electrons, etc., which cannot be studied by man without being disturbed by his observation. The electron is so affected by the photon of light that it must give or take in order for us to locate it, that we are prevented forever from being able to measure both its location and its velocity at once. But these are the two measurements we must have for an exact causal science. We cannot reach such science, then. Of course, it is possible to make mathematical allowances for the uncertainties in these measurements, so as finally to arrive at a science of statistical probabilities, upon which usable predictions can be based. But once again this is not a science of absolute certainty. Heisenberg also argues that nature itself, and whatever ultimate elements it may be made of, are in the last analysis hazy anyway. This ultimate vagueness in nature and in our knowledge of it, however, will prove to have significant uses for dynamic meaning and value.

3. The Place of Qualitative Knowledge. Now DR finds what SMR did not exactly deny but at least was uninterested in: that there can be the ordinary kind of scientific knowledge, based on repetitive connections, about certain aspects of qualitative experience considered as such. We saw that SMR tended to confine the sensations permitted as sources and verifiers of knowledge rather narrowly to touch and sight which were best at reflecting apparently external reality. Practically all of physical science is rooted in vision, primarily because the most precise measurements available to man are those gotten via the eyes. By the use of instruments, scientists strive to force most phenomena they care to study to cause some kind of visible effect that can be measured — on meter-sticks, graph recorders, microscopes, etc.

Other senses, as well as the sheer aspect of qualitative enjoyment or disenjoyment in vision and touch themselves, tended to be ignored by science both because quantitative measurement is difficult to apply to them, and because qualitative feeling cannot be directly communicated or compared between different feelers. That is, for instance, I can never know whether your internal experience of the quality "red," or a feeling of joy, feels just as mine does, nor how they compare in degree. A real direct, empirical comparison would presumably involve some kind of hookup of my nervous system to yours, so that I would be feeling your actual feelings, alongside my own, and such a hook-up would be presumably impossible.

Scientists, then, have tended to assume that they used the senses only in their aspect of discriminating spatial and temporal boundaries and gradients to which quantitative measurement can be applied in some way. Even SMR's psychology and social science try to confine themselves to measurable observable motions of some sort — muscle movements measured by kymographs, nerve currents measured by electrodes and dials, observed pecking orders, etc. — and are suspicious of any conclusions based on introspective awareness of the immediate quality, enjoyability or preferability of feelings, sensations, ideas. And, of course, any statements derived from such preferences that go on to assert "oughtness" would be even less scientifically knowable, since they go beyond descriptions of repetitive sequences.

But there seems to be something rather anomalous about this exclusion of qualitative and preferential aspects of sensation from the knowable. Whitehead says,

> The question of the proper description of the species of qualities termed "sensa" is important. Unfortunately the learned tradition of philosophy has missed their main characteristic, which is their enormous emotional significance. The vicious notion has been introduced of mere receptive entertainment, which for no obvious reason by reflection acquires an affective tone. The very opposite is the true explanation.[6]

The obvious truth that all sensation, experience, thinking is invariably accompanied by feelings of enjoyment or non-enjoyment, it seems, ought not to be ignored by knowledge method.

Actually, there was no real reason, even in SMR's method, why at least any lawful, repetitive connections between internally felt qualities and preferences, and any other observables, could not be studied to produce scientifically verified propositions (with the qualifications already discussed under number 1 and number 2). The inability to communicate directly our qualitative experience does not, as a matter of fact, make certain kinds of quantitative comparisons between them impossible, nor prevent the discovery of some regular connections between them and other factors. To begin with, men can certainly arrive at a consensus whereby they all use the same word, e.g. red, for the same part of their environment, even though they do not directly know whether that part feels the same internally to each man. The same holds for feelings of pleasure and pain. In addition men can also communicate about degrees of these feelings, whether something is redder than another, whether they felt more or less pleasure. Such measurement will be imprecise for these experiences, but it is still measurement and not different from ordinary visual measurement in lacking absolute precision, except that it lacks it in larger degree.

On this basis, then, there seems no reason why men cannot consider any kind of sensory experience or feeling in verifying the presence of repetitive, lawful sequences or connections between it and other factors. If smell, hunger, fear, pleasure, or even ideas of approval and disapproval are regularly connected to other factors of any kind, there can be a science of those connections.

The social scientist or psychologist, then, might study the sensation of red not only as a sign of some hypothesized object (an acid with red litmus paper), but also as something that is enjoyed or preferred. He might establish a connection between a shade of red and the preferences of a certain class of people — women versus men, Latins versus Northerners, etc. He would here be counting (measuring) in the realm of evaluation itself. Of course, he would not actually be producing statements of what was actually or absolutely "better," nor determining that some shade of red "ought" to be preferred. He would only be measuring existing opinions and preferences, and finding more or less regular connections between them and various cultural or background factors. Ugly shades of red would be as much subject to such study as beautiful ones.

Now what if some stable and repetitive features turn up in all or most experience that people label "good"? It seems that a scientific theory of factors associated with high evaluations or with satisfaction should be able to be worked out at a sufficiently general level. This theory undoubtedly would have to satisfy itself with a greater degree of imprecision than many in physical science, but again that would not make it different in kind from such theories, only in degree.

The kind of knowledge that would result from considering this preferential aspect of experience might be differentiated from the more usual kind of science, sometimes called knowledge of the "external world," which comes, as we have seen, from sensations considered apart from their enjoyability. However, it is doubtful whether the distinction can be pushed very far. At any rate, this kind of qualitative knowledge we have been making room for will turn out to have a special bearing upon our problem of knowledge of meaning, value, significance and God. We have not said that it determines what *is* best, or what ought to be done, or why things are as they are. It is still "what" and "how" knowledge, really, though it tells something of the antecedents and effects of satisfaction.

Is "why" and "ought" knowledge then still excluded from the scientifically knowable? Are the greater theories of philosophy, metaphysics, religion beyond the verifiedly known? We will now discuss whether DR can go further toward such knowledge through its second basic kind of correction upon SMR's theory of verification.

4. Correction of the Atomistic Error: The Coherence Test. The same correction which we discussed under Sources and Construction leads DR to think more seriously about the place of holistic relational awareness in verification, and also about tests of design, patterns as such. What happens to the thesis that knowledge depends upon repetition of natural or experiential sequences, when we recognize that these sequences contain within them assembling and organizing of many factors into unified configurations? Synthetic wholeness occurs both in the field of sensation itself, where awareness can be of spread-out fields or continuums just as much as it can be of parts or discriminations; and in the operations of the mind, which can synthesize hypotheses or constructs as well as analyze and distinguish ideas.

Now in this synthesizing work of thought, scientists do use criteria which are quite another matter from mere correspondence of thoughts to observations. And these criteria are simply various aspects of our old friend, the Coherence test of truth, which DR accepts from SIR and emphasizes more than SMR did. The probability of a theory is held to be increased when it is found to fit coherently with other theories that have been verified as above; or when the theory itself, if adequate empirically, is felt to be "simpler," neater, more "elegant" than competing theories.[7] And it is within this process of synthesizing complex structures of thought, with internal logical relationships of "requirement" that we begin to feel that we are dealing with reasons *why* the details are as they are. For we can see that the whole system requires its partial aspects to take their places as they do; that is, we can deduce by logic and mathematics the particular phenomena and their measured functions from it.

Actually, correspondence and coherence testing are already intertwined in the work of science when in later cycles, the hypothesis-making step III builds up more and more complex generalizations. Before the final empirical testing of the hypothesis is

128

undertaken, the principle of parsimony, which is part of the coherence criterion, may be used to help decide what constructs are most worth bothering to test empirically. It is also used *after* the empirical test, as it was in deciding that the Copernican theory of the sun-centered solar system was superior to the Ptolemaic, though both more or less corresponded to observation. Of course, only theories that can pass the correspondence bar thus will come up for final comparison on the coherence criterion.

Complex hypotheses that incorporate other formerly verified theories into their system can presumably count the empirical verification of those theories toward its own verification. But then scientific method calls for this new hypothesis to have some further deductions drawn from it, and empirically checked, so that its coherence may be supplemented in turn by more correspondence. That is, every part of the complex hypothesis must pass the correspondence test independently; and then the whole theory must pass it. For example, Einstein started with Michelson's observations on the velocity of light near earth, together with much accumulated data and theory on electro-magnetism, gravitation, light, etc., all of which had been verified separately. He then spent years organizing a conceptual system from these data which would bring them all together in the "simplest", coherent system (and, contrary to the layman's impression, relativity theory was as simple as he could get it). This system in turn implied slight differences in some of the empirical observation that had formerly led to Newtonian theory — for instance, that stars whose light passed near the sun should be seen at a little different place than older theory implied. Observations during eclipses, as every one knows, "corresponded" to the implication.

Thus scientific verification combines both empirical and rational criteria. Facts and theory are interdependent. Science proceeds by a back and forth movement between them, which is to say between correspondence and coherence testing.

Reality is conferred jointly by the process of fitting new parts into an already existing structure of ordered conceptions and by the process of empirical validation.[8]

All philosophy is an endeavor to obtain a self-consistent understanding of things observed. Thus its development is guided in two ways, one is the demand for a coherent self-consistency, and the other is the elucidation of things observed.[9]

These two criteria of correspondence and coherence, we shall find, represent the two factors (the "most" and the "least") that turn up in all evaluation, not only that of truth. (Chapter XVI).

Now we come to the question what additional kinds of things this holistic approach may permit us to know. Well, first, there can be no doubt that we have a kind of *subjective* experience and knowledge: we can experience and feel the development of these patterns of thought, and the experience is enjoyable. It includes the early phase of feeling or realizing the disorder and disconnection among sensations and ideas, and also intimations of what direction might be promising to resolve the disorder. The mind may utilize bits of formerly verified knowledge concerning partial processes involved in the present process, and arrive at prior estimations more or less precise of what "is called for."

On the subjective level this felt tendency may constitute desire, aim, motive or plan. Activity will follow and the plan be "confirmed" in the pragmatic sense if the results are as wished.

On a more *objective* level (though the ego-centric predicament remains to be discussed in the next section), the mind's creation of hypotheses or constructs by which to connect its sensations and experiences of an "external" world, would not differ essentially as regards being an intimation of a direction to move, an activity to perform, utilizing former knowledge, the synthesis being *felt* with enjoyment both when it first appears, and when it is successfully confirmed.

Notice here that prior to the final confirmation by pragmatic-correspondence test, we have a basis for a kind of tentative knowledge of unique or novel events, not entirely dependent upon repetitive natural sequences. It is partly informed by repetition of some formerly experienced part-processes, but the present experience may, as a whole, be a new combination never before experienced; yet we can have a sense of the tendency of the whole dynamically developing system, and make an "educated guess" about its nature. It is within this picture that we shall later find a place for knowledge of creative purpose which is not just positivistic knowledge of deterministic sequences. (Chapter IX.)

Of course such knowledge of unique new events will eventually be confirmed, at least to a degree, by subsequent experience of results, whence it then takes its place as "verified knowledge" to be used in later experience.

Next, concerning the more "objective" constructs, we must understand more about DR's correction of SMR's analytic approach, both as to what individual objects and real things are in themselves (assuming for the moment that they do exist outside the mind); and how they are connected into more and more inclusive systems. Now DR finds that every thing is actually an intersection of many qualities, quantities, processes, laws; in short, it is a concrete whole combining many aspects, arranged, organized and related in a real synthesis. But SMR takes these wholes apart, either in actual dissection, as in biology; or at least in mental analysis, as in much of physics and astronomy, where the scientist focusses his attention on selected aspects. The partial aspects focussed on were, in earlier science, the most definitely visible and touchable ones. The arrangement, organization and relations themselves are often not so visible or touchable; and upon dissection, they vanish into thin air, having no continued material existence at all. But the *parts* themselves often seem to continue as sensible objects. For instance, when a beautiful vase is broken, its pattern disappears, though its fragments remain, in the full measure of its original weight. This leads to SMR's tendency to consider the parts more real than the relations or the wholes. Yet, obviously, in such a case as that of water, the molecule is quite a different thing than the atoms of oxygen and hydrogen that went into it: its qualities of liquidity, freezing at O degrees Centigrade, making plants grow, etc., are simply not present in the gases. But SMR is tempted to deny this point, and to insist that "wholes are nothing but the parts." SMR's analytical fallacy thus becomes the "reductive fallacy," which will be illustrated under SMR for every topic in this book.

A related fallacy is that of abstraction, reification or hypostatization, also called by Whitehead the "fallacy of misplaced concreteness." This occurs when the parts or constructs which thought has analyzed out of the original gestalt (e.g. "mass", "atom", "glandular secretion") are imagined to be themselves real separate things, more real than the original totality in which they were merged in a pattern of process. The colors, facial differences, feelings, characters, etc., etc. that are combined in a unique pattern in each human being, differentiating him from any other, are all ignored by Physics, as it finds that his body behaves like

131

any lump of matter as far as the laws of mass and motion are concerned. But we find people trying to think of themselves as essentially pieces of matter with mass, as though the physical aspect of their bodies had been proven to be their only real aspect.

To affirm the combinational and holistic nature of real things then, is one route of escape from the mechanical purposelessness that SMR implied.

Next, let us see how the recognition of holistic relations, when carried still further toward understanding systematic connections among objects and events, can get beyond merely *descriptive* knowledge of the what and how of things, to *explanatory* knowledge, which begins to show "why" things are as they are. As the interrelated system of concepts becomes more and more inclusive, we pass from bare understanding of what exists and *how* it operates, to understanding how it fits into great patterns of relationship that *require* it to be so.

For example, let us start with Kepler as he contemplates Brahe's observations of the positions of Mars: a collection of figures showing at first sight no rational relationship. He needed a hypothesis suggesting some plan of orbit that would call for these positions. He tried different guesses until he struck the ellipse, and on testing found that the measurements fitted. He had now explained "how" Mars moved; but also, in a sense, he had got so far as to explain "why" the measurements had turned up as they had, insofar as the elliptical form *required* them so. But why should it be that planets follow elliptical orbits? So far this is an arbitrary fact that just *is,* without our understanding any reason *why.*

In the meantime Galileo, as we have seen, had found a formula that called for the measured positions of balls rolling down inclined planes. We next have Nèwton contemplating the data and theories of both Kepler and Galileo, which, together with additional data (an apple falling on his head from a tree, the legend goes), constitute *his* data. Then on a new cycle of the method, he comes to step III and conceives the more inclusive hypothesis of gravitation from which both of the previous hypotheses can be deduced. He can now "explain" why the measurements of Mars are as they are, not only by deducing them from the ellipse, but in turn deducing the ellipse from the laws of gravitation. We might go on and discuss how Einstein, starting with these observations and hypotheses as *his* data, makes a still more inclusive hypothesis from which he can "explain" why the law of gravitation is as it is. Thus we seem to answer "how" things occur in terms of precise measurement; and then to progress toward ever more complete explanations as to "why" they occur that way, by subsuming them under more and more inclusive concepts, which provide the relationship of *requirement*.

Now, as this synthetic, explanatory, systematic work of science proceeds, more and more reality is ascribed to the invisible, imagined constructs that have been verified, by confirmation of more and more deductions from them. If the hypothesis involves the use of any imagined, unobservable construct, such as electron or "gene", most scientists agree that this also receives a tentative kind of reality, even though it has not been observed itself, but only some effects of it that were predicted. Even more puzzling are some of the constructs in quantum theory, which are not imaginable or picturable in any way whatever, but are nothing but certain mathematical expressions. Margenau, however, argues that even these (for example the *phi* state) must be given a tentative "reality," since predictions that can be drawn from it are confirmed.

SMR itself had to admit that there were "laws" of nature, which weren't exactly visible, touchable *things,* but rather matters of relation between the things. DR in general is much more conscious of the manner in which nature conforms to intricate, and invisible mathematical relationships — relationships which cannot possibly be pictured in terms of solid particles moving in space and time and affecting each other individually. In fact, the relationships, the patterns, bid fair to become so much the locus of reality as to make it a major difficulty in DR to work out any doctrine of ultimate units or particles at all! (See Chapter VIII.)

Margenau discusses the "ascending order of 'whyness'" that is associated with this increasing complexity and inclusiveness of theory, always insisting, however, that it is a never-ending order, and that science arrives at no *ultimate* why.

Thus it turns out that the distinction between the how and the why is primarily a logical one . . . the problem of "description vs. explanation" . . . We have previously drawn attention to the variations in "distance" of constructs from the plane of perception; concepts can be related to Nature by very obvious rules, and in the other extreme they can be quite abstract. We mean by a *descriptive* theory one which involves constructs of the former sort; and *explanation* involves a further progression into the constructional domain. We explain by going "beyond phenomena."[10]

The inductive approach via selected experiments has historical importance. . . . Yet it may be said . . . that there comes a time when the necessity for organizing knowledge suggests an alternative approach, a logical approach from the side of basic axioms. Only when this is conjoined with the inductive story will the whole picture emerge. . . .[11]

Here is a thrilling picture of science groping its way, by inductive methods, to a piece-meal knowledge of facts and causal relationships. Gradually it ascends to higher and more inclusive and more integrated theories. At this point, all that had looked at first so fragmentary and meaningless begins to take its place in a system. In biology, for instance, we look at the bits of knowledge about primeval one-celled creatures, amoebas, then colonies of cells, then primitive multi-celled organisms and then the whole panorama of evolution up to man. We probably get an impression of blind groping, aimless trial and error change, finally issuing "accidentally" (according to SMR at least) in man. And yet, once we understand the nature of the final effect, man, we can turn around and understand that it would have *required* just such an evolution if he were ever to exist, in balanced relation to his environment and all the other creatures, plants, cells and chemicals upon which his life depends. In general, causes may seem to produce their effects non-purposively; and yet once we understand the effect, we can always reverse our point of view and understand that that effect required that kind of cause if it was ever to exist.

Is there then any essential difference between scientific theories built together into super-theories this way, and philosophical and religious theories? Were the positivists wrong in excluding metaphysics from the realm of meaning and verifiability? If there is no essential difference except degree of complexity, then our only problem would be the increased difficulty of verifying broad philosophical theories. On the other hand, if the verification of all the sub-theories that are incorporated into the grand theory counts toward verification of the latter, it may have pretty solid grounds already.

Thus the method of philosophy is empirical. Our theories must spring out of experience and be tested by experience. A crucial test in the physical laboratory may not be possible, but in the laboratory of life the hypothesis must find its verification. . . . A philosophical theory that comes into conflict with no accepted principles of science or philosophy, that is self-consistent, and that has been formed only after the most careful and impartial analysis of all the factors involved and after the widest appeal to human experience, is to that extent verified. Its wide appeal, its satisfactory working, even the prestige which it may have because of the successful scientific achievements of its proponent, are all steps in the process of verification.[12]

Some theorists would argue that this process of creating more and more inclusive hypotheses may be carried finally to the level of concepts of God. The idea of God would be a construct to be confirmed in the regular way. Well, it does seem that the concept of God is no more imaginary and invisible than that of electron, only more complex. Our definition of God as Cosmic Purpose for Good (Chapter II) might be considered such a hypothesis — *the source of deductions found in the DM section of each chapter, which we will be trying to show as verified in every DR section.*
Some positivists, however, still exclude metaphysics from the realm of knowledge, specifically refusing to define it in terms of such integrated theories as we have been discussing.

I do not include in metaphysics those theories — sometimes called metaphysical — whose object is to arrange the most general propositions of the various regions of scientific knowledge in a well-ordered system; such theories belong actually to the field of empirical science, not of philosophy, however daring they may be. The sort of propositions I wish to denote as metaphysical may most easily be made clear by some examples: . . . The Materialists say: "All that is, is in its essence material," but the Spiritualists say: "All that is, is spiritual.". . . .[13]

Carnap goes on to say that such ultimate statements are meaningless because unverifiable in the empirical sense. No proposition can be deduced from them which would assert any perception or feeling whose appearance or non-appearance would either confirm or unconfirm the metaphysical belief. Meaningful, verifiable statements are confined to the elements or parts of a system; and cannot be made about the whole system as such.

Carnap may be right about metaphysics as he defines it. However, is metaphysics in that sense involved in our task of showing how the world of dynamic science is "meaningful" — "why" it is as it is — by comparing DR with DM? We have said that what we must do is to carry on philosophy as the system of the sciences until we have an inclusive, coherent theory of all facts, which already begins to give us requirement, or "whyness" for the details within the system; and that then finally we must show the *requirement of this system by a concept of value*. Only this move will give us the real and ultimate why. But can we have *knowledge* of such an ultimate concept of value?

Now many scientists and philosophers have been holding that the final generalization of inductive science, more general even than Einstein's Relativity theory, is the idea of process or creativity, which we shall study systematically in Part III. Such philosophers then go on to make logical statements of requirement of many things we observe from the concept of process; for instance that the sheer fact of the existence of individual things is logically required by the concept of process. They also hold that the idea of organic process is as far as science can go; it is the ultimate idea from the side of empirical observation, giving the ultimate "why" for science.

But I have said that any ultimate reason "why" would have to be a concept of value. That is, we would have to be able to show that the correct idea of value "requires" reality to be organic process.

But it is just at this point that many positivists would deny the possibility of scientific knowledge of what value essentially is. Now we cannot complete our discussion of knowledge of value until Part IV, but will remark here that the kind of knowledge of quality and feeling which we argued above under point 3 was possible, will be involved in completing our project of systematizing all knowledge, and showing that value logically requires all that is found out through correspondence and coherence testing. The remainder of this book is concerned with this task.

A last point under our present point of holistic knowledge is DR's finding a place in its theory of verification for SIR's *intuition,* in a certain sense. We have found intuition in step I as the original vague awareness of reality; in step II as the direct awareness of sense data; in step III as the mind's ability to create hypotheses to explain its observations. Bergson suggested still another meaning for intuition as a kind of feeling of reality in all its dynamism and wholeness that is more "true" than any of science's analytical knowledge. Scientific knowledge was "dead" knowledge, knowing only the dissected parts and abstractions *from* reality itself. Reality itself can only be known in the direct consciousness of the moment, where one seizes the on-going, concrete reality itself. Bergson tends to imply that this direct insight is the truest knowledge and that it is independent of ordinary verificational methods.

However, the majority opinion is that though such synthetic, dynamic insight is an important final moment in the knowledge process, it should not be understood as being able to dispense with verificatory methods, because too often such vividly grasped "truths" have turned out not to be true after all. But, *after* the verifying has been properly done, we do find a place for this intuition as a direct grasp of living reality in all its concrete quality, and it is more truly *knowledge* than any amount of scientifically verified, but abstract and dead theory. This is also the point that mystics of all ages, especially in the East have made. Northrop in *The Meeting of East and West* points out that eastern thought has always emphasized immediate awareness of aesthetic, qualitative data as the most real reality; and that this includes direct awareness of divinity. Let us call this aspect of experience *intuitional appreciation;* it is *not* to be considered as a "source" nor as verification of knowledge at all, but rather as a final *awareness* of the integrated and verified product of all the preceding struggle to know. In this sense, intuition is called by Wheelwright "post-ratiocinative" intuition. (Cf. p. 98). This is

> . . . a direct grasping of a situation by the whole mind, a final "sizing up" of evidences and values in a unitive mental commitment. . . . The deliverances of preratiocinative intuition are notoriously unreliable.

Post-ratiocinative intuiting, on the other hand, is unavoidable as the crowning aspect of every process of discovery. When all the evidence is in hand, when all the rational deductions have been made, there is still the culminating step which may be expressed by the exclamation, "Oh, I see!"[14]

Now, the pragmatic theory of knowledge which was one of the main roots of DR's theory, was one-sided in its exclusive emphasis on problem-solving as our only concern. DR's conception that the achievement or "composition" of integrated patterns of ideas and actions is the very substance of the knowing or any other process, makes a place for awareness of the achieved designs or arrangements as the final moment of the knowledge process.

> The functions of consciousness and reason are not exhausted in meeting novel situations and controlling behavior by a reference to the future. When I am engaged in aesthetic con- templation of nature or art, when I am enjoying the com- panionship of a friend, when I am contemplating the logical symmetry, beauty and impersonal grandeur of some scien- tific or mathematical construction . . . my consciousness, keen, vivid, and expanding, may have no reference to my own future behavior or that of anyone else. The human spirit lives not by deeds of adjustment to external and future situations alone. It lives deeply in pure contemplation and free imag- ination.[15]

We must insist, however, that this enjoyment of contemplation of pattern, according to DR, *can never come except as the out- come of a process of building that pattern. The contemplation at all times includes the enjoyment of remembering when the pat- tern was not, and of realizing how expertly or beautifully that pattern has succeeded in resolving what was not at first resolved.*

5. But how have these features of DR's approach affected the problem of subjectivism? Can we know that the qualities and feelings, the systematic relations, the intuited dynamisms which we have found to be knowable in the senses discussed so far, exist objectively beyond our minds? If we know values and purposes within ourselves, can we know that they exist elsewhere too?

Twentieth Century philosophy has reacted widely against subjec-

138

tive idealism and toward realism. We haven't space for a complete presentation of the grounds for believing in an external world, so will mention only a few most related to the dynamic, holistic approach. Of course there are all the arguments based on how our different senses converge and mutually support one another to explain which it seems so much easier to assume external objects simultaneously affecting them. This does not really get around the solipsist argument; yet on grounds of parsimony we might justify accepting it as the simplest explanation. Then we experience such a clear distinction between occasions when we ourselves are producing ideas or imaginary pictures, and those when something else beyond our control seems to be producing them in us willy-nilly. This something else seems so strongly to be pursuing an economy of its own independent of our minds that again it seems simplest to suppose it exists.

Belief in the existence of external things might also be defended pragmatically as leading on the whole to better results in the process of living than solipsism. Another defense has been based on the dynamic approach to knowledge, with its claim that our most immediate and direct experience is of our being in an interactive process, incorporating elements from beyond ourselves into our processes, and having effects on external things when we act. It is said that we directly know ourselves to be seeking ends in a world beyond us which is often resistant to us. The whole knowledge process is only an offshoot of this compositional process. We start, not with sensations mirroring an inert, hypothetical world, but with the awareness of seeking ends in an environment.

The sheer spectacle of the intricate structures of things, especially of organisms, sometimes seems to the author to be his strongest reason for believing that there is a world of processes and adjustments and strivings that exists in its own right, not concocted by his own mind.

Now assuming we believe in an objective world whether these points absolutely prove it or not, we have the question whether it is at all like our ideas of it. But if all that really concerns us is whether our mental process enables us to gain sufficient control of things so as to increase our success and enjoyment in life, we begin to wonder if it matters much whether or not there is some additional reality beyond what we find ourselves able to know. And one who accepts the dynamic philosophy finally wonders whether our experience of creative adjustment isn't after all "what nature is really like." Can we really care about knowing anything more?

If we know only our own ideas directly, how can we ever be certain that our "knowledge" is knowledge of the "real"? For the (newer) naturalistic point of view this problem does not arise. If our scientific theories are experimentally corroborated, if they enable us to predict future experience successfully, and can be applied technologically, it is idle to ask whether this knowledge is "real" knowledge. To say that it is knowledge of "ideas" rather than "things" is only a verbal distinction. For the critical naturalist knowledge is itself a natural phenomenon. Man is a part of nature, not somehow an external spectator of it, still less an external spectator with smoked spectacles that he cannot remove from his nose. The activity of knowing is as much an event as anything else.[16]

Finally, on what basis is DR to believe that not only objective things exist outside our minds, but also that those subjective value feelings which we know within ourselves exist elsewhere? We have discussed how DR can build up a science of regular connections in the realm of feeling; but how can it know that such feeling really exists pervasively in an outer world? When Whitehead, for instance, universalizes feeling as existing within any energy field, what are his grounds?

Actually, far from any one of us having direct evidence for feeling in all energy, we do not even have direct evidence for it in another human being. We know within ourselves that the search for desirable feelings is the reason for most, if not all of our activity. But we cannot know this by direct empirical verification for any other creature, for that would involve our actually feeling the feelings of the other creature. Our belief in others' feelings and values, then, turns out to depend upon the "argument from isomorphism." This means (1) that we notice other processes have observable external features parallel to our personal process in our organism; (2) we know that we feel qualitative feelings accompanying such observable movements (e.g., smiling, crying, etc.); (3) we conclude that the observable movements in the other creature are accompanied by similar feelings as our own are. Not all modern realists follow Whitehead in applying this isomorphic argument to all compositional processes, holding, for instance, that even atomic processes feel. But it is a real question whether the burden of proof is on those who affirm or deny it.

It is along all these lines, then, that DR claims knowledge of a reality beyond ourselves which is essentially a realm of value and purpose: the dynamically felt organizing process that the dynamic idea of good requires.

And now here at the end we can perhaps find a place for James' conception of the pragmatic test, in the sense of successful production of satisfaction, beneficial results in life, "spiritual health." Such an appeal to a philosophy's power of giving hope, motivating constructive conduct, leading to survival may have something to do with verifying the truth of a whole system, which Carnap (p. 135) said was beyond the other tests of truth. Of course, since creating a great system of coherent ideas out of a prior state of confusion is itself the supreme example of compositional process, which DR claims both the mind and nature to be engaged in, it will presumably be accompanied by a supreme feeling of consummatory satisfaction, i.e. dynamic good. One will be tempted to believe that this great theory *must* be true, when so much slips so beautifully into place in it. But of course each part must have hurdled the correspondence test first; and then the criteria of coherence and simplicity. After that, however, James' test might be used, for instance, in deciding between solipsism and objectivism, or between atheism and theism. If a nihilistic atheism or a self-centered solipsism should appear to confuse a person's life or to lower people's stamina and cause social decay, we might consider their apparent unworkability for human affairs as some testimony to their falsity. They would not seem to fit into the nature of life if they regularly led to collapse and degeneration. However, we could not take a religious belief's ability to give stamina to some people as itself a verification if the belief flew in the face of any ordinarily verified facts or involved internal logical contradictions.

Now at the end there is also a place in DR's theory for authority. It has a similar status to the above satisfaction — it can only supplement the other tests. When something that has passed those tests also turns out to have been universally accepted over long periods of time, by large numbers of reputable minds, we feel that its truth is that much more established.

And yet, finally DR must once again confess that no structure of knowledge is ever final, perfect or certain. DR has to admit that the inaccuracy of the senses, human proneness to errors in logic, and emotional biases remain to keep man forever from perfection of truth. And even if perfection were achieved, the minds would tire of it. Actually, contemplation always eventually becomes aware of incompleteness, of new problems arising, as they must if zest in knowing is to continue. None of the methods of verification nor all of them put together can give man in this life final truth. Thus there is a place for skepticism at the very end. DR can never let down its critical guard, must continue on the lookout for possible improvements of our beliefs. Knowledge must keep changing in some degree forever.

Comparison of SM and DR: For SM, this conclusion of DR's is entirely dismaying. Upon being told that the old Newtonian science, for instance, which had seemed to be humanity's first success in finding a truth that could be proved to everyone's satisfaction, has been overthrown, the certainty-seekers ask what reason have we to place any confidence in the new science. The answer is that the new science does not exactly negate everything in the old; it *refines* it. Men did not waste their time for three hundred years on a tissue of hopeless errors. In fact, Newtonian science remains roughly valid for certain relatively rough purposes. But it is now understood as describing for us only average or statistical results, rather than basic relationships. The more refined science has uncovered phenomena which carry quite different implications, however, for our final metaphysical conclusions about the nature of reality.

SM also asks how man can live without certainty, at least on the matters of God, Immortality and the Moral Law. DR answers that he must and can act on knowledge that is only probable. In fact, at the core of scientific method is the necessity for the scientist to act on his hypothesis even though it is only a guess. This action then leads to more substantiation of the hypothesis afterwards. By analogy, DR suggests, strangely more sincerely that SIR itself, that religious beliefs must be based on faith rather than absolute knowledge. And it means by faith precisely readiness to act without certainty.

On the other hand we could argue that DR does permit, in its holistic knowledge based on a final intuitional grasp of many, many things fitting together and pointing in one direction, a kind of general certainty in the meaningfulness of things, though not a certainty in specific outcomes or exemplifications of that meaning.

142

Implications of DM and Correspondence to DR: The dynamic idea of value obviously implies that the verification process should be what we have found it to be: a constant improving and refining of our ideas, a constant building of them into more and more inclusive structures of thought. The enjoyment that is associated with the successful testing of bits of knowledge, and the successful building of them into coherent structures is one of the greatest examples of dynamic good itself. Man must be in a situation of striving to resolve disorder and enjoying partial attainment of organized pattern. He may be allowed to "appreciate" the beauty and grandeur of great designs of knowledge — but only to a degree. For his appreciation of them is a function of his having experienced struggle in attaining them; and his future enjoyment of contemplation will depend upon his now entering another creative struggle. Thus every present attainment *must* reveal, presently, scope for further striving and building.

DM also clearly implies both the objective and subjective sides of the knowledge process. There must be the subjective enjoyment or feeling by a "feeler" (#1.1, p. 53); but there must also be the objective contribution of ingredients to enter (in relative disorder) into the composition process (# 2.2. p. 53). There must be an objective world that hands us the miscellaneous materials with which we must grapple in building up our ability to control them and to appreciate them.

Our final word under epistemology, is the conclusion of the theory of how we can *know* the meaningfulness of reality. DR, we saw, arrives at scientific theories of *process* and *feeling* as the culminating concepts of its work. We have maintained that scientific method can go so far as to verify a theory of the nature and causes of "good" feeling, or enjoyment. Would it now be possible to show that an understanding of good or value incorporating these facts, would provide an ultimate theory of theories from which all the lower theories of science could be deduced, *including* that of process? That is the question for the remainder of this book.

PART III

ONTOLOGY: THEORIES OF REALITY

(THE PROBLEM OF MECHANISM)

CHAPTER VII

THEORIES OF SUBSTANCE AND CHANGE

Having some idea of the methods of study by which man approaches his notions about reality, we now move to the study of those notions about reality themselves.

The first two divisions of this study of the most basic features of reality — the stuff and the units (in this and the next chapters) — must be thoroughly understood before we can go on to the more momentous questions of causation and purpose in Chapter IX and the following. For it is necessary to understand the different ideas of substance and units in order to understand the different ideas of causation; and whether causation by purposes and aims is possible or not will depend on how causation in general is conceived. The difficulties men have fallen into on these problems involve essentially the relation between wholes and parts, or units. We shall, then, consider what each of the philosophies indicates on each of these topics.

SM with SIR.

Implications of SM on Substance and Change: Mentalism. Why has there always been, in the history of philosophy, a great reluctance on the part of many thinkers to admit that material substance, or matter, and change are real? The layman may wonder how anyone could waste a minute on trying to deny things so obvious, and yet he probably dimly realizes that Plato, who many feel was the greatest philosopher of all, was definitely not happy about the existence of matter and change, and would have been glad not to have to deal with them in his philosophy. For he could find no meaningful reason why they should exist, though he did not go so far as his predecessor, Parmenides, in flatly denying that change exists; or as some of his modern heirs (Berkeley, Hegel) in denying that matter exists. We also recall

147

the widespread tendency of men to despise the matter in their bodies. Some Hindus seem to desire nothing so much as to punish their bodies out of existence; and some early Christian ascetics carried out Plato's antipathy toward the body much farther than Plato did himself.

But why have philosophers wished to cast doubt on the importance and reality of change and matter? What is so bad about process and material?

Well, there are some obvious but superficial reasons: men are lazy and imagine that they would enjoy calm rest above all things. As Rome decayed, men became so exhausted with disorder and violence that only the fixed and effortless appealed. It was out of this condition that Christianity arose, with its favorite themes of peace, casting burdens on the Lord, waiting for a static heaven to eliminate the struggles of this world.

Pretending to despise matter also offers a convenient out for one's sins: he can blame them on the material body while keeping a belief in the purity of his "spirit."

However, there is a conceptual reason deeper than any of these, which neither ancient nor modern commentators have made very explicit, underlying all discounting of matter and change. And of course it is a *value* reason that is the real source of the desire to deprive such apparently obvious facts of some or all of their reality. It has always been, both in Asia and the West, precisely the static idea of value that has made men hate matter and change, and crave as the only *meaningful* world that could be expected from a cosmic purpose for such value, a world of unchangingly perfect thought.

We have already hinted in Chapter IV that there is a connection between the static idea of good, and the expectation that reality should consist of nothing but mentality or thought. It is easy enough to see why there need be no process or change to embody static value; but in order to show why there would need be no *matter* I have to jump ahead a little to what will be clearer when we come to DM below: that an integral connection exists between the ideas of process, structure and matter. As we shall show, process requires *structure*, which is defined as such arrangements of rigid and flexible parts as make effective motion possible. Especially to be noticed is the necessity not only of flexible and fluid parts (which is obvious) but also of some relatively *rigid* parts, if there is to be process. The flexible parts must have solid anchorages, leverages, etc., or their motion will be ineffective. It is from this concept of rigidity that we can derive the idea and necessity of matter or material substance.

But we have seen that the static idea of value does not require process, and thence structure or matter. And this is the real root of the antipathy to matter in earlier philosophy.

The implication of the static idea of value as to what substance reality should consist of, then, is that it should be a realm of processless concepts or thought essences; or, to use a term that the Greeks invented, a realm of *mental substance*. Secondly, this realm should be unchangingly perfect, for there is no reason in the nature of static good, why it might not exist in complete conceptual fullness at all times, since it in no way requires growth or process as part of its being. Therefore, a Cosmic Purpose might as well, nay, definitely should have established it absolutely at the first instant of time, supposing there is any time (which however itself is not required by the static idea of value). Reality should be a timeless, perfect system of ideas or thought.

That this rather odd picture has not been concocted by the author merely to fill out a place in his scheme is easy enough to prove, for it has been defended explicitly by perhaps more thinkers and theologians than have attacked it, at least as a description of God's own reality. Whether they can manage to believe that world is static mentality or not, such great minds as Aristotle, Plotinus, St. Augustine, etc., have insisted that God is. Even Aristotle, dynamic though his theory of the world may be, never questioned that the cosmic Absolute itself was a motionless and perfect Being whose experience of perfect value implied that it could not even be aware of the dynamic world it had created, for that would introduce imperfect thoughts into its consciousness. It had nothing more to do than timelessly contemplate its own perfect thinking. As Dewey puts it:

> And while Plato took, comparatively speaking, a pessimistic view of change as mere lapse, and Aristotle a complacent view of it as tendency to realization, yet Aristotle doubted no more than Plato that the fully realized reality, the divine and ultimate is changeless.[1]

Adjustments of SIR: Monism, Dualism. The earlier theory of Reality, SIR, noticed that Reality does not clearly conform to

149

the above implications of SM. Change and material substance are so insistent that even the strictest devotees of the above line of thought feel obliged to provide some sort of further explanation. As we have seen, two main tacks are pursued in this emergency:

1. The theory of Appearance or Illusion. By this device some Idealists believe they can return to the strict implications of SM. The contradictory evidences of the senses are dismissed as unreal or "Non-Being," and a monistic theory of unchanging mental essences as the one real substance is regained. Belief in an absolutely cosmic purpose for (static) good is again possible. Some forms of Hinduism are possibly the purest example of this tack; also the beliefs of the American religious group known as Christian Science.

There are various ways by which these "Illusionists" purport to disprove the existence of matter and change. In recent times, the familiar epistemological approach (See Chapter VI) has been used against the former. Another approach impressed Parmenides and Plato — a mathematical one. They were devoted to the superior certainty that mathematics seemed to possess as compared to any kind of sensory experience. The senses often fooled us, and the world that they revealed was dismayingly unstable and contradictory. But mathematical relationships never changed, and if 2 x 2 equalled 4 when you thought of it to-day, it still equalled 4 when thought of next week. This mathematical interest was a source of Greek philosophy's tendency to conceive of reality as a static perfection with timeless relationships on the model of the fixed axioms of Euclidean geometry. Parmenides and his follower, Zeno, presented the famous paradoxes that seemed to prove logically that motion and change were self-contradictory and therefore impossible. On such bases, Plato believed that unchanging mental concepts, such as mathematical ideas, were "more real" than material things, because they were not so fleeting. Greek philosophers after that habitually measured Reality (or "Being") as proportional to unchanging stability. Matter was always "becoming" and thus obviously had less "being," thus less reality. This passage from Dewey just precedes the one above:

Wherever there is change, there is instability, and instability is the proof of something the matter, of absence, deficiency, incompleteness; these are the ideas common to the connection between change, becoming, and perishing and Non-

150

Being, Finitude and Imperfection. Hence complete and true Reality must be changeless, unalterable, so full of Being that it always and forever maintains itself in fixed rest and repose.[2]

2. Dualism. The more frequent adjustment is reluctantly to grant the existence of the second realm of change and matter, but to keep it dependent upon, or subordinate to, the static mental realm. But since no reason can be found in the static idea of value why this realm should exist, dualism, in purest logic, must relinquish our "cosmic" factor, that is the "omnipotence" of God. Plato is the great exemplar of this view, admitting that God did not desire nor create matter, and that he has no complete control over it. Christianity also took the dualistic tack, yet tried to retain omnipotence with its theory of the material universe being "created out of nothing." It seems fair to say however, that Christianity has never succeeded in settling men's minds with its explanation of why God created a material world at all—let alone the evil material world that it is—and that this weakness in its philosophical foundations is making more trouble for it today than ever.

The dualist solution, as we shall see in later chapters, has also brought with it what modern psychologists would insist has always been an unhealthy attitude toward the body. The matter-vs.-mind, body-vs.-soul, flesh-vs.-spirit dualisms that stem from the basic dualism, many are saying today, not only have kept philosophy in confusion, but are the root of much of the pervasive neuroticism of our age.

SM with SMR.

Findings of SMR: Matter. As we explain the essential features of the mechanistic, materialist view of early modern science, its contradiction of every expectation of SM will be apparent to the student with only brief reminders from the author.

We recall that SMR's theory of the sources of knowledge, in assuming the mirror analogy for human knowing, restricted itself to those sense organs that are especially adapted to receiving or reflecting data from the external world; and was directed at first to the more available and obvious objects in the environment—

151

the larger, or "macroscopic" things, that seem so manifestly to be made of "solid" matter. And finally, what these senses seemed to convey about these objects (their solidity, their inertia, etc.) was taken at face value — the more so, the earlier in the history of science. As Jeans notes, the practical struggle for survival forces us to store up a degree of expertness in knowledge and skill about handling normal-sized objects. The concepts of rest, motion, push, pull, hard, soft, impact, etc., arise out of our everyday activity. Early science had to start with ideas men already had — their ordinary interpretation of their sense experience, their ideas of number and quantity. The sense of touch, taken at face value, makes us believe in forces, tensions, pressures, hard or soft stuff and is thus the source of most of the basic ideas used in mechanical explanations. Our notions of shape and motion root more in the sense of sight, which thus is the source of geometrical explanations. Putting these two together gives us the ordinary idea of matter and motion, upon which is based SMR, mechanistic materialism.[3]

The notion that Nature is made of material, that is, some solid "stuff" or substance is actually as old as any idea in philosophy — older, even, than the "mental substance" ideas of SM-SIR. Everyone knows that the first Greek philosopher, Thales, coming forward with the early attempt to explain things by some unified, intelligible concept (rather than by the arbitrary will of demons or spirits) took it for granted that his job was to find some one "stuff" from which all things came. He chose water, and inaugurated the various pre-Socratic suggestions of what kinds of materials the world might be made of. Only Heraclitus resisted this assumption of "stuff," trying to put more emphasis on change as the basic concept. But even he, like all the Greeks, found it impossible to think without the idea of some stuff, so he tended to embody change in the rapidly moving "element" of fire.

The main stream of thought from the Greeks through the medieval period, as we have seen under the dualistic theories above, granted a world of stuff or matter, but never gave up believing that this stuff was informed with purposiveness in some sense. Aristotle, for instance, insisted on a doctrine of "substance" but all substances contained in their essence inherent tendencies toward goals. Everything had a natural potency toward its own most perfect fulfillment.

However, when the source of knowledge is restricted as it

was for early modern science, it is apparent that this inner purposiveness, this feeling, desiring element cannot be allowed as
real, because the senses of hearing, touch, vision, do not distinctly
reveal it as existing in ordinary material objects. And so, the concept of matter that resulted in early modern science (it had
already been worked out in Greek times by Leucippus and Democritus), was that it is a stuff that has only the touchable and
seeable characteristics of solidity, extension (that is, it occupies
space), and motion. Newton added (see quotation below) one
other characteristic of matter, inertia. This meant that matter
was entirely passive, and could never initiate any motion or change
its state of motion from within itself. It could only begin to
move, when not moving, or change its rate of motion, if moving,
when something else acted upon it — either another piece of
matter already in motion must collide with it, whereupon the
motion would be transmitted according to a fixed law; or (and
this was a later concession of SMR) some kind of attractive or
repelling force must act on it across "empty" space.

The story of how all qualitative aspects of nature were removed
from matter is the familiar one of the primary and secondary
qualities. Galileo made this distinction early in the history of
modern science. It seemed obvious that such experiences as
colors, sounds, smells, etc. could not be said to be "in" matter,
for they only arose when our minds somehow reacted to matter.
Galileo called these the "secondary qualities" and dismissed them
from science as merely "subjective." Number, figure, magnitude,
position, and motion he considered "primary" and to be really
"in" the matter. His criterion for "reality" was mathematical;
these qualities were able to be measured and used in mathematical
formulae. In this manner the whole qualitative and feeling side
of experience was ruled out of the realm of matter, that is, ultimately, out of reality.

Whitehead discusses this concept of matter as a neutral stuff
under the term "vacuous actuality"; this means to assume that
reality, in its ultimate nature, is "devoid of subjective immediacy."[4] The materialism of earlier science is

. . . the fixed scientific cosmology which presupposes the ultimate fact of an irreducible brute matter, or material, spread
throughout space in a flux of configurations. In itself such
a material is senseless, valueless, purposeless. It just does

what it does do, following a fixed routine imposed by external relations which do not spring from the nature of its being.[5]

Now, under the topic of Substance, we have also to make clear how the philosophy relates its notion of substance to the static-dynamic issue. We have already seen that mechanistic materialism starts off granting the existence of *motion*, at least: matter can change to that extent. Matter (or its units, see Chapter VIII) is constantly swirling about, colliding, transmitting motion according to Newton's three laws of motion. However, as we have just said, it is always passive in this motion; it never initiates motion itself. So this is one static feature of this view. In addition, there is a sense in which the motion of this matter never *does* anything, never really accomplishes anything, or creates a new reality. A full understanding of this point must wait till the discussion of the Whole-Part relationship in Chapter VIII.

Contradictions between SM and SMR; Recourses: Obviously, instead of SM's substance whose essential nature is to exemplify purpose and values, we have a substance that seems utterly separated from any possibility of exemplifying ideas, purposes, values, feelings.

The desperate measures Idealism resorted to in this emergency are familiar — the Illusionist and Dualist escapes. Descartes is the great exemplar of Dualism; Berkeley and Hegel of Illusionism. Descartes saves purposiveness in his mental realm while he delivers the body over to mechanistic materialism. His attempt to connect the two through the pineal gland, then, notoriously erred in both empirical and rational respects. Berkeley makes both the mental and the objective worlds spiritual. By Spirit, he means an undivided active being whose two principal activities are creating and perceiving. Reality is thus essentially mental and purposive. But the objections to the Idealist solution (p. 118 f.) drive us on to a more basic criticism of SMR itself.

SM with DR.

Findings of DR: The Revolution in Science. All authorities in the field of science grant that there has been a revolution in science during the last century; and laymen know that something of a striking nature must have occurred in science to issue in such cosmic powers for man as are signified by the word "atomic."

But the layman is apt to be entirely unconscious of the ideological side of this revolution. For him atomic power is just another in the series of technological inventions that have issued from "science" — the same science, supposedly, that has always existed ever since "modern times" began. Few realize that the concepts that enabled the invention of the atom bomb must result, in a few centuries, in everyone's feeling quite differently about "Nature" in general than they have felt since Newtonian ideas seeped down into their blood and bone to shed that impersonal and mechanistic aura about most things which we all, *now,* take for granted. Most of us assume that our feeling that the "physical world" about us is mostly an inert, impersonal, purposeless, place is the only possible attitude man can take to it — native to human nature as such, age-old. But actually it has only recently become wide-spread. Not until the Industrial Revolution began a century or so ago, did men at large begin to find "machine-like" a widely applicable characteristic. During about 99% of its history, man-kind has habitually felt that almost everything that existed was "life-like" rather than "machine-like." All animals, of course, seemed clearly to be filled with purposeful life, dim though it might be. The vegetable kingdom too, was thought of as guided by still dimmer, yet certainly not mechanical spirits. Thunder-storms, sunsets, breezes, etc., were always thought of as planned and purposed by either demons, spirits or God Himself. The notion of all these things being the non-intentional products of automatic material causes was simply not around during most of man's history. And strangely enough, this idea is not going to be around much longer either; if it is not eliminated by the atom bomb itself, along with humanity, then it is going to be eliminated by the implications of the theories behind the atom bomb. For it was not until science dropped its picture of the solid, inert, material atom that could not have *real* relationships, or continuity, or fusion into wholes with other atoms, that it could proceed with the theorizing that finally released atomic power.

Many professional scientists are not too much ahead of the layman in understanding these implications. Many still stubbornly use the word "mechanism" for their basic category, even though they vaguely realize that they are debarred from considering "matter" in any of its older, more usual senses and from think-ing of atoms as in any sense solid nuggets. If they have let themselves be pushed to conceiving atoms as little solar systems, they may light on the electron and other sub-atomic "particles" as their new solid nuggets. When told they may not conceive of these either as solid nuggets, they will probably subside into facetious acquiescence but continue to try to work out pictures of electrons "pushing" other electrons.

This revolution in science, after all, did not happen in a thunderclap, but was spread out over a period of time — about a century if you date it from Darwin's Evolutionary theory in 1859, through the laying of the main foundations of Relativity and Quantum theory during the first quarter of our century, by Einstein and others. Thus it may not have been so much a revolution as an evolution, so that people are not very conscious of it. In this book space requires us to try to confine ourselves to contrasting the earlier ideas with the final ones, and to neglect all the hybrids and compromises that were conceived while the change was slowly going forward.

As a brief preview of some of the ingredients in this evolution, we may mention first, that as usual, the Greeks had already suggested some main features of the dynamic view. Among the very first thinkers to guess at explanations of nature in terms other than personal wills or spiritual agents was Anaximander (611-546 B. C.) with the first hint of a doctrine of evolution. Heraclitus, a little later, put such an emphasis on change as the basic reality that he is usually taken by dynamic naturalism as its spiritual father. Hippocrates and Empedocles, early thinkers in the areas of biology and medicine who contributed to organismic ways of thinking, led to Aristotle, whose thinking also was primarily conditioned by biological studies. Rather than taking "stuff" or "substance" as his primary category, as other early "physicists" had, he took *generation* or growth as his basic idea. This meant, in Greek terms, that he gave "Becoming" an importance it had not had with Plato, for whom static "Being" had been the essence of reality. Aristotle still used the term "Substance" — in fact was the first to give it a clear meaning. Substance was for him the basic identity of any thing that continued throughout all its changes, so that it could still be considered itself, and yet the nature of any substance was its ability to take on changing forms. "Substance" is thus divided into "matter" and "form." But he defined "matter" essentially as formless potentiality, as the stuff that was able to be formed. "Form" was as real as matter, being the source or cause of matter's becoming formed. But we are not to consider form as separable from matter at any time — it cannot exist as disembodied "Idea" in Plato's sense. Matter developing toward form, then, seems the essential concept in Aristotle, so that we may say "Process" or "development" was his basic idea of "substance" or "stuff." And yet, he seems to have retained enough of Plato's way of thinking to suppose that, although no form ever existed without being the product of a process of development from matter, still the possible forms that could be developed were already somehow existent and prescribed. He returned to the "static" in this sense: conceiving reality as a realm of repeated developmental processes continually producing and reproducing the same allotted forms. New forms as such were not evolved. Also he apparently allows that any particular developing process can succeed in fully and perfectly reaching its final form; and that it can then enjoy existence in this form without further development. We have already seen that Aristotle's God is in this condition: He is completely "at" his perfect form, has nowhere further to go. In Aristotle's thinking this also means that he has no "matter," that is, anything *un*formed, in Him. He is "pure form."

Thus it is that we could refer to Aristotle above (p. 149) in illustration of static ideas; and that the medieval philosophy, which was ultimately based mostly on Aristotle, can always be included in our early static philosophy, SM and SIR.

Nothing new was added to Aristotle's analysis of development, then, until the "Darwinians." The mechanistic theory that occupied men's attention in the intervening period was curiously even more static than Aristotle's. Finally the theory of evolution of species, crystallized by Darwin after much preceding speculation by others, was undoubtedly more instrumental in forcing philosophy over toward dynamic categories than any other event in the history of thought. The key change from Aristotle is already apparent in the name of the theory: evolution of *species,* that is, of the Forms themselves. When this concept was expanded in modern thinking, to include the possibility that nothing whatever in the universe, or in man's thought about it, is finally fixed, that everything is constantly being modified, developed, created, we are in the realm of DR.

Nevertheless, we must not forget that a period ensued characterized by attempts to combine mechanistic explanations with evolutionary theory, resulting as we will see in Chapter IX, in the conclusion that evolution *does* nothing real. In fact, Darwin's theory was taken at first as a final clinching keystone for mechanistic theory, enabling it, at last, to explain the origin of life. In this book, this phase of thought — mechanistic evolutionism — will always be included with SMR rather than with DR. Eventually one feature of Darwinian theory (the "struggle for existence") proved an opening gun for demolishing mechanistic theory.

But it was not until Physics itself found it necessary to change its old concepts of solid, inert matter and mechanistic, atomistic causation, that the foundations of SMR really began to crumble. The very first threat to SMR was probably back with Newton himself, when "action at a distance" to explain gravitational phenomena, arose as a difficulty for the pure mechanistic theory of causation as push and pull between material bodies *in contact*. Newton tried to escape any such suggestion of immaterial "forces" operating across space by resorting to the idea of a material "ether" pervading all space to transmit the pushes and pulls. But such "dynamic force" notions kept recurring, in Chemistry, for example, to explain attraction and repulsion of atoms and electric charges.

> Until the most recent times, various hybrid combinations of substance and dynamics were developed, but gradually the constructive dynamic properties of matter displaced its substantial ones and rendered them superfluous.[6]

However, with the help of the idea of "ether" and others, the materialistic, mechanistic theory seemed to be successfully extended from its original area of macroscopic bodies, to more subtle phenomena, such as those of heat, electric currents, light waves, etc. All of these phenomena could be thought of as the motions of particles either of ordinary matter, or of ether.

Development of the Concepts of Energy and Field in Electro-Magnetism, Light, Gravitation and Atom: It was in the study of electricity and magnetism that the materialistic mechanistic theory met its first decisive defeat. Faraday and Clerk-Maxwell's work resulted in a new kind of mathematical equation: one that described the conditions obtaining *between* the particles, instead of the state of the particles themselves. A glimmer of what the

158

problem is can be got by the layman if he thinks of the familiar magnet and iron filings. Something invisible makes the filings fall into oval patterns around the magnet. Materialistically, we would have to suppose that some sort of material substance is coming out of the magnet and pushing or pulling the particles into their places. No such stuff can be detected by any sense-organs or instruments, however. It might be put off onto the ether, which was defined precisely as a stuff too thin to be detectible, which yet can transmit pushes or pulls. But this commits a methodological sin which we set ourselves against (p. 119) appealing to a non-empirically-verifiable idea. The problem becomes worse, anyway, as soon as we learn of the behavior of electricity in the vicinity of a magnet or, vice versa, of the behavior of magnetism in the vicinity of an electric current. When either type of "force," if we allow ourselves to use the term, *moves,* the other one springs into existence at right angles to it. If electricity is flowing down a wire, then a magnetic needle held nearby will point perpendicularly to the wire. Or if a magnet is moved back and forth perpendicularly to the wire, electricity will flow in the wire. In addition, the force of the reaction, instead of depending only on the mass and the square of the distance, as in mechanics, also depends on the *velocity* of the action. No satisfactory picture of material pushes and pulls, by the particles themselves, or transmission by an ethereal medium around them, has ever been found to explain how particles pushed or pulled in the direction of their motion could give rise also to forces pushing or pulling to the side, proportional to the velocity.

It is interesting to study Maxwell's first attempts to explain these phenomena by equations relating exclusively to the particles or electrons themselves, their masses, directions of motion, etc., assuming they followed the inverse square law for attraction between material bodies; and how he was gradually pushed to equations relating to the pattern and "strength" of the "field" of space between the electrons.[7] This meant a change from explaining phenomena in terms of causes located in the material particles, to causes located in the spread-out continuum or field surrounding the particles. There was still a hope of considering the field as "made" of an elastic material ether of some sort, but when Relativity theory (see below) found reasons to eliminate such an ether, electro-magnetic theory was glad to let it go and to move on to an immaterialistic concept of the field as in some sense pure "energy." We now speak of the "electro-magnetic field" that pervades all space.

The old mechanical view attempted to reduce all events in nature to forces acting between material particles. Upon this mechanical view was based the first naive theory of the electric fluids. The field did not exist for the physicist of the early years of the nineteenth century. For him only substance and its changes were real. He tried to describe the action of two electric charges only by concepts referring directly to the two charges. . . . In the new field language it is the description of the field between the two charges, and not the charges themselves, which is essential for an understanding of their action. The recognition of the new concepts grew steadily, until substance was overshadowed by the field. It was realized that something of great importance had happened in physics.[8]

We move then, to the second blow to materialism, Einstein's Special and General Relativity theories. His thinking began in the branch of Physics dealing with light. Materialism had tried to explain light in either of two ways. Newton had preferred his atomistic approach: light should be streams of tiny particles moving through space until they collide with other material particles agglomerated in solid matter, and are thus stopped or bounced back (reflected). This explained light's seemingly never bending around corners, and certain other light phenomena. It did not explain other light phenomena however, especially interference — cases where different beams of light thrown on the same area cancel each other out, producing dark bands. A wave-theory of light as a vibration was required to explain this: if light were like water-waves, for instance, and two series of waves came together in such a way that the crests of the first waves met the troughs of the second waves, the result would be for water, a smooth surface; for light, absence of vibration, therefore darkness. But materialism demands a material "something" to vibrate, and therefore the material ether was again called upon to transmit the vibrations of light, in addition to its other tasks of transmitting the "forces" of gravity, and of electro-magnetism.

However, as everyone knows, the famous Michelson-Morley experiment, supplemented by others, proved, in finding that the speed of light was the same whatever direction you measured it relative to the earth's direction of motion, that the hypothesis of a motionless material ether carrying light waves, through which the earth moves, was unverifiable. Einstein felt obliged to conclude that light would reveal the same velocity (186,000 miles per second) no matter what the velocity of the observer might be relative to the source of the light. If a light beam is assumed to be flying past you at 186,000 miles per second while you are standing still, it will still be flying past you at exactly the same rate if you should start flying toward it on a rocket at 20,000 miles an hour.

The only way out of this impossible contradiction was the desperate measure of supposing that all objects, including all measuring devices, contract in the direction of their motion, and all time keepers change their rhythm just enough to eliminate any trace of the addition or subtraction of velocity that would be expected.

A host of unexpected implications came out of this odd conclusion. Some of the main ones for our present subject of "substance" besides the above elimination of the material ether are as follows. It was discovered that the equation (the "Lorentz transformation") that tells just how much the above contractions must be, indicates that the amount of force necessary to increase the velocity of any object depends on the velocity or the kinetic energy involved. This was what was found for electro-magnetic forces (p. 159) but supposedly not for mechanical ones, where the force was proportional only to the *mass* of the material in the object. However, relativity theory was proved to be correct. Since the need for the increased force only becomes appreciable at high velocities — near those of light itself — it had been too minute at ordinary velocities to be measured. But what have we just said? Velocity, or kinetic energy, behaves like mass in this respect: it resists change of motion, or requires extra force to accelerate it just as mass does! Pursing this hint, Einstein ultimately made his famous declaration that mass and energy are equivalent and should be transformable one to the other. The equation for their equivalence was $E = mc^2$, meaning that mass is multiplied by the square of the speed of light to find its equivalent energy. Obviously a little mass contains an enormous amount of energy! The main point, however, is that the "matter" and "energy" of the older physics are somehow unified, and that the two laws of "conservation of mass" and "conservation of energy" become *one* law of "conservation of energy." Once again, solid, dead matter loses "reality" to something seemingly less solid yet more alive!

A second line of implication, arising in the Lorentz equation, which we will not explain at length, led to considering Time as inseparable from Space in such a manner that the figure for Time, in relativity equations, can always be treated quite interchangeably with any of the three measurements for Space. This leads to the term "four-dimensional Space-Time Continuum" as an essential description of the nature of reality.

Taken together with the additional reasoning of the *General* Theory of Relativity, which added gravitational phenomena to the electro-magnetic, mechanical and optic phenomena already unified by the Special Theory, Einstein at last found himself thinking of the "Space-Time Continuum" as a field of energy entirely analogous to the field concepts that had appeared in electro-magnetic theory. Space-Time was now considered as a spread-out immaterial unity with an inner geometrical structure or pattern or organization, which controlled or guided the various objects or events that took place within it. Explanations once again are based more on the "space" between units of matter, than on the units of matter themselves. Instead of trying to think of light for instance, as "caused" by vibrating particles, then transmitted in straight lines through a sympathetically vibrating jelly-like ether, we think rather of a structured Space-Time that constrains the light energy to follow paths according to the Space-Time's own pattern. And instead of thinking of the planets as somehow pulled by forces localized in the sun, we think of them as "fitting into" the field patterns of the solar system, or helping to achieve some proper balance or symmetry in the overall unity. Rather than "forced" by influences emanating from individual bodies, they follow the curves of the Space-Time field as a whole.

The third decisive blow against materialistic theory came from microphysics, dealing with the very small in Quantum theory (in contrast to relativity theory dealing with macrophysics and the very large). These findings relate more to the topic of "Units" in the next chapter, but we can point out here that this same factor of control of the "parts" by the energy fields surrounding them appears in quantum theory as does the equivalence of matter and energy.

Summary of the Nature of Energy, Field, Matter: We find the terms "energy," "process," "field," "Space-Time," "functional," etc., all used in trying to get at the nature of the basic reality, stuff, or substance. There is a strong tendency to drop the concept of "substance" or "matter" entirely, although the latest that we hear from the physicists is that matter has not entirely disappeared yet. The "unified field theories" keep trying to eliminate it, and to find equations involving exclusively field concepts that will hold all the way into the core of those high concentrations of energy called "matter." But there still seems to be something different in those concentrations from what obtains out in the "thinner" fields in space.

At any rate, the presumption is that "energy" is the more basic reality, whatever it may be.

> . . . if we ask what energy is, we are told that it is the . . . capacity for *doing* something. . . . We see work done and we can measure it — and those measurements are our data for the construction of our science. It is not *being,* but *process,* to which we are always led. Things *are* what they *do.* We cannot know what energy is; we can only know what mathematical ratios prevail in its various manifestations.[9]

> . . . The modern interpretation of atomic events has very little resemblance to genuine materialistic philosophy . . . modern physics is in some way extremely near to the doctrines of Heraclitus. . . . Energy is in fact the substance from which all elementary particles, all atoms and therefore all things are made, and energy is that which moves.[10]

> . . . the notion of *mass* was losing its unique pre-eminence as being the one final permanent quantity. Later on, we find the relations of mass and energy inverted; so that mass now becomes the name for a quantity of energy considered in relation to some of its dynamical effects. This train of thought leads to the notion of energy being fundamental, thus displacing matter from that position. But energy is merely the name for the quantitative aspect of a structure of happenings. . . .[11]

Energy, then, is such a general idea that it can hardly be defined, or imagined as such. It means the *aliveness* of reality, the source of motion, change, power. And although it is capable of concentrating into portions of "matter" which attain a degree of stability, or identity, and shape and structure — still, apparently, it is only a *degree*. The most inert-appearing matter is still in constant change, losing, receiving energy; and internally, it never stops being a cauldron of whirl and tension, though the whirls may be more or less kept in one "place" for some eons before they escape to the outer field.

This energy is such stuff as can constitute "fields." This means that, however much it may be divisible into parts (see next chapter) still it is also capable of fusing into spread-out unified states which have *properties* extended over the whole. Einstein explains how the field concept was first used by Maxwell as mere representation, to help the human mind think out the behavior of magnets and electric currents. But

> Starting as a helpful model, the field became more and more real. It helped us to understand old facts and leads us to new ones. The attribution of energy to the field is one step further in the development in which the field concept was stressed more and more and the concepts of substances, so essential to the mechanical point of view, were more and more suppressed.[12]

> We summarize: A new concept appears in physics, the most important invention since Newton's time: the field. It needed great scientific imagination to realize that it is not the charges nor the particles but the field in space between the charges and the particles which is essential for the description of phenomena.[13]

Matter, then, is as we have indicated, thought of as highly concentrated energy, where the "mass" that all energy has anyway, becomes thousands or millions of times greater than it is in other parts of the field. Theoretically however, there is no separation between the matter and the field around it; it is just a matter of the field becoming rapidly, and yet gradually, stronger at this or that place. This "knot" of concentrated field strength, nevertheless, changes the pattern of the nearby "thinner" field around it, or, in other terms "curves" the nearby space more than it is curved farther away. This is shown by the fact that when other concen-

164

trations of energy, or "matter," pass by the first concentration they take a curved path. The curve is immeasurable except for the very "thin" objects passing very "thick" ones — such as starlight passing by the sun. This has been measured as curving according to prediction.

Related to this constraining characteristic of fields is one other feature of field physics which promises to be useful for the purposes of dynamic meaning. This is the concept of "strains"[14] as used in the branch of physics known as the physics of "continua." Strains occur in the deformations of fields, and are defined as displacements of a point in a continuum or field to another place than its normal position. In such a case, as when the pattern of a field is distorted by some interfering body or force, the field reveals a tendency to pull back into its more symmetrical or balanced form. It seeks "equilibrium." Either it finds the "best" form it can in the presence of the foreign object, or it works to eliminate the object so as to reach the "better" form. Applying this idea to the universe, someone has said that gravitation results from the universe's constantly trying to "straighten itself out." This concept is very useful for the concept of causation in Chapter XI.

Philosophical Conclusions: *The Concept of "Process," "Creativity"*: Now we find that philosophers of dynamism, of whom Alfred North Whitehead is the most eminent, meditating upon these findings of physics, and also considering hints from biology, believe that this bare idea of energy in fields always "straining" toward equilibrium, or symmetry is not quite a complete description of the basic nature or "stuff" of reality. The term *"Process"* is preferred for the most general and inclusive concept of all science, for it adds to the bare idea of energy, the notion of incorporation of ingredients, of building them into structures, of development and passing on into more inclusive accomplishment. Energy means hardly anything more than that there can be motion and change transmitted according to known equations. Process means in addition that this motion and change can accomplish definite products, that it can add up to some creation; or contrariwise, that it can produce a definite dissolution and dispersion. The term "creativity" is also used, apparently applying only to process that builds or organizes. Instead of a "matter" that may sometimes be entirely motionless and separated from change, and at other times related to motion and change, we must understand that only change or

165

process really exists. Sometimes it achieves relative stability which must probably be conceived as repetition of a pattern of process, but the relationships between the part energies or ingredients involved are always changing.

Whitehead analyzes the idea of process as including the "data," which are the existing energies in formerly achieved structures that are moving into the current unit of process; the "form" which the actual change takes; the "transition" which is the fact of change itself; and the "issue" which is the outcome, the new structure achieved after those ingredients have moved into their new organization. But there is no stop here; new ingredients immediately swim into the process and a new episode of organizing takes place showing the same phases over again.

> Too much attention has been directed to the mere datum and the mere issue. The essence of existence lies in the transition from datum to issue. . . . One main doctrine . . . is that "existence" (in any of its senses) cannot be abstracted from "process." The notions of "process" and "existence" presuppose each other.[15]

It is thinking of data or issue as stopping places, or as "things" temporarily or permanently free from process, that gives rise to the idea of static "matter." Whitehead insists that there are not even "points" in the process to be analyzed out and fitted together. There is nothing but the constant merging, continuous rather than cinematic.

In another place Whitehead says

> In all philosophic theory, there is an ultimate. . . . In the philosophy of organism this ultimate is termed "creativity."[16]

> "Creativity" is the universal of universals characterizing ultimate matter of fact. It is that ultimate principle by which the many, which are the universe disjunctively, become the one actual occasion, which is the universe conjunctively. It lies in the nature of things that the many enter into complex unity.[17]

"Creativity" is another rendering of the Aristotelian "matter," and of the modern "neutral stuff."[18]

We see in these passages again the idea of "composition" which was so useful to us in explaining the knowledge process. (p. 98) Whitehead suggests that the most advantageous concept to take as our ultimate for explaining the nature of reality is this concept of a process of putting parts together into structural unities. "Organization" is another term covering about the same idea; and "organism" is a term for the result of such a process, or rather for the structure that is continually "doing" such process. Thus, Whitehead decided to label his whole philosophy "the Philosophy of Organism."

Feeling: A last question arises as to what connection, if any, reality-as-process, as we have come to understand it on the basis of empirical objective studies of physical processes observed "from the outside," has to *qualitative feeling*. We saw that SMR's conception of matter was utterly un-connectable to any realm of appreciative feeling. Is energy-field or process any better off? Well, we still seem to be debarred from any direct observation of *feeling* as such in other processes than our own personal one — even in the case of other people. In chapter VI, we saw how "isomorphism" of structure and behavior is the basis of our belief that other people and animals do have inner feeling, which is the explanation "why" of most of their actions. Whitehead is famous for extending this argument from isomorphism to *all* organizing processes from atom on up to man, so that he claims that inner feeling is always present wherever process is.

The key notion from which such [cosmological] construction should start is that the energetic activity considered in physics is the emotional intensity entertained in life.[19]

So we see that no concrete happening or act or process is without private, internal tone or without public imprint.[20]

The philosophy or organism seeks to describe how objective data pass into subjective satisfaction, and how order in the objective data provides intensity in the subjective satisfaction.[21]

167

In *Process and Reality* (p. 476) Whitehead also suggests that "strains" in the field are identical with feelings in the subject.

In summary terms [Whitehead's philosophy] is an interpretation of the workings of nature on the pattern of a unity of process capable of caring for quality, rather than on the pattern of pellets or energy quanta which care for nothing.[22]

Whitehead repudiates "the notion of vacuous actuality, which haunts realistic philosophy. The term 'vacuous actuality' here means the notion of a *res vera* devoid of subjective immediacy."[23]

It is true that not many philosophers follow Whitehead in this rather strange notion that atoms, grass, viruses and men all *feel* their processes. It is also true that none of them can draw any sharp line, in the hierarchy of organisms, where inner feeling should be supposed to disappear from process. Does everything above the reptile have feeling, but nothing below it? Or above the earthworm? Or the clam? Or the amoeba? Or the virus (a favorite division point, although it obviously is not really one)? Or the molecule? Or the atom?

However this may be, we at least know that our own bodies are made of this energy, and that they take it in and give it out, and are able to feel such processes. Energy is at least the sort of thing that can enter into feeling processes *in oneself.*

And so the *substance* for DR is energy-in-fields, or process, which can at times, concentrate into a relatively stable condition known as "matter," and which *may* be identical with feeling, or at least can come into close relationship with feeling.

Comparison of DR with SM: This reality of DR's may not seem very close to what SM wants reality to be — a realm of thought and pure form. And yet this idea of energy — invisible, almost infinitely rapid, insubstantial — is surely not as antipathetic to SM as SMR's heavy lumps of dead solidity. It is not so hopelessly unrelatable to our feelings and consciousness either. It might almost be the "stuff" that thoughts are made of. It is certainly "as quick as thought."

The difficulty is that SM would not know what to do with the *changeableness* of this energy. The notion of unending process is a horror to the static idea of value. Why should there be this eternal restless creativity, this "divine discontent"? Why should energy-in-fields be forever straining to get into "better" shape?

Why must any attained equilibrium always be immediately disrupted by new ingredient energies, giving rise to further strivings to organize inclusive harmonies?

DM with DR.

Implications of DM and Correspondence to DR: We have already shown (Chapter III, p. 53 #2.1, 2.4), the deduction of process and disequilibrium from the dynamic idea of value as *feeling* of organizing process. The necessity of feeling and of feelers is quite obvious in the definition (# 1.1, p. 53), though we admit that it is not quite clear that *all* processes, no matter how simple, must have feeling within them. However, having deduced the necessity of human minds as feelers, it seems that we may thence deduce the necessity of all the other processes of nature as potential ingredients in the processes of such minds. And so, what DR finds reality to be in fact *does* correspond to what our new idea of value implies *should* be fact.

Now, although these new theories of reality have greater affinity than SMR's to concepts of value, it has not yet become fashionable for scientists, philosophers or men in the street to talk like medieval theologians. All things and events are not yet widely felt to be universally suffused with divine purpose, required to be as they are by an intelligible cosmic design for value. The new universe of energy, process and existence has been tied in with value theory by many thinkers, and statements in the form of "The concrete event *is* value," or "value is in process," are familiar. Yet the prevalent empirical habit of mind has led to a curious way of wrapping up event and value in an indissoluble conceptual package, obscuring the order of requirement which we are maintaining, and which brings such advantages to thought. This order has at least the advantages of simplifying and clarifying relationships between concepts of value and fact; and as we shall see, it has also the advantage of permitting stronger statements with regard to cosmic purpose than process philosophies usually make.

Process philosophies have generally not settled the question whether process or value is metaphysically the more ultimate concept; they have either not asked the question at all, or have implied that the two concepts are so closely intertwined that it is meaningless to assign priority. The tendency is, if anything, to take process itself, the summary conclusion of all empirical observation of fact, as ultimate, the final reason for all lower details. Why are all things, including values, processual? Simply because reality happens to *be* process. Process just *is*.

That both layman and philosopher feel this type of statement fails to make existence "meaningful" is apparent. The layman instinctively looks to the occasional successes of process — the accomplishment of some good, the resolution of some chaos — and wants to say that the meaning of the process is *to* solve these problems or *to* create these goods. But the philosopher forces him to notice that processes just as often miss, and sooner or later always end in disintegration; and both return to contemplating an eternal seething that just seethes. Besides, he might ask the layman, even if the process always did succeed, why should not good be given immediately? Why must there be problems at all? The idea of good itself, he suggests, assuming the static interpretation, does not explain why it should always be separated from us by a prior period of striving for it. Existentialists, for instance, beating themselves into accepting a life of struggle and decision, are quite clear that such a life is not what could be deduced from any idea of cosmic value. Again, it just blindly *is* such, and they undertake to gird up their loins knowing not the reason why.

No, it is not generally held that we can derive the entire dynamic universe from an idea of value. And that, of course, would be a necessary prerequisite for any theory of divine cosmogony.

The present manner of using the dynamic idea of value adds, for the author at least, a great deal in the way of appreciative feeling about the meaning of things to any philosophy that takes process itself as the last underivable ultimate. Some of that sacramental flavor is brought back which moderns could well envy the medieval man for possessing, a flavor whose lack impoverishes our evolutionary realisms. And the order of requirement from this idea of value, of which we have begun the outline, opens up a dimension of significance for facts which the cheerless positivisms and the brave existentialisms of nausea and absurdity have too soon rejected.

It has been objected to the dynamic idea of good that it only reconstructs our concept of value to the specifications of the analysis of process, and that when we thereupon derive the totality of dynamic reality out of our idea of value, we are only drawing out of our ultimate what we had carefully put into it. But the dynamic idea of value is, to begin with, at least a more accurate description of our actual psychological experience of value (see chapter XIV), and not merely concocted out of metaphysical demands. And if this empirically derived notion turns out to provide a concept of value that can be understood as logically prior to the notion of process itself, a major metaphysical step would be before us. Especially would it be important to take this step, if the concept of value could be seen to *imply* everything science knows about reality, both constructive and destructive. For this would give that additional sense of *requirement* that we must have for real meaningfulness. It would answer on a level moderns generally despair of penetrating, "WHY" things are as they are.

Another objection would be made by existentialists and Schopenhauereans. They might still shrug that to be told value essentially consists of and requires striving process is no better than to be told Reality simply *is* striving process. They would be as impatient with a God who arbitrarily decreed of Value, as with One who arbitrarily decreed of Reality, that they have such will-o'-the-wisp natures that nothing can ever be permanently *had*. It may legitimately be suspected that these people's problem is less philosophic than psychiatric. A certain psychological maturity is probably required before one can stop philosophically demanding gifts on a platter.

Now I am not prepared to work out the deductions of the more detailed and technical aspects of process: why, for instance, the processes of the universe should obey Einstein's stupendously complex equations for relativity, or why the speed of light should be 186,000 miles per second instead of anything else, etc. Some statements of "requirement" of this nature are appearing in the work of the students of physical reality themselves, as we saw in Chapter VI (p. 132, 133).

There is one deduction, however, of great significance to be made at this point: the deduction of "structure" from the idea of "process." And since we have already deduced process from value, we shall have shown the necessity of structure for value. In so doing, we will have gone a long way in solving some very ancient philosophical puzzles, especially the mind-body problem. In fact, the author believes that in this step of thought we have found the reason for "matter," and will have said the most significant thing that can be said about it.

We saw under SM how static good did not require structure, defined as arrangements of flexibilities against rigidities, permitting

171

the leverage, push, motion, articulation, etc. upon which motion depends. "Material," i.e., structured, bodies were nothing but a hampering of the good. Thus material structure was not derived from God or Good, but had to take its place as a happenstance due to the unfortunate fact that the second world of matter or non-being happened to be there. The world of structured objects is thus essentially unexplained.

I define structure in just these terms — an arrangement of more rigid and more fluid (or elastic) parts in such a manner as to enable movement, change or *process*. Process could not exist in a totally homogeneous world. It is easy enough to see that if all reality were homogeneously solid or rigid, there could be no process; but more difficult to see that the same would hold if all reality were homogeneously fluid. Effective movement or process requires more rigid parts to provide anchorages, leverages, resistances, etc.; and more fluid parts to move against them. Therefore if the universe were essentially fluid energy (as we are told it is) some of this energy must arrange to stiffen up, as it were.

Here then is the essential reason for "matter," and also, perhaps the best suggestion for conceiving its nature. It is "stiff" or relatively rigid energy, and it appears in order to make "process" possible in the energy continuum of reality.

Thus, in contrast to SM we find a place for "material" — or at least relatively rigid substance. But in contrast to SMR we do not make that rigid energy the essence of reality. The dynamic idea of good clearly implies what DR finds: that the living, feeling energy is the basic reality; but also that it is required to develop heterogeneous differentials between fluidity and rigidity before it can create any *effective* process.

What we have in this philosophy, then, in regard to the "stuff" of reality can be said to be a monism in the sense that only one ultimate "substance" is appealed to — energy. If we give this an inner feeling aspect and an outer material or "public" aspect, we come back to something like Spinoza's "double-aspect" theory, except that we might question whether his word "substance" is the right one to use when referring to "energy."

On the other hand, we can also admit pluralism into this philosophy insofar as we admit that this energy can be broken up into units, or can form itself into individual things. This takes us to the next great topic in ontology, in the next chapter.

In summary, the two most significant features of the revolution in science would seem to be:

The change from static to dynamic concepts. This will prove to be especially helpful in dealing with the problem of good and evil in Part IV.

The change from atomistic to holistic concepts. This bears more especially on the problem of mechanism vs. purposiveness, to which we now turn.

CHAPTER VIII

THEORIES OF UNITS; THE PART-WHOLE RELATIONSHIP

SM with SIR.

Implications of SM: Indivisible Wholes: We may start this topic as we did the preceding, by noticing what the layman might think a strange tendency that has cropped up from time to time in the history of philosophy: a reluctance to grant the division of reality into parts or units of any kind. There is a special anxiety to deny any parts in God. Plotinus, in crystallizing some of the implications of Plato's philosophy, called God, who was "perfect Being," "the One."

> The One has no parts, and, thus, cannot be taken apart or destroyed. . . . It must be eternal, for time involves a succession of moments, but the One has no parts to succeed each other and, thus cannot be temporal. It involves no conflicts, because it has no parts which can conflict. . . . Such perfection has no relations, for relations entail separation, and, therefore, plurality. Perfect unity is without any plurality whatsoever.[1]

Hinduism comes to the same conclusion wherein existence is thought of as ultimately a "perfect, eternal, indivisible, attributeless unity called Brahman."[2] We remember, also, Plato's argument in the *Phaedo* that the soul must be an indivisible unity without parts.

Why this unpopularity of parts or units? Well, Plato's motivation in the *Phaedo* was to find a proof of immortality, and we can understand why he would wish to believe in that. If the soul has no parts, it cannot be taken apart, therefore it cannot die. As for keeping God partless, this is an outcome of the curious tie-up which we saw in the preceding chapter between the ideas of Being, Perfection and Changelessness. If God is to be perfect, he can not desire anything that he lacks, therefore he has nothing to work for or change toward; therefore he need not, indeed must not, change. And the best way to insure his not changing is to deny him parts which might change their relationships with one another.

We can see here again what the real root of the disparagement of parts is: the static idea of good; good can exist, in fact would exist pre-eminently, as an unchanging state of complete fulfillment. Thus it would require no process in its essence. If there need be no process, then there need be no parts; for it is *process that would require things to have parts!* For change or process can have no meaning except as changing relationships among parts as they move and rearrange themselves.

Therefore, the pure implication of the static idea of Meaning is that reality should be a seamless unity without parts.

Or if individual minds are granted existence at all, they too will be considered as seamless wholes that elect their Ideas as a unit. Desiring the Mind to be self-caused, not dependent upon anything below itself, Idealists are inclined to deny it any parts also. We might say, then, that Idealism has a native tendency toward emphasizing causation by *Wholes,* to the exclusion of any causation by Parts whatever; and this is just the opposite to what we shall find in SMR.

The early Greek thinker, Parmenides, our great examplar of static logic, saw that if you assume only stuff without parts, then you cannot have change; and he stuck to this logic, holding that reality is a single, solid, motionless sphere of stuff without parts.[3]

Adjustments of SIR: Few other philosophers have been so bold as to deny that there is a very insistent appearance, at least, of parts and units of some sort. The first recourse of SIR, Illusionism, has not failed to be applied to this problem, and all parts placed in the realm of Appearance. Brahmanism, for instance, allows that the indivisible unity, Brahman, manifests itself in individual souls as "Atman", yet staunchly insists that it has not *really* become plurality. The Atman is "Unity that pervades all plurality." But souls somehow begin to believe that their plurality is real, and thereupon experience rebirths until in mystic or yoga practices they can realize that their individuality is illusory and unreal. They then are reunified with Brahman and experience Nirvana

175

which is freedom from the "lesser reality" of individual separateness.

Plotinus worked out a similar theory of how the One "emanates" from itself an illusory "many," but the many are imperfect and therefore "non-Beings."

In modern times the above kind of talk has seemed so scandalously "double-talk" to idealists as much as realists, that some degree of reality is allowed to units and parts, although, as Butler remarks, the problem of the One and the Many is an "extremely difficult problem of Idealism . . ."

> Is there just one substance and only one . . . i.e., Universal Spirit or God? Or are there many separate and distinct individual selves . . . ? If an idealist takes his stand in an affirmative answer to the first of these questions, saying that Universal Mind is unimpeachably the supreme reality, he would seem to disregard the reality of individual finite minds, rob them of uniqueness, and do away with immortality as a continued personal existence after death. But if he answers the second question affirmatively, saying that individual selves are unimpeachably real, he would seem either to make God a sort of collection of individual selves not having much unity, or else a finite God who, while having somewhat more power than others, is yet just one among many individuals.[4]

He goes on to show how variously idealists solve this problem: Aristotle, Leibnitz, J. A. Leighton being early and late examples of the more pluralistic, atomistic emphasis; and Plotinus, Hegel and Bosanquet examples of the more monistic. Butler concludes, "the whole-part relation is the most basic of all relationships."

Now, granting any reality to parts or units, Idealistic philosophies will fall into various classes according to whether they are monistic or dualistic under the first topic of Substance. If monist, allowing only one, mental, substance, their units if any, will be of course, mental; first individual, finite minds, and secondly individual ideas, thoughts, concepts, etc. within those minds.

If they are dualistic in the doctrine of substance, then they will presumably have both mental units and material units. There also arises the problem of where the mental units — the ideas, forms, concepts — exist: only in individual minds, or only in God's mind, or in both places, or in a special realm for forms? Plato sometimes sounds as if the latter is the case, although the special realm may really be in God's mind. He also seems to mean that an idea in this special realm is "copied" by the idea in an individual mind, when he thinks that idea; or perhaps the idea in both loci is somehow one and the same unit. However the ideas may exist, they seem to be capable of joining together into systems of ideas which are themselves new units. But there is an ultimate idea that seems to include all the others in some hierarchical sense, the Idea of Good. Finally these mental units must have some relation to the units of matter, though Plato never clearly works out a doctrine of material units. Aristotle is clearer in his doctrine that every unit is both mental or "formal", and material. Northrop points out that when Idealists are especially enamored of *mathematical* ideas and relationships, as Plato and Descartes and some modern Physicists are, they always show a tendency to move back toward monism and to conclude that only the mathematical, conceptual units are real, and that we can, after all, drop the concept of material or physical parts.[5]

SM with SMR.

Findings of SMR: Atomism. We have already seen (p. 175) in discussing SM that the idea of change or motion necessitates the idea of parts or units. It was Leucippus and Democritus who first carried out these two assumptions of stuff and change to a logical conclusion: Nature must be made of moving bits of stuff, that is "atoms." Leucippus also saw that if the bits of matter were to be separate and distinguishable from one another, and if they were to move in relation to one another, there must be a third feature in Reality: Space. And thus the "kinetic atomic" theory was born, to which early modern science returned, when it dropped all the idealistic methods of denying full reality to matter and change, and decided to take what our sense organs seemed to report at face value.

No one shows more clearly than Newton himself that the conception of material atoms follows directly from taking our tactile and visual sensations at face value — we simply divide up the solid matter so known into small pieces:

We no other way know the extension of bodies than by

our senses, nor do these reach it in all bodies; but because we perceive extension in all bodies that are sensible, therefore we ascribe it universally to all others also. That abundance of bodies are hard, we learn by experience; and because the hardness of the whole arises from the hardness of the parts, we therefore justly infer the hardness of the undivided particles not only of the bodies we feel but of all others. That all bodies are impenetrable, we gather not from reason, but from sensation. The bodies which we handle we find impenetrable, and thence conclude impenetrability to be a universal property of all bodies whatsoever. That all bodies are movable, and endowed with certain powers (which we call the vires inertiae) of persevering in their motion, or in their rest, we only infer from the like properties observed in the bodies which we have seen. The extension, hardness, impenetrability, mobility, and vires inertiae of the whole result from the extension, hardness, impenetrability, mobility, and vires inertiae of the parts, and thence we conclude the least particles of all bodies to be also all extended, and hard, and impenetrable, and movable, and endowed with their proper vires inertiae.[6]

The atoms, thus, are solid (which includes the ideas of rigid and indivisible), impenetrable, movable and inert. They cannot be conceived as having any feeling, desires, purposes within themselves. The familiar analogy is with billiard balls — so that SMR is sometimes called "the billiard ball view of the universe." Nothing happens within Reality but the moving and colliding of these tiny balls according to the three laws of motion.

Now, it is crucial to understand this point: that the materialistic notion of atoms makes it impossible to conceive of *wholes* made of such atoms as having operative reality, or effective unity in themselves. The best way I know to show this is to ask the reader to imagine a group of billiard balls, the analogues of material atoms. Suppose six of these balls to be arranged in a hexagonal pattern on the table. It is immediately clear that the hexagon (the whole) as such has no efficacious control over its parts (the balls). Although the balls are together, they remain dynamically independent of each other. If you roll one ball away, the others are unaffected. If you roll another ball into the pattern, only those balls actually hit will be affected. There is no reality in the hexagon itself that would make *every part* of it respond relatedly, whenever the pattern is affected by any force. Much less can you suppose that the hexagon itself has any initiatory control over the balls, that *it* can direct or cause them to rearrange themselves according to its desires or intentions, supposing it could have any. Similarly, imagine a heap of sand made up of grains of sand. We do not believe that the heap as such controls its grains, or makes them take up certain fitting positions. The heap is just the accidental outcome of the motions of the sand particles. It can be said then, in both these cases, that "all causation is from the parts alone; none is from the whole." The whole is simply the passive result of however the parts happen to have fallen together, following whatever laws or forces happened to affect them separately.

Another approach to this eternal separateness of the atoms in SMR is by way of Whitehead's discussion of the "Fallacy of Simple Location." By this he means that the units are conceived of as having their existence or reality confined exclusively to the exact point in Space and Time where their solid matter is here and now located. This means that their relationships to other bits of matter has no reality in itself; their "being" in no sense extends outward in the space around them, or intertwines with other units. There is no sense in which they can "fuse" with other units into any new unity that is real in itself. All this is obvious if you keep in mind the analogy of billiard balls or grains of sand, with their definite boundaries where their solid matter stops. This sort of atom can never have any "togetherness" to use another of Whitehead's terms.

Still another and perhaps a simpler approach to understanding why SMR cannot take the design or arrangement of the parts in a whole seriously as a reality, is merely to notice that the arrangement of a group of parts does not itself have any additional *weight,* momentum, etc., over the sum of the weights and momenta of the parts. In short, the *pattern* as such is not quantitatively *measurable,* at least by the means of measurement early scientists were accustomed to. And they had become so habituated to believing only in what they could touch, weigh and measure that the reality of weightless organized design escaped them.

And so Newton had stated a doctrine of parts that was to allow science to advance rapidly for several centuries, but which (as we shall see) was ultimately to ruin philosophy, demolish theology, and give rise to endless futile writhings by thinkers to escape its

179

proof of the meaninglessness of reality. Today, science itself has dropped this theory of parts, and man is free to return to an inspiring *and* valid meaningfulness. Unfortunately, very few men understand the route and most of them continue to waste their time with Newtonian presuppositions and either the nihilistic conclusions or the invalid escapes from them.

Contradictions between SMR and SM; Recourses. We must wait until the next chapter to understand fully how fatal this conception of the units or parts is for all meaning and value, though we can dimly grasp it already. When thought, ideas, form or value was excluded from the units, *and* the units were enjoined from forming wholes that might contain these things, it ultimately proved impossible to get value back into reality in any satisfactory way.

But, of course, Idealism got it back in by either of its two usual methods. Descartes, of course, preserves mental and purposive units in his mental realm. Leibnitz, a monist in his theory of substance, was a pluralist in his theory of units, working out a "Spiritual Atomism" where the units were called "Monads" conceived as living spiritual forces or units of energy. Each Monad was "absolutely simple" and did not interact with other Monads, but only mirrored their activities within itself. Spinoza, a monist in regard to substance, was also a monist, apparently, concerning units, allowing only one substance, God, with material and spiritual aspects. In Berkeley's subjectivism, material units became illusory, and only the impressions and ideas remain as units. Hegel's view is difficult to classify. All that exists belongs to the Absolute which is a network of developing ideas in an integral unity. Apparently there are parts in some sense in this Absolute, as would be implied by its being an evolving, changing unity.

However, since Physics itself has completely revolutionized its theory of units, these recourses have lost their point in recent thought.

SM and DR.

Findings of DR: Energy Quanta. The approach to DR's theory of units is so extraordinarily difficult that one wonders how it can ever become common currency and reduce the amount of nonsense that is talked by would-be mechanists, positivists and materialists. However, Newton's theory once seemed as difficult, but is second nature to most of us now: while Aristotle's theory, which was once second nature to most men, now seems incomprehensible to most of them.

In selecting from the mass of material, we will keep the whole-part question before us as a guide. The first roots of the change go back almost to Newton himself, when attractive and repulsive forces began to be admitted as centering in the hard, material atoms. And then

Hardness and impenetrability of the atoms gets replaced by the repulsive forces with which they interact and by the law according to which this force depends on distance. . . . The atoms become "centers of force" . . . Kant . . . constructs matter out of the equilibrium of attractive and repulsive forces. The purely mechanical interpretation of nature is replaced by the physics of central forces.[7]

Then the solid atoms of the old chemistry — the supposedly irreducible particles of each element — broke up and became little solar systems for awhile, consisting mostly of empty space with nuclei and orbiting electrons. And then the nuclei broke up and revealed a new list of ultimate "atoms:" protons, neutrons, mesons, positrons, etc. The Curies and their study of radium, Rutherford and Bohr are great names pioneering in these developments. The ultimate particles of this new list could not very well be imagined as hard, inert bits of matter, although this was not for lack of trying by many materialistic-minded students. In general, this replacing of hard material atoms with energetic interfusing forces organized in unified atomic patterns weighed on the side of continuity and holism. And when Huyghens' wave theory of light won the day, with Fresnel, over Newton's particle theory, while Maxwell's field theory took over Electro-magnetism, the physics of "discrete systems" (i.e. of particles) seemed to be losing out.

But then atomism won a resounding victory when energy and light themselves suddenly revealed undeniable particle characteristics. Max Planck, in 1900, showed that energy must occur only in irreducible units called "quanta," which would seem to be something like tiny "puffs" of energy. It is these, apparently, that now become the ultimate units for modern science: units of energy rather than matter.

181

This assumption that energy and light would not transfer themselves from or to atoms until they had built up to definite minimum quantities, at which time they would "jump" all at once, explained a number of phenomena that had contradicted mechanistic expectations. It was in studying the radiation of incandescent solids, which failed to fulfill predicted intensities, that Planck first worked out the idea of quanta of energy. Then Bohr applied it to the facts of spectroscopy with great success, showing incidentally that radiation or light occurred in the same quanta as energy itself did. Mechanistic theories, picturing electrons as material particles orbiting the nucleus, had called for them to increase their frequency of revolution, spiral inward to the nucleus, and collapse into it, all within a fraction of a second. This means that atoms should radiate during their whole short existence, and at continuously changing frequency. Actually, however, atoms can last for long durations, radiate only when excited, and then at fixed frequencies, as shown by the spectroscope. All this would be explained by supposing that electrons remained in a stable state until their energy was either increased or reduced by the amount of a quantum, at which time they jumped into another state, simultaneously radiating or absorbing the quantum of energy in a wave with a fixed frequency. Only, as Margenau remarks, "the whole substance of classical physics was traded in exchange for this success."[8] For there was nothing in mechanics, or conventional electrodynamics either, to explain how a particle could orbit a nucleus and be in a "steady state" without energy change of any kind.

A third kind of evidence for the atomicity of radiation was found by Einstein in 1905, in the photo-electric effect. When ultra-violet light falls on a metal surface, a stream of electrons is "knocked" out of the metal. But instead of the *energy* of the escaping electrons being proportional to the intensity of the light, the *number* of electrons shot out is. If the light is very feeble, a very small number of electrons are dislodged, but each one moves with the full energy associated with that wave-length of light. All this implies that the light is composed of particles with a definite energy, rather than of waves, so that if fewer light particles (that is, "less intense" light) hit the metal, then fewer electrons will be struck, but if struck at all, they will be struck full force. It was also found that any electron that is dislodged has absorbed exactly one full quantum of energy. These light "particles" were named "photons;" they are the same as quanta, applied particularly to light radiation. Light then, for awhile, was again pictured as Newton had, as a stream of particles, colliding with electrons like billiard balls.

Particles versus Waves: But now the picture veers again, and the wave, or continuous nature of radiation received new evidence. Just as light, the former stronghold of wave-theory had betrayed particle characteristics, now the electron, the former stronghold of particle theory, betrayed wave characteristics. First de Broglie in 1924 predicted mathematically that electrons *ought* to have wave characteristics; and then various experimenters found that electrons could be diffracted, made to show interference phenomena, and polarized — all phenomena that had always required wave-theory to explain.

Physics was now in the desperate situation of seeming to have to conceive all of its units — of matter *and* energy — as simultaneously particles and waves, which seems meaningless. The ways out of this dilemma that have been suggested have been as incomprehensible as they have been numerous. Mostly we are told to give up trying to picture the ultimate units at all, to give up ordinary Space and Time for subatomic events, and to be satisfied with complex mathematical formulae dealing with probabilities.

The phenomena that forced these strange speculations were patterns of light and dark smudges on photographic plates at which beams of photons, electrons or other sub-atomic "particles" are shot under various arrangements of screens or gratings. There is some evidence for behavior as particles; but not particles that behave according to mechanical laws. An individual particle seems to have some freedom to diverge from mechanically predictable lines of motion; but on the other hand it seems to be constrained by some unvisualizable factor to land in such a way as to make up a predictable pattern together with all the other particles. And this holds even when the particles are "shot" separately in sequence, so as to rule out the possibility of simultaneous mutual influence. Margenau even suggests that, if we try to preserve any particle picture at all, we must suppose that each particle has some "inherent disposition for forming the pattern which the whole aggregate only was able to realize."[9]

Giving up, at least for the moment, the effort to form a Space-Time picture of these sub-atomic entities, physicists saw that at least they had a measure of the probability of the location of a "hit." The probability was greater in the dark bands, less in the light ones. If you wondered where a single quantum of radiation was going to land you could measure very exactly the percentage of probability for each point in the pattern. You could never say for certain where it *would* land; you could only say for sure that millions of quanta would take this distribution. We see here why it is said that quantum physics is essentially statistical in character: it cannot exactly predict for individual entities; but it can for crowds of them, just as the insurance business does in connection with deaths in the population.

Another approach was Heisenberg's taking Bohr's measurements of spectra by themselves, and eliminating all mental picturing of atoms with orbiting electrons, that is all mechanical "models;" then he simply tried out all kinds of mathematical equations until he found one that could correctly calculate or predict the measured positions of the lines in the spectra of different atoms. He found that his equations, when finally worked out, were in the same form as those already worked out in pure mathematics as the algebra of matrices; so his theory was called matrix machanics, which hints again of the surrounding conditions or matrix controlling the units. It was afterwards generalized by Dirac and Von Neumann and called "Quantum mechanics." It now seemed impossible to visualize any mechanical model that could produce the amazingly complicated mathematical relationships of these equations. If there were any basic units in nature, they were certainly not simple particles pushing one another according to ordinary laws of action and reaction; they were impalpable somethings that "knew" how to fit themselves into endlessly intricate mathematical patterns. Or rather, what seemed to be appearing, was that intricate patterns of some sort had sufficient reality to guide their constituents into their required places.

De Broglie finally supplied some models for these incomprehensible mathematical relations that helped a little to visualize them. It turned out to be fundamentally a wave picture from which something like particles could be derived as points of concentrated energy within, and guided by, the wave. He also assumed that any particle phenomenon in nature must have accompanying wave characteristics, or an undulatory principle spreading continuously in all directions from it. The laws of wave propagation were fundamental; and the laws of dynamic particles could be deduced from them. De Broglie called the electron, or photon, conceived as a tiny sphere of spreading waves, a "wave-packet."

184

Schrödinger went ahead to suggest dropping any idea of a material oscillator to initiate the waves and to satisfy ourselves with the waves alone. He worked out a mathematics for De Broglie's picture which was shown to be equivalent to Heisenberg's matrix equations, and called it "wave mechanics."

The following quotations may help bring out significant aspects of this new conception of the units.

Neither the traditional continuous nor the traditional discontinuous theory will suffice. . . . The traditional procedure of starting with constituent microscopic atomic parts and building up chemical elements and their interactions out of them has failed. An adequate theory of atomic and optical phenomena must conceive of them as a single system in which the propagated light determines the motion and behavior of the particles as much as the particles determine the nature of the radiation. . . . Just as [relativity theory] forced science away from the doctrine that all relatedness between physical objects [depends] on microscopic atomic notion, so . . . the relations between atoms . . . cannot be regarded as the mere effects of a simple compounding of electrons and protons. The wave or macroscopic aspect and the corpuscular or microscopic aspect are both parts of a single system. . . .

Briefly, the purely analytical approach to nature has broken down. The relation of the microscopic atom to light and to its neighboring microscopic particles is as fundamental as the particle itself. . . . Field or macroscopic as well as atomic causes are present.[10]

Photons are no longer independent individuals, but members of a single organization or whole — a beam of light — in which their separate individualities are merged, not merely in the superficial sense in which an individual is lost in a crowd, but rather as a raindrop is lost in the sea.[11]

. . . particles will appear as regions of reinforcement where *constituent waves* overtake each other at nodal points to produce *group waves* or matter . . . matter is composed of energy-knots or boundary singularities in the field.[12]

. . . the electrons [are] manifestations of group waves accompanied by a train of waves which the particles are compelled to follow. Here the *guiding waves* show the electrons where to go, as it were.[13]

Since all physically important properties of an elementary material particle . . . belong to the surrounding field rather that to the substantial nucleus at the field center, the question becomes inevitable whether the existence of such a nucleus is not a presumption which may be completely dispensed with. This question is answered in the affirmative by the *field theory of matter*. According to the latter, a material particle such as an electron is merely a small domain of the electrical field within which the field strength assumes enormously high values, indicating that a comparatively huge field energy is concentrated in a very small space. Such an energy knot, which by no means is clearly delineated against the remaining field, propagates through empty space like a water wave. . . . There is no such thing as one and the same substance of which the electron consists at all times.[14]

From the point of view of a consistent field theory, the whole mass, that is, the whole energy, of an electron is the energy of its field; the bulk of its strength is within a very small sphere, and away from the "center" of the electron it is weak.[15]

More complex units — atoms, molecules, etc. — must now be conceived as complex wave systems too. Concepts are beginning to appear to explain how vibrations at one level of complexity, focussed in many centers of that magnitude (atoms, for instance), compound into some higher pattern of vibrations (a molecule, say) which resolves tensions that had appeared at the lower level. The "lower" entities whose vibrations had been colliding or interfering in some awkward manner probably lose their identity entirely in the "higher" pattern. When the hydrogen and oxygen atoms are together in the water molecule, to take an overworked analogy, they no longer exist as themselves. The molecule is a new unity with its own symmetrical pattern of waves. Thus patterns of waves become "food," as it were, for more inclusive patterns of waves. The same logic is then carried to all the stages of evolution up to living organisms.

186

The *ultimate* units — the sub-atomic particles — seem to be vibratory phenomena that are intrinsically interlinked with other vibratory phenomena. Reiser, above, speaks of them as "constituent waves" which are controlled and directed by "guiding waves." The point is that we have come to the same sort of idea that we did in relativity theory: the conception of a surrounding medium or field that interacts reciprocally with the unit or "body" and partly, at least, guides it into its "proper place."

The Units as Events, Organisms: In such a philosophical generalization upon these physical theories as Whitehead's, he feels that certain other specifications need to be added to the doctrine of units: particularly an emphasis upon their nature as real give-and-take of *attainments*. The unit should be thought of, he thinks, as an episode of transaction of energy from one center to another. The emphasis should be upon the continual incorporating of existing things into newly emerging things, and upon the fact that what emerges are new patterned unities. Therefore he names his units, variously, "events," "actual occasions" or "actual entities" all of which mean any instance whatever at any level of complexity where any kind of ingredients (atoms, cells, foodstuffs, air, thoughts, feelings) come together or "ingress" to form some "concrescent" structure, or pattern (in the same order as above: molecules, organisms, tissue repair, oxidation, problem-solving, satisfaction). From the point of view of the achieved structure, his unit is called "organism," which emphasizes the fact that all existing things are structured transactions between parts and wholes in this manner.

Science . . . is becoming the study of organisms. Biology is the study of the larger organisms; whereas physics is the study of the smaller organisms. . . . The organisms of biology include ingredients the smaller organisms of physics. . . . We are faced with the question as to whether there are not primary organisms which are incapable or further analysis . . . a theory of science which discards materialism can (give) only one answer. . . . We must start with the event as the ultimate unit of natural occurrence . . . a non-materialistic philosophy of nature will identify a primary organism as being the emergence of some particular pattern as grasped in the unity of a real event. Such a pattern will also include the aspects of the event in question as grasped in other events, whereby those other events receive a modification, or partial

187

determination. The concept of organism includes, therefore, the concept of the interaction of organisms.[16]

The Whole-Part Relationship: It is already clear that DR differs from both SIR and SMR on this most crucial of relationships. SIR always tends to emphasize the whole and to eliminate causation by parts entirely. SMR wants to trace all causation to the parts and to ignore the reality of the whole. We now have a reciprocal relationship between whole and parts that is very difficult to conceive precisely, and yet all branches of science find themselves forced to work out ways to do so. Maxwell's field equations for electro-dynamics have already been discussed as the first appearance of holistic causation in physics. Relativity theory and wave-mechanics reveal the same sort of equations. Organismic theory in biology and gestalt theory in psychology represent the same movement in those fields.

As biological science developed, the concept of *organization* was forced upon men's attention more and more as posing a major difficulty for mechanical concepts. It seemed more and more difficult to believe that atoms and molecules arranged themselves by chance into living organisms. But the biologists' and psychologists' call for holistic concepts was not widely influential — even among themselves — until physics itself suddenly discovered the need for them. Some of the most basic equations in modern physics refer to phenomena that could have no existence if the ultimate particles and their summative forces only were real. The various "minimal" principles, the most familiar one being the "Law of Least Action," are most important.

This sort of law was first formulated by Fermat (1601-1665) as applying to the path that light takes through refracting and reflecting media — it takes the quickest or shortest route. Maupertuis (1698-1759) is responsible for the term "Least Action," and also for the feeling, which physicists themselves resist, but others of us like, that the principle smacks of purposiveness, divine wisdom, or ethical necessity. Euler and LaGrange worked to improve the formulation of the principle and Hamilton finally perfected equations for it. The principle of least action "has the strange distinction of being perhaps the most fundamental and yet the most imperfectly understood law of physics."[17] The "action" referred to in the principle is a curiously non-mechanistic concept, being the product of the distance a body moves times its velocity while moving that distance. There is thus a larger "quantity of action" when a body is covering a distance speedily than when it is covering the same distance slowly. In Hamilton's more perfected statement, however, the concept of energy is used, indicating that bodies move from one place to another by a path and with a velocity that use a minimum of energy. Or more technically,

> When an event that requires energy is taking place in the physical universe, it must take place so that the mean value of the difference between the kinetic energy and potential energy involved, in the interval of time required for the event to take place, must be as small as possible.[18]

Jeans illustrates the concept by considering a planet trying to get past the sun, and assuming that closer to the sun's gravitational field more energy is expended. The shortest route to the other side would be straight through the sun, but this increases the energy expenditure over what it would be if the planet took a longer curved route around the sun, and rushed faster where the curve was nearer to the sun. It turns out that an elliptical path, with greater velocity where it comes near the sun is the "cheapest" route the planet could take in terms of energy, and this is the route it *does* take.

This principle is at the foundation of almost every equation in physics, and was taken as the one unalterable assumption in the reasoning that led to relativity and quantum theory. When Bohr began to make his atom model to fit quantum theory, he first postulated that the principle of least action should be preserved. And Einstein, Davis says, in creating his theory of relativity preferred to leave this principle alone and alter the nature of space and time instead. The principle of least distance appears also in the geodesics of relativity theory, the study of shortest paths in curved Space-Time.

The main point is that this principle again is a matter of the structure of a whole field compelling the individual object to behave in a manner that "fits" the overall pattern.

Margenau discusses the "exclusion principle" of quantum theory, discovered by Pauli in 1925, in similar terms. The original example of it was in the behavior of electrons in atoms, but it was rapidly applied to a host of unexplained mysteries afterwards. The principle explains why sub-atomic particles stay in "proper" relations to each other, do not collide or get into random patterns, but abide eight-to-a-shell, etc. Two electrons in an atom can never be in "the same state of motion," have the same velocity or position; in fact something makes them be as different from each other in these respects as possible. In a hydrogen atom, the single electron is free to move in any way permitted by quantum laws. But in a helium atom

> *. . . the presence of the first electron forces the second into a different state of motion.* It is as though the second electron "knew" the first was there even though it does not interact with it by forces of the familiar [mechanistic] kind. The helium atom thus owes its characteristic properties to a nondynamic interplay, a sort of tactful avoidance between its parts.[19]

. . . the essence of mechanistic reasoning is seen to cluster around two beliefs: first that entities . . . are divisible into parts, and second that these parts are localizable in space and time. . . . Prior to [the time when the exclusion principle began to illuminate the scientific scene] all theories had affected the *individual* nature of the so-called "parts;" the new principle regulated their *social* behavior. With respect to a single particle it has nothing to say. . . . Mechanistic reasoning, already far behind, has gone out of sight as a result of this latest advance. . . .

Not too far ahead lies the field of biology with its problems of organization and function . . . modern physics . . . possesses in the Pauli principle a way of understanding why entities show in their togetherness laws of behavior different from the laws which govern them in isolation. . . .

Emergence of new properties on composition is a rather general phenomenon in modern physics and owes its occurrence to the exclusion principle. . . . In the process of constructing a crystal from its atomic parts, new properties are seen to emerge, and these properties have no meaning with reference to the individual parts: among others, ferromagnetism, optical anisotropy, electrical conductivity appear, all "cooperative phenomena" . . . which owe their origin directly or indirectly to the exclusion principle.[20]

Margenau also points out how similar the exclusion principle is to relativity theory, in explaining behavior of bodies, not by pushes and pulls, that is "dynamic forces" operating in the line of action by Newton's laws, but by reference to the geometrical patterns of the surrounding Space-Time field.

On the basis of such facts as these, dynamic naturalism condemns SMR's excessively discrete explanation of units. The concept of field and radiation proves that all things are indissolubly connected to realities or energies beyond their apparent boundaries. Everything is intertwined with everything else in existence. It is obvious, for instance, that something from every star in the heavens exists at the point where your eye is, simply because you can see it there. Rays from the entire universe must come together where your eye is, or where any eye is, therefore each star and each electron must fill the universe with its radiations. And so, in opposition to "simple location," we must insist on "togetherness," to use Whitehead's terms, or connectedness as equally real with separateness. This possibility of a real togetherness must be established before we can go on to the ideas of real processes that produce real attainments; for real attainments could only exist if the new patterns that were put together from old parts or units could be themselves real unities and not just collections of the old parts continuing as their original selves.

> The ultimate metaphysical principle is the advance from disjunction to conjunction, creating a novel entity other than the entities given in disjunction. The novel entity is at once the togetherness of the "many" which it finds, and also it is one among the disjunctive "many" which it leaves; it is a novel entity. . . . The many become one, and are increased by one. . . . Thus the "production of novel togetherness" is the ultimate notion embodied in the term "concrescence."[21]

Finally togetherness must be real if the attained pattern is to have the power to guide its parts into their "proper places" which the pattern itself requires. In short, togetherness must be real, if we are to have real, operative wholes. Whitehead's most famous passage on holistic causation follows:

> The doctrine which I am maintaining is that the whole concept of materialism only applies to very abstract entities,

the products of logical discernment. The concrete enduring entities are organisms, so that the plan of the *whole* influences the very characters of the various subordinate organisms which enter into it. In the case of an animal, the mental states enter into the plan of the total organism and thus modify the plans of the successible subordinate organisms until the ultimate smallest organisms, such as electrons, are reached. Thus an electron within a living body is different from an electron outside it, by reason of the plan of the body.[22]

Comparison of DR with SM. DR's return to a doctrine of wholes should be amenable to SM. But its insistence that these wholes change and therefore must have parts or ingredients with which they are in reciprocal dependence, does not fit SM's expectation of unchanging, undivided wholes. But DR resists such a notion of wholes. DR insists upon the stubborn concrete reality of individual things, each made up in its unique pattern of ingredients. However spread-out fields of energy are, the fact remains that they *do* focus into relatively distinct centers of energy or finite organisms. SM would not quite know what to do with this concreteness and finiteness of individuals, preferring as it does the abstract and intellectual essences as the most real.

DM with DR.

Implications of DM: We have now to show the logical derivation of the whole-part relationship and of the units from the dynamic idea of meaning and value. It is interesting to note how empirically minded thinkers will discuss the reverse relationship: they will notice how the organizing of parts together into wholes often *produces* value, empirically; how the existence of parts in structures does factually give rise to processes. But very rarely do we find these statements turned around into statements of requirement: "Value requires organizing of parts into wholes"; or "Process, in order to take place, requires structure with parts." These are the sort of statement we claim it is legitimate and vitally important to make, under DM.

First let us recall our basic definition of dynamic value as "feeling of organizing process" (p. 53). Among other things we deduced from this (# 2.4 p. 54) the necessity of emerging order or pattern to be felt. Thus we already have deduced from DM the concept of organism which DR had arrived at empirically. From the concept of developing organism we can now, in turn, show the requirement of finiteness or limitation. It can be understood that the organism or pattern cannot be infinite, if it is to be continuously in creative process. If it already included everything, then it could no longer grow and develop; if there were no more order to attain, then there could be no further organizing process, and therefore value would no longer exist. Whitehead has made this sort of statement:

> All value is the gift of finitude, which is the necessary condition for activity.[23]
> Process and individuality require each other.[24]
> Restriction is the price of value. . . . Thus as a further element in the metaphysical situation, there is required a principle of limitation.[25]

We can go on now to deduce the necessity of smaller parts or units to be incorporated into the larger units or organisms. The necessity of parts if there is to be any change has been familiar to philosophers ever since Parmenides. It is also clear that the very idea of pattern, meaning an arrangement or design, intrinsically involves the necessity of parts to be so arranged. Also #2.41 (p. 54), the notion of Disorder, equally requires parts that can be in disorder.

But the dynamic idea of value also requires that these parts, while separate enough to be in disorder and to rearrange themselves into order, must also be *together* enough so that the relationship among them of disorder or order can itself be *felt*. "Felt disorder" requires parts to be in disorder, yet they must also somehow make up a whole that feels their disorder. To feel discomfort is to feel awkward *connections* among part energies. The feeling is *of* the pattern of relationships, not of the entities taken separately. The feeling is always *of* the changing whole-part relationships.

Correspondence with DR: DR's theory of parts or elements which we have been studying, seems pretty well to fulfill these requirements. The older, Newtonian science's conception of the elements — its solid, inert, material atoms — did not fit these requirements since it precluded any kind of real togetherness. The heap of sand does not become a real, operational unit in its own right, that "knows" or "feels" its parts in their relationship. Quantum theory's elements, on the other hand, whatever they may partake of particle or wave-like characteristics, at least show strong hints of an ability to fuse into new unities, to have relations to other units so real as to be conceivably "feelable" as awkward, unbalanced relationship or as comfortable, symmetrical relationships.

The feeling of good must have a matrix in which to inhere, and this is the reason why finite structure and pattern exist. The feeling of good is a feeling *about* articulated design. Dissatisfaction-satisfaction cannot exist without disorder and order of structures, which in turn are impossible without movable parts.

Finally, Whitehead has a statement joining our deduction of Process in the preceding chapter, and parts and wholes in this chapter, into his final and ultimate philosophical concept:

> "Creativity," "many," "one" are the ultimate notions involved in the meaning of the synonymous terms "thing," "being," "entity." These three notions complete the Category of the Ultimate and are presupposed in all the more special categories. . . .
>
> "Creativity" is the universal of universals characterizing ultimate matter of fact. It is that ultimate principle by which the many, which are the universe disjunctively, become the one actual occasion, which is the universe conjunctively. It lies in the nature of things that the many enter into complex unity.[26]

194

CHAPTER IX

CAUSATION AND PURPOSIVENESS

We are now in a position to study the requirements of the notion of purpose, how it is interpreted under the static and dynamic ideas of meaning, and what the static and dynamic ideas of reality allow to be true concerning its existence and its relation to sensation. The treatment will be divided according to the more antecedent aspects of purposive activity — the prior needing, desiring, and aiming; and the more subsequent and consummatory aspects. The question of freedom or determinism of purposive activity can be taken up afterwards in the next chapter. Then we can go on to more concrete applications in the succeeding chapters on life and evolution, bodily structure and mind, and environment, considering their relevance to purpose. Also, in Part IV on Value theory, we will have occasion to refer back to the present analysis of the phases of value-process.

I. Antecedent Aspects of Purposiveness.

Under each position the material will be arranged, to aid comparison, according to the following sub-heads:

1. General conceptions of cause and purpose
2. The subject
3. The need or urge
4. The object
5. The consequent meaning of desire, aim, motive, purpose.

Of necessity, most illustrative material must be taken from the human level, though at this point we are not necessarily assuming that our points might not apply to organisms at other levels. Under DR at least the whole hierarchy of organisms can be under consideration as "subjects," although it is not until Chapter XIV on Evolution that we will have introduced the organisms higher than atoms and molecules.

SM with SIR.

Implications of SM: 1. General Conception of Cause and Purpose. Once again the strict implication of SM to causation and purpose is quite odd. If value can exist in a state of fulfilled perfection, where no process or change is needed, where, in fact, the latter would only damage perfection, then what scope could there be for causation *or* purpose? If nothing need ever move, then there is no need of anything to cause it to move. And what content can the idea of purpose have, if there is no want, no lack, and therefore nothing desired to aim at?

And sure enough, examples are not lacking of thinkers who would defend the thesis that where static value fully exists — that is in God — there is no place for desiring or purposing, or even causing. Aristotle's Absolute is something like this: it does not desire; it only contemplates itself. Of course, it "causes" in a way: the Absolute is the cause of the motions of all creatures in that its perfection attracts them toward it. It arouses desires and movements in all imperfect creatures, but the Absolute itself has no desire and exerts no effort as it causes the creatures to do so.

Obviously, the question why such a perfect Absolute should ever have introduced a situation containing lack and consequent desire, followed by purposed and caused change, now comes up. And it has been recognized throughout the history of philosophy as a question that cannot be answered in SM's own terms. A world of change can not be derived from a changeless ultimate. Only by appealing to other independent principles have static philosophies been able to make any sense of a striving and purposing world. Christianity appeals to the extra principle of "Love." God is love and therefore wants something to love and to be loved by. But in allowing this, Christianity has already contradicted the implications of its own idea of God's fulfilled perfection: why should God want anything? Hinduism has no real explanation why the fully satisfied Brahman should have allowed the whole business of unpleasant illusory life to develop at all. Plato, A.E. Taylor says, suggests that God "was perfectly good, and for that very reason did not want to keep his goodness to himself, but to make something like himself."[1] But in saying this, Plato has admitted that goodness implies a process of sharing, and has departed from the strict logic of the static idea of good.

2. The subject: The present point, that no causing and no pur-

posing are really implied by fully static assumptions, is consistent with the preceding one (Chapter VIII) that no units, parts, or individuals are implied. If no creative interaction is necessary, then no individual subjects to interact with one another are necessary. Nor would a variety of specific causes be necessary for such individuals to be influenced by or to deal with. All existence might as well be a seamless unity without part causes or individual feelers.

3. The Need or Urge Aspect: SM is especially blank on this subdivision of the problem. Static good obviously does not imply lack or want at any point in the enjoyment of good. It conceives desire not as for something to satisfy an existing need, but as a mere attraction to the essence, ideal or form that is presented to the contemplating mind. What this means is that SM emphasizes the *end* phase to the exclusion of the beginning, need phase of experience.

4. The Objective Factor. Not clearly implying a doctrine of need, SM consequently fails to imply a doctrine of objects or materials to fulfill the need. Again, conceiving existence intellectualistically as it does, SM imagines that it is enough to mention the essences which in themselves are expected to produce satisfaction in the mind by mere direct contemplation. Existence might as well be a purely mental traffic of ideas, not involving concrete objects at all, but only the essences of thought as such.

5. Desire, Aim, Purpose. Purposing, then, becomes a mental adoption of the envisaged essences. Or, assuming we allow any individual subjects (contrary to # 2), minds "desire" the essences by a kind of surface attraction, not related to any propulsion from existent need. There is no place for any kind of causes or conditions requiring the mind to discover a resolution for them. The mind has only to elect the essence according to its idle preference.

Adjustments of SIR: 1. General Conception of Cause and Purpose; The Four Causes. As always, specific processes and subjects and causal conditions force themselves on men's attention, and static idealism must deal with them. Purposing and aiming have hardly ever been denied, even by the Illusionists. For them, the monistic world of mental substance is fully purposive — in fact, for some views, to the exclusion of causality, if by the latter is meant impersonal factors enforcing effects according to natural laws. SIR would prefer to believe that *all* causation is by mental purposes only, by minds contemplating the realm of ideas, and then in quite unconditioned freedom, electing whichever ideas appeal to them. In a pure monism, the only ultimate desire, or purpose of the mind, as it elects ideas would apparently be to form some kind of harmonious system of ideas that is "right" or perfectly consistent; after which it finds supreme value in "ecstatically" contemplating that system in all its symmetry and order.

However, the more common picture — not only for the earlier static idealism, but for the man on the street today — is the dualistic one where minds freely adopt ideas which thereupon somehow incite actions in the material world (the body) to execute or embody that idea in things. This is more or less how Plato conceived cause and purpose. He allowed that the material, bodily realm could resist the influence of ideas, but it could never *initiate* or "cause" anything. Only the mental realm of purposes could do that. This view also tends to believe in the existence of a special faculty of the mind called the "will," as a self-caused, independent source of purposed action.

Aristotle elaborated the doctrine of causation into his famous fourfold classification. Taking an example, such as a man building a house, he argued that the final house resulted from four sources: (1) the "material cause" — the materials used in the house, wood, plaster, etc. — was the least significant. It was quite passive and did not really "cause" anything to happen; it had to wait until the more active causes worked on it. (2) The "efficient" cause was the man's exerting effort on this material to move it about and get it into its place; the application of force or energy to the matter. But this still told us very little about what kind of house finally appears. (3) The "formal" cause was the shape and plan of the house which direct the man in his movements and determine just where and how the materials are arranged. But this still did not tell why that particular form or plan is chosen. (4) The "final" cause was the *purpose* or use to which the house is to be put, and *this* is the reason for the particular plan or form that was selected. A similar analysis was applied to developing and growing creatures. The material cause of the oak tree is made up of the substances that go into its growth; water, minerals, etc. The efficient cause is formed by the powers of nature, perhaps the sun's power, that makes the growth go on. The formal cause is the shape of the oak tree in which the materials are finally arranged. The final cause, in the case of developing things, tends to become identical with the formal. It is conceived as a sort of pre-set goal which the thing strives to approach and conform to, already existent somehow in the germ (or in the acorn). Apparently Aristotle himself did not think of final causes as the enforcing agent that caused the growth — this was the efficient cause. The final cause did not "make" things grow; it was only that into which they did grow. However, some medieval and more recent thinkers tend to confuse final causes with efficient causes, speaking as though ends could themselves act as causal forces.

2. The subject. SIR takes the existence of individual purposing minds for granted. In fact, earlier thought considered most events as emanating from some kind of subject motivated by final causes, with their mental and purposive flavor. Rocks fell to earth because they knew in some quasi-mental way, that they "belonged" there. The winds of the air, volcanoes in the earth, etc., were caused by the purposes of quasi-personal spirits, imps, demons, etc., inhabiting the phenomena.

3. The Need or Urge Aspect: SIR remains unclear about any factor of depletion or dynamic disharmony as a prior source of directed forces or readiness to respond to something. It continues to think rather in terms of the mind chancing to envisage an essence and then gravitating toward it by attraction. The mind is not thought of as being propelled by anything until the vision of the essence, or of the formal and final causes, descend out of the blue to start up a desire within it. None of Aristotle's causes mean exactly what we will mean by "need." SIR thus still considers only the *end* phase of process and remains rather unclear about the beginning phase.

4. The Objective Factor. Even Plato, on this point, recognized that as a matter of fact, man usually has to work with materials when he wishes to enjoy values. This was true, however, only because of the inexplicable happenstance that the material world intruded between man and pure form and unfortunately forced him to deal with it. Aristotle conceded that the forms could exist only in concrete objects. The material cause, of his four-fold theory, means that there must be some objective thing for the efficient and formal causes to work upon by way of reaching the final cause.

5. Desire, Aim, Purpose. In summary SIR conceives purpose as an intellectualistic adoption of pre-envisaged ideas or essences from a realm of forms; or else, as in Aristotle, a pre-set form

which guides processes as "final cause." In either case the purpose is not definitely associated with feelings of maladjustment in the preceding situation nor with desiring objects to fulfill it. We should also remember that the whole-part relationship is presumed in any of these concepts of purposiveness — the parts of a purposive being are under the control of minds, ideas, forms, emanating from the whole.

SM with SMR.

Findings of SMR: 1. General Conception of Cause and Purpose: Mechanism. How causation must be conceived, given such parts or units as have been described for SMR, is obvious. Everything that happens can only be the result of the motions of the bits of matter as they collide with one another and transmit motion from one to another according to fixed laws. Burtt, speaking of Galileo, who perhaps has the best claim to be considered the modern founder of SMR, says:

> . . . the primary realm . . . for Galileo is identified with material atoms in their mathematical relations, the *how* of events being the sole object of exact study. . . . The real world is simply a succession of atomic motions in mathematical continuity. Under these circumstances causality could only be intelligibly lodged in the motions of the atoms themselves, everything that happens being regarded as the effect solely of mathematical changes in these material elements.[2]

Aristotle's formal and final causes could find no locus in this picture. Only the efficient and material causes, now identified, were left. "Push" accounted for everything now; "pull" in the sense of attraction by ideals, "forms" molding motions toward desired outcomes, were all now unthinkable.

The question arises whether we are confined, in SMR, to considering actual bodily contact, or collision, between these bits of matter as the only mode of causal efficacy. Certainly, this is the simplest way of conceiving it.

> An explanation in any other than mechanical terms would seem incomprehensible to [the ordinary man] as it did to

200

Newton and Huyghens. . . . When he wants to move an object, he pulls or pushes it through the activity of his muscles and cannot imagine that Nature does not effect her movements in a similar way. The essence of a mechanical explanation is that each particle of a mechanism experiences a real and definite push or pull.[3]

And yet, the early thinkers were soon aware that bodies seemed able to affect one another at a distance across empty space. This was especially apparent as soon as the law of gravity was proved to hold between heavenly bodies which never came in direct contact with one another. However, Newton found the conception of "Action at a Distance" impossible.

It is inconceivable, that inanimate brute matter should, without the mediation of something else, which is not material, operate upon, and affect other matter without mutual contact. . . . That gravity should be innate, inherent, and essential to matter, so that one body may act upon another, at a distance through a vacuum, without the mediation of anything else, by and through which their action and force may be conveyed from one to another, is to me so great an absurdity, that I believe no man who has in philosophical matters a competent faculty of thinking, can ever fall into it.[4]

For this reason Newton accepted the ether, filling all space, as a substance to transmit forces between ordinary material bodies not in direct contact.

As mechanistic theory moved on to trying to explain chemical and electrical phenomena, it had to make more and more use of the ideas of attractive and repulsive forces emanating from the solid atoms and passing through "empty" space to affect other atoms.

The next point to consider is plurality of causes. SMR was naturally tempted at first to consider only "trains of single causes," since that is so much simpler to conceive. On the model of one billiard ball hitting the next, and that hitting the next, and so on, all transmitting forces from one to another by absolute necessity, SMR tried to conceive of everything as the necessary result of "chains" of collisions. However, it was obvious that two or more causes or forces might come together simultaneously, especially if we allow the attractive and repulsive forces acting simultaneously at a distance between many atoms. This, in fact, would make situations involving single causes exceedingly rare, if not non-existent. Even in the case of struck billiard balls, the forces coming from the supporting table, friction, its inner structure etc., etc., are acting on it simultaneously with the force of the striking ball. Thus SMR had to develop a theory of "total" cause. One could hope to uphold the necessity or determinism of causality only by showing that a given total effect necessarily followed from a given total causal situation. Or, alternatively, one could state mechanistic determinism in terms of partial causes, if he added a statement that all other causes in the total cause remain constant.

However, this concession of SMR did not mean that it gave up thinking of total causes and their effects *additively*. Effects were still the necessary, and unpurposed, outcomes of the several partial forces that happened to come together to produce the geometrically predictable "resultant." Prediction still required only knowledge of the position and velocity of all the component causes, figured out individually and added together. Until Clerk-Maxwell originated field concepts, all forces were still lodged in individual atoms, remaining always distinct and separate forces, however much they may interlace with one another in the space between. Remember also that the *effects* could not be considered as new unities in any sense, as we have shown in the discussion of the whole-part relation (p. 188).

According to Newton's laws, any particle A in the world will be subject to forces from any or all of the other particles B, C, D. . . . These forces may come from contiguous particles, as when two billiard-balls collide — or from distant particles through gravitational attraction — as when the sun and moon raise tides in the ocean. In either case the amount of force at any instant depends only on the positions which the various particles of the world occupy in space at that instant.[5]

Next we come to the question of the extent of application of this mechanistic analysis. It originated, we saw, in taking our sensory experience of ordinary objects at face value. At first, there was no thought of extending the theory to the human being —not even his body, let alone his mind. But then Descartes conceded that our bodies were made of mechanical parts. Next Hobbes boldly began the application even to the mind — though only on a speculative basis.

As for experimental science, it more slowly pushed the theory beyond its origins in astronomy and in Galileo's experiments with ordinary material objects, into chemistry, electricity, biology. Right up to our own century (when the whole theory rather suddenly collapsed) some scientists hoped it would provide the final explanation of all things, including human personality, though we might wonder why anyone would desire such an unattractive outcome for thought. Incidentally, one of the main reasons why some have desired this is simply that mechanism promises a relatively *easy* or simple, explanation of things. As Einstein puts it:

> With matter and force as our fundamental concepts, we can hardly imagine simpler assumptions than that forces act along the line connecting the particles and depend only on the distance. But is it possible to describe all physical phenomena by forces of this kind alone?
> The great achievements of mechanics in all its branches, its striking success in the development of astronomy, the application of its ideas to problems apparently different and non-mechanical in character, all these things contributed to the belief that it *is* possible to describe all natural phenomena in terms of simple forces between unalterable objects.[6]

And so, as late as the 1920's we had the Behaviorists trying to make mechanism do as a complete explanation for the human being. As Whitehead characterizes the view, preparatory to criticizing it:

> . . . Each molecule blindly runs. The human body is a collection of molecules. Therefore, the human body blindly runs, and therefore there can be no individual responsibility for the actions of the body. If you once accept that the molecule is definitely determined to be what it is, independently of any determination by reason of the total organism of the

body, and if you further admit that the blind run is settled by the general mechanical laws, there can be no escape from this conclusion.[7]

But all this is only what Hobbes had already worked out at the beginning.

"There can be no cause of motion, except in a body contiguous and moved."[8]

Commenting on this passage Burtt writes:

Having carried through the new conception of causality to a decisive statement, having also, in his doctrine of the relation of the human mind to nature, made such a strong bid for a consistent materialism, there was no temptation for him to return to teleology in his psychological analysis. He was not able to develop a psychology in terms of mathematical atoms, but he strayed no farther from this method than was necessary; he described the mind as a compound of elementary parts . . . produced in the vital organs by the clash of inrushing and outpushing motions, and combined according to simple laws of association. . . . This treatment . . . set the fashion for almost the whole modern development of psychology. . . . From now on it is a settled assumption for modern thought in practically every field, that to explain anything is to reduce it to its elementary parts, whose relations, where temporal in character, are conceived in terms of efficient causality solely.[9]

Thus purposiveness — as wholes directing parts in the light of chosen values — was driven out of its last abiding place, the human mind.

2. The subject. While putting its extreme emphasis upon the individual part as against SM's failure to suggest the need of any parts, SMR certainly does not thereby arrive at individual subjects. The atoms in themselves have no inner feeling, no purposive, subjective aspect; nor can they make real wholes that might have these features, as we saw in the preceding chapter. SMR can provide no entity or subject to contain ideas or desires for goals.

3. The Need or Urge Aspect. We have seen that SMR, in contrast to SM, emphasizes the origin phase of processes, finding the prior disconnection and unrelatedness of parts to be essential and final reality. Thus it might be expected to find the need aspect more real than the later consummation aspects. And indeed it is typical of mechanistic psychologies to focus on primitive instinctive urges as more significant than developed goal-ideals. And yet, the lack of any locus for feeling logically prevents SMR from speaking of "needs" as having any qualitative or preferential aspect. It develops, rather, a doctrine of urge as mechanical force propelling the organic machine into trial and error motion until quiescence is more or less accidentally achieved. Of course, there can be theories of conditioning to explain how the activity may become less blind through experience and memory. But nowhere is the behavior conceived as primarily for the sake of qualitative achievement; it is always only a matter of blind causes issuing in inevitable effects for no reason except efficient production.

4. The Objective Factor. Reversing SM's disconcern with material objects as wherewithal for satisfying needs, SMR is only too ready to consider the object to the exclusion of any aiming at ideals or essences by the subject at all. The object, like the need or urge, is conceived as a mechanical stimulus (from "outside" rather than "inside" the organism) which propels it into deterministic activity. The need state of the organism and the properties of the object are *both* thought of as measurable physical and chemical causes that will interact and produce some predictable result. The organism passively reacts to the stimulus. All reference to its expectations, to the "meaning" of objects for the organism is thus eliminated. The object cannot be spoken of as "liked," "attractive," "preferred," etc.; it can only issue its inevitable causative forces upon the subject.

5. Desire, Aim, Purpose. To summarize the anti-purposive features resulting from the materialistic conception of atoms: First, these atoms, considered individually, are inert and have no inner feeling or desire. Next, their motions are entirely determined, precluding any choice of action in terms of evaluated purposes. Thirdly, their solid, impenetrable nature prevents them from constituting real wholes that might have had these features. Conceiving the organism as an intersection of currents from inner and outer stimuli and currents to responding mechanisms, as in a

telephone exchange, SMR cannot understand the organism as an entity in itself with qualitative desires choosing values toward which to organize its behavior.

If such logic seems to deny experience too queerly, SMR attempts a doctrine of conditioning to explain how the organism can seem to search out "desired" objects. In the first instance of satisfying an urge, there might not be any envisaging of an ideal or goal; there would only be the random trial and error behavior. But on later similar occasions, conditioning and memory might enable the organism to select what it "wants."

Contradiction between SMR and SM-SIR: SM itself, we said, did not clearly imply desire or aim for a different condition than already exists, but rather mere permanent order or perfection of activity. SMR might seem to fulfill this in its doctrine of universal obedience of atoms to the laws of motion. But SM certainly meant that its perfect order should be the intention of *mind*. Newton, then, found his picture of an eternally repetitive clockwork universe suitable to illustrate divine purpose, though it had no room within it for purposive creatures. However, it was not long before the purposelessness of creatures was seen to involve the purposelessness of the whole. The universe could just as well have been caused by the blind motions of atoms from all eternity, and never have been intended and created by a divine mind at all.

Moving to SIR's interpretation of purpose as involving aim, or intention, conceived as either disembodied idea chosen by mind which then wills behavior to conform to it; or as form somehow inherent in the process that molds it toward a preordained outcome: SMR obviously makes all this impossible. We have just seen that the material atoms themselves cannot envisage aims or ideas; nor can they make a whole that might envisage them. Nor do they allow a locus for the more Aristotelian concept of formal or final cause. Wheelwright expresses this point as mechanism's "Principle of Telic Neutrality":

> Any given process, and the motions of which it consists, are to be explained by reference to previous spatial motions, never by reference to a tendency inherent in the process itself [an "entelechy"] nor to a cosmic mind or purpose.[10]

Recourses to SM: Idealism tries to escape these dismaying

conclusions about purpose by its ancient devices. We have seen how Descartes revived Plato's dualistic escape, trying to preserve SM's kind of purpose in a separate mental realm; and how Hobbes soon weakened this defense. It has therefore been the illusionist escape that has been most used in modern thought. We have seen Leibniz's and Spinoza's monisms where the one existing reality was a substance that was somehow essentially mental or force like; and no matter how apparent its material "aspect" might seem, it was nothing more than an aspect. Leibniz allowed this two-aspected substance to be divided up into plural purposive individualities while Spinoza was more interested in its single, unified nature.

We remember Berkeley's argument that the whole mechanistic theory itself was only the product of mentality in the first place; and that it was based on sensory experience which no one could prove to originate in external material objects at all. Kant adopted the suggestion that since we could never know what nature in itself was, beyond the screen of our ideas, there was no necessity of believing that it was as mechanistic as it had been so gratifyingly simple for our minds to figure out. German philosophy, following this lead, made itself the most popular philosophy all through the nineteenth century as "German Idealism," and much of Christianity adopted this kind of defense. Men in general happily accepted this leave to believe in the mental and purposive nature of reality. But the Industrial Revolution kept changing the "feel" of life for masses of people more and more toward the materialistic. Later this illusionist escape was less successful in quieting doubts. Many could not help asking why there should be such an insistent *appearance* of material causes in life, if they really have no part to play in God's design? Especially when modern biology began to pour out such an infinity of detail about the material structure and causation within animal and human bodies, did the question become overwhelming: why, if Ideas are all that need be real, has this amazingly complex and toilsome structure of bodies been necessary? So that, currently, Idealism has lost its popularity, and most philosophers do not feel satisfied that they are really facing up to the problems of thought unless they start with granting genuine reality to the complex "material" structures and causes that face them wherever they study nature. To just dismiss it all as "Illusion" seems too easy; too much a matter of first conceiving your wishful dream, and then, if nature doesn't fit your private preference, telling nature to get lost.

Whitehead remarks that, trying to believe in human purpose while science seemed continually to confirm nothing but choiceless determinism in nature has, during recent centuries, "enfeebled" the whole human enterprise of thoughtful maintenance of a healthful and creative culture.

A scientific realism, based on mechanism, is conjoined with an unwavering belief in the world of men and of the higher animals as being composed of self-determining organisms. This radical inconsistency at the basis of modern thought accounts for much that is half-hearted and wavering in our civilization. It would be going too far to say that it distracts thought. It enfeebles it, by reason of the inconsistency lurking in the background. After all, the men of the Middle Ages were in pursuit of an excellency of which we have nearly forgotten the existence. They set before themselves the ideal of the attainment of a harmony of the understanding. We are content with superficial orderings from diverse arbitrary starting points.[11]

In short, no way of trying to save purpose and aspiration in the face of SMR has seemed to achieve complete satisfactoriness for either philosophers, seeking intellectual consistency; theologians, seeking strong bases for religious inspiration; psychologists, seeking bases for healthy human attitudes; or sociologists seeking bases for progressive and creative societies. Of course Communism puts on the appearance, at least, of inspiring purposive behavior in individuals on the basis of a philosophy that partakes of a good many features of SMR. We shall discuss in Part V why we think they derive their dynamic from different sources than their ostensible Marxian materialism.

Our thesis is that no philosophy that grants the essential assumptions of SMR can ever be the source of healthy, purposive aspiration and staunch effort on the part of any individual or culture based upon it. If science should ever have succeeded in establishing SMR as *the* philosophy of reality, humanity would have been doomed to a long regression, to an inert cynicism and despair.

Providentially, science itself has moved away from SMR. We

are no longer stuck with it as our starting point; no longer confined to these rather feeble and foredoomed attempts to escape from it. A new theory of reality is widely accepted to-day.

SM with DR.

Findings of DR: 1. General Conceptions of Cause and Purpose. It is supremely important to remember that neither SM nor SMR prepared us for understanding how desires and consequent experiences of purpose consist in the relations of a plurality of parts to wholes, i.e., upon planning and scheduling multiplicities into patterned unities. SM expected single value essences to produce value experience; SMR finds single impulses dominating over others and then mechanically producing their effect.

Now we have seen that in DR, the basic "substance" is energy which might conceivably be the locus of feeling that is capable of caring for quality. We have also seen that its units can fuse into unified fields which are realities in their own right, and which can thereupon control the units of which they are composed (Chapter VIII). This seems to give us some of our basic requisites for purposive functioning. But is there anything in this picture that bespeaks of *aim,* foresight, prospicience?

To answer this, we may go back to the concept of "total cause" which we found in SMR (p. 202f.), to discover that it makes room for something that SMR never noticed. SMR recognized that nature reveals no cases of single causes enforcing single specific effects.

> . . . the causal order is not a set of parallel chains but a spreading network. Every event, the closer we examine it, produces many effects. And equally, every event has many contributory causes. There is no "the cause" of anything. What caused the landslide? A series of heavy rains, a gradual increase of the weight of vegetation on the slope, a bit of an earth tremor, frost . . . ; omit any one of these factors and it would not have occurred. . . . Evidently the causal context splays out from any event in both directions; the descendants multiply and so do the ancestors, the more deeply we look.[12]

But SMR did not recognize the significance of the fact that the many causes, in coming together, might fuse into a field of energy in which *strains* would appear, pointing to a future pattern of organization or integration that would resolve these strains in an equilibrium. SMR's mechanistic reasoning could only find "concatenation" or "assemblage" in the effects, all the partial causes and their laws remaining essentially unchanged by their togetherness. Effects are conceived as mere sums of separately acting causes, passively determined by those causes. But now we have the conception of causes as waves, or patterns of energy which, as soon as they come into contact, are immediately together in such a way that tension, imbalance, "bad-fitting" exist, setting up dynamic tendencies or pulls toward more inclusive, symmetrical patterns wherein these energies *would* "fit." The *arrangement* has reality now in a way that was lacking in SMR.

This picture of energies in awkward relationships, *straining* toward other relationships that would resolve tensions, begins to resemble what we mean by "aim." Something is wanted, desired, pointed to. Imagine a network of rubber bands, all tied together in a pattern and stretched between rigid supports. Make it a hexagonal pattern such as we imagined for the billiard balls (p. 178) and let the rubber bands be analogues for our new energy units, as the billiard balls were for our old material atoms. Now pull our hexagonal network askew. We know that when we let it go, it will snap back "into place" — in the pattern that holds its internal forces in the most symmetrical, balanced condition possible. Now, while it is being held askew, can we not imagine that the network, then and there, is aiming at the hexagonal shape? that the potentiality of the hexagon is somehow contained within the present lop-sided, unbalanced state? The pattern of the whole, here, is operative and real in a sense that the pattern of the billiard balls was not. Aim seems to arise out of this situation where holistic strains appear from a group of energies (causes) that have flowed together, pointing to some new arrangement they must achieve in order to "fit."

In fact, causation itself may now almost be seen as "the effect" of holistic strains, at least in some kinds of structures. Whitehead, in a remarkable passage tieing causation to value, suggests that causation or "power" arises out of this fact of wholes pulling themselves together:

> . . ."actuality" is in its essence "composition." Power is the compulsion of composition. Every other type of composition

210

is a half-way stage in the attainment of actuality. The final actuality has the unity of power. The essence of power is the drive toward esthetic worth for its own sake. All power is a derivative from this fact of composition attaining worth for itself. There is no other fact. . . . It is efficient cause maintaining its power of survival. It is final cause, maintaining in the creature its appetition for creation.[13]

Causal "force," Whitehead hints, may not be so much a matter of bits pushing bits, as of fields pulling ingredients into satisfactory places.

It remains to remind ourselves of the place of feeling within this picture. The notion of holistic energy strains does not quite become the notion of purposiveness or aim, until it is understood to contain feelings, desire, or the ability to *care* about disorder and resolution, and about value. Can this factor be shown, by scientific method, to exist within all causal, compositional processes? We have seen (p. 167) that the answer to this question is apparently that the observer cannot know that there are feelings or desires in the processes he observes external to himself, by any direct empirical or sensory means. But such thinkers as Köhler, Whitehead, Reiser etc., conclude by the logic of "isomorphism," that is, from the similarity (iso) of form (morph) of externally observable processes to internal experiences, that inner feelings do so exist.

2. The Subject. We have now before us all that is needed for a theory of the feeling and aiming subject: the holistic organism is the center of feeling which can desire and then aim at the solution of its desire.

3. The Need or Urge Aspect. DR makes it more explicit than either SM or SMR that value processes arise out of need, and that need itself must be understood as *felt* dynamic disorder, strain or depletion. This notion in turn requires our whole-part relationship to be such that certain parts can be somewhat out of adjustment within some kind of whole which can feel that non-adjustment. Instead of either SM's essences mystically calling forth purposive effort, or SMR's individual instincts blindly pushing activity, we have the notion of some variety of field strain selectively pointing toward some presumptive activity-with-objects.

The prior phase of need, then, arises (1) from disorders and vaguenesses within the organism itself; and (2) from new data ingressing from outside into the organism and disrupting it. In either case, holistic strains arise, accompanied by feelings of discomfort, with vector forces already pointing the way toward, or at least ready to respond to, objects that will help resolve the tension. The strains of Physics and the feelings of psychology give us the essentials of a doctrine of need and urge. Reiser summarizes these ideas:

> The potency of organizing fields of influence is required to bring the parts together in the right times and places if products are to emerge, and these force-fields provide the closure principles which operate in nature. The lowest organisms such as atoms, have minds (field-unity) analogous to those of higher organisms, such as man, based on gestalt synthesis. The hunger for whole-ness is the spiritual aspect of nature.[14]

4. The objective factor. DR recognizes more explicitly than SM or SMR the necessity of objects for the existence of value purposes. Value feeling is found to exist only within processes of interaction; the feeling subject thus must have something to interact with. The need situation above requires the feeling subject to enter into processes with other and additional energies in order to bring the fulfilling process in which value inheres into existence. This is the essential meaning of the object.

5. Desire, Aim, Purpose. We now have the notion of field strains toward unity informed with feeling, *caring* for what is done. But have we yet got conscious aiming, previsioning, goal-envisaging? First, we might note that some recent thinkers suggest that aim may exist with or without consciousness (cf. Laird and Whitehead); that in lower organisms there may be "unconscious" aim, which must mean that field strains press toward resolution without any kind of previsioning or planning. Conscious purposiveness, then, with goal-envisionment, would arise as an enhancement of this aim factor. It would represent nature inventing more complex ways of guiding process more efficiently toward consummations, and of increasing the vividness of good feeling. But conscious previsioning would not necessarily involve any principles fundamentally different from or unrelatable to field strains. It would be solidly ensconced in the existing energy-patterns; it would be a kind of tentative rearranging, by neural

212

brain surrogates, of existing elements in the situation. We prevision our *presently existing* materials in another pattern.

But how is imagination interpolated into the perception-memory-conception cycle to produce the unity of purposive behavior, — especially at its highest level of creative activity? If the mind is an emergent from the brain, *how can an "emergent" change the pattern of causality in the matrix from which it emerges?* The solution of this riddle may be found in the concept of the *self-field.* Physicists are now considering the possibility that particles and field, *and their interaction,* must be treated as equal partners. . . . The macroscopic field of consciousness emerges out of its microscopic constituents, but in turn it lives to dominate the subordinate rhythms through an electro-magnetic bond of fealty which unites body and mind.[15]

Perry distinguishes among the related terms, drive, purpose, and need as relating to a complex process:

As the term "drive" calls attention to its forcefulness and treats it as a *vis a tergo,* the expression "governing propensity" refers to its continuing control of the intermediate stages of the process (subordinate acts, stages, etc.). The term "purpose" emphasizes the peculiar role of the terminal or culminating phase as determining its antecedents — in short, the teleological character of the process; while the term 'need' refers to the impulsions created by a deficiency in the existing situation — which may be an urgency or "pressing need."[16]

Both the "forceful" character of the drive and the "urgency" of the need would be explained in our terminology as a matter of field strains or forces within the unbalanced whole-part situation.

To explain how specific desires and aims arise out of needs and urges, we would require, of course, a theory of learning and memory. The first time any need is experienced, we may suppose there is no goal-envisaging, especially none of SM's electing essences from some non-natural realm, since there has not yet been any experience of what kind of goal or object can satisfy that particular kind of need. Random trial and error may be the only mode of solution. On future occasions of the same or similar needs, the memory would supply a pre-visioning of objects or goals which the organism has learned to be salutary for that need. We way now speak of "desire" or "interest" as a positive attraction toward selected objects prompted by the underlying need. In this way needs and urges would develop into desires and aims. The term "desire" is intermediate between need and aim-motive-purpose: it suggests a mind conscious of need, knowing what objects are wanted, but not necessarily yet definitely intending or planning what activity might attain the objects. The latter terms add this latter content.

To explain disappointment, failure, frustration, of course, we must assume a feeler sufficiently developed to conceive aims or purposes, and to experience their obstruction. Also there is the fact that the ability to conceive an aim vivifies value feelings when the aim is successfully achieved, though as we shall continually insist in Part IV it is not necessary to have aimed and been fulfilled in order to feel value. Satisfactions may come that were never desired or planned for; there was only an obscure "need" or readiness for them. Aim is thus essentially an enhancing factor.

Above all, we must never forget that DR finds all goal-achieving to be partial, finite and revelatory of new goals to achieve.

Comparison of SM with DR: Purpose As Involved in Present Factors. The last point above, of course, would not please SM. But more particularly neither would DR's insisting upon aim as involving *felt* need, thoroughly involved in present conditions. SM's conception, we have said, was that of the mind freely electing an idea or essence out of the blue, unrelated to any causes in the past history of that mind, or in its present circumstances. The mind was to operate *"ab extra,* and out of a detached spontaneity of its own,"[17] somehow inserting itself as an efficient cause into a creature's process and causing its subsequent behavior independently of all conditions. But the idea of causation as "composition," the creating of organized wholes out of ingredients, never loses sight of the fact that the wholes *are* composed of concrete ingredients and not of disembodied ideas. There is no place for idea as an outside entity coming in and regulating the parts. In a proper understanding of the whole-part relationship, the whole *is* the order or pattern of those parts

214

in that whole, satisfying the field-energy relationships. There is no further "force" beyond what those parts themselves supply.

What about Aristotle's revision of the notion of cause and purpose so as to do away with Plato's disembodied ideas causing effects? His formal and final causes are indissolubly tied to matter, somehow molding it toward a future shape that it was "meant" to take. This idea became later the conception of the future ends as a kind of force causing the present effects.

Patrick in his great chapter on purpose in nature seems to wish to revive this last conception:

> Let us make the daring experiment of thinking that the end actually determines the means. This certainly seems to be the case in the organic world. It seems as if the parts of the eye come into existence in the process of evolution, not because of some material motions among atoms and molecules, but because they are *indispensable* to the act of seeing. . . .
>
> It is form and structure, not matter, which are real . . . and they are final causes. . . . Viewed all along the evolutionary line there is creative synthesis issuing in novelties and new and higher values; but the reason why the things which we have been accustomed to call efficient causes appear is because they are indispensable to the new realities. . . .
>
> To put all this very bluntly, is it Push, or Pull, that drives or draws the world onward? It is the . . . push from behind, that our habitual nineteenth-century mechanistic habit of thought has always emphasized. And yet in humility we realize that even the manner of this push, to say nothing of the *reason,* is unknown. So perhaps after all the world is pulled, not pushed . . . [by] an *attractive* force.[18]

Yet DR would be about as resistant to this upsetting and hopelessly non-empirical conception of the future as cause of the present as would SMR. To suppose that that which does not yet exist is causing events is much too mystical for science. All causal laws have as their first essential, that time runs in an irreversible direction, and that from known and existent factors we hope to be able to predict future ones.

But there is also a certain internal inadequacy in the above ideas, insofar as they hint of the non-evolutionary notion that the future can consist only of forms or essences which are already somehow in existence. To suppose that things can only run through pre-set schedules to pre-set outcomes tends against any thought that the present is genuinely *solving* problems, genuinely *creating* novel harmonizations.

DR would prefer a doctrine that present "unsatisfactory" strains or disequilibria press toward, and ultimately succeed in achieving a resolution of problems. This may seem still rather a "push" picture, but it is really a kind of simultaneous push and pull: the partial energies are pushing or "jostling" one another, but the whole field is at the same time constraining or "pulling" them all into pattern. The pattern may not be pre-set, but a real creation of something really new.

But the development of the eye in the embryo, long before it has had to solve any "problem" of seeing, gives us pause. This seems at first sight to force us to some doctrine of the "future" causing the present. However, Reiser offers an explanation that keeps within the realm of ordinary causation from present to future without falling into any theory of chance.

> In our theory . . . mutation is the process whereby directed changes accumulate to the point where a new level of organization makes its appearance. And if, as Bergson argues, the vertebrate eye appeared in order that the organism may see, the genes which produce the eye must contain the potentialities for precipitating the mutations which direct evolution . . . even before the mutations become useful as survival factors.[19]

We have then, the idea that the eye *first* did appear as a "solution of a problem." We can suppose that cells slowly "learned" to be sensitive to light, then to shape themselves into some crude globular structure with a small focussing ability, then into a better form, etc. The older theory was that "mutations" gave rise to better structures by pure accident, leading to survival according to Darwinian theory. But recent theory tends to suggest that mutations are really field phenomena, being holistic "snappings together" of some sort of strains into new resolving patterns. In any case, once the eye was created, whether by accident or not, nature has the gene mechanism for passing that solution on to descendants. Thus the eye in the embryo develops before it ever solves any problem of seeing; but it is not being "caused by the future"; it is being caused by presently existing genes. Recent embryology, incidentally, is stressing more and more that bodily structures develop through some kind of *combination* cause, involving *both* the gene, and exercise or use. The embryo does roll its eyes about before birth, and this modicum of "problem solving" does seem to have something to do with the final shape of the eyes.

In general, we conclude that DR would favor the idea of causation by present field strains rather than by future states, or by disembodied ideas.

DM with DR.

Implications of DM and Correspondence to DR: 1. General Conception of Cause and Purpose. The dynamic idea of good clearly implies that purpose must be a matter of "handling" existing ingredients or forces. It must be saturated with the feeling of present tensions; it must be a precipitate of the existing factors in dynamic strain. There is no call for the appearance of independent essences hanging in mid-air, unconditioned by existent energies. Rather, DM requires "causes," conditions, materials to be grappled with and felt, the aim coming out of their midst as the implication of their tensions. Nor has DM any use for the notion of a pre-set form pulling things through pre-set routines. If Aristotle were correct, that nothing ever happens but the attainment by creatures of goals that were already somehow existent in the germ, we are left asking the creator why he doesn't simply place the creature in that desired shape to start with. We see no reason for the endless weary repetition of the same old developments. From this point of view, even Whitehead's and Santayana's effort to retain "essences" or "eternal objects" loses point. DM then, perhaps, would not necessarily have to readmit any sort of realm of pre-existent essences or ideals. Processes may create their forms anew each time; and if the same form is created over and over, it may be a real creation from its own point of view for all that. "Purpose" then would always have to do with what a presently existing field of energy under strain is here and now pointing to, and not with floating pre-existent essences.

217

2. The subject. We have already explained DM's implication to the necessity of a center of feeling. (# 1.1 p. 53).

3. The Need or Urge Aspect. SM's notion of a mere repetitive order, offering no place for lack or need, obviously could not, according to DM, embody purposiveness. There must be the feeling of dissatisfaction in disorder (# 2.41, p. 54) to give purpose a foothold. Since dynamic value can be experienced only in the organizing of disorganized factors, we need a principle that can get the process going, a "drive" to save the process from being either Aristotle's perfect but idle functioning that accomplishes nothing, or a mere chaotic tumbling about without direction. This requirement is fulfilled by DR's concept of purposive urge as field stress.

4. The Object can easily be deduced from # 2.62 p. 55, the requirement of further energies to interact with and incorporate so as to resolve and fulfill the need.

5. Desire, Aim, Purpose. We found under DR that holistic ordering tendencies are real in nature. But it was not clear that they are necessarily conscious or evolved to the level of definite prospicience and planning. Also we saw that having consciously aimed at a certain outcome is not absolutely necessary in order to feel or enjoy it, though the aiming can *enhance* the enjoyment. We are usually more vividly thrilled when we get what we had dreamed of, but we can also enjoy a sudden glimpse of a sunset or an unexpected meeting with a friend that comes to us unforeseen. Does DM require any more than this?

Well, if good is defined as the feeling of organizing process, it would seem only to require that holistic feelers should be able to feel whatever organizing processes they possess, whether aimed at or not. But it would also seem to require that the holistic field should strain toward resolution, should "seek" release however unconsciously, so as to avoid a world that in having no tendency toward order would achieve it only rarely and by accident. This much "purpose" there must be. For more conscious and efficient aiming and planning to rise out of this native tendency in things, accompanied by more intense feelings of fulfillment could be easily deduced from some of the subsidiary principles such as Novelty and Definiteness (# 2.32 p. 54; #2.7 p. 55), and others to be discussed in Part IV.

II. Subsequent Aspects of Purposiveness. Moving from the need and aim aspects of purposive functioning, we come to the instrumental and consummatory aspects, which we will consider under three heads:
1. Theories of Transition and Integration of Parts.
2. Theories of Means.
3. Theories of Ends, Attainment, Satisfaction.

SM with SIR.

Implications of SM: 1. Transition and Integration. We are now familiar with SM's failure to imply the existence of any process of satisfying needs or achieving purposes. Thus it cannot imply that a center of feeling, consisting of partial factors more or less disorganized and lacking needed factors should have to appropriate additional factors, pass through processes of organizing and unifying these factors, and attain a new felt condition. What SM does, in effect, is to consider final ends (the essences, forms) alone as though they constituted a complete doctrine of purposiveness in themselves.

2. Theory of Means. Thus SM lacks real grounds for any doctrine of means or instruments. However, if we depart from strict logic enough to admit the notion of an end-seeking that utilizes means, then SM inclines to a doctrine of a fixed hierarchy of means and ends, where all existing objects should be precisely the means required, no more and no less, for accomplishing those ends perfectly. All that exists, all causes, all conditions should be pre-planned, indispensable means, perfectly adapted to the ends. Lower in the hierarchy, all environmental objects should be just the proper means for supporting animal and human life; the animals in turn should be means to human ends. The parts and structures of bodies should appear as called for by the creatures' mental desires and aims. And creatures, including man, must be requisite means to some end of the Creator.

3. Theory of ends. The ends, of course, should be ultimately reached to the full, issuing in some kind of totally consummated state where nothing more should need to be done. There is certainly no implication that new ends should appear, new forms created indefinitely. Rather it is expected that a perfectly definite plan exists to be fulfilled, and there are precisely enough of the

219

proper means to fulfill it. Nothing need be left over, accidental, wasted or useless. More strictly, of course, the perfect ends should exist first, last and always, not needing to be "fulfilled."

Adjustments of SIR: 1. Theory of Transition and Integration. SIR always admits that there seems to be a process of development, though SM gives it no reason why. Aristotle worked out a theory of potentiality and activity, as we know, though he was not clear on the part-whole, organizational nature of it.

2. Theory of Means. SIR accepts the less rigorous implications of SM above. It assumes that ends were first conceived by the divine Mind, and all things created in the form required by those ends. Creaturely minds select and use objects in their environment for their purposes; and those objects were placed there by the Creator specifically for those uses. None of the phenomena of existence are thought of as mere blind outcomes of automatic causes. Minds may even create the bodily parts they are going to need in their living. The eye, for instance, is not the accidental effect of causal processes, but is a purposively created device "to see with." It was "meant" to be the means for seeing. Every feature of the earth was specifically created to be used as a means to some intended end. The medieval sacramental feeling about existence, which we have described, involved this conviction that there are no "loose ends," no useless, unplanned objects playing no required part in the great purposeful drama.

3. Theory of Ends. The crucial point should be emphasized: that in both the more Platonic and more Aristotelian concepts of the end, the goal of final form was conceived as already existent in some sense; either in a realm of disembodied forms, or else in the germ or seed. All growth was conceived as the unrolling of something already set, the following of a given model or prescribed routine.

SIR, of course, takes for granted what DR has to make explicit against SMR — that accomplishment, creation, solution are really possible. Goals must be achievable or creatable in principle if any creature is to be held responsible for striving for them. SIR however assumes what SM implies: that purposes can be *fully and perfectly* fulfilled. Although Christianity, for instance, resigned itself to the absence of perfection in this life, it still expected it in the next; and less insightful views have always strayed into a careless acceptance of some objects and outcomes in this life as "perfect." SM-SIR thus have always set men up for disappointment whenever perfection failed more markedly than usual to put in its appearance.

SM and SMR.

Findings of SMR: Reductive Analysis. 1. Theory of Transition and Integration. It is already clear how SMR makes the notion of creative process impossible. There may be *motion* of the parts, there may be rearrangement of their relative positions; but this never adds up to a genuine creation of anything new. There is never any real fusing of the parts into new unities or wholes. And of course, there can be no feeling inherent within the process of organizing wholes from parts. In later chapters we will apply this by now familiar analysis more specifically to life, evolutionary theory and the growth of the human organism, ideas, and values.

2. Theory of Means. Clearly, in SMR *causes* can never be thought of as means to ends. They are blind pushes and nothing but blind pushes. As we will understand more concretely in the next chapter, the means-end relationship is denied by SMR at every level. The environment is no longer a carefully planned means to the life of specially created creatures. It is simply an accidental concatenation of materials out of which evolved forms of life that it "fits" only because all forms that it didn't fit died off. The creatures' own bodily parts are the result neither of their own intentions, of purposive final causes, nor of divine planning; they too are merely the blind outcome of causal forces. Nor can the creature as a whole, or man, be thought of as a means to some divine purpose; he is once again merely the accidental outcome of blind atomic motions.

3. Theory of Ends. And so we come to the final negation of SMR: its denial of the possibility of ends, in the first place, for any means to subserve. Our study of the whole-part relationship in SMR prepares us for understanding that it can grant no reality to ends in the sense of real creations, accomplishments, solutions. Even if purpose were conceivable in the antecedent senses above, we now discover that the unreality of wholes for SMR means that no purpose could be fulfilled in any case. Process or evolu-

tion can never really *do* anything, develop or accomplish any improvement or fulfillment of purposes. For the only meaning that "accomplishment of a purpose" or "creativity" can have is the organizing of various factors, conditions, parts that were formerly disconnected, unrelated or disordered into a new arrangement which is a real new entity in itself. But in SMR, parts can only shift about from one conglomeration to another, and reality remains quite unaffected by their arrangement as such. One arrangement is as good or insignificant as another; the only realities are the separate atoms, whatever arrangement they may be in. We have the idea of motion or process that never accomplishes anything more than an eternal tossing about of atoms from one grouping to another, nothing ever becoming real except the atoms themselves.

That this strange notion is not merely the author's following a logical idea to absurdity is shown by the prevalence of the famous *Reductive Fallacy* among both the older mechanistic philosophers, and the current man on the street, whose thinking has in recent times caught up with the former. Statements in the form, "The product of this organizing process is nothing but those low-down parts and origins from which it started," are still very common. "Man is nothing but an ape," or "Man is nothing but a collection of chemicals and several pails-full of water" are probably the two most familiar examples, illustrating the two main forms of the fallacy: (1) reducing the outcome of a process to some earlier stage in that process; or (2) reducing a patterned, organized whole to the parts that may be analyzed out of it. In short, reducing present developed and synthesized wholes to past disconnected parts. It is clear that in either form the fallacy results from the mechanistic theory of atomic causation, which cannot allow that anything new and real is ever genuinely created when a process of development organizes parts or elements together into patterned unities. Examples of the reductive fallacy in every topic of thought will be given under SMR in later chapters.

There is one other feature of SMR which many assume is its most absolute contradiction of anything SM and SIR may have hoped for: the famous Second Law of Thermodynamics, or the theory of entropy. This seems to prove that whatever episodes of growth and creativity appear to exist in certain phenomena of nature must be dismissed as essentially insignificant eddies in what is the true, fundamental current of reality: a downward tendency toward final disintegration, toward an utter randomness of distribution of particles, toward the "heat death." All creative process, it is shown, depends upon statistically improbable differentials between energy levels, and invariably ends by reducing the amount of differential, leaving nature with a more statistically probable distribution, which means a more random and inert distribution, of the ultimate particles. The presumption is that, far from organizing process being the fundamental character of reality, disorganizing process is. This gloomy thesis would seem to blast DM's implications as much as, or more than, SM's.

Contradiction between SM and SMR: The absolute denial of SM-SIR's view of the electing and attaining of perfections through the use of exactly suitable means by SMR's theory of purposeless motions is obvious. We will omit a discussion of recourses tried by modern Idealism and go straight to DR's way of recovering meaning for means and ends.

SM with DR.

Findings of DR: 1. Theory of Transition and Integration. We are now considering the later phases of process, the transition as such and the result or issue (though we must keep insisting with Whitehead that only transition ever really exists). For DR, the transition, however, is a real integration which creates real products, though the latter proceed onwards into new processes. DR's theory of the part-whole relationship underlies this possibility.

> . . . how can new or unprecedented material events occur if the same causes always operate? These are the two main theses of materialism: that all realities are material, and that the functioning of the material universe is machinelike . . . devoid of genuine novelty. . . . According to this classical conception, an effect cannot "contain more" than its cause; nor can it be "qualitatively different." In other words, a cause must be "equal" to its effect.[20]

But a truly empirical attitude would be troubled by such apparent denials of plain experience. Causes so obviously produce effects that are different in quality from themselves and contain "more." They may not contain more material, mass or energy, but they surely contain more and different kinds of properties and ways of behaving. DR, then, takes account of these facts in its theory of emergence or causation as generation. Newton's *Principles,* Whitehead says, gives "no hint of that aspect of self-production, of generation . . . which is so prominent in nature."[21]

> Realization is a gathering of things into a unity of prehension. . . . A prehension is a process of unifying. Accordingly nature is a process of expansive developments, necessarily transitional from prehension to prehension. What is achieved is thereby passed beyond, but it is also retained as having aspects of itself present to prehensions which lie beyond it . . . the event (is) one entity, and not a mere assemblage of parts or ingredients. It is necessary to understand that Space-Time is nothing else than a system of pulling together of assemblages into unities.[22]

From the present standpoint, the notion of "chance" is clearly inapplicable to the creation of higher organisms. Democritus' and Russell's famous characterization of the human organism as an "accidental collocation of atoms" assumes a situation where eternally isolated and distinct atoms fall into random groupings by "chance." Chance here is opposed to purposive intention, though not to determinism, for the atoms are following their inexorable laws obediently enough when they meet. The new theory, however, understands the pattern of the organism as something that really accomplishes a resolution, that "succeeds" in a struggle to harmonize the awkward but real relationships that obtained between the atoms at first. The field equilibrium that is gained among partial energies that had been in tension is not random, but is called-for. It solves a problem, brings some sort of benefit.

Taking this idea back to the atoms, we may suppose that an electron unites with a proton in a hydrogen atom because it achieves some real relaxation, or completion of fields or "smoothing" of wave-patterns by so doing. Then the hydrogen and oxygen atoms fuse into a water molecule because the pattern of the molecule eases tensions; or allows wave-patterns that were colliding at awkward angles to slip into some symmetrical, mutually reinforcing combination with each other. This combining of patterns into more inclusive and complex patterns must continue, as evolution proceeds, producing the hierarchy of living forms.

A question arises at this point whether the conception of merely eliminating tension between wave-patterns is a sufficient principle to explain nature's advance to the immeasurable complexities of design that she achieves. One finds himself reaching out for some doctrine of *positive* nisus toward complex and interesting forms and structures for their own sake. A definite search for the novel and vivid experience, and a tendency to invent forms and structures that will efficiently subserve such experience is so strongly suggested that we can hardly resist belief in it. At any rate, the dynamic theory of reality is aware that nature's tendency toward complex organization requires a much more adequate principle of explanation than SMR's "chance." SMR was content simply to ignore what Reiser calls the "ever-baffling riddle of why nature is not satisfied to remain on the first level of manifestation (hydrogen atoms) but insists on climbing up"[23] the ladder of evolution.

But before we can go further with this kind of talk about nature, or her living forms "seeking" more vivid experience and therefore inventing novel and ever-improved structures to contain it, we will have to consider the mechanistic features of evolutionary theory more carefully in Chapter XI.

2. The Theory of Means. In the light of DR's approach to creative process, it should not be difficult to find a meaning for instrumental means. The center of feeling obviously must be continuously interacting with objects in order to make the process go forward. There must thus be an environment of some kind supplying means to the organisms. However, what can DR say as to whether this environment and these means are "planned" in any sense? Is there any sense in which SM's feeling that the purposive order is over-ruling, that everything that happens or exists is a specific means to some human or divine purpose, can be defended? Is the causal order specifically arranged as a planned means to definite, pre-conceived purposes?

Again the notion of the ends pre-arranging their own means rises from Idealistic thought to tempt us back to "final causes."

[The organism's] vital activity and its development are

225

made possible only by these definite organs and their no less definite functions. But these definite organs and functions are, in turn, only possible in this organism. Hence the whole, which causes the effect, determines the parts which are required for it. They are only in it; and it is possible only through them. In this reciprocal dependence of the whole and the parts Kant has given us the classic definition of an organism. A watch is a whole that may be put together out of pre-existing wheels, etc. But the organism must itself produce the parts of which it is to consist. From this we get two fundamental types of the construction of a whole; the mechanical and the organic. In the one the parts themselves are conditioned by the whole and are only possible in it. In the organic whole, therefore, the end, which is to come out of it, determines the beginning.

This latter formulation is at first sight too much for ordinary views of causation. The determination of the beginning by the end seems paradoxical and impossible. That the pre-existing should determine the present seems natural enough, though it is not quite so self-evident, as it seems at first sight; but how can the future, which does not yet exist, do anything? How can it itself determine the process of an event to which alone it will owe its existence?[24]

Windelband goes on to defend this apparently impossible idea of the future end constraining the causal order to produce just what that end is going to need, with the help of Kant's view of the time-relation as merely one of our mental thought forms that does not legislate as to what nature-in-itself might be able to do.

However, as we have seen (p. 215), DR finds it both more factual and more meaningful to retain SMR's one-way causal order, from past to present to future, but to hold that the whole field creates resolution-patterns here and now out of what the causal order brings to it. DR places both cause and aim, as it were, in the present. It is willing to grant a relative blindness to the partial causes. We can admit that Nature throws together various forces "by accident." It doesn't much matter what ingredients flow together. But once together, then "purpose" arises to see what it can do with these factors. It is not necessary that the future purpose be somehow already marked out, thereupon

226

demanding that prior conditions be just so. Purposiveness need only begin to work upon what is given, to see what it can create then and there. If it succeeds in creating something interesting or "successful" from these ingredients, *then they will acquire the status of having been "means" to that end.* But the end does not have to be pre-existent in any sense. We do not have "future ends" preparing "means" for themselves. We have, rather, *solving of current problems.*

To what extent this idea may be applied to the evolution of new forms or organisms will be discussed in the next chapter: whether "nature" is solving current problems when she invents a new creature.

Once an organism's structure is evolved, however, it seems that it will be able to select objects from its environment as means to its budding purposes in a more ordinary sense. This phenomenon may extend downward to the bottom rung of organisms: The oxygen atom "selects" the hydrogen atom as fitting into its "desire" for the more comfortable state of the water molecule; it rejects other kinds of atoms as not fitting. The analogy to man's selecting some substances to eat and rejecting others seems complete. The developing pattern "knows" what kind of additional ingredients it needs for its completion. In higher organisms, this selectivity develops into the ability to envisage future patterns and thence to a more adequate selecting, seeking and finding of external ingredients to add to the organism's own processes so as to bring about the future state. But no future end had arranged for those ingredients to be there. They just are or are not there, and the purposing organism snaps them up if they are, and misses them if they aren't. However, they are apt to be there, for the organism originally evolved from this sort of environment, and thus naturally uses the sorts of ingredients that it supplies. Evolution also increases the organism's ability to move about and find and even to create the needed means, in case they are not immediately at hand.

3. Theory of Ends. A few other features concerning the attainment of ends may be added to what was said under # 1, particularly concerning creative attainment as including, not replacing, the past. Hartshorne has steadfastly insisted on this feature of creativity. Criticizing Cassirer, he says

227

But the drift of his discussion tends to minimize the asymmetry of time. He would like to think of causal order as applying equally and in the same way to retrospective and prospective relations. Thus he exhibits what I call the prejudice of symmetry, which was so neatly embodied in the old saying, "The cause must be equal to the effect." . . . If causality is ultimate, it must be so either in the form, the cause greater than the effect, or in the converse relation. Which is it? The answer is again given by simple analysis of meanings. In a causal transaction in which, for the set of conditions C issues a result E, we have first C alone and then C *and* E. Thus the total result of causation is in every instance an enhancement of reality, the creation of a new whole. The more comes from the less. This (crudely sketched) is Bergson's and Whitehead's idea of process as creation. . . . I incline to believe that logicians will eventually, though some of them reluctantly, accept the theory of asymmetrical creativity as ultimate. But this acceptance, when and if it comes, will be a vast intellectual revolution whose consequences can only in part be forseen. . . .[25]

This conception of asymmetrical, cumulative time is obviously crucial for the dynamic idea of value, which requires simultaneous feeling of the contrast between present resolution feeling and past tension feeling. (See below). It is also necessary in our dealing with the problem of evil (cf. p. 505f.).

As for the question of permanence and finality of attainment, the above point makes room in a sense for the retention of attainment in future episodes of process, for past states can be included in new ones. But it also implies that the attainment has permanence only within new and further creative events; it does not constitute a final end to process.

There is also the by now familiar point that it is form or structure only that shows any persistence of being. "Matter" which SMR was so sure was the permanent reality, is, strangely, the most impermanent thing about any organism, from electron up to man. Apparently the "stuff" or "energy" of all these units is incessantly being exchanged. Their persisting identity is an identity of form only.

It is not by finding compounds which hold themselves fixedly

228

together by their chemical bonds, after the manner of the inorganic stone, that the persistence of the living organism has been achieved, but by the continuous breaking down and reorganization and reassembling of chemical constituents . . . the findings are in a way the direct opposite of what chemical theory alone would lead one to expect. According to the theory of atoms upon which chemistry is founded, the persistence should be in the entities, and not in the structure. [But] the chemical constituents of the living organism are in continuous motion and flux, and it is the relatedness which persists.[26]

Whitehead explains endurance or permanence, which for his philosophy becomes something of a problem, as *reiteration* or repetition of a form of process on the part of the one organism itself, and also on the part of other organisms surrounding it. Since organisms exist by the giving and taking of energy from one another according to definite forms of process, if there is a portion of space containing nothing but similar organisms, they can only keep giving and taking the same form. Thus a rock or any seemingly permanent "matter" consists of a vast number of similar organisms, i.e., atoms, which can only repeat the same form of process until something new (e.g. sulphuric acid organisms) comes in from their environment to start them off in some other pattern of process.

A piece of "dead matter" itself, then, is a collection of such organisms which are prevented by certain circumstances from evolving together into a more inclusive and more "living" organism. The rock itself is not an organism as a whole, but "a confused aggregate"[27] of small organisms. The rock's behavior follows laws which are the result of statistical effects. A human body weighing the same as the rock, and perhaps containing a similar assortment of chemicals, is, however, a new unit or organism in its own right, for now holistic field forces operate *over the parts,* and they are fused into a real whole.

With this background we arrive at a final understanding of what matter really is and why it exists in the world. Matter may be nature's way of preserving past dynamic accomplishments as bases for future advances. Matter consists of repeated processes holding a relatively fixed form upon which other higher processes are founded. Our more complex life processes, for instance, depend on the processes of our bones, and of the earth upon which we move, maintaining a high degree of fixity.

This property of emergent evolution of turning time (function) in to space (structure) by congealing the products of evolution into the "matter" of the next higher level is, for us, what makes it necessary to adopt a non-Aristotelian logic and metaphysics.[28]

But now, what has DR to say about the second law of thermodynamics, which would seem to imply that these preservations of past accomplishments by means of material structures are at best only temporary? For obviously bodies all finally disintegrate and die, and thus apparently return to the more basic tendency in nature: the inexorable march toward the structureless, random distribution of energy which SMR has told us was to be the final fate of existence. All accomplished ends, then, are sure to be undone eventually.

Well, DR has to admit that all creative process "lives" by appropriating energy from environmental sources; that there is no perpetual motion organism; that all living creatures obey the laws of heat, consuming substances of high organization and energy, leaving waste products of less organization and energy. But it is not clear that the eventual "undoing" of a creative process means that the creativity did not exist when it existed, or that creativity must be considered negligible and insignificant just because subsequently it is discontinued. Also, DR is not sure that, just because all that physics has studied so far obeys the second law, therefore it has been proved absolutely to hold for the entire cosmos and for all time. There are the "steady state" theories of the universe on the other side — daring to suggest that an equal and opposing tendency toward higher energy levels exists at the root of reality. There are "cosmic epoch" theories, suggesting that, if the present epoch is one of deterioration, there is nothing to prove that it might not be followed by one of up-building. We can be sure that there is no absolute principle upon which a deductive proof could be based, that such a reversal could never be. Hinduism had already suggested, millennia ago, such an "in-breathing and out-breathing" of Brahma.

Be the facts as they may, we will discover, under DM, how dynamic value might suggest a possible need for a law of entropy

230

anyway. And in the chapters on the problem of evil, more will be said about the reasons for death of created structures.

At any rate, we have seen how DR escapes from SMR's reductive logic. Calling the new patterns that arise out of composition "nothing but" the components is now clearly fallacious: the "reductive *fallacy.*" The components are not to be conceived as sitting side-by-side in the whole, retaining their original natures; rather they have utterly lost their separate identities within the new identity of the whole. Thus *ends* can come into being.

Comparison with SM-SIR: Thus DR attains to a kind of means-end purposiveness, but not in SM's pre-planned sense. It is a much more experimental, exploratory picture than SM likes. There is less guarantee of success, more risk, more demand for constant creative effort. How our existentialists and infantile writers hate this fact!

DM with DR.

Implications of DM and Correspondence to DR: 1. Theory of Transition and Integration. The implication of DM to organizing process is now familiar (# 2.1 p. 53). Nothing more needs to be said at this point.

2. Theory of Means: DR retains something of SMR's picture of causes as "accidental" and not necessarily pre-ordained means to pre-ordained ends. But DM does not find this antipathetic to purposiveness, when purpose is conceived dynamically. Dynamic purposiveness would imply, not building the pre-illustrated house out of pre-fabricated panels; but an experimental creative struggle to see what you can do with what you've got. We can thus come around in an unexpected manner to the sort of statement that SM wanted to make: "The end requires such means," or "the purposive order requires the causal order to be as science finds it." For DM actually requires that a loose, miscellaneous causal order should first throw things together "by accident"; but after that, DM requires a principle in nature whereby field forces should always immediately go into action to try to pull the random ingredients into something of interest. DM can grant that whatever nature pops up with, out of her ingredients, need not be pre-planned in the sense of being required to fill some specific place in a blue-print envisioned in advance by God. Rather God would have intended a rich, somewhat haphazard causal order

231

supplying ever new problems and materials for ever new and interesting solutions.

But *now,* once the purposive process has taken place and created something, it is legitimate to say that *that loose world of causal ingredients and process was required in a general way as means to that kind of creativity.* The world may seem gropingly to produce "mind" for instance, by accidental emergence. SMR is suspicious of turning around and saying that "mind" requires such a groping antecedent world. But DM believes it is legitimate to do so. Mind does requires precisely that experimental, trial and error reality in order to be evolved.

The causal order as we find it — accidental in respect to what ingredients it happens to assemble, but orderly and holistic after they are together — is required by purposiveness, dynamically conceived. Such a causal order is the only kind of "means" that such ends could use.

3. Theory of Ends. Next, in regard to purpose as involving the possibility of *attainment of value,* it goes without saying that the dynamic idea of meaning requires such a possibility. But, of course, it implies the attainment of value in a different sense from SM. The latter expects the full and complete attainment of the static essence that was aimed at, and this means the bringing into full existence of a definite, final state of things, the pre-conceived idea of pre-set form. Static thinking can never see why the attainment should not follow immediately on the conception, except that stubborn reality arbitrarily prevents it.

DM, on the other hand, implies that value will exist only as the process of composition is in the act of resolving tension and approaching organized wholeness. Thus it does not require the arrival at a final finished stasis, a perfect consummation. True, a *degree* of resolution is needed — perhaps moments of relative relaxation and rest; but new tensions must appear, new ingredients to incorporate must impinge to prompt a further episode of felt organizing. Of course, there must be *feeling* accompanying those moments of relative attainment and rest: feeling of consummation. We have seen then that DR allows exactly this real, though partial, attainment of organized products, objectively; and on the argument from isomorphism, that subjective feelings of value may accompany such attainment. The organizing of the electrical energy of the universe into evolving structures and functions is conceivably identical with the feeling that *is* dynamic value.

Finally, we may roughly suggest a possible reason for the second law of thermodynamics. The dynamic idea of good clearly implies that there must be a problematical situation, a strain, a maladjustment and that effort must be made to resolve it, in order for value to be *felt*. This picture seems to preclude that resolutions should come automatically, without struggle, search, procuring and using of additional objects and energies. A continuous source of depletion, then, seems required, and also the wherewithal to refill that depletion. The unending loss of heat, or dispersion of energy, then, could be the necessary guarantee, demanded by the notion of dynamic value, that creatures should recurrently fall into needs, requiring efforts to resolve them. Creatures could not be perpetual motion machines, and experience value. Without entropy, we would have no source of problem and difficulty; we would be wafted along in a life of unending repletion, with no real stimulation to effort, no real threat to our sustenance to make us think and move.

So, whether science will ever prove that all things must end in a heat death we cannot say; but short of that, we can see why there must be, at least in individual beings, a continuous consumption of energy and a dispersion of heat, if they are to experience dynamic value.

CHAPTER X

FREEDOM AND DETERMINISM

SM with SIR.

Implications of SM: Fatalism. One line of thought takes us from the static idea of meaning to the notion that all things and events should be laid out or pre-planned from the beginning. Recoiling from any notion of a genuinely creative process-in-time that can continually give rise to new possibilities and new achievements, static thinking naturally gravitates to the supposition that all reality should be present before any process has taken place. If there are to be any events at all (though the logic would find no reason why there should be) they must all somehow be already present in original reality. *Fatalism* expresses this thought in terms of an *impersonal* prior plan which, as it is unrolled, all things are fated to follow. Clearly, most prophecy, fortune-telling, astrology and palmistry etc., depend upon this assumption for their cogency.

Predestination is a very similar conception, except that the prior plan is considered the intention of a *personal* divinity. In either case, there is no scope for freedom on the part of individual creatures to alter the plan. Practically, of course, fatalistic views have not usually been held in purely logical forms, and, as with Greek mythology, men and gods on occasion seem to be able to turn the course of fate.

Both of these views are types of determinism, man's behavior being determined by something other than his own will. Thus, strictly speaking, they cut the ground from under any doctrine of individual responsibility, though Calvinism, in adopting predestination, arbitrarily insisted upon man's responsibility for his sinfulness anyway.

Indeterminism: Seeking better grounds for individual responsibility, another line of thought leads from SM to Indeterminism. Assuming that we depart from SM enough to grant any process of purposing or willing at all, we arrive at the notion that minds might as well be able to choose ideas or essences instantaneously, entirely free from and undetermined by any other causes than themselves. For Plato, the individual mind contemplates the realm of forms and then freely elects whichever idea or purpose pleases it, expressing in so doing its own essential character. We cannot suppose that it is forced to that choice by any other causes than itself, or we should clearly have lost any basis for praise or blame, that is, for responsibility.

As for right and wrong, better and worse, and the *obligation* to pursue the right, the basis for these is of course simply the intrinsic value of essences or ideas, which are good in the static sense of value. The mind or will, being entirely free to do so, "ought" to choose the good or perfect idea or essence, and the will "ought" to make the creature conform to it. This question of evaluation and obligation will be studied more thoroughly in part IV.

Adjustments of SIR: For earlier periods of thought, and also for the naive person to-day, the connections between one's supposed "free" choices and the innumerable circumstances of his past experience, his needs, the present state of his body and glands, etc., are not likely to be fully present in his conscious memory. His tendency is to assume that the implications of SM are upheld: that he simply elects, or freely chooses his acts; that some attractive idea pops into his mind and that he thereupon causes his bodily parts to behave accordingly by "free will." He feels certain that he could have chosen otherwise if he had wanted to; he has no notion that habits, ingrained fears, etc., produced by past experience, or perhaps merely the atoms of his body, may have enforced that and only that act. One form of SIR, then, confirms SM's expectations on free will. Other forms, of course, accept SM's fatalism or predestinarianism.

Of course, SIR's free will form recognizes that there is much failure to choose rightly, or to attain the ideal if it *is* chosen rightly. It deals with these facts as well as it can. The illusionists merely tell us to work to get rid of our state of illusion that is making us imagine these failures. A dualist like Plato utilizes his realm of Matter to explain our evil choices; matter not only causes the original separation from good but also our failure to see the Idea clearly and to choose it definitely, and also our difficulty in moving toward it when we do choose. For Matter is resistant and recalcitrant to the realm of ideas. Christianity works out an elaborate theory of Fall and Sin and Pride. None of these views, however, depart from the basic picture that causation is exclusively by purposes or ideas freely chosen from a realm of forms and essences.

SIR thus confirms and upholds SM's bases for obligation, oughtness, requirement. Having granted that existence has departed from SM's implied perfection, it has no doubt that minds can know what they ought to choose to aim for.

SM with SMR.

Findings of SMR: Mechanistic Determinism. In the preceding chapters, we could not discuss how SMR's view of the atom precluded any reality for purpose as aim without already mentioning the deterministic aspect of atomic motion. But here, we need to emphasize this aspect for its own sake. Early modern science certainly did not understand these solid atoms as being random or free in their motion. Luckily for human knowledge, they seemed to abide by certain fixed laws: Newton's famous three laws of motion. But this only completes the picture of the particles as purposeless, passive, blind things; not only do they have no inner feeling or qualitative character, but they have no ability to choose their actions in the light of such quality, supposing there was any. They must either stick in one place inertly, or fly along at a fixed rate of speed in a straight line, totally unable to initiate any change in their own state, until a force or forces from other atoms do something *to* them (first law). And when some force does hit them, it is preordained exactly how much they must speed up or slow down, and exactly what new direction they must take (second law). And when two atoms (or any larger pieces of matter) bounce against each other, each is just as helpless as the other, and in the rebound, they have no choice but to have action and reaction exactly equal (third law).

. . . the movement of two atoms after their collision is determined by their movement before . . . the laws of conservation of energy and momentum . . . determine the motion. . . .[1]

These conclusions concerning atoms are, of course, extrapolated to all creatures made of atoms, including man.

> This brought a beautiful simplicity into inanimate nature, but it also threatened to bring a most unwelcome simplicity into human life. . . . If, then, the world of atoms worked with the inevitability of a machine, the whole race of men seemed to be reduced to cogs in the machine; they could not initiate but only transmit. Exhorting a man to be moral or useful was like exhorting a clock to keep good time. . . . We could not choose our paths for ourselves; these were already chosen for us by the arrangement of the atoms in our bodies. . . . Yet, on this imagined freedom man had built his social system and his ethical code; it alone gave a meaning to his ideas of right and wrong, of purpose and moral responsibility. . . . But if human conduct was only a matter of the push and pull of atoms, all this becomes meaningless.[2]

Contradiction between SM and SMR: This mechanistic determinism might seem to correspond with the fatalism or predestinarian interpretations of SM, which are also deterministic. But actually, mechanistic determinism is purposeless in a far more thorough sense than they are. Both fatalism and predestinationism can still believe in plan and purpose on the part of fate or God, at least. They usually even believe that man experiences purpose and aim, even though his purposes and aims are pre-set by fate or God. In mechanistic determinism, however, as we have seen, there is nothing to experience plan or purpose. There are only atoms, blindly determined by inexorable pushes, neither able to aim nor to choose nor to feel.

The contradiction with SM's indeterminist interpretation is more serious. For obligation, oughtness, requirement are made impossible, at least in SM's interpretation of the words. In SMR, there can be no comparative evaluation of different goals, both because there is no entity that can evaluate, and there is no basis for a criterion of better and worse in a world without feeling or design. There can be no praise for the course taken or for the effort involved in taking it, for it must have been taken auto-

237

matically. There can be no blame for taking a worse, or easier course for the same reason. The whole realm of evaluation, obligation, responsibility loses its foundations and its reality.

Recourses: Descartes preserved freedom of the will in his mental realm, not, however, without raising an insoluble problem of how the mental realm could make contact with the material realm and affect it without interfering with its deterministic laws of motion, and the law of conservation of energy.

Spinoza then gave up freedom of the will, and tried to learn to live with a monistic determinism. He gave his one substance mental and rational characteristics, but the mental aspect was now just as necessitarian as the purely material world had ever been. He managed to have "an intellectual love of God" on this basis, paradoxical though this might seem to anyone who has not followed his system through to enjoy its beautiful, if static, consistencies. The determinism in the *mental* aspect appears as our experience of logically necessary implication between ideas; in the *material* aspect, it appears as causally determined events. Spinoza is confident that the causal order is a completely rational expression of, or "the other side of," the logical mental order. There was no free choice in either aspect; therefore there would seem to be no obligation, unless one might be blamed for resisting one's tendency toward rational clarity, and responsible for pressing toward it. Yet it is unclear how one can be responsible for thinking his way through to rational clarity, if his doing so really depends upon prior causative forces.

Leibniz was aware enough of these difficulties to work out a much more teleological theory, where all existent things, from particles up to trees and men, were entirely self-caused, purposive "monads," so far from being at the mercy of atomic pushes and pulls, as to be "windowless," i.e., totally independent of all causation external to themselves. German Idealism followed Leibniz, struggling to get freedom and responsibility back into reality in idealistic ways. But none of these ways has proven convincing enough to the modern mind to prevent our literary and scientific leaders from still subscribing, in large part, to deterministic views. Again, the revolution in science inclines us to devote our attention more to the new theory of facts which makes these older "escapes" more or less outdated.

We now have all the essential ontological contradictions between SM-SIR and SMR before us, as studied in these four chapters. All the ways in which SMR prevents any reality for purposiveness and meaningfulness may be summarized briefly: It begins by disallowing feeling or quality in its basic substance; then by conceiving its units as similarly lacking in feeling and purposiveness in themselves; and as incapable of forming wholes that might contain them. Thereupon any doctrine of subjectivity, need, desire and aim becomes impossible. Next we saw how any notion of means to ends, and of the attainment of ends becomes meaningless. And now finally freedom of choice or any other basis for responsibility is prevented. In short, SMR allows nothing but blind causes which preclude purposive functioning and creative accomplishment.

Let us now consider some of the general reactions which have appeared among men over the last few centuries, as they faced this threatening outcome of SMR.

First we have those who tried to live on the basis of complete acceptance of these negative conclusions, frankly admitting that it renders aspiration and effort futile, and life and the universe meaningless. Such men have occasionally taken the name "nihilist" from the Latin word meaning "nothing." Something of this element seems to remain in modern existentialism, though this is not entirely a static mechanistic view. Predictably, a good deal of irresponsibility and succumbing to isolated, atomistic impulses, often of a destructive sort, have accompanied this philosophical adjustment. The great novelist, Dostoievsky, specialized in depicting characters of this type. Our current "Beat Generation" seems not to have gotten much further in its understanding of the nature of things than this view, similarly stressing the passing impulse, determinism, consequent irresponsibility, and the futility of all effort.

Secondly, there are those who would argue that men can build a decent life on this basis, can actually get a certain inspiration out of the vision of puny man facing an oblivious and entropic universe and proudly defying it, refusing to let it discourage him. Bertrand Russell has made the most familiar statement of this feeling:

The world which Science presents for our belief is purposeless and void of meaning. . . . That Man is the product of causes which had no prevision of the end they were achieving;

239

that his origin, his growth, his hopes and fears, his loves and his beliefs, are but the outcome of accidental collocations of atoms; . . . that the whole temple of Man's achievement must inevitably be buried beneath the debris of a universe in ruins. . . . Only within the scaffolding of these truths, only on the firm foundation of unyielding despair, can the soul's habitation henceforth be safely built.[3]

But the majority of philosophers and laymen find such a suggestion too paradoxical to take very seriously. How can we demand from man, here declared to be a purposeless automaton, resulting from blind atomic collocations, such a brave determination to defy the universe's corrosive hostility and somehow choose to create noble character and decent living for himself? The presumption is that, debilitated by the gloomy and uninspiring metaphysics, having no faith that there is any goal worth striving for, or that nature would support him if he *did* strive for it, men will rather succumb to decay and discouragement. And the history of human affairs during the period when this philosophy has been chipping away at faith seems to confirm that presumption.

The idealistic escapes have therefore been invoked frequently also. The evolutionary process that seems so blind and pointless in SMR was finally incorporated into idealism by Fichte and Hegel, giving the conception of reality as an evolving, purposive *thought* process. In the latter's "dialectical idealism," God himself became a constantly evolving mentality known as the "Absolute." He does his thinking by what someone has called a waltz-step dialectic where opposed theses and antitheses eternally yield syntheses. In fact, some of Hegel's theory is very close to DM. However, this great system of thought suffers from the usual idealist weaknesses: insufficient attention to the structural realities of the world; lack of contact with the detailed findings of empirical science, and a tendency to fall back to an Aristotelian belief that there are pre-set forms or goals to which everything is moving, upon the achievement of which the dialectic may come to rest. At any rate, for Hegel, history seemed to arrive at a final stage in the Prussian state!

Marx attempted to correct the excessively speculative, idealistic flavor of Hegelianism by transforming it to a dialectical materialism. But he retains the Aristotelian notion of final goals fully attained, only now it is the Communist, rather than the Prussian, state that is final. He also readmits the reductivism of SMR, explaining the evolution of societies in terms of blind material causes, denying any real effectiveness to purposive ideals. Still, the Marxists derive a good deal of enthusiasm from their conviction that the evolutionary process itself will infallibly carry their system of society to the top of the wave, willy-nilly, whether they aspire to growth or not.

This attitude toward the mechanistic processes, as deterministically guaranteeing eternal improvement and enforcing ultimate perfection, was the most optimistic response that thinkers found. Herbert Spencer expressed the idea for English philosophy. But this lifted hopes so high only to dash them down again. Pessimistic reactions followed when perfection did not soon arrive. Schopenhauer's is the name most closely associated with the pessimistic repudiation of Hegel's optimism. For him, all process and striving was a cheat and a weariness to the soul. H. G. Wells comes to mind as a Spencerian optimist who ended up as a black pessimist when perfection delayed its appearance too long.

What, then, can DR do for us in these extremities?

SM with DR.

Findings of DR: Total Cause. We have studied DR's conception of the whole-part relationship, and how it makes room for a concept of purpose or aim as residing in present holistic strains. Now the question arises whether these wholes that take over and govern the part causes that have converged in them, aiming at better organization, have any freedom of choice in their aiming. Or are they determined by those very parts that have constituted them to be one and only one kind of whole which can behave in one and only one way?

Science feels that in order to exist at all, it must have deterministic causal laws that can be depended upon, so that predictions may be made and man can win control over the conditions of his life. And yet such determinism, in SMR, leads to a denial of choice and obligation in man. How can we have determinism where we need it without losing obligation in human affairs? Many have sought escapes from mechanism's blind necessity as the only hope.

Hume worked out one famous argument against determinism, based on his extreme empiricism. He pointed out that man could never prove "necessary connection" between any of his impressions of the world, because he had no sensory knowledge of causal forces between objects to begin with, being able to sense only *sequences* of sensations. Nor could he ever have absolute knowledge that such sequences would invariably hold for all future cases just because they had for all past ones.

However, science has found it possible to drop "forces" from its thinking and still retain causality by reformulating it as a problem of finding all the conditions "in the presence" of which a certain effect invariably follows, with no mention of causal "force." Newton had already confessed to knowing nothing of the forces themselves that caused, for instance, gravitation. He knew only an equation describing *how* bodies moved, not *what* moved them. And Einstein has side-stepped puzzling over what "forces" might operate in the heavens by speaking only of bodies following Space-Time curves.

Notice that the impossibility of proving necessary connection remains, even in this non-force conception of cause. This is because the necessary "following" of an effect upon a group of conditions would depend upon nature's never changing, but repeating herself undeviatingly: that is, upon the unproved and unprovable postulate of the Uniformity of Nature. There are some grounds for suspecting slow changes in Nature's laws. Dirac and Jordan suggest that even such a rock bottom law as that of gravitation may be slowly changing.

None of these considerations has interfered on a large enough scale with science's practical success based on the assumption of causal determinism to make it give up the assumption. Another difficulty arises from the "total cause" problem. Hume was still thinking of the single cause as "an object precedent and contiguous to another." Even in that case, we could neither sense nor know "necessary connection." What are we to do when, with Laplace, we admit that absolute prediction of future motions depends upon one's knowing the positions and momenta of every particle in the universe at a certain moment? A god knowing that, he said, would be able to predict the entire future of the universe as following necessarily from the motions and collisions of the particles. But no human can hope to know such a thing, so what becomes of causal determinism? Well, science has also slipped by this, for practical purposes, by being satisfied with what it calls "closed systems" limited enough so that an observer *can* measure every relevant factor. Nature more or less allows this, since the energy relations between things drop off very rapidly as their distance from one another increases. Although everything in the universe supposedly does affect everything else in it, the effects beyond a short distance are so small as not to matter in ordinary equations.

With these qualifications, scientific determinism can be defined in terms of total cause in J. S. Mill's words:

> The cause, philosophically speaking, is the sum total of the conditions positive and negative taken together . . . which being realized, the consequent invariably follows.[4]

Or as Thomson puts it: ". . . a certain collocation of antecedents and no other will result in a certain collocation of consequents and no other."[5] The same definition can be restated in terms of "partial" causes, as by Margenau: ". . . if all other causal factors remain constant, a given partial cause invariably produces the same effect."[6]

Indeterminacy; Principle of Uncertainty: But now a more serious threat to determinism came from sub-atomic phenomena, which began to suggest that the individual particles, such as electrons, were not determined by ordinary Newtonian laws to follow predictable paths. One of the first signs of this was in the disintegration of radioactive substances. Einstein, noticing that they disintegrated at a fixed rate, no matter what the external conditions were supplying as possible "causes," decided that individual atoms must sometimes disintegrate spontaneously, without specific cause. The overall rate of disintegration is exceedingly stable, but apparently there can be no law indicating exactly which particular atoms are due to disintegrate next, in order to fulfill the quota.

> We know, for example, that in 1600 years half of one gram of radium will disintegrate, and half will remain . . . but . . . we have no power to designate the individual atoms condemned to disintegration. The fate of an atom does not depend on its age. There is not the slightest trace of a law governing their individual behavior. Only statistical laws can

be formulated, laws governing large aggregations of atoms.[7]

The phenomena of the electron microscope were another source of the suspicion that sub-atomic particles are not determinately pushed or pulled by forces having definite locations and velocities according to Newtonian laws. Again, it was a matter of being able to get predictable patterns when large numbers of electrons were hitting the photographic plate; but being quite unable to say exactly where any single electron must land, beyond giving a figure for its probability. This probability will be greater at the distances where the dark bands are found, less for the light bands (see p. 183).

Now the methods of statistics are able to find regularities or laws for the behavior of aggregates of these particles, just as they can for actuarial problems for insurance companies, or for thermodynamics. The behavior of large groups of men issues in predicable statistical figures for human births, deaths, job choices, etc., and yet actuaries cannot tell exactly what a single individual will do; nor have they proven that intelligent, goal-seeking behavior and free will do not exist on the part of the individuals concerned. Thermodynamics can predict what temperature will hold for a group of moving molecules — that is, what their average motion will be — without being able to tell what any particular molecule is doing.

There is a difference between these two kinds of statistical science and quantum physics nonetheless. The former presume that there *are* individuals behaving in definite ways. Thermodynamics assumes that its statistical information is a precipitate of the movements of particles each of which is following the laws of motion, and has a definite position and velocity at every instant. But quantum physics can never have knowledge of the exact location and velocity of individual particles from which to start, even in theory.

This is for two reasons: the first is a matter of epistemology — what it is possible for man to *know* (observe and measure) about sub-atomic particles. Man can observe such a particle only if it gives off or absorbs a photon of light; but the "particle" is so similar in magnitude to a photon, that such an interaction with a photon will disrupt its behavior. This makes it impossible for us ever to determine the location and velocity of the particle simultaneously. Now since deterministic causality was supposedly based on knowledge of position and velocity of particles, quantum physics would seem to be prevented from attaining to it from mere epistemological difficulties. Although the actual behavior of the particles might be deterministic enough, we simply could never observe, measure and know it. This is one basis for Heisenberg's famous "uncertainty" principle.

But there is a second *ontological* reason why quantum physics seemed debarred from determinism: those indications which we have given that the particles may have no actual definite position and velocity in the first place; that they may exist, at least some of the time, as spread-out waves; or more likely, that there may not be any actual transmitting of forces between colliding bits, or any transporting of bits across space at all.

Heisenberg insists that his principle of uncertainty, or theory of indeterminacy does not mean merely that our method of knowledge is fated to a certain irreducible vagueness; but that the ultimate units themselves possess a kind of vagueness, or freedom of choice as to whether they will or will not appear in certain places at certain times. In his latest book[8] he indicates that in all experiments in quantum mechanics, you start with a measurement of an electron which will involve uncertainties of position and velocity. But a "probability function" can be calculated from these figures. Secondly you let time elapse. Thirdly you make a new measurement, still with the uncertainties, but they will be found to be within the area allowed by the probability function. In the middle step, we must understand that determined motion, according to classical physics, is not taking place at all. Heisenberg believes that during that period, the new physics allows for genuine "potentia" in Aristotle's sense. The electron is not determinately located anywhere, and has no more than a "tendency" to end up where the probability function generally indicates.

> This concept of the probability wave was something entirely new in the theoretical physics since Newton. Probability in mathematics . . . means a statement about our degree of knowledge of the actual situation. . . . The probability wave of Bohr, Kramers, Slater, however, meant more than that; it meant a tendency for something. . . .[9]

And yet, it seems that capriciousness and disorder is not the result of this "freedom" of the ultimate particles. There is some kind of control in nature that makes these individual entities, uncertain though they seem to be themselves, take, all together, a thoroughly predictable and law-abiding overall pattern. They seem "determined" to come out, as a group, in one and only one way. Jeans remarks that the "waves" show determinism, if the particles don't. All phenomena that appear highly deterministic concern large aggregates of particles where the theories of quantum mechanics reduce to Newtonian theories because the uncertainty aspects of the single ultimate particles are damped out in the mass.

We seem to have, then, units which possess a certain freedom *until* they are taken up into wholes which then cause the units to obey orderly laws. DR finds it necessary to incorporate into its theory of causation concepts that deal not merely with repeated routines where causes produce effects equal and of similar nature with themselves — mechanistic theory confines itself to these — but with the phenomena of organization of patterns or wholes, and the emergence of new properties, new types of lawfulness in the new levels of organization. As between any two levels of complexity of organization (ultimate particles, atoms, molecules, cells, organisms, man, societies) we might find some freedom in the lower one which yet results in some stability, orderliness, lawfulness in the higher one. This could happen in two ways. First, assuming the units continue as relatively distinct and free individuals (as the molecules in a gas, or the above human individual in a group), stabilities, order, repetitive lawful phenomena might appear in their aggregations due to statistical effects. Secondly, if the units "fuse" into a real dynamic field, then new forces would appear for the higher level of a field nature, and the lower units would now be determined in their behavior by the field forces, losing their freedom. But the new field would have a degree of freedom of its own, at least until it entered into a higher field.

As we have said (cf. p. 188), after the parts have come together into a dynamic whole, *they* no longer control the whole according to their own laws or characters. The whole now controls them according to *its* laws and character. True, the parts may determine what kind of a whole can be constituted by them — it may be predicable that, given water and sulphur dioxide, sulphuric acid must be the effect. But once this whole has appeared, it takes over the direction of its constituents in all subsequent behavior and cannot now be said to be controlled by its parts.

All the energy or being that the whole can have is what its parts give it; but the whole directs or combines or focuses those part energies, so that they can only exert their energy through the whole, though the whole has no energy or causative force of its own additional to that given it by its parts.

Margenau concludes that causality, defined as "temporal invariability of laws," has been restored in quantum physics, even in the absence of determinism of position and velocity of particles. Although quantum mechanics can never distinctly observe what it is trying to measure, having, rather, to make many approximate measurements, then calculate probability functions, it still is able to set up equations relating prior states to later states which are always fulfilled by nature. That is, it finds laws and predictability in atomic matters. But the uncertainty and probability aspects underlying this lawfulness give leeway, so to speak, for lower level units to organize themselves into new creative patterns with new and undeducible properties. These latter now reveal a new lawfulness of their own.

Comparison of DR with SM and Recourses: We know that SIR thinks of purpose as a matter of unconditioned, uncaused election of ideas. The prevalent tendency in the history of western thought has been to assume that freedom of choice or freedom of the will is an essential basis for purposeful, responsible living. It seemed clear that human responsibility to choose and behave according to high values would be impossible if man could only do what his parts made him do.

Some representatives of the dynamic theory of reality have felt obliged by this logic to seek an escape from SMR's inexorable cause-effect relations between the material atoms by way of a radical revival of SIR's Indeterminism. They have granted that the universe does not always follow the laws of motion, and that pure chance events occur occasionally. This has driven such leaders of this view as William James to a pluralistic ontology, meaning that reality is not one single order of law, but contains numerous more or less independent realms which may have differing laws of nature, or no laws at all. And here and there among these different realities there can be true *spontaneity,* or uncaused effects.

Our sense of "freedom" supposes that some things at least are decided here and now, that the passing moment may

247

contain some novelty, be an original starting-point of events, and not merely transmit a push from elsewhere. . . . So the commonsense view of life, as something really dramatic, with work done, and things decided here and now, is acceptable to pluralism. "Free will" means nothing but real novelty; so pluralism accepts the notion of free will.[10]

Another support for indeterminism seemed to come, as we have seen, from the physicists' study of sub-atomic particles. But this was only as long as we were erroneously trying to picture the ultimate units as independent particles. With a better understanding of the whole-part relationship, we ended with a somewhat more deterministic picture of surrounding fields or waves that do follow formulable and predictable laws, although they are not mechanically visualizable. We seem to have units of energy that emerge from and are guided by fields of energy; but also a hierarchy of energy or field pattern arising from the fact that "lower" wave-patterns can fuse together into "higher" (that is, more inclusive and complexly organized) ones. There are regularities in these emergings; they are limited by certain laws so that only certain kinds of wholes can come from certain kinds of parts. "Chance" does not seem a proper term to apply to this emerging at all. And once a whole has emerged, it follows laws of its own nature. Its existing parts, and also any new parts or energies impinging upon it are now apparently determined, partly at least, by the nature of this whole, its pattern, its field stresses. Of course, a very powerful part force — say a tornado — will still determine my organism's movements willy-nilly; but a smaller one — say a cold wind — can only determine me to start some activity; but *I* determine the form of this activity; putting on a coat or going in the house.

Perhaps the term "cause" is not the most suggestive one for the part energies, the sub-fields, that merge to form the new whole, or impinge upon it after it is formed. "Ingredients" may give a more proper feeling for what nature is doing in her cause-effect relationships. Causes are really supplying *materials to be built* into felt patterns. But DR would resist any implication that the whole is completely free in picking and choosing which ingredients or causes it will use in its self-building. We cannot get away from the point that the ingredient causes determine some limits at least as to what kind of whole can come from them.

248

Hydrogen and oxygen atoms determine that the whole which comes from them shall be a water molecule, although once the molecule has arisen, it "takes charge" and the atoms must now behave as this new whole or field requires them to. But then, remember, there are some other possibilities at that, even at this simple level: hydrogen peroxide for one. Is there "free choice" as to which of these patterns of behavior H and O might take? Apparently not. For the "total cause" of H_2O_2 includes the definite experimental conditions that determine hydrogen and oxygen to take that pattern instead of the water pattern. Once in that pattern, however, the constituents are now controlled or determined by that kind of molecule to exist and behave differently than by the water molecule.

By analogy then one who knew absolutely all the conditions bearing upon a man at a certain moment — his entire history of influences, habit building, etc., the entire current situation he faces — could predict a "necessary" response. His behavior will be the product of his self-field, with control over his parts, making them cooperate as is required to support the whole. This seems to release us from mechanistic determinism by parts. But the pattern of this whole itself seems to be the necessary precipitate of the kind of part causes that went into its formation. The sort of "self" he has was determined by the total causes ingredient in him, though now that it is in existence we grant that *it* controls those parts, and selects (to some extent) what new parts or ingredients it will accept from its environment. Have we advanced at all, then, toward "free choice" of alternative patterns of behavior by this self?

A kind of evidence that is often cited for the possibility of freely choosable alternative patterns of the same assortment of part causes, is our experience of inhibition of action while we deliberate or consider alternative courses of action (and this means to consider alternative ways of combining a number of factors in our lives into patterns). When you are considering whether to get a job in a garage or to go to school, do you *really* have free choice of these patterns? Suppose you decide to get the job and take the more immediate rewards; put the longer term project off to a possible future. If determinism were the rule, why would you have stopped to deliberate? Why would not cause push right through to some inevitable effect immediately? These alternative patterns seem equally possible.

249

But the determinist, without being a mechanist, can still argue that a full knowledge of the pattern of your existing personality would have enabled him to predict that you would finally take the more short-term decision; that this is the sort of personality pattern you have, that it has expressed itself in this manner in many other instances. Granted that what you have decided, and your subsequent behavior — including the motions of your parts (arms and legs, etc.) — will all be the expression of your total self, rather than of your parts operating in isolation from one another; yet this was the only course you could really have taken. The inhibition of action for deliberation meant only that it takes time for field forces to jostle themselves into equilibrium. The pattern of the equilibrium would be in principle as predictable as the pattern of an electro-magnetic field when strengths of currents and angles of incidence are known.

Thus, although DR safely escapes from *mechanistic* determinism by blind, isolated parts, it does not clearly repudiate determinism by wholes or fields.

In this situation, can DR find any reality for obligation or oughtness? SM, we remember, based its theory of obligation on its notion of pre-existent ideas or forms which were inherently right in the sense of the static idea of value. The will was free, and therefore obliged, to choose the inherently right and good. SMR, on the other hand, could find no basis whatever for value nor for the obligation to pursue it. It could not even find a basis for the simplest relationships of requirement: for our experience of feeling that some things "belong" with other things, that some ideas require other ideas or fit into logical systems, that some colors or sounds are harmonious and others are not. For all those things are, fundamentally, matters of design, of patterns of dynamic energies fitting or not fitting with each other.

Now we have already studied DR's criticism of intuitional and static theories of essences. DR has no place for ideas that are merely contemplated. In the world of energy and field, all realities must take the form of processes resolving strains toward equilibria. But in this conception, we already have something that reveals affinity to the notion of obligation or requiredness. Köhler, the gestalt psychologist, has suggested how "rightness" may fit into a field, or gestalt theory of reality.[11] Field and gestalt phenomena disclose "closure forces," the tendency of a broken or interrupted or unsymmetrical portion of energy to work toward some more completed, rounded-off, or symmetrical shape, eliminating interfering objects, or incorporating other objects, whichever contributes best to the "smoothing" of pattern. Gestalt experiments in vision provide familiar instances. Broken figures, such as circles missing a small sector, are flashed momentarily before observers who are asked to reproduce what they see. A strong tendency to reproduce complete circles suggests that the observers' eye strains to fill out the design and remove dissymmetries. Such hints as these are broadened into the theory that nature in general contains a principle of "closure" or balance in its fields. The shapes of flowers, the spherical tendency of heavenly bodies, the beauty of some of the higher animals come to mind as examples of nature's tendency to achieve form. But all these phenomena remind us again of field equations in physics, which have already told us how small and large units are constrained toward pattern.

Our inner experience of rightness, or of "requiredness" in Köhler's term, shows "isomorphism" with these externally observed phenomena. The final suggestion is already obvious: The sense of obligation may arise from this field tendency toward patterned wholes. Our sense that we "ought" to do something would involve our feeling that there is a certain possible pattern of acts that would organize the factors in the situation we are facing most inclusively and smoothly. "Ought I to take a job in a garage, or go to school this year?" You answer this question by considering which act will incorporate the largest number of your needs, desires, hopes. Taking the job will give more money to spend, perhaps allow immediate marriage, satisfy your mechanical interests; but threatens to impoverish your future and cut you out of advancement and more cultured contacts. Going to school means immediate penury, putting off marriage perhaps, but eventually will bring these goods in even greater measure, *plus* the others. If you decide on the job, you will feel some guilt, some sense of "oughtness" defied, and it will arise from your vague sense that you have chosen a pattern that excludes potentialities, that does not organize everything in your potential as well as it might.

But have we still found any place for *free choice* of whether we shall or shall not include any given factor in our aim; whether we shall be more or less inclusive; whether we shall or shall not strive harder? If a person takes the easier and less inclusive path,

251

was it because his native store of energy dictated that he do so? Could he have put forth a little more effort and taken a broader path if he had decided to? Can we choose to make more or less effort?

In terms of inner psychological experience, most of us would feel that we can "will" to exert ourselves more or less. Most of us would agree, however, that we ultimately arrive at positions where, although we can envisage even more inclusive and difficult lines of action that might bring even better long-term results, we still conclude that we can do no more, and we settle for something more immediate.

But I am not sure how we could prove that we had the energy and freedom to choose to make more effort than we did. Even without such freedom, we may have a place for the sense of obligation as above explained. We have gained the element of being able to feel that some present situation "requires" some future pattern as a resolution. A determinist may conclude that we thereupon had no choice but to move in that direction, or, if we have been "born" without the required energy, to give it up; but "oughtness" still has some meaning in this situation.

Hartshorne finds a basis for a stronger doctrine of free choice in the concept of creativity.[12] However, I will leave the subject on the above minimal ground, and go on to consider what DM logically requires on this topic. Does DM require the unconditioned free choice that was one of SM's implications?

DM WITH DR.

Implications of DM and Correspondence to DR: All that the dynamic idea of value clearly calls for, in the present connection, is centers of feeling (# 1.1 p. 53) to be able to feel, as wholes, the changing stresses among their parts as they shift from awkward, uncomfortable energy relations toward more symmetrical, balanced, comfortable ones. Whether these shifts are determined or not seems somewhat irrelevant, as long as there are real wholes feeling them. *Mechanistic* determinism, by feelingless parts incapable of forming feeling wholes, of course, is prohibited. Is DM entirely satisfied, then, with DR's rather equivocal pronouncements concerning freedom of choice? First let us notice a few respects in which DM would seem to require a measure of determinism.

DM does require a process that *improves* order in some sense. This means a presumption in favor of some kind of regular tendency in nature toward organization. Now we have seen that science is thinking of cause-effect regularity more and more in terms of field tendencies toward organized pattern. So this requirement bids fair to be satisfied.

Next a presumption in favor of *regularity in the causal order* comes from the thought that creatures who can experience good only as they build patterns of order, would require an environment reasonably orderly, so that they would not be lost in a chaos where they could never trust any laws of accomplishment, or learn how to build order. And Nature reveals this degree of orderliness.

Next, DM clearly requires "causes" in the sense of "ingredients." SM's notion of free floating ideas that cause behavior quite independently of conditions is empty and meaningless for dynamic thinking. There has to be a concrete order of things that constantly throws up "material" to deal with, to organize. In fact, the whole problem of purposiveness is reconceived by DM as not so much a problem of idly "choosing" ideas, as one of creating patterns out of givens that are first in felt strain and disorder.

Similarly "indeterminism" in the sense of allowing "chance" events is a quite needless idea for DM. There is no significance in novelties just popping into existence arbitrarily. The only novelties DM is interested in are ones that creatively solve given problems and tensions, that accomplish some task that has been set in the prior conditions. There is nothing particularly admirable about William James' "spontaneity" if it means an effortless leap from anything to anything else. Only a wrestling with difficult twists or distortions to straighten them out is worthy of admiration.

The uselessness of indeterminism for the theory of education has often been discussed. In education we are trying as it were to introduce certain "causes" or "ingredients" into the processes of the students with the full expectation that they shall have intended effects. We rely, in short, on reasonably dependable cause-effect relationships to get the behavior that is desired. If indeterminism were the case, so that any kind of act could freely and arbitrarily follow our causal efforts, education would be futile.

It is not even clear that indeterminism is quite what is wanted for moral responsibility. For an act to be to a person's credit, it seems that it should be a reflection of what the person really is; it should be "typical" of him, express his "nature." Indeterminism would imply that any kind of person might be freely and spontaneously able to choose any kind of act, quite independently of what sort of character he may have been building. In this case what would be the point of trying to build a "good" character? The term "self-determination" is being used for this concept that a person's acts should be the natural product of his personality pattern, and not mere happenstances issuing from no cause at all. And this term means, essentially, "determinism by one's whole" rather than blind causation by his parts.

But we still have not definitely secured that the pattern of one's personality is self-chosen, his own responsibility. It may still be only the precipitate of all the causes that have entered into it. In that case, what scope can there be for obligation? We have said that DM does not necessarily require freedom of choice; but does that mean that it does not necessarily imply responsibility, obligation, oughtness?

At present, the most we can say is that DR permits that we can envisage and consider possible patterns of factors, can guess that one of them harmonizes all ingredients better than others, can feel that we "ought" to work for that pattern, can then aim at it, can organize and control our parts and select means to help bring it into existence, can feel and enjoy it as it comes into existence. But DR does not clearly prove that we could have finally decided for any other pattern than we did.

There are, of course, religious views that find it immodest in man to suppose that his successes in resolving conflicts and attaining patterns are to his own private credit. They advise us to give God the credit and the thanks for what we become. They also advise that for us to blame men who fail to reach our standards is unjustified; that pity is the proper response. Psychiatry and penology take this line, and move constantly toward less and less use of blame in treating the inadequate. Punishment is less and less thought of as vengeance, more and more as a matter of supplying needed causes or ingredients in the life-processes of wrong-doers that will result in their reaching more inclusive and balanced personality patterns. These attitudes would imply that we may not want to claim too unreservedly free choice and total responsibility for what we are. It may be enough to have the power of feeling our disorganization, aiming at resolution, and feeling the accomplishment, thankful to the Creator who gives it all to us. Have we come back around thus to "predestination"? We have at least found grounds against overweening pride, and against unloving blame.

CHAPTER XI

EVOLUTION AND LIFE

With the present topic we move toward a more concrete application of the concepts developed somewhat abstractly in the preceding chapters. We also move toward what DR considers to differ from the preceding topics (concerning matter, energy, atoms, molecules, etc.) essentially only in the increasing complexity of the units or organisms involved. The static positions, of course, distinguish the subject matter in other ways.

In studying purposiveness and mechanism in this area, the positions will be presented under five subdivisions, of which the first is:

1. *The Nature of Life.*
SM with SIR.

Implications of SM: We are accustomed to SM's way of implying that all realities should partake of the nature of static essences; should consist in mental ideas. "Life," then, since it seems at least to the modern mind inseparable from the notion of growth and development, would presumptively be difficult for SM to deal with. In strictest logic, SM would thus fail to imply the existence of life at all, in the sense of a constant series of activities of structured organisms; and would point rather to its usual world of motionless contemplation of essences. But with relaxation of logic, the more usually accepted implication is to some type of what today is called "Vitalism," which attempts to conceive of Life as itself an essence. Life is expected to be an entity in its own right, a substance which living things are to contain along with whatever else they contain, and which reveals its presence in them by certain characteristics. There is, of course, no implication that this Life should be embedded in matter. Life itself might be a special thing that could exist independently in itself. This use of the term Life leads to the supposition that we have explained something when we have given a name to a mystery. We imagine that we can answer all questions about living phenomena by simply announcing that the mystic essence "Life" has caused them and made them behave as they do.

Adjustment of SIR: The keynote of SIR is, we have seen, that it recognizes the existence of dynamic development (however un-required by SM), but interprets it always as an effort to return to, or bring into full flower, the already existing essences of SM. Thus Aristotle's thinking was capable of a still useful theory of growth of the individual creatures within species, but he was notoriously unsuspecting that species (or forms, or essences) themselves developed. "Life" for Aristotle belonged to the realm of formal and final causes: it was the thing that made matter proceed toward its predestined form. Aristotle's word "entelechy" means, precisely, the manner in which the form or essence propels the growth process toward itself as an outcome. "Life" then, still may be conceived as an entity in its own right that takes hold and controls matter. SIR's theories of the nature of life are thus still vitalistic, with Life considered as a mystic substance in itself. This sort of theory was almost universal in human thought until recent times.

> Vitalism is the view that living organisms owe their organ-ization and distinctive characteristics to some principle or element not found in non-living things. There is a life princi-ple, a capacity, an entelechy — something in addition to the chemical and physical properties — that gives direction to the process.[1]

SM with SMR.

Findings of SMR and Contradiction to SM-SIR: In all the topics of the present chapter, the contradictions between SM-SIR and SMR are especially glaring. The most acute part of the "conflict between science and religion" is now before us.

We already have everything that is needed to understand the "mechanistic theory of life." This theory most particularly rejects any form of vitalistic view urging that life is some kind of mystic, purposive entity entirely different from matter in motion. For that way of explaining, we must agree, commits the verbalistic error typified by Molière's gentleman who thought he had an explanation of how opium puts one to sleep when he learned the term "dormative property." Confining itself rigidly to the non-qualitative atomism which we have studied under SMR in Chapters VII and VIII, SMR must interpret life as "nothing but" certain complex motions of material atoms. Democritus of ancient Greece, and Hobbes of the Age of Reason had already extended the mechanistic theory of atoms not only to the workings of the body, but to those of the mind. La Mettrie and Holbach in France carried to its greatest length the thesis that man was entirely explicable as a machine. Perhaps the last attempt to defend the mechanistic theory of life in its most Newtonian, atomistic form, was Loeb's in his *Mechanistic Conception of Life*.[2] All these views make life an "epiphenomenon" of matter, a purposeless, feeling-less outcome of blind atomic motions.

A common way of expressing this view is to say that it holds that life can be explained in "physico-chemical" terms, or that it "obeys the universal laws of physics and chemistry." These phraseologies do not seem to the present author as revealing as that which defines the mechanistic view in terms of non-qualitative, material atoms which negate any theory of whole-part relationship. We would also object to C. J. Herrick's and others' retention of the term "mechanistic" for a theory that makes "mechanism" cover energistic views incorporating a theory of feeling and consciousness.[3] This seems a careless use of words that blots out important distinctions of meaning which should be kept clear. In the present book, at any rate, mechanistic theory (SMR) will continue to refer only to views that explain all phenomena in terms of mindless, non-purposive atoms enforcing effects conceived as passive, necessary, unappreciated outcomes. "Explained in physico-chemical terms" then, would mean: explained in terms of parts which follow blind laws of motion.

SMR's theory of life may thus be expressed finally in Democritus' and Russell's famous phrase: "an accidental collocation of atoms." Usually the story of the monkey of infinite longevity typing forever on a typewriter is now told: somewhere in infinite time he could "accidentally" type out all of Shakespeare's plays. Analogously, in infinite time the atoms, blindly colliding by the laws of motion, might knock themselves into the shapes of living bodies "by accident."

Recourses to SM: There have been persistent attempts to revive some form of vitalistic theory of life as the failure of mechanistic theory to explain the organizational, self-preservative, *striving* aspects of living creatures became clearer. The best known names in "neo-vitalism" have been Hans Driesch in Germany, Henry Bergson in France, J. S. Haldane in England. They all tend to resort to some kind of "vital principle" thought of as an extra factor additional to the matter-in-motion of SMR. Driesch calls it by Aristotle's name, *entelechy;* Bergson by the term *elan vital;* Haldane by the phrase "regulative principle." These and other views fall more or less into the pattern of thinking of their peculiar life principle as a mystic agency in itself, which administers directive control upon the world of matter. To the extent that these views do this, they would inherit the typical weakness of dualism, particularly its conflict with the law of conservation of energy (see next chapter) and its verbalistic fallacy, whereby a puzzle is explained by coining a fine sounding word. The scientific mind abhors such solutions because they set up a principle of explanation which by definition is beyond empirical observation and test.

DM with DR.

Findings of DR: The dynamic idea of reality does not need to resort to the vitalistic *deus ex machina* to hurdle the problem of mechanism, since its theory of energy, field and the whole-part relationship enable us to understand life as inherent in the basic nature of reality, and not something that must be artificially imported into a world of dead matter as an additional mystic principle. Instead of taking the most inert phenomena as our fundamental model as does SMR, and wondering how to get living development out of it, we take energy organizing itself in fields as our model — and then, we must admit, run into a problem of explaining all the seemingly inert things. But they turn out, as we saw in Chapter VII, to be things that are changing very slowly, or "reiterating" themselves; and under certain conditions they prove themselves amenable to being incorporated into more speedily developing things. The inert bit of hard candy can enter into the life processes of a child; the rock of ages can crumble, become soil, and enter into the living processes of a tree.

DR looks over the hierarchy of organisms from electrons, atoms and molecules, through super-molecules, viruses, and protozoa, to multicellular organisms, plants, animals and men; and it asks SMR just where it proposes to draw any absolute line between "living" and "non-living." Nature reveals no sharp line. It suggests rather a perfectly smooth continuum of organisms, increasing gradually in complexity, with new functions, properties, abilities added accordingly; but no spot where the utterly dead and inert suddenly changes over to the self-moving, developing and alive.

Of course, if we wish, we may agree on some conventional definition of "Life," including under it only organisms above a certain arbitrary level — probably the virus. But we must not forget that below this there is only a shading off, and no radical jump. The usual list of characteristics supposed to differentiate Life from the inorganic may be appealed to in settling on the virus as the boundary, but there is more and more doubt that these characteristics do differentiate very distinctly:

1. The will to live; the urged, striving characteristic of life.

2. The reciprocal relationship between parts and whole, including such phenomena as re-development of parts that are lost.

3. Metabolism, the incorporating of needed and eliminating of unneeded materials from outside or inside of the organism.

4. Growth and development itself.

5. Irritability, or ability to be stimulated.

6. Adaptability to environmental conditions.

7. The ability to learn by experience, and retention of learned methods of adaptation in *memory*.

8. Reproduction.

9. And finally, the inner feeling, desiring, aiming and appreciating aspect of at least man's level of life.

We have space only to hint at some of the reasons for suggesting that these characteristics might extend further down the hierarchy than has been assumed in the past. 1. Whitehead wonders whether, if we were able to follow the entire life history of a particular molecule, we would not find it to involve struggle, will to live, etc. 2. We have found reciprocal relationship between parts and wholes to be universal for all DR's units or organisms, however small. 3. When molecules incorporate atoms into, or eliminate them from, their patterns, is this essentially different from metabolism? 4. Certainly all electrons and atoms show the tendency to come together into larger groupings, that is, to "grow." 5. Many "inorganic" compounds seem to be irritable, able to be made to glow or change color, for example, when various kinds of energy are thrown upon them. 6, 7. There is evidence that viruses and protozoa possess some analogue to learning and memory; that the laying down of patterns of nuclear material in genes is somehow related to memory in developed nervous systems. 8. Some "super-molecules" not heretofore considered as viruses seem to show something like reproduction. In fact if the ultimate particles — electrons, protons, photons, etc. — are to be conceived as flashes of energy, could it be that they are "reproducing" themselves at that enormously rapid rate we would expect for such minute entities? 9. We have already discussed in several connections how far feeling, desiring and appreciating may be imputed to the very nature of energy as such.

Thus, the felt organizing of increasingly complex patterns of function becomes the essence of life in DR; and it extends throughout all that exists. There is nothing dead to which a "vital principle" needs to be added.

A living body contains no mysterious entity called a vital principle, or vegetative or sensitive soul. It is not a soul or vital spark in living organisms which causes life — or gives rise to the power of growth and reproduction. These properties are the outcome or organization and structure. . . .

. . . The *theory of levels* has thrown much light on the problems of life and mind. Electrons and protons are organized into atoms, atoms into molecules, molecules into cells, cells into living bodies, and at each new level of organization new qualities appear, which are in the nature of new creations, since they cannot be inferred by adding together the qualities of the elements which are organized. Oxygen and hydrogen are organized into a molecule of water, which possesses properties that do not belong to oxygen or hydrogen, and that could not be predicted from the completest knowledge of these two elements. . . .

Thus life is not due to the presence in the living organism of any mystic "vital principle," or "life force." It is the evolutionary product of organization.[4]

Perhaps the best and best-known passage on these matters is

Whitehead's, parts of which we have already quoted in other connections:

> Tennyson goes to the heart of the difficulty. It is the problem of mechanism which appalls him.
>
> " 'The stars,' she whispers, 'blindly run.' "
>
> This line states starkly the whole philosophic problem. . . . Each molecule blindly runs. The human body is a collection of molecules. Therefore, the human body blindly runs. . . . The traditional way of evading the difficulty — other than the simple way of ignoring it — is to have recourse to some form of what is now termed "vitalism." This doctrine is really a compromise. It allows a free run to mechanism throughout the whole of inanimate nature, and holds that the mechanism is partially mitigated within living bodies. I feel that this theory is an unsatisfactory compromise. The gap between living and dead matter is too vague and problematical to bear the weight of such an arbitrary assumption, which involves an essential dualism.
>
> The doctrine which I am maintaining is that the whole concept of materialism only applies to very abstract entities, the products of logical discernment. The concrete enduring entities are organisms, so that the plan of the whole influences the very characters of the various subordinate organisms which enter into it. . . . Thus an electron within a living body is different from an electron outside it, by reason of the plan of the body. . . . But the principle of modification is perfectly general throughout nature, and represents no property peculiar to living bodies . . . this doctrine involves the abandonment of the traditional scientific materialism, and the substitution of an alternative doctrine of organism.[5]

The argument whether organisms can be sharply distinguished from machines is still raging. And with the development of cybernetics, the science that studies the operations of calculating machines and brains under one set of concepts, it might seem that the mechanists were one up on the organicists. We now have electronic hook-ups that seem to imitate the directive, purposive actions of organisms to the last degree. "Negative feed-back" devices are used in rockets, for instance, capable of keeping the rocket focussed on its target however the target might dodge about, for all the world as if the rocket had a positive lust for the target like any swallow chasing mosquitoes. But we may perhaps risk the assumption that the *lust* is exactly what the machine will never have, however many of the other characteristics of organisms it may imitate. An ardent mechanizer of life, Warren McCulloch, cockily whips through the organism-like functions he believes are or will soon be done by machines:

> The circuit in a servomechanism may include, as we hold it does in a man's head, complicated machines of calculation. Turing showed that one having a finite number of parts and states, scanning, marking, and erasing one of four symbols at time on an infinite tape, can compute any computable number. . . . Pitts and I showed that brains were Turing machines. . . . Memories, general ideas, and even Spinozistic consciousness, the idea of ideas, can thus be generated in robots. These robots, even simple ones having but half a dozen relays, may, without inconsistency, show that circularity of preference, or of choice, called the value anomaly. . . .
> Elsewhere I have shown that computing machines by playing chess may not merely learn to play better than their designers . . . but that they may learn the rules of the game when these are given only ostensibly. This insures their ability to generate their own ethic — not merely to be good, like the virtuous savage, because they are so made that they cannot break the rules, nor, like the gospeled or inspired, because they were so instructed by their fellows or their creator . . . that we can design ethical robots, who may even invent games more fun than chess, is enough to prove that man's moral nature needs no supernatural source. . . .
> Hence the crucial question: Can machines evolve? John von Neumann suggests that we are familiar only with simple machines that can make only simpler ones, so that we suppose this is a general law, whereas, in fact, complicated ones can make others still more complicated. Given a suitable Turing machine, coupled to a duplicator of tape and to an assembler of parts from a common store, it could make one like itself, put in a duplicate of its own tape, and cut loose its replica ready to make a new one like itself. . . . Variations compatible with this reproduction, regardless of their sources, will lead to evolution. . . .[6]

263

Mechanical robots, then, he specifically suggests, could live ethical lives, and not merely in SM's sense of following a given set of rules, but practically in DM's sense of creatively solving problems and attaining higher levels of behavior. And they could conceivably be made to reproduce themselves and evolve. But he has not yet said that these machines could *feel* these accomplishments, *care* about solving problems, *strive* persistently in the face of pain and frustration toward *desired* resolutions. But McCulloch boldly presses on to this quintessential point:

> In 1953, in the symposium on consciousness of the Institute for the Unity of Science, Wilder Penfield used the term . . . to mean precisely that his patient at a later date bore witness to what he also bore witness to as having happened then and there. Of course we can make machines do that. The questioner meant "Was the patient aware that it was he himself that did it?" which is self-consciousness, requiring but simple reflective circuitry. . . . A psychoanalyst explained to me that "a patient is conscious of what he once felt only if at a later time he can verbalize it" — which is to say, "he is conscious of those things of which he says he is conscious" — and this requires only a machine that sometimes answers "yes" to this question. That is too easy. . . .[7]

McCulloch thereupon grants that we may mean by consciousness something more internal than these or other "objectivist" definitions. Even so:

> Granted that we have objective knowledge of others, and substantial knowledge only of ourselves, this only proves us to be like every other thing, and divine, if you will, only as a part of all that exists. It does not demonstrate the metaphysical self-sufficient mind or soul with the unique property of perception. However one defines feeling, perception, consciousness, substantial knowledge — so the definition be finite and unambiguous — each and all are well within the tricky scope of circuitry.

But this hardly seems to dispose of the question. Under DR we certainly are not trying to restore the "metaphysical self-sufficient mind or soul" as an essence additional to the structure of energy in organisms. But we are saying that the factor of feeling, of being able to *care* about what happens, is probably the best locus for an absolute distinction between organism and machine. We can grant that organisms are equipped with innumerable mechanical devices, and that the mechanistic may penetrate far into the brain. But the manner in which all of these structures feed "ingredients of feeling" into the central feeler, which derives all its infinite variety of felt qualities out of their mixing and compounding, would seem to be beyond the bounds of the mechanical.

One of Whitehead's names for this irreducible factor possessed by organisms and not by machines is "self-enjoyment."

> Life requires a certain absoluteness of self-enjoyment. This must mean a certain immediate individuality which is a complex process of appropriating into a unity of existence the many data presented as relevant by the physical processes of nature. . . . The process of self-creation is the transformation of the potential into the actual, and the fact of such transformation includes the immediacy of self-enjoyment.[8]

Other ways have been sought to distinguish between machine and organism, one of the most important being Kohler's distinction between machines which utilize rigid structures to "compel events to take a certain course" and the more organic situation, where "dynamical self-distribution" takes place in a field of energy without rigid walls, channels, levers, etc. Organisms contain both sorts of situation, but machines do not contain the second kind. Presumably, however mechanical many parts of the organism may be, there are at least some areas in the nervous system or elsewhere which are complexly structured fields of energy, possessing qualitative feeling.[9]

It has also often been pointed out that in a machine the rigid structural parts are permanent. But in organisms no "matter" remains permanently in place; only the structure and form persist, while the "matter" or energy is constantly replaced.

For *DR*, then, life is a felt process of organizing many structured functions together, focussing them into various combinations each of which has a unique feeling quality.

Comparison with SM-SIR: This manner of distinguishing between life and the mechanical is thus non-vitalistic. Life is a pattern of energy-function not a mystic entity added to the energy.

DM with DR.

Implications of DM and Correspondence to DR: The deduction of life from the dynamic idea of good, as a felt process of incorporating ingredients into accomplishments, hardly requires further discussion at this point. Life, as DR understands it, is almost synonymous with dynamic value.

2. *The Origin of Life.*
SM with SIR.

Implications of SM: Considering life as the indefinable essence discussed above, the most typical expectation as to how it would first appear is that the divine mind should (1) *purposively* conceive it; and that it should then (2) *instantly* be. The theory of creation by instantaneous, purposive "divine fiat" is illustrated approximately in the book of Genesis, which reports that

> God said, Let there be light: and there was light. . . . Let the waters under the heavens be gathered together unto one place, and let the dry land appear: and it was so. . . . Let the earth bring forth living creatures after their kind, cattle, and creeping things, and beasts of the earth after their kind: and it was so.[10]

Of course, Genesis allows some days for the process of creation, and harmonizers of religion and science tell us we may consider "day" to mean any length of time, so that we cannot accuse the scripture of describing an entirely static or timeless manner of creation. However, it is difficult to believe that the writers of the book were envisaging God's creation as spread out through all time; there is a strong flavor of the presumption that Life, and all other existences, spring into being instantly upon God's conception of them. The process of developing is not itself the focus of interest, but only the fully developed product. At any rate, the purest logical implication of SM would be, assuming that anything is to be created at all, that is should be created fully at once.

Adjustments of SIR: SIR accepts SM's implications on the origin of life and species through instantaneous, purposive divine fiat; it merely adds the theory of development of *individuals* within the preestablished species. Although a kind of evolutionary theory had been hinted at by early Greek thinkers (e.g. Anaximander) it was ignored during the ages of SIR's predominance.

SM with SMR.

Findings of SMR and Contradiction to SM: Under SMR, we might place, first, some rather primitive theories of spontaneous generation, which tend to conflict with SM-SIR's theory of the divinely purposed creation of fixed species. The materialistic poet of Roman times, Lucretius, had already suggested that living creatures came directly from "dead" matter. Until Pasteur disproved some of the supposed cases, by proving the presence of seeds or eggs emanating from previous life, it was commonly believed that worms were generated directly from warm earth, insects from stagnant water, germs from dirt, maggots from dead flesh, etc.

The view that life came from other planets as microorganisms or spores in meteors, suggested by Helmholtz, Kelvin and others, is hardly worth mentioning, since it does not really deal with the question, merely putting the origin of life off into an unavailable part of the universe.

What we hear most about to-day is the primeval ooze and the warm soup oceans which existed billions of years ago on earth, in which it is said that certain atoms found it possible to unite into complex molecules. We also hear of chemists synthesizing organic compounds in test tubes. SMR would, of course, interpret all this exclusively in terms of the ultimate units, the atoms or electrons, and speak of their following the laws of their own natures when they choicelessly hook up in the early "living" compounds. Then, by "chance" some large molecules would appear that possessed the property of reproducing themselves. From here on we would have the endless succession of "accidental" developments that led to the single cell plants and animals, cell colonies, and the whole sequence of multicellular organisms. We come, then, to the theory of evolution, which might be placed here as part of the theory of origin of life. We will study the details in the next section under the theory of kinds of life. Here we may conclude that SMR's theory of the origin of life certainly denies the second feature of SM-SIR's theory: the *instantaneous* nature of creation. For it obviously holds that all forms of life have gradually developed throughout all time, and that many have died out. And secondly, SMR denies the *purposive* feature, in seeming to prove that the long-drawn-out process is wholly haphazard and non-purposive.

Notice that, as explained in Chapters IV and IX, we are discussing here the earlier interpretations of Darwinism, although evolutionary theory is also considered to be the root of DR. But we have already begun to understand how, when evolution was formulated with Newtonian atoms in the background, it yielded the belief that evolution can neither be aimed nor consummated. In short, we get the theory of an "evolution that does not evolve."

The standard presentation of evolutionary theory as built upon the findings of Darwin, Mendel, Weismann, and DeVries, looks mechanistic enough at first sight, as will be seen below. We have a picture of blind, atomistic parts — genes and cells — "accidentally" producing the various forms of life.

SM with DR.

Findings of DR: There is little to add to what has been explained in the more abstract chapters preceding. When the first more complex molecules synthesized in the primeval mud, DR would presume that it happened organismically, accompanied by some experience of attainment and success. It was no more a matter of blind atoms accidentally coming together than any other part-whole event. Neither is it so if it happens in a modern test-tube.

But DR clearly continues to contradict SM-SIR's expectations of an *instantaneous* creation of all living things as much as SMR did. Only it is not as sure as SMR that the earlier steps of the gradual process were *purposeless*. DR's conception of the whole-part relationship permits a doctrine of evolution as real accomplishment, not to be reduced to its original components.

DM with DR.

Implications of DM and Correspondence to DR: If we define this topic as covering only the first or lower levels of synthetic process, it raises no issue essentially different from the general concept of life under #1. The origin of life would already be implied in DM's presumption that all things should be life-like or amenable to organizing process anyway.

3. The Kinds of Living Things.
SM with SIR.

Implications of SM: In Chapter XIV we will point out why SM does not really imply a *variety* of kinds of value or of anything else. But waiving that point, and assuming a variety of species, SM sees no reason why God should not have set out the entire range of species just as he intended them to be in his original instantaneous act of creation. Since the time process of creative development itself does not count for anything in value or knowledge, God must have known from the beginning — if he is the perfect Being SM implies — just how everything should be arranged to embody perfect value. Therefore, as Genesis' account strongly implies, He must have created every needed species of plant and animal in its final form immediately, no more and no fewer than were required by his omnisciently foreseen plan for earthly life. There is no expectation that these species should need to evolve and change; and certainly not that new and different species should be added from time to time or old ones dropped. This latter picture would smack too much of God's not knowing what He wanted, of constantly revising his plans which should have been perfect from the start. This way of thinking has been called the "Theory of Special Creation," emphasizing that each species was immediately created by God for a special purpose, fitting requiredly into its place in the design.

Adjustments of SIR: If SM fails clearly to imply different kinds, SIR frankly admits their existence and goes on from there. Historically, there was no doubting, until after SMR's and DR's theories were developed, SM's expectation that God has set out the one inevitable assortment of species at the beginning, and that it would persist as long as this life continued. We have just seen how Aristotle did not believe in evolution of forms or species; and up through the first part of the 19th century such a concept was felt to be impious.

SM with SMR.

Findings of SMR and Contradiction to SM: In contrast to this belief in a pre-ordained series of species, mechanistic evolu-

269

tionary theory seemed to prove an entirely random accumulation of species who survive mainly by lucky accident. The four parts of Darwinian theory will now be presented systematically, with the modifications of the "neo-Darwinians" incorporated.

i. The theory of variations. This takes account of the fact that offspring may differ from their parents in various slight details. Darwin himself did not attempt to prove a theory of the source of these variations, but assumed that natural causes would do to explain differences. An example: the minute changes inherent in bisexual reproduction whereby offspring in possessing a mixture of parental characteristics, could not exactly resemble either one. Such differences, however, would have been so small as to require enormous amounts of time for establishing a distinct new line. Lamarck was anxious to insert purposiveness into this part of the theory by arguing that a parent's efforts to develop some ability in his organism would cause a variation in his germ plasm so as to pass on this modification of himself to the offspring. The ancestor of the giraffe, for instance, by trying very conscientiously to reach for leaves in the trees to eat, would be rewarded by a slight stretching of his own neck, and this accomplishment immediately recorded in his genes, would be passed on for the benefit of his offspring who would be born with longer necks to start with. This is the theory of "inheritance of acquired characteristics." Weismann, however, seemed to eliminate the possibility of even this much purposiveness by proving that the germ cells in organisms are isolated from and unaffectable by whatever happens to the bodily cells. No amount of self-development during an individual's life time could ever either improve or deteriorate his genes. The germ cells pursued their own economy according to Mendelian mechanics alone (see part iv below).

De Vries perfected the mechanical theory of variations by showing that the most effective source of gene changes were the wholly unplanned mutations, the entirely accidental results of such forces as radiation impinging upon the germ cells. A small minority of such accidental changes improved the offspring's structure or functioning; the vast majority were destructive. Much supporting evidence has made this mechanistic theory widely prevalent today.

ii. The theory of struggle for existence. This was Darwin's special contribution, with the help of the grim population theories of the economist Malthus. The result was highly contradictory to Christian belief in a loving God, for it pictured a ruthless world

270

in which there would always be more creatures seeking sustenance from the environment than there was sustenance to be had. Creatures reproduced themselves so as to increase numbers in geometrical ratio, while the food supply could not increase in more than arithmetical ratio. The only answer was for creatures to struggle for the insufficient food and for those who lacked the strength or the wit to win it, to die. This was the darkest portion of the theory, but curiously enough, it was also the least mechanistic. For mechanism, in the last analysis, had no means of explaining how there could be creatures with desires and the will to struggle. (See DR).

iii. The theory of the survival of the fittest. It was Herbert Spencer who coined this phrase, managing somehow to derive an incorrigible optimism from it. In the light of the whole theory, this fitness never seems to be the purposed intention of its possessor, nor the deserved reward of effort. It is only the result of lucky accident under step i — fortuitously receiving mutated genes for some favorable variation. Besides, just what kind of "fitness" it took to win out in the struggle for existence remained to be clarified. Some saw in this whole mechanical picture a guarantee for eternal "improvement" of species, and thus waxed very hopeful. But it was not at all guaranteed that fitness meant improvement in character, Christian virtue, nor cooperativeness. In fact, the presumption at first sight was that fitness was liable to consist merely of increased strength and ability to destroy one's competitors ruthlessly. What this line of thought led to in moral and social behavior will be studied in Part IV.

iv. The theory of heredity. It was obvious that the offspring of the members of a species inherit a form and characteristics closely resembling that of their begetters. The "fit," then, having survived, pass on their accidental superiority to their offspring. The mechanism by which they do it was studied first by Mendel, and it was sufficiently mechanical: the familiar theory of chance assortment of genes from each parent. This guarantees that the offspring has the basic characteristics of the species, but allows him to inherit special characteristics according to a random statistical law. Nothing that the parents can do of a purposive nature can affect the *biological* nature of their offspring. After many generations of survival and increase, this "fit" variation may become a new species.

And so by this largely mechanical process, rather than by purposive design of God, SMR suggests that all species in existence have come about. There may be some tendency toward "improvement," at least in the sense of efficiency in surviving the battle for food; but certainly not an aimed-at or intended improvement.

SM with DR.

Findings of DR: DR must admit, with SMR, that all species were not immediately created in their final form for all time; and that their distribution over the earth has a somewhat hodge-podge appearance, depending merely on adaptation to and survival of the conditions around them. But DR notes, too, that however many instances of *de*volution appear — degeneration, return to simpler form, loss of powers, (viz., the parasitical forms) — the major trend, at least for this planet, has so far been toward greater complexity of structure and function.

> Evolution . . . refers to the general theory of development by orderly, progressive changes. By progressive changes we usually mean those in the direction of greater complexity and a higher degree of organization . . . of greater differentiation of function.[11]

Whitehead makes the same point together with a criticism of SMR:

> The aboriginal stuff, or material, from which a materialistic philosophy starts is incapable of evolution. . . . There is nothing to evolve, because one set of external relations is as good as any other set of external relations. There can merely be change, purposeless and unprogressive. But the whole point of the modern doctrine is the evolution of the complex organisms from antecedent states of less complex organisms. The doctrine thus cries aloud for a conception of organism as fundamental for nature. . . . The organism is a unit of emergent value.[12]

DR, then, recognizes this seeming "wish" for greater complexity of structure and function in nature, however much it may be opposed by SMR's entropy. The fact remains that, at least for a time, any organism in nature (from atoms on up) experiences this "struggle" toward inclusion and organization. One aspect of nature, at least, is this nisus toward novel and more adequate structures apparently accompanied by more vivid and varied feelings.

But how can we talk of nature's "seeking better forms" in the face of SMR's apparent demonstration of the mechanistic nature of evolution? There is Weismann's prohibition of "improvement" of genes through any efforts one might make upon his own body; and De Vries' theory of mutations still suggesting that new forms fall out by mere accidental disturbance of nuclear material in germ cells.

Well, for one thing, there is some evidence that mutations themselves take place holistically, involving at least sometimes, a general re-gearing and smoothing of all parts and relationships in a mutated form. A change in one feature of a body calls for changes in many other features to fit. If a bone is reshaped, then all the muscles and nerves related to that bone have to be re-designed as well. There may be a pressure in germ plasm toward better balanced design. Also it has been suggested that the form of an organism results from more cooperation between hereditary predispositions, and use and effort by the individual himself than was supposed. Then, the theory of sexual selection also makes a place for a factor of evaluation of design and beauty that has surely been responsible for increased beauty in fish, birds, men.

Besides, we could leave the theory of heredity and variation somewhat mechanistic perhaps, and still safely claim the theory of *struggle for existence* for non-mechanistic theory. A little thought discloses that the notion of a machine whose behavior must be the passive resultant of the movements of its parts, and the notion of struggle, are mutually exclusive. The meaning of struggle is inseparable from the notions of desire for existence, effort-making, persistence — even purpose and aim. A collection of dead parts cannot be conceived as possessing any of these features. In short, it is the third factor in evolutionary theory that is hopelessly beyond mechanistic explanations, even though it is also the one that makes more trouble for the problem of evil.

We may have to grant, then (as far as any facts we yet possess go), that novel and improved organic structures appear more or less by accident. But, be that as it may, once an improved or more efficient form appears, its native tendency to live, strive, seek fulfillment is all we need for planting purposiveness firmly within nature.

But we can do better than this: there are some things that can be said on the basis of DM below about why evolutionary nature would *need* to have traits passed on from parent to offspring by a more or less fixed and deterministic mechanism; and why Weismann's isolation of germ cells from anything the individual can do may be more suitable to a meaningful view than Lamarck's belief in the inheritance of acquired characteristics.

Comparison with SM-SIR: SM can suggest no reason why there should be this endless progressive change of structure and function. It all suggests to SM only that any God who might exist does not know what he really wants, and is in some kind of eternity of futile tinkering and experimenting toward a needlessly postponed goal.

DM with DR.

Implications of DM and Correspondence to DR: If we consider this topic to concern essentially the question of increasing complexity of organic structure and function, we may make explicit a somewhat distinct point in the deduction from dynamic good. The evolution of forms toward greater complexity is implied by the principles of Novelty (# 2.7 p. 55) and Inclusiveness (#2.6, p. 55), which were shown to be intrinsic to the definition of dynamic value. In order to continue to exemplify or feel value-as-organizing-process, nature must seek ever fresh and more challengingly complex organisms or modes of process. Or, in respect to an individual organism, it must grow and increase the definiteness and inclusiveness of its own processes in order to continue to experience zest in life. In short, if the principle of evolution may be derived from the principles of inclusiveness and novelty which were in turn derived from DM, we thus find the "why" of evolution.

It is most important to realize that in the scale of evolution from atoms → molecules → living cells → multicellular organisms → humanity, this time-direction is not relative. The test of growth is absolute, being in terms of complexity of structure and unity of function.[18]

As for DR's having to accept some of SMR's mechanistic aspects of the evolutionary process — the accidental nature of mutations, the chance assortment of genes, etc. — DM is not necessarily consternated. For in the more dynamic, experimental conception of purposiveness, these features can find a place. The mutations would become simply one of the devices by which nature (or God) "throws new ingredients together" to see what creative purposiveness can do with them. In order to get such a product as a successful animal form, adaptable to the changing conditions of the environment, we can see that some sort of source of variant forms is needed, and that they must be tried and tested through dynamic interaction with conditions.

Hartshorne makes a related point.

> As Bergson and Peirce were among the first to see, even a world purpose must be indeterminate as to details. . . .
>
> Nevertheless, the idea that adjustments are the result of natural selection among unpurposed or blind variations is not incompatible with that of cosmic purpose. For the maintenance of the general conditions under which chance and competition will produce evolution may itself be purposive. Darwinism derives generally higher forms of interadjusted species from lower; but interadjustment itself and as such is assumed, not explained. . . . Theism can explain order as a general character of existence; can any other doctrine? . . .
>
> Why should the dinosaurs be any less satisfying to God or to us because they were not specifically predesigned? What after all did the old teleology accomplish, except to swell the problem of evil to impossible proportions, and to make an enigma of the process of human choice? Chance, the non-intentional character of the details of the world, is the only remedy for these two difficulties. But, as Darwin repeatedly declared, chance cannot explain the world as an ordered whole of mutually-adapted parts.[14]

Another reason for a mechanism of heredity is to preserve attained levels as a basis for future advances. When nature achieves some great success of design, it would not do for this immediately to be dispersed into chaos again at the whim of the individual. Advance requires that achieved positions be retained, for the higher rests upon the lower, uses it, needs it. Man's life, as the most varied and vivid experience yet created by nature, requires the primitive organisms in rocks to be stable and repetitive; and the vegetable world to keep repeating its dull routines; and the bacteria to do their dull work at the roots of plants and in intestinal tracts. A mechanism of heredity, then, would necessarily have to keep forms reasonably similar; and the mechanism of variation should not disrupt it too much.

And now, in regard to the Lamarck-vs.-Weismann issue: that the source of new forms should be independent of the wishes and efforts of existing forms (the parents) seems not too unreasonable, at least from the offspring's point of view. For it might well prefer not to be at the mercy of its parents' aims, decisions, efforts, or *lack of efforts.* "Ay, there's the rub:" for if Lamarck felt it would be fairer of nature to allow parents to benefit offspring directly through the germ plasm by their improvements upon themselves, then he must also accept that parents can hurt their offspring hereditarily by careless deterioration of themselves. From the point of view of personal responsibility, then, it seems that Weismann's doctrine of the independence of the germ cells from the body cells is what we need. We might end up wishing nature could have made the germ plasm even *more* safe from the tamperings of the parents than she has: for they can still do a few things to hurt their children's endowment, such as keeping their own blood pickled in alcohol, or choosing to be atomic scientists in highly radioactive environments.

4. *The Evaluation of Life.*
SM with SIR.

Implications of SM: It is already implicit in what we have said, that Life in all of its species should be perfectly good, should fit some inevitably "right" plan. Genesis follows each step of God's creation with the phrase "and God saw that it was good." The Garden of Eden story obviously implies that the first phase of creation consisted of a state of perfect adjustment of all things and creatures among one another. Some feel that the Bible implies that insects and carnivores did not begin their destructive ways until after Man had fallen and brought general calamity throughout nature.

Adjustments of SIR: SIR accepts SM's implications as to the original goodness of life and all of its forms. But it must recognize the appearance at least of subsequent evil, of insect nuisances, of life living on life, etc. It deals with these facts, as we shall see in Chapter XVIII, by its usual devices of dualism or illusionism, and by other ways of defending the existence of universal divine providence.

SM with SMR.

Findings of SMR and Contradiction to SM: It is the second of the four points in Darwinian theory that makes the trouble under this topic, and caused a good part of the fanatical fear and resistance which has not even yet died out on the part of upholders of traditional religion. What would the Loving Father of traditional belief be doing in constructing nature so as to enforce a dog-eat-dog manner of life? Darwin himself, though he ends *The Origin of Species* with a rather feeble attempt to recommend his view to religious believers as enhancing the glory of God, cannot avoid writing in the grim third chapter on "The Struggle for Existence":

> We behold the face of nature bright with gladness, we often see superabundance of food; we do not see or we forget, that the birds which are idly singing round us mostly live on insects or seeds, and are thus constantly destroying life; or we forget how largely these songsters, or their eggs, or their nestlings, are destroyed by birds and beasts of prey; we do not always bear in mind, that, though food may be now superabundant, it is not so at all seasons of each recurring year.[15]

Certainly, the Darwinian picture is far from Genesis' Garden of Eden; far from Rousseau's idyllic Nature, far from the romantics' benign, if wild, forests; far from Christianity's lion lying down with the lamb. What can be added to Tennyson's universally quoted lines in *In Memoriam,* which puzzle so fretfully over why God has made Nature "red in tooth and claw"? SMR, as usual, in discovering the nature of the original phases of the world process concludes (in agreement with SM) that they tell of the essence of things for all time; only now (in contradiction to SM) the essence is found cruel and "evil" rather than gentle and good.

277

What kind of life might be attained through creative problem-solving is of no concern, for, as we have seen, the outcomes of process have no significance or reality for SMR.

SM with DR.

Findings of DR: DR has to recognize what SMR discovered about the evolutionary process: that it is full of cruelty and destruction as well as progress and consummation. But it notices one thing that SMR discounted: that the cruder, more violent and forceful modes of survival, which SMR assumed were fostered by the very nature of things, are not necessarily the last word in adaptation. Cooperation or mutual aid between creatures is acknowledged, and far from being a recessive feature of life, occurring only during temporary lapses of the Malthusian fate where some species happens upon a fresh abundance of food, it would seem to be, if anything, more prevalent than competition. And also more successful. Once they looked for evidences of it, men ran across a plethora: species with one of the best records of survival were the cooperative bees and ants; the peaceful herbivores always exist in larger numbers than the cats and wolves; in human affairs the meek sometimes seem to inherit the earth — only too often, Nietzsche thought — from the predatory nobles and heroic fighters. SMR may look upon these facts convinced that mutual aid is only a negligible fluke in nature's affairs, certain to be dropped as soon as the more typical state of near starvation is restored. It also insists that *between* the cooperating groups the competition is as ruthless as ever; that the individuals cooperate only as an incidental means to destroying life beyond their group the more completely. But DR asks in retort, why does the scope of cooperation tend to grow then? Why does nature evolve forms (particularly man) who learns to hold larger and larger groups of individuals together without internal slaughter?

But the central point is that even if there is always some outer boundary to groups across which the friction and destruction is as great or greater than ever, the fact remains that a process indubitably exists in nature whereby creatures do learn to survive less clumsily, with less mutual breakage, with smoother and less painful relationships, and SMR is not being faithful to the facts when it ignores it. And if you still complain that bloodshed and

278

life-consuming-life has not been utterly eliminated by this refinement, DR answers that this fact does not render the partial improvement, as far as it goes, entirely unreal.

The materialistic philosophy . . . directed almost exclusive attention to the aspect of struggle for existence in a fixed environment. . . . It is folly to look at the universe through rose-tinted spectacles. We must admit the struggle. . . .
But during the last three generations, the exclusive direction of attention to this aspect of things has been a disaster of the first magnitude. The watchwords of the nineteenth century have been, struggle for existence, competition, class warfare, commercial antagonism between nations, military warfare. The struggle for existence has been construed into the gospel of hate. The full conclusion to be drawn from a philosophy of evolution is fortunately of a more balanced character. Successful organisms modify their environment. Those organisms are successful which modify their environment so as to assist each other. . . . A single tree by itself is dependent upon all the adverse chances of shifting circumstances. The wind stunts it; the variations in temperature check its foliage: the rains denude its soil. . . . But in nature the normal way in which trees flourish is by their association in a forest. . . . Also, the lions and tigers are not the successful species. There is something in the ready use of force which defeats its own object. Its main defect is that it bars cooperation. Every organism requires an environment of friends.[16]

Comparison with SM:
Of course neither SM nor SMR are happy to find that there is no unlimited "goodness" in nature, but that it remains much mixed up with heartlessness. SM would prefer a nature of pure "good;" and SMR is still suspicious that the "badness" is somehow more basic (since it is earlier) than the goodness. But DM, of course, shows both why the goodness must be only partial, and must come as a subsequent reaction to the badness, never entirely wiping it out.

DM with DR.

Implications of DM and Correspondence to DR: It is only here that we can complete the discussion of whether life is purposive and good. DR technically can only consider what can be taken as factual, without being able to state categorically whether it is good or not. Under DR we discussed the *fact* that nature contains a trend toward more cooperative, less crude ways of surviving, and toward more complex, adequate structures and functions. Now, on the basis of our postulate that good is the feeling of organizing, resolving process, and that it is proportional to the inclusiveness and complexity of factors being incorporated, we are in a position to say that the kind of evolutionary process DR finds *is* good; that is, it is what value requires. It is what one would expect a Cosmic Purpose for (dynamic) good to create. As for the destructive and painful features that the life process still reveals, even at best, and as for the fact that death and disintegration are never eliminated, these are aspects of the problem of evil which we are reserving for discussion in Chapter XVIII.

5. *The Status of Man.*
SM with SIR.

Implications of SM: Applying the idea of special creation (#3) to Man, the expectation of course is that he should be separately created, with no relationship to any lower species. Genesis puts particular emphasis upon Man's independent creation — it comes on a different "day" from that of the animals, and Man is immediately given dominion over all other species; but most important of all, only Man is created in the Image of God. This last point involves an application of #4 to Man: he is expected to be not only "good" as all the other parts of the creation but better — even unto likeness to God. The effect of SM's approach is to habituate men to supposing that honor for man requires as much separation of his essence from animalhood as possible.

Adjustments of SIR: During the ages of SIR's predominance scientific scrutiny had not yet noticed anything to cast doubt on the faith that SM was supported by the facts in its implication to the special creation of man. Man's rationality, his possession of a "soul," were appealed to in maintaining his absolute distinction from any animal in spite of his obvious possession of an enormous number of features in common with animals.

280

SM with SMR.

Findings of SMR: It was Darwin again who in his second book, *The Descent of Man,* rubbed the noses of his dismayed readers in this fact: that man himself was part and parcel of the ruthless evolutionary process, indissolubly related to the animals. And, with some sort of poetical justice, it must needs be that ugliest and most ridiculous of genera that he "descended" from: the monkeys and apes. As if the injury under the preceding points — that nature and human nature are basically cruel and destructive — was not enough, the insult under the present point was added to it — that man is nothing more than a simian. Perhaps this point gave rise to even more resistance than that one. At least the most notorious of conflicts between science and religion — that legal event in a tiny Tennessee village, which has produced a legend, a play, a movie, innumerable books and just lately research pamphlets[17] — has gotten itself labeled "The Monkey Trial." The devotees of old-time religion desperately tried to keep Darwin out of the public schools, and when we read of the trial, it does seem that what they hated most in Darwinism was not its hard-boiled implications concerning the nature of man's *spirit,* but its humiliating aspersions upon the sources of his *body.*

But behind the whole furor, we must be clear, is the perverse twist of thought and feeling that results when SM and SMR touch upon one another. For it is SM that makes men so concerned about their origins as the only revelation of their essence; as though it was not so much what they did creatively in their own lives and out of their own powers that gave honor to them, as what they passively receive from their ancestors. And it is SIR that encourages men to believe their origin was high and perfect. Then it is SMR that contradicts SIR and discovers the "lowness" of men's origin and in the bargain proves that they can never surpass it. Darwin himself was enough under the spell of static thinking to label his book the "Descent" of man, as though if there were to be any process or evolution, it must necessarily be downwards from the antecedents. The familiar conclusion was "Man is nothing but an ape."

Contradiction to SM: Thus SMR contradicts SM's assumption of the special creation of Man in God's image and suggests that Man like all other life is only the haphazard outcome of the blind squirmings of atoms and molecules in primeval mud, by way of the particularly repulsive assemblage known as "the ape-like common ancestor."

SM with DR.

Findings of DR: Almost the whole of what DR has to say about man's relationship to chimpanzees can be epitomized by asking Darwin why, oh why did he not think to name his book "The Ascent of Man." Clearly the facts as DR sees them thoroughly justify his doing so, at least provided we define "ascent" as involving the development of a structure capable of increasingly flexible and complex movements, and a center of feeling capable of increasingly inclusive organizations of function and appreciations of richer quality-feelings. No doubt man still retains many connections to the "lower" animals, but an adequate grasp upon the marvels of his being (which we shall try to express more completely in the next chapter) might conceivably be enough to create admiration and honor for him.

Comparison with SM: But the mind imbued with SM's expectations is seemingly crippled for feeling any emotional glory in man as long as he does possess these animal features, and is capable of the wretched behavior that he often sinks back to in company with his animal forbears. There are many men and religious groups who still today feel it incumbent upon them to deny the whole theory of evolution — in spite of its being the best supported of all scientific theories — so unable do they find themselves to feel it anything but disennobling to man. And among the philosophically sophisticated we can find such statements as the following from Joad:

> Is man, objectively considered, such an achievement that his devising could have constituted a purpose which Divine Omnipotence would consider an adequate motive for creation? Looking at the world he has made and his behavior in it, it is difficult to say that he is.[18]

DM with DR.

Implications of DM and Correspondence to DR: On the basis of dynamic idea of value, as we have already begun to see and

282

will discuss more thoroughly in the chapters on Evil as such, the imperfection of man can form no proof that he is not a divinely intended creation. Here let us concentrate more on the question of whether his relationship to other animals degrades him or not.

One thing that immediately suggests itself for a view that can admire growth rather than fixed being, is that more credit would be due to a creature who *attains* higher qualities out of "lower" states, and who has to *maintain* them in resistance to temptation back to "animalhood," than to a creature who merely receives its high qualities passively from God in the first instant. From this point of view, man's connection to apes would be no disgrace at all. In fact it becomes inconceivable how we could know or appreciate man's greatness except in its contrast to and superiority over what he formerly was. As for the fact that animality continues as part of man still, this would be no reason to mock him as though he was permanently dishonored by his attachment to animal parts; it becomes rather the only grounds on which we could conceivably admire a man who succeeds in retaining his *human* perquisites in the face of the pulls of his animality. There could be no other ground for honor, dynamically speaking. SM-SIR's picture of a marionette cut to the designer's pattern, with no choice but to be a perfect doll becomes a relatively trivial one compared to DR's evolutionary view.

But on what grounds can DM evaluate man as "better," greater, more significant, more important than other creatures? There has been a tendency in DM-DR to sanctify all things as being equally creative energy embodying dynamic value. Each atom, amoeba, snake, cow is a center of value-feeling and therefore significant and holy. Are there any grounds for saying that these "lower" creatures should be considered significant more in their aspect of serving to enrich the experience of the "higher" creatures (men) than in their own subjective aspect? Or must the human sphere relinquish any favored position and take a humble rank as merely one among many patterns that have been evolved? If self-consciousness appears only at the human level, it would merely be an incidental development intensifying feelings and aims that exist at the other levels as well. Like the Jains, vegetarians and Schweitzer we would not exalt the human level as the special purpose of the Creator, but would anxiously avoid killing and using other creatures for our benefit, flies and bacteria included.

But the corollary which we derived from the dynamic idea of

good (#2.63, p. 55), the proportionality of values to the complexity of factors organized, may suggest some special status for the most complex creature in any epoch. And it is obvious that the experience of such a creature depends upon its making use of the less complex (or "lower") ones for its own sustenance and diversion. A fish is not only a little organism living out its own dim purposes here and now; nor is it only the potential ancestor of some higher form a billion years hence. It is also a means to sustain human life now, and to provide one variety of sport. The highest conscious form needs the lower forms, requires them to be relatively inert, stable, assimilable. Their meaning, then, might be primarily to be ingredients in the life of the most complex form.

In this sense human existence might conceivably be a special purpose of a cosmic Creator, and not necessarily SMR's "accidental" product of an insensate evolution. Supposing the drama of personal experience were the point of the universe, we can now ask on dynamic grounds how else one would expect God to go about embodying it. Not by SM's method of precipitating a fixed form into existence by immediate fiat. But by an agelong experimentation such that a delicately complex structure could be in a balanced interaction with a maximally varied and interesting environment. Such a creature could live only immersed in a world constituted of its former stages and thus assimilable to it. Thus the human drama might be in a real sense the final cause of phenomena so far; i.e., the reason for all preceding events, and not merely the accidental outcome of blind strivings.

This does not necessarily imply that the human must be the last and final form. Logically we might maintain only that the highest form in any given epoch possesses metaphysical uniqueness, even though it is continuous with other forms and has evolved out of them. The other forms acquire significance as potentials to its experience. The lower forms explain the appearance of the higher in terms of efficient cause. But once the higher are evolved, they explain the lower as their final cause, or reason. If there were such a final cause, there is no other way it could be embodied.

Taking such account of the hierarchy of organisms would help to restore to man his inviolable importance, the sense of which our age has lost through war and massacre. The dynamic idea of good puts an end to contempt for man on the grounds of his not being perfect; and the organismic view relieves us of having to think of him as a purposeless automaton. Now the idea of a hierarchy of complexity offers a basis for treating man as distinct from other creatures in his metaphysical significance.

Our argument does not of course demonstrate that man *is* the final purpose of the present epoch. There are all the difficulties of determining what constitutes the "highest" form and the suspicion that it might be only human egoism that concludes we are especially important in the scheme of things. On the other hand, that there is a scale of inclusiveness and complexity of organization seems clear enough. And as we have said, DM leads us to expect nothing different from what we find, supposing there were a cosmic purpose aiming at embodying dynamic good.

Now, having arrived at man through the process of evolution, we may go on and study his nature somewhat more in detail.

CHAPTER XII

MAN, MIND AND BODY

We are now in a position to tackle that worst failure of the modern attitude which we characterized in the first pages of this book: the feeling that man, particularly in his bodily aspect, is essentially ridiculous, repulsive, nasty and low. If the dynamic idea of value seems most helpful in showing how man may be considered a meaningful creature in spite of his lapses into evil, that victory only clears the way for a second victory in the present connection: it can also show why he must be the partly mechanical bodily creature that he is. The dynamic idea of value originally arose in the author's mind as a way to restore to bodily man that reverence and nobility to which former ages were sensitive but our age is mockingly oblivious. All that we have done in this Part III is involved in understanding why man must be a structured creature. In the present chapter as in the last we are engaged in a more concrete application of those concepts.

The chapter is divided into the usual topics of the Mind-Self, the Body and the Relationship between them. Much of what is said under these topics might be supposed to apply to other kinds of organisms, running down the hierarchy of organisms as far as might be thought feasible. But we will naturally be thinking preeminently of the human level in this chapter.

1. *The Nature and Meaning of the Human Mind or Self.*
SM with SIR.

Implications of SM: What was said under SM for the nature of life could be repeated almost verbatim here, substituting the term "Mind" or "Soul" or "Spirit" for "Life." The way of thinking, as usual, is to expect Mind to be an essence, appeal to which will explain all mental phenomena without further analysis. Mind or

Soul should be its own kind of substance — and we have already studied what sort of substance under the first topic in Ontology, Chapter VII. For there we learned that SM actually implies that there should be nothing else in existence but this mental substance, an unchanging and indivisible container or awareness of all ideas. SM also expects mind to be essentially *rational*, unhamperedly cognizant of perfect truth. And, in Part II on Epistemology, we learned how SM expects mind to be a spectator, a passive mirror or contemplater of ideas, rather than a doer, problem-solver or creator.

Adjustments of SIR: The two main devices used by SIR to make reality "fit" SM, Dualism and Illusionism, were discussed in Chapter VII. Plato, as a dualist, admitted that Mind is always, in this world anyway, attached to a material body. He also suggested some subdivisions for the mind, each of which he located in a part of the body. Besides the rational part, located in the brain, there was the feeling part, in the breast or heart, and the desiring part, in the abdomen. Descartes restated this dualism, making the mind its own independent substance, lacking extension or any other physical property, and again consisting of pure thinking or rationality. Then, as we have seen, he defined the body in terms of extension and mechanics and struggled unsuccessfully to figure out a way to relate his two substances (see #3 below). The man in the street still widely believes the Mind or Soul to be some definite thing located in a part of the Body.

The illusionistic device used by the subjective idealists has already been explained, whereby matter and bodies themselves become ideas. On the present topic it seems that Aristotle deserves to be placed in DR rather than SIR, for he had moved quite far toward a functional view of the mind.

SM with SMR.

Findings of SMR: A. Static aspect: Hobbes, trying to make Newton's law of Action and Reaction do for mental phenomena, light-heartedly identified qualitative perceptions with quantitative motions of material atoms, with never an apology for self-contradiction:

The cause of sense is the external body, or object, which

287

presses the organ proper to each sense, either immediately, as in the taste and touch; or mediately, as in seeing, hearing, and smelling: which pressure, by the mediation of nerves, and other strings, and membranes of the body, continues inwards to the brain . . . causes there a resistance, or counterpressure, . . . to deliver itself: which endeavor, because *outward*, seems to be some matter without. And this *seeming*, or *fancy*, is that which men call *sense*; and consists, as to the eye, in a *light*, or *color figured*; to the ear, in a *sound*; to the nostril, in an *odor* [. . . etc.] All which qualities called *sensible*, are in the object that causes them, but so many several motions of the matter, by which it presses our organs diversely. Neither in us that are pressed, are they anything else, but diverse motions; (for motion produced nothing but motion.) [1]

Thus, in one paragraph, Hobbes says that nothing exists but matter in motion, and that motion produces only motion; but that motion also produces qualitative perceptions which, we might point out, are not motions but qualitative perceptions. Hobbes goes on in the second and later chapters to apply Newton's law of inertia to the imaginative and rational activity of the mind, consistently showing that the mind can never *do* anything really creative, but can only passively react to material causes. The spectator view of the mind is thus carried over from SM in a different form. In this respect SMR's theory continues essentially static.

B. Analytical aspect: We remember that SMR always reveals a second aspect: one related to the part-whole relationship. To illustrate SMR's denial of SM's expectation of an indivisible mind or soul substance, we cannot avoid again quoting (cf. p. 86) David Hume's famous confession, in the section "Of Personal Identity" in *The Treatise of Human Nature,* that he found himself to be nothing but a sequence of unrelated impressions:

There are some philosophers who imagine we are every moment intimately conscious of what we call our *self;* that we feel its existence and its continuance in existence; and are certain, beyond the evidence of a demonstration, both of its perfect identity and simplicity. . . . For my part, when I enter most intimately into what I call *myself,* I always stumble on some particular perception or other, of heat or cold, light or shade, love or hatred, pain or pleasure. I can never catch *myself* at any time without a perception, and never can observe anything but the perception. When my perceptions are removed for any time, as by sound sleep, so long am I insensible of *myself*, and may truly be said not to exist. . . . [The mind or self is] nothing but a bundle or collection of different perceptions, which succeed each other with an inconceivable rapidity, and are in a perpetual flux and movement. . . . They are the successive perceptions only, that constitute the mind.[2]

This statement does not go quite as far as Hobbes in trying to demonstrate that the mind, like all other things, is only a swarm of solid, material atoms complexly colliding with one another (see p. 288). Hume allows himself to speak of "impressions" or "perceptions" as his units, rather than atoms, but consonantly with SMR, never gives up thinking of them as separate elements.

Both Hobbes and Hume hotly criticize and specifically reject SM-SIR's concept of the mind or self as a separate substance with a unified wholeness of its own. Nothing exists but the train of elemental impressions, giving rise in turn to sequences of ideas. True, they were forced to a doctrine of "association" of these elements. Hume found three laws of association: resemblance, proximity in time and space, and causation. But he never meant that the elements ever left off being elements; they merely became closely tied to one another or habitually connected; they did not fuse into new qualities in any sense.

Modern Behaviorism follows this lead, and "scientific" physiological psychology during the first part of the present century made itself a curiosity by smart statements to the effect that there is no qualitative awareness, no self-consciousness, no private thought and feeling, no internal purposiveness. Only what could be externally observed by an onlooker was allowed reality, and this turned out to be stimuli and responses, primarily muscular or visceral-chemical. Connecting stimuli and response was the reflex arc, which becomes the elementary unit for modern mechanistic psychology. This concept results partly from the objective study of nerve physiology and partly from objective experimentation with muscular and glandular changes in animals and men. Behaviorism remained consistently elementalistic in its explanations, refraining from any statements about unique qualitative experience that may accompany different patterns of reflexes. Significantly, the two homes of the theory were in Russia, where dialectical materialism fostered founder Pavlov's leads, and where even yet Communism finds the theory of man as reflex automaton useful; and America, where founder John Watson emerged from the world of business advertising, with a natural interest in how to manipulate people like robots by materialistic stimuli. The theory of conditioned reflexes tries to explain all learning behavior by the associating of substitute stimuli to responses, reminiscent of Hume's associationism. An organism comes to respond to an associated, "learned" stimulus as it first responded to the original stimulus: the dog salivates to the ringing bell as it first salivated to the sight of food. Presumably we are not to imagine that conscious thought or quality is involved; or that anything like "meaning" or an understanding grasp of the total situation ever becomes intrinsically involved. It is merely that separate nerve branches get hooked up in such a way as to enforce a series of unfelt actions, once the auditory nerve has been hit by the sound waves. The experimenters like to "prove" this, by cutting out all of the dog's brain where "self-consciousness" or "thought" may have been imagined to exist, and showing that the saliva glands can still be conditioned to salivate when the sound waves collide with the ear. The thought is then transferred to human beings and everything from "instinct" to philosophical questing becomes the blind outcome of reflexes which get pasted together one by one, and remain separate units throughout.

It has been noted that Behaviorism was not particularly interested in the problems of motivation or need, or in the nature of consummation. Stimulus, as a mere physical or chemical push, seemed sufficient to explain the start of action; response, as a necessary outcome, a quiescence satisfying the law of conservation of energy, seemed sufficient to explain the terminus of action. That is, neither *felt* need, nor *felt* satisfaction entered into the theory. Only the mechanical transactions in between did.

Freudian psychoanalysis devoted its attention to the missing realm of motivation, but in many aspects retained an atomistic, deterministic approach. Dividing up the mind into Ego, Id and Super-ego, Freudian phraseology often suggested a quasi-mechanical interaction between these entities, as though they were each blind forces hitting out some resultant motion. The modes in which they reached their mechanical equilibrium were even labeled "mechanisms" and we get the feeling that the person is only a passive stage upon which these impersonal forces thrash out their actions and reactions. The greater part of the adjustment was done unconsciously; and "consciousness" retains the epiphenomenal status given it by Hobbes and the Behaviorists. Freud also commits a biological reductivism, where the causes of the individual's acts are not his whole, present self, but biological and chemical part-forces coming out of the past. He was anxious to show that every action, however trivial, was the necessary product of definite cause in the past; and the further back in the past, the more determinative. All the life history of a person should be implicit in his earliest years, in the birth trauma, or even in the womb.

Among later philosophers, we find Bertrand Russell similarly reductive:

> We know much more than we knew formerly as to the causes of desires. Sometimes they are to be found in the working of the ductless glands, sometimes in early education, sometimes in forgotten experiences, sometimes in the desire for approval, and so on. In most cases a number of different sources enter into the causation of a desire. And it is clear that, when we make a decision, we do so as a result of some desire, though there may at the same time be other desires pulling us in a contrary direction. . . . The idea of a wholly uncaused act of volition is thus not defensible.[3]

Thus he lists a number of separate, unpurposing parts and origins as causes. He does not go on to make anything of this fact of multiplicity of sources, and thereby misses the clue. The only way he would think of the multiplicity is as an added sum of causes, the final effect being the mechanical resultant. But in the latter part of the quotation he has ignored multiplicity entirely and has slipped insensibly back to single determining desires. When Haldane maintains the existence of personality as a unifying principle, or of a quality of wholeness having its own causative function, Russell answers that he sees

> . . . no reason to regard this as true. . . . If one man is choleric and another phlegmatic, the difference is usually traceable to the glands, and could, in most cases, be oblit-

erated by the use of suitable drugs. The belief that personality is mysterious and irreducible has no scientific warrant.[4]

That is, personality *is* "reducible" to its parts — the glands and thence to the atoms. Causation runs one-way only — from the parts.

> . . . if our bodily actions all have physiological causes, our minds become causally unimportant. . . . The practical issue . . . may, perhaps, be stated as follows: Are our bodily acts determined by physico-chemical laws?[5]

Thus SMR works to eliminate mind, in SM's or any other sense, from reality.

Contradiction to SM-SIR and Recourses: The contradiction to SM's theory of the mind as a mystic, indivisible substance is obvious. We cannot stop for discussion of modern attempts to revive mentalistic theories. They take the same form as the neo-vitalism mentioned in the preceding chapter (p. 259). Kant's theory of the mind as a "synthetic unity of apperception" is already on the way to DR's non-substantive view. He criticized the substantive view of the mind, and questioned whether it could ever become an object of knowledge. He had a theory of reciprocal causation between parts and wholes, and understood the self to be an organic unity transcending its separate experiences.

SM with DR.

Findings of DR: Under the theory of the Mind, DR's dynamic correction to SMR is represented by the Functional, Instrumental theories of the Mind; the whole-part correction by the Gestalt movement in psychology, and other related schools such as the holistic, organismic, personalistic psychologies.

A. Dynamic correction: Aristotle had already moved toward a functional view of mind. He resisted Plato's extreme dualism and denied that the forms, the mental essences, could exist independently of material structure. Their nature became closely associated with the developing process that all matter engaged in. Mind was the locus of the formal and final causes which gave direction and organization to the potentiality of matter.

But it has been since evolutionary theory became basic in

modern thought that the functional view of mind has become widespread. The mind is not thought of as a specific organ in the body, dissectible as a heart or liver, but as an aspect of the total functioning of the organism. William James, in his great *Psychology,* and John Dewey in many works pioneered in expressing this view. The latter specifically sets it against the substantive view of SM-SIR:

> There is no separate "mind" gifted in and of itself with a faculty of thought; such a conception of thought ends in postulating a mystery of a power outside of nature and yet able to intervene within it.[6]

Commenting on this passage, Titus writes:

> Mind and thought become functional aspects of the interaction of natural events. Mind is intelligent behavior. . . . Man is not part body and part mind. Dewey rejects all dualisms and the spectator view of mind.[7]

B. Part-Whole Correction: The foundations for understanding holistic phenomena were given in Chapter VII and VIII. Some of the best explications of the concept as applied to the mind have come from the Gestalt psychologists, Wertheimer, Köhler, Koffka, and their followers. They made explicit what was wrong in the analytic and atomistic methods of SMR's psychology. But they are very clear about not returning to any kind of vitalism or mentalism that sets off mind dualistically against matter. Mind is always conceived as the organized unification of the partial energies that flow within it; not as a separate agency in addition to its part energies. But that its part energies do fuse into holistic states is proven by the gestaltists in many kinds of carefully devised experiments. These experiments are one of the best ways of waking an analytical mind to what is meant by saying that "the whole is more than the sum of its parts." They reveal phenomena that cannot exist or be conceived in terms of parts. Much of the experimentation deals with vision, but in proving that the retina of the eye does not behave as a mosaic of permanently separated parts, it opens the way to the presumption that the rest of the nervous system may very well not do so either.

Köhler criticizes SMR's theory that sensory experience must

begin with purely local stimuli, must pass through isolated nerve pathways as in a telephone exchange with a fixed system of interconnections, and issue in purely local elements of experience; and that sensory experience is what it is independently of emotional attitudes or "meaning" deriving from the total situation. It had been supposed that

> By enumerating the actual properties of all elements at a given time we give an exhaustive account of the presented field. This is what has been called the summative, or mosaic, character of sensory experience. . . . The organization of processes in the field is excluded because order must be explained by functional separation. Specific function, dynamically extended over an area of the field is excluded for the same reason; we have to deal with a purely *geometrical* pattern of *local* processes.[8]

In this way of thinking, the organism is nothing as a whole. It contributes nothing to the

> . . . monotonous elementary currents conducted compulsorily from a point of stimulation to a point of reaction. So it becomes an indifferent stage for actors indifferent to the stage as well as to each other.[9]

However, psychology has turned up examples of reactions that could not conceivably take place on any such basis. The Gestalt experiments show organisms reacting differentially to figures whose difference is not a matter of stimulation of local cells at all. Lines in two figures may be exactly alike, stimulating the same number of retinal cells. Yet our resulting experience is of lines of different length; and it is due to something in the background, to the state of quite other retinal cells, although these are supposed to be isolated from the ones being tested. The specific properties of the experience thus belong to *extended wholes* and do not exist in local elements. We have already cited the "closure" plenomena shown in flash card experiments (p. 250). They show that the retina and nervous system do not react exclusively in terms of their parts which have been actually stimulated, but also in terms of their own field forces straining toward holistic symmetry. Or the familiar experience is pointed to in which we can immediately recognize a melody played in one key as being identical with the same melody played in another key, though no specific auditory nerve which was stimulated in the first case may be stimulated in the second case. That is, we are able to "know" the holistic form of the melody though an entirely different set of specific parts is involved.

By these and other experiments the same conclusion is reached for nervous functioning that the field physicists reached for atomic functioning: that there are realities which have no being in terms of parts or collections of parts but are related necessarily only to new unities of parts, or to "the area between the parts."

This construction invalidates Russell's claim that mind must rate as "causally unimportant" just because we can analyze physiological causes prior to its own action. He touched upon the clue to the problem (p. 291 f.), but paid no attention to it: the fact of many causes as such. Russell's demand and his findings are both misconceived because of his inability to attribute significance to plurality of factors. He imagines efficacy of mind as involving unconditioned mental choice of one definite decision out of the host of alternatives. He finds determined enforcement of one choice by a dominant desire, itself determined by the past. But actuality reveals neither of these cases. We find usually, not an arbitrary election of one thing and rejection of all others, but the emergence of optimum patterns from a concatenation of factors presented simultaneously. Meaningful, enjoyable experience is embodied in playing with a group of items, shifting them about, trying out arrangements, fitting this to that, estimating coordinations, until the materials slip into their places in a way best calculated to accomplish a plurality of aims neatly. The possibilities considered do arise from partial interests: from hunger, sensations, glandular emotions, habits, hopes. But no one of these automatically produces an inevitable effect. Each must present itself before the bar of the mind and plead its case, then accept compromise with the other elements. The decisions of the mind are certainly not uncaused. But neither are they caused only by the constituent fragments. The mind then can rate as "causally important" in its regulating, organizing function.

This does not, as we have admitted in Chapter X, prove the existence of free will. Granted that the mind or personality has a unique part to play in harmonizing its contents into balanced patterns, still the balancing might remain a matter of producing a necessary mechanical resultant. Be that as it may, we have still gained for the mind a reality additional to that of its ingredient parts.

From this point, the new holistic, personalistic psychologies move to their over-all theories of the nature of mind, self and person. Jung and Adler and later psychoanalysts have made this correction upon Freudian theory; Allport, Lewin, Goldstein, Murray and others for personality theory. From a review of recent theories of personality we select a number of relevant passages:[10]

Elementarism in personality theory usually takes the form of a reductionism which says that personality is "nothing but" the abstracted entities or events forming the basis of the theory in question . . . an aggregate of discrete parts which associationist theory has never been quite able to put together in a really convincing manner. (p. 318).

Lewin (1940) refers to his approach as "field theory," based on the ideas that "(a) behavior has to be derived from a totality of coexisting facts, (b) these coexisting facts have the character of a 'dynamic field' in so far as the state of any part of this field depends on every other part of the field. . . . According to the field theory, behavior depends neither on the past nor on the future but on the present field. . . . This is in contrast both to the belief of teleology that the future is the cause of behavior, and that of associationism that the past is the cause of behavior." (p. 314) (Cf. SM and SMR).

Henry A. Murray's *Explorations in Personality,* which appeared in 1938, has proved to be one of the truly great landmarks in the development of the science of personality. . . . . For Murray personality is the dominant unity of brain processes. Those coordinating, controlling processes in the nervous system which integrate behavior and experience on the highest levels of complexity occur in the brain. . . . Further, in the regnant brain processes the past experiences of the individual are conserved, the future is anticipated, and past, present, and future are bound together in continuity of purpose. The unity of regnant brain processes is temporal in function, it is "time-binding." . . .

To account for the purposes which often dominate men's

activities, Murray postulates the development of inferred (not directly observable) brain processes, drives toward certain general goals, persistent trends in the individual. Such must exist in order to account for the fact that individuals may and do use a variety of means to achieve the same goal; those means which lead to adjustment being used over and over again. . . . Tensions originate within the organism out of cyclic bodily changes, interaction with the physical environment, interpersonal relations, etc., and the need is a resultant regnant brain process which coordinates, mobilizes, and directs the actions of the organism in its tension-reducing activities. This is a dynamic rather than mechanically behavioristic or teleologically purposivistic conception of human experience and activity.

. . . Living is a process wherein the organism is continually seeking equilibrium out of conditions of disturbance brought on by internal and external factors. (pp. 348-350).

Functions of Personality: Tension-reduction. — A function of the regnant processes is the reduction of need-tensions during both katabolism and anabolism (the energy-building phase of metabolism). After the anabolism of sleep the individual deliberately seeks expenditure, rather than conservation of energy; he wants thrills, he welcomes exertion. This formulation covers both positive and negative need-systems. Sometimes need systems develop images of remote goals, and here it becomes a function of the regnant processes to provide *serial programs,* outlining sub-goals to be achieved as well as the order of their achievement leading to the final goal. . . .

Self-Expression. — An extension of the tension-reduction principle is the general *need for activity* which characterizes all human beings. . . . Because of their relations to the various psychological functions they might be termed *mode pleasures* to distinguish them from *end pleasures,* toward which workful striving is often carried on. (p. 351).[11]

Reduction of Conflicts by Scheduling. — Another function of the regnant brain processes (personality) is the process of choosing. . . . But seldom is the situation of an either-or nature; it is usually a matter of deciding which of many purposes is to be served first and what the order of achievement will be from that point on. (p. 352) (Cf. our discussion in Chapter IX, p. 209 ff.).

(Other applications of the notion of regnant brain process follow).

One of the more notable concepts of Murray's theory is that of needs. This contrasts sharply with the prevalent concern of American students of personality with acts, motor and verbal, which occur in response to needs . . . (p. 354).

It is becoming increasingly clear in both the natural and social sciences that whatever occurs is a function of a complexity of forces, conveniently abstracted in the concept of *field*. Today's physics is dynamically nuclear, not elementarily atomic. Today's biology is becoming ever more chemical and physical in this new field sense. The age of atomic particles and rugged individualism is past. The individuality of events and persons is now seen in terms of the continuous relations between internal and external forces . . . (p. 355).

Regnancy, then, is a principle at home in a world generally described in terms of field theory. . . . On the neurological level the functionally central or focal area of personality is the brain. This corresponds to what on the psychological level has been referred to variously as *the ego, the soul, the self, the psyche,* etc. (p. 356).

The earlier view of personality as a kind of substance with inhering properties or traits is giving way to a dynamic conception wherein personality is viewed not as a thing, entity, or substance but as a complex of functions of interactive forces which may be studied within various abstractive frames of reference — physical, chemical, hormic, neurological, psychological, social and cultural. (pp. 357-8).

From these and other sources, we may itemize the main aspects of the mind, self or personality which become understandable on the basis of holistic field theory. The order takes the same sequence that has appeared in chapter IX.

A. There is a center of feeling, a "focal area" which holistically feels the relationships among various kinds of part energies or feelings. This was called "the subject" in Chapter IX.

B. This center of feeling feels the first phase of processes as "tension" or "need;" such feelings are based in field stresses, where a complexity or plurality of energies impinge upon the center, from inner or outer sources, and put it into some strained state.

How this strained field gives rise to desire and aim has already been studied in Chapter IX, Section I, items 3 and 5. It is not a matter of causation by the past nor by the future, but by forces existing in the present field. It usually involves planning patterns of many factors to satisfy a cluster of needs. This aspect of mind is a significant addition that DR makes to SMR, which lacked any theory of felt need and desire.

C. Mind next is a feeler of stimuli from objects which may be used as means in the processes of resolution that it thereupon directs. This relates to item 4, the Object, in Chapter IX, Section I and item 2, Section II, the Means. For SMR, the theory of stimulus was all there was to explain the initiation of behavior.

D. Mind is a feeler of its own integrating processes as applied to the above contents, and issuing in the responses below. This aspect relates to the process or transition as such, item 1, Section II, Chapter IX. Here the mind feels the partial forces as they rearrange themselves within the holistic field situation, reducing the tension or strain by an innumerable variety of ways, such as scheduling. Thinking itself, which SM-SIR tended to emphasize to the exclusion of the other aspects, comes here. It is to be conceived as a continuously felt process adjusting the constituents of the emerging field into a good "fit." What the functionalists and pragmatists have to say of the mind as instrumental belongs primarily under this item.

E. Mind is a feeler of the Responses, the actual motions in muscles and other tissues that follow the integrative work. This item takes care of the pragmatist stress on the mind as *doer,* in contrast to both SM's and SMR's spectator, mirror view. This was the final item in SMR's S-I-R theory; but DR adds other aspects:

F. The center of feeling finally feels a degree of resolution, consummation, relaxation, as a result of the responsive movements. Some recent theories call this the "Reward," emphasizing that it differs from the concept of Response. It is the appreciative, or affective function of the mind, and relates to item 3, Section II, Chapter IX, the "End." This feeling, DR discerns, cannot exist except as the preceding feeling of strain (# B) is somehow realized in simultaneous contrast. Therefore the mind must possess:

G. Memory, or the "time-binding" ability. Just as item B has a reference to the future in time, the present item has a reference to the past in time. Memory must include both some kind of continuing feeling of the original pain and its contrast to the present relief; and also a function of preserving attainment. The unique pattern of personality that results from all the experiences of the personality is retained and gives its own flavor to all subsequent operations of that organism. In a sense, then, the "habit-building" factor of mind belongs under the present head. Personality, then, as a unique personal unity, distinct from all the parts of which it is composed, and built up from habit and memory, has come back into psychological theory, after the era of standardized reflexes.

We have, then, a somewhat expanded list of aspects of mind under DR. Instead of SMR's stimulus-integration-response alone, there is:

Motivation
Stimulation
Integration
Response
Consummation or Reward
Products: Memory, Habit, Personality.

We might call this the M-S-I-R-C-P sequence.

Comparison with SM: The student may work out the contrasts between this dynamic, motivational view of purposive mind, and SM's theory of mind as an essence electing essences.

DM with DR:

Implications of DM and Correspondence to DR: There is nothing essentially new to mention at this point. The six aspects of mind just itemized have already been deduced from the dynamic idea of value in other connections:

The center of feeling in # 1.1 p. 53 and item 2, p. 218.

The Motivational (need-aim) aspect in the 2.-1 items, p. 53 f. and in items 1, 3 and 5, Chapter IX, p. 207ff.

The stimulus-object factor in # 2.22, p. 53 and item 4, Section I, Ch. IX.

The process-integration-response factors in # 2.1, p. 53 and item 1, Section II, Chapter IX.

The resolution or consummation factor in the 2.-2, items, p. 53 f. and item 3, Section II, Chapter IX.

The Mind as the unique, resulting pattern or personality was deduced implicitly in Chapter IX, Section II, item 3, ends, under the theory of retaining former accomplishments as bases for subsequent ones.

2. *The Nature and Meaning of the Body*

The present text will stop longer on this topic than most, because it was preeminently meditation upon the structure of the body, and experiences in biology laboratories that opened up philosophy for the author, giving rise to his first fruitful questions and to answers which turned out to be answers to many other problems as well. It was dissatisfaction with the modern habit of belittling the body and ridiculing particularly its sexual and excretory functions that started him thinking. Perhaps a Puritanical ancestry endowed him with its typical extremity of contradiction: between deep conviction that life is divinely meaningful, and equally deep prudery, which finds life basically dirty and repulsive. The modern resolution of this conflict is to drop the first part, and to sink into smug self-satisfaction in one's unshockability by any extreme of irreverent mocking, frivolous degradation, vicious despoiling of the body. But both the Puritanical attitude, and the "hard-boiled" attitude are equally entrapped in the inadequacies of the static views which we have been explaining. In fact, our framework of positions was developed more than anything else in order to explain and correct the profane attitude toward man which we referred to in the first chapter as one of the sicknesses of the modern mind most in need of cure. This attitude was better expressed in Krutch's *The Modern Temper* than in any other American book I know of, though it pervades almost every work of modern literature, however ephemeral or great.

> Casually [the modern man] accepts the spiritual iconoclasm of science, and in the detachment of everyday life he learns to play with the cynical wisdom of biology and psychology, which explain away the awe of emotional experience just as earlier science explained away the awe of conventional piety. . . . In love, he calls upon the illusions of man's grandeur and dignity to help him accept his emotions, and faced with tragedy he calls upon illusions to dignify his suffering; but lyric flight is checked by the rationality which he has cul-

301

tivated and in the world of metabolism and hormones, repressions and complexes, he finds no answer for his needs. . . . In the grip of passion he cannot, as some romanticist might have done, accept it with a religious trust in the mystery of love, nor yet can he regard it as a psychiatrist, himself quite free from emotion, might suggest — merely as an interesting specimen of psychical botany.[12]

If one turns to the smarter . . . novelists . . . to, for example, Mr. Aldous Huxley or Mr. Ernest Hemingway — one will discover in their tragic farces the picture of a society which is at bottom in despair because, though it is more completely absorbed in the pursuit of love than in anything else, it has lost the sense of any ultimate importance inherent in the experience which preoccupies it. . . . To [them] love is at times only a sort of obscene joke. The former in particular has delighted to mock sentiment with physiology, to place the emotions of the lover in comic juxtaposition with quaint biological lore, and to picture a romantic pair "quietly sweating palm to palm."[13]

Here is a conviction that there can be no holy meaningfulness or dignity in human life after it has been found to have a basis in the materials that scientific biology has unearthed. In Krutch and Huxley we see a revulsion against bodily structure; a judgment that divine purpose could not possibly have required machinery so solid, particular, laborious, arbitrary and specialized. The discovery that intricate nerve paths and glandular secretions should function at the basis of every sublime spiritual experience comes as a pointless shock. Huxley is an especially good example of one who re-adopts SM, hook, line and sinker, including its ascetic attempt to annihilate the body, in the mystical books that followed his earlier expressions of SMR's disgruntlement.[14]

But in this book I undertake to show that dynamic meaning can recover a feeling of reverent wonder for these immediate and palpable realities that biology reveals underlying spiritual experience; can show that a cosmic purpose needed elaborate mechanisms of cell, gland and nerve-pathway to embody "soul," must operate through such solid shapes, strangely arbitrary though they are. Here we are, thrown irrevocably into a two-legged, five-fingered form, our bodies the most intricate tangle of non-inevitable structures and arrangements, our persons tied to a peculiar selection of functions. But it can be understood why this must be so.

To render the body meaningful and sacred, we must both believe it real and be able to derive the necessity of its reality and also of its specific nature from an idea of meaning and value. But the most prevalent belief during the ages has turned this around: men have found the body not to be of the proper nature, being evil and mechanically purposeless. Then they have neatly side-stepped this difficulty by denying the other stipulations: by saying that things and bodies are unreal and illusory; and that value does not require their reality anyway. But in the dynamic positions I undertake to fulfill *all* the stipulations.

What, then, is the idea of meaningfulness behind such complaints as Krutch's and Huxley's? What do they demand ought to be true?

SM with SIR.

Implications of SM: Their presuppositions are of course based on the static idea of good and its implication that spirit should be a kind of stuff in its own right having no essential need of matter. All that comes into consciousness, in the youth of the race and of individuals, is the awareness of immediate desiring and willing. Even today most men know little of the past antecedents of their habits of desiring and willing, nor of the physiological structures that are going off in correspondence with their thoughts. The idea has always arisen, then, that one's real self is this idealike consciousness which seems to control itself and freely choose what it wants the body to do. The body is a tool which the spirit handles — the soul being quite able to carry on an existence of its own apart from the body. There is certainly no reason for the body in which the spirit is located to have any part in the making of it, for it does not need to be made, except by God, in its first instant. If there can be experience of good without channels and limitations for a process of overcoming obstacles and building structure, then man might as well, or better, be a formless cloud, an essence always in direct contact with the given good. Plato, of course, feels that the body is only an encumbrance, a needless hampering of the spirit. Certainly

303

the body whose intricacies have been disclosed in the laboratories of science is not called for by SM.

Adjustments of SIR: But bodies very obviously exist, and SIR sometimes acknowledges their reality. Christianity, thanks to its unanalytical Jewish heritage, never dreamed of concrete things and creatures being unreal. God must have some purpose for them, and the usual conclusion is that he gives the body to the soul as a tool to manipulate to its purposes. The question was not asked why the soul should have to manipulate anything. The problem of evil gradually appeared in the Bible, but not the problem of individual structures as such. It was the Greeks who first raised the question why God should create concrete structures when presumably He must have been perfect and satisfied in Himself without them. Jewish thought also did not consider the body as a main source of evil; the Old Testament always speaks of it and its functions with naturalness and reverence, and the Creation story implies that the body is fundamentally good. Ordinarily, then, Christianity should enjoy a full sense of the sanctity of concrete things and bodies; the sacramental idea, wherein bread and wine, sexuality, bodily death, etc., were elevated to the estate of holy affairs, is still the best model for what we are trying to recover.

Christianity, however, did not escape entirely the Greek antipathy to the imperfect world of desire and material embodiment. The spirit-matter dichotomy entered into its fundamentals, and with Paul there was the temptation to track down the always perplexing evil to an origin in the flesh. An ascetic revulsion followed, and is still a deep current in such an attitude as Krutch's and Huxley's. The explanation of the meaning of the body that is now favored, is that God gives the spirit thereby a battle to fight. The body exists only to be denied and punished.

When the material body began to take on the nature of mechanism in early modern thought, Descartes relegated it to one half of his dualism, where it could be mechanized and degraded as much as you wanted, since purpose and meaning still reigned in the other realm.

All these sources must have gone into the Puritanical assumption that the body should be concealed as much as possible; that "shame" was the proper attitude to take to it; that many of the words dealing with bodily functions belonged to profanity never to be uttered before polite ears; in general, that the body must not be enjoyed but disdained and kept out of one's thoughts.

These feelings, however, psychiatrists told us afterwards, led to a burden of neurosis and inhibition that was almost more than human nature could support. The practical results of SM-SIR's line of thought can hardly be considered a testimony to their adequacy.

But SMR's ways of escaping from this impasse, we shall see, though they gave an escape from the inhibition, did not give a healthy one.

SM with SMR.

Findings of SMR and Contradiction to SM: We have studied how profaned matter encroached into the realm of mind or spirit and SIR's dualism broke down. The spirit no longer seemed to be the body's independent superior director, but the helpless slave of the body. Evolutionary theory and physiological psychology, reductively interpreted, made man nothing but an ape; both ape and man nothing but collections of organs, glands, cells; cells nothing but chemicals; and chemicals nothing but dead material molecules and atoms. This exhaustive involvement of what were formerly thought to be unconditioned spiritual experiences with bodily structures was a completely unexpected and meaningless discovery. Exalted spiritual beings could only be dishonored by the taint of supposedly common and sodden matter. Thus Krutch is utterly dismayed to find love embodied in glands and mechanisms. After millennia of looking down on matter as profane, man functioning as a physical organism seems paltry and inane compared to man as noble spirit.

All this, of course, relates primarily to the mechanistic aspects of man-as-body. We should remember that the problem of evil also enters into the despising of the body: the evil behavior that despoils bodies, the diseases that disfigure them, the age that withers them, the death that decomposes them. This part of the problem must wait until Part IV for a completer discussion.

But now we must notice a considerably less significant, but probably more immediately influential reason for the inability to feel significance or sanctity in the body: what is apparently merely a contingency having to do with one of the senses: the olfactory sense. For the thoughtless, it is merely the body's possessing processes that give rise to "unpleasant" odors that prompts most of their derision. Now it is readily understandable that the processes of the body (which can be deduced from the dynamic idea of meaningfulness as we shall see) intrinsically involve waste products; and that the waste products require not to be attractive to the in-taking structures of the creature. And it has so developed that the olfactory sense has been charged with the larger part of the task of prompting withdrawal from the waste poisons: excreta, sweat, drying saliva, etc. The odors may not be intrinsically bad; creatures learn as infants to consider them bad on pain of sickness if they don't. The visual sense takes over some of this task too, and we learn to consider excreta, sores, etc., repulsive looking as well as repulsive smelling. Those people, then, who react only to the simplest immediate stimuli rather than in terms of understanding, impute these incidental repulsions to the very essence of the creaturely body, and as we know spend lifetimes in an incessant magnifying of these aspects, clearly intending to express in their "frank" speech a conviction that man himself has no more importance or meaning than the kind of impression some of his parts and excreta leave upon the nose. Ambiguous feelings about the sexual parts of the body, too, are due largely to the fact that proximity of the bodies involved brings out odors for which that other part of the body, the olfactory glands, may have developed an un-called-for aversion, perhaps through distorted upbringing.

However, I suspect that any lifetime conviction that man is a degraded and meaningless monster will add at least vague beliefs anent the problems of evil and mechanism to these superficial olfactory impressions.

Now SMR's inability to believe that effortful development ever affects the significance of things, explained in the preceding chapters, produces especially vicious consequences in the present connection. The typical attitude which shows up in all our literature, in the unspeakable practices of concentration camp functionaries, Nazi doctors, and in our own people under warfare and other abnormal conditions, is this perverse deduction from SM combined with SMR: that if bodily life is not automatically, naturally, essentially safe from dirt, smell, undignified postures, and mechanical accidents, then it can never have been meant even to be saved from these things through some sort of *dynamic effort and care*. The modern mind has at last carried SM's thought to its last implication: if God or Nature do not guarantee the body to be always in a state of beauty and dignity, then it is not for man to select and train toward such states; no! we must be "realists" and this means we must stress the unreconstructed states, wallow in the dirt, exaggerate the smell, celebrate the undignified, and degrade the body by smartly triggering its various partial functions to prove its ridiculously mechanical nature.

Our literature is endlessly preoccupied with depicting the repulsiveness of bodies at their best, and with seeking out bodies at their worst, dwelling on the impious attitudes and heedless acts that make them so. The modern return to torture has perhaps a special note of fascination with one's ability to force the body of another to perform mechanical indignities in spite of the other's will, belief or principles. The expert jibe in the ribs that makes him soil himself with vomit; the squeeze that makes him emit an animal grunt; the invasion of his brain with innumerable mechanical contrivances from drugs to painful stimulation so as to get responses that seem to prove his not being a responsible will, but only a collection of manipulable reflexes. Making prisoners live with their excreta in the prison cell is a favorite modern expression of the belief that excreta fundamentally discredits any claim of man to noble significance.

Most men through all the ages up to the present have, without question, *taken the pains* necessary to reduce the body's potential offensiveness, even though SM never implied such tasks. Things have been done to make the body's sexual economy, for instance, as acceptable as possible — at least having intercourse in private. People have washed themselves and not felt that the body's need of washing dishonored it. Sanitary facilities have been worked out as solutions to the repulsions incidental to the problem of waste and few, other than earlier too logical devotees of SM, have argued that man was to be despised because he had to take steps to separate himself from his excreta.

It was left to the modern period to be so strictly logical in SM-SMR's terms as to conclude that since excreta and animalistic sex are real, they must therefore be paraded in their crudest form; that since nature herself does not hide these things, therefore man should not. Now we have shown all through this book that DR implies that effort to "change nature" is a part of nature; thus the presumption of DR would be that, if the body untended creates problems of dirt, smell and indignity, then it behooves us to find solutions to these problems. But SM can give no reason why we should have to "rectify" reality thus; and SMR declares it would not count if we did. This then is what is really behind modern "dirtiness;" people pride themselves on being "honest," "free," when they ostentatiously drop Puritanical prudery. They are proving themselves to be "regular guys" when they show they can tell dirty jokes that top those of the most lost slum delinquent. They are being "realists" when they refuse to hope for or dream of the possible beauty and attractiveness that might be created in the body, and force themselves to dwell on its sores, freaks and faeces instead.

Now I do not mean to argue that the Puritan reaction to absolute concealment of the body was the ideal attitude; or that the movement toward greater frankness and acceptance was not justified in a certain respect. Obviously the Puritan attitude came close enough to SMR in considering the body essentially dirty and not really a meaningful part of the divine plan. Notice that this implies that the ordinary modern "free" person, comfortably telling his dirty jokes, is actually not a whit less disdainful of the body than the Puritan prude. He merely imagines himself more toughly honest when he faces up to, frankly looks upon the dirtiness rather than hiding it as the Puritan did. Neither view makes any progress toward grasping the true significance and wonder of the body to which all reverence is due.

Recourses of SM: The romantic attitude toward the body was a paradoxical one. Believing in man's natural goodness, romantics tried to believe in the natural goodness and beauty of the body too. Love reached heights of idealistic glory, but had to be carefully confined to the spiritual and formal aspects of the lovemate. The spiritual grandeur and ideal beauty of human beings was the constant theme. At the same time, there was the accompanying phenomenon of extreme sexual shame, bodily concealment, keeping the animal functions of the body behind the scene. The romantic glorification of man stopped short of including the "insides" of his body, which imposed a heavy strain on the mind. Man's dignity was juxtaposed to the nastiness of certain aspects of him. The conflict waxed acute in the familiar Victorian attitude, and most intense at the point of sex, where the grandest of spiritual experiences insists on being intimately tied to the most blatant operations of the animal body. Thus it was not man in his immediate and real being that was felt noble

308

and holy; but a vague conception of him purified in the direction of spirituality. And it was this view in particular, which in being disappointed, produced the current plunge back into SMR's exaggeration of the unromantic aspects of bodily life.

What then can fully dynamic thinking do for our attitude toward the body?

SM with DR.

Findings of DR: First, it is important to see that DR does not at all deny the reality of bodies, of their parts, of their waste products, of their mechanical aspects. In fact, it insists upon the concreteness of reality and of its particular structures more fully, if possible, than SMR; always understanding the absolute necessity of bodily structure for process. But, of course, the newer organismic science and philosophy, while retaining a vivid awareness of the concrete parts which have been analyzed in man, refuses to allow reductive statements that man in his functioning wholeness is no more than the aggregate of these parts. Man is what he is and not an itemization of glands and chemicals.

On the other hand, that he has a definite structure is not forgotten. His every idea and emotion is conceded to be based on laboriously wrought molecular and cellular structures. He is a system of channels and limitations which, in excluding formless potentiality, permits definite activity. The newer science is no more inclined than the older to suppose that an unstructured spirit exists independently of this body merely governing it externally. Man's thoughts are not an inevitable set of universals planted in him independently of particular experiences, but are such thoughts as result from his being a hand-eye-minded creature, being bisexual, not having wings, etc. We are impressed that our flights of imagination have as their basis a special pattern of nerves and muscles that was obliged to arrange itself in space with the most toilsome ingenuity in order to keep from getting hopelessly tangled up. This world of hard-wrought shapes is too real to be ignored and relegated to the realm of illusion. How should illusion produce the careful moldings and complexity of parts that make the voice and ear and thought?

It takes a peculiar wide-awakeness to become surprised at that most obvious fact of our consciousness: that our personal selves are attached to a mechanism whose shape has no universal necessity about it but is really strangely arbitrary. We eat and we communicate with our fellows by means of a single complex apparatus of mouth and throat, but it is by no necessary logic that these two functions should be so joined. Our hands have no simple, obvious, symmetrical shape. Most people, if they experience this surprise at all, may experience it in connection with the uro-genital apparatus, since that is not so ubiquitously in view as the hands or mouth, and besides particularly forces our awareness of its mechanical aspect; it also performs functions somewhat more remote from the immediately personal than other bodily structures. Why should what SM-SIR thinks of as personal souls require to have such tubings, syringes, bladders, hydraulics as this attached to them? And the logical unrelatedness of the two functions served by the uro-genital structure is particularly insistent. The questioning that may arise in this case is also of course peculiar in being more accompanied by the ambiguous feelings of prurience and disdain mentioned above.

But if these examples do not waken the surprise, how about the fact that the brain, which SM might assume should be the most spiritual part of us, is threaded through with blood vessels? Why should *thought* be mixed up with *blood?*

The structures and functions of the body are classified in various ways, but we might list the main ones in the following groups, roughly following the M-S-I-R-C-P sequence.

A. The brain as center of feeling.

B. All tissues of the body which can be depleted or fatigued or strained in any way so as to give rise to "needs." This would include preeminently parts of the alimentary system; but also sensory tissues, muscles, sexual parts, etc., insofar as they prompt desires for other states. We cannot quite consider this class identical with "internal organs" because "external senses" can also be in states of fatigue or boredom regardless of their relation to external objects.

C. The external sense organs in their aspect of receiving stimuli from external objects to aid the search for the wherewithal to satisfy the need feelings of # B.

D. The nervous system and such parts of the glandular and chemical systems as are involved in integration of the preceding classes with one another and with the following classes. Includes the brain as *integrator.*

E. The bone, muscle and gland systems in their aspect as

310

responding to all the preceding so as to accomplish what needs to be done to procure and use the objects that will bring satisfaction. (The muscles also have an aspect # B as prompting need feelings; and the glandular system has aspects under # D and # F below.)

F. All parts of the body in their aspect of being fulfilled or consummated.

1. The digestive and circulatory systems considered as prior users of what has been secured under # E, satisfying basic needs of # B. Includes the sustenance, tissue-building and repair which must be accomplished before the following consummations can exist.

2. The remaining tissues of the body, including the brain, as bases for other satisfactions of sensation, creative work, sex, etc. Of course, satisfaction can be felt anywhere in this sequence from # C on whenever integrations of any kind take place, however preparatory they may be as "means" to more ultimate integrations or resolutions.

G. The whole body and brain in their aspect of growth and preservation of accomplishment and embodiment of personality.

H. The reproductive system in its aspect of creating new organisms. (Its aspect as supplying satisfaction to the individual is in # F2.) This system, of course, involves structures from all the preceding classes.

But after listing all these parts of the body, our more central concern remains the mystery of our having bodies at all; or, more precisely, granting that we have bodies, that they should be so peculiarly special, that out of all the kinds and shapes of bodies we might have had, it is just this one arbitrary shape that we are consigned to and no other. Can this peculiarly concocted apparatus be what cosmic purpose would have had to create in the interests of meaningfulness? Is there some reason why Universal Mind might have had to settle upon some particular invented structure?

Comparison of SM and DR: As far as the author can see, most students of anatomy, physiology, medicine, physiological psychology, are kept, by an unconscious fixation upon SM, from having much experience of mystical appreciation of the meaning, the *why* of the body. It is assumed that if they cannot dissect

311

out SM's "soul" as a definite entity, then there is no other way for a God to reveal His concern with bodily man. Glandular, nervous, pharmaceutical research goes on with always strong implications that each new specific cause or cure reduces by so much any place for a divine creator's activity. We hear excited reports on single causes — viruses, chemicals, etc. — for cancer, schizophrenia, etc.; and search for specific drugs which will enforce cures of anything from bodily measles to spiritual malaise. A psychiatric group dismayedly concedes that their science's assumption that *personal understanding* is involved in mental cure has been badly shaken as mere chemicals seem to be saving souls today. How much more must the devotees of prayer be concerned then! All this amenability of the body to man's efforts and to natural influences is taken as a proof of the non-existence of spiritual reality and purpose; for this would act, it is assumed with SM, only as an external essence unrelated to concrete energies.

Now DR's conception of the whole-part relationship does allow a place for partial causes, and for administration of part-ingredients to influence the field-energies of the whole organism. For the wonder drug, LSD, for instance, to be able to stimulate memory and insight to the hastening of mental adjustment, or for penicillin to be able to enhance the body's battle against microorganisms is not unexpected. But DR would also have predicted what the theorists of LSD and even of sulfa drugs and penicillin have recently confessed to be true of their wonder-chemicals: that they do not enforce cure by themselves, but that internal, synthesizing effort and thought on the part of the patient is still needed to bring mental health; while a bad state of mind can keep even penicillin from bringing bodily health. All the causes and drugs take their place under DR's concept of "ingredients" in the holistic pattern-building, but the pattern-building is the final locus of significant reality and value.

SM, however, does not imply even this much place for the part causes and cures. And so the scientists continue to believe that their discoveries invalidate cosmic purpose, while SM religionists, like the Christian Scientists, still hanker for divine cure which shall be utterly independent of all specific natural processes and human efforts whatever.

I believe it would be fair, too, to say that most devotees of the SM-DR philosophies — the pragmatists, existentialists, positivists, etc. — continue with the profane attitudes toward the body that result from SM's failure to imply its meaningful requirement. The smarty, wise-cracking customs permeate the representatives of these schools known to the author, at any rate. I know of no attempt like the present one to find grounds for the reverent attitude toward the body by means of whatever creative efforts, reticences and decencies may prove useful for the task.

How will DM make us feel about the body?

DM with DR:

Implications of DM and Correspondence to DR: We have already worked out the derivation of individual creatures, structures, parts from the idea of process in Chapter VIII; and the idea of process was of course derived in turn from the dynamic idea of value. It remains to try to convey a more vivid impression of how this may affect our feelings, our ability to grasp emotionally the wondrous meaning of man as structure.

We understand, then, that dynamic good requires both individuality — the separated centers of activity that are to interact with one another; and that the individuals should be structured out of parts, containing channels of limitations which concentrate forces into accomplishments and save them from undulating in futile homogeneity. Considering the human body in this way, Whitehead finds two ways in which it is necessary: feeling and expression. Concerning the latter he says, "The Human Body is that region of the world which is the primary field of human expression."[15] For example, anger issues into bodily excitements which are publicized in words and gestures. This idea of the meaning of the body, as a means of expression, is sufficiently familiar. The Bible, the Greeks, St. Paul are all inclined to think of the body in this aspect only: as a tool for the spirit to use in expressing its deeds — a rather poor tool at that. The spirit has an existence of its own in addition to that of the body, which it simply manipulates.

But the body is also necessary for feeling, that is for the very existence of the spirit. For "spiritual" experience of value can only exist within process which can only exist in structure.

. . . the universe is a process of attaining instances of definite experience out of its own elements. . . . Accordingly any given instance of experience is only possible so far as the antecedent facts permit. For they are required in order to constitute it. . . . The limitations are the opportunities.[16]

Here we see the logical connection between the idea of experience of value and the necessity of limited definiteness. The body is a collection of "antecedent facts" which supply the material or data of new experience; these data must include dissatisfaction, tension or pain, too. But besides holding in itself the unresolved data, the body also provides the channels and mechanisms through which the process of resolving them can operate. The body, then, is not merely an external tool for expressing the spirit. It is necessary for the very making of the spirit in the first place.

Now what can be said about the deduction of the body in its specific detail from dynamic value? We can see that some sort of structure is required; but can we see why it is this particular structure with its particular group of felt functions instead of any other? Well, it seems easy enough to deduce the general list of structures under DR (p. 310 f.). They each follow from the mental functions (p. 298 f.) which were already deduced (p. 300). But the precise, specific nature and shape of the structure and function seem to the author at least, to be ineluctably contingent.

A. The brain structure is surely the center of feeling which is required to feel the strains and resolutions among the part energies. But why should it be necessarily the odd horse-shoe-crab-shaped thing that it is, with this crease here and that bulb there?

B. The depleted tissues: that the body should contain a variety of tissues that can supply needs, or felt strains and discomforts, is easily deducible — from the notion of Variety (# 2.7 p. 55), and of Disorder (# 2.41, p. 54). But I don't see that we can explain why the body supplies just the particular qualitative needs that it does: the four basic elements of taste, the particular quality of thirst based in desiccated mucous membranes, the special feeling of cramped leg muscles, etc. Of course these feelings relate to the kinds of objects the earthly environment happens to provide — the body has arranged to use and enjoy the chemicals, light rays, types of surface, movable objects which are "there." But why, then, should just those particular kinds of objects be provided? We can explain why *some* sort of materials must be provided,

314

but not why the particular ones that are. Whitehead always suggests the possibility of other universes built on other ingredients and other laws. But we are touching on the topic of the next chapter concerning environment.

Granting what our particular environment does happen to supply, we can then see that the body develops to suit. It develops seeing and hearing apparatuses, for instance, to make use of the sound and light waves that exist. Granted their existence, the theory of dynamic value can then explain why they begin by feeling disorder in their area of phenomena; can go through a process of unscrambling and ordering; can feel emerging order within the light or sound situation and convey enjoyment of it.

But the felt needs of hunger, thirst and breathing seem peculiarly significant. Why does the thinking man have to have a stomach and the other supposedly less elevated parts of his body dealing with self-maintenance? Why is he obliged to incorporate parts of the environment within himself or die? Why can't he just be the contemplating mind, realizing the "higher" values of art and thought, that Plato wanted him to be? Well, for one thing, the whole eating process can be understood as a source of a whole gamut of qualities of feeling, and DM can always explain increased variety of qualities. The digestive system is a repeating provider of one kind of the tension and pain that are necessary prerequisites of good feeling. But this particular process of hunger, eating, and digestion seems especially important as a kind of basic guarantee that the organism will remain in the striving process that value requires. It is having to feed ourselves that gives real seriousness to life and forces it to be something more than frivolous play. A large portion of the millions of value experiences, including many of the more profound ones of morality and compassion, would have no scope if men could never fall into desperate hunger and risk of life.

We catch a hint here, too, why man's brain — to SM's confounding — has to be a self-feeding, self-repairing thinkery, with a blood system second in complexity only to its nerve pattern itself. For the brain is part of an organism with a job of self-preservation to do.

If we understand why we must be creatures with wants who must keep building themselves from environmental materials, we may then move toward the deduction of the other parts of the organism. C, the external sense organs, obviously now arise to

315

search for the needed environmental objects. D, the integrative system, is easy to deduce from the concept of "organizing process" itself (# 2.0 and 2.1, p. 53 f.). E, the motor system, is simply understood as necessary for moving the organism over to the relevant objects. F, the digestive and circulatory systems and other consummatory tissues, come from # 2.52, p. 54. G, the growth of individual organisms is obviously related to # 2.6, p. 55 "increasing complexity." H, reproduction, together with the necessity of death, are deducible from the principle of finiteness itself (Chapter VIII and this chapter, p. 314) and will be discussed more thoroughly in Chapter XVIII on evil and death.

Thus dynamic value shows us why man must be finite and why he has a bodily structure; but, as I have confessed, I do not see that we can say that he must have only the particular *kind* of structure that he happens to have. Of course, biologists do have significant points to offer concerning certain superiorities our body does possess: how bi-lateral symmetry, specialization of the head end, support on the hind appendages leaving the fore appendages free, the opposable thumb, etc., are all "improvements" upon former bodies. Schrödinger has an interesting statement of requiredness concerning the size of the body: how the statistical nature of the sub-atomic particles requires aggregations of about the magnitude of our bodies before necessary regularities of function can be attained. All this is relevant, yet does not dispose of that feeling of surprise at the arbitrariness of our shape.

One very significant point about the body was that mentioned under DR: how the same part or structure is often used for two or more tasks which may not have any close relationship at all: the mouth cavity for eating and speaking; the uro-genital for elimination and reproduction; the rib cage for breathing and for anchoring the arm muscles, etc. What we see here are astounding instances of "killing several birds with one stone," which, we shall argue in Part IV is of the essence of value experience: the combining and organizing of factors in efficient, harmonious ways. It is in this respect that the body is "beautiful," concentrating a maximum of possible experience or feelings into a minimum of parts, which manage to be aesthetically balanced besides.

Actually, I think the dynamic logic can be shown to imply the very contingency of the body. For finiteness implies that we leave the realm of limitless possibilities and adopt something in particular. This particular will have to be, in a sense, arbitrary, though

316

we can go on to make statements about its adequacy and efficiency in accomplishing its varied duties. The human creature is an organism that exhibits abilities to function in this kind of terrestrial environment, to utilize light and sound vibrations, air and water, to reproduce itself, to live socially, etc. Its success in organizing itself for these multiple functions can assuredly be deemed stupendous and wonderful.

Students sometimes faint when they are initiated into the procedures of the operating room; a reaction of disillusionment is common upon the first encounter with the biological analysis of the body. It comes as a shock to discover the chemicals whose flow is experienced as sexual passion; the nerve pathways in the brain to which willing and thinking are assigned. The decision to move an arm can be located in a bit of matter in the cerebrum; kindness is expressed by a strange pattern of facial muscles. We are accustomed to believing that man should be a spirit, a sacred, untouchable entity which ought to be beyond the reach of analysis. But the laboratories break creatures up into their parts, and the students cannot but ridicule the members, made meaningless by their disarray. The analysis inflicts a myopia on the student, crippling his imaginative grasp of the miracle which these parts composed when they were in the whole.

But with further study and synthesizing meditation, men can recover from this disillusionment. They can regain an appreciation of the whole organism in all its breath-taking complexity, and they end with a more tremendous awe than the old doctrine of disembodied spirit inspired. Wonder increases that man's mysterious self should possess this one shape; that his voice should issue from vibrating flesh and flexible sound-chamber; that his eye is a round hollow marble pulled about by tiny strings; that within his skull churn electrical currents to correspond with his every intention, while other currents of blood intricately feed his thought. Even the formerly defiling excreta can now be accepted as playing a metaphysically meaningful part. So one returns from analytical curiosity to synthetic appreciation of man as a whole, infinitely more than a machine. He is a marvelous structure devised for the embodiment of meaningful experience.

3. The Relationship between Mind-Self and Body.

The traditional collection of Mind-Body theories usually make up an extended chapter in philosophy. However, since we have expanded on the concepts of Mind and Body separately above, there is not a great deal left to be said under the present topic. We will merely distribute the conventional theories according to our positions with a few comments.

SM with SIR:

Implications of SM: Psychical Monism. We have already explained why SM does not imply the existence of material body at all, and would expect mind to be the only Existent. Therefore there would need to be no theory of mind-body relationship.

Adjustment of SIR: The monist adjustment, of course, forcibly conforms itself to SM's implications by dint of denying the existence of the seemingly existing matter and considering all material things, including the body, to be appearance only. Berkeley was the first modern thinker to revive this way of thinking and there are later idealistic philosophers who are ready to defend it: Lotze, von Hartmann, Paulsen, C.A. Strong, etc. The view is variously called mentalism, spiritualism, subjective idealism, etc.

The dualistic adjustment, in admitting the existence of both mind and matter, must then provide some theory of their relationship. There are two main theories:

Interactionism. This is probably the most popular of all views of mind and body. It is presumably the usual view of the ordinary man, and seems to have been assumed by men from the earliest times. The body seems so obviously a material thing; and one's inner consciousness seems so obviously different from it that the notion of the two quite different entities mutually affecting one another has been normal from the earliest time. Descartes gave the view a philosophical presentation at the beginning of modern philosophy, stating that his mental substance, immaterial and consisting of pure thinking, could cause events in his material substance, and vice versa. This seemed to fit the facts: for it was obvious that by thinking and willing we could make things happen in our bodies; and that accidents and diseases in the body could make our minds unconscious or sluggish, drugs operating on the body could produce strange mental experiences, and injuries to the brain (which belongs on the body side) had distinct effects upon our mental life.

But from the point of view of science there were insuperable difficulties for the theory, especially its apparently running afoul of the law of conservation of matter and energy. If the phenomena in the material realm were completely accounted for by this law, it seemed impossible to suppose the mental realm could do any causing of material events without unbalancing the equations for material processes by introducing or subtracting energy of some sort. But no sign of such extraneous energy changes could be detected by the usual measures applied to the material realm.

And in any case, the interactionists offered no explanation of how two such entirely disparate substances could act on each other. How could pure thought act on physical stuff? Descartes tried to answer this by offering the pineal gland, to which no other use had as yet been assigned, as the spot where the mysterious transaction took place. Later physiology, of course, proved this impossible.

Parallelism. Leibniz saw no way out of this dilemma, assuming we must accept dualism, than to suppose the two realms, mental and material, always produced simultaneous effects, but that there was no causal relationship between them. Whenever something happened in the body a corresponding something happened in the mind, but only because God had sent the two realms off in a "preëstablished harmony." They would be like two synchronous clocks which always ring at the same time, but not because one directly causes the other to; only because they happen to have been wound up and set running in time with each other. Thus there is no conflict with the law of conservation of energy in either realm.

Obviously parallelism is only a desperate effort to make dualism work; it does not offer the least hint why the two realms should need to exist, and why the mental realm would not be enough by itself.

The double-aspect theory. Spinoza's theory seems to be an effort to combine the monist and dualist theories; and it is a question whether it should come under SIR or SMR, since we know Spinoza as a mechanistic determinist in many aspects of his thought. However, he posits an unknown *substance* (and his use of this word keeps his theory from going under DR) which has both an external, objective aspect, and an internal, subjective one. All things are made of this substance and therefore have both aspects. The substance itself becomes Spinoza's God, who is thus present in all things in a pantheistic sense. This solution obviates the difficulty as to how two completely different substances can interact, and preserves the law of conservation of energy. But critics feel it is a verbal solution only, not really explaining how the inner, mental aspect can seem to operate teleologically and purposively, while the outer, physical aspect seems to obey the laws of mechanics.

SM with SMR.

Findings of SMR: Epiphenomenalism. From what we have said under SMR for Mind and Body, it is obvious that SMR can only consider mind an unreal, or at least inefficacious something without any causative power over matter; and that all causation must emanate from matter and body only. The mind is at best a "shadow" of matter, which is the exact meaning of "epiphenomenon." Hobbes, Hume and the Behaviorists all assume this theory, though the name was first used by Thomas Huxley.

Contradiction to SM: As usual, SMR's theory is the exact opposite of SM's implications: instead of psychical monism we have a material monism.

SM with DR.

Findings of DR: In discussing Hobbes under #1, we touched on the main weakness of SMR's material monism: its flying in the face of its own rule of empiricism when it either denies the existence of what is plainly experienced: subjective, qualitative feeling; or else tries to redefine it by a verbal twist as "matter in motion." We have also explained how DR recognizes this qualitative experience as real.

All theories under DR are perhaps double-aspect theories in a sense, taking Energy, rather than "substance" or "matter" as the single basic reality, and assuming that Mind has to do with a more fluid form of this energy, and body with rigid or semi-rigid states of it. On this basis we have two possibilities:

The Emergent Theory. According to this approach, Mind would appear some time subsequently to the first synthetic organizations of energy; only at a certain level of organization could we begin to speak of Mind. The way of thinking would be the same as we have discussed in the preceding chapter under the emergent theory of Life — Mind being conventionally agreed upon and defined as applying only to certain higher levels in the hierarchy of organisms, though we would realize that there would be no sharp and definite boundary in Nature itself where Mind would be supposed suddenly to emerge. Once it has emerged, it would be what we have already discussed under #1 above as the functional and holistic theory of Mind-Self.

Pan-Psychism. The other possibility would be to assume with Whitehead, Laird, Hartshorne and others, that the subjective aspect is present in all energy, whatever its level of organization, and that what we have is a continuously increasing complexity of subjective experience (as well as of external structure) from atom up to man and beyond. For some it seems logically necessary to conclude that if energy as organized in man has the inner, feeling aspect, then this aspect must be native to energy in its essence; that it is contradictory to suppose that the absolutely non-mental could produce the mental; that is, that the effect could contain more than the cause. But for the Emergentists this does not seem contradictory, and Mind takes its place along with all the other emergents as merely the last or highest emergent. If the characteristics of water emerge at the molecular level, and reproduction at the virus level, and learning at the protozoa level, etc., why not Mind at the animal level?

I am impressed, however, with Hartshorne's argument that Mind cannot be considered as merely a parallel to other emergents:

> . . . I am unimpressed by the fashionable notion that mind has emerged from mere matter. First show me the mere matter. . . . It is not that particular qualities, including qualities of feeling and thinking, cannot emerge unpredictably, or be created. But since any quality, to be known, must become a quality of experience in some form, sensory or affective, mind as such cannot be a mere species of quality; rather, it is the universal correlate of quality and of quantity as well. It follows that the analogy between any known instance of emergence and the alleged emergence of mind is tenuous in the extreme. . . . Starting with the notions of structure and process as involving an essential aspect of creativity or novelty, we can predict that new structures will keep arising, the novelty varying in degree or extent. However, that something which is not merely spatio-temporary configuration, but the enjoyment, awareness, of configuration, should arise, this is

on the premises not only unpredictable, it cannot even be stated without introducing a whole new language. . . .

Many will say, you forget that mind has been shown to be simply structure and behavior; hence the emergence of mind is merely the appearance of somewhat new modes of behavior. Here is a nice dilemma. If mind is just behavior, then there is no emergence of mind from mere matter, there is only mere matter, though sometimes it is more complex, and moves about and transforms its shapes in especially elaborate and intricate ways. . . . The other horn of the dilemma is, mind is not merely behavior; but then there is simply no analogy at all between its alleged emergence and any established case.[17]

In either case, Mind is not thought of as a second, entirely different substance added to matter. It is rather a certain way in which energy functions. Or at least, the Body is known to be composed of energy in certain patterns of organization, and for it to "feed into" the Brain its various ingredients, and for the Brain to be able to feel these ingredients as a field of energy does not require a dualistic mode of explanation. The Mind is not here thought of as distinct from the body, and the law of conservation of energy is thus not contravened.

A good formulation of the relation between mental experience and bodily causes is Köhler's.[18] He begins with an analysis of "requiredness," that is, our subjective experience from the inside of meaningful connections between things, of oughtness, rightness, fittingness. We distinguish between harmonious and awkward lines in art, between right and wrong behavior. But behavioristic, mechanistic psychology, confined to the idea of isolated causes enforcing effects, has been unable to find in its theory of causes anything like these phenomenological convictions. Its necessitarianism precludes anything like "oughtness." But the field theory of physical forces in elastic contact, issuing in vectors and patterns, has at least an *isomorphic* correspondence to ideas of oughtness. Köhler means by this term that although we cannot establish by empirical method that a feeling of requiredness is actually present inside a physical or nervous process which we observe from the outside, still we can recognize a parallelism in their respective form and sequence. We experience thoughts combining together to establish a decision we consider right. In physics and neurology

322

we now discern dynamic self-distribution, where an aggregate of forces strains toward orderly patterns. Köhler asks whether this analogy is not convincing enough to permit the belief that brain, on the matter side, is after all capable of implementing purposive mind, on the idea side. Our sense of requiredness would then be the inner feeling of those events that science studies from the outside. Physical forces and mental experiences of purposing, striving and resolving, then, would be two aspects of one series of energy events, isomorphic with each other.

Comparison with SM: The difference between DR's findings and SM's expectations are obvious and will be left to the student to work out in detail if desired.

DM with DR:

Implications of DM and Correspondence to DR: For the mind to be such a thing as can focus and feel the processes of the body in togetherness is what DM obviously requires. Our deductions of the necessity of a feeler, and of a structure of ingredients and processes under the preceding headings leave nothing further to work out in this place.

It has seemed to the author that the above deductions of the necessity of finite, structured, feeling organisms belong logically prior to the deductions of the environmental realities: the immediate environment, world, universe, Space and Time. Therefore these latter matters must come last in our treatment of the nature of Reality. And so we move to a final chapter under this division.

323

CHAPTER XIII

THE ENVIRONING WORLD

In the preceding chapters we have dealt with some of the most basic aspects of Physics, Chemistry, Biology and Psychology in our ontological project of understanding the fundamental nature and possible purposiveness of reality. There remain some ontological questions related to the remaining sciences, sometimes called "mixed" physical sciences, of Geology and Astronomy; and the sciences that connect physical and biological phenomena, Geography and Ecology. We might say that these all deal with the environment within which purposive creatures are placed, and they raise the fundamental question whether this "inanimate" part of the universe is of a nature that could be deduced as required by an idea of value.

We do not have space for more than a few sample features of these subjects, and the present chapter will consist mainly of hints as to the direction further philosophizing might take.

Our course of thought in this Part III has in general been moving in the direction of larger and larger "organisms," starting with sub-atomic particles and atoms in Chapter VIII and moving up the hierarchy of organisms to man. In this chapter we could think of ourselves as moving in the direction of larger and larger *aggregates* of *simpler* organisms (atoms and molecules), as they come to constitute the larger and larger chunks of "matter" in individual rocks, portions of soil, bodies of water, etc., then in the earth and other planets as a whole, then in stars and solar systems, galaxies, super-galaxies and universe in toto.

Thus we will begin with questions relating to geology and geography, having to do with the earth as man's most immediate environment.

1. The Earth
SM with SIR.

Implications of SM: In our discussion of Means, in Chapter IX, we saw that if SM grants a place for means at all (which it does not in strictest logic) it expects a world of pre-planned means perfectly adapted without excess or deficiency to human and divine purposes. It also implies, not a world of constant development and change, but one that is laid out in the first moment in some inevitable, proper plan for all time. The Garden of Eden story tells of an environment of plants and animals perfectly adapted to the needs of life and man. All earlier conceptions of the world proposed a much simpler and more symmetrical arrangement than was ever found, as we see in any ancient map. The early Jewish conception was of a simple flat land area surrounded by a band of sea; with a hemispherical bowl of sky above it, supposed to be solid, the "firmament," which kept the waters above the earth from deluging it except when it let the water through the star-holes as rain. Of course, once again the story in Genesis is not completely static, It says that the first thing God created was a "void" (Gen. 1:2) and that afterwards he took the necessary steps to shape things up by separating the water from the land, creating the firmament, etc. This implies some process of creative adjustment during the first few days of creative activity. But presumably he soon got the world into its necessary form, after which, if he did the expert job SM implies, it should remain fixed.

Adjustments of SIR: As usual, the existence of earthly and climatic catastrophes has to be recognized: earthquakes, volcanoes, deserts, droughts, ocean storms, etc., etc. These are part of the problem of evil and will be further discussed in Chapter XVIII. We will only remark here that SIR strives to preserve by any means available its belief in the divine purposiveness of the earthly environment, its special providentiality, that "God's in his heaven and all's right with the world." One of its tacks often has been to assume that all environmental catastrophes come as specific punishment for some definite sin or crime by a human individual or group. Certain devotees of SIR can still be found to populate the entire environment with quasi-personal forces, demons, imps, etc., who see to it that every tidal wave, every sunny day, every gold deposit eventuates in proper relation to divine plans and human deserts.

On the other hand SIR may recognize with the Bible that "the rain falls on the just and the unjust"; but then most traditional religions expected whatever was not rightly portioned in this life to be made up for in the next. And of course, most of them expect environmental factors to be influenced by prayer. This would mean going so far toward a dynamic view as to believe that God has not got everything settled in His mind already, but in some respects waits to see whether man's pleading accompanies sufficient devoutness to deserve a special adaptation of the environment to his needs. The whole belief in miracles would be based on this presupposition, and indeed is a main aspect of SIR's theory of the environment. On the other hand, stricter interpretations, such as Calvin's, might doubt whether the Omnipotent would allow that much contingency, and might advise that the safest kind of prayer is "Not my will but thine be done."

Nor does SIR usually suspect that the earth continuously evolves through infinities of time. It was still capable of believing, with Bishop Usher, that God created it instantly in the year 4004 B. C. And, since the main era of SIR came before the Age of Exploration, we may suppose too that it was not as aware of the arbitrariness of the world map as later ages were.

SM with SMR.

Findings of SMR: We noted in Chapter XI that Darwin's hard-boiled theory of survival shocked many people and created great resistance to its conclusions. Another reason why his theory of evolution was resisted was its appearing to confirm SMR's contention that, far from everything in the world being a divinely created means to some intelligible purpose, as SM-SIR believed, absolutely nothing had been so created. Of course, mechanism had always implied that all events were "pushed from behind" and thus nothing could ever be shaped according to any future purpose. But in the realm of Biology and life, this notion seemed to contradict plain experience so violently that there, at least, it appeared positive that mechanism was an insufficient principle of explanation. Animal structures were plainly "designed" to enable certain purposes to be achieved; the whole environment of the earth was clearly designed for the support of the animals; and both in turn for the support of man.

But now the theory of evolution provided a way of understanding how, given any kind of environment that "accidentally" happened to exist on a planet, animal forms might evolve by accidental mutations and unplanned survival of the fittest, for whom this environment would then appear to be "adapted." Most mutations were useless and the possessor and his offspring died out. Rare mutations were accidentally adapted to the conditions and allowed the possessor to survive. Man got an efficient hand, or a big brain, not because he or a God envisioned them and strove for them, but because some ancestor sprang from the womb with just such an accidentally mutated hand or brain, and the peculiar kind of forested earth then happening to exist enabled him and his offspring to flourish.

As for earthly catastrophes, they become for SMR merely the necessary results of impersonal causes. And once one reluctantly gives up the faith that all events relate to human desert, it is easy enough to find innumerable instances where arbitrariness rather than providence appears to be the case. It happened that the earthquake and tidal wave which destroyed Lisbon in 1755 occurred just when European thinkers had been enough primed by SMR's philosophy to entertain the thesis that it might have been merely accidental, as far as human deserts were concerned. Probably the main discussion between the defenders of SIR and SMR took place in that connection, with the most familiar record of it for modern readers to be found in Voltaire's *Candide,* where he ridicules some Inquisitors who assumed there must be specific human criminals around Lisbon whom God wished to punish, though the Inquisitors do not ask why He should kill thousands of innocents in the process, unless all inhabitants be assumed guilty enough via original sin.

For SMR, then, attempting to influence rain storms, fire and earthquake by prayer is the height of foolishness. And the attempt to argue that there is a God who designed this environment in precisely the form that is required for His good purpose is an utterly lost cause. The theory of miracles was strenuously fought by SMR's zeal for an absolutely law-abiding universe.

Under SMR also were made the first discoveries of the true age of the earth, and the first presumption, with the geologist Lyell, that the earth followed orderly laws of change and evolution.

The contradiction between these billions of years and the Bible's thousands was one of the sharper blows to traditional beliefs.

Finally, we may point to the aspect so much reinforced by early explorations: the utter arbitrariness of the world's map, with continents, oceans, islands strewn at random over its surface; with dead polar regions, useless expanses of salt water far exceeding land surfaces, deserts exceeding arable land, species dying out, glaciers wiping out forests, etc. Nothing could seem more miscellaneous and accidental to minds imbued with SM's expectations.

Recourses to SM: Here we will only mention as one example, Hegel's effort to interpret the whole of the universe and earth as the gradual clarification of the thought processes of the Absolute. Hegel has, in fact, much help for DR's similar project, without however, enough emphasis on the felt process as such, nor on the concrete nature of the compositional process and its requirement of ingredients to be incorporated into organic structures.

More popular evidences of the nostalgia for SM-SIR are the numerous sectarians to-day who still desperately and futilely deny the geological findings, still prefer praying for rain to seeding clouds, criticize explorers as "daredevils" venturing where God never meant man to go.

SM with DR.

Findings of DR: In this field, by and large DR accepts SMR's findings. It seems more difficult to argue here that the larger "aggregates of organisms," i.e. chunks of "matter" as such, should be reconceived in organismic terms; that earthly geological processes, for instance, follow any internal, subjective aim of their own. Even Whitehead, though he argues that all such chunks of matter ultimately consist of small organisms repeating their forms of process for long stretches of time, does not argue that the chunk as such is a "living" unity in any sense; or that the earth itself is an organism living out its own aims.

DR must accept the possibility of arbitrary accidents in the environment (that is, arbitrary from the human point of view; law abiding enough as to physical laws). It of course accepts the theory of long ages of constant change in the earth. And it cannot deny the miscellaneousness of the terrestrial map.

Comparison with SM: It is already clear that this picture is not what a cosmic mind aiming at static value could have intended. But is it entirely unthinkable that it might be what a cosmic mind aiming at dynamic value might have intended?

DM with DR.

Implications of DM and Correspondence to DR: The deduction of the necessity of the environment from dynamic value would seem to have to follow that of the necessity of structured organisms. Thus the present chapter must follow the preceding. It is from our conception of a feeling, structured organism which must engage in creative processes utilizing additional energies or objects from outside of itself in satisfying its needs and building itself up, that we get to the necessity of an environment. If the creatures must incorporate new ingredients into their experience, then there must be an environment to supply the ingredients. And if the creatures' zestful value experience requires that they solve real problems, create real novelties, experience real variety, then the environment must be not entirely predictable, but provide a maximum of problems to solve, surprises to enjoy, variety to explore; yet also provide the possibility of accomplishment. The lawfulness of nature could be understood as necessary so that feeling creatures would not be hopelessly engulfed in chaos and quite unable to find the experience of building order. But the ineliminable vagueness of Nature, and its sudden changes and catastrophes would also be required as an eternal supply of problems. If the earth had been entirely symmetrical, so that some simple key to its arrangement could be found, and all its problems immediately understood, SM might have thought this desirable, but DM is clear that it would have left man suffocating with ennui.

This thought opens the way to answering the prevalent objections to the earth's not being that neatly right creation that medieval man expected it to be. DM sees no reason why oceans should not cover as much of the earth's surface as they wish, for learning how to sail the great expanses can provide profundity of feeling in having conquered a difficult environmental hazard. The crookedness of coast lines only provides the more scope for exploration. It is quite possible to rejoice in the existence of deserts as guaranteeing wide open spaces for those who like room, and as inspiring unique religious feelings within its dwellers. Also, learning how to irrigate deserts is an interesting problem many have enjoyed hugely. There are some who fear that men will learn how to irrigate them only too well, removing one barrier to overcrowding.

As for the problem of the evils, destructions and agonies this environment can cause for its evolved offspring, we will find in the chapter on evil that much can be said to rationalize them. Already we can see that adventurous souls, the greater human spirits, would object strenuously if there were no risk on earth, no challenge. There are some who would rather that tornadoes exist to fill us with awe and exciting dread, at the possible price of death, than that the weather should be unendingly tepid and safe. Only the half-alive, the hopelessly tame people, object to the earth's occasionally providing spectacle, terror and catastrophe.

Thus it seems we can understand some of these general features of our environment as necessary to provide a variety of puzzles and of the wherewithal to solve them. But as remarked in the preceding chapter, it seems doubtful that we can show why the environment should necessarily be what it specifically is. Why should earth be predominantly green rather than pink? Why should two-thirds of the globe be water and one-third land? This class of questions has no answer in terms of requirement as far as I can see. We may only be able to show that there must be *some* sort of environment to provide some sort of problems and materials. This one would be good enough to supply grist for dynamic value's mill.

On the other hand, some might wish to argue that we can go further in deducing the necessity of specific features of this particular environment. Biologists may some day have resources to show that this particular environing universe has some intrinsic superiority for value-production. Physical scientists may be ready to show "why" some of the physical laws must be just what they are for any possible value-producing world. For instance Schrödinger shows why size of electrons must bear the ratio it does to the size of biological organisms.

So the world as we find it is not necessarily different from what we would expect from dynamic good. But does this prove that a cosmic purpose has planned it for us? Is there a cosmic mind behind these blind upheavals of mountains, this inert downhill flow of water carving its interesting shapes, this growth of the planet by attracting cosmic dust? Well, we still get a strong impression of blind mechanism in these movements, and yet they turn out, as indicated, in an environment no one thoroughly imbued with the dynamic idea would necessarily complain about. How else, then, should a cosmic purpose go about preparing an interesting value-life? From this angle it seems impossible for the atheist to prove that there is some other way it should have been done.

DM and DR do not clearly restore to us that *personal* communion with brooks which were transformed nymphs, with trees that contained dryads, with winds thought to be God's breath, that SM-SIR sometimes had. We cannot exactly believe that there are purposive spirits in Nature responding to our spirits. But it may be that we can look upon the environment as *generally* planned for us by a Cosmic Spirit to use in our constructive experience. In this sense DR can think of the environment as a *means* to the evolution and sustenance of creatures in the sense we discussed in Ch. IX (p. 225 f.). Granting that what is required is an experimental creature seeing what it can do with what is given, we do not require anything more than the rather miscellaneous environment that is given, never too assured, always somewhat risky, not entirely predictable, though reasonably so. It is not preplanned in SM-SIR's sense, or in the old sense of specific providence. Yet, since all the organisms originally evolved from it, it tends on the whole to supply the sorts of things they need for life and growth, albeit without guarantee.

2. *The Universe.*
SM with SIR.

Implications of SM: Applying the same ideas suggested under the preceding topic to the universe, SM would expect it, too, to be a perfect, symmetrical, simple design, all exactly adapted to some preconceived plan of God's. And assuming that man's fate is the center of God's plan, then the universe would be centered around man. The most familiar specific example illustrating these expectations is the Ptolemaic astronomy upon which the medieval period based its beliefs, and which Dante took as the basic structure for the Divine Comedy. The interest is clearly in having the universe conform to some presumably inevitably right system of things. Dante is fascinated with the idea that God would make all things fit a proper, mystically necessary number scheme. The universe will naturally arrange itself in threes — the sacred trinitarian number — and fours, the perfect square, and sevens, the sum of three and four, and nines which is three threes, etc., etc. The Universe is symmetrically built up in seven spheres (the perfect form), and God surely has some mysterious purpose in having the three infra-solar planets (Moon, Mercury and Venus) and the three supra-solar ones (Mars, Jupiter and Saturn), together with the Sun add up to seven. This preoccupation with number symmetries of course goes back through Plato to Pythagoras and to pre-history.

The response of a medieval mind to Galileo's discovery of the satellites of Jupiter vividly reveals this static conviction of SM that God *must* have laid everything out in some fixed and perfect pattern:

> There are seven windows given to animals in the domicile of the head, through which the air is admitted to the tabernacle of the body, . . . two nostrils, two eyes, two ears, and a mouth. So in the heavens, as in a macrocosmus, there are two favorable stars, two unpropitious, two luminaries, and Mercury undecided and indifferent. From this and many other similarities in nature, such as the seven metals, etc., we gather that the number of planets is necessarily seven. Moreover, these satellites of Jupiter are invisible to the naked eye, and therefore can exercise no influence on the earth, and therefore would be useless, and therefore do not exist. . . . Now, if we increase the number of the planets, this whole and beautiful system falls to the ground.[1]

Adjustments of SIR: One modification upon SM's implications that the Ptolemaic astronomy makes is to admit that the spheres do move and revolve (in fixed patterns, however), though SM would have expected a motionless pattern of the heavens. The epicycles had to be added too, unwelcome though they were to SM's wish for simpler spheres. Other exceptional movements also had to be admitted, such as shooting stars, comets, etc. SIR as usual interprets these as specific acts of God designed to be signs of something of concern to human deserts. In fact, we might place the whole of astrology under SIR as the age-old effort to believe that the whole universe is centered upon the lives and destinies of individual men.

Randall mentions another amusing adjustment of *SIR*: how the

Aristotelians were so disturbed by discovering the moon's surface to be rough and pock-marked instead of perfectly spherical, that they resorted to supposing there must be some invisible crystalline material filling up the valleys and craters to make the sphere. Galileo responded to this insistence upon static perfection thus:

> I can listen only with the greatest repugnance when the quality of unchangeability is held up as something preëminent and complete in contrast to variability. I hold the earth for most distinguished exactly on account of the transformations which take place upon it.[2]

SM with SMR.

Findings of SMR: The Copernican, Galilean and Newtonian astronomy retained more of SM's belief in fixed perfections in this field of thought than in some of the other fields. Although Copernicus replaced the earth with the sun as center of the universe, he still, like a medieval man, wrote masses of material trying to find mystic meanings in the new arrangement of heavenly bodies. When Kepler replaced heavenly circles with ellipses, there was objection to the arbitrariness of the elliptical form, but Newton was glad to discover a beautifully simple law of gravitation which, in requiring ellipses, restored something of the old idea of a rationally planned heaven. So, we still have a beautifully lawful clock-work universe though it is not as symmetrical and focussed on human destiny as SM-SIR desired. Newton was still able to enthuse over its marvelous rationality. But, as we have seen, his worship of such a universe soon gave place to the more typical reaction that, however law-abiding it might be, the universe was after all forbiddingly cold, meaningless and inhospitable to man's interests. SMR became more aware of meteors that smack helter-skelter into the earth; stars that blow up; suns that grow cold; moons that are more thoroughly dead than anything that had ever been imagined.

SMR was fond of assuming that the life that accidentally appeared upon this particular planet earth was absolutely alone in a universe that had no basic concern for life. Sure that there was no communication between the positions of heavenly bodies and human fate, it assumed that any other kind of communication

333

between other parts of the universe and man could never exist. And most obvious of all, this universe allowed no place for heaven to be located, still less for hell. Telescopes revealed no God among the stars; nothing but an infinity of useless empty space. SMR could only ask why, if life or human development were the point of things, should it be so insignificant in size amongst the contents of the universe. SMR's emotional reaction to the discovery of the size of the universe, is a reinforcement of its conviction of the puny unimportance of man with which it had already been engulfed from its physical and biological discoveries.

Recourses to SM: Astrology, of course, has not died and disappeared since the advent of SMR. Heaven-and-hell religion shows an incredible ability to keep going on even in the midst of the age of space exploration. On a more serious level, idealism and traditional religion have tried to acclimate themselves to this enormous expansion of space and time as well as possible; but one wonders if they do not do it mostly by refraining from contemplating the universe that has been revealed. Tennyson's *In Memoriam* is perhaps the top ranking expression in English of the religious mind reeling before these discoveries, trying to regain its footing.

> "The stars," she whispers, "blindly run;
> A web is woven across the sky;
> From out waste places comes a cry,
> And murmurs from a dying sun;
>
> "And all the phantom, Nature, stands —
> With all the music in her tone,
> A hollow echo of my own —
> A hollow form with empty hands."
>
> And shall I take a thing so blind,
> Embrace her as my nature's good;
> Or crush her, like a vice of blood,
> Upon the threshold of the mind?

SM with DR.

Findings of DR: Perhaps the most notable change that DR makes upon SMR is a greater emphasis upon development and

334

evolution as applied to astronomical bodies. SMR was still, we said, somewhat under SM's influence in presenting a clock-work universe eternally revolving in fixed paths. For DR, of course, there is not even that much permanent design, and even the "fixed stars" which once had promised to be the one empirical observable to live up to SM's hope of something unchanging, have now been found to change their mutual positions. The North Star, we hear, graduated to the estate of determiner of our directions within historical times. We also now hear of the "birth, life and death" of stars, and the blue, white and red stars are assigned different ages. Theories of the birth and death of the universe as a whole are commonplace in the newspapers to-day; most well informed people know about nebular gases condensing into stars and planets; and old stars, called "novae" exploding back to nebular gases. There is also the strange story of the expansion of the universe, with the outer galaxies retreating from us at almost the speed of light.

Recently it rather suddenly became usual to assume that "life" is at home all over the universe, and that earth-like planets capable of evolving life similar to ours abound. I have not heard much speculation about this except in terms of the assumption that the presence of life elsewhere depends upon whether a similar set of circumstances to the earth's exists anywhere else: the same proportions of oxygen, nitrogen, water, gravitation, heat, etc. But DR's presumption would be that if the tendency toward more complex organization is native to energy throughout the universe then more complex organisms might be evolved from quite other combinations of elements under other sets of conditions. Does anyone know what silicon and chlorine and . . . might not do under different circumstances of gravitation, light, heat?

With man moving outside of the earth's immediate atmosphere in recent years, SMR's emotional conviction that the universe is entirely hostile to and empty of life has faded. We need not be so certain of its cold meaninglessness any more. Of course man is still just as tiny in comparison with astronomical distances as SMR found him to be. In fact new telescopes have added several billion more incomprehensible light years to the visible extent of things. But these increased distances do not seem to have increased the sense of insignificance for man much over what it already was under SMR.

Comparison with SM: In the present field, it seems that DR has widened the breach with SM, if anything. SM may not have liked SMR's mechanical universe and its unconcern over human destiny; but at least it ran according to a fixed system. But DR's chaotic universe, swirling drunkenly about, with galaxies and stars strewn in a hodge-podge, and expanding wildly, may seem even more horrifying.

DM with DR.

Implications of DM and Correspondence to DR: I can only hint at a few lines of thought here. There is, of course, a rough correspondence between DR's universe so saturated with development and change, and DM's requirement of change. Whether specialists in the field of astronomy will ever be able to go further in showing requirement from the idea of value to specific features in astronomy only further thought and study will tell. The present author is not competent to do so.

DM would tend to imply that an infinity of kinds of organizing process might as well exist all over the universe, as just the one kind on earth. It would expect *all* reality to be generative of value-process.

On the problem of man's supposedly insignificant size compared to that of the entire universe, DM indicates that it is not necessarily size that determines value and importance, but complexity. Man perhaps could regain some sense of his greatness in challenging anyone to prove that there is anything more complex than himself in the universe. Some statements have been made too (as early as Pascal) that man may not be so small after all, if you take his size in comparison to that of both universe and electron. From this point of view he may be about half way in size. It may be possible some day to show a relationship between man's size and complexity and the necessity of a universe of the size of ours, just as Schrödinger has suggested the necessity for man to be of the magnitude that he is in comparison to the size of sub-atomic particles.

Bertrand Russell complains that too small a quantity of purposive mind has been produced in the universe to suppose that it constitutes the reason for all things.

336

If it is the purpose of the Cosmos to evolve mind, we must regard it as rather incompetent in having produced so little in such a long time. . . . It may seem odd that life should occur by accident, but in such a large universe accidents will happen.[3]

By what logic, however, does he assume that the universe's success in embodying purpose requires it to fill up all space with a solid mass of minds? Is it so obvious that there should be fewer tons of inert matter, and fewer cubic light-years of empty space per rational mind? Who is to say that God ought never to have allowed, as one of mind's possible experiences, the contemplation of expenses of space much larger than itself? Who resents that there is available to us on this planet, and maybe on others, a relatively huge amount of "lifeless" matter to use in various ways, or simply to look at in wonder? Dynamic good certainly contains no implication that feeling creatures ought to occupy some other proportion of space than they do.

At the present stage of human thought, it seems that we are safest in saying that SMR was too cocky in supposing it could prove the insignificance of man in this universe; and that if we look hard enough, we might find more requirement in things, for the production of dynamic value, than we think.

3. Space and Time

For lack of space, I have not planned an adequate discussion of this supremely abstruse topic, and will give only a few hints of possible lines of thought.

SM with SIR.

Implications of SM: We have already had occasion to remark in several connections that SM does not strictly imply the existence of Space or Time. In not implying process, it implies no need of any room for the process to take place in; nor certainly of any time for it to elapse in. SM's "mental substance" was always defined as spaceless, or in Descartes' terms, as not "extended." And SM's favorite concept, "Eternity," has often been explained as the contrary of time: it is not to be conceived of as infinite time, but as the time*less*. Aquinas's and Dante's Empyrean was definitely spaceless and timeless.

Adjustments of SIR: What this must be should be obvious: the existence of a world of Space and Time is admitted; and it, of course, exists only for the purpose of leading up to and issuing in the spaceless, timeless eternity. The perfect value of SM is to exist preëminently in this utterly processless, and therefore timeless, Paradise.

SM with SMR.

Findings of SMR: Newton's doctrines of Absolute Space and Absolute Time should be referred to here. They are not necessarily implicated with each other: his space is conceivable without time, his time without space. It is often said that in Newtonian mechanics, time counts for nothing, for the motions that take place in time have no cumulative aspect. We have discussed how, with the lapse of time, the atomic motions create nothing, generate nothing, produce no real change. For Newton Time is a sequence of self-contained instants, not necessarily involved with one another. A frequently discussed aspect of the Age of Reason is how both space and time became widely measured for the first time; how clocks became widespread outside of monasteries (where the desire for a scheduled day had first appeared), and people began living in terms of precise divisions of the day.

Contradiction to SM: The last point above undoubtedly made SM-SIR's concept of timeless eternity more difficult for the common man to understand, while the conception of infinite time-flow became easier. The traditional hope for a moment when this world's time and space should be ended and the earthly drama brought to a glorious end becomes somewhat more difficult with SMR suggesting an infinity of time. Otherwise there does not seem to be much specific evidence of conflict to point to.

SM with DR.

Findings of DR: Einstein's Space-Time continuum is extraordinarily difficult to explain. We will confine ourselves to remarking that the concept seems to imply that Time and Space are implicated with each other, and neither can be conceived of as

338

existing without the other. The figure for time can be interchanged with the figure for space in the equations for relativity theory; while simultaneity in time can only be defined in terms of spatial positions. The general effect is to make time more integral to reality than it was in SMR.

Philosophical reactions to this fact have been a new insistence that the time process is cumulative and creative. An earlier theory was Bergson's concept of "Duration," interpreting time as more than the Newtonian sequence of snap-shots, or succession of self-contained instants. Time is genuinely cumulative, in some sense taking up into its later moments the preceding moments. Whitehead followed this lead in his doctrine that successive occasions of experience, that is events, must be thought of as including earlier ones, rather than as annihilating or replacing earlier ones. Feeling, as the basic reality, is a compound of the earlier and the later, a simultaneously felt contrast of past and present, and perhaps even future.

Comparison to SM: There would be no implication from SM to such a taking up of past into present as DR has here hinted at. For this is not the timeless eternity of complete fulfillment SM looks for.

DM with DR.

Implications of DM and Correspondence to DR: The only idea that the author wishes to defend here is that the idea of Process is prior to the ideas of Space and Time, in the order of requirement. The prevalent opinion is perhaps the other way around: that man first becomes aware of Space and Time, and then realizes that their existence entails the concept of Process. It may be argued that relativity theory supports this order, when it discovers that the measurement of Time and Space requires the measurement of processes. Samuel Alexander implies that Space and Time are the most ultimate concepts, even more ultimate than the concept of Deity, and that the concepts of process and of the development of deity follow secondarily.

To the author, however, it seems clear that the order of logical requirement is from process to Space and Time. Then, since the idea of process has been deduced from the dynamic idea of value, Space and Time become second-level deductions from the dynamic idea of value. Unlike the static idea of value, then, the dynamic idea requires the existence of space and time. It would also seem clearly to require an infinity of time, rather than an ending of time in static eternity.

4. *The Beginning and the End.*
SM with SIR.

Implications of SM: In the light of what was said under the preceding topic it is clear that SM does not imply a beginning in time of any structured reality; and thus, of course, no end. The point that was made concerning the origin of life in Chapter XI holds on the present more general topic of Creation as such: SM implies no creation of a world additional to the world of essences. There should be only the timeless world of eternal contemplation of essences by minds, or, most strictly, by Universal Mind.

Adjustments of SIR: Since SIR accepts the existence of a time process, whose only purpose, however, is to return to the essences from which it departs, it has to have a doctrine of the beginning of this process. The doctrine of instantaneous creation by divine fiat then may be applied to things in general here as it was to Life in Chapter XI. Traditional religion, at least in the West, usually holds that creation takes place at a certain date of time. Orthodox Christianity defended the theory of "creation out of nothing" at that date so as to obviate the Platonic notion that matter had already existed, uncreated by God. What existed before this creation puzzled theologians as much as it puzzles the child who asks "who created God?" but the usual answer is the doctrine of timeless eternity mentioned under the previous head.

Likewise, traditional thought looked forward to an ending of time. The Judaic religions were all apocalyptic, producing prophecies and descriptions of how God will bring to an end his epoch of creation. What follows the end is, of course, again the timeless eternity. In popular thought, however, what follows the end of this world is a heaven which continues to contain life and events of a less strenuous nature than those of this life. Even St. Paul seems to envisage the need of some sort of "body" — a "spiritual" one — for the next life. But we are treading on the last topic of the book, Human Destiny.

340

SM with SMR.

Findings of SMR: Newton and the Deists clung for awhile to the First Cause argument, which implies that there must have been a beginning of the clock-work universe, and that the notion of an infinitely enduring mechanical process is impossible. But critics soon decided that infinite time was no more difficult a concept than that of a beginning with its equally unthinkable notion of the nothingness prior to the beginning. Thus SMR in its later phases usually prefers the notion of infinite time with no beginning or end, and consequently no need of creator or terminator.

Contradiction to SM-SIR: This idea of an infinite mechanical process is only another of the dark, comfortless aspects of SMR which traditional religionists long to escape. Actually, there seems to be no absolutely conclusive reason why the machine might not have a beginning and end after all; at any rate believers have kept on believing in them.

SM with DR.

Findings of DR: We hear much of how the expansion of the universe at present seems to imply that it must have begun expanding as a smaller entity, presumably with energy or matter packed tightly together. One hears discussions of the "creation of the universe" that take off from this point, and thus do not deal with their title topic at all, since they do not tell us how the tightly packed ball of matter got started. The "steady state" theories apparently repeat the earlier retreat from creation theories to infinite time theories, and give us an eternal universe.

The second law of thermodynamics has already been discussed as seeming to indicate an ending of existence; and yet it cannot be said that anything in this area has reached the state of unequivocal, demonstrated knowledge. Both theories, of a beginning and end of time, or of infinite time, seem equally in the running at the moment.

Comparison with SM-SIR: Thus there can be no conclusive statement at this time whether DR contradicts SM-SIR as to beginning and end or not.

Implications of DM: There may seem to be a presumption from the dynamic idea of good to the necessity of a never-ending process, at least as long as value is to exist. But then, who can say anything about whether value should exist forever or not? Also it seems impossible to demonstrate that dynamic value might not logically permit one universe to come to an end and another get started. I think the general effect of the concept of dynamic value is to focus our attention on the present, and to see to it that we are managing that properly for the production of value. The first beginning and the final outcome, as we have said in several connections, are not necessarily involved in deciding whether value *now* exists sufficiently to allow us to conclude that the world is meaningful.

With this suitably terminal topic we come to the end of the ontological part of the book, the attempt to characterize the fundamental nature of things, or of the operations of things in regard to their causal and purposive characteristics. We claim that the dynamic positions have been able to relieve us of the problem of mechanism insofar as it had seemed to preclude the existence of anything like purposiveness. We now come back to a more thorough treatment of the nature of value itself, and to the third great problem, the problem of evil. Let us close with D. H. Lawrence's prose-poem which seems to incorporate within its short length almost all of our sub-topics:

The Work of Creation

The mystery of creation is the divine urge of creation,
but it is a great strange urge, it is not a Mind.
Even an artist knows that his work was never in his mind,
he could never have *thought* it before it happened.
A strange ache possessed him, and he entered the struggle,
and out of the struggle with his material, in the spell of the urge,
his work took place, it came to pass, it stood up and saluted his
    mind.

God is a great urge, wonderful, mysterious, magnificent
but he knows nothing beforehand.

PART IV

AXIOLOGY: THEORIES OF EVALUATION
(THE PROBLEM OF EVIL)

CHAPTER XIV

THE VARIETIES AND FACTS OF VALUE EXPERIENCE

We have now found the general structure and mode of nature's functioning, as understood by dynamic science, to be very close to what is implied and required by the dynamic idea of value and meaning. The problem of mechanism has been relieved, not to say solved by science itself as it refined its own observations and concepts and found a place for something like purposiveness in the whole-part relationship.

With no flat interdiction placed upon our search for meaning by a non-purposive view of reality, we may now dare to assault that even more ubiquitous cause of doubt — the problem of evil. Many among today's humanists and agnostics, mentioned in the first chapter, are kept from any very sustained efforts to rationalize evil by their conviction that meaningfulness is already a lost cause because of the problem of mechanism. Why should we expect a mechanical universe to be beneficent to man in any case? However, with the universe now looking unexpectedly purposive in so many ways, we may feel like reopening the problem of evil, and searching again with as much persistence and faith as Job did, in the days when the non-existence of God was so unthinkable that he felt obliged to seek out some hidden reason for His allowing evil.

But before we can intelligently tackle the problem, we must attain a more thorough knowledge of what good is, and in what ways it might be expected to be embodied in reality. This means that we must apply our structure of discussion to a more detailed treatment of the field of values than we could when first introducing our distinction between the static and dynamic ideas of value in Chapter III. This part of the book will then culminate in an application of the framework to the various views concerning evil.

The analysis just completed provides us with powerful tools for

explaining and assuaging the almost fatal confusion and negativity about values into which much modern thought and literature
have fallen. Man seems to have arrived in our time at one of
the great divides in intellectual history, commensurable with such
eras as the crystallization of higher religions in the 500's and 600's
B. C., the development of other-worldliness around the time of
Rome's fall, or the inauguration of the scientific world view
during the Renaissance. It is a time when the conflicts between
the staticisms of fact and value which we have been studying can
no longer be obscured by the age-old devices, and a final despair
is becoming explicit as the utter valuelessness which is the
logical outcome of the failure of dynamic experience to fulfill the
implications of static value is more and more clearly revealed.
Those who can bring themselves to give up the old dream of a
static heaven, however, will receive in return a world meaningful
in dynamic terms, and a new reality for evaluation and for "high
things."

Our framework, together with the proper breakdown and sequence of sub-topics, should help disentangle the confusion in the
field of value. However that task would be too great for the space
remaining in the present book, and will be left for another. In
this book we can present an outline of sub-topics to all of which
the framework might be applied, but will stop to work it out for
only those that are important for our present theodicical task.

I. The Varieties of Value Qualities. The best starting place for a
study of the value question, I would suggest, would be an empirical canvassing of the whole field of value experience in its
concrete variety, with suggestions for a basic classification of the
kinds. For our framework, the main issue would be what the implications and findings of the types of philosophy are concerning
the fact of variety as such. We will confine this topic to mere
notes except for DM-DR:

SM with SIR:

Implications of SM: None to variety, since that would involve
parts, which SM never implies. Emphasis on unity, or a single
highest good, such as love of God, or Plato's Idea of the Good.
Adjustments of SIR: Limited types of value, e.g., Truth, Beauty
and Goodness. Aristocratic disdain of "lower" values.

Findings of SMR: The analysis of SMR's atomistic determinism, in the preceding Part, prepares us for understanding its fundamental inability to take account either of value in general or of specific types of values and qualities. In strict logic, all qualitative distinctions must be unreal, or at best epiphenomena, having no significance or efficacy in the purely quantitative world of reality. However, empirical experience forces qualitative differences upon SMR's attention and, from Democritus and Lucretius to Hobbes we find the same sort of glossing over of the problem of deriving the qualitative out of an atomic theory that has specifically excluded the qualitative from the nature of the ultimate units. Hobbes passes as blithely from his "motions" occurring in the "strings" of the nerves to his reflected sensory "phantasms", as Lucretius passes from smooth, round atoms to sweetness and pleasure. In neither case is there any attempt to deal with the obvious fact that the notion of reflected motions has no kind of relationship to the notion of sensory quality; nor the notion of smooth roundness to pleasant sweetness.

Typically, those steeped in the quantitative approach of SMR will ignore or minimize the evidences of concern for quality among nature's phenomena, always finding such evidences only incidental or accidental accompaniments of what are taken to be essentially mere efficiencies, mere productions for the sake of blind production, mere issuings of causes into effects. The "beauties" of Nature are of no basic significance for the nature of things. If birds show a genus-wide penchant for developing gorgeous plumage, varied songs, elaborate sex-dances, SMR puts it all down as incidental to sexual selection, as merely serving the blind survival of the species. The factor of sheer enjoyment for its own sake, far from being made a central end for which these processes are developed, becomes at most an epiphenomenon of a blind evolution that evolves only for the sake of evolving. Nature's endless production of new varieties and refusal to repeat anything exactly is classed as a sort of accidental result of the multiplicity of factors. And the trend in nature toward complexity and increased richness of reaction is also made a matter of survival only. Why do animals and man develop a greater range and variety of color vision, or refine their taste discrimination? Only because increased powers of discrimination will presumably enable more accurate avoidance of threatening objects or poisonous substances, and thence greater survival. The fact that more varied enjoyment accompanies these increased powers is an irrelevant happenstance.

If SMR does undertake a classification of qualities, it is apt to take the form of a list of instincts or urges, conceived again more as quantitative forces "pushing from behind" than as qualitative attractions. Analogously to the Newtonian atom, they operate separately and deterministically, the accompanying qualitative feelings being strictly inessential. The organism's behavior will be thought of as a kind of passive result of these unsynthesized forces batting it about.

If this doctrine of multiple instincts is somewhat analogous to SIR's multiple essences, though the two views are poles apart in their conception of what these entities are, SMR also has an analogy to SM's single Good, equally different in conception. That is, SMR inclines toward a monistic ultimate value, or rather, since SMR cannot, technically, speak of value, "result" or "effect," which all the instincts are to serve: self-preservation, or will to power, or pleasure, as various sub-schools may label it. Bentham's psychological hedonism aspired to the reduction of all value to measurable quantities of the latter, where qualitative differences were irrelevant, though pleasure itself would seem to be too qualitative in nature for SMR to deal with. Nietzsche takes the even less qualitative concept of will to power as the one real urge.

Recourses to SM-SIR: Attempts to restore values and qualities as essences attracting the mind or placing it under obligation are not wanting in recent thought. The extreme intuitionist, Ross, returns to SIR's characteristic acceptance of a limited list of "higher" value essences and specifically denies the legitimacy of trying to derive them, arbitrary as they may seem, from any unitary principle that might show why God chooses to constitute the realm of value thus rather than any other way. He finds "three main things that are intrinsically good — virtue, knowledge, and, with certain limitations, pleasure."[1] He also finds a variety of "prima facie duties" but they are not to be derived from any general conception of value. These miscellaneous duties arise out of certain kinds of prior circumstances: the fact of having made promises yields the duties of fidelity; of having done something wrong, the duties of reparation; of having received benefits, the duties of justice, etc. Ross explicitly rejects any appeal to consequences in felt quality as a rationale for these duties. When

348

Perry complains about the non-inclusiveness of the list of duties and the lack of systematic relationship to any unified concept, Ross answers:

> His assumption, then, is that there must be some single sense of 'valuable' in which the word is always used, and his contention is that a subjective theory alone will serve to assign such a single meaning and to show the relations between the various specific kinds of value. And under the heading of 'valuable' he includes both things which would not naturally be described as being valuable at all, and things which we can surely recognize to have value only in fundamentally different senses. . . . It is not a hasty assumption to assume that [obligatoriness] is an instance of the same kind of thing of which moral goodness or beauty is another instance? And is it not clear that what we call economic values are merely instrumental values, different in kind from the goodness of virtue or of pleasure? The assumption that there must be "a general theory of value" applicable to value in all the senses of that word seems to me to be unjustified.[2]

This curious readiness to leave value theory in a state of disjunction and arbitrary restriction is evidently related to conceiving values as a collection of independent static essences. DR will prove able to recognize the true extent and variety of value qualities, yet find a unity behind them and principles for due subordination and distinction between various phases or levels.

SM with DR.

Findings of DR: A greater fidelity to empirical experience leads DR to question SMR's tendency to make unreal the qualitative side of it and to suspect, as we have seen, that SMR's purely quantitative reality results from an excessively analytical, selective and abstract method. The qualitative aspects may not be merely rarities or insignificant by-products as SMR indicated. Do male Lyre Birds develop their elaborate tails only because accidental mutations produce them, females happen to prefer them, the Australian environment happens to be so favorable that the efficiency-reducing tails do not prevent survival, and so such males get to reproduce themselves? Is the beauty, that is, just SMR's "accidental epiphenomenon"? But a prominent question remains: why should the female develop a taste for such beauty at all? If mere survival is the only real point, why not always do it with a minimum of paraphernalia, exclusively efficient? It becomes a significant question why efficient processes should ever be accompanied by qualitative feelings at all. Why might not organisms just as well be pushed into survival by mechanical devices alone, without any associated feelings? We are developing driverless airplanes with "feed-back" mechanisms that avoid obstructions without having pain feelings, and reach their goals without feelings of triumph. In short, why should enjoyment and non-enjoyment be attached to processes at all?

We begin to glimpse the possibility, then, that SMR may have the cart before the horse when it assumes that efficient processes exist first, and are incidentally accompanied by qualitative feelings. Could not variety of quality be the prior idea, when varied structures, incidentally serving survival, were called into existence to develop the ever more complex processes required for such variety? DR is clear, at any rate, that if there were to be varieties of dynamic feeling, there would have to be varieties of structured process in any case; and that if there were to be increasing richness of quality, there would have to be increasing complexity of structured function.

This last reminds us of a significant fact: that when processes associated with certain qualitative feelings merge into larger, more inclusive processes, the associated feelings correspondingly merge into new feelings which are qualitatively unique — that is, they are not mere collections of the old feelings. For instance, suppose we hear the tone of middle C sounded, followed by the tone of E. Then suppose both are sounded together. An unbiased empiricism must admit that what we now hear is not an experience of two separate tones just the same in quality as they were when heard separately. We now hear a major third, as a unique new quality, a new unified experience of a harmony. Thus combinations of varieties of quality produce new varieties of quality, and this holds not just within one sense organ, but between and among sense organs, muscular feelings, thoughts, etc., coming from most of the tissues and structures in the organism. This provides for an infinity of distinguishable quality-experiences.

The search for varieties of value, quality, feeling, then, may be the central reality, the point from which our thought should start in trying to understand the meaning of reality.

But now, DR finds a monism behind this infinite plurality, though very different from the one SM implied. This is simply what we have meant by the dynamic idea of value: every kind of value quality, whether involved in self-preservative struggles or in mere non-practical awareness, can be felt, enjoyed, only as some organizing process somewhere in the feeling organism underlies it; or, for the negative and unpleasant qualities, as some disintegrative process underlies them. Whether it is succeeding in finding food to keep us from starving, or merely observing a painting, the factor of process from some sort of depletion, tension or disorder toward some sort of resolution and organization will be present below any value enjoyment. This point will be illustrated in greater detail in subsequent chapters, but to allay skepticism in those who would find it fantastic to speak of resolution of tension in connection with some simple qualitative enjoyment, such as seeing a red color, I will point out now that such an experience at least involves a transition in the retina of thousands of cells from a state of miscellaneous stimulation to a unified "red" field; and also point out that the enjoyment of the redness does not persist much after the nerves may be supposed to have finished their transition.

We have, then, a common factor of dynamic attainment in every kind of qualitative experience, with enjoyment existing only within the dynamism itself; and the pluralistic factor that this dynamic attainment takes innumerable specific forms, each accompanied by its own identifiable quality.

At this point a more or less exhaustive classification of value types should be worked out, as a sort of panorama of value-reality, against which to check our generalizations under the following heads, to see whether they truly apply to every kind of value. Our list (which we cannot discuss thoroughly here) could take as its main principle of sequence, inclusiveness or complexity. Several other principles of sequence tend to fit this one. The order from instrumental value toward intrinsic or ultimate value would correspond roughly, though, as we shall discuss later, DR does not make as radical a distinction between these categories as the static positions do. DR finds every value experience to have both aspects, though instrumentality decreases and intrinsicality increases as we move upward on our main axis of inclusiveness. To some extent, then, we can say that no later value on the list could arise until the earlier ones had been achieved; but that the later ones are the reason why the earlier ones are sought at all. But this cannot be pushed all the way, since all earlier values can be enjoyed in themselves too; and sometimes a later value can be seen to have instrumentality for earlier ones. Human experience is too intertwined for any linear sequence of items.

Our order by complexity may also correspond with an order from "lesser" to "greater" value, though intractible problems, to be discussed in the next chapters, lie in the way of our evaluating what is lesser and greater. The order of cumulation would naturally correspond, in the sense that later items tend to require, include and organize all preceding items into unifiedly felt value-experiences.

We must remember that for DR value itself is the feeling of an organizing process, thus necessarily located within a feeler. Thus any objective or instrumental aspects of value that may loom prominently in any of our classes can only be considered as derivative from or auxiliary to some eventual felt organic process.

Our sequence of value or quality-kinds, then, follows.

A. Physical, biological values, including enjoyment of food, sex and other bodily feelings.

B. Sensory values, restricted to enjoyment of immediate sensory qualities without consideration of their use under the following classes.

C. Cognitive value. Although, according to the dynamic idea of value, the most exact locus of value in this class must be in the satisfying *feeling* of gaining knowledge, solving cognitive problems, etc., the tests of cognition (see Part II) enter into the situation in a special way, as an application of the general criteria of any value (see Chapter XVI).

D. Practical (or Productive) values, including the main body of human doing, making, working, with its large factor of extrinsic instrumentality, but always with some degree of intrinsic enjoyability, too.

E. Political-economic (or Distributive) value, mainly concerned with the area of social science, and the distribution of what is produced under class D to provide individuals with the wherewithal of value-experience.

F. Social-personal values, including all enjoyment of immediate social relations, from family up through interracial and international contacts. The locus of the main part of individual ethics.

G. Recreational and Aesthetic value.

H. Philosophy and Religion as the most inclusive of value-processes.

For the remainder of Part IV on Axiology, the headings undertake to be applicable to every one of these types of value. Under each heading, illustrations from every type should be given. However, for brevity's sake, we reduce the types back to the traditional three, cognitive, aesthetic and ethical, and here will say a little about how they are related to the longer list above.

1. Cognitive value, where Truth was the traditional standard and Logic the technique, consists, for DR, in the enjoyment of processes apparently located in the higher centers of the brain, though connected to processes in many other parts of the organism, including sensory organs and muscles. As studied in Part II, this kind of value is tested or evaluated by the empirical correspondence test, which may be rather different in nature from the criteria we shall discuss later (Chapter XVI) as applying in all areas; and yet the confirmation of hypotheses by observation constitutes a kind of resolving-process-with-feeling that shares the same basic sequence of phases that all other value-processes possess (see section II). The fact that the cognitive enterprise is involved in all other kinds of value, at least from class C on (since getting the mental contents to "fit the facts" is a needful step in all) is already taken care of by the principle of cumulation. I think it is adequate to say that the two preceding classes (A and B) as defined consist of direct enjoyments not involving cognition.

2. Aesthetic value, where Beauty was the traditional standard and Art the technique, has been distinguished from cognitive value by many as concerning a "pattern-arranging" kind of mental activity as opposed to the "puzzle-solving" kind in cognition. For the latter, the original desire is said to be "curiosity," or a sense of the unknown and puzzling; and the satisfaction lies in confirming correlations, theoretical explanations, etc. For the latter, the problem is some disorder, vagueness, disarrangement among some kind of objects or entities, and the satisfaction lies simply in rearranging them into patterns satisfying some principle of organization.

If the term "aesthetics" is taken to cover this aspect of design, or patterned order, wherever it is involved in any area, then it too will have an application beyond the special class G. For instance, the test of Coherence, which we agreed in Part II was an essential one in the realm of cognitive value, would represent the present general aspect of value entering into that class. The aesthetic, in this sense, comes into Practical Arts (D) in many ways, both in the design of specific structures, and in the planning of complex projects in engineering, city planning, etc. There are even those who would consider ethics itself to be ultimately a matter of aesthetic order within our acts.[3] The special relevance of the aesthetic to class G, then, would arise merely from the fact that bodily movements and external materials are peculiarly suitable to processes of patterning for its own sake. Most forms of recreation, such as games, set up prescribed orders of interaction with objects (balls, opponents, etc.) through which the muscles and nerves are to move, first raising tensions, then providing routes toward relaxation and order, usually in rhythmically repeated time-patterns. The forms of art differ only in utilizing other nerve tracts and muscles, and other objective materials, which usually happen to permit greater complexity of developing order to be experienced. The philosophical and religious experiences (G), too, are essentially similar, carrying the experience of pattern-building (here the "materials" are more ideational) to ultimate levels of complexity.

Every one of these types of value, however, reveals all the phases of the MSIRCP sequence underlying the experience of them. The analogues of the phases of need, disorder, or tension, of aim, of transition, and of consummation can be found in more strictly cognitive value processes as much as in more strictly aesthetic ones.

3. Ethical value, where Good was the traditional standard, and Morality the technique, has narrower and broader meanings similarly. In the broadest possible sense, the term "ethics" has been used to cover the general theory of evaluation (comparing any kind of values as "better" or "worse"). If evaluation within any special area of value experience is considered an application of general theory, then ethics would enter every one of our classes as the evaluative function, distinguished from the sheer fact of enjoyment or qualitative experience itself. It would also include evaluating *between* classes — directing choice, for instance, between pursuing a bodily versus a cognitive experience when time allows only one. This is Perry's use, when he says that morality

354

does not deal with a new and special kind of value of its own. It is rather the organizer of all other values.

> If human life be likened to a garden, then morality and its institutions represent the fencings, spacings, and arrangements by which the plants, such as truth and beauty, and divers special and personal interests, are enabled to flower most abundantly. . . . To consider morality as the supreme end in and of itself reflects a profound misunderstanding of its role. Its values are compounded of other and prior values; its claim to control rests on its provision for these values, and for their several forms of perfections.[4]

However, it so happens that at least in class C and class G, cognitive and aesthetic value, the evaluative function is, in ordinary language, included in the meaning of Logic and Aesthetics, and not considered an aspect of Ethics. So, a narrower meaning of Ethics seems to cover the task of evaluation only in certain selected classes: A (ethics of bodily care, etc.), D (ethics of workmanship, etc.), E (social ethics), F (personal ethics). Finally, a narrowest sense tends to consider class F the preeminent locus of ethical behavior, as we have noticed, for most of the general and altruistic virtues would come under that head (though such a virtue as honesty seems to have more general applicability to other classes).

In summary, I feel that the best way to conceive the relationship of these three more general value concepts (cognitive, aesthetic and ethical) to the classes of value quality is this: Each special class is to include both the sheer enjoyment or experience aspect of its value or quality type; and also the application of evaluative theory in that area. The general theory of evaluation may be placed in class H. In being applied to the special classes, it enters into different ones with somewhat different emphases, which have received the three traditional labels. The cognitive type of evaluation first appears in class C, but is used instrumentally in the following classes. Aesthetic evaluation apparently also arises in class C (as Coherence theory) and has applicability in class D, perhaps none in classes E and F, but preeminently in classes G and H. Ethical evaluation has the broader and narrower applications discussed above.

In the following chapters, then, illustrations will be given from classes C, G and F in this order, and from their factual, experience aspect, or their evaluative aspect, as needed.

Returning now to the fact of variety as such, we become aware of a certain arbitrariness about the list of value-kinds. Why would any divine planner of the universe lay out just this peculiar selection of possible qualities? If we considered values at a more specific level we might feel this question even more acutely. Why is it the specific odors of apple-blossom, smoke, pine needles, hydrogen sulfide, etc., that make up our olfactory experience instead of other unknown kinds? Why is it the feeling of walking on two legs that is ours, instead of any of an infinity of other motion-feelings that we might have had? Why the special mixture of social consummations, faux-pas, and anguish that comes to us? Looked at this way, life may seem essentially a completely miscellaneous, senseless collection of arbitrary qualities and feelings of all kinds. This impression would correspond to the similar one we felt in Chapter XII, in contemplating the peculiar and non-inevitable selection of parts, faculties and functions our bodies consist in.

All that DR can suggest is that variety of qualitative feeling seems to be the most immediate and pressing of facts, and that SIR and SMR were inadequate in their grasp of this fact, while SM failed to give any reason why this strange variety exists.

DM with DR.

Implications of DM and Correspondence to DR: But DM, as we have already seen (Chapter III) implies novelty and variety. We have shown how the dynamic idea of good requires variety and freshness of quality; how feeling, enjoyment, good, can exist only when strains and dissatisfactions are felt passing into orders, and how these orders must necessarily be felt as distinct qualities, as new, real solutions to real problems. They must not be mechanical repetitions of the same old thing, and in order to be experienced as new, they must have new distinguishable quality.

Just as we could not see that DM implied any particular assortment of bodily parts, however, so it seems doubtful that we can show that DM implies just the particular kinds of qualities we find life to contain. It only implies that there should be *some* rich variety. Perhaps others may some day be able to demonstrate that our particular variety in this life is especially suitable, but I doubt it.

The most ultimate of ideas, then, may be that the dynamic idea of good requires that quality-kinds should exist; and that process-kinds, thence structure-kinds, must exist to undergird them. Also that new qualities should be able to be created and enjoyed through effortful, compositional process. And this is exactly what we find in DR.

II. Empirical Approach to Value Experience. The next question in value theory, after the preliminary overview of all the kinds, is the descriptive formulation of whatever can be empirically observed of value experience. Physical, biological, psychological and social data must be organized for whatever it may contribute to our effort to state the general and universal features of value-reality. The framework could presumably be applied to each contributory field, but the psychological would be most crucial, having most to do with our conclusions on such central questions as: whether rational decisions, or altruistic ones, can exist, or whether value is essentially hedonistic, or formal, etc.

The phases of purposive process distinguished in Chapter IX offer themselves for our basic breakdown on the psychological foundations of value theory. The framework could be applied to each sub-head, such as Subject, Need, Object, Aim, Integration, Means, Ends, etc., but we will group these items, together with some from the MSIRCP sequence of Chapter XII, into a smaller list: Motivation, including the factors of subjective need, objects and stimulation, and desire and aim; Integration, including means and response; Consummation or ends; and Product, or habit. Even under this more generalized list we will discuss only some of the positions of the framework on only a few of the most relevant points. Some of the types of philosophy do not recognize the relevance of every one of these subtopics for the meaning of value, of course.

A. Motivation. The most important point in this area is the question whether motivation is by desire for objects and acts as such, or by desire for the feelings expected to result from the objects and acts, or by knowledge of duties that exist in regard to objects and acts, that is by rational will.

SM with SIR.

Implications of SM: None to these categories (See Chapter XI) at least in the strictest static logic, where nothing needs to be desired or changed. Less strictly, motivation should be by static attraction to pure essences or ideal forms.

Adjustments of SIR: The conflict between impulse and rational will has to be recognized, and SIR must defend the possibility of control by the latter.

SM with SMR.

Findings of SMR: Mechanical instinct and conditioning theories render rational or altruistic concepts of duty impossible as real motivation.

Recourses to SM-SIR: Modern intuitionist and rationalist theories of motivation by concepts of right and duty.

SM with DR.

Findings of DR: Applications of concepts from Chapter IX to a theory of organismic motivation in which rationalism and organismic feeling theory are assimilated:

Concerning the question whether the object of desire is the thing, or the satisfaction (pleasure) that accompanies interacting with the thing, we can now understand that the militantly antihedonistic rationalists as well as some more dynamic interest theorists go wrong because they fail to keep value in the interactional process itself. They all feel obliged to deny that pleasure or happiness is the only object aimed at, and hurry to list the infinity of other kinds of objects that are definitely desired. But it seems clear that the pleasant or satisfying feeling is not in the same category as the other kinds of objects, but a factor that accompanies them all. And since pleasant feelings cannot be had except in interaction or in the thought of interaction with varying objects, and interaction with objects cannot constitute value without producing pleasant feeling at some level, it is hard to see why the disjunction should be insisted upon. It would seem impossible for us to aim at either object or feeling separately; we can only aim at enjoyable interaction with the object. The error seems to be a case of what G. C. Fields considers the inappropriate degree of analysis and distinction logical minds seek to apply to value theory. Because they can mentally distinguish the concepts of object, feeling, interaction, etc., they assume nature itself must be similarly divided, when it might not be, in dynamic reality.[5]

It is DR's conception of the whole-part relationship, however, that gives us most help in saving what SIR wanted to save from SMR without going back to tools SMR can always destroy. When DR makes more explicit than either SIR or SMR that there is usually a *multiplicity* of needs and objects, giving rise to numerous simultaneous desires and drives, it can then find, in the consequently required planning of complexly organized patterns of behavior a place for rational feeling. Motivation turns out to have to do with this organizing of a plurality of factors so as to satisfy a plurality of desires at once.

This thought is to be contrasted with SIR's and SMR's treatment in terms of single dominant essences or instincts overcoming and excluding the rest, and thus becoming single causes of behavior. Of course we cannot exclude cases of specific desires for more or less single or simple qualitative enjoyments, especially in infant organisms, or in developed ones whenever they run across a new sensation or other attraction. I have argued, however, that even in the simplest value experience — as for instance in enjoying a single color — we have a process of organizing many factors — numerous retinal and optic nerve cells in this case — that were in miscellaneous states of stimulation, into one unified field of color. With further cycles of the MSIRCP sequence, then, desires, and motives come to concern, more typically, complexes of needs or urges seeking patterns of activity with complexes of present or sought objects that will resolve most or all of them optimally. And experiencing the working out of such patterns becomes itself a main locus of value enjoyment.

We have already studied in Chapter IX how, on the basis of this recognition of plural needs and objects, we can have a conception of motivation which escapes SMR's mechanistic theory of causation by blind part-urges and gives us genuinely purposive goal-seeking, without having to appeal, as SIR does, to an isolated faculty of non-natural reason or rational will. It is out of this compositional field, or gestalt situation, then, that what SM-SIR thinks of as the faculty of reason, and the motivational power of thoughts of duty, would come. These would arise as repeated cycles of the MSIRCP sequence incorporate more and more knowledge of cause-effect connections and means-consequences relations, etc., into the person. The central moral conflict between "irrational impulse" and the "sense of moral obligation" would require for its understanding the theory of the whole-part relationship, where the part force can sometimes break through the holistic field force; and the holistic field force can sometimes inhibit the part force, or at least keep it in place. We can admit that all motivation involves desire for good feeling, but that good feeling can be had not only through resolving processes in one specific part of the organism giving a more localized, perhaps "physical," pleasure; but also through resolving processes which integrate many processes in many parts, giving the pleasure of rational order. The difference between "desire" and "rational motive" would not be so much whether or not they seek satisfying feeling, as in their degree of complexity. Having a motive to duty opposed to impulse or desire would not be a matter of having a feelingless, desireless thought opposed to a felt desire, but feeling a desire for more remote but more inclusive feelings of resolution opposed to one for nearer, more immediate and partial feelings of resolution.

When one acts from a sense of duty "regardless of cost to himself," as Kant wishes us to do, it seems impossible to deny that however much he may be thinking of general social imperatives, rather than immediately personal pleasure, he is still feelingly attracted to the meaningful pattern of society he believes his dutiful act will fit into. Are not the rationalist and the hedonist theories of motivation genuinely fused in this idea that good feeling accompanies organizing process? Obeying the dictates of rational will is precisely to try to organize factors consistently and this itself produces satisfying feeling. If anyone seems to reject "duty" and live for more immediate and selfish satisfactions, it can only mean that his organic structure has not yet developed ability to grasp more inclusive groups of factors, to feel distress in their disharmony, and to aspire to more complex organization for the broader satisfaction it can hold.

> . . . if we were pure reason without any desire or feelings, we should not, as Kant thought, act in a particular way, but we should simply not act at all.[6]

The illustrations of the dynamic, compositional nature of desire and motive in our three main areas of value must be confined to mere hints. Cognitive motivation is clearly a matter of aiming at intergearing of multiple ideas into consistent (coherent) theories or systems. The desire to have these ideas "fit" only logically was enough in the pre-scientific age; scientists have added the desire to have the system "fit" observation, but both sorts of fitting are alike in being expected to produce feelings of satisfaction.

In aesthetic value, the aim is to seek a pattern into which one's multiple materials will "fit" to the enhancement of feeling and effect: colors, lines, subject matter in painting; main and subordinate themes and developments of themes in music; movements and strategies in games and dancing, etc. There may be an analogue for the concept of duty as the call of inclusive organization in the artist's anxiety to attain a certain level of perfection in his work.

In the realm of ethical value, it seems safe to say that motives are concerned with the patterning of multiple acts, personal and social. Our discussion of the psychology of motivation and duty has indicated that DR can understand how men might be motivated either by desires for some immediate physical sensation; or by desire to arrange acts referring only to himself in some rational pattern, to reduce mutual interference and cancellation among his own various needs and interests both to increase the amount of satisfaction of each several desire, and also to enjoy the building of the rational pattern as such.

But the most hazardous question in the psychological foundations of ethics is the question of the reality of social, altruistic interest. We come to the age-old discussion whether or not all social duties must be based in the end on self-interest before they can be motivated. Can DR, with the above admission that individual satisfaction at a certain level is involved in all "dutiful" behavior, escape from SMR's crass egoistic hedonism?

Egoism in social relationships, sometimes called the power motive, in its cruder manifestations produces obvious efforts to exploit others for one's own benefit. But the defenders of egoism argue that even the less obviously exploitive human relationships are only more subtle manipulations of others for one's own benefit, entailing less risk of retribution afterwards. Most of us, however reluctant to accept egoism, know how to discern the possible selfish motive behind the most altruistic seeming act: The mother who sacrifices her own ambitions to foster those of her child really wished to exploit her child's success. The martyr who dies rather than betray his party or belief is really avoiding the painful self-hatred that would result from saving his life through recant-

361

ing. Psychologists may point out that individual happiness is possibly more dependent upon social acceptance than any other single factor; so that therefore all obedience to society's demand for considerateness may be essentially for the purpose of maintaining one's own inner peace and self-esteem.

In these and other ways, then, the defenders of universal egoism make their point. Many of them go on to argue that there is no necessary difference between the behavior they could recommend on egoistic grounds and behavior desired by the most other-regarding altruist. They merely point out that one could decide to be generally considerate of others in the expectation that this would foster the best future results for one's own happiness: by encouraging a general tendency in society to return considerateness to oneself, by making oneself popular, by enriching one's social relations, etc. Or they can hold that men tend to be conditioned so that the sight of suffering in others produces unpleasant feelings in themselves, so that they will be kind to avoid this discomfort.

Other ethicists, however, feel it important to show the existence of altruistic motivation in a deeper sense than this, free of any egoistic component whatever. We might wonder at the outset why they should be unsatisfied with the apparently adequate sources of benignity presented by the egoists. One reason is Kant's, that the very notion of ethical action excludes self-regarding motivation. To be concerned in the slightest degree with the benefits to oneself is to fall from the province of morality into that of mere prudence and calculation. There is also the conviction of many that to admit an egoistic component in all behavior is to lose any dependable guard against a presumed inveterate tendency in human nature to sink into the narrowest selfishness, no matter how much the egoist may preach that a longer-term prudence counsels the tenderest regard for others.

For these reasons a search is undertaken for a psychological basis for pure altruism. The first resort may be to "instinct": man must have a native impulse of compassion, as Rousseau claimed. But aside from the fact that instinct theories risk the fallacy of supposing that labelling a mystery with a word explains it, this theory does not avoid saying that because of being constituted with an altruistic instinct, man must satisfy it in order to be egoistically happy. The theory that man becomes conditioned to sympathy for others, so that he desires to be genuinely unselfish, also does not avoid saying that he has now so constituted himself

362

that unselfish action brings him the greatest satisfaction. Mothers-head remarks, at this point, that the egoist may be caught in a circular fallacy:

> Altruism for the sake of self-interest is a contradiction in terms, for an act is altruistic by definition only if it is not performed for the sake of one's self. In saying that your nature is such that you will be happy only if you are unselfish, we are not persuading you to help others in order to be happy yourself; for if you do this, you will not really be unselfish and hence will not enjoy the happiness that comes from helping others unselfishly. . . . Don't we urge you, help a fellow man in trouble because it will make you feel righteous. This is the formula for priggishness. . . . Help him because you want to get him out of trouble.[7]

And yet, if you do desire to get him out of trouble, you will certainly enjoy succeeding in the task. You might also be wishing to avoid feeling ashamed of yourself for ignoring him.

It seems we must say, then, that, psychologically speaking, it is true that the enjoyment we can feel in giving others benefit and happiness can be enhanced if we genuinely intend to help them in terms of their own, and not our, needs. And it seems psychologically possible for such an intention to motivate us. But we cannot escape from that enjoyment within ourselves that does result if our kindness does thus help them, leading, perhaps besides, to pleasant relationships of gratefulness and friendship. Now it seems doubtful that foresight of this self-satisfaction, conscious or unconscious, can be actually excluded as an inevitable *part* of our prior motivation. Nor does it seem necessary to do so for ethical purposes, though this is another question to be considered in later chapters on evaluation and obligation. However, our theory of the reality of desire for and enjoyment of inclusive, ordered patterns of interaction can give sufficient reality to genuinely social motives for our purposes. These will be desires for those more complex, thence more satisfying, processes that are possible only through relations with the most complex available objects, other people, which in being sincerely considerate, will be unhampered by suspicions, in the others, of selfish or exploitive motives in ourselves. But the inevitable self-enjoyment that will accompany these processes, both in ourselves and in the others, though it is surely part of our motivation, does not reduce the whole situation to pure selfishness. Reese still further clarifies the distinction between self-interest and selfishness here, using our same criterion of inclusiveness:

> The contention of universal selfishness starts from the undeniably true statement that all action is done in terms of one's self. But we have seen how the self is a compound of feeling, sensation, idea and purpose. One may have a narrow range of loyalties or purposes; another may have an extremely wide range; whatever the range, they are part of, and define the limits of, one's self. And to be sure, one is always acting in terms of the interests of this self. The doctrine of self-interest is innocent enough, until it is confused with selfishness. At this point 'selfishness' should refer only to selves which support a very narrow range of loyalties. . . . Man *can* act from selfish motives shading all his actions; and man can act from more general motives; in either case he will be acting from self-interest; but he may not be acting selfishly.[8]

By a similar argument, DR can oppose SMR's tendency to suppose that only the more material desires and pleasures are "real" and that the more refined or "spiritual" desires are illusory — mere sentimental pieties. For if the basic desire is for more satisfaction which is based upon more complex and inclusive processes, then philosophical and religious interests are as solidly founded as are the desire for satisfaction of hunger and sex. The field forces of the brain are no more content to lie about in a disconnected welter than are the tissues of the stomach to shrivel up in thirst.

Comparison with SM: Thus DR, while getting away from SMR's blind, deterministic instincts, does not come back to SM's disembodied essences hanging in the air, elected by the mind, but not essentially involved with needs and concrete objects. The aims and purposes that guide human behavior are inextricably related with the particular kinds of field imbalances (needs) which ongoing life dumps upon the creature. The value-experiencing organism is not externalistically appropriating values out of the blue; rather it is constantly creating value feelings by resolving its *needs* through organizing and scheduling activity-with-objects.

Mediated interest must be conceived, however, not as dwelling in a world apart, aloof from the physical and vital processes of nature, but rather as a superimposed and more advanced stage of complexity. There are antecedent and underlying levels, and there is a threshold which marks the advent of cognition, and hence the level of interest "proper," that is, intelligent or expectative interest.[9]

DR can find a place for rational duty, but it is never separated from desire for concrete satisfaction.

DM with DR:

Since this chapter is only adding applications of the theory of need, object and desire of Chapter IX there is nothing fundamentally new to deduce from DM at this point. If dynamic value is defined as proportional to increasing complexity and order of creative process, then a development of the ability to plan and make habitual more "rational" modes of behavior is certainly implied.

B. Process, Development, Integration. Of the mass of material we might go into here, we will again select what bears upon one main point.

SM with SIR.

Implications of SM: Static value, of course, implies no necessity of integrating process. The individual should contain a fixed knowledge of values in intuition or conscience from birth. There should not need to be any problem of corrupt motivation and behavior needing to be elevated to higher levels. A processless contemplation of unchanging value essences or perfections is all that should need to exist.

Adjustments of SIR: SIR allows for the processes of achieving specific values that have been desired, though it conceives the process as imitative, as striving to conform to given codes of rules, to virtuous models, to the "true" self. The values themselves, of course, exist only at the end of the process of attainment. SIR developed no clear theory of the integrating of multiple desires as the prime locus of value experience.

SIR must also allow for "bad" behavior and the problem of reforming desires. The former becomes a somewhat inexplicable lapse from those fixed virtues implied by SM as built into human nature; and the latter a return to what was already implicit in one's instincts, a restoration of "true" nature. The process of returning as such is essentially meaningless, nothing more than repairing an accident which "never should have been." Only the final state of finished adjustment, of serene awareness of the perfect whole, has significance.

It cannot be too often repeated that this way of thinking is what is embedded in the minds of most of our writers, no matter how much they repudiate it on the surface. It is just because they persist, perhaps unconsciously, in demanding this picture of things, that they remain so bitter when either SMR or DR reveal the facts to be far otherwise.

SM with SMR.

Findings of SMR: Applying to the present material what we learned of SMR's inability to take development as really creative (Chapter IX) we can understand why it would be difficult to say what "fulfilling desire" or "creating value" could mean even in the case of a single urge. As for the merging of many motives and values into more complex patterns of behavior with new and "higher" value feelings, SMR cannot appreciate the significance of it. But that interests and desires should be modified by circumstances — both for the individual and for the culture — is only too explainable by SMR's unqualified relativism. It expects the preferences of individuals, groups and races to be as variable as the innumerable causative circumstances of different environments could make them and, of course, sees no grounds for evaluating any as better or worse than any others. (This statement treads upon evaluation, the topic of a later chapter.)

Most important to study at this point is why the notion of "higher development" of instinct and desire becomes meaningless. SMR, we know, can find no more significance in the process of creating values than can SM-SIR, though again for an opposite reason. It is now the beginning states that constitute reality, and to which process is irrelevant, rather than the end states, as in SM. This leaves SMR preoccupied with the primitive, original

366

instincts and drives that it focussed upon in the preceding head, to the exclusion of concern about what those drives may become. The most familiar example is early Freudianism's reducing all personality values to their origins in unsavory infantile preoccupations with eroticism in mouth, anus and urethra. Only social pressures, supposedly forced men away from their first modes of pleasure. Later activities were still, somehow, essentially identical with the infantile ones in value. No matter what a man expressed consciously, in any attempt to appear rational, his *real* motive remained the irrational original urges, sneaking past the repressions society has forced upon him as well as they could. The social pressure, moreover, which is the only source of inhibition or modification of the atomistic urges, was considered, at least by many Freudian camp-followers, as essentially unjustified in its demands. It only forced the personality — conceived mechanically enough as a group of separate parts, ego, id, and super-ego — into an unnecessarily tortuous jostling of its parts through the "mechanisms" of adjustment. If there is any central feeling, purposing and organizing self at all, it seems mainly a passive and helpless experiencer of the collidings of its parts. Thus much of the early "cure" of psychoanalysis consisted of flouting the social pressure so as to allow the fatalistically accepted instincts to go their own way.

A special feature of SMR's value psychology, which results from its atomistic approach, needs to be emphasized above all others: the unresisting readiness to push any isolated impulse to its limit. We have said that SMR has no more basis than SM for understanding why the essence of life might be the organizing and scheduling of many factors together in holistic patterns of function. The mere existence of an instinct or an urge, propelling one toward the kind of activity that satisfies it, is sufficient reason to believe that one neither can nor should resist the impulse, wherever it may carry him.

Now, in succumbing to fragmentary impulses, three psychological facts are discovered: first, that increasing the intensity of stimulation of a more or less sharply localized tissue can, up to a point, increase the vividness of sensation and pleasure experienced. But, second, in order to repeat such pleasure, the intensity of stimulation must be constantly increased. And, third, a "hangover" effect, which also constantly increases, is the price that must paid. These facts can be shown to apply to all those specifically sensational pleasures, not involving increased inclusiveness and organization, that SM and SIR call "sin" or "dissipation," and SMR calls "living it up": drunkenness, violent and exaggerated sexual activity, drug-addiction, sadism, etc. In all of these there is a first step of anaesthetizing the more holistic, organizing functions of the organism, which otherwise tend to keep the partial energies and currents at low enough levels of intensity so that they will not disrupt the order of the whole. Alcohol, stupefyingly repetitive music, self-hypnotism, etc., are ways to dull the higher centers of the brain. Now some partial impulse can capture the energy of the organism for its own purposes, at the expense of other needs. The drunk or addict can now pursue sexual impulses, or desires for revenge to extremes of violent feeling. The third fact, however, is sure to overtake him: destruction, "burning out" of tissue, or some other kind of irreversible disintegration of structures appears on the outer fringe of these extreme intensities of reaction.

SMR, however, in having no doctrine of balanced organization of the many part energies into patterned wholes, can have no reason for guarding against this disruptive pursuit of partial urges to the limit. And when the necessary consequence of illness and breakdown (that is, essentially, interference and colliding among the unaligned parts) follows, the devotees of atomistic determinism can only conclude that life is a cheat. This is one of the most persistent themes of current literature: the insistence that extreme states of fragmentary sensation are the only point of life joined with the bitter complaint that they lead to destruction. The disconcern with connections and subordinations among impulses is endemic in our writers. The famous Hemingway style of writing rejects subordinate clauses, purposely stringing details together by long series of "ands" and confining itself to primitive dialogue in order to express its rejection of life's long-term connections in favor of its highly charged, isolated instants. All instants are equally important or equally meaningless. We are advised to live like moths, burning ourselves up in the vividly flaming moment, rather than to work at relating our moments for the sake of longer-term satisfactions.

Comparison with SM: Thus SMR comes to conclusions poles apart from SM. The latter counsels total suppression of the vivid but risky impulses in favor of a passionless serenity of wholeness. The former loathes this ideal as suffocatingly dull and plumps for the corrosively intense fragmentary passions. Neither view directs our attention to the locus of true enjoyment that entails neither boredom nor hangover: the process of creatively organizing many factors into dynamic design, enjoyment rooted in the assembling, resolving, synthesizing as such. It is perhaps fair to say that "classicism," under the influence of SM, emphasizes the consummatory stage too exclusively; and "romanticism," though an attempt to escape from SMR back to SM, under the influence of SMR, emphasizes the initial, fragmentary stage too exclusively.

SM with DR.

Findings of DR: Perry states that every interest or value involves "a specific form of consummatory activity,"[10] utilizing some part or parts of the bodily structure plus objects of some sort. He calls the interaction with the object the "dealing." One object may be dealt with in different ways, in which case we have different interest or value experiences upon the same object. An apple may be enjoyed as food, as a beautifully colored object to paint, as a source of income to vendors, etc. Perry does not quite say what I would: that the dealing is the real locus of value, rather than the object that is dealt with (which "has value" in his usage), though I agree that the particular kind of object is necessary in order to make the dealing the specific kind of felt quality that it is.

DR, of course, recognizes the reality of many kinds of change that SM failed to imply: single desires giving rise to single strands of creative process (though we suggested on p. 351 that the simplest enjoyments must actually involve many elements or cells in the body); complex desires prompting complex patterns of action producing both consummations of separate part needs, as well as the over-all consummation of achieving the pattern itself; change of preference and evaluative criteria with individual growth and experience; and change of cultural standards with history. But we have said enough under the DR position in previous chapters to explain why such facts need not lead to SMR's conclusion that none of the changing standards can be any better than their origin. Nor can developed values be reduced to "original drives." We may give Perry's refutation of the reductive fallacy in this connection:

In this context the Atavistic Fallacy consists in supposing

369

that the Biological Drives continue to provide the driving power which the Social Drives merely canalize. This would mean that the original drives are the only independent drives . . . if they ceased to operate the wheels of action would cease to turn. This is plainly contrary to the fact of development. . . .

It is . . . important to know what drives are the most powerful and deep-seated; but this again, does not depend on innateness. Indeed it is characteristic of man that many of his most powerful drives, such as patriotism, ambition, and love of money, are clearly acquired. Drives may *become* deep-seated, in the sense of perseverance and mastery. Hence it is not in the least prejudicial to man's higher or more idealistic purposes that they should have been developed rather than original. Human interests can rise above their source. Indeed it might be said to be the very essence of man that both phylogenetically and ontogenetically he *does* rise above his source.[11]

Running over our three types of value, the "dealing" or "process" aspect of cognitive value would include such matters as we took up in chapter V on constructing knowledge, emphasizing that the enjoyment of thinking is in feeling the puzzles becoming clarified, feeling the bits and pieces of theory begin to fit together into systems, feeling the mathematical procedures issue in their symmetries and q.e.d.'s.

For aesthetic value, our approach would naturally be dubious of such a statement as Morris makes in commenting on Whitehead's aesthetics:

For aesthetic purposes, it is wise to distinguish as clearly as possible the process from end at which it is aimed; the achievement resulting in "satisfaction." There is some warrant for distinguishing between the process as art, conceived fundamentally as an activity, and the end as beauty, the satisfaction aimed at.[12]

Whatever may be the uses of considering beauty as a terminal state, we would have to insist that aesthetic enjoyment itself can occur only as we experience beauty *coming into being.*

Other statements of Whitehead's warn us of stagnation and destruction in Aesthetics, related to the problem of evil:

A static value, however serious and important, becomes unendurable by its appalling monotony of endurance. The soul cries aloud for release into change. . . . Great art is the arrangement of the environment so as to provide for the soul vivid, but transient values. . . . This element of transition in art is shown by the restlessness exhibited in its history. An epoch gets saturated by the masterpieces of any one style. . . . Yet there is a balance in things. Mere change before the attainment of adequacy of achievement, either in quality or output, is destructive of greatness.[13]

Art thrives in dissonance, but a dissonance ultimately resolved in consonance. Where it is unresolved, we have frustration or discord. Discord is aesthetic destruction. . . . The destruction which does not lead on to the production of new aesthetic wholes is evil, the ineradicable loss of value.[14]

In the realm of ethical value, let us deal with DR's rectification of SMR's excessive emphasis on the intense but fragmentary passion. The thesis that enjoyment resides preëminently in organizing multiple needs throws a different light on SMR's resentment that single passions cannot be pushed to their limit without punishment, and its suspicion that morality is mere inhibition and killjoy.

Of course, even the Freudians allowed that specific passions could be "sublimated," that is satisfied indirectly through other kinds of activity than whatever they originally drove toward. Other psychologies have analogous doctrines of the modification of "innate tendencies" by social demands for substitute activities. There is frequently the feeling, however, that the social and cultural forces that force the satisfaction of "basic needs" to take only certain selected forms are entirely inhibitory in significance, possessing mere nuisance value for the individual himself. We noticed this attitude in the less reconstructed Freudians under SMR above.

But with DR's conception of the whole-part relationship we know that added enjoyment comes from discovering patterns of behavior that "kill many birds with one stone." Therefore, when an individual finds a way to satisfy his sexual needs which at one

371

and the same time achieves personal love with a partner, the enriching complexities of family life, community esteem, the promise of contentment in old age, etc., his incorporating society's standards into his behavior has more than the significance of mere inhibitory nuisance value. It is clearly enhancing and multiplying value enjoyment for the individual himself, quite apart from society's demands. The sum of value enjoyment in behavior that integrates all these varieties of feeling is unarguably greater than those fleeting moments of intense sexual tickle to which the sexual monomaniac confines himself. If we admit that the risk of mismating, frustration, maladjustment with wife and children are also increased when one conforms to society's preference for the complex pattern of monogamy, we grant what is only the obverse of our coin, that enjoyment is proportional to complexity.

If the Freudian still argues, "but why might not society just as well change its requirements so that we can have promiscuous sex and social esteem both, and thus still more enjoyment?," the answer might be that society only fosters what human experience has found to be intrinsically best for long-term enjoyment anyway: that the relationship with one partner, developed in depth for an extended time, including experiences of trust and faith and shared memory, is inevitably superior to flitting through a repetitive routine of ephemeral affairs. That is, what society approves can be argued to be on the average, far from merely inhibitory, actually the most rewarding mode of process anyway. In other words, many of the taboos which have survived millennia of human experience might be defended as intrinsically conducive to better experience for the individual, even if society were not enforcing them at all. I say this recognizing that there are always repects in which society's views might be improved, though I suspect that most of those advocated by pseudo-Freudians and "realistic" litterateurs may not be among them.

Comparison with SM: This swirling world of constantly created values, merging and mixing concrete contents into fresh qualities of feeling, thus again escapes SMR's bitterness that isolated passions cannot be given uncontrolled reign. But it does not approximate to SM's expectation of rigid conformity to pre-set essences.

DM with DR.

Implications of DM and Correspondence to DR: With this

372

topic we are at the very center of the dynamic idea of value. The requirement or organizing process is contained in the original formula of definition from which we started (Chapter III).

But there remain some points to be clarified about the relation of consummation to process.

C. Consummation, Satisfaction. On this phase, rather than give the whole schedule of positions, we will discuss only a clarification of DM-DR's refusal to place value in any state of final perfection of achievement. Of course, for SM, the identification of the seeking mind with the essence sought is the only essential phase. "Contemplation" becomes the supreme and only meaningful state, conceived as a motionless regarding of essences, somehow eternally thrilling in itself. Unless indeed, like Plato and the Buddha, we grant the possibility that the state of perfection will contain no emotion or pleasure, and that we will not miss these temporal feelings.

What does DR mean, then, by saying that dynamic value exists only in the process and not at the terminus of activity? It seems impossible to deny that satisfying feeling is associated more especially with the later moments of a process; in some cases almost with the final moment, the last rapid resolving, or slipping of factors into place. In cases where what we desired was some definite simple object — a diamond ring, say — it might seem that the satisfaction was entirely located in the moment when we took hold of the ring and had it. However a little thought reveals that the enjoyment here is still intimately tied up with the preceding experience of not having, dreaming, desiring; or at least with previously knowing that diamonds were valuable (in cases where one had hardly aspired to owning one, receiving it as a surprise). Our continuing to experience value from the ring for any length of time then requires us to keep going through processes: putting it on the finger, holding it out for effect, showing it to others, etc.

For more complex, but still material, objects, such as a house, it is more obvious that the satisfaction lies in process. Here the sense of satisfaction is spread out over the many steps it takes to produce the house: the inspection of the plan, dreaming how it will be to live in it, enjoying each step in the building, etc. Probably we still would feel that the satisfaction increases in intensity during the finishing steps, and during the actual moving in; though on the other hand we often feel some letdown at the final attainment and it turns out the greatest satisfaction was somewhere earlier in the process.

As for less material objects — the satisfaction of rational and moral behavior, for instance, it is even more obvious that the meaning and satisfaction is spread through subordinate episodes in the steps of thought or the schedule of behavior that is attaining some moral success. Of course we can again admit that feeling may become more acute at special climactic moments of resolving.

Even if we were forced to admit that there are times of actual *possession* of satisfaction, of fulfillment that is *complete,* we would still maintain that such satisfaction involves, then, a simultaneous holding before the awareness of the former contrasting period of lack or threat. Or, perhaps more accurately, there may be a kind of oscillation of attention between the present consummation and memory of the former lack. Realization of great moral value — heroism, sacrifice, etc. — certainly involves the continuing thought of the former risk and tension that was faced and overcome.

In summary, we hold that value as the satisfying feeling of organizing process integrally involves all phases of the process, though it may well be felt more acutely in some phases than others — insofar as living process can be broken into phases at all. Actually the units of process probably do not have absolute breaks, especially no sharp division between a period of change and one of absolute rest. Anyone who wanted to place value preeminently in the latter state would not be able to find it in existence. However, there is no doubt that processes are not homogeneous throughout, and that there are moments of more rapid resolution associated with more intense satisfaction feeling.

It remains to clarify just what this consummatory feeling is, particularly how it is related to the hedonists' pleasure, happiness, etc.

Pratt argues that the hedonist should not be allowed to define "pleasure" so broadly as to include any sort of "satisfying feeling," as we just done. This renders the hedonistic thesis merely tautological, he feels: obviously no one can be motivated by anything but the desire to satisfy desire. This might seem a complete concession, if we assumed that such satisfaction would always consist of some sort of "pleasant feeling," but Pratt argues steadfastly that "satisfaction" does not have to mean either feeling in general or pleasant feeling in particular.

First, he even questions that one with a desire necessarily desires the satisfaction of the desire.

When one is very thirsty and longs for a drink, is it the ending of the state of thirst, or the drink that one desires? A Scotch proverb says, "It's fine to be hungry and ken a'meat."[15]

The first of these instances seems to illustrate the absurdity of the analytical fallacy often mentioned particularly well. On the dynamic theory one can only desire the felt interaction with the drink, and the disjunction between object and feeling (relief of thirst) becomes only a mental distinction, not significant for the nature of the actual process. The Scotch proverb so little illustrates not desiring satisfaction of desire ("kenning" the meat surely consists of anticipating its enjoyment) that mention of it seems frivolous.

Pratt goes on to make quite explicit this thesis that the term pleasure should be confined to one specific kind of feeling. This arbitrary narrowing of its meaning then, of course, makes hedonism very easy to refute. Pleasure

. . . is most commonly used as the psychologists use it, to mean a quality of sensation and images — a quality not ultimately definable (because not further analyzable) but recognized by all. . . . Unfortunately the word is often used . . . to mean the sense of satisfaction of desire, the realization of the achievement of purpose. The desire or purpose in question may be of any sort. . . . This use of the word has no justification and is most unfortunate.[16]

There is a breath here of the rationalistic supposition that pure intellectual "realization of the achievement of a purpose" is quite outside the category of feeling, which DR finds to be unfactual. However our problem now becomes mainly a matter of definition. If the term "pleasure" is to be used to cover only a certain class of sensuous feelings, we may agree upon the definition. In that case we will need another word to cover the entire genus of consummatory feeling. Any hedonism worth considering at all has always meant its term for pleasant feeling — "pleasure", "happi-

375

ness" or whatever else — to cover the whole genus. For Pratt (and most anti-hedonists) to insist upon a conveniently narrow definition, thereupon easily upsetting the theory, does not signify much.

In any case, we need to understand that satisfaction *feels* satisfying. It is a feeling, and not the merely mechanical adjustment of urge to object, or object to object that Pratt often seems to envisage. Dynamically, it can only be a felt resolution of some kind of felt dynamic tensions, and this feeling will surely be pleasant. So I conclude that the dynamic idea of value leads to a type of hedonism, if the term for pleasure is conceived inclusively enough.

Moritz Schlick makes an interesting distinction between "motive feeling" and "realization feeling."[17] Realization feeling, of course, comes under the present heading; motive feeling under the first heading on motivation. We can accept that there is feeling in that earlier phase of the process, for we hold that any phase of the process is felt as good whenever any feeling tissue is moving toward greater order; and in enjoying one's prior desiring or planning, there are certainly nervous tissues that are in the act of going through organizing processes. But the realization feeling would usually be a stronger feeling simply because it would involve many other tissues besides just brain tissues feeling the solving process.

What is the consummatory aspect for our three kinds of value? For cognitive value it is clear that the verifying of the hypothesis, or the solving of some mathematical puzzle is accompanied by pleasant feeling. But many would be most chary of the implication of our theory that this feeling itself *is* the value in the situation. Certainly the feeling itself, at least that in the particular knowledge episode, does not seem to be the determiner of the *truth* of the knowledge — in the scientific age it has been carefully excluded as any *test* of truth or validity. Here, however, we verge upon the topic of *evaluation* of values, which belongs under a later heading. That topic relates to the present one (whether the *value* of knowledge lies in its aspect as a satisfying feeling of organizing process) only insofar as the development of improved tests of truth renders it necessary for one cognizant of them, who wants to experience knowledge-value to feel that he is succeeding in satisfying those tests. It may once have been possible to enjoy a belief simply because it was immediately comforting (i.e., consisted of some sort of mental organizing) whether "verified" or not. And today "knowledge experiences" in people who can believe regardless of the improved tests may still be a pleasant feeling process for them, and thus valued; only now, under the evaluative head, we would rank them as "low" values ("poor knowledge"?). An educated scientist today, however, might not enjoy such knowledge at all, because any knowing process that does not satisfy the new tests simply would not constitute a real experience of resolution for him any more, and therefore would not be enjoyable, or a value.

We are saying, then, that the value in knowledge lies in the pleasurable feeling of the process of gaining it, and not in the circumstance that a set of ideas "corresponds" to fact or "coheres," although the latter enters in integrally as a criterion of whether we *are* gaining it or not. The intellectualism of both SIR and SMR has always discounted this feeling experience that accompanies the building up of truth, and led men to suppose that the final state of pure "knowing" was the significant thing, the enjoyment of resolution only a peripheral accompaniment. But our approach would see much more point in the fact that reality is so constituted as to require men to acquire past knowledge through the *learning process* and new knowledge through the *creative thinking process*.

For aesthetic value, our approach would lead to more emphasis on the moments just before the pattern or design has crystallized in the artist's or spectator's mind. It is not in contemplating the finished pattern that the value consists, but in feeling our sensorium slipping into it out of the confusion that preceded. Our illustrations in our first presentation of dynamic value (p. 49) were drawn from different kinds of aesthetic and recreational experience and may be referred to here.

For ethical value, the ever-present threat of possible imbroglios in human relations would be integral in the value-feelings involved in virtuous behavior. Just as in the cognitive case, value itself would not be in the standard of evaluation, but in feeling the process whereby we approach that standard out of less adequate ways of acting. And the standard itself would be justified in terms of its tendency to produce longer-term satisfactions.

Comparison with SM: This emphasis on feeling in the consummatory moments is quite different from SM's way of thinking, where it is assumed that possession of the final essence or form by the mind will be instantly, statically and permanently satisfactory in some purely intellectual manner. DR is not reluctant to

377

admit, as SM is, that pleasant feeling is the point of all existence. For this does not necessarily mean that the world is run by selfish, low-grade pleasures. We have begun to see some of the means DR has to escape from this threat, and will see more in the chapters on evaluation.

DM with DR.

Correspondence of DR with DM: DR's thesis that satisfaction is a matter of feeling of process naturally corresponds with the dynamic idea of meaning, since the latter takes its rise from just this ultimate finding of the dynamic idea of reality (DR).

This forcing the factor of qualitative feeling in processes out into the open, upon which our philosophy rests, is surely the supplementation most sorely needed by our age of blind quantity and goal-less efficiency. The answer to those who are perplexed by the failure of our much vaunted quantitative "progress" to produce proportional enjoyment lies in this declaration that reality is not primarily for mere cause and effect, mere production for production; but that it is for organizing and patterning processes to be tested by their success in producing good feeling.

D. Product: Memory, Habit, Virtue. On this last topic under value facts we will run over the positions very sketchily.

SM with SIR.

Implications of SM: SM would incline to expect minds or souls to come already outfitted with all necessary knowledge of values built into the memory or conscience, fixed in habitual routines of action (if there is to be any action at all). All creatures should be endowed with virtue at the outset, built into memory and habit.

Adjustments of SIR: Traditional thinking was aware that virtue was not automatic, and that a great deal had to be done to develop it. Of course, once again, the training of virtue was conceived as a "return to true nature." Aristotle discussed the difference between doing right by an arduous act of will and doing it easily, happily from virtuous habit. And the Middle Ages had much to say about the saintly life as one where virtuous behavior had become almost automatic, no longer requiring effort. Thus the saint had returned to and now occupied his original status as unalloyedly good.

SM with SMR.

Findings of SMR: SMR's theory of learning by the conditioning of reflexes achieved its greatest success in the explanation of habit building. But of course all habits thus produced would have to be deterministic, and no habit can be evaluated or prescribed as virtuous and obligatory for anyone to develop. Habits are considered largely from the point of view of their usefulness in enabling the organism to behave more efficiently and quickly.

Contradiction to SM: There is no place in SMR for SM-SIR's notion of the virtues as somehow already implanted in men. The infant is considered to be practically bereft of any fixed modes of behavior, and every habit that he is ever to possess must be learned and developed from scratch. In the instinct theories of SMR, habit may have more of an inborn nature, but certainly not in the sense of virtue. A recourse of SM might be the romantic's attempt to rely on "naturally good instincts" as the source of virtuous behavior. This recourse would then receive its disillusionment by evolutionary theory in the usual way.

SM with DR.

Findings of DR: The most useful way of thinking of habits and skills is to relate them to our theory of the preservation of attainment (Chapter IX, DR, Ends). They are ways of holding or preserving achieved levels of value-process so that an advance to more complex ones may thence be made. In fact the whole realm of habit-building might come under the same category as material structure. The factor in nature that causes atoms, molecules and cells to fall into the repetitive routines that undergird the maintenance of the "material" structures that are necessary for advanced organic processes is the same factor that appears in the repetitive routines of the nervous system that undergird memory and the more advanced complexities of behavior. This approach relieves DR of the threatening dilemma of having to accept repetitive habit as a very pervasive characteristic of life, while it wants to insist that fresh creativity is more centrally significant. The repetitive habits become in this way quite integral means to the fresh creativity. They are exactly what allows life to be something other than the solving of the same old problem over and over. A problem once solved may thenceforth be relied upon to solve itself habitually on future occasions while the attention moves on to some new activity made possible by that stable habit.

The building up of habitual modes of reacting, when taken all together, results in the personality pattern as a whole — that unique holistic design recognition of which, we have argued, helps DR to escape from SMR's mechanistic determinism by separate part forces.

As for modern developments in the understanding of the nervous processes that undergird habits — the nerve-nets et al. — we cannot take space to deal with them.

Comparison to SM: The student may work this out for himself.

DM with DR:

Implications of DM and Correspondence to DR: The deduction of memory and of preservation of accomplishment through habit was detailed in the chapter on Mind and Body (XII).

So much for our suggestions on a few points in the factual theory of value experience. We now proceed to the task of summarizing and defining the nature of value on the basis of these facts, taking up a few of the controversies in the topic, which have waxed incredibly complex in the modern history of philosophy.

CHAPTER XV

THE NATURE AND DEFINITION OF VALUE

On the basis of a thorough study of the factual phenomena of value experience (only a small part of which we have had space for in the preceding chapter), we may suppose ourselves to be ready for our summary conclusions as to the general nature and definition of value. The present chapter will be constructed according to the framework, taking the same schedule of sub-topics under each position for comparison. This gives us a pigeon hole for most of the material on this vexed topic, though again, for lack of space, we will not necessarily develop every sub-topic under every position.

We have already discussed a main question as to the nature of value, when we introduced, in Chapter III, our basic distinction between the static and dynamic ideas of good. In this chapter we will be especially concerned with how that distinction bears upon these other distinctions in the area.

The schedule, with some preliminary explanation, is as follows:

A. *Fundamental Distinctions in the Approach to Definition.*

1. *Use of Language.* One controversy in modern axiology concerns whether or not the philosopher should be allowed to redefine words in his effort to reach some inclusive and consistent system of understanding, or whether he must confine himself to clarifying "ordinary meanings."

2. *The Question of Intrinsic Value.* It will be convenient to state at the outset, under each position, what it tends to hold concerning the distinction between intrinsic and instrumental value, and whether the former is best conceived as "Right" or "Good." The following heads, for SM and SIR refer to Intrinsic value.

3. *Canons of Definition.* Under this head we mean to consider

many of the distinctions that have been made (especially by those seeking "recourses" from SMR back to SM-SIR) to guard against illegitimate identifications of meaning in defining Intrinsic value. In modern logic, different kinds of terms are found to be susceptible to different kinds of definitional status.

    (a) Simple vs. Complex terms.

    Simple terms are said to be indefinable because:

      i. they are ultimate and can find nothing beyond themselves in terms of which to be defined, all other terms being defined in terms of them.

      ii. they have no parts to be enumerated.

      iii. they refer to immediate qualities, like colors, which can only be pointed to. E. g. we cannot define "red" for a blind man. To be known, it can only be directly observed.

    Complex terms can be defined:

      i. in terms of more ultimate terms.

      ii. by enumerating their parts (which may be simple terms).

      iii. by indicating necessary relations in which they stand to other ideas or things.

    (b) Analytic vs. Synthetic definitions.

    The definition of a complex term may be:

      i. Analytic, when it merely brings out aspects of meaning already contained in the term itself, logically and necessarily related to the concept, as "A triangle is a three-sided figure." It adds no information about it.

      ii. Synthetic, when it adds knowledge about the thing which is discovered to be invariably part of it, as "Man is a mammal."

    (c) Non-natural vs. Naturalistic definitions.

    A synthetic definition may be:

      i. Non-natural, when the additional information is not a matter of empirical discovery, but can be intuitively known *a priori*. And, according to many rationalists, non-natural definitions also include cases where the term can be analyzed into some natural and some non-natural characteristics.

      ii. Naturalistic, when the information is empirically discovered, and the term can be analyzed into naturalistic terms without remainder.

(d) Finally there remains the question whether the invariably accompanying characteristic is merely "common" to the thing but not "peculiar" to it or "sufficient" to define it; "peculiar" to it but not "sufficient" to define it; or absolutely identical and synonymous with it and sufficient to define it.

B. *Conclusions as to the Nature of Value.*

Under headings 4, 5, and 6, we itemize some further distinctions that have been involved in value controversy, concerning the kind of characteristics named in the definitions.

4. Relational vs. Non-relational Definitions. How value is conceived with regard to essences, qualities, things, events and relations.

5. Deontological vs. Teleological Definitions. If relations are allowed, what part if any do relations to ends or consequences play?

6. Objective vs. Subjective Theories. If relations are allowed, what part if any in them does subjective feeling play? Particularly subjective feeling of needs, aims, processes, consummations?

7. Summary statement of what value is said to be.

8. Adequacy. Prior hints (to be developed in later chapters) as to main strengths and weaknesses of the theory, the latter prompting transition to the next theory. The main problems are how successful it is in dealing with the facts; and with obligation and responsibility.

SM with SIR.

Implications of SM: 1. Language. Our use of the concept, "static idea of good," as essential to SM is obviously a product of special thought, and not merely an analysis of "ordinary language," though we do hold that it is implicit in a good deal of traditional thought, and of much "ordinary" thinking still today. Our efforts to develop what is logically entailed by the idea may sometimes carry us to notions that no one ever seriously defended; but many times, as has been seen in the book, we can find examples of "ordinary thought" in the past that exactly illustrate some strict implication from the idea. To what extent Parmenides, Plato and Aristotle were merely analyzing ordinary language when they sent philosophy off in the static direction would be a moot question.

383

2. Intrinsic Value. Intrinsic value (the "good in itself") conceived statically has, of course, no implication to instrumental value at all. For SM, intrinsic good would simply be the static idea of good itself, which can conceivably exist independently of process, parts, means, instruments, as we have repeatedly seen.

3. Canons of Definition. The static idea of good is, for anyone who has made the distinction between it and the dynamic idea, a "complex" term since it makes a connection between the idea of value and the idea of static. For the traditional devotees of the idea, however, it may be considered a "simple" term that cannot be defined, being ultimate, or a simple quality without parts. Or it may be treated as complex and capable of an analytic definition in terms, for instance, of "rightness" (see below). Or perhaps it may be given a synthetic, non-natural definition in terms of the theory of static being, perfection, etc. A naturalistic definition in terms of psychological processes and feelings is less common, though I have included definitions in terms of permanent states of satisfaction under the static idea of good.

On the whole, I think it is fair to say that the static idea of value tends toward indefinability. Modern rationalists often stress this indefinability for their purposes. It would stem from the underlying failure of the static idea to imply process, and thence parts and relations as intrinsic to good. The most usual criticism of the static intuitionist view of value concerns its lack of concrete content.

4. Status as to Relations. Most strictly, of course, the static idea of good means (a) that value should be an unchanging essence, concept, idea, quality, not essentially involved in development, embodiment or relations. And if a variety of specific values is envisaged (contradictorily to SM's basic logic, as we saw in Chapter XIV) they would also be such essences.

(b) Less strictly, SM might allow value or values to be definite qualities located in, embodied in *things,* almost as substantial entities attached to objects. Things could then just "be" good, preeminently when they fulfill perfect form and thus no longer need to change. But if they do change for the worse, decay, disappear, the value would not have changed, rationalists have argued; value would still mean the *concept* of the beauty or the color or the truth or the virtue that the thing had formerly possessed.

(c) Still less strictly, values might be embodied somehow in *events,* acts, behavior, but, as we said in Chapter III, only when these are conceived as perfectly harmonious functioning, according to some fixed rule or routine.

(d) We have seen in many connections that the static idea of value does not imply relations among entities. We shall find, under Recourses below, how often modern rationalists recur to this reluctance to define intrinsic good in terms of relations. In fact, "intrinsic" is sometimes taken to mean, precisely, independence of relations; to refer to things that are right or good in themselves, and would be so "if nothing else existed in the world."[1]

5. Status as to Consequences. In implying no process, the static idea of good obviously cannot imply that relations to consequences have any essential part to play in defining intrinsic value.

6. Status as to Minds. There is no implication that the essences or the qualities in objects or acts need to be known or felt by minds in order to exist. Thus there may be some presumption from SM in favor of objective theories of value: that value essence can exist independently of whether any minds are knowing or feeling it or not (unless its independent existence is conceived as being in the mind of God). In the preceding chapter and Chapter IX, we noted that the static idea implies no relation to the need or process aspects of the feeling process, only possibly to the consummatory aspect, not necessarily conceived, however, as felt satisfaction.

7. Conclusion on the Nature of Value and Standards: Absolutism. Intrinsic value statically conceived, then, is a self-existent essence carrying no implication to process, relations, consequences or feeling. "Absolutism" is the usual name for the theory of standards consonant with SM. The good or the right is independent of all circumstance and relation. "Perfection" thus becomes a meaningful term for SM, in fact the very nature of value.

Paradoxically, at the same time that Absolutism purports to be so certain of exactly what the good is, it actually finds it impossible to give specific content to it. We shall find that this debility forces SM to shy off from explaining value or standards themselves; and to resort to its intuitional or authoritarian methods of *knowing* value as though they were somehow themselves the standards.

A related tendency is, in the absence of a usable explanation of the *nature* of value or good, to take "right" and "duty" as root, underivable concepts, more fundamental than value. The latter would then be derived from rightness, considered normally as conformity to the model essence. In the days of custom and authoritarian rules this would have been an easy way to conceive the situation. Intuitionists might be conceived as trying to make it do for later days when customs and rules more often conflict with one another.

8. Adequacy. If SM has always been appealed to as necessary for a firm foundation for moral obligation, we might remark that it does not really imply any process so that obligation could have any scope. But the main inadequacy of SM is always its failure to fit facts. Rather than extend a discussion of its weaknesses here, we will first present SIR's efforts to accommodate it to actual experience.

Adjustments of SIR: 1. Language. Traditional thought depended very largely upon the method of analyzing "ordinary language." It was certainly Aristotle's basic method; and it is often said that throughout the Middle Ages, including the Thomistic synthesis, philosophy and theology were closer to the layman's understanding than they have ever been since. In much traditional thought the concept of value as such may hardly emerge from the details of logical, aesthetic and moral rule-making. Thus when modern students try to make generalizations concerning the traditional concept of value as such, they may perforce depart from ordinary traditional language. However, they usually claim that in some sense they do not depart from its "essential import," etc.

2. Intrinsic Value. The distinction between Intrinsic and Instrumental Value had to be made early in traditional thought when it had to be recognized that men, for some reason unknown to SM, are under the necessity of striving and using practical instruments in order to approach the fixed essences. And so a whole department of axiology must be added to anything SM implied: the theory of instrumental values, their infinitely complex interrelationships, their order of precedence, or the "hierarchy" of values, and how they are related to the highest value, the "summum bonum," an old name for intrinsic value. Intrinsic "higher" values are now kept carefully uncontaminated, as pure, contemplated thoughts, from instrumental values, always sullied by their close involvement with matter, change and struggle. All instrumental activity and work are significant only insofar as they lead to the being of the higher essences; they are not significant or valuable in any sense for themselves. The problem remains

how to identify and define intrinsic value so that it may serve as a guide for the instrumental activities.

3. 4. 5. 6. I will postpone discussion of SIR's preferences on these topics until the "Recourses" section under SM-SMR.

7. Conclusion on the Nature of Value and Standards. SIR, then, differs from SM mainly in adding a theory of approach to SM's theory of fixed essences. Many forms of SIR follow SM in finding "rightness" a more fundamental concept than goodness. SIR supports the Absolutism SM implied; and also reveals the typical inability to say what value is in concrete situations, falling back on its authoritarian and intuitional theory of knowledge for all specific content.

8. Adequacy. We will study SM-SIR's adequacy in more detail under Recourses. Under SMR we will find some of the "facts" that make trouble.

SM with SMR.

Findings of SMR: 1. Language. In earlier phases of SMR's value thinking, there was a great readiness to ignore "ordinary meanings," and to explode and debunk them in terms of the implications of its mechanistic assumptions. The "good" could be defined in terms of instinct, pleasure, desire, etc. (see items below) with never a question whether most people meant such a thing by the term or not. But with the criticisms of the rationalists on this point thinkers are more hesitant nowadays about importing unusual meanings into value terms; so that even the positivists, undertaking to import the strangest meaning of all, can be heard dismissing older identifications, such as the hedonistic, because they do not correctly analyze "ordinary language." Ayer, for instance, writes:

> . . . we reject utilitarianism and subjectivism, not as proposals to replace our existing ethical notions by new ones, but as analyses of our existing ethical notions. Our contention is simply that, in our language, sentences which contain normative ethical symbols are not equivalent to sentences which express psychological propositions, or indeed empirical propositions of any kind.[2]

387

On the whole, however, SMR's interpretations of value continue to be radically different from ordinary meanings.

2. Intrinsic Value. We already understand why SMR naturally confines its attention almost exclusively to Instrumental Value, and technically can have no theory of intrinsic value at all, exactly opposite to SM. In fact, it is a question whether it can have a theory of instrumental value either, insofar as we have seen that it cannot strictly admit a place for feeling, quality or attainment in any genuine sense. However, there are certain typical theories of value associated with SMR in spite of this. They will seek to formulate value as fact, in terms of efficient activity or production, of empirical sensations, of individually experienced pleasure. Thus things might be considered "good," if they perform their function efficiently or successfully, producing their proper effects. Also, the primarily instrumental character of their "goodness" appears here. An example can be found in Spinoza's ethics.[3]

But I will also include under SMR theories that try to deal with intrinsic value in a certain sense: as what is factually desired and enjoyed as a matter of empirical psychology and sociology. Values may be conceived as analogous to sensation or emotion, as empirical experiences, epiphenomenal to material processes though SMR is inclined to consider them. Thus the desires and enjoyments by which good is defined will be as various as the pluralistic material and social causes make them. These will not be absolute intrinsic goods in SM-SIR's sense, as providing grounds for ultimate evaluation and obligation. They will be merely whatever preferences have been actually thrown up by different circumstances.

We saw in the preceding chapter, however, that SMR may attempt more monistic theories of good as pleasure, power, or evolutionary success.

3. Canons of Definition. The usual kind of definition of value for SMR, then, is synthetic and naturalistic. It associates the good with some existent empirical phenomenon and concludes that the good *means* that characteristic. The identification can be in the area of biology, with given instincts or with evolutionary trends; or in psychology with existent desires as determined by heredity or early environment; or in sociology with customs as culturally determined. All these types agree that value relates to the factually existent rather than to the prescriptive.

4. Status as to Relations. SMR will naturally have difficulty in

locating value (if there be any such thing) anywhere but in material things. We have seen how unreal relations between parts and wholes must be for mechanistic thought, and therefore how non-relational its theory of value will tend to be. Events and acts, too, would, strictly speaking, be too insubstantial to be real locuses of value. So we find attempts to make value a non-relational quality of things which is received by some special sense, analogously to the way light sensations are received by the organs of sight. This way of thinking may be extended to acts, by attempting to conceive the goodness of acts as some quality in them which is picked up by a "moral sense." The special sensation caused in the perceiver may be called "approval" or "pro-feeling."[4] G. E. Moore's famous theory of good as an indefinable non-relational quality, immediately perceived, might be mentioned here as an attempt to reinstate value as a reality within SMR's world-view in this manner, though his anxiety to avoid the naturalistic fallacy would place him under the Recourses section below. Still, Moore shows SMR's typical reluctance to make the *felt* process of interaction between subject and object the basic reality, and wants to keep value as a non-relational, external something which is merely registered upon the sensorium in a passive, or reflective manner, just as SMR conceives sensations to be. As Pratt says of Moore: Value is

. . . a quality which certain things and acts possess in themselves, entirely out of relation to what anyone feels or wants or likes. . . . Similarly Mr. Moore insists that certain things, situations, acts are good in themselves no matter what anything else may be or do, or what anyone may wish or feel.

This quality of goodness or beauty, and (in more general terms) of value as such, is as directly observable as any quality of anything is observable. In asserting this, the Moore-Laird position would seem to be as far removed as possible from that of Hartmann. For value, being directly observable in things, is conceived as an empirical, not as an a prioristic quality.[5]

Moore yielded, afterward, on his claim that good is quite analogous to an immediate quality like "yellow," and admitted that there is some difference between intrinsic qualities, like colors, and value. For one thing, there was no specific sense organ for good or value as such. But still rejecting any relational status for value, Moore confessed he could not say what the difference was. SMR's lack of an adequate doctrine of the whole-part relationship, I suggest, was his main difficulty.

5. Relations to Consequences. Although much of what Utilitarianism has to say on value theory belongs under DR, J. S. Mill was accused by G. E. Moore of an SMR-like "naturalistic fallacy," for having offered, as a proof that happiness in consequences is the criterion of desirable goods, the fact that people actually desire it. This, Moore argues, confuses two meanings of "desirable": "able to be desired" and "ought to be desired." Mill, using the first meaning, does not see that it fails, in itself, to establish the second meaning. This does, perhaps illustrate in a sense SMR's typical making value to be what actually happens without any theory of what ought to happen. Bentham's exclusion of qualitative differences in the consequences from value measurement, considering only quantitative aspects of pleasure, also smacks of SMR, but J. S. Mill, of course, admitted qualitative criteria too.

More typical of SMR, however, than any form of consequence theory is what was mentioned under # 2: taking existing, fragmentary desires as sufficient to determine value, without regard to their relations to other desires, or to further consequences.

6. Relations to Minds. Although SMR might be presumed to favor objectivism, with its lack of an adequate theory of feeling, and its focus on the objective processes of external nature, we find subjectivist, relativistic theories associated with it in value theory. The biological and sociological theories mentioned above are objective in a sense, in endeavoring to explain what factual causes have led to the tastes and moral attitudes in certain groups of individuals. But in the last analysis, value experience itself is seen as a matter of subjective desire and satisfaction, however much the modes of desire and satisfaction may be the result of those causes. And, of course, the subjective modes will be entirely *relative* to those cause, as against SM's hope of absolutism. SMR's satisfaction, too, will tend to be interpreted as physical pleasure only.

7. Conclusion on the Nature of Value and Standards. Value can be conceived by SMR only by departing from the strictest implications of its atomistic and non-affective foundations. Thereupon it will conceive value as an epiphenomenal, non-relational,

subjective experience analogous to sensation; or as an instrumental efficacy. In all senses value will be assimilated to the factual and existent rather than the prospective and evaluated. Thus SMR will not try to derive intrinsic good from intrinsic right. Of course, for the individual within a particular society, there might be a "right" or "duty" with respect to the demands of that group. Hume, for instance, defines the good as what is "approved by most men." Individuals, then, "ought" to do what is approved by most men. But this leaves the content of good or rightness, as Broad notes,[6] to be settled by a statistical survey of most men's opinions, in whatever state they happen to be, with no basis for criticizing that state itself.

8. Adequacy. It is obvious what weaknesses of SMR's value theory prompt the desperate efforts of rationalists to refute it and to reinstate something of SM-SIR's absolutism. The relativism seems to destroy any genuine evaluation. It makes any notion of obligation meaningless. It obscures the distinction between means and ends, bringing into doubt the existence of any final ends or intrinsic goods. The battle against SMR's relativistic naturalism and subjectivism is carried on along all the lines which we have itemized, many of the points purporting to defy DM-DR as well.

Recourses to SM-SIR: 1. Language. Many modern rationalists, defending ways of thinking related to SM-SIR, take as basic philosophical method the analysis of "ordinary language" or accepted meanings of terms. One finds them refusing to follow not only the SMR theorists who identify value with fact, but any value theorist who, for reasons of theoretical consistency, or in the light of more dynamic categories, suggests that value ought to be identified with some systematic structure of concepts. For, they say, "It isn't what we mean by value." By "we" is meant the ordinary man, and by "mean" is meant the general consensus of such ordinary users of the language. If "men," then, are still thinking of value as a static quality attached to substances, then the philosopher apparently must also.

W. D. Ross, in taking "right" (as against "good") as his ultimate unanalyzable concept, constantly appeals to what "plain men" think.

> When a plain man fulfills a promise because he thinks he
> ought to do so, it seems clear that he does so with no

thought of its total consequences. . . . He thinks in fact much more of the past than of the future. What makes him think it right to act in a certain way is the fact that he has promised to do so — that and, usually, nothing more. . . .[7]

Ross goes on to appeal to intuitional self-evidence in support of the plain man's lack of concern about consequences.

In fact it seems, on reflection, self-evident that a promise, simply as such, is something that *prima facie* ought to be kept, and it does *not* on reflection, seem self-evident that production of maximum good is the only thing that makes an act obligatory. . . .

It would be a mistake to found a natural science on "what we really think," i.e. on what reasonably thoughtful and well-educated people think about the subjects of the science before they have studied them scientifically . . . the man of science must appeal from these to sense-experience itself, which furnishes his real data. In ethics no such appeal is possible . . . the moral convictions of thoughtful and well-educated people are the data of ethics just as sense-perceptions are the data of natural science . . .[8]

Here the plain man has changed to the thoughtful, well-educated one, but otherwise we have the same demand that we take certain immediate intuitions of a vaguely specified group of thoughtful people who, however, are not said to have devoted special effort to thinking out value systems, as our final arbiter to the exclusion of analysis, testing and systematizing by those who have made special efforts to clarify the field.

2. Intrinsic Value. The rationalists return to putting a great deal of emphasis upon the difference between instrumental and intrinsic value; they then stake their whole case for the objectivity and absoluteness of value upon the latter, from which they hope to derive obligation and duty. It is rescued from the contingencies of empirical experience by every means available, most of which occur here among our items.

3. Canons of Definition. The standard statement of intrinsic value as a simple, indefinable term must be G. E. Moore's. For

him, any attempt to define good in terms of any other properties
— that is to identify it with them, to say it *means* them — is to
commit the "naturalistic fallacy."

. . . if I am asked "How is good to be defined?" my answer
is that it cannot be defined . . . propositions about the good
are all of them synthetic and never analytic . . . if I am
right, then nobody can foist upon us such an axiom as that
"Pleasure is the only good" or that "The good is the desired"
on the pretense that this is "the very meaning of the word."

. . . My point is that 'good' is a simple notion, just as
'yellow' is a simple notion; that, just as you cannot, by any
manner of means, explain to any one who does not already
know it, what yellow is, so you cannot explain what good
is. . . .

And many people appear to think that, if we say "Pleasure
and intelligence are good," or if we say "Only pleasure and
intelligence are good," we are defining 'good.' . . .

It may be true that all things which are good are *also*
something else, just as it is true that all things which are
yellow produce a certain kind of vibration in . . . light. . . .
But far too many philosophers have thought that when they
named those other properties they were actually defining
good; that these properties, in fact, were simply not 'other,'
but absolutely and entirely the same with goodness. This
view I propose to call the "naturalistic fallacy." . . .

My dear sirs, what we want to know . . . is not how people
use a word; it is not even, what kind of actions they approve . . . what we want to know is simply what *is* good. . . .
When they say "Pleasure is good," we cannot believe that they
merely mean "Pleasure is pleasure" and nothing more than
that. . . .

'Good,' then, if we mean by it that quality which we assert
to belong to a thing, when we say that the thing is good,
is incapable of any definition, in the . . . sense . . . in which
a definition states what are the parts which invariably compose
a certain whole; and in this sense 'good' has no definition
because it is simple and has no parts. It is one of those innumerable objects of thought which are themselves incapable
of definition, because they are the ultimate terms by reference

393

to which whatever *is* capable of definition must be defined. . . .[9]

Ewing goes on to argue that to keep good undefined and unidentified with any natural or subjective factors is necessary if obligation to pursue it is to be defended. First he restates Moore's thesis in terms of the illegitimacy of "reducing ethical terms to non-ethical ones."

> . . . I see that "good," "right," "duty," "ought," "morality" are just not the sort of concepts which can ever be analyzed completely in terms of psychology. . . .
> . . . this is . . . only to exclude the possibility of reducing the central concept of ethics to non-ethical terms . . . such statements . . . may be correct descriptions but they are not definitions, at least in the sense under discussion. . . .
> What is it that is missing from any naturalist or subjectivist account? Well, I should not like to say the only missing element but at any rate the most important one is the concept of obligation. "Good" in its non-natural sense or senses carries with it the notion that the good thing *ought* not to be wantonly sacrificed but, other things being equal, pursued.[10]

He next itemizes the various kinds of naturalistic "definition" of good — that it is a certain kind of emotional feeling, or the object of desire, or an exclamation expressing emotion, or what is approved by most people, etc., — and shows that obligation to pursue any of them is not deducible from their conception.

The argument is, then, that the only way to get the ethical "ought" indissolubly tied in with the meaning of "good" is to include it in a non-naturalistic definition.

4. Relations. Perhaps Ross's statement of the non-relational status of intrinsic good is as uncompromising as any.

> . . . most theories of value may be divided into those which treat it as a quality and those which treat it as a relation between that which has value and something else — which is usually but not always said to be some state of a mind, such as that of being pleased by the object or desiring it or approving of it or finding its desire satisfied by it. And it

seems clear that any view which treats goodness as a relation between that which is good and something else denies
that anything is intrinsically good, since by calling a thing
intrinsically good we mean that it would be good even if
nothing else existed.[11]

He proceeds to criticize objective theories which identify value
with harmony or coherence between parts. But this already commits the naturalistic fallacy; and to say that what is good is
good because it is coherent does not tell us what good itself is.
He objects in particular to assuming that good can be identified
with any *one* other characteristic, coherence or otherwise.

. . . it is just likely, initially, that conscientiousness is good
because it is conscientiousness, and benevolence good because
it is benevolence [as that they should] be held good by virtue
of the coherence of [their] elements. . . .[12]

After rejecting such objective types of theory, Ross passes to
the subjective types with a statement which comes close to
describing our theory under DR:

. . . is it not clear that even if most and possibly all pleasures are complex, it is not on account of its being a complex united by the relation of coherence, but on account of
its having the felt character of pleasantness, that it is judged
to be good?[13]

But he argues also against such a subjective reference. (See under
#6) Ross finally relinquishes the task of finding a common kind
of relation in all cases of value, and settles for a multiplicity of
intuitional judgments, which he believes will better secure the
existence of certain absolute goods.

. . . the more important question for philosophy, is whether
there is not a sense of good in which it can be applied to
things not as meaning that . . . they are instrumental to a
good beyond themselves, but as meaning that they are good
in themselves. And it is surely plain that when we state, for
instance, that courage is good, this is what we mean. . . .[14]

Intrinsic good, then, belongs to the quality side of Ross's original distinction between qualities and relations.

Ross is even more concerned to prove the non-relational character of rightness than of goodness:

> But the *reason* for an action's being right is evidently not the same thing as its *rightness* . . . the view that productivity of maximum good is not the definition of 'right' but another characteristic which underlies and accounts for the rightness of right acts. . . . Anyone who is satisfied that neither the subjective theories of the meaning of 'right', nor what is far the most attractive of the attempts to reduce it to simpler objective elements (Moore's), is correct, will probably be prepared to agree that 'right' is an irreducible notion.[15]

5. Relations to Consequences. If intrinsic good is the quality that is present when the consequences are in hand, are achieved and present, then in itself it would not be defined by consequences. In quoting Ross for illustrations under #1 and #4, we have already seen his view that consequences are not involved in knowing our *prima facie* duties: the "plain man" does not think of consequences when he keeps his promise.

Broad, using "ordinary language" method, denies Hume's appeal to remote or "total" consequences as much as his appeal to immediate ones, as a rationale of good — justice, in this case.

> A particular act of justice may be extremely unpleasant to the agent, who may have to deprive his friend of something which the latter values. It may be extremely unpleasant to the person on whom it is exercised. And it may be detrimental to the general happiness. All these conditions might be realized in carrying out the provisions of a will which was correct in point of law. Yet we should certainly approve of those concerned if they acted in accordance with the law. . . . Hume's general solution of the difficulty is as follows. If we confined our attention to this particular act and its immediate consequences we should disapprove of it. But, as rational beings, we cannot confine our attention to this very restricted object. We shall inevitably tend to think of its remoter consequences, of the consequences of acts

like this becoming prevalent, and so on. . . . The happiness of mankind is enormously increased on the whole by there being a set of acknowledged and rigidly enforced rules about . . . property. . . . The whole utility of having rules depends on the fact that they are known to be invariable; and, if you begin to make exceptions in hard cases, this utility will very soon vanish.

. . . Is [Hume's theory of Justice] adequate? . . . Plainly this is not the whole of the matter. We say that one set of rules is, on the whole, "more just" than another. . . . Now the question whether one set of rules is juster than another seems to be quite different from the question whether the former makes on the whole for greater human happiness than the latter. It seems quite conceivable that one set of rules for distributing property might be far less just than another, and yet that the first might stimulate production so much more than the second that a community would be happier if governed by the first.[16]

Broad concludes that such a conflict as this between two distinct goods, justice and utility, cannot be resolved by appeal to utility, assumed to be the more ultimate concept. We can only have mixed feelings, approving equally of both. He also doubts that consideration of total consequences can explain the original estab-lishment of a system of rules of justice, since primitive people would not have been capable of such abstract considerations. Also in most cases of present obedience to such rules, he can't believe that many people think about the total consequences. Rather, he thinks, they appeal to a more immediate sense of "fairness."

Thus the rationalists strive to make their immediate intuitions about good things and actions final, prohibiting any calculations concerning consequences that might lie behind their intuitions.

We should keep in mind, however, the distinction between the good which is present here and now in an experience; and the good it may lead to in the future, for possible use under DR.

6. Relations to Minds. Returning to Ross's argument against relations in general (#4), he proceeds also to deny relations to feelings in minds as essential to defining good, taking R. B. Perry's theory of value-as-object-of-interest as his quarry.

397

It is surely clear that when we call something good we are thinking of it as possessing in itself a certain attribute and are not thinking of it as necessarily having an interest taken in it . . . surely . . . it had its goodness before we attended to it and could have had it if we had not attended to it. And again it is evidently possible to think that some of the things in which an interest has been taken have nevertheless been bad. . . . The view, therefore, that 'good' and 'object of interest' stand for the same notion must be given up. . . . We may claim that we are directly aware that conscientious action, for example, has a value of its own, not identical with or even dependent upon our or any one else's taking an interest in it.[17]

Another statement of anti-subjectivism is Bertrand Russell's:

To explain what we mean by Good and Bad, we may say that a thing is good when on its own account it ought to exist, and bad when on its own account it ought not to exist. . . . When a thing is good, it is fitting that we should feel pleasure in its existence; when it is bad, it is fitting that we should feel pain in its existence. But all such characterisations really presuppose the notions of good and bad. . . .
. . . when a thing is good, it ought to exist on its own account, not on account of its consequences, nor yet of who is going to enjoy it. We cannot maintain that for me a thing ought to exist on its own account, while for you it ought not; that would merely mean that one of us is mistaken, since in fact everything either ought to exist or ought not. Thus the fact that one man's desire may be another man's aversion proves that *good,* in the sense relevant to ethics, does not mean the same as *desired,* since everything is in itself either good or not good. . . .
It is important to realise that when we say a thing is good in itself, and not merey as a means, we attribute to the thing a property which it either has or does not have, quite independently of our opinion on the subject, or our wishes or other people's.[18]

This statement contains some good examples of static phraseology,

398

in assuming good is a "property" of "things"; and using the verb "exist" to mean merely to persist in being, not necessarily involved in genuine transforming process.

Ross, in the article just quoted, gives a detailed discussion of *whose* interest or desire may be appealed to as defining the good: that of any single person, of the one who is judging, of the majority of persons in some class, of a majority of mankind, or of all mankind. He refutes all of these, primarily by pointing out that, even for the fifth case of all mankind, we recognize cases where what all mankind approved might turn out to be wrong when they became aware of a new evaluation which no one ever thought of before.

C. A. Campbell, however, finds himself forced to concede a subjective element in all values (knowledge, beauty, etc.) *except* moral ones, but manages to restore a measure of objectivity by suggesting that human nature as such may possess certain permanent "likings." What the intuitionists take for "intrinsic" goods, independent of subjective preferences may, then, be values which are "good for man," in the sense that there is a universal tendency in human nature to like, prefer, benefit from those values.

> When goodness is predicated of such things as knowledge or aesthetic experience, the Objectivist holds that we are using, or may be using, the term goodness in an absolutely simple, unrelational, unanalysable sense. I contend against this . . . that actually there underlies the predication of goodness in all such cases the conception of a certain relationship between the things and the emotional nature of man as we know it . . . the things are objects of independent, integral, and relatively permanent liking to human nature.[19]

The last terms, "integral" and "permanent" derive from a theory of *organization* of the multiple likings of men, as essential to understanding what human desires are, that becomes, of course, central to DR's theory. Campbell points out that his subjective referent, "human nature as such," was not included on Ross's list of insufficient ones, since his fifth, "all men" is not the same as "human nature" in general. The latter has more permanence and, Campbell thinks, obviates the difficulty of subjectivism's ordinary implication that the good comes and goes with the changing likes of individuals or groups. Human nature's liking

399

for integrated experience is permanent. The article continues with a labored reminder to Objectivists that even Knowledge, which they are so sure is an absolutely objective good, would not really matter, if there were no entities in the universe capable of being curious and caring about knowing answers. It is good for a pragmatist, who is so accustomed to recognizing this feature of knowledge and other values, to be reminded, in reading Campbell, of how patiently and tactfully one who has been immersed in the intuitionist atmosphere feels it necessary to treat his confreres to persuade them of so obvious a truth.

Even Campbell, however, cannot give up a special objectivist place for moral value. And then, oddly, he ends the paper perfunctorily with a hint of doubt even about moral value. DM-DR, of course, will find no need for even this exception.

7. Conclusion on the Nature of Value. All this stubborn refusal to let good or right "mean" any other characteristics they may be associated with, however universally, in experience, is motivated by the desire to have permanent, unchanging standards, unaffectable by necessarily changeable feeling and experience. The intuitionists also assume that, since a naturalistic identification of value with SMR's type of phenomena not only destroyed permanent values, but even made temporary evaluations of better and worse meaningless, any other kind of naturalistic definition will do the same. But our question must be, was it not so much naturalistic identifications as static, atomistic presuppositions in both SM and SMR, that destroyed evaluation? Will the seating of value and evaluation within compositional process permit stable standards, evaluation, and obligation even when we let value be a matter of natural experience?

8. Adequacy. The main strength of static objective theories is said to be that they are the only safeguard against the relativism which naturalistic subjective theories are supposed to be open to; the only basis for a solid theory of obligation. But, as remarked under SM, the extreme objectivist theory of value, which tries to explain values without reference to our experiencing of them, has always suffered from an inability to say just what the values-in-themselves are, and thus just what we are obligated to. It is left with intuition and self-evidence as its only answer to what the specific content of value is, and we know what the fate of these sources of knowledge has been in other fields of knowl-

edge. Many presume that their fate will not be better in the field of value. Instead of seeking a retreat to SM-SIR, let us push on to DR.

SM with DR.

Findings of DR: 1. Language. Perhaps a justifiable claim is that in DM and DR we allow the Coherence criterion of truth to take precedence over "ordinary language," when there seems to be a need for changed meanings of terms. We certainly do not assum that the "plain man" has necessarily succeeded in making the language take care of all the facts and relationships that may be discerned in the value realm by those who take special pains to sharpen their awareness in the area. I would agree with Aiken's statement:

> But even if we should . . . agree for the nonce that the primary purpose of analytical ethics is to determine the conventional meaning of ethical terms, many vexatious and imponderable questions remain. Consider, for example, the almost universal use of last-ditch appeals to "intuition" or, which comes to the same thing, our "sense of language." What are these but the contemporary semantical hangover of the discredited rational intuitionism of the seventeenth century, with all its antique gear of "clear and distinct ideas," its "self-evident truths," . . . Is it not quite apparent, however, that the disclosures of "language sense" are at least as corrigible as those of the "natural light"? . . .
> I see little hope of, at present, advancing our understanding of the problems of ethics by analyzing the common meanings of individual words such as "right" or "good."[20]

Aiken goes on to define "evaluation" as having to do with satisfactions in a way that agrees with my use. His appeal for a more empirical approach to the whole area and for more experimental research would also agree with our arrangement of material, where the preceding chapter on the empirical facts *did* precede the present and the following ones on interpretations and comparisons of value.

2. Intrinsic Value. In finding value to be a feeling-quality that exists only while organizing and resolving process is in the act of

401

happening, DR will naturally be unable to use any concept of value as a quality that is merely possessed by things, merely "had", merely persistent in being. The direction of the process, the question whether the next moment (the most immediate consequence) or more future moments (the long-term consequences) will increase organization or not becomes inseparable from stating whether there is any value. If we wish to preserve what the theorists of intrinsic value may have meant to defend — that value after all must be actually possessed some of the time, that it cannot always be put off to future consequences — then we will have to say as we did in the preceding chapter (p. 373 f.), either that intrinsic value is the feeling of getting satisfied to the extent that it is actually happening in each moment of the process; or else, if it must be defined as possessed satisfaction, then that it requires simultaneous memory of preceding contrasting need in order to be known and felt. It will presumably be present more or less vividly throughout all parts of the process where resolving and organizing is succeeding to any degree. But all parts of the process will simultaneously have an instrumental aspect with respect to their bearing on the sequel.

Dewey has constantly maintained that there is no essential distinction between means-value and end-value. He considers ends as merely longer term goals, but, when reached, just as much means for something still beyond as ever. He argues that to require end-values to have an intrinsic, immediate or inherent nature in the sense that they are not to be judged by what they lead on to, is to invite laudation of irresponsibility.

> Discrimination between . . . respective shortsightedness and farsightedness is made precisely on the ground of whether the object of a given desire is viewed as, in turn, itself a conditioning means of further consequences. Instead of taking a laudatory view of 'immediate' desires and valuations, common sense treats refusal to mediate as the very essence of short-view judgment. For treating the end as *merely* immediate and exclusively final is equivalent to refusal to consider what will happen after and because a particular end is reached.[21]

This statement may seem to rob "intrinsic values" of the certainty SM-SIR desires, since present possessed satisfaction seems always to have to wait for something in the future before it can be sure of itself. Still, it is clear that there is no place in DR for intrinsic value as a terminal state, existent only when the transforming or striving ceases. It will have to mean the satisfaction felt in a process as it is happening and yet somehow be qualified by what that same process and feeling lead to later. How this may be done will be discussed under #5. It seems so far that every moment of value must have both intrinsic and instrumental aspects.

3. Canons of Definition. Ross had already admitted that a term we think at first to be simple and unanalyzable might turn out to be complex and definable.

It appears as if we cannot avoid recognizing that there is such a thing as using a term which implicitly refers to a certain complex, while yet the complex is not explicitly present in our minds. And in principle this might, it seems, be true of 'good.'

The absence of an explicit reference to a complex in our ordinary use of the term should therefore not be taken as necessarily implying that the term is indefinable, nor [non-relational]. . . . The method should . . . rather be that of attending to any proposed definition. . . . If it is the correct definition . . . we should be able to say, "yes, that is what I meant by 'good' all along, though I was not clearly conscious [of it]. . . ."[22]

Ross and Ewing then proceed to announce that no definition of good or right presented to them has ever caused them to say this 'yes.' They remain conscious of the additional indefinable meaning of good that cannot be identified with any proposed accompanying characteristic.

G. C. Fields comes to the conclusion that the supposed indefinable meaning of a simple term may be merely the original vague idea we have of it before coming to more precise knowledge of its characteristics which can then be put into a definition which does advance our knowledge about it. If the presence of another factor — the simple undefinable quality — is still insisted upon, he will not object, but considers it a relatively trivial aspect of good compared to some of the invariably accompanying characteristics we may be able to discover in it. He concludes:

The distinction, therefore, which Dr. Ross so frequently insists on, between the attribute which we mean by the term and the further attribute or attributes necessarily connected with it, seems to me an unreal one. Partly, it smacks too much of the sharp distinction between essence and properties which we are agreed in abandoning. But it also seems to me to misrepresent the nature of ethical investigation. What we *mean* by "good" (or "right" or any other moral term), in the first place, is the vague indefinite idea with which we start. But this only sets the problem. What we are trying to find is the nature of the facts that we must suppose to exist in order to account for the way in which we think about these matters. And anything that we can say about them may equally be taken as a part of the definition, in the only sense in which definition is possible in ethics at all.[23]

W. W. Frankena goes on to show that Moore and the others have extended the Naturalistic Fallacy so far as to make *all* definition impossible. If we refuse to allow two terms — whether naturalist *or* non-naturalist — ever to mean the same thing, then non-naturalist definitions become as illegitimate as naturalist ones.

But do those who define ethical notions in non-ethical terms make this mistake? They will reply to Mr. Moore that they are not identifying two properties; what they are saying is that two words or sets of words stand for or mean one and the same property. Mr. Moore was being, in part, misled by the material mode of speech, as Mr. Carnap calls it, in such sentences as "Goodness is pleasantness" . . . etc.
    . . . if Mr. Moore's . . . [naturalistic fallacy] rules out any definitions, for example of 'good,' then it rules out all definitions of any term whatever.[24]

In DR, then, we will not refrain from considering some of the aspects of process and feeling that invariably accompany value experience to be important features of its definition.
4. Relations. Santayana once delivered a blow against non-relational views, as represented by Russell (see quotation, p. 398) which the latter once confessed[25] kept him from writing on ethics again for many years, Santayana also notices how much Russell presupposes the static idea of good.

Pleasure, and its rivals, are not synonyms for the abstract quality "good," but names for classes of concrete facts that are supposed to possess that quality. From this correct, if somewhat trifling, observation, however, Mr. Russell, like Mr. Moore before him, evokes a portentous dogma. Not being able to define good, he hypostatises it. "Good and bad," he says, "are qualities which belong to objects independently of our opinions. . . . We cannot maintain that for me a thing ought to exist on its own account, while for you it ought not; that would merely mean that one of us is mistaken, since in fact everything either ought to exist or ought not." Thus we are asked to believe that good attaches to things for no reason or cause, and according to no principles of distribution. . . .

That the quality "good" is indefinable is one assertion, and obvious; but that the presence of this quality is unconditioned is another, and astonishing. . . . Green is an indefinable predicate, and the specific quality of it can be given only in intuition; but it is a quality that things acquire under certain conditions, so much so that the same bit of grass, at the same moment, may have it from one point of view and not from another.[26]

In a footnote, Santayana remarks that Russell and Moore evidently take their views from Plato's *Philebus,* emphasizing the more static statements we considered in our introductory chapter III. But Santayana feels that Plato, if he hypostatized the good, still made the power and directional tendency of nature and human nature integral in the concept, so that good can have some relevance to reality.

If the good were independent of nature, it might still be conceived as relevant to nature, by being its creator or mover; but Mr. Russell is not a theist after the manner of Socrates; his good is not a power. . . . The hypostasis accomplished by Mr. Russell is more serious . . . : In the realm of eternal essences, before anything exists, there are certain essences that have this remarkable property, that they ought to exist, or at least that, if anything exists, it ought to conform to them. What exists, however, is deaf to this moral emphasis in the eternal; nature exists for no reason; and, indeed, why should she have subordinated her own arbitrariness to a good that is no less arbitrary? This good, however, is somehow good notwithstanding; so that there is an abysmal wrong in its not being obeyed.[27]

Ewing and Broad admit, as part of the essential nature of good, the objective relationship of "fittingness" within the situation, or coherence among the parts of a whole. With these by-your-leaves, and in the light of our study of all the phases of value experience as found out by empirical observation, DR will adopt a relational theory of value, perhaps better called an "interactional" theory. The term "organizing process" in our basic formula indicates immediately that value is inherent in the relations among parts that are being organized. It can have no existence except within emerging patterns of ingredients. We may agree that the relations are not identical with the qualitative feeling that is value; yet they are involved in such a way that value cannot be understood or theorized about at all without reference to relational interaction.

5. Relations to consequences. Regarding Broad's and Ross's point that neither primitive men nor the "plain man" to-day always consider consequences in deciding on rightness, I can see no reason for not accepting the explanation forthcoming from the psychology of habit and attitude building. Broad (p. 396) cannot believe that primitive man could have originated justice by thinking out the complex and abstract utilitarian grounds of it. But surely primitive men could think out immediate and simple consequences and complain when some rule led to unfair deprivation. Systems of justice could then have been put together piece-meal throughout ages of experience of new consequences, and indeed do seem to have arisen in that manner. These conclusions can then enter into social habit (custom) and individual habit, and at last seem self-authenticating. Yet they would really have arisen from utility, and be traceable again to it by current thinking when need be.

And the "plain man's" belief in keeping a promise simply because he made it in the past, or admiration of courage and conscientiousness without thinking of their consequences, could be (and the psychology of attitudes finds that they are) emotional habits either taken over from group attitudes, or built up through earlier individual experiences of consequences, until now they

406

operate without consideration of results. Both Broad and Ross admit that the actual thought of consequences may drop out of consciousness leaving only a sense of reverence for the virtue itself. Now I would argue that the admiration or reverence inspired by any virtue arises largely from our sense of it as a kind of behavior that is steadfast in the face of difficulties. But difficulty can only be defined in terms of complexity of ends to be achieved, shorter term temptations to be avoided, etc. In the case of courage, for instance, our supposedly "intuitive" sense of its unconditioned rightness cannot be separated from our knowledge of it as behavior that, avoiding easier, more immediate pleasures, maintains with risk, sacrifice and effort a set toward more far-sighted goals. And to be directed toward inclusively beneficial goals is intrinsic to its nature, for we call it foolhardiness if it is not, in addition to being risky, also wisely calculated as to results.

When Ross remarks that courage and conscientiousness must have possessed "goodness" all along, whether anyone was observing them or considering their consequences or not, he is in the first place not clear that these virtues exist only as characteristics of *actions,* processes, and not as *things* possessing the attribute "goodness." As actions or processes, they cannot be conceived except as tending toward certain kinds of results; or even if virtues are considered primarily as attaching to motives, motives still cannot be defined except in terms of aimed-at consequences. But more damaging is the fact that neither of these virtues is necessarily always good or right absolutely. There is such a thing as over-conscientiousness, being hindered by too refined a conscience. And to evaluate when conscientiousness has hypertrophied into preciousness or rampant guilt complex, we would have to look to results. To tell when courage has become foolhardiness, we would have to do the same.

For DR, then, the nature of consequences is intrinsically involved in identifying virtue and any other kind of value.

But now we must clarify more than we have so far how good as a present and possessed quality of feeling (intrinsic value) can be affected by the consequences that it leads to. We have so far suggested (in discussing consummatory feeling in the preceding chapter) that immediate good feeling involves consequences in the next few moments, insofar as they must be "organizing" in order for the feeling to be good at all. But what of cases (if there be such) where a felt enjoyment of immediate organizing

407

consequences itself happens to cause some later bad consequence? E.g., conviviality under alcohol leads to a hangover, perhaps eventually to alcoholism. We seem thus to have cases where the dynamic idea of good must start by admitting something is a value (the social process, enhanced through alcoholic relaxation is accompanied by increased good feeling) and then end by denying it was a value in the light of subsequent experience.

Dewey is especially committed to denying that "antecedent enjoyments" are assuredly values until after they have been tested by resulting experience. A statement of his that includes typical characterizations of SIR and SMR is: For naturalistic theories,

> . . . emotional satisfactions occupy the same place that sensations hold in traditional empiricism. Values are constituted by liking and enjoyment. . . .
>
> I shall not object to this empirical theory as far as it connects the theory of values with concrete experiences of desire and satisfaction. [This] is the only way known to me by which the pallid remoteness of the rationalistic theory . . . can be escaped. The objection is that the theory holds down value to objects *antecedently* enjoyed. . . . Operational thinking needs to be applied to the judgement of values just as it has now finally been applied in conceptions of physical objects. . . .
>
> The contrast between experienced and known objects was found to be a temporal one. . . . Consequences of operations became the important thing . . . escape from the defects of transcendental absolutism is not to be had by setting up as values enjoyments that happen anyhow, but in defining value by enjoyments which are the consequences of intelligent action . . . enjoyments are not values but problematic goods, becoming values when they reissue in a changed form from intelligent behavior. . . .
>
> . . . the difference between the enjoyed and the enjoyable, the desired and the desirable, the satis*fying* and the satis*factory*. . . . To say that something is enjoyed is to make a statement about a fact, something already in existence; it is not to judge the value of that fact. . . . To assert that it is satis*factory* is to define it in its connections and interactions. . . .[28]

He is saying that felt enjoyments are not known to be values until after we have let time elapse and ascertained their consequential success in "fitting" with other things.

Our question, then, is: how can we ever know that we have actually possessed value when, consequences being presumably endless, a remote adverse one may at any time reverse our evaluation of both the "antecedent enjoyment" and of its less remote consequences? There appear to be two alternative answers.

First, we could agree with Dewey, that the present seeming intrinsic values of enjoyment *can* be rendered a disvalue by later developments. Then we would have to hold that for most cases, life indicates "natural" boundaries for a unit of experience — a roughly recognizable beginning and end after which the consequences become too remote for practical consideration. At this terminal time, then, we would decide whether or not the antecedent enjoyment, and also the consequent enjoyment, if any, was really value.

The second solution may seen at first sight more consonant with the dynamic idea of good: we could consider felt satisfaction as always constituting possessed, intrinsic value, whenever it occurs (and as always testifying to the presence of some degree and kind of organizing process underlying it); but we would have always to *summate* the amounts of organizing and feeling and their reverse over certain durations of process in order to tell how much value we have in the end. This approach would also have to use the "natural boundaries" of the preceding view in order to find a point to "settle accounts." At that time the summation would be performed and we would decide whether the unit of process as a whole was value or not, though we would already know that the early enjoyment was value as far as it went. On this view, we could avoid having to admit that apparent intrinsic value at one point can be "undone" by later untoward consequences; we would only have to say that it could be "outweighed" by later bad feeling, resulting in the whole sector of process being evaluated as negative on the balance.

Both theories would have to admit, of course, that the conclusion is tentative, and that we may decide we have to extend the terminal boundary, take into consideration still later consequences, and revise our evaluation. This is only what all science has to do.

The second approach however has a possible disadvantage equal to its advantage of knowing intrinsic value when it has it: what if the bit of known organizing and pleasantly felt process is of such a nature as to guarantee a succeeding moment of destruction and pain? Suppose our man who is enjoying increased conviviality under alcohol *is* an alcoholic so that this pleasure is bound to be followed by threatened destruction of his career? How can such a deceptive pleasure be classed as true value in any sense?

For this difficulty, it is clear that, if we are going to hold that consequences are essential in determining value, the second approach is obliged to show that possessed enjoyment can never in itself be the direct cause of subsequent disorganization and pain. It might try to argue that it is not such pleasure, and the strand of organizing process in the situation that it must be based on, that is the actual cause of later bad consequences, but rather it is some other concomitant strands or factors which invade to upset what was a good enough value-process in itself. In the alcoholic's process, it would not be the strand of relaxed, successful social intercourse, and its accompanying positive value-feeling, as such that causes his later destruction. It would be the fact that other maladjustments pressing forward for resolution did not happen to be included in that pattern of behavior, and *they* finally destroy his organization. The social success in itself would be all to the good. It would not be *its* fault that the other disorders come in to produce final disintegration. Would this tack relieve us from having to say that something which necessarily produces bad consequences is yet a positive intrinsic value?

The trouble is that it is not clear how we could prove that pleasure can always be thus absolved of being the direct cause of later inadequacy of adjustment. The age-old problem of "evil pleasures" gives us pause. Can a process which fails to incorporate into its pattern what requires to be incorporated at that juncture be called "good" at all, though it does permit a certain limited strand of satisfying interaction? Is the "relaxation" of the alcoholic really an "organizing process" in any genuine sense, though it gives him pleasure? (A counter question occurs here, though: is it the relaxation as such that gives the pleasure, or the released activities?) Does not the alcohol give the alcoholic pleasure precisely by means of a deceptive and spurious "resolution" of his conflict accomplished merely by dint of blotting out some of its elements rather than by genuinely resolving them? And is not this kind of process and pleasure the very cause of his subsequent disintegration, the very reason why he never grapples with his real problem, never encompasses all the factors that he must encompass if he is ever to achieve a valid resolution? If these things are true, then such "good feeling" is indeed itself the cause or part cause of bad consequences, and cannot be admitted as intrinsic value. On the other hand, if it were possible to reduce every case to a matter of side-forces causing the pain rather than the enjoyment itself, we could use this view with its advantage.

But it may be safer to go back to Dewey and allow that antecedent enjoyments may be rendered non-values if they themselves cause later ills. But this admission could be harmonized with the dynamic idea of good in this way: We note that the meaning of the term "organizing" intrinsically involves duration; and therefore that, if value depends on organizing process, the meaning of value must involve duration also. We can then go back to our point above that the decision as to the presence or absence of value, and how much there is, cannot be made except by considering a certain minimum duration of process — that "natural" unit of experience which we said life usually indicates, admitting that the boundaries occasionally need to be revised and thence the evaluation. Our basic definition of value then has to be qualified. Two ways of stating it occur to me. (1) "Value is the satisfying feeling of organizing process which is not in itself, within certain natural limits of time, the direct cause of disorganizing process and dissatisfying feeling greater in amount than itself." This phraseology is to make room for cases where there may be directly caused subsequent pain but no more than would incline us to accept as valuable the unit of process and such good feeling as it may have contained earlier. For example, a non-alcoholic, having good grounds for believing that it does not doom his whole life, may decide that the hangover is not too much of a price to pay for the prior socializing and enjoyment, etc., and thus evaluate the whole episode as primarily valuable, though it ends in discomfort. (2) "Value is the satisfying feeling of a unit of organizing process, of a certain 'natural' duration, in which the amount of organizing and good feeling exceeds the amount of disorganizing and painful feeling." This phraseology may be more adequate and less cumbersome though it does not point to a time of actually possessed value as much as the first one.

These definitions perhaps would tend to bring value theory more into line with most definitions in the modern dynamic world-view, in that they take a "differential" form, stating relations over periods of time.

6. Relations to Minds. Under this head in the Recourses section, we saw that Campbell was one rationalist who felt constrained to grant a subjective element in all value except moral value.

> Among conventionally accepted good things there is one whose goodness we feel it quite peculiarly repugnant to identify with any relation to subjective interests. I refer to moral virtue. . . . When a man in defiance of strong temptations rises to what he recognises to be his duty, it seems merely inept to suggest that his dutiful act derives the value which we all regard it as possessing from any subjective feelings that are entertained toward it by anyone. . . .
>
> . . . "We may claim," writes Dr. Ross, "that we are directly aware that conscientious action, for example, has a value of its own, not identical with or even dependent upon our or any one else's taking an interest in it. . . ." But note how immeasurably (this claim) would be weakened in its effect if, instead of the *moral* value of 'conscientiousness,' we were to insert some non-moral value — even one of the so-called 'intrinsic' values like 'knowledge'. . . .[29]

But under the preceding head we have seen that conscientiousness definitely does have to be evaluated in terms of the consequences of good or ill it is aimed at. The delinquent's knife slash for the glory of the gang is "conscientious" enough but highly in need of further evaluation as to its consequences. And the consequences, then, for DR, must ultimately be evaluated in terms of the feeling they give rise to in sentient subjects — for moral as much as any other kind of value.

DR claims, then, that empirical observation shows that *all* value exists within *felt* interaction; and this requires that a feeling subject be in interaction with structured objects or energies from beyond or within itself. This interaction is more than mere perceiving or knowing.

> This relation . . . is not the simple relation involved in perceiving or knowing. An object or experience that is valuable . . . bears some specific relation not only to the pure

412

perceiving or thinking aspect of the subject, but to the will or the feelings or both. If a thing is to have value it must be desired, liked, or appreciated.[30]

This statement of Pratt's, however, is still trying to speak of value as being somehow in the *objects,* though only if they are reacted to by subjects. Perry's well-known theory of value as the object of any interest leans in the same direction. Another statement of the same sort is Ducasse's:

> . . . *beauty is that property of an object which consists in the capacity of the object to cause pleasure in a subject who contemplates it.* Beauty, that is to say, is a character of some objects, but a *relational* character of them. . . .[31]

The fully dynamic theory would avoid this kind of definition as awkward in any case; but such a definition also loses the supreme advantage of the dynamic idea of good as a property of the interaction itself: its ability to make all dynamic existence a meaningful implicate.

Parker's more idealistic formulation avoids this staticism of speaking as though values were *had* by things and clarifies the derivative nature of "objective values."

> . . . values belong wholly to the inner world, to the world of mind. The satisfaction of desire is the real value; the thing that serves is only an instrument. Not the bread but the appeasement of hunger; not the physical "work of art" but the satisfactions of the imagination which it provides are values; . . . A value is always an experience, never a thing or object. Things may be *valuable,* but they are not values. We project value into the external world, attributing it to the things that serve desire; just as we project sense qualities there, as if things were themselves independently colored or sweet . . . but the value resides in the mind, even as color and sound and taste reside there. We should, therefore, distinguish between value as an attribute and value as an experience, with the understanding that the experience is primary and the attribute a projected derivative. It is convenient to speak of things as *having* value, but *it* must not be forgotten that this is only [a way of speaking]. . . .[32]

413

The phrase "values belong wholly to the inner world" is perhaps a little too exclusively subjective. If we say that values exist only in the interactive process between the subject and aspects or energies emanating from objects, then the objects become more essential than Parker's phrase might suggest.

We should remember what we have noticed in several connections, that the "desire" and "aim" factors in subjective feeling are not universally necessary for the existence of value, nor integral in its definition, though I have argued that "need", as including everything from desperate lack to mild disorder, is. Aiken, taking "satisfaction" as the essence of value, clarifies the point.

> . . . I do not mean by the expression "satisfaction" . . . either "object of interest" or "realization of the object of interest." The reason for this is empirical. The occurrence of satisfactions is dependent in the last analysis not upon achieving results that we think we want, but upon actualizing consummatory behavior patterns which, in many instances, occur without any preparatory or anticipatory activity whatever."[33]

He points out that desires, or foreplans, *may* help us toward satisfaction, but that they can also fail to do so; thus they are to be understood only as tentatively instrumental to value. Only actual satisfaction, with or without preceding aiming, constitutes value.

> As here conceived the primary value-fact is satisfaction itself. Upon it, therefore, all other modes of value and all ascriptions of value to objects ultimately depend. By "intrinsic value," then, I here mean simply "satisfaction."[34]

Of course, we have granted, under the preceding head, that this satisfaction itself stands under the judgment of future consequences in a sense. Aiken goes on to discuss a concept of "inherent value" as distinguished from intrinsic value, to cover value that is ascribed to objects in Perry's manner. But this "remains by definition derivative and extrinsic."

Aiken also makes some important remarks about how a subjective satisfaction theory of value corrects the tendency of naturalistic and interest theories to evaluate anything as automatically good if it fulfills interests or desires, even though the fulfillment may turn out to be unsatisfying or destructive.

414

. . . to forget the end for the sake of which alone . . . causes or objects are worthy to exist is to run the risk of substituting achievement as an end in itself without regard to the human well-being from which achievement derives its inherent value . . . interest theories involve us in a violent functional inversion of ends and means, and require us to regard as a final and inviolable value-fact *any* goal-object to which the organism happens to direct its energies, however ill-suited it may be to satisfy the organism's wants. From a moral standpoint, moreover, such theories require us to regard achievement as such as an end in itself and the ultimate desideratum of the moral life the widest possible realization or even the creation of goals, no matter how pointless they may be from the standpoint of happiness.[35]

This reminds us of the plight of our civilization, with its hypertrophied production, doing and making, without notable increase in human contentment.

Finally, as to the place of subjective pleasure in value, we concluded, under Consummation in the preceding chapter, that for the dynamic theory of value, the "feeling" in terms of which it is defined is surely pleasurable, considered in as inclusive a manner as need be, and not excluding the all-inclusive notion of "satisfaction."

7. Summary. Parker's statement of all the factors in value comes close to what I would feel correct:

(a) The appetition, wish, desire, interest, defined as "impulse toward a goal." (I would prefer the term "need" as explained above.)

(b) The concept and/or presence of an object and the judgment of its relevance to (a). Parker suggests that this factor may be missing in some rare kinds of value — for instance music. But I wonder why music should be said not to have an object, for sound can be an object, something that is interacted with. And if internal chemicals etc. are included under objects, I think we can make this factor universal.

(c) Process. Parker has also adequately recognized the process aspect of value:

Now satisfaction is no instantaneous or eternal fact; but a

415

process in time, a duration, an action. The good or objective of desire is not the object of desire, but action upon the object.[36]

(d) Pleasure. Parker's statement on the place of pleasure in value is largely acceptable, though he still makes "desire" too central:

> Finally, every value contains an ingredient of pleasure; for as desire is satisfied, pleasure arises. This has been questioned on the ground that there are satisfactions, like those of tragedy or morbid compulsions, which are unpleasant; but a subtle analysis shows that even in such cases there is pleasure on the whole; the unpleasantness arising from the frustration of subordinate accompanying impulses. In other words, so far as there is satisfaction of impulse there is pleasure. . . . Pleasure is not, as hedonists have claimed, identical with value; it is only one factor in value. Value is the complex experience of satisfying desire with all the complexity involved in that process; it includes pleasure, but cannot be identified with pleasure.[37]

Our formula that value is the feeling of organizing process does not, I think, diverge from this.

(e) Finally, Parker recognizes the cumulative aspect of value experience, which I have been discussing under the term "product."

> But value is not a process that arises and maintains itself only in the present of the individual. On the contrary, it brings into operation his entire past. . . . Every stage in the process of satisfaction leaves a residuum of satisfaction which is conserved to enrich the next stage; and each instance of the satisfaction of an impulse revives something of all past instances.[38]

This thought has something to do with DR's ability to compare values as to their complexity, one of its main bases for evaluation.

Comparison with SM: Since we are saying that DR's empirical theory is the source and support of the dynamic idea of value, and since obviously the static and dynamic ideas of good are contradictory, our conclusion here must be that DR does not "fit" SM. But we will not review the contradiction any further here.

DM with DR.

Implications of DM and Correspondence to DR: Our procedure at this point is familiar by now. We adopt DR's concept of value, derived as it is from factual experience, as the supreme concept of Metaphysics, central to the definition of meaningfulness. Obviously then, DR will find what DM implies. It is at this point, where the ultimate *empirical* fact, the final conclusion as to the actual nature of value, becomes the ultimate *metaphysical* concept, that the direction of thought is reversed: from formulating facts, it turns to deducing those facts. From observing the detailed processes of nature producing value, we turn to deducing the necessity of those processes of nature from the idea of value. In the first approach those facts of nature seemed contingent, groping, miscellaneous, succeeding in producing value almost by accident. But in the second approach, understanding what value is, we can see that just that kind of facts of nature are required to be as they are in order for that sort of value to exist.

For the sub-topics of this chapter, it is hardly necessary to work out the deduction in detail. On (1) Language, DM obviously does not hesitate to go beyond ordinary meanings. On (2) intrinsic values, we have explained how dynamic thinking uses the concept under DR. The type of definition (3) is synthetic and naturalistic. On (4) DM requires a relational status for value, better named interactional, since it seats value in processes of relational organizing. The relevance of consequences (5) needs no more discussion. On (6) the dynamic idea of good has a necessarily subjective aspect along with a necessarily objective aspect. On (8) the adequacy of the theory, we will now proceed to see how well it can solve the problems of knowledge of standards and evaluating of better and worse, and of obligation.

CHAPTER XVI

NORMATIVE KNOWLEDGE OF STANDARDS
AND EVALUATION

In addition to the question of what value is, there is the question of evaluating better and worse, or the normative problem of knowledge of standards and degrees of value: how to *prove* what should be taken as standards and how to apply them to measuring amounts of value. The differences of opinion on how the problem should be stated, and whether or not it can be solved, however stated, are legion. Our framework could bring some order to the subject, but in the present book we will not undertake a complete coverage of the material. We will concentrate on some features of SMR's denial that there is any such thing as normative knowledge, and of DR's basis for believing that some things are better than others, mainly for the purpose of leading up to the problem of evil and what the dynamic view can do with that.

This topic can be divided into four sub-topics, the first three of which will be treated in this chapter, the fourth in the next.

1. How (or whether) we can formulate a standard or standards of value; and how they (if any) are related to the nature of *value* itself, as studied in the preceding chapter, and to *fact*.

2. How (or whether) the standard or standards can be "known," that is, proved to be true.

3. How (or whether) different things, acts or events can be comparatively evaluated as better or worse (possibly by use of the standard or standards).

4. How (or whether) "rightness" is related to "betterness" as thus evaluated, and thence "known."

Some of the views deny the possibility of knowledge or proof at one or more of these points. Also some of them may deny one or more of these distinctions. For instance, for SM and SIR, the first two questions tend to fuse into one: the method of knowledge that is adopted (intuitional, etc.) in itself almost constitutes the

418

standard as such. They also tend to deny the dependence of question 4 upon question 3, as we noted in the preceding chapter. SMR's theories may undertake to state some concept of standard (#1) but to deny that any such concept can be proven "true" (#2), and thence that there can be any real answer to #3 and #4.

Some of the familiar theories of value, then, seem to refer more to the way of knowing or finding out (or denying) standards and what is right and wrong: "Authoritarian," "Intuitionist," "Positivist," etc. Others seem to refer more to the nature of standards as such: "Absolutist," "Relativist," "Naturalist," "Formalist," "Teleological," "Hedonist," "Self-realizationist," etc. All of these will find their place in our schedule in these chapters.

SM with SIR.

Implications of SM: On all three sub-topics, SM implies more or less the same theories implied under Epistemology: built-in, intuitional knowledge, or knowledge from divine or other authority, equally fixed and unchanging from whatever source.

1. The *standard* will be identical with the absolute values indicated in the preceding chapter, whose specific content, however, cannot be stated apart from the immediate intuitions or authoritarian pronouncements.

2. Knowledge: The absolute standards will be perfectly knowable, provable with certainty by these methods.

3. Evaluation: In strictest logic, SM would not imply a task of comparing values since, as we saw under the topic of varieties, it does not imply a plurality of values to be compared, nor degrees of attainment and complexity if there were. It implies only absolute, final, complete rightness and goodness, without degrees. Less strictly, the expectation would be for a hierarchy of value essences, culminating in the summum bonum of perfect good itself. What places one value above another would be its intrinsic quality, its given nature, whose "betterness" would be divinely revealed, intuitively known, etc. The idea of Good, and the lower essences would all of course be absolute and unchanging. Evaluation would be a matter of comparing the degree of conformity between the evaluated thing and the pre-established model essence, or the codes of rules derived from them.

419

Adjustments of SIR: 1. Standards. SIR accepts SM's implications to absolute, pre-existent standards and essences.

2. Knowledge. SIR, of course, is forced to recognize the existence of apparently non-valuable or anti-valuable *facts*. It discovers a distinction between what is and what ought to be. It notices the realm of material structure, apparently functioning according to laws that are not necessarily value-oriented. SM, of course, can supply it with no reason why such gaps between actuality and the essence of value should exist. So SIR resorts to its dualist or monistic outs here as on every other topic. But it does not yet understand that there is any problem of conflict between factual and value knowledge. Traditional thought was not fully apprised of the facts of psychological development of desires and value concepts, nor of the history and sociology of changing standards. If the Greek Sophists, for instance, recognized the relativity of value ideas to circumstances, their observations did not keep Plato from reinstating SM's absolutism of standards toward which these relative values were to be conceived as tending. SIR's received methods of knowledge — the same authoritarian, intuitional ones SM implied — do not preclude a direct, rational certainty of what is good, true and beautiful, no matter what the relativistic appearances. In fact, a thinker as far advanced in empirical method as Locke still believed that it was easier to know what is good than to know what is real.

3. Evaluation. In allowing for a process of attaining SM's absolute terminal values. SIR finds more need for a theory of comparing values than SM implied. It follows the looser interpretation of SM, then, in assuming that we must distinguish instrumental from intrinsic values, and must locate their established place in a permanent hierarchy of values. The higher values will be known to be so through the usual avenues of knowledge — custom, authority, divine command or intuition. The "human" is higher than the "animal"; the "soul" than "body"; "reason" than "baser appetites," etc. This "higherness" is not derived from any further systematic relationship, but simply accepted. Failing to give any further reason, SIR may strike rebellious minds as arbitrarily snobbish in its condemnation of "low pleasures," "crass materialism," etc.

On this basis, SIR characteristically seeks to deduce exhaustive codes of rules from the primary essences or divine commands, etc. Comparative goodness will then be determined by noting

420

the degree of conformity between the evaluated thing and the pre-established model essences (standards) or the rules derived from them.

We can only briefly suggest examples of this approach in the three main areas of value (1) Cognitive: If SIR's static, substantial "Truth" exists in divinely revealed or self-evident premises, all that needs to be developed is the deduction of detail, conforming carefully to pre-set patterns of thought rules. Aristotle's syllogism models as used by medieval imitators might illustrate the desire for pre-existing stencils, as it were, for every possible situation the mind might ever meet.

(2) Aesthetic: SIR develops SM's implications into "Classicism," for which Art is a matter of applying a system of fixed rules to various kinds of subject-matter. The rules are derived from earlier movements in art, especially, for western civilization, the Greek, presumably in more direct touch with the original essences. One must arrange his materials to fit these inevitable forms. How rather arbitrarily the Greeks settled on their rules, only later antiquarian studies revealed. For Tragedy, for instance, Aristotle took Sophocles' practice, recently though it had been stabilized — as the final canon. In spatial arts, there is much concern to root the rules in certain mathematical fixities, such as the golden section, etc., conceived to be somehow inevitably "right."

(3) Ethical: The ethics of fixed customs and codes, implied by SM, was exemplified by SIR for millennia before being forced to other adaptations. The Pharisaic and Talmudic tradition in Judaism was perhaps the most persistent attempt to solve the problem of ethical evaluation by an exhaustive system of rules for every detail of life. The rules supposedly followed from the perfect and unchangeable origin, the divinely given Ten Commandments. The rules, typically, take a negative rather than a positive, creative form.

The by now familiar weaknesses of customary ethics — their irrational origins in *post hoc ergo propter hoc* fallacies, or in primitive fears, atavistic emotions like revenge, and trivial points of etiquette, their sanctifying the average and condemning the exceptional, and their mutual contradictions — at last push SIR, in ethics as in epistemology, to intuitional or conscience theories. There is no further point to be made under the present topic of comparing values beyond those made on preceding topics, since intuition, or divine command, or other authority, unsupported by

421

any further appeal to degrees or measurements, settles ranks of value as immediately as it settles ultimate criteria. We are now familiar with the great weakness of this view, which even its defenders had to admit: that consciences of different men, or different divine revelations and authorities do not agree, and since the theory lacks any concrete concept of the nature of the standard, it has no means of judging between differing divine revelations, authorities and consciences, or of single consciences in case they may have become warped and need to be realigned.

SM with SMR.

Findings of SMR: 1. Standards. As seen in the preceding chapter, SMR strictly speaking can have no genuine theory of felt qualitative value as a reality. And since it has no theory of creative process moving toward syntheses not yet existent, but eventually to be real, then it can have no real theory of a standard that requires to be aspired to, beyond whatever may already exist. Its theory, if any, will have to be thoroughly relativistic and naturalistic, always tending to recommend one's accepting whatever fragmentary or unharmonized situation he finds necessarily existing now, relative to all the causal forces that have determined it.

2. Knowledge. Following from its restricted theory of knowledge, studied in Part II, all theories under SMR will have to return in one way or another to the dictum that only repetitive sequences of cause and effect can be "known" or verified. This means that all value statements that prescribe action that "ought" to be done, referring to future events not known to be in regular connection to past events, cannot constitute knowledge. Also, the standard or standards that such "ought" statements may recommend approaching, or conforming to, are said not to be in the category of verifiable effects, in any sense, and thus can never be the subject of anything more than relativistic personal opinion or taste.

In Part II we saw how authority and intuition were demolished as ultimate sources of knowledge or bases of proof by SMR's requirement that all that is to be considered as "truth" must pass the bar of sensory verification. And since the senses are conceived as collections of isolated parts or elements, whose relations in togetherness can add nothing to what they are in separation, while the feeling aspect is also ignored, SMR, strictly speaking, can have no theory of experience as the feeling of temporal development, of the growth or improvement of patterns in unified wholes. Knowledge, then, can concern only sequences of self-sufficient snapshots, each snapshot itself being essentially a mosaic of self-sufficient parts. Visual experience will be an incessant stream of separate flashes of light following one another for no discoverable reason; auditory experience a series of vibratory pops. Of course, SMR appealed to "association" to explain how we got impressions of unified objects or of patterned sequences out of our popping, flashing sensations, but never really succeeded in explaining what, for instance, our experience of a musical melody is, nor what it was that experienced the melody, what entity feels the melody as a connected, qualitative experience rather than as a sequence of arbitrary tones.

In spite of this lack of theoretical basis for any real theory of value knowledge, however, some materialists talk of it anyway: as something in the realm of repetitive fact, observable by such senses; something that concerns what *is,* not what ought to be. This approach leads ot the "naturalistic" theories that make values out to be some variety of empirically observable phenomena, some kind of deterministic cause-effect relationship. The various kinds of naturalistic theory were mentioned in the preceding chapter: subjectivism, instinct theories, psychological hedonism, evolutionary ethics, etc. All these theories hold that value statements are genuine, descriptive assertions of fact which can be empirically known to be true. "That object is good" is a factual statement that can be verified, in subjectivism, by noting whether the object is actually desired by any subject. "That act is good" is a statement that can be verified, in evolutionary ethics, by noting whether it has led to survival; or, in an instinct theory, whether it is propelled by some instinctive urge.

But such proved statements, of course, are certainly not statements of absolute standards in SM's sense. All such "proved" values are relative to the causal factors, the social and environmental backgrounds or evolutionary processes that have produced them. Statements about "morals" can only be statements about "mores," about what various groups happen to be habituated to thinking better and worse. There can be no knowledge of a good that holds for all cases and circumstances, or that requires to be aspired to *out* of whatever conditions one finds himself determined in, or pursued beyond what a society may arbitrarily demand.

There is another group of theories which apparently should be placed under SMR: those of some of the Logical Positivists. They realized that value statements refer to something more than existing fact — to perhaps wished-for but not yet existent conditions; but, still maintaining the empirical criterion of verifiability for knowledge (and for meaning itself), concluded that statements about value could never come into the realm of knowledge at all, i.e., they could neither be true nor false. These theorists differentiate themselves from both the SIR and the above SMR kinds of theory, which are alike, they say, in considering ethical statements to be *assertions*, though SIR theories make only "non-naturalistic" assertions as against SMR's "naturalistic" ones. But, they declare, *normative* value statements are not assertive in either sense, for the terms that refer to values and goods have no referent of either the absolutist essence sort (non-naturalist) or of the empirical sensory sort (naturalist).[1] Such normative value statements are only "emotive" which means that they only *express* or "evince" feelings, which is not the same as asserting that the feelings exist. Therefore they cannot be factually verified, and thus have no knowability, meaning or sense.

We are challenged, then, to show that such statements as "Toleration is good," or "Killing is evil" are more than mere explosions of private feeling, accidentally put into propositional form. There may be much feeling attending our belief in normative criteria, but surely, one believes, that feeling arises from, or is almost constituted by, what one *understands* about the criterion and remembers of past experience in using it. Are there no reasons for our feelings about what is good?

Would we, then, in going to dynamic, consequence theories, which can speak of "the desir*able*" in contrast to "the desir*ed*," have advanced at all toward showing that "normative" value statements have more than mere relativistic feeling and opinion behind them? Actually, it is at the point of *applying criteria* to either aimed at, or experienced, results, that the distinction between descriptive and normative statements returns to frustrate us; for although it may be verified whether a given act succeeds in satisfying a desire, or in producing happiness, we still have not "proved" that *satisfaction in the results* is the only possible conception of ultimate value. Feigl has given a pointed expression of the point:

424

As long as disagreement in morals depends merely upon differences in opinion or belief regarding the efficacy of contending means, such disagreement is in principle capable of settlement by empirical method. . . . The question raised (and sometimes answered negatively) by metaphysicians, "Is the satisfying of human interests morally valuable?" is therefore not a factual question at all. . . . The ever present possibility of asking the question "but is this really good?" shows that no descriptively delimited locus of valuableness forces its acceptance upon us as an ultimate criterion.[2]

Ayer thus concludes that there can be no rational argument about ultimate criteria; these are chosen arbitrarily in terms of feelings conditioned by social and environmental happenstance.

In short, we find that argument is possible on moral questions only if some system of values is presupposed. . . . Given that a man has certain moral principles, we argue that he must, in order to be consistent, react morally to certain things in a certain way. What we do not and cannot argue about is the validity of these moral principles. We merely praise or condemn them in the light of our own feelings. . . .
. . . there can be no way of determining the validity of any ethical system. All that one may legitimately enquire in this connection is, What are the moral habits of a given person or group of people, and what causes them to have precisely those habits and feelings?[3]

Can we find any way past this interdict, that "no locus of valuableness forces its acceptance upon us as an ultimate criterion"?

There is reason to suspect that this unhelpful conclusion results less from the logical and semantical necessities which the positivists believe they have followed so faithfully, than from static and mechanistic assumptions lying still deeper behind their thinking. I believe it can be shown that they commit the two kinds of error we have always found in the SMR position: the static error and the analytic (whole-part) error; and that they do not adequately utilize the conception of reality as compositional. Thus I believe it is fair to place much of the positivistic work under SMR, as exemplifying the overly static and analytic approach of mechanistic thought. This thesis will be defended under DR.

425

3. Evaluation. Having no real theory of a standard nor of knowledge of it, SMR can hardly have much to say on ranking of goods. It cannot even rank existent objects and desires in value, let alone tell us of a future *best* to be aspired to. The lack of a theory of whole-part relationship at least makes it impossible to rank value experiences by their degree of wholeness, inclusiveness, order, etc.

Actually, if SMR undertakes to evaluate at all, it is driven to favoring the more partial, isolated experiences over the integrated ones insofar as these tend to rate high in the one quantitative scale of intensity. As we studied SMR's psychology of value experience in Chapter XIV, we found that there is a certain association between sharper, more intense thrills and more violent stimulation of circumscribed parts of the organism; while more integrated processes involving the organism more wholly may be associated with milder but more lasting good feeling. SMR, then, will tend to indulge unreservedly in the intense but fragmentary sensuous experiences, and this amounts to using just one of the criteria which we will find DR using but keeping in balance with the others: intensity.

The use of this one criterion exclusively naturally leads SMR's devotees to angry rebellion against SM-SIR's fixed hierarchy of values. The grounds for this hierarchy now seem quite arbitrary, if not actually mainly snobbish, and it seems designed primarily to inhibit most joys of life. So the materialists love to shock the traditionalists by breaking their rules and indulging in the so-called "lower," though more intense, pleasures. They celebrate the second term in all the dualisms — body, matter, animal, appetite, etc. — as more intensely "real" than the pallidly non-material first terms — soul, spirit, human, reason, etc. The "lower" values, however, all share the characteristics of non-inclusiveness and threatening dissolution ("hangover"), so bitter an anomaly to SMR, and so meaningful to DR.

Reflections of this approach in (1) Cognitive value were seen in Part II: primarily in the emphasis on isolated facts based on specific observations, the suspicion of complex mental constructs involving unobserved systematic connections, the tendency toward specialization and disinterest in evaluating among "truths" as to their relative triviality or importance.

(2) Aesthetic. In this area, where synthesizing, including, organizing, and harmonizing would seem most obviously at home,

we have seen for almost a century now, the most persistent attempts to base an art upon SMR's analytical and fragmentary approach. The cry has been to "reduce" art to "barest essentials," to exclude content, complexity and concreteness in favor of desiccated abstractions and dead, analyzed parts of things.

The two usual inadequacies of SMR permeate current art and literature: first, its making unreal the whole-part relationship, and thence, second, creative effort for and dynamic development of greater wholes. More related to the former are such frequently noted characteristics as the overstress on special techniques, the intensification of isolated sensations, the obliviousness of differences between the organic and the mechanical. The prevalent deflation of love to mere accounts of sexual physiology illustrates, in literature, the concentration upon a single part of a complex experience. Writing is "simplified" from overflowing wealth, personal idiosyncrasy and varied emotional tones to a neutral journalese. Architecture is "simplified" to neutral, machine-like buildings as though no other human interest should be permitted to be satisfied than pure efficiency. Painting denies the possibility of coherence and, as Mumford says

   . . . surrenders to the accidental. . . . To gaze piously into this ultimate emptiness has become the last word in art appreciation to-day.[4]

The more static side is illustrated in the rejection of complex, long-term, effort-taking creativity and development as either method or subject-matter. Simple swipes of pure paint, casual dashes of decoration, lazy improvisations are called as "great" as intricately inclusive designs. Few writers care to undertake the presentation of regenerative experience, which would involve so many greater difficulties of technique, interpretation, explanation of concepts, than does the mere recounting of disintegration and failure.

   In despair of conquering the machine and humanizing the environment, because this would involve an act of self-regeneration which they are incapable of making, or even, it would seem, of conceiving, they turn upon man himself and deface his image.[5]

A large part of the creative as well as the critical fraternity has steadfastly maintained for decades that the fragmentary, destructive and cynical is bound to be greater than the hopeful and

427

constructive, mainly because it is sure to be more "realistic." Any distinction between playing tricks and hoaxes, and valid creativity, is pretty much denied. They are granted "greatness" if only no one has thought of doing them before. The result of confining art to such wearisome and trivial antics is, as our theory of "increasing dose" (p. 367) would predict, that to escape the suffocating boredom of mere repetition of simple sensuous stimuli, the artists can only resort to more and more violent and shocking (i.e., intense) sensations.

One prevalent defense of this art is that it "faithfully reflects" the disintegration of human experience in the world at large. That disintegration is, of course, itself a reflection of non-resistance to SMR's philosophy, helped along, I am convinced, by this very art itself. It therefore reflects, to a considerable extent, what itself has caused, in habituating us all to capitulation, and, so far from reminding us of the ways and means to creative grappling with disorder, and inspiring us to undertake it, working in every way to thrust such determination back into the unconscious.

A related argument is that modern art is justified in denying the traditional assumption that organized beauty is its essential concern, because ugliness, being as "real" as beauty, is just as worthy of expression. But it would seem fair to say that modern literature and art concentrate on ugliness almost to the exclusion of beauty, which is only to be expected since, if ugliness is defined as broken pieces left in a state of brokenness, and SMR denies that organizing them toward some ideal pattern can be "real," then only ugliness can ever be real. Art, then, can only be judged by how faithfully it reflects what "is"; it cannot aspire to reorganizing what *is* toward beauty.

The inapplicability of SMR to aesthetics is trenchantly expressed by Whitehead:

> . . . the assumption of the bare valuelessness of mere matter led to a lack of reverence in the treatment of natural or artistic beauty. Just when the urbanization of the western world was entering upon its state of rapid development, and when the most delicate, anxious consideration of the aesthetic qualities of the new material environment was requisite, the doctrine of the irrelevance of such ideas was at its height. In the most advanced industrial countries, art was treated as a frivolity.[6]

(3) Ethical: Perhaps the kind of ethics most exactly consonant with SMR is what Pratt calls "Amorphous Egoism," the doctrine that we "ought" to try out every impulse or desire no matter what it is. Rimbaud among poets is famous for pioneering this doctrine for modern intellectuals, and remains the model for many of them, though he himself gave it up as soon as he emerged from adolescence. Freudianism seemed to provide a rationale for this view in its doctrine of non-repression of urges, and was enthusiastically adopted by the literary world in the early part of this century. The latest literary movement, the "Beats," seeking some fresh way to shock the world, seem merely to have repeated this philosophy for a fifth or sixth time in a century, under the new name of "kicks." Thus SMR inspires ever new attempts to prove that existence should be handled as a collection of disconnected but maximized impulses, evaluated exclusively by intensity and never rejectable as "bad" simply because they will not fit into any rational pattern of life.

But existence insists on being so inter-involved that some experiences, especially at exaggerated intensities, cannot be had without making other, probably "richer," experiences impossible. Pratt mentions the young murderer who found he could not "try everything once": he could not try both murdering for fun, and living beyond the electric chair. Pratt also points out that this theory cannot be modified by saying "If complete satisfaction of all desires be impossible, make the best combination," for that statement calls for a criterion of "best" which SMR cannot supply, since it has no basis for considering wholes of behavior patterning a multiplicity of impulses and objects to be real at all, and therefore certainly not "better" than the separated impulses alone.[7]

The more familiar "psychological egoism" is less identifiable than the above with SMR's typical approach, though it has an atomistic character. For it does not necessarily preclude that the individual can include and organize his interests, and can choose to do so, even perhaps incorporating pseudo-altruistic interests, as explained in Chapter XIV. Ethical egoistic hedonism, of course, goes beyond psychological facts, and states that the individual *ought* to pursue only his own happiness, and thus as a normative theory can hardly be placed under SMR's naturalism, atomistic though it also is. Besides, as Mothershead says,

Hedonism in this ethical sense would be superfluous if psychological hedonism were true, that is, if would be pointless to assert that we *ought* to seek pleasure if in fact we were unable to do otherwise.[8]

Still less, then, could any altruistic ethical theory, hedonistic or otherwise, fit under SMR. If SMR cannot even tell the individual to include and organize a more complex pattern of behavior for himself, it certainly cannot tell him to include consideration of others' wants in his purview. SMR and its literature, then, are notoriously blank on the subject of social obligation. Our prevalent literature almost never treats altruistic behavior, either as an empirical phenomenon that can actually exist (all apparent evidences of it are generally debunked) nor as an obligation that can be defended in any valid way.

And so SMR cannot draw from its deterministic naturalism any real directives for the future, nor any measures of approximation to such directives.

Contradictions to SM-SIR, and Recourses: 1. Standard. Modern efforts to revive SM-SIR continue in the inability to give systematic or concrete content to the standard, resorting again to intuition to tell us what to do in each case. (Cf. quote from Ross, p. 395.) This topic, then, merges with the second.

2. Knowledge. Kant gave the rationalistic theory of value knowledge its best known modern presentation, rejecting any appeal to consequences, and seeking unchanging a priori categories as a basis. Further remarks on his theory will be placed under the ethical illustrations below.

Pratt points out convincingly the futility of the rationalist appeal to absolute intuitions, as stated by Ross:

. . . Ross . . . defends the view . . . that rightness and wrongness of acts is not derived from or knowable through their consequences or their other relations; but that acts are somehow right and wrong in themselves, in the sense that they are inherently appropriate or the reverse. . . .

If right is not to be known by definition, nor to be distinguished from wrong by reason or by any objective methods but by intuition only, it is of the utmost importance for ethics to know with considerable exactness what these intuitions are. . . . Is there any reason to believe that they are always trustworthy. . . . ? Not even Ross would claim that they are. He admits that the intuitions of different men, or at least their moral judgments based on their intuitions, may differ, and that therefore some of them may be mistaken. One takes altogether too simple a view of the moral life who "ignores the fact that in many situations there is more than one claim upon our action, and that these claims often conflict, and that while we can see with certainty that the claims exist, it becomes a matter of individual and fallible judgment to say which claim is in the circumstances the overriding one. In many such situations, equally good men would form different judgments as to what their duty is. . . ." [Quoted from Ross's *Foundations of Ethics,* p. 63.]

This looks very like an admission that intuition cannot with any certainty distinguish right from wrong. It is useless to respond that other ethical theories, such as those which judge the objective goodness of an act by its probable consequences, often find it equally impossible to decide which of several courses is the best. For the difficulty faced by these teleological forms of moral theory arises simply from [practical difficulties in judging consequences], whereas the difficulty in the case of Ross's theory [is that it does not offer even a theoretical way of deciding].

In short, the admitted divergence between different men's intuitions is . . . fatal for Ross's theory . . . intuitions (in the form of "prima facie obligations") are neither the basis of right nor the means of knowing what is right. . . .[9]

3. Evaluation. To recapitulate, SM suggests fixed, non-empirical standards and value-levels, justifiable and provable only through authority and intuition. SMR demands a basis in experience but so construes experience as to rob standards and value-levels of any reality. SIR counsels striving for ideals far above us and perhaps rather pallid. SMR counsels settling back into whatever we find already in existence, no matter how far it may be from SIR's ideal. SM neither suggests, nor does SMR find that reality for value and evaluation could be found in the creation of not yet existent harmonies among plural factors.

The Romantic and Idealistic movements of the 19th Century were, of course, attempts to recover values and standards more or less in SM-SIR's sense. Aesthetically, the Romantic Period

431

strove to bring artistic feeling back to the center of life, but it has often been remarked of romanticism that it remained under the influence of atomistic mechanism enough to issue in an art of bits and patches, of momentary inspirations, of short lyrics in poetry, imperfectly integrated programmatic music, and fragmentary "Impressions" in art.

Mumford concludes that romantic art is an unsuccessful rearguard action against the machine. The romantics looked backward too much for their inspiration. The poets and artists, who could work with Christianity "at its dogmatic worst" could not do so with the mechanistic age, and not being philosophers could not create an adequate new foundation for aesthetic endeavor.[10] The "Art For Art's Sake" movement epitomizes this disjunction between SM and SMR at the same time that it embodies SMR's separatism and specialization.

In ethics, it is the Kantian, formalistic type of theory that falls in this place. Aspects of SM-SIR that are revived in this theory are the emphasis on intellectualistic rationality without a clear doctrine of feeling; the emphasis on duty and on the rules to which the duty is owed; and the failure to state exactly what the content of values and standards, and thence of duties, is while assuming that whatever it is, it is fixed and absolute. Kant specifically rejects appeal to consequences in judging the rightness of acts, on the grounds that any such appeal immediately renders acts prudential and non-moral. The only motive than can make an act moral is the willingness to follow reason; therefore the source of ethics must be a rational rule independent of inclination. It must also be capable of holding for all rational beings equally. These specifications lead to the familiar rule, the categorical imperative: act so that the maxim by which one acts can be universalized, or adopted by all men, without *logical* self-contradiction. Only by conscientiously willing to obey such a rule, Kant feels, can *Goodwill*, the only essentially good thing, be manifested. For any thought of happy consequences to enter into the motivation would be to nullify its ethical character. Lying, then, would be wrong not because it tends to lead to bad results, such as confusion and disruption of the interrelated system of human affairs by distrust, but only because of a logical contradiction involved in its nature, whereby it cannot be universalized as a rule for all to follow.

The thought of degrees of goodness or rightness, and the ranking of values typically does not appear very explicitly in the theory, since duties are expected to be quite absolute. Ross, however, applies himself to the problem of ranking variant duties on the intuitionist basis. He naturally opposes any concrete measurement of empirical factors in experience (by such scales as Bentham's, for instance) in favor of immediate awareness of the precedence of one duty over another.

It may be said that besides the duty of fulfilling promises I have and recognize a duty of relieving distress, and that when I think it right to do the latter at the cost of doing the former, it is . . . because I think it the duty which is in the circumstances more of a duty. . . .

When I am in a situation, as perhaps I always am, in which more than one of these *prima facie* duties is incumbent on me, what I have to do is to study the situation as fully as I can until I form the considered opinion (it is never more) that in the circumstances one of them is more incumbent than any other. . . .

It may be objected that our theory that there are these various and conflicting types of *prima facie* duty leaves us with no principle upon which to discern what is our actual duty in particular circumstances. But this objection is not one which the rival theory is in a position to bring forward. For when we have to choose between the production of two heterogeneous goods, say knowledge and pleasure, the "ideal utilitarian" theory can only fall back on opinion, for which no logical basis can be offered, that one of the goods is the greater; and this is no better than a similar opinion that one of two duties is the more urgent. And again, when we consider the infinite variety of effects of our actions in the way of pleasure, it must surely be admitted that the claim which *hedonism* sometimes makes, that it offers a readily applicable criterion of right conduct, is quite illusory.[11]

This seems a frank enough confession of what Pratt accused Ross of (see p. 431) that the intuitionist view (in either Ross's 'duty' form or Moore's 'good' form) offers no better basis for the ranking and choice of duties than unsupported opinion. The remark about hedonism's failure to offer a "readily applicable" criterion would apply to the theory to follow under DR, but has little weight, since no one necessarily has a right, in science or

433

axiology, to demand an *easy* method of measurement; but as science does, axiology must do as well as it can with difficult methods. And, as Pratt said, a teleological theory's problem is just a matter of practical difficulties in applying the method it possesses; whereas the intuitionist problem is in not having a method even in theory to apply.

Other usual criticisms of formalistic ethics may be mentioned:

1. Rigidity: the lack of a standard for modifying rules when they are clearly maladapted to situations.

2. Conflict of rules or duties: as just illustrated, there is no real method of selecting among rules pointing in different directions. Critics argue both that many rules can be universalized, yet still conflict, and that no rule can be universalized.

3. Negativity: the lack of positive content. It is easier for rules to indicate what should not be done than what should be done. Kant admitted this, but hoped that one could get to positive duties by eliminating all the alternatives that could not be universalized.

4. Lack of specific content. It has been said that whenever Kant tried to give specific directives, he fell back on consequences himself.

5. The tacit appeal to consequences. This seems so obvious to a non-intuitionist when he thinks of Kant's imperative or Ross's *prima facie* duties, that he wonders what makes the intuitionist so want to call a halt to thought in mid-career, arbitrarily ignoring the results that so patently lie just beyond the duties, principles and rules. Of course, they usually assume that the pragmatic appeal must necessarily contract to a short-sighted expediency, and that only rigid rules can guard men against corruption, especially in times of threat and temptation. The teleologist, however, sees no reason why he cannot adopt such rules for that very purpose, without in the least affecting the fact that the ultimate justification of the rules themselves must be in terms of their tendency toward long-term benefit. As for the categorical imperative of Kant, it is not absolutely clear to everybody how it can be said to avoid self-contradiction in a sheerly *logical* sense; and even if it does, why that rather "top of the head," intellectualistic circumstance should be selected as so much more significant than the more massive fact that it avoids *practical* self-contradiction. That is, to follow maxims that can be universalized to all men would appear to be a very promising method of decreasing mutual frustration and cruelty and thus increasing the general benefit. So

434

why should we refrain so strictly from considering this utility of the rule in favor of considering only its logical character? It seems impossible not to ask how mere logical consistency can matter to men, if it has no bearings upon satisfactions that are *felt*.

DR can waste no further time with these rationalist attempt to distinguish better from worse or right from wrong by unanalyzed intuitions, avoiding the "dirty work" of detailed, concrete measurement. As science has had to do, it undertakes the difficult work of distinguishing the factors involved and finding scales upon which to compare them.

SM with DR.

Findings of DR: 1. Standard. The entire analysis of dynamic creativity and of the whole-part relationships as conceived by DR in Part III underlies the possibility of stating a standard, knowing it to be true, and comparing and ranking value experiences according to it. Only if wholes can be developed, organized and real can experiences differ in degrees of inclusiveness, order and wholeness, and in degrees of accompanying feeling.

We have established that for DR, value is the feeling of satisfaction that accompanies or is embodied in these processes that are in the act of organizing various energies into patterned unities. Such value becomes the *standard* for activity when we say that it is to be maximized; or that experience is better the "more" of such feeling it produces. We will discuss the apparent appeal to quantity a little later. We will now discuss briefly how this standard can be "known" or proved to be the one man must and should live by.

2. *Knowledge.* Does this approach provide any way around the avowal that "no descriptively delimited locus of valuableness forces its acceptance upon us . . . ?" (Cf. Feigl, p. 425) We have insinuated that the positivists are still too much under the influence of static, analytic modes of thought. On the first, or static, error, the form of expression, "that object is good," is still prevalent with them, as though the Aristotelian subject-predicate language had never been questioned as to its adequacy for a dynamic reality. If value turns out to be dynamic, that language would presumably be inadequate for it too. Also, when Ayer says ethical words are only "used to express feeling about certain objects" we

435

smell the old static way of thinking that the mind passively regards objects or essences which then elicit a mysterious factor of "feeling" as a sort of mirror reflection. It does not suggest that the feeling is a complex with specific properties verifiably related to aspects of the objects and to the processes which the objects prompt in the feeler. The words "emotive" and "feeling" are used in a manner reminiscent of the old faculty psychology.

On the second, whole-part, kind of error, the positivists are surely too analytic when they assume value theory is a matter of analyzing single propositions like "Killing is evil." How might the problem be changed if reality were "proved" to be essentially the organizing of a plurality of factors toward felt patterns? Would it be as possible to reject such a general concept as "increasing organization of wholes" as an entirely arbitrary "locus of valuableness," as it was to reject some of the more specific criteria ("benefit of others," "satisfaction of one's needs" etc.) Feigl may have been thinking of?

This emphasis upon assemblage, scheduling, patterning of many parts into wholes, of many factors into unity — makes misconceived all such statements as Schlick's:

> One can act only toward that end whose idea is most pleasant for one, and this means in the direction of the strongest impulse. [12]

Bertrand Russell is another who speaks of motivation as a matter of one strongest desire overcoming others:

> And it is clear that, when we make a decision, we do so as a result of some desire, though there may at the same time be other desires pulling us in a contrary direction.[13]

Perry has made a clear correction here:

> Morality is man's endeavor to harmonize conflicting interests . . . the solution of the problem created by conflict — conflict among the interests of the same or of different persons. . . .
> Interests are integrated by reflection. . . . From reflection there emerge decisions which fulfill, in some measure, the purpose of harmony: plans, schedules, quotas, substitutions,

and other arrangements by which the several interests avoid collision and achieve mutual reinforcement.

The personal will which emerges from reflection is not, as has sometimes been held, merely the strongest among existing interests, prevailing after a struggle of opposing forces. It is not a mere survivor, other contestants having been eliminated. It does not intervene on one side or the other, but takes a line down the middle, analogous to the resultant or vector in a field of forces.[14]

We are saying, then, that value lies in the satisfying feeling of processes that organize a plurality of factors into schedules and unities; and that *the standard is the amount of such feeling based on the amount of such inclusive order.* Does *this* "descriptively delimited locus of valuableness" force "its acceptance upon us as an ultimate criterion"?

I will organize my answer around two points, which relate to what was said in Chapter VI concerning two basic kinds of verification: correspondence (which is the only one the positivists explicitly recognized) and coherence (which itself emanates from the whole-part situation).

The empirical-correspondence part of the verification of the above statement would apparently have to take the form of finding the hypothesis — a complex system of concepts concerning the relations between good or happy feeling and the organizing of needs and processes toward harmony — describes more correctly and adequately than alternative hypotheses what all value experience and evaluating is observed to be. It would be relevant for verifying a theory of value criteria, to show that men can only and do only evaluate as the theory asserts they do. And it might well be — indeed we might rather expect — that the best verified theory of the nature of life and reality itself would be involved in verifying something so ultimate as a theory of value. In this sense, I believe that when one traces the nature of valuing sufficiently far back to the really general features of it (which I don't feel any of the positivists do), he will find it rooted in the general nature of creative process which *does* force itself on him as a "locus."

To show, then, that the whole theory of dynamic good and its implications to evaluation are better supported by empirical observation not only of how men actually do evaluate, but of innumerable other phenomena as well, than any other theory, would be relevant for verifying it as the ultimate standard. This would require detailed demonstration for an indefinite number of instances as inductive science always entails. One would have to take up other theories of standards and show that behind or beneath them this one is actually operative, obscured from recognition only by neglecting to pursue the implications as far as it is open to do. One would have to deal with apparently contradictory cases, such as those of seeming desire or approval of pain and destruction, showing them, in the usual ways, to be, *factually,* searches for resolving growth in some sense, only blocked and diverted by colliding factors; and, *valuationally,* approved only in terms of some greater benefit implicitly appealed to. (See, for instance, quotation from Parker, p. 416.) One would have to take up all the peculiar local standards of different times and areas, and show their actual derivation from this theory, only narrowed and truncated by limited experience and thought development. But I cannot do the whole task in this book, though some parts of it have already been done in various connections. And of course, even if the task were undertaken exhaustively, it could hope for no more final certainty than inductive science ever achieves, even in the physical realm. (One might, perhaps, ask those inveterately critical minds whose prime enjoyment is in breaking down theories by searching out recalcitrant cases, to contribute some creative and constructive interpretation of such cases for themselves.)

Be that as it may, we still have the other ground for preferring one theory over others: the test of coherence. If dynamic good is accepted either as the metaphysical reason for all things (as we have been arguing in the earlier parts of the book) or as the source of evaluation (as we are arguing in this part), it will be accepted because a larger amount of empirically tested human experience and knowledge fits logically and harmoniously with it than with any other concept. In fact, the feeling which the positivists say is the source of our ultimate choice of standard will itself be largely constituted from our sense of the fitting of many factors into the unity of our system. If we ultimately accept our standard on account of feeling, then, it is only because the feeling itself is a reflection of our grasp of coherence in our belief.

We now have the question whether, in saying that as a matter of fact, men cannot experience value, aspire or evaluate by any other standard than dynamic good, we have not returned to a naturalism, saying that whatever is or has to be is the good. This however makes no sense, since contained within our "what has to be" is reality for dynamic evaluation and choice as it is not in the ordinary naturalism. That is, our theory is not confined to prior impulses and urges as given by nature, but recognizes the possibility of comparing alternative courses of behavior as to amounts of value: priorly, in the estimated results, choosing accordingly; then latterly, in the verified results. So we cannot be criticized for trying to get an "ought" out of an "is" (like trying to base ethical hedonism on psychological hedonism) by saying that one ought to do what he is forced to do anyway by deterministic impulses.

But if it is said that we are trying to get an "ought" out of an "is" in the sense of stating that man ought to evaluate by this method, because that is the only way he can or ever does evaluate, perhaps we are guilty. The case lies more like this, however: we are saying that men can only and do only evaluate by this method, but they do it in a confused way, failing clearly to trace their decisions to this ultimate basis, stating instead all kinds of unclear and partial intermediate principles and rules, sometimes to the detriment of adequate behavior; but that men *ought* to evaluate by this method much more clearly and adequately than they do, learning and practicing to become expert in it. This "ought," though, lies outside the theory itself, and could only be justified pragmatically in a sense to be mentioned below.

Can we still ask, then, about this criterion, "But is it *really* good?" In a later writing, Feigl has made new specifications as to what is required to confirm ultimate norms which are not violated, I believe, by my treatment. He now finds two fundamental types of justification, which correspond somewhat to the coherence and correspondence tests: *validation,* which refers to the rules of deductive and inductive inference and regulates such parts of evaluation as showing some stated criterion to be logically dependent upon some more ultimate criterion; and *vindication,* which refers to the empirical and pragmatic results of adopting the (logically validated) norms or sub-norms. He then writes:

> . . . the supreme norms of a given ethical system provide the ultimate ground for the validation of moral judgments. No matter how long or short the chain of validating inferences, the final court of appeal will consist in one or the other type

of justifying principles. . . . Disagreement with respect to basic principles can thus only be removed if the very frame of validation is changed. This can occur either through the disclosure and explication of a hitherto unrecognized common set of standards, i.e., still more fundamental validating principles to which implicit appeal is made in argument, or it can be achieved through the pragmatic justification of the adoption of an alternative frame, or finally, through sheer persuasion by means of emotive appeals.[15]

What he requires us to do in justifying our theory, then, is to show that it stands logically behind any other criteria stated by anyone; and that to adopt it will bring empirically experienced advantages of some sort. This has been our general line of approach.

Feigl then asks whether ultimate ethical norms will ever be found, as universal as those of cognition. But what seems to be fixation of his attention upon cultural norms at a certain specific level keeps him from moving back to the general characteristics of *any* organizing process, as we have done, and leaves him tentatively relativistic with Stevenson and the emotivists.

> But in view not only of the stark realities of group and culture-centered ethical standards, but also because of the ever present quandaries regarding the priority between the several supreme standards . . . within a given group or culture we can scarcely expect a universal unanimity of purposes which would vindicate a set of unique standards and a rigid order of priority among them for any and all questions of moral decision.[16]

A discussion follows, granting the necessity of an empirical reference for all value statements in addition to their emotive aspect, so that they do become "knowledge-claims" subject to validation "by virtue of their accordance (or non-accordance) with the supreme norms of a given ethical system." The norms themselves must have empirical content, and are not purely logical principles as the rationalists would have them. But, still staying at the level of specific cultural norms rather than of creative process in general, he does not find these norms empirically verifiable in any ultimate sense. However, he finally does touch on this possibility, in listing eight possible meanings of "Objectivity" in the moral domain, the sixth and seventh of which are:

440

(6) The conformity of the norms with the basic bio-psycho-social nature of man, especially as regards the preservation of existence, the satisfaction of needs and the facts of growth, development and evolution. (7) The degree of universality with which certain moral norms are actually or potentially embodied in the conscience of man within given cultural groups or perhaps in cultural groups of all times and places.[17]

These specifications are just what I suggest dynamic good as fulfilling. The variant special norms of particular people and cultures would result either from confusion and failure to think out the complexities of the application of the standard with similar degrees of completeness; or from the fact that, when the general idea is applied to specific constellations of circumstances, it does imply varying solutions. The next division will give more idea of where the seeming relativism comes from, though we do claim the existence of a universal dynamic norm.

In summary, we find the following identifiable kinds of thought in the value realm:

1. Empirical (sociological, psychological, etc.) knowledge of actual human evaluations.
    a. Descriptive (merely reporting what is observed).
    b. Explanatory (analyzing causal relationships in a.).
2. Definitions of value terms and logical analyses of value sentences (presumably in the light of the data in 1).
3. The adoption of value criteria or norms.
4. "Normative judgments," or the comparison of motives and achievements with norms.
5. Judgments of obligation, rightness, oughtness.
6. Exhorting or inspiring persons toward higher values.
7. Instrumental applications.

We hold, with Perry, that Nos. 1, 3, 4, and 7 of these kinds of thought are all descriptive and verifiable. Only the sixth clearly belongs under the positivists' category of emotive communication and influence. It seems obvious by now that our beliefs under 3 and 4 can produce emotive power under 6 only if we do *not* accept them as mere groundless feelings.

It will be noticed that Part IV on Axiology has been organized in this sequence. No. 7 is not taken up at all in this book.

3. Evaluation. DR's complete theory of ranking goods is very complex, and in this book we must confine ourselves to only a few suggestions. The problem is, how to apply the standard of dynamic good to the evaluation of specific experiences in the various areas of value as listed in Chapter XIV.

It seems that we get from the mere knowing what the standard is to the ability to use it in actually measuring values, both by (A) considering the amount of good feeling itself, either as (1) estimated and aimed-at, or (2) as subsequently experienced; and (B) by taking cognizance of certain observable aspects of the process that underlies the feeling. The estimation of the amount of feeling itself must remain rough and subject to much correction. But there seems no reason to deny that we might increase the accuracy of our evaluation by taking account of factors in the process which can be observed and counted in other ways than by immediate feeling. The analogy to sight or hearing seems complete; we can make a direct estimate of shades of color or intensity of sound from our immediate sensing; we can supplement it by measuring frequencies and intensities of the objective light and sound phenomena by the more exact methods of physics. In the case of value, however, it is clear that we will never be able to measure these factors in the process to as great a degree of precision. Even so, we would have in these graded, if not easily gradable, characteristics of the underlying processes a meaning for "greater" and "less" value to correspond to our direct feelings of better and worse.

We have implied here that there may be more than one factor or dimension involved in value experience, and the underlying processes, so that measures on a plurality of scales might be foreseen. This is only to carry the analogy to light and sound further: just as there are measures of frequency, intensity, saturation, etc., for them, so there is a plurality of dimensions and scales for the measure of value.

Now the objection has often made that if we, like Bentham, admit other dimensions of measurement, such as duration, intensity, fecundity, etc., we are displacing dynamic satisfaction feeling itself (or happiness, etc.) from the position of ultimate criterion, in favor of these other criteria. Broad's denial of this argument as put against Hedonism will also serve for the dynamic idea of good:

No sane Psychological Hedonist would deny that a pleasure which is believed to be longer and less intense may be preferred for its greater duration to one which is believed to be shorter and more intense. Nor would he deny that a nearer and less intense pleasure may be preferred for its greater nearness to a more intense but remoter pleasure. And this implies that duration and remoteness are in some sense factors which affect our desires as well as pleasantness and painfulness. This complication may be dealt with as follows. There are certain determinable characteristics which every event, as such, must have. Date of beginning and duration are examples. There are others which an event may or may not have. Pleasantness, colour, and so on, are examples. Let us . . . call them respectively "categorial" and "non-categorial" determinable characteristics of events. Then the accurate statement of Psychological Hedonism would be as follows. No non-categorial characteristic of a present or prospective experience can move our desires for or against it except its hedonic quality; but, granted that it has hedonic quality, the effect on our desires is determined jointly by the determinate form of this and by the determinate forms of its categorial characteristics.[18]

The other dimensions to which satisfaction is proportional, then, do not displace it as the actual value and standard.

Another remark is worth making at this point, concerning the assumption implicit in what we have said so far, that the standard is actually the *amount* of value or satisfaction feeling, as directly felt, or as measured from a balance of all the scales. This may offend some as a curiously quantitative approach to take to evaluation, risking running afoul of all the criticisms of Bentham's pleasure-calculus, particularly that it makes a "pig philosophy" bound to approve the "lowest" pleasures, if only they exceed in quantity. However, I feel clear that if evaluation is to be rescued from the arbitrariness of the rationalists' intuitions, it will be a virtue rather than a vice of our method, if it succeeds in anchoring the comparison of values in some sort of quantization. And when we have all the scales before us, I think ours will escape having to acquiesce in any kind of behavior however "low" if it only contains "more" pleasure. I would, in fact, push Moore's suggestion in the following quotation the whole way, maintaining that all "highness" of values may be construed precisely in terms of quantitative superiority in the various scales taken together.

It is, for instance, commonly held that some pleasures are higher or better than others, even though they may not be more pleasant. . . . And, of course, even those who hold that actions are right because of the quality of these pleasures, might quite consistently hold that it is *as a matter of fact* generally right to prefer higher pleasures to lower ones, even though they might be less pleasant . . . on the ground that higher pleasures . . . do, if we take into account all their further effects, tend to produce more pleasure on the whole than lower ones. . . .[19]

He goes on to discuss whether this greater quantity of pleasure, thus arguable as the sure result of the "higher" values, is only a *sign* of rightness (or goodness), or the actual reason *why* of them. In my view, if quantity covers inclusiveness, complexity, fecundity, and the other measures, then it is not merely the sign, and the why, but the very content of higher value and rightness.

A last preliminary, before the actual task of building up a list of dimensions, would be to point out that if value experience involves all the phases of process studied in Chapter XIV, Section II we should not be surprised if measuring value embroils us in a forbiddingly complex business of measuring prior states in subjects, characteristics of objects, characteristics of aims and motives, and subsequent states in subjects and objects. And if the ultimate measure must be of the process itself, i.e., of the "advance," then we might expect to have to look for the difference between the measures of prior and subsequent states, that is, perform some analogue of subtraction of the former from the latter.

But now the intuitionist will feel sure he has us cornered, because it is really too obvious that no one goes through this endlessly complex process in deciding on his evaluations. But we have the answer in our theory of holistic mental operations and "post-ratiocinative" intuition (see Part II, p. 137). A holistic, intuitional grasp upon facts, theories and meanings is a normal final phase of the knowledge process in other areas. It may be more or less informed and refined by prior analysis and precise measurement, being improved the more of this there is, but not having to wait for any final perfection of analysis before it operates. Such intuitions are, of course, subject to further testing when needed or possible.

Now presumably the brain has a general tendency to "pull together," whether or not we are consciously willing it or have made absolutely explicit every element that goes into the final impression or decision. But, if we wish to, we seem to be able to analyze into explicit awareness more of the specific elements that are involved in the synthetic work of the mind. Now the intuitionists, as Field remarked (p. 403), would quixotically prohibit this analyzing what underlies the final sense of intuition or decision, so as to make the latter self-authenticating. We admit that much evaluating is done by such intuitional product of unconscious synthesizing of the factors, but hold that, as in any scientific knowledge process, the analysis and testing may be done if one wishes to take the trouble, and that demonstration is not forthcoming unless we do take such trouble. That it takes a great deal of trouble indeed to do this analyzing and measuring in the field of value is no grounds for avoiding it as our final appeal in favor of the facile intuiting. Men resisted the onerous work of precise science in the physical realm for millennia, trying to solve its problems by self-evidence and intuition, but they came to it at last before they could get beyond the stubborn disagreements among the intuitively "certain."

Next should come a discussion of the various parameters that can be identified for value experience, and how they might be measured and summed to arrive at maximal optimum values. We would start with Bentham's pioneer suggestions of some respects in which value, or at least pleasure, might be measured, even though most succeeding theorists like to reject his hedonic calculus as absurd. What was really called for, I believe, was constructive criticism and improvement rather than outright rejection. We thus find very few other authorities to study for further improvement of the measurement, since again most axiologists seem to have spent their efforts in finding reasons why there can be no empirical criteria and measurements of value. Only a few have got down to the dirty work itself. Perry and Whitehead contribute a few suggestions.

However I do not have space for a detailed discussion of the parameters, and will go straight to my main suggestion as to how to reduce the complexity of value measurement. A year or more

445

of stumbling about among a jungle of incommensurable parameters (duration, fecundity, contrast, inclusiveness, intensity, etc., etc.) preceded the discovery of a rough formula. The first hint for it came from the idea of "advance," which suggested that any measurement of dynamic value-in-process would have to "take a sounding" at two points in the process, the difference between the two measures indicating the actual amount of value. But how are we to handle our welter of intertwining criteria in measuring the two points?

The second hint that proved most helpful in reducing the confusion was forthcoming from that idea of "least action" or "least energy" which, as we have seen (p. 188 f.), constitutes both the most universal law in basic science, and also the one that hints most of something evaluative in nature, of some kind of perfection of efficiency. Could it be that in measuring value in every other realm we are trying to measure the success of processes in attaining the "most of something for the least of something else?" And incidentally, is there also a hint in this starting point that what many feel is the most value-contradicting law of science — the Second Law of Thermodynamics — may fit the requirements of dynamic value after all? Can it be the guarantor that all processes in this universe are pressed to seek the most efficient way, and cannot count on boundless supplies of energy for them to waste in excesses of consumption and form?

We have, then, the notion that value may be proportional to be "most" — to some quantity that may be countable — which however is limited or "judged" by another opposing quantity, which is to be kept "least." It will not do merely to add factors indefinitely, calling the "most" the "best". The collection must also satisfy some criterion of form and efficiency. One remembers that satisfaction arises preëminently from finding creative patterns that "kill two birds with one stone," or attain a "both-and" where one had thought himself sentenced to an "either-or."

I resorted, then, to a quasi-mathematical formula that would picture this "most" and "least" in a usefully simple, if mathematically dubious, way. Let X stand for quantitative aspects in the "most" — to incorporate, we might foresee, such criteria as Bentham's fecundity, duration and extent, and Perry's inclusiveness, however these might be interpreted and counted in different types of value. Then let us use Y to cover any aspects of quality and intensity that we may want to maximize or optimize and include

446

under the "most" that is sought by the process. Many of the other criteria (contrast, order, etc.) will go into this, raising, I admit, great problems of measurement and commensurability. Z, finally, will be for everything involved in the minimization — usually the energy utilized, but also, we will find, counts of basic principles, rules, aspects of design and form. If sub-1 indicates measures for the conditions at the start of a segment of process, sub-2 for conditions at the terminal measure, and S the ultimate amount or satisfaction or value, we have:

$$(X_2 + Y_2 - Z_2) - (X_1 + Y_1 - Z_1) = S \text{ (max.)}$$

This formula indicates roughly that it is "good" or "better" to do anything with X, Y and Z, before and or after the segment of process to be measured, that will maximize the first parenthesis, minimize the second, and thus maximize the difference between them, or S. This will usually mean to increase X_2 and Y_2 (or at least their sum), as compared with X_1 and Y_1, and to decrease Z_2 as compared with Z_1. But, notice that the formula easily provides for cases where we purposely "make the situation worse before we make it better" — e.g. wait till we are hungrier before we eat, or set up difficulties to overcome in games, or create discords in music — in the expectation of increasing value-feeling in the succeeding resolutions. In such cases we would be widening the gap between the first and second terms of the formula by decreasing X_1 and Y_1 and increasing Z_1 *before* we start on the ultimate increasing of X_2 and Y_2 and decreasing of Z_2. The formula directs us to seek the largest amount of transition toward inclusive complexity at optimum quality-intensity possible for any amount of energy. Is this possibly what "organizing process" means?

Of course, many fine points about this formula are not settled. Should any of the terms have exponents? Should X and Y be a product rather than a sum? The mutual involvement of the terms is not shown: the fact that increasing inclusiveness in X itself tends to decrease intensity in Y, etc. There is also the problem of incommensurability among the different factors, much discussed by Perry. He admits the impossibility of many kinds of comparison and decision, but argues that inclusiveness takes precedence over preference (quality?) and preference over intensity, though there are cases where it cannot be decided whether one outweighs the other or not. In using my formula I must undoubtedly admit the same difficulties, though I assume the mind does "add up" these incommensurables anyway in its rough, intuitive way. I believe the formula expresses in a crude though clarifying way what the mind is doing when it evaluates.

Aside from these difficulties, the formula does seem to express rather well why evaluation never does become or will become a final static figure. The three main figures mutually affect one another in such a way that the finding of their optimum values which will make the total maximize must remain a continuous task. Too much inclusiveness may begin to lower quality-intensity and raise energy use, so as to lower the total value. We cannot aim at a simple maximizing or minimizing of any figure without making the others change in a possibly undesirable way. Yet we can have an absolute knowledge whether the first is greater than the second, though we have no absolute, fixed essence as a standard to compare with.

The actual amount of dynamic value attained is shown by the application of the entire formula with its measures of both prior and subsequent states and their difference. It might thus be able to indicate more value existing when a person of poor attainment or maladjustment grows or improves considerably, than when one with high development at the start does not advance much, though the first does not arrive at as inclusive development as the second starts with. But also, the single expression $(X + Y - Z)$ by itself can always be applied to single states of objects and subjects, for measuring their "objective value" in the derivative sense, or for comparing their existent states with those of other objects and subjects, always remembering that value does not become actual until such objects are interacted with by feeling subjects, or such subjects proceed beyond such states. Thus used, it could show the second person's state as absolutely more complexly organized than the first's at a given moment.

As to specific ways of measuring the X (quantity), Y (quality) and Z (energy expenditure) for different types of value, we have space for only a few remarks.

Z, the energy factor, is to be minimized, we have said, but we are guarded against having to say that any amount of reduction of it (laziness?) is sure to yield more good. For it is the expression as a whole that is to be maximized, and if reducing Z beyond a certain point means that X and Y vanish entirely, we would not have done that. Z might conceivably be increased, if that should lead to such greater increases in X and Y as to increase the whole. In many kinds of value, Z would be the energy available, required or consumed in a part or all of the body involved; especially in physical, sensory and practical values (classes A, B and D, p. 352 f.) and also many personal and social ones. The problem may often be not how to minimize Z but how to maximize X and Y for a given Z. For other types of value, Z will consist of minimized numbers of axioms, rules, classes, themes, elements, etc., which are being utilized in cognitive, aesthetic, recreational and ethical processes. We would be estimating how many deductions, confirmations, plays, variations, consequences (X) could be related to how few axioms, rules of correspondence, rules of games, basic themes or materials, ethical rules, etc. (Z). All such rules, principles, etc., fundamentally concern how much energy, physical or mental, is going to be required to handle how much organizing process and enjoyment. Rules, may, at first, *increase* the energy requirement of the processes that abide by them; but this greater energy should still be minimal for the increment of value-experience that it instigates. In some cases, nature itself seems to set the rules, as in cognition. In others man artificially creates rules, and even oppositions (as in games), in order purposely to raise the tension and energy requirement, thus decreasing the value of $X_1+Y_1-Z_1$ (cf. p. 447). But this is done only, of course, for the purpose of enabling more resolving process to come into being ultimately. Setting up standards thus both instigates activity, calling for more energy (Z), but also gives content to X and Y, which often consist precisely of experiences of "fitting" standards. "Better" criteria or rules, then, though they may call for more energy than no rules at all, still lead to more experiences of consummation in X and Y per amount of energy.

Now every *type* of value (Chapter XIV, section I) will call for its characteristic meanings for the parameters included in the X, Y and Z measures. This sketchy presentation of DR's method of evaluation, then, brings us to a few illustrations of its use under the types. I will include remarks on one or two of the other types on the "long list" (p. 352) besides the basic three.

A and B. For simple bodily and sensory feelings, the X, Y and Z counts might have to do with characteristics of the light or sound waves being sensed, or metabolic states in cells and organs.

C. Cognitive Value. It is easy enough to see the application of the formula to measuring the *amount of enjoyment* taken in the process of thinking, solving problems, confirming hypotheses, for it is made up, like any other process, of a prior need state (the curiosity, the puzzlement), the object (the cognitive problem), the aiming, planning (the hypothesis and projected test), the process (the experimenting and observing) and the consummation (the successful confirmation). Complexity (X), novelty, precision, etc. (Y), and reduction of basic explanatory principles, i.e. Occam's razor (Z) are all involved in the prior feelings of dissatisfaction and the subsequent ones of triumphant solution.

But does the *truth* of the knowledge as such rest upon these criteria? At this point I might mention such a discussion of criteria of "good" hypotheses or "constructs" as Margenau's.[20] He lists six "metaphysical requirements on constructs," non-empirical criteria which are ineliminably involved in evaluating the adequacy of theories.

1. Logical Fertility: constructs should be stated so as to be able to enter into "more" logical relationships and implications.

2. Multiple Connections: Closely related to the preceding, this item points more to the construct's implications to subsidiary rules and to testable observations — the "more" the better.

3. Permanence or Stability: The correlations between the constructs and what they stand for should not change so often as to lose usefulness.

4. Extensibility: this refers to what we discussed in Chapter VI as Systematization, or ability to be extended into other sciences and other bodies of data.

5. Causality: Success in showing invariability of connection or sequence among phenomena.

6. Simplicity and Elegance: This criterion includes the traditional principle of parsimony, and the sense (which Margenau confesses is very difficult to conceive any measurement for) of almost aesthetic "neatness" in concepts.

Now half of these (1, 2 and 4) are obviously matters of increased number of connections or observations which are to be connected to the construct or principle whose "truth" is being evaluated. Both numbers of confirming observations and of intervening theorems or connecting principles might go into the X count. #3, Permanence and Stability, is similar to Duration which we have also considered an X factor. #6, Simplicity, seems plainly to be Z, for cognitive value, the minimization of basic explanatory concepts which we hope will "efficiently" explain the materials under

X. The "Elegance" perhaps is what goes into Y, for cognitive value, including such matters as symmetry, precision, etc.

The remaining item, #5 Causality, seems to be that special quality or nature which constitutes the content of cognitive value, as colors or sounds constitute it for sensory value. That is, what is usually to be counted under X for cognitive value is the number of correspondences between the implications of the constructs to regular sequences in nature, and actual observations of such sequences.

What our formula roughly indicates, then, is what is quite generally agreed upon by epistemologists: that the "amount" of truth is proportional to the number (X) of confirmations or independent data that are correlated by the theory (the correspondence test); and to the "simplicity" of the theory (Z) (the coherence test). Fecundity, as part of the inclusion, is also considered, when we hold all truth to be subject to indefinite correction in the light of future results; or when we talk of "fruitful hypotheses" as being "better" than barren ones.

D. Practical Values. No particular difficulties in the application of our formula arise in this area. X in productive value is specified as the "output," measurable in various ways for different kinds of work. Z is called the "input," and is ordinarily kept at a minimum: the amount of fuel used, the number of man-movements, time, etc. There is usually some evaluation of quality, too, for Y.

E. Social-Political Value. This class of value must be slighted in this book, though I will remark that I have found the formula applicable to the famous problem of distribution of happiness which is always thrown at hedonism.

F. Personal Values will be considered at the end, under Ethics.

G. Recreational and Aesthetic Value. Since for DR value is felt in the process of interaction between a feeling subject and objects, the nature of the process will naturally be a function of the nature of the object. Therefore, Art criticism tends to become a matter of evaluating finished art objects alone, suppressing the fact that actual art value lies only in the felt process such objects may instigate in subjects. Therefore, we would obviously have to know something about the subject's degree of training, receptive ability, etc., before we know how much *actual* value that object has instigated in this subject. However, there is nothing to stop us from evaluating the objects by our formula, ignoring the abilities of particular subjects, as long as we remember the derivative nature of the resulting "values."

Yet we cannot seem to get away from having to evaluate appreci-ators in order to evaluate art objects. "Good art" is sometimes de-fined as whatever an eminently qualified connoisseur enjoys. But qualified appreciators are identified as those who enjoy "good art." So we land in the well-known circle of criticism. However, since the real locus of value is in the interaction itself, it is at least theoretically meaningful to say that *its* value will be highest when the most complex, etc., appreciator is being most fully and satis-factorily activated by the most complex, etc., object.

For practical purposes, however, it is obviously easier to evaluate and measure aspects of the object than of the subject. To some extent, then, we could count the inclusiveness or complexity of the object, its Y factors, and its simplicity of design (Z) and presume its value to be proportional, whether certain subjects could feel its goodness or not. But artistic fineness, intensity, contrast, etc., can be so subtle as probably forever to escape exact measurement, leaving us with the "taste" of connoisseurs as our arbiter on whether the art object, complex as it may be, remains a clumsy aggregate, or possesses ingenious pattern and symmetry and tight organization. Dare we suggest that some Mahler and Bruckner symphonies, for instance, though they are inclusive and lengthy enough, tend toward tepidity of effect because of insufficient contrast and in-tensity (Y) and too flaccid organization (Z) as compared with Beethoven or Brahms? Each criterion can be thought about separ-ately, and the connoisseur mentions now one and now another. But he can also feel the whole together. In the end, perhaps "Duration" has the final word considered not only as how long the connoisseur continues to enjoy the work, but how long the work remains popular culturally and historically.

The principle of ordered inclusiveness would tend against some kinds of abstract art. To the extent that exclusion is a leading principle in such art, or reduction to single abstract aspects such as the planar or cubistic aspects, it would risk lowering X so much that its concomitant lowering of Z would not rescue the work from triviality. Ephemerality has indeed characterized much of this art and would seem to confirm this evaluation. Other things, i.e. Y and Z factors, being equal, there seems to be no reason why many other parts of our experience — memories, social ideals, emotional associations, etc., — might not be included in the art experience in addition to mere perception of lines, or perception of mathematical relations between sounds. The passion for "pure form" of much modern art and music suggests SMR's analytical, fragmentizing approach. Although such works may achieve some value due to their raising some one criterion to a great height (something in Y perhaps, though there may be a high X count in some one respect — number of notes, or lines, etc.), still a readiness to include many kinds of materials or subject matter might be a surer way to greatness and richness. Operas, for instance, are often superciliously rejected by "art specialists" as mongrel hybrid forms. Some operas, of course, may not reach greatness because they are so low in form and quality that no amount of inclusion of musical, poetic, narrative, personal and emotional materials can make up for it. But with reasonably adequate formal qualifications, greatness and profundity of feeling are more likely to be communicated by them than much more "formally perfect" works that involve only a few superficial nerve tracts in the top of the brain. The connoisseurs who scoff that such older "great" music bores them should not confuse mere excessive familiarity with poorness, nor the mere differentness of the new music with greatness; that is, they should not use the criterion of novelty to the exclusion of all the others.

DR, then, although, it cannot evaluate aesthetic value with much precision, is not at all bound to deny our daily experience of realizing that some beauties are greater than others. The theory of wholes which can differ from one another in inclusiveness and organization provides the ground for believing in these impressions even though we may not be able to prove them.

For recreational values, our formula is well adapted to take care of the fact that most or all games begin with *lessening* the value of X + Y — Z purposely, moving from the tepidity of ordinary experience to the threatening but exciting tensions of the challenge. The setting up of opposing teams, of rules of games, the shuffling of the cards, the tossing of the dice, etc., are all methods of reducing order, setting up random disorder, increasing tension, at the start. But of course, this is only to allow a process of creating new order to get under way. The application of the formula to the various kinds of order that are created from these starting points will be left to the student as we move on to the crucial test of DR's evaluative methods.

H. Ethical Value. Under the DR position in Chapter XIV, we mentioned broader and narrower coverages for the field of ethics. We concluded that the term was best used for evaluations within only certain ones of the varieties of value-process: certain individual personal ones concerning the care of one's person, the choice of one's goals, the apportionment of one's time, etc.; and secondly and more expecially, evaluating acts in connection with their effect on others, that is, evaluating in the realm of social relations.

It is obvious that DR's ethical theory requires us to consider consequences of processes or acts, either as aimed at or as attained, when we are trying to determine the amount of value, or "advance." DR's ethical theory, then, will belong to what is usually called the "teleological" type, though it must, of course, resist the tendency of the ordinary teleological theory to suppose that terminal states tell the whole story. It is the nature of the process itself that defines value. But since, in order to ascertain the nature of a process we must cut into it at several points to find out whether the later phase is "improving" over the earlier, we will find ourselves measuring one or more terminal "states" anyway, for this purpose. So our theory remains teleological in that sense.

Now we have explained in Chapter XIV in what sense the dynamic idea of good is hedonistic in its theory of psychological fact; and in Chapter XV and #1 above in its theory of the standard. A good many objections to hedonism in ethics could be discussed at this point, with our lines of defense against them. But aside from warning that "pleasurable feeling" or "happiness" must be conceived inclusively enough, we will pass them over to concentrate on the most serious one: the difficulty any ethics based upon feelings of satisfaction in feelers has to find a basis for altruism.

> Here we face the problem that many consider the crucial problem of ethics: the advance from the egoistic to the general point of view, from the purely subjective to the objective. If . . . we base our ethical theory on values, and if we define values as those things and experiences which individuals desire and like, how is it going to be possible to go on to the conclusion that the individual ought to take into consideration other values than his own?[21]

We have considered the factual, psychological aspect of this question in Chapter XIV, finding it possible for the self to love others or wish to help them genuinely for their own sake, with whatever enjoyment the self gains through this loving and helping not to be

454

considered as rendering the behavior essentially selfish. We have also seen how society can motivate any additional altruism it may need by sanctions. Our present question, however, is whether we have grounds in our method of evaluation for holding such genuinely altruistic behavior as either "better" or obligatory, as compared to self-regarding behavior.

Of course, on a strictly egoistic basis, we could evaluate altruistic behavior as better by maintaining that in the long run larger amounts of benefit (more X) should tend to redound to the agent for less exertion on his own part (Z) from associates encouraged to similar behavior by his own. But it is said that we must have a basis for holding altruism better and obligatory quite apart from any benefit to the agent; or even for commending behavior that helps others at the *expense* of the agent as better than any other kind. The presence of any self-regarding interest, in fact, is said to remove acts from the realm of altruism in the first place. Now we have said that genuine altruistic motivation is psychologically possible; but on what grounds can we say it is *better?* Is there any reason why one ought to do this which he *can* do? Or ought he, perhaps to inhibit any inclinations to consider others' welfare over his own?

One basis for approving the fostering of others' happiness as equal to or greater than seeking one's own is to point out that if we say that value-as-satisfying-feeling is good at all, we are saying that it is good wherever it exists. The egoist cannot say that "only *my* satisfying feeling is good" without contradicting the general thesis. Therefore, if such feeling is adopted as our criterion of evaluation, the "more" of it that exists in many feelers is "better" than that existing only in one. Our formula, then, might be applied by letting X_2 include the values felt by multiple subjects which results from the action of one of them, thus easily showing the greater value of acts that produce happiness in many rather than in only one.

This measure, however, seems to give us no basis for deciding on relative distribution of value among the individuals concerned, especially in cases where an individual might serve the good of his neighbor or of society, but only at the cost of sacrifice, pain, or at any rate some lesser good for himself. The acts of Horatio at the bridge or of Christ on the cross have usually been considered "best" though there was apparently no positive value felt in the agents' own experience. But how, on the basis of a theory that centers "betterness" in the greater complexity, etc. of processes in the feeler, can we especially approve of that feeler's concern for others' feelings over his own? It would seem crude to insist with egoism, as suggested above, that such potential benefits for the self as ending up a hero praised by beneficiaries, or avoiding self-hatred and social shame which are commonly the alternative to acting helpfully or sacrificially, will invariably be available, and will be the only reason why the generous or sacrificial acts are good. This seems to reduce all such acts to mere selfish prudence. Can we account for men's tendency to ascribe credit to an agent just to the extent that he is *not* motivated by prudential considerations?

Must we say perhaps, that the value of disinterested sacrifice can only be measured from the point of view of the beneficiaries, and that its very meaning depends upon its risking producing negative value for the agent himself, or at least a definite comparative loss? Is this the only way of avoiding reducing all agape or risk for others to selfish prudence? But, if so, how can we explain such acts ever being motivated at all, let alone develop any theory of their betterness from the agent's own point of view? Is society's demand for such acts the only basis for either explanation?

At this point, thinking again of our thesis that satisfaction is proportional to some kind of inclusive organization, we may wonder whether the unselfish one or the martyr, no matter how much he resists the above sort of prudential considerations, can be entirely without an awareness of the benefits to others his act will foster, and whether such thoughts about inclusive and facilitated social results can fail to produce in him satisfaction-feeling at that level, perhaps even enough to outweigh competing desires for personal ease. Would admitting this drive us back to a kind of prudentiality in all sacrifice and unselfishness?

To admit such a broad type of satisfaction in the agent from his unselfish act would certainly simplify our explanation of how such acts come to be done, and also enable us to retain the use of our formula for measuring such value even from his own point of view. But the satisfaction which we would be saying is maximized in this sense, *for the agent* can hardly be equated with selfishness. For, to be able to take satisfaction in that sort of comprehension of inclusive social benefit, even if it implies some trouble at another level for oneself, is just about what we mean by unselfishness. The

456

agent, then, can be said to "enjoy" his unselfishness at the level of thinking of its social results for others. This would mean that the negative value he may feel more personally in going through the fires, does not outweigh the positive value he feels in a consistent course of action.

With these few hints of a dynamic method of evaluating or ranking value processes, we must conclude, leaving the defense of other virtues and decisions to a more specialized book.

Comparison of SM with DR: Although DR thus reinstates value as possibly pervasive throughout reality, and finds values, standards and ranks to be knowable, to SM's satisfaction, its suggestion that this knowledge is creative and experimental is not all what SM looked for. This is nothing like that intuitive certainty of final absolute values that SM wanted, and it leaves authority and custom as sources of value knowledge far behind.

DR supplies a sort of absolutism in its theory that all value experiences whatever involve increasing and harmonizing of factors. But it does not use SM's notion of fixed criteria against which all creatures must be judged and condemned. Rather, we have a sort of "sliding" absolute standard, as expressed by Dewey:

> No individual or group will be judged by whether they come up to or fall short of some fixed result, but by the direction in which they are moving. The bad man is the man who no matter how good he *has* been is beginning to deteriorate, to grow less good. The good man is the man who no matter how morally unworthy he *has* been is moving to become better. Such a conception makes one severe in judging himself and humane in judging others. It excludes that arrogance which always accompanies judgement based on degree of approximation to fixed ends.[22]

DM with DR.

Implications of DM and Correspondence to DR: 1. Standard. 2. Knowledge. It is hardly necessary to continue to work out the correspondence between the implications of DM and the factual findings of DR. Obviously the dynamic idea of good implies what DR has found concerning the creative, experimental manner in which we know value.

We might say at this point, however, that if the critic is still doubtful that we have "verified" under DR what value is and what standard it implies, we could now say under DM: "Then postulate and adopt the dynamic idea of good; and upon doing so, notice how much experience and knowledge fits its implications." This concept of value cannot be deduced from any more ultimate concept above it, and perhaps must be taken as "self-evident" in that sense. If it should be asked "Why does God choose to make value dynamic instead of anything else?", we would confess to having arrived at that level of ultimates which must simply be accepted.

However, I believe that we actually arrive at an understanding of the nature of dynamic value from empirical experience. We then carry the concept thus produced in DR over to the DM side, to use as the ultimate idea from which all things may be "re-deduced."

3. Evaluation. The implications of DM to some of the parameters of measurement were presented at the outset in Chapter III. We saw there the derivation of differentiation, order, inclusion, contrast, advance, etc. We might add here that there is an implication from the concept of dynamic value to multiplicity of parameters as such. For to have to balance a multiplicity of factors which stand somewhat opposed to one another would conduce to a more permanently dynamic situation than to be able to come to rest in pushing some one criterion to its ultimate limit. We cannot, thus, push either inclusiveness or intensity to extremes without losing so much of the other as to lower the sum (or product?) of both. One must balance his plans for incorporating more elements with both his plans for attaining vividness and with his available energy.

The dynamic idea of value also explains why human evaluations should evolve and change, as we found they do.

> Conduct which in one environment and at one stage produces its measure of harmonious satisfaction, in other surroundings at another stage is destructively degrading. . . . Thus the notion that there are certain regulative notions, sufficiently precise to prescribe details of conduct, for all reasonable beings on Earth, in every planet, and in every star-system, is at once to be put aside.[23]

> The theory of "eternally valid values" leaves no room for creation in the moral sphere.[24]

458

CHAPTER XVII

THEORY OF RIGHT, OBLIGATION AND INCITATION

Of the remaining branches of value theory — Right and Wrong, Obligation or Duty, Rights, Laws, Instrumental Values, Social Values, Virtues, etc. — only the first two are of such fundamental theoretical importance as to require treatment in this book. The vast detail of the other topics (in applied ethics), if ever to be treated by the present author, will be treated in a less systematic book than this.

The theory of Right and Obligation is placed latterly in this chapter because for DR it is a dependent topic, and our basic order is determined by DR. For some of the static positions, as we saw in Chapter XV, this topic is more fundamental or underivative.

The closely related topic of Incitation, Inspiration, Dynamic, or Motivation (whatever it be called) will also be discussed in this chapter. It forms the transition to the last part of the book. We begin, then, with the first topic.

1. *The Meaning of Rightness and Obligation.*
The question here is distinguished from that of the second part of the chapter as being concerned with the *intellectual* rationale for calling anything right and obligatory, and what the relationship between these two concepts is; as against the *psychological* problem of how to get anyone to accept his obligation and act upon it. Some theories place a still more subtly distinguished category between these two: the question of what to answer anyone who, upon intellectually understanding what duty or responsibility he is obliged to, still asks, "Why should I do my duty?" This is not the psychological question — how to make anyone *feel* like doing his duty, or to incite him to undertake difficult obligations; it is still on the intellectual side, asking for "proof" of why one should go on to perform the duty that has been ascertained. We will

include this question when it is admitted, under the present topic.

In some theories (e.g., the Socratic) the second question (incitation) is not distinguished from the first; in others (e.g., the Pauline) a separate problem of incitation arises when it is recognized that people can understand and admit their obligation yet still fail or refuse to exemplify it.

The problem of freedom and determinism from Chapter X is obviously involved in these questions. And in Chapter XIV we have given some of the factual psychology. And concerning the most important application of this topic — our basis for demanding of an individual, as his duty, that he consider the welfare of others as well as that of himself — we have presented most of the foundations. So there is nothing more to do here than to round out loose ends.

SM with SIR.

Implications of SM: We explained (in Chapter XVI) why SM implies that intuitively known rightness should be more fundamental than value or goodness, the very source of value and goodness in fact. The right should not be derived from any calculation about value-results, but should be conformity to some established essences, divine commands or built-in habits and customs. We will leave further discussion of subtler points till the Recourses section.

Knowing what the right is, then, what does SM imply as to why one should *do* it? But, of course, SM hardly implies any doing; certainly no resistance against the right. The spirit should just naturally seek the essences, supposing it had ever got separated from them at all, which SM does not imply in the first place.

Adjustments of SIR: Again, in stating SIR's theory of value above, we had to state its theory of rightness, since they tend to coalesce in static thought.

As for the question why one should do his duty, it was not very explicit for the earlier customary, intuitional, etc., theories. One simply followed the custom or obeyed the authority without thinking. Mere habit, or tribal ridicule, must at first have made people ready to do what it was taken for granted they "ought" to do.

As soon as there is any occasion to question custom or rebel against authority, the problem of obligation comes out into the open. The authority is asked for a reason why one must or ought to obey it. At this point the divine origin of the commands may seem enough reason why they should be obeyed. Various strands of Christian thought make this explicit in holding that God's arbitrary will is the source of right, and of our obligation to conform to it. There can be no further justification of God's decrees than His sheer will, for His will creates all standards and all justification.

Next, when men come to seek standards behind God's willing — criteria according to which He Himself must have willed — and resort, with Plato to a realm of absolute essences or standards, man's obligation to seek and conform to these essences again more or less goes without saying. The very nature of life is felt to be the desire to come nearer to the form of good, to obey one's "conscience." It is inconceivable that men should learn that there is a true state of things to reach, without undertaking to reach it. Socrates assumed that to know this truth is to desire and accept the obligation to strive for it. Knowledge is virtue. Or, SIR may supplement this belief with a doctrine that greater happiness will result from conformity to principle, as Socrates argues against Thrasymachus. Paul, of course, did not believe either kind of knowledge would necessarily lead to action.

SM-SIR's theories of freedom or predestination which support or fail to support these ideas of responsibility and obligation were discussed in Chapter X.

SM with SMR.

Findings of SMR: Deterministic anthropology, of course, soon proves how dependent all motives, all consciences are upon the relative backgrounds and experiences of the individuals. SMR especially likes to show that a conscience which SIR might have thought a model one can very well be exceedingly unhealthy, like the Victorian one, deserving to be unendingly rebelled against. Freudism and other strands of SMR are inclined to consider conscience as essentially an inhibitory function built up from social causes, which ought to be rooted out in favor of the more direct impulses and instincts, however irrational.

Nothing more needs to be said here of SMR's lack of basis for speaking of anything as "right," except insofar as individuals might be conditioned to think that what their particular society demands of them is "right." There can be no deeper grounds for obligation when mechanistic determinism, as we have seen, rules out choice, standards, and any meaning for evaluating any thing as better than any other. We find the expected positivistic view in a statement by Ayer.

When one comes to pursue the psychological inquiries which constitute ethical science, one is immediately enabled to account for the Kantian and hedonistic theories of morals. For one finds that one of the chief causes of moral behavior is fear, both conscious and unconscious, of a god's displeasure, and fear of the enmity of society. And this, indeed, is the reason why moral precepts present themselves to some people as "categorical" commands. And one finds, also . . . that a society tends to encourage or discourage a given type of conduct by the use of moral sanctions according as it appears to promote or detract from the contentment of the society as a whole. And this is the reason why altruism is recommended in most moral codes and egotism condemned. . . . [The essential defect of each of these theories] is that they treat propositions which refer to the causes and attributes of our ethical feelings as if they were definitions of ethical concepts. And thus they fail to recognize that ethical concepts are pseudo-concepts and consequently indefinable.[1]

Not that thinkers in the tradition of SMR can not be found telling us that we "ought" to follow our impulses or instincts; or that SM's standards, now seeming arbitrary and non-empirical, "ought" to be flouted; or that society's deadening restrictions "ought" to be rebelled against. This only represents SMR's evolutionary, instinctivist type of determinism conflicting with its social determinist form. None of these "oughts," of course, asks us to resist the "natural," however it is conceived, or to make effort to shape ourselves toward some more complex mode of behavior, evaluable as higher than what happens to be given. Certainly there is no more asking us to be "rational," or to conform to any "spiritual" essence already within us; these things are not discovered to exist *now*, empirically, in the ordinary human being, and we cannot, then, be obligated to develop them.

Recourses to SM-SIR: Rationalists seek to restore absolute rightness and obligation by all the methods we itemized in Chapter XV on the nature of Value. The appeal to ordinary meanings, and the repudiation of synthetic, naturalistic definitions can be seen in

462

the following passage from Ross where he approves of Moore's revised theory that right cannot, any more than good, be said to "mean" any other characteristic, no matter how universal an accompaniment.

> But the *reason* for an action's being right is evidently not the same thing as its *rightness,* and Professor Moore seems already to have passed to the view that productivity of maximum good is not the definition of 'right' but another characteristic which underlies and accounts for the rightness of right acts . . . obviously a criterion of rightness is not rightness itself. . . .
>
> . . . [therefore] 'right' is an irreductible notion.
> Nor is this result impugned by inquiries into the historical development of our present moral notions from an earlier state of things in which "what is right" was hardly disentangled from "what the tribe ordains." The point is that we can now see clearly that 'right' does not mean "ordained by any given society." And it may be doubted whether even primitive men thought that it did. . . . "It is the custom" has been accompanied by "the custom is right," or "the custom is ordained by some one who has the right to command." . . . for the nature of the self-evident is not to be evident to every mind however undeveloped, but to be apprehended directly by minds which have reached a certain degree of maturity. . . .[2]

The point of insisting on the indefinability of rightness is thus to deny SMR's allying it with any existent state of things. This is supposedly the only way to gain the ground for saying that the right might be some future, as yet unattained, state of things. We have been holding, of course, that it is possible to "measure" some hypothetical future complex as "better" without the use of any absolute standard, and that the right would be what would conduce to such a complex. But we know that Ross will not allow right to have reference to such future results either (p. 395 f.); and that this leaves him without any general scale for measuring the degrees of goodness or rightness, but only a list of *prima facie* duties, the precedence of which we can only see intuitively when the occasion arises. Our discovery of the inner complexity and variousness of different situations involving virtue and duty in the

463

preceding chapter should reveal how arbitrarily truncated this analysis of the nature of duty is.

Passing to the question of *why* one should do what has been ascertained (in whatsoever manner) as being right, the rationalists take as their main thesis Kant's, that obligation or oughtness excludes acting from desire. The phrase "categorical imperative" reminds us how central the present topic is for Kant. One's duty can only be to conform to the rational or self-evident right, usually in opposition to desire. For Kant, obligation rests on the assumption that man's nature is essentially rational, that he is obliged to develop this rationality, and therefore to conform to the supremely rational concept, the principle of universality.

> It is . . . because of his dual nature that man is subject to obligation. Nonrational beings such as the animals have no obligation, and it would be a misuse of language to attribute obligation to any purely rational beings such as God is conceived to be. Obligation is a command arising from one's own rational nature which one recognizes as binding, but which runs counter to one's nonrational inclinations. It is the *necessity* of acting in universal, *objective,* fashion if one is to be true to one's own inmost rational nature.[3]

Notice here SM's finding no need for obligation in the state of pure (static) goodness (God's); also the split between separate faculties of reason and inclination as against DR's preferring to distinguish between the non-inclusive vs. the inclusive *desire.*

Prichard develops this type of view, with special focus on the question "why should we do what we agree is our duty?"

> . . . the reason 'why' is usually stated in terms either of the agent's happiness or of the goodness of something involved in the action. . . . The formulation of the question implies a state of unwillingness or indifference towards the action, and we are brought into a condition of willingness by the answer. . . .
>
> The answer is, of course, not an answer, for it fails to convince us that we ought to keep our engagements; even if successful on its own lines, it only makes us *want* to keep them. . . . The advantage of [the other] appeal to the goodness of

something consists in the fact that it avoids reference to desire, and instead, refers to something impersonal and objective. In this way it seems possible to avoid the resolution of obligation into inclination. But . . . to be effective it must neither include nor involve the view that the apprehension of the goodness of anything necessarily arouses the desire for it. Otherwise the answer resolves itself into a form of the former answer by substituting desire or inclination for the sense of obligation.

Perhaps, however, the best way to see the failure of this view is to see its failure to correspond to our actual moral convictions. Suppose we ask ourselves whether our sense that we ought to pay our debts or to tell the truth arises from our recognition that in doing so we should be originating something good, e.g. material comfort in A or true belief in B. . . . We at once and without hesitation answer 'No.'[4]

Now when Prichard wants us to confess the absurdity of saying that "wealth for A" is the source of the obligation to pay our debt, it is to get us to admit that it is not such a consequence, but the prior act of promising to pay that creates the obligatoriness, and that this is understood by intuition. But "wealth for A" (as a static state) is not the significant consequence for this case; rather the continued working of the system of loaning and paying that was invented for its practical efficacy in furthering the wherewithal of life and enjoyment. In Kant's terms we cannot universalize non-repayment without cancelling the system of loaning itself; but the whole point of the system is its furtherance of human benefit, both egoistic and social. How can obligation be unrelated to this *general* consequence of preserving a beneficial pattern of behavior?

If we argue, as we did in the preceding chapter, that the individual cannot avoid taking a certain amount of "non-egotistic" (as well as egotistic) satisfaction in fitting his behavior to this "rational" system of loaning and paying, we seem to have committed what to Prichard is the supreme error of "resolving obligation into inclination." But to make the mutual exclusiveness of duty and desire as absolute as to reject even satisfaction in being rationally inclusive seems pointless.

SM with DR:

Findings of DR: The conception of compositional process allows DR to consider rightness to be derived from naturalistic experience of value without being caught in an ultimate relativism. Without more ado, I identify the right with whatever is evaluated highest by the method of the preceding chapter. To the extent that that evaluation is an estimate for aims, motives and means, and verified for consequences and virtues, or revised for further consequences, then the right is estimated, verified or revised. To the extent that we have provided for different evaluations from different points of view, or for more ideal evaluations by more adequate feelers, then the right will be different in more practical or more ideal senses. "Right" would thus never be found in actual life in an absolute sense; but neither must its meaning evaporate into utter relativism. There would be scope for a constant "improvement" in our ideas of rightness, as we progress to an ever increasing grasp on ways of organizing complexes of activities that will produce the most "life" with the least waste. We could distinguish, more or less clearly, what is "more right" from what is less, though we had no model of absolute rightness. Even the greatest minds' idea of the right could take account only of a finite amount of complexity and fecundity; and everyone would need to improve his competence in making evaluations and finding the "most right" behavior possible under the circumstances.

If we resort to "rules" as an aid (perhaps especially for less reflective minds) in deciding on the right, we would have to remember that, though one succeeded in conforming perfectly to a rule, and was "right" in that respect, the rule itself must be evaluated for rightness in terms of the more ultimate criteria. As Perry expresses it:

> According to the theory here proposed, 'right' means conduciveness to moral good, and 'wrong' means conduciveness to moral evil: the one to harmony and the other to conflict. So construed, right and wrong are dependent and instrumental values. That which is right or wrong may, however, like all objects of dependent interest, come to be loved or hated for its own sake, and thus acquire *intrinsic* value. . . .
> . . . it should be noted "the right thing" or "the wrong

thing" do not derive their ultimate meaning from intentionality, but from the nature of the *consequences* intended. . . .

There are certain generalized rules of conduct which experience proves to be conducive to harmoniousness . . . and an act may be judged according as it does or does not conform to them. The word 'right' suggests alignment, and it is therefore peculiarly applicable to the relation of an act to a rule. . . . But if the act is to be morally right the rule to which it conforms must be . . . a rule the observance of which conduces to moral goodness. . . .[5]

After finding the "right" in this manner, we come to the question of obligation, how we pass to the ought; the question "why should I do the right?" The content of one's duty comes down to this in our view: to take sufficient care to reflect and think out the evaluations as adequately as possible; and then to perform what one has thus evaluated as best or right. We are asking, then, why one should bother to reflect thus and then act thus? In short, why "ought" one to live by the dynamic idea of value?

Of course, to consider such a question at all presumes that we have settled the question of freedom of will in the affirmative, finding men able to do what we say they ought: to choose to reflect further, and to include more in their purview. Now in Chapter X, we admitted to some uncertainty whether field forces should still be considered as operating deterministically; or whether man had freedom to choose how much he would deliberate, and how many factors to include and what pattern to put them in. In the first case, obligation would have to be only a misnomer for a naturalistic field tendency, or for an irresistible urge toward a one possible state of wholeness. Does this approach give some ground for, or eliminate the possibility of a categorical imperative? Do we adopt our duties because existential field forces compel us to, or because of a free choice to be more or less "rational" (inclusively harmonious)?

A statement by Parker allies obligation with field forces, but is unclear on our question:

The "feeling of oughtness" and the judgment that I ought are expressions of the 'will' or 'go' of a system of tendencies to action in competition with some impulses of "lower order" which it is trying to bring within its scope. We should never feel that we ought were there not such a system operating within us in the direction in which, as we say, we ought to move. . . . There is, therefore, no 'ought' without presupposition, the presupposition of a system of desires.[6]

Pratt, in making the statement that "the sense of *oughtness* (is) an urge to be consistent with oneself"[7], seems to be assimilating obligation to the natural force of compositional process also, but he works this into a defense of the categorical imperative. This would seem to have to mean that he believes that there are alternative ways of being "consistent with oneself" among which we are obliged to choose the "best" or most rational; or that we are free to be consistent with ourselves, or not to be, but are obliged to choose the former. The field forces then would not be determined to push through to one outcome.

Dewey's familiar way of defending responsibility, even when freedom of choice within the field process is doubted, is to say that the sheer holding of a person responsible for what he has done in the past will make him behave accordingly in the future. That is, whether he could help what he did in the past or not, being blamed or praised for it in the present will enter as an "ingredient" into his field and determine it as desired in the future. This is almost to make determinism a servant of responsibility or at least determinism from *social* praise or condemnation.

If, on the other hand, we allow more freedom of choice as to how much one can, prior to action, deliberate or consider the consequences, etc., then we could hold him responsible in a more genuine sense for making conscientious efforts to estimate results in terms of inclusiveness and harmony. Man could then be "blamed" for insufficient effort to keep his partial urges "in gear" with the whole. "Sin" would have meaning as a non-necessitated one-sidedness of behavior, an unfated laziness about considering enough of the data and possibilities. We would have grounds, too, for explaining how any one might not only undertake to act in as inclusive a manner as he is now capable of, but could aspire to further inclusiveness, to higher tastes, to self-improvement, or even feel obliged to do so.

A statement by Broad seems to me to come closer to what actually happens than any I know of. The sense of right and the sense of obligation both appear in his "moral emotion" which is a deposit of many ingredients fusing together through a gestalt or "closure" tendency into belief, readiness to act, and assuredly feeling.

What is happening when a person is said to be feeling a *first-hand* moral emotion towards an act in respect of his belief that it is right or that it is wrong? . . . It *seems* to me that in such cases I do not first recognize or think that I recognize a quality or relation of rightness or wrongness in the act, and *then* begin to feel a moral pro-emotion or anti-emotion towards it in respect of this knowledge or belief. What I seem to do is to consider the act and its probable consequences under various familiar headings. "Would it do more harm than good? Would it be deceitful? Should I be showing ingratitude to a benefactor? . . ." In respect of each of these aspects of the act and its consequences I have a tendency to feel towards the act a certain kind of moral emotion of a certain degree of intensity. These emotional dispositions were largely built up in me by my parents, schoolmasters, friends and colleagues; and I know that in the main they correspond with those of other persons of my own nation and class. It seems to me that I call the act "right" or "wrong" in accordance with my final moral-emotional reaction to it, after viewing it under all these various aspects, and after trying to allow for any permanent or temporary emotional peculiarities in myself which may make my emotional reaction eccentric or unbalanced. By the time that this has happened the features which I had distinguished and had viewed and reacted to separately have fallen into the background and are again fused. They are the real mediating characteristics of my moral pro-emotion or anti-emotion; but I now use the omnibus words "right" or "wrong" to cover them all, and say that I feel that emotion towards the act in respect of my belief that it is right or wrong.[8]

I would not, of course, confine the "ingredients" that fuse into the sense of rightness and the emotional readiness to accept obligation and to act, as much to the rules of one's nation and class as Broad seems to. A fresh evaluation of consequences, inspiration by model persons, etc., might be other contents. But all these factors would "feed into" people's sense of rightness and duty, finally fusing into the feeling and propulsion itself. The "intuition" and "self-evidence" of the rationalists *is* this resulting holistic conviction. But the fact that it is finally felt as an undivided sense of right does not at all remove the evaluation of the separate ingredients by the usual criteria from the position of the ultimate basis of the rightness.

Human opinion abounds in categoricals and unconditionals which signify only the limits of knowledge. Most opinions have this absolute character not because there *is* no ulterior grounds, but because it is forgotten or ignored, or is a yet undiscovered, or lies beyond the capacity of the person who holds the opinion.

Thus a man's opinion that he ought not to lie is for most persons a simple mandate, with no "why or wherefore." This does not imply, however, that there *is* no why and wherefore.[9]

Comparison with SM-SIR: DR, then, gives us a real meaning for right and obligation to seek higher integrations of behavior, as against SMR's "obligation" to follow the compulsions of one's fragmentary urges. But we do not have the duty to elect SM's fixed essences, nor the rationalist's duty to obey unanalyzed intuitions, nor the Kantian duty to exclude desire from the picture. The dichotomy between rational will and desire does not come up, at least as a conflict between two different faculties. The rational will can only consist of the tendency toward more inclusive harmony of organizing process, which cannot be without a sense of satisfaction at that level. If opposing partial desires still operate and sometimes override the "rational" desire, it will not mean a conflict between desire and duty, but between short term vs. long term desires.

Now rationalists may still insist that under DR we have discussed only the factual, psychological forces that account for the sense of right and duty, and for the tendency to adopt duty and act on it; but that this is still not tantamount to "proving" that one ought to do his duty (cf. Prichard, p. 464.) I am not convinced that there is any very important point here, but we can perhaps answer it by saying that we must move on to DM before we can make such a statement.

Implications of DM and Correspondence to DR: Under DM, then, we could place the act of adopting the dynamic idea of good and its implications. We could then say, "On that basis, then, you ought to do your duty, which is to increase dynamic good, which requires that you reflect to the best of your ability, seeking the most inclusively adequate course of behavior that you can, and then perform it as best you can."

On the question of freedom or determinism in the compositional process, DM would seem to imply that reality *should* contain a native tendency toward increasing inclusion and organization; but not one that is guaranteed at all times and without fail to overcome partial urges without any trouble. The battle between short term and long term "desires," i.e., between desire and rational will in the older terminology, with the possibility of the former causing error and pain, *should* exist. The discovery of longer term obligations would originally be prompted by the experience of the pains resulting from falling into the errors of short-term desires.

But this opens up the fateful topic of improving desires or inspiring the adoption of long-term duties by perhaps other methods less wasteful and destructive that merely to allow the "painful" consequences to go through every time for every individual.

2. Incitation.

The present topic lies at the center of our book. It is the problem of elevating human motives and behavior, getting men to adopt higher obligations, which the opening chapter placed at the root of civilization, its health or decay. It is in no longer being able to supply humanity's need here that traditional thought fails us; in being unable even to recognize the problem that mechanistic thought threatens us; and in promising new foundations for dealing with the problem that dynamic thought gives us hope. It is to the extent that the possibility of higher and more difficult levels of behavior is admitted, and the consequent problem of a dynamic to raise men to that level is recognized, that interest in religious bearings upon ethics is likely to follow. Thus the present topic forms a transition to the last part of the book.

471

SM with SIR.

Implications of SM: Since SM does not imply value process at all, it of course does not imply struggle for higher values, or need of "improvement" and effort. It expects perfect thoughts first, last and always. It does not even imply ends to be *accomplished*, but rather pre-established ones. This approach has, I suspect, throughout history tended to keep the problem of inspiration from becoming entirely explicit. Men have derived inspiration from their myths and heroes and mystical experiences, but have so taken it for granted that when a non-inspirational philosophy like SMR comes along, men never understand exactly what it is that they lose through it.

Adjustments of SIR: As we have seen in many connections, although SIR recognizes the existence of a process of attaining to SM's essences, it is in the nature of a return to "true nature" rather than a genuinely creative effort. Actually, SIR paid a good deal of attention to ways and means of inspiring higher motives, though all of its methods tend to be statically contemplative, imitative or punitive. Contemplating the essences, or the heroic and saintly exemplars of them, is expected in itself to call forth higher desires and efforts to improve. Plato's ideal forms were to do this, whatever other difficulties they might make for understanding.

Conscience, too, in the older theories, was an intuitive organ that not only explained how man knows the ideals, but also explains what makes him strive for them. The other theories of knowledge of value also had their incitational aspect: divine revelation, social custom, authority, etc.

Socrates and St. Paul divide sharply on the present issue, though both would belong under SIR. Socrates, of course, assumes that knowledge of the essences in itself will incite virtuous behavior automatically. St. Paul confesses that though he knows what he should do, he still does not find it possible to do it on his own strength. This is the great entering wedge for the remainder of Christian belief, which takes its place primarily as a solution to the problem of incitation of moral behavior. The whole theory of salvation, immortality and rewards or punishments in the after life, whether emphasized or minimized in various religious views, seldom loses its character as motivational to higher morality in this life.

472

Another characteristic of traditional incitation is the reliance upon repetitive exhortation as a source of dynamic. Many still feel,
assuming fixed rules of morality, that the main task is to scold
people into following them, rather than explaining and evaluating
consequential benefits with increasingly subtle adequacy. An arbitrary threatening with authorities and punishments is still so
much the predominant way of both determining the right and
inciting conformity to it that a rebellion to equally arbitrary modes
of behavior, no more carefully thought out as to consequences, is
routine in the younger generation.

SM with SMR.

Findings of SMR: Unable to find any doctrine of better or worse,
or any reason why man should strive to make more effort than
"what comes naturally," SMR obviously has no reason to be concerned with sources of inspiration for undertaking effortful growth.
Complacently fearless of any untoward consequences resulting
from not trying hard enough, SMR is unworried (or was until
modern rediscovery of human weakness) that its whole line of
thinking disproves the possibility of any source of greater strength,
such as a divine healing and saving power in the universe. And
when disintegration and breakdown do turn up as the result of
its carelessness, SMR can only react with disgruntled bitterness,
finding such results only further proof of the meaninglessness and
succorlessness of reality. It is inspired neither by Socrates' faith
in the realm of perfect essences, nor by St. Paul's call to prayer
for salvation.

Materialists are inspired, in a way, by the call to rebel against
SM-SIR. They feel a kind of bravery, a noble individualism, in
daring to indulge their fragmentary impulses against the supposedly arbitrary prohibitions of society and authority. But it
often seems the last perversity of life to these "pioneers of the
moment" when they end up as unadmired bums, perennial ado-
lescents, disinherited isolates, while stuffy bourgeois society absorbs all and marches on its stolid way unimpressed. It seems
fair to say, however, that they are not quite honest with themselves when they imagine that indulgence in anti-social urges is
necessarily so creative and intrepid an act. Actually there remains,
at bottom, a factor of easiness in "daring" the fragmentary urge.
The truly difficult and brave thing would be to strive for a higher

rather than a lower integration than society currently approves.

SMR may claim hedonism's great advantage of the in-built motivational dynamic forthcoming from the desire for happiness. However, if happiness is construed as above — as the immediate pleasure only, with no need of effortful subordination and organization of desires — then it still offers no dynamic for advance, for altruism, and for developing the more complex "spiritual" levels of experience.

The natural outcome of these ideas appears on an ever broader front: the increasing dishonesty and corruption throughout business and political life; the pervasive shame for *being* ashamed — the apologies for being so sentimental as to refrain from taking advantage of people's credulity out of the weakness of old-fashioned integrity; the careful avoidance of aspiring to create anything "great" or "elevating." The thing to do is to confine one's ambitions to the surface glitter, to sensational tricks, to sophisticated nonsense, to the passing lascivious urge.

Recourses to SM-SIR: The romantic indulgence of emotion seems to be a kind of abortive combination of SMR's approval of the fragmentary feeling, and SM's ready-made ideals. The romantic trusts his feelings, however untrained, to take him unaided up to the heights of the ideal. Then he is embittered when such feelings, unevaluated at SMR's behest, turn out to be rather infantile and disgusting ones after all.

Kant made an effort to escape SMR's leveling, and found a prominent place for God, Immortality and the Moral Law as inspirational factors. He may not be absolutely clear that such enthusiasm-prompting beliefs contribute something that sheer rationality in itself cannot do, but his pietistic background suggests that he knew what religious inspiration was meant to accomplish. Positivists and others continued the Enlightenment's assumption that "feeling" or "enthusiasm" was so far from being the point of life as to require to be eliminated not only from research but from existential life itself.

There is a claim, which we must consider seriously under DR, that an ethics of fixed rational principle will provide a more stable defense of high motives than a teleological ethics.

And though the point is somewhat moot, let me suggest that the view which spends all its time looking to consequences is for the safe, secure, gradually constructive days.

474

In times of peril it is integrity that counts. And there are such times. This is, of course, just the reverse of what we most often hear: unhappily, integrity is often thought a luxury for the safe and pleasant days when nothing threatens; an anxious weighing of consequences is selected as the needed instrument for times of danger. . . . I suspect those who have done most to save what can be saved within an age — those called heroes, saints, and martyrs — have been able to command themselves, even in dangerous times and despite the consequences to themselves, to stand on principle.[10]

We have already discussed whether the will to follow rational principle is not ultimately a *desire* for the satisfaction to be had in fitting behavior to a consistent order. But although we cannot agree that the heroes and martyrs are not considering consequences, we may find a use for this idea of sticking to a principle.

SM with DR.

Findings of DR: We have explained how DR can evaluate better and worse, and arrive at a tentative idea of what is right to aim at, aspire toward, be motivated to. We have found a gestalt, closure force tending to cause organisms to adopt what seems consistent and right for them. But, on the less deterministic interpretation, it seems that it is not guaranteed that they will adopt the most inclusive organization of behavior conceivable, or that they will not fall into some more partial, "wrong" behavior, even if they are shown a more adequate, inclusive way. In other words, it is not guaranteed that they will accept an "obligation" to a "higher" mode of behavior, even if they understand what it would be.

Aiken, whose "satisfaction" theory of value has been discussed as very close to ours (p. 414 f.), has made a sharp distinction between the present topic and the preceding. He considers everything we have studied in Part IV up to the present topic to come under the "appraising" function — finding out what is best and right; but the question of how to get people to *accept* and *act* on this right is the "normative" function of value theory. The first of these is entirely empirical; the second is not, and cannot be deduced from or enforced by the first. But he does not mean by this split between the normative and empirical what is usually meant, that you cannot base rightness on facts; he only means that you cannot compel *psychological acceptance* and readiness to act by any amount of intellectual proof of what is right.

. . . empirically tested evaluations will tend to have some normative appeal or urgency. . . . But it is of the utmost importance . . . to an understanding of the problems involved in the normative use of appraisals, to realize that there is nothing inevitable in this. Unquestionably the most serious theoretical error of any axiology which accepts [an interest or a satisfaction type of value theory] . . . is the assumption that evaluations are *ipso facto* normative. The price to be paid — and, for my part, gladly paid — for a theory of valuation which identifies value descriptively with satisfaction (or interest) and which treats appraisals as bona fide empirical judgments is the recognition that the normative function of "ethical" or "practical" judgments and their appraisive or evaluative function cannot be reduced to the same thing. . . .

It follows from this that even in principle there is no process of analysis or dialectical manipulation by means of which we can deduce norms from values or normative statements from mere appraisals of value. . . . The former . . . is incitive and rhetorical in method, even when it appears "rational." . . .

. . . the controversy [over the emotive theory] is secondary and not fundamental to the question of norms . . . no matter how "value" or "right" or "duty" may be defined, and no matter what conception we may have of the relations of cognition to interest — whether we agree with Hume and Perry and Stevenson that "reason is the slave of the passions" or with Kant that there is an autonomous rational moral will — there is no way whatever of deriving the obligatoriness or imperativeness of any statement, ethical or otherwise, from an analysis of its descriptive meaning.[11]

Aiken applies this last generalization even to scientific and rational truth: mere logical or empirical demonstration does not compel anyone to "accept" it and believe it. Their decision to do so comes from other psychological factors. The point is that we cannot by argument compel a person to adopt rationality itself as obligatory upon him.

476

The reason, I think, is clear: the relation between cognition and motivation, in any theory of motivation whatever, is a causal, not a logical relation. There could, therefore, always be a logical possibility that the cognition of good would not cause us to favor it.[12]

Sellars agrees that the mistake of Prichard, Ross and other "deontological intuitionists"

. . . almost inevitable in view of their rationalistic background, was to suppose that it is merely by grasping the conceptual logic of the "language of norms" that we become conscious of having obligations.[13]

All this implies that we have to do other things than merely argue or demonstrate evaluations in order to get people to *act* on them. Not that clarifying what is best or right is said to be entirely without any motivational influence; it is only said that the logical proof as such does not compel action; and that if it *does* influence action, it is by psychological, causal influence, not by rational. This means, I take it, that rational argument, taken together with other kinds of influence, will act by gestalt-closure forces within the brain-field. In the light of the latter concept, however, I find myself still wondering whether a rational demonstration that was really thorough, respecting the whole situation of him who is to be persuaded, would not, as Socrates argued, inevitably issue in his adopting the implied course of action. If anyone rejects "the enterprise of rationality," would it not be because the suggested program is not really encompassing all of the forces — including whatever neurotic blocks he is up against — that exist in his situation and therefore cannot really be called "rational" for *him?*

Be that as it may, we would still have the problem of finding enough inspiration, enough dynamic, to energize the "blocked" person to the often very arduous labors of analyzing and dissolving his block; or any other person to the difficulties of surpassing his present level of inclusive adequacy. For if "betterness," as SM never implied, and SMR never admitted, means more comprehensive and harmonious patterns of behavior, then it means more difficult ones, and these will require more energy and focus to start with. Now though our theory claims that there will be more satisfaction or good feeling within the more complex process in the end, it still has to admit that these difficulties — the longer period of struggle, the greater possibility of intervening frustrations, etc., — definitely calls for more energy and effort. This character of existence, then, is what faces us with the problem of incitation, that is, how to make the longer-term, but often immediately less attractive, motive to "greatness" prevail over the shorter-term, but often temptingly vivid one.

This is surely the most crucial point in our whole project of analyzing the inadequacies of SM and SMR and trying to show how DR can adequately rectify them — at any rate the most crucial for practical human affairs. For if reality and life are actually arranged so that a factor of inspiration to aspiration is integral to their proper functioning, then any theory, such as SMR, which issues in obliviousness of this fact will not only be untrue, but dreadfully dangerous, since it destroys the essential guard against painful and miserable disintegration. In a sense, our whole analysis has been heading for an adequate recognition of this problem, and has been incidentally constructing a solution for it, insofar as we have been succeeding in finding solid grounds for a unified scientific-religious belief that will provide inspiration. The last chapter of the book will round out this theme.

Now in providing for a dynamic that will raise men above their existing levels of interaction, DR would rely primarily on this synthesizing philosophical work itself; after that, it would draw upon the ways and means used throughout human history. Religious belief has, of course, always been intended to be a unifying system of beliefs that would help to reduce the amount of internal conflict and mutual cancellation of an individual's impulses, thus releasing and focussing his energies for "higher," that is, more integrated, value attainments. But the scientific-philosophical-religious scene to-day is so confused that neither one alone nor all together succeed in producing much unifying of energies for modern man. But we would claim that our framework in this book, disentangling static and dynamic confusions, could conceivably be a major help toward that "seeing the meaning of things" which, being based upon an underlying harmonizing of organic and mental energies, has always in the past led to more enthusiastic and energetically constructive behavior. Whether our own attempt to clarify a consistent structure of thought that places most current knowledge in meaningful relationship proves "inspiring" to anyone or not, the fact remains that DR points to the need of some such effort if men are to be raised above mediocre aspirations.

Short of a completely satisfying philosophical or religious system, there are, fortunately, other ways and means to incite efforts toward higher values. Some may find a theory of values or ethics by itself (not necessarily the implicate of a larger system of ideas) enough to inspire effort. If the essential problem is to win people away from that easy indulgence of partial urges so excused by SMR, to the more difficult but also more permanently satisfying wholeness implied by DM and DR, perhaps the mere understanding of this point itself could turn many toward the search for integration. However, we have to reckon with the enormous drawing power of the partial and destructive urges: we have to recognize, as the traditional views did so much more wisely than SMR, the factor of "temptation." For the pull of the nearer, easier, more immediately pleasurable urges is undoubtedly always stronger, before training and effort, than the desire for wholeness and integrity. This is, of course, exactly why we have the problem of incitation. All the recognition in the world that the larger interests will bring broader happiness does not in itself make us here and now desire them with the passion we have for the immediate thrill at hand, even when we remember, in the face of our partial selves' desire to forget, the hangovers and shame that will follow it. Thus, almost a century of literature which has concerned itself with nothing but the "low" and violent passions, and with the disintegration and misery it has been honest enough to inform us invariably follow them, has not made an iota of progress in inspiring anyone — writers or readers — toward higher modes of integrated behavior. Clearly, the mere naturalistic reporting of meaningless passions has not only not halted, but even contributed to larger and larger sectors of our society descending into the same fragmentation.

Actually, what DR indicates is that what we have seen throughout to be the implication of the dynamic idea of good is true: that involved in the process of resolution is not only an escaping from tension and pain, but an approaching to a desirable harmony. Therefore men need to know not only of the threatened debacle but of the vision. Creative effort is simultaneously "pushed" from behind by the pain and revulsion, and "pulled" from ahead by the attractive hope. SMR can never get beyond diagnosing the past or present disintegration, and this, in itself does not prompt growth. The modern mind must have grounds for taking quite seriously the dream of possible beauty and grandeur — though it must always be ready, too, for only partial attainment. Men will not move at all, however, without both propulsions. I am convinced that the literature of the twentieth century, insofar as it has confined itself to diagnosis of ugliness and decay, can never rank with the greatest art. A complete art must find out not only how to represent the ideal, to which SIR's was perhaps too confined, or the exact nature of the depths of reality with SMR; but it must be able to reveal how to transfer from one to the other, being quite as unsqueamish as SMR about the facts, but, still more realistically, showing us what can be done about them.

We have said, then, that the understanding of an ethical theory as such may add some constructive motivation to the mere understanding of the psychological facts of partialized indulgence. It might not be guaranteed to yield corresponding ethical behavior, though it might make some minds more hospitable to other means to that end.

> Not that the reading of treatises upon ethics . . . is necessary for moral living. Many a good man has never done [this]. But there can be little doubt that in a world no longer simple, a world in which situations frequently arise that are not easily classified under old and conventional categories, reflection upon . . . the nature of good and evil will be a necessary prerequisite for the wisest and the most nobly moral decisions. Hence it is not unreasonable to hope that a study of ethical principles will enable a man to become, not perhaps a more devoted, but a more efficient servant of righteousness and of his fellows than he would have been without it.[14]

Pratt goes on to discuss the psychology of habit building, with mention of William James' advice that it is good to exercise our spirits by making a little gratuitous effort from time to time. There is such a thing as moral athleticism that can be trained, just as our bodies can be, by making efforts, small at first, but growing gradually more strenuous. Thus the developing of "virtue-habit" is relevant to the topic of elevating motives.

There are many other psychological aids for raising aims: such old-fashioned ways as keeping the attention in likely areas, by reading books that do something other than inflame the most short-sighted passions; or seeking out people who might conceivably be character models rather than those possibly "exciting" but usually impotent "crazy, mixed-up kids" of our café society, etc., etc. Then there is no reason why DR cannot make use of Bentham's social sanctions. DR has rejected SMR's assumption that whatever society demands by way of individual inhibition as being generally conducive to welfare, is *ipso facto* namby-pamby or arbitrarily restrictive. If an individual either will not or cannot grasp the longer-term plan internally, society may be allowed, with qualifications, to try to motivate it externally by economic, political or penal sanctions, and social ostracism and ridicule.

DR may also avail itself of SIR's disciplinary rules and codes as a practical means of at least keeping people's motives from deteriorating. Although we know that specific rules derive their value ultimately from the appeal to consequences, they perform an exactly analogous function to the actuarial tables used by insurance companies to shorten calculations. They do not, however, provide answers in new and unique cases. For these, the actuary and the moralist both have to know the theory from which the tables or the rules came.

Social convention, or following customary rules, have another function besides saving time — more especially related to our problem of dynamic. For there is no doubt that no force is so strong for keeping an individual above the narrowest levels of behavior than shaming by his fellows. If society can be got to accept some "higher" ethic, then there can often be a rapid spreading of this improvement to individuals who might not have adopted it on their own. Courage, kindness, family loyalty, etc., are motives that might not be as wide-spread as they are but for their having become socially approved and disregarding them socially disdained. Of course, society can lag below certain moral pioneers; the great task is to get the group up to the level of the pioneers, so that the above kind of spreading of his insight to the rest can take place.

So our problem of incitation to higher motivations comes back to the individual and how he is to conceive and adopt higher aims, often in the face of preliminary social ridicule. At this point, the intuitionist school may claim that it can motivate higher aims

481

than any teleological theory. A mystical enthusiasm from the conscience will, they say, be surer to keep the martyr to his principle, or the saint to his sacrifice, than any figuring about the good results of his actions.

We might grant that what the saint may be most conscious of is some internal shaming by his conscience which will not let him settle for the easier life; or some commandment of scripture or church authority which he dares not break; or that his brotherhood will despise him if he softens. Psychologically this may be so. But nevertheless, his conscience, commandment or brotherhood are themselves to be justified by their conduciveness to good value-process; and he himself is surely not without some sense of the benefit to mankind that ought to be forthcoming from his obedience. Nor will his conscience, his commandment or his fellows be able to adjudicate new and unique cases without some fresh estimate of consequences.

When the individual grasps the larger view, we know that the very nature of his whole-seeking organism will not let him feel fully satisfied until he can enact a plan that incorporates what he has grasped. If this plan runs counter to other factors in the field — embroiling him in social opposition, perhaps — it must become a problem of comparative strength of forces. Is the individual's internal pull toward unity stronger or weaker than the opposing forces toward partialization? Will "internal-unity-with-social-mal-adjustment" make a "stronger field" than "internal-disunity-with-social-comfort"? Presumably the individual who envisages a finer life, though his fellows are disinclined to take the trouble it entails, and so would like to silence him — this individual will either work for his vision at the expense of trouble with his fellows, maybe even unto death; or he will avoid conflict but keep working guardedly for his vision at a slower rate; or he will completely relinquish all public and private work for his vision, to escape any social disapproval. All three courses of action will include their mead of certain satisfactions and certain pains. If the vision is genuinely "higher" than the accepted views of the society (and DR can tell in principle whether it is or not), we would feel the above three courses of action to be arranged in the order of decreasing "highness"; that the first and second are more "inspired" than the last.

We are saying, then, that a teleological value theory, hedonistic in the carefully guarded sense that we have discussed, is quite adequate for incitation; the strengths of the other theories can all be incorporated in this one as either psychological aids not in any basic contradiction to this theory; or as beliefs that root back in this theory ultimately anyway.

Why, after all, do we continue to be ashamed of a man who gives in to an urge, let us say, for some perverted sexual passion, even after SMR has told us that he cannot help it factually, and therefore that he should not even try to help it, and, in fact, is rather the more admirable if he flouts society and ostentatiously refuses to help it? Take one of that burgeoning new class in our cities: the brazenly heedless homosexual. If we feel ashamed of him, are we merely confessing our own prissy fear of our own passions? Are we merely resistant to the unusual, the different? A whole literature has been trying to convince us of this for a half century. But what about that sense of softness, of fibreless capitulation, of resistless flabbiness that so inveterately accompanies perversion that it would be curiously inconsistent of militantly factual SMR if it failed to note the fact?

No, we are not merely *shocked* by the strangeness, or repulsed by some unknown nastiness we obscurely suspect, as SMR would have it. We are truly *ashamed,* for we feel repelled by an unjustified immaturity, an unresisted fragmentation, a failure of integrity. What we really feel is that one part of this man is leading the rest of him around by the nose; that he has been content to be, in a degree, an automaton at the mercy of a single passion; that he has not had enough seriousness about his life to balance and complete it. His "sin" is not that he is in *advance* of philistine society in his "freedom" to express his urges; but that he is *behind* society in being less well-balanced than its norms are. He is arrested at an early stage of growth when the further riches of mature, parental life are not yet encompassed. We feel uneasily that he is not a unified soul in charge of himself, but a robot trailing behind a sex gland. This would explain what I have generally noticed: that sexual perverts by and large give an impression of soft emptiness, are found in the easier jobs, share a generally frivolous attitude toward life, know nothing of staunch conviction or firm principle not only on sex, but on any other issue. I grant that they range on a scale from the silliest light weights to great geniuses capable of much application. But however admirable the work of the genius, his irresponsibility about his sexual life neither improves the work nor is excused by it.

Comparison with SM-SIR: Although traditional thought learned much about how to inspire high and great character and action, it did not explicitly recognize such effort as the very essence of the meaning of existence. In traditional Christianity, inspiration to salvation-seeking arises only as a makeshift that God introduces afterward to repair an unlucky accident in His design. In the perfect world of His original creation there would have been no need for constant work to raise creatures above their existent level of functioning. DR however indicates that all value is on a basis of proportionality to effortful creativity. The creature's business of aspiring and finding energy for reaching new heights would have to be the very intention of any God interested in sublimity.

DM with DR:

Implications of DM: The dynamic idea of good clearly implies that life should be an adventure seeking inspiration to dare for greater aims. If good is proportional to the complexity of process, there is a clear implication to a problem of additional energy procurement. We would expect any God who desires such good to exist, to place his creatures under the necessity of seeking such energy through some kind of inspiration.

With this, we complete our review of the field of positive value. We are now in a position to understand what evil is in fact; and to deal with the toughest problem of all: why it should exist. The problem of human evil stems from "the inherited inertness of our nature"![15] for that is the root of our reluctance to give forth the effort that adequately inclusive organization of our lives requires. Sin and vice are essentially "one-sidedness"; they result from aims so narrow that pursuing them guarantees collision with and destruction of other processes that need to be included. Can the dynamic approach tell us why we should be exposed to such possibilities? Before we can finally reap the inspiration of a meaningful world-view, integrated through the idea of dynamic good, we must go to the center of the problem of evil, grappling with it less superficially than we have so far.

CHAPTER XVIII

THE PROBLEM OF EVIL

We are now ready to bring together all the aspects of the problem of evil, many of which we have unavoidably touched upon in various preceding chapters. Our study of what good is in this third part will make it possible for us to define evil more clearly, and to make a final assault on this toughest block to belief in meaningfulness with all the resources of the dynamic idea of good.

For each position we will summarize the aspects of the problem under three heads:

1. The status of fact and value in existence.
2. The nature of man in respect to good and evil.
3. The nature of the environment, natural and social.

SM with SIR.

Implications of SM: The expectations, the unconscious demands of our cynics, the disappointment of which causes their cynicism, are, it should now be quite clear, derived from the static idea of good. Only if good is assumed possible in a state of timeless being without process can it be demanded of any God there may be that He place perfect, uninterrupted, substantial goodness (or else perfect "activity") into the creation from the beginning. There is no implication, from within the concept of static good, that evil need exist in any sense whatever: as vagueness, discomfort, disorder, tension, want, dissatisfaction, pain. In Platonic terms, the real should be a state of finished Being, so replete with perfection as to require no improvement.

On the first of the three questions, the status of value in existence, SM implies that Good should be "rooted" in nature in the sense that it should suffuse the original state of things, be present as a prior deposit and then continue unchangingly throughout eternity. It should be present in the "natural," in instinct, in the primitive.

Secondly, as applied to human beings, static good implies that they should be perfect in their origins — both racially and individually: primitive men in general, and children in particular should be naturally good. There is no intrinsic reason why men should have any weaknesses, or why they should need transformation or growth. Genesis follows these implications in considering Adam and Eve, at creation, to have been entirely innocent of any perverse impulses. Plato also envisages the possibility of human perfection in his omnicompetent philosopher-kings and guardian caste.

Thirdly, as applied to environmental and social realities, SM implies that nature should be entirely beneficent and idyllic; and that Utopia should be the normal state of society. Frustration and tragedy caused by arbitrary external forces, natural or social, has no possible rationale on the basis of static good.

Adjustments of SIR: Here we come upon all the traditional ways of trying to explain the stubborn differences between the world as observed, which seems so full of evil; and meaningfulness as conceived in terms of the static idea of good. First, what will evil be for SIR? In general it will be defined as a departure from the essence or form of good, frequently but not necessarily accompanied by pain. Human evil tends to be seen as a purely gratuitous perversity defying God's perfect plan; natural evil as a falling away from the divine routine. The latter may be explained in terms of rebellion by quasi-personal agents, such as angels, imps, devils, etc.; or may be traced back to the former as having been initiated somehow by man's Fall. Also evil, once initiated, will be directed by God to the punishment of human sins. The essential nature of evil, then, is the flouting of the fixed standards or essences of SM. Evil is evil because of the denial of the essences, not because of the pain and unhappiness that may result. The latter are only punishments of the former.

How, then, does SIR explain this contradiction of the divine essences, which is so entirely unnecessary in SM's logic?

First, we remember that all older views believe implicitly that the kind of creation called for by SM had actually once taken place. Premodern views invariably believed in primeval golden ages, perfect gardens of Eden. God's own work had indeed been perfect in the sense of the fullness and completion of this distinct

486

state or substance called goodness. So the problem becomes to explain what happened after that to bring in the evil.

It is significant to notice here at the outset that this static idea fails to give us a real sense of meaningfulness or holiness quite regardless of any contradiction between it and later science. This picture of a world of pure bliss in itself lacks the seriousness and momentousness that are definite parts of holy meaning. We will see, now, that whichever way men turned in the effort to save belief in a good God in the static sense, they lost some one or other of the requisites of meaningfulness: cosmic, purpose or good (see Chapter IV).

The traditional Christian view explained evil by blaming it on man. God had created the perfect world, and man in his own image. A difficulty immediately arises: how could this perfect creature do evil? The answer was that it was necessary to give man free will (so as to make his obedience to God other than merely automatic), whereupon man disobeyed God and brought evil (both human sin and natural evil) into the perfect world. God then agreed out of his grace to enter into a struggle to save man from his own wrong-doing, and the Salvation drama was begun.

It is only now, incidentally, that the fullness of purpose and holiness appear. We now have that serious "urgency" which Otto, for one, finds integral in holy feeling and which was lacking in the world of passive contemplation of perfection. And yet, it seems that for Christianity, this latter world has only appeared accidentally on account of something man inadvertently did. God did not mean it this way, but would have preferred everything permanently good from the beginning and forever.

But now, granted that free will was necessary to man's perfection, a difficulty arises concerning the source of man's inclination to use it wrongly. God is still not safely absolved of the responsibility for having created man so that he actually did choose evil. Joad analyzes several difficulties here:

(1) If God is omniscient he knew man would misuse freewill and bring evil into the world. The universe before the creation of man was wholly good. God therefore wittingly connived at introducing evil by man's agency into a painless and evilless world. (2) If God is omnipotent and omniscient, everything must happen by His plan anyway, and man cannot really be free as this view requires. (3) How can we conceive of man choosing

evil if he is not already a partially evil being? When you trace this back through heredity you arrive at last at God's creation again. (4) In any case, this alleged necessity of free-will to do evil holds only for the world as it is.

A universe could be imagined which did not carry with it this disability. Such a universe would surely be superior to our own in which pain and evil are freedom's necessary concomitants. To God, we are told, all things are possible.[1]

Thus the Christian explanation is really unintelligible. Perhaps even deeper than any of the above objections is the thought that the reason for the necessity of free will would supposedly be that man needs to be partly responsible for achieving his goodness. But we have seen that there is no implication from the static idea of good that there should be any achievement of it. Besides, Christianity usually insisted that all credit for achievement of good should go to God anyway. Christianity, then, managed to preserve the deepest possible sense of the holy importance of things in its idea of Salvation, but without a secure logical foundation.

At this point SIR resorts to either of its two familiar outs: first, dualism, the appeal to a second independent principle in the universe in addition to the good God, such as matter or the devil. The evil in man, like that in all of nature, might come from his material aspect, into which God is trying to introduce goodness. It is obvious which of our elements of meaningfulness fall now. The *cosmic* dimension is lost, with God entangled in a world of matter he did not intend; also the goodness and meaningfulness of concrete things, individuals and bodies is given up. This explanation may preserve a realm of meaning in a mystic somewhere, but loses the integrality of this world. Christianity usually refuses this way out, maintaining the Biblical belief in the goodness of real things. Still, this strand of thought has got into the modern mind anyway, producing the distaste for material bodies.

Secondly there is Illusionism once more, the distinction between appearance and reality, banishing evil into the realm of illusion. But this weakens the element of *goodness* in God, who might seem to be playing tricks; and it again robs the immediate realm of things of importance and reality. The idealisms would all fail in solving our task in these ways.

None of these variations of the Christian explanation, however, has entered into modern expectations as much as a fourth, to which their unsatisfactoriness drove thought; the return to pure SM in spite of all evidence — to the Pelagian and Rousseauan belief that man and nature are, after all, basically good and perfect already, with only temporary accidents hiding the fact. This is what almost all of our writers were taught to expect of the world, and it is in the light of this demand that they remain so unimpressed by what they find. Rejecting Christianity's illogical idea that God's perfect creation, Nature, and his perfect creature, man, could have "fallen," a search begins for the self-identical good stuff which must exist at the core of things, however overlaid by seeming corruption.

Concerning the first of our three sub-topics, the status of evil in existence, pre-evolutionary romantics imagined that goods, which must really inhere in development (DM says), were *original* realities. They began to delve into nature expecting to find pure goodness at the bottom, fixed and dependable. They turned to nature, expecting to find embedded in it fixed standards to take the place of those which had become doubtful in the wranglings of scholastic opinion.

> . . . "reality" is what existence would be if our reasonably justified preferences were so completely established in nature as to exhaust and define its entire being and thereby render search and struggle unnecessary.[2]

This trend of thought is illustrated, under the second head, the nature of man, by Rousseau's conception of man. While Christianity knew in practice that man had not been automatically good to begin with, but that a great struggle to become better had transformed an originally barbaric creature, Rousseau now taught men to expect man to be somehow naturally good. The Renaissance and Age of Reason had found themselves with many good people and many fine cultural products, thanks to the ages of Christian inspiration and training. Men found themselves in the midst of these fruits, forgot the roots which had caused the flowering, and assumed that the fruits were total and original realities in themselves. Christianity's idea of good and evil was inverted. Instead of an imperfect creature needing to be curbed and formed into a good one, they thought they saw an automatically good one being perverted by restraints. What need is there to restrict a creature which will naturally unfold in goodness if left completely free? Randall's comments on Rousseau perfectly illustrate the idea:

> The whole aim of education should be . . . to preserve the natural man, and ensure that the habits he forms are not the artificial ones of custom and tradition and reason, but rather those in which his nature will flower of itself. Rousseau's elaborate scheme of education, recounted in the *Emile*, is to preserve the child from any formal teaching by other human beings. It is primarily negative, consisting "not in teaching the principles of virtue or truth, but in guarding the heart against vice and the mind against error." If this endeavor is successful, the real education of the child will come from the free development of his own nature, his own powers, his own natural inclinations. . . .[3]

Here is the most explicit repudiation of aspiration and effort in favor of a reliance upon automatic nature, which is thought to be impregnated with good already. Rousseau gives no more explanation of the origin of the evil customs that pervert naturally good man than to blame the human effort for advancement through competition itself. He would prefer men to return to the passive, effortless life of the savage.

Primitive nature, then must be explored to find truth and standards of value. If man is naturally good, then his natural instincts must be dissected and studied as standards. The "natural" is the original and primitive, what existed before any human effort interfered. The myth of a primitive golden age was unquestioningly adhered to.

Under the third head, the goodness of the natural and social environment, we have the well known story of utopianism, expecting this perfect condition to return. The only evidence of God's existence would have to be evidence that He is succeeding in removing the unnecessary and meaningless evil. It is left unclear how things got away from God, but as long as He is going to show His power by restoring the pristine state of perfection, men can be quite enthusiastic over their lot. Men dream of this paradise, and their hearts are filled with praise for the idyllic world that originally was and soon will be again. The present human state of problems, trouble and struggle is a meaningless accident, to be forgotten as soon as it is superseded. Whether it will have meaning or not will be determined by whether the future brings perfect success or not.

Herbert Spencer heralds the inevitable end of trouble:

Progress is not an accident but a necessity. What we call evil and immorality must disappear. It is certain that man must become perfect. . . . The ultimate development of the ideal man is certain — as certain as any conclusion in which we place the most implicit faith; for instance, that all men will die. . . . Always toward perfection is the mighty movement — toward a complete development and a more unmixed good.[4]

There could not be a clearer expression of the static idea of good, nor a more glaring failure to answer the lurking question why, if perfection is so inevitable, either a divine creator or a world machine should cause a preceding period in which goodness is absent. The period of struggle is left without metaphysical significance.

SM with SMR.

Findings of SMR: "Realism." Following Rousseau's lead, that we must expect to find standards of value only in the most primitive origins, SMR proceeds with evolutionary tools to analyze origins and causes more thoroughly than they had ever been before. It thus discovered the real nature of the beginnings. But we now understand why SMR can only conceive these beginning states as SM had conceived the end-states: as self-identical and non-implicated with succeeding process. The process that grows out of these beginnings and leads to other conditions is no more relevant to their being than it was to that of the endings in SM. But SMR had assumed, with SIR, when it started research, that the beginnings would reveal the essential nature of things, which later development only obscures.

And now the beginning phases were discovered to be "evil"! That is, they were certainly not in accord with SM's criteria of good. The second factor of Darwinism, the struggle for existence, carried with it a picture of bloody, ruthless Nature, in complete contradiction to the static expectation of what a God of Love would make. Freudian psychology found the famous polymorphous-pervert child completely other than Rousseau's Emile. Marx presented the selfish economic man in complete contrast to what the Utopians looked for.

Now, connecting this picture with SMR's doctrine that no process ever really changes anything, no developed whole ever contains anything different from its parts in their original disorder, we reach the conclusion that Good does not factually exist at the beginning, and cannot come into existence afterward. The reductive fallacy now appears in its final viciousness: no achieved good is ever real; it can always be reduced back to the evil which it had seemed to overcome. More accurately, SMR, since it cannot evaluate at all, as explained in previous chapters, can actually neither call the prior state "evil" nor the latter state "good." It can only insist that the latter state is not essentially different from the former state, whatever that be. This is what our prevalent literature unendingly declares to us, as it tirelessly peels off "veneers" of goodness to reveal the wretched human realities beneath.

Contradiction to SM: We are now ready to understand the fatally debilitating conclusion that results from combining SM with SMR: the source of western culture's ill-health to-day. Our corrupt literature and our lack of aspiration, characterized at the beginning of this book, are based on the present issue of our whole analysis from Chapter III onwards. It can be summarized thus:

1. According to the static idea of good, if good is to exist at all, it must exist by original deposition in the nature of things, in primitive instinct, almost as a "stuff" whose reality can be shown only by dissecting it out of those original states.

2. SMR finds the origins fundamentally "evil," or at least not in conformity to SM-SIR's standards.

3. SMR makes any developmental or evolutionary improvement from those origins unreal.

4. Therefore good, in SM's sense, cannot exist, since it does not exist at the beginning, and cannot come into being at the end.

5. The last and worst doctrine results when Rousseau's (SIR's) *normative* doctrine, that we "ought" to return to our (supposedly good) origins or essence is combined with SMR's belief that the origin is actually crude and cruel. This results in the ethical dictum: "You ought to return to your (evil) origins." This is the

source of current literature's search for disintegration, perversity and degradation as both *fated, and a moral duty;* and it is the essence of the Nazi philosophy of cultivating the human brute. Let us now take our three expectations in order, to illustrate these conclusions a little more in depth. First, the search for fixed standards of good rooted in Nature turned up the opposite. The earliest and most primitive origins of things were *less* good than any later stages. Human values faded away and resolved themselves into crude, undignified origins. Joseph Krutch, for example, is amusingly dismayed at finding that modern romantic love is a recent invention of man:

. . . such tacit evaluations as that set upon love are accepted as matters of fact, almost as something established by the scheme of nature. . . . (But) the savage — the American Indian, for example — knows comparatively little of what we call romance.[5]

Love is, then, not a fact in nature of which we become aware, but rather a creation of the human imagination. . . .[6]

Standards are imaginary things, and yet it is extremely doubtful if man can live well, either spiritually or physically, without the belief that they are somehow real.[7]

So accustomed is he to thinking that values can be real only by being fixed routines established in nature, that for them to turn out to be intentions and conclusions in human experience is to make them imaginary and unreal. Value, then, is unfounded in Nature, has no solid being within the universe.

Secondly, the imperfection of man was discovered, and the primary pillar of Rousseauan optimism was shaken. The results of SMR's discontinuance of religious aspiration began to come in, too, and the feebleness of the secular substitutes in regenerating character became visible. Biology found the battle for survival of the fit; psychology found a basic narcissistic egoism that reduced all altruism to a thin veneer; social science found a selfish aggrandizement as man's sole motivation. Men's higher ideals and levels of moral behavior were shown to be illusory by pointing out the economic and selfish motives that either at present underlie them or formerly did so. Present cultural attainments did not reveal the essence of man; only his behavior at the primitive level of superstition and tribal ruthlessness told the truth about him. Saintly character was meaningless in the face of the fact that at the level of nature the law of tooth and claw operates. Thus man was not naturally good as the Utopian view expected; but neither was he a sinner by his own free will, as the orthodox view decreed. He was a sinner, a neurotic, in more than an accidental or temporary sense, as against the liberal, humanist view; and was forced to be so by determined causes in his parts and origins, as against the orthodox view.

Now the static way of thinking issues in its usual ominous conclusion: instead of interpreting this primitive bloodiness and selfishness, this neurosis and abnormality in the best of us, as an indication of work to be done, it takes it as an indication of the essential and final nature of man. Having expected nature to supply the goodness to start with, and having discontinued the striving in which alone good can inhere, this view feels betrayed by nature when man thereupon relapses. It proceeds to mock at those engaged in the process of regeneration, when it discovers that those who are not so engaged become monsters of evil. Human nature cannot be changed, it concludes. Finally, still believing that standards are only to be found in origins, and finding origins to be evil and selfish, they conclude that nature calls upon them to be evil and selfish — to follow instinct in all of its brutishness and disregard for the rights of others. Morality and culture are dismissed as weakness, as unnatural. In the absence of cultivation of virtue, the brutishness increases and conditions worsen, which only proves all the more that the universe is evil and meaningless.

Utopianism's and humanism's glorification of man and worship of his beauty now changes to a perverse interest in mocking and degrading him. The uglier and more worn of human beings are selected as most representative of the nature of things. There is a fascination with the dirt and waste products of the body, and the nastiness associated with them is imputed to the whole creature. Literature hypostatizes the ugliest parts of life in its realism. Humanism's ungrounded affirmation of man's worth seems a mockery in the face of the misfortunes he causes in the godless world. The spectacle of men turned into beasts by their panic and discontent kills all inclination to admire them. How individual men become worth nothing while the mythical state is erected in the place of the ultimate is a topic I need only suggest. Men are misguided enough to take one of themselves as absolute leader, hoping illogically that he will save them. But of course the leader's own cynical thinking leads him to massacre his followers if he finds therein some trivial advantage. The luminous and reverent feeling for each creature as the beloved child of the cosmic father is quite lost. The butchery of human souls is of no consequence.

And so finally, it appears that the third expectation of the Utopians, Utopia itself, the actual basis of their idea of Meaningfulness, is not going to arrive. They themselves may be among the sacrificed, thus cheated out of the meaning. Men awake to the stubborn presence of all kinds of evil, natural and social, from which they had hitherto averted their eyes. Joad makes an interesting confession:

> I am claiming no credit for this conclusion. On the contrary it is ground for humiliation to have come to it so late. There has always been evil in the world, and it is only poverty of imagination which refuses to accept its significance until it struts prominent and repulsive upon the stage of one's times.[8]

Whereas the traditional religion somehow could make just these events of catastrophe and tragedy the source of their deepest and most poignant experience and belief, our culture, on the basis of the Utopian expectation, finds them both the most direct reason for not believing in God, and the most futile of problems when He is not believed in. There is nothing to do about it but to hope that one can avoid bad luck, and to avert one's notice from those who are caught. Of course, the utopians never did have anything to say for those who lived, suffered and died in all pre-Utopian times. Krutch in his chapter called "The Tragic Fallacy" shows how unable our culture is to cope with tragedy.

> When its heroes (sad misnomer for the pitiful creatures who people contemporary fiction) are struck down is not, like Oedipus, by the Gods that they are struck but only, like Oswald Alving, by syphilis. . . . Their so-called tragedies do not end and cannot end with one of those splendid calamities which in Shakespeare seem to reverberate through the universe, because they cannot believe that the universe trembles when their love is, like Romeo's cut off . . . despair becomes intolerable because it is no longer even significant or important.[9]

495

And so trouble and tragedy were discovered in reality which are not illusory (Idealism), accidental (Utopianism), nor man's fault (Orthodoxy). The obvious conclusion: it is not good, but evil which is given, implanted in nature. And thus static, substantial ideas ended by producing a complete contradiction between the two sides of our basic question: (a) the description of the world and (b) the idea of meaningfulness. So utopianism sinks helplessly into a cynical atheism, and men discern in life and nature only a dreary profaneness.

We need a word of clarification here about the relationship between the problems of mechanism and evil in contradicting meaningfulness. Evil in itself seemed enough to the Utopians to contradict cosmic purpose. The religions of the ages, however, have always known of its existence, yet believed in God. For the existence of a God or gods had always been the primary, necessary postulate to explain why anything existed and moved at all. We have to take the existence of evil in connection with the notion of mechanism to explain why it clinches the disproof of God's existence. For mechanism seemed to provide an alternative explanation of why and how things move and function. To the mechanist it was no longer necessary to endure searchings of heart and mind to learn what God might be trying to teach by His chastisement. Evil is only to be expected in a blind, mechanical universe.

SM with DR.

Findings of DR: We said at the beginning of Part IV that the problem of mechanism has been relieved, not to say solved, by DR's science itself as it refined its own concepts; and that it remained to see what DM and DR between them could do about the problem of evil.

First, then, we have two relatively easy parts of the problem, which SM and SMR between them had made inexplicable: why any evil at all exists; and why, existing, it must be assuaged. Then we will come to the more difficult problems: supposing it is conceded that *some* evil must exist and can be assuaged, why, then, must there be *so much* evil, even unto death, which apparently can not be assuaged?

Considering SM with DR, then, we understand that the conflict between the theory of the facts, and the implications of the theory of value has been softened in regard to the problem of mechanism and purposiveness, although we have found that DR does not correspond quite perfectly with the implications of SM even there. Now, on the problem of evil, we find that the conflict remains as obdurate as ever. For the organismic view of reality is no less "realistic" about the existence of evil than SMR — in fact it can recognize evil more genuinely and sincerely than SMR could. For SMR can find no difference between a patterned unity and a jumble, since the arrangement of things does not count for it. No arrangement of atoms can be any better or worse than any other arrangement, though some arrangements might involve more pain and destruction (whatever these might be) than others. (Of course, though natural processes might seem confused from the point of view of human desire, they still were supposed to be following the laws of motion in an orderly enough manner.)

DR, however, can explain what evil is; it can take account of strains in the field, to make such distinctions as that between equilibrium and disequilibrium. It can speak of degrees of order. It can also accept the possibility of feelings of pain in the disorganized energy fields. Also, for DR, any order that exists is sure to be one that has *developed* from conditions that were less ordered. DR further doubts that any such thing as a permanent, undeviating routine of orderly functioning exists anywhere in nature. And any order that has developed will not be a "perfect" order in any sense; even supposing a perfect order ever were attained, it would be guaranteed to be disrupted almost immediately by new factors or energies impinging upon it.

Evil, for DR, then, must be defined as dynamically as good. It will, of course, be the painful *feeling* that accompanies processes of disintegration; and "things," "people," "means," "motives," etc., will be evil derivatively in the same sense that we have understood their goodness — in terms of their conducing to disintegrative processes toward destructive consequences. The measures or criteria of evil will be the same one we used for good, except, of course, that the "lower" figures will measure evil. Or in terms of our final measure of "advance" evil would be revealed in a negative figure (indicating "retrogression") which would show that the degree of inclusiveness, harmony, etc., in a later phase of process was less than that in an earlier phase.

DR, then, recognizes the reality of evil, and objects even more genuinely than SMR to the idealistic pretense that evil and disorder are not real. They are just as real as order and satisfaction. Dewey, for instance, insists that the precarious and the stable are equally real in experience:

> As against [the] common identification of reality with what is sure, regular and finished, experience in unsophisticated forms gives evidence of a different world and points to a different metaphysics. We live in a world which is an impressive and irresistible mixture of sufficiencies, tight completenesses, order, recurrences which make possible prediction and controls, and singularities, ambiguities, uncertain possibilities and processes going on to consequences as yet indeterminate. They are mixed not mechanically but vitally like the wheat and tares of the parable. We may recognize them separately but we cannot divide them, for unlike wheat and tares they grow from the same root. Qualities have defects as necessary conditions of their excellencies; the instrumentalities of truth are the causes of error; change gives meaning to permanence and recurrence makes novelty possible. A world that was wholly risky would be a world in which adventure is impossible, and only a living world can include death.[10]

The latter part of this quotation passes into statements of requiredness belonging more properly under DM below.

Whitehead expresses the same preliminary observation. Disorder, evil, error are inexpugnable parts of experience.

> In some sense or other, things go wrong. . . . It is a temptation for philosophers that they should weave a fairy-tale of the adjustment of factors; and then as an appendix introduce the notion of frustration, as a secondary aspect. I suggest to you that this is the criticism to be made of the monistic idealisms of the nineteenth century, and even of the great Spinoza. It is quite incredible that the Absolute, as conceived in monistic philosophy, should evolve confusion about its own details.
> There is no reason to hold that confusion is less fundamental than is order.[11]

Disorder and evil then, are presented to us by the realistic, naturalistic view of the world. We are barred from pretending that they are unreal. However, DR in contrast to SMR of course grasps

498

that there is a real process which, sometimes anyway, can have a real success in resolving this disorder, and can really create an order which can have associated good feelings. DR never finds values to be "rooted in nature" in the sense of being pre-established or already deposited. They are found only within resolving processes. Nor is man found to be perfect to start with in any sense. Every aspect of him, from bodily structure through mental development to goodness can only be the product of experimental process. This would apply similarly for all social arrangements.

DR in respect to the problem of evil presents two main findings:

(1) The reality of evil and disorder.

(2) The reality of processes that can sometimes really resolve evil and disorder and produce value.

Comparison of SM and DR: Does DR's world of creative process help us with the problem of evil? We now have a growing, alive world in which man is more or less at home, for it cooperates with him as he works to achieve some of his desires. The difficulty caused by the older mechanism in asking us to imagine a nature of dead particles where purpose was unthinkable is greatly eased. It does enable us to see that good is supported and produced on occasion by the process; evils are transmuted sometimes. It may possibly support the hope of progress in good. Does this give meaningfulness?

In answering, I will begin by quoting objections from two who are or have been well-known unbelievers. Bertrand Russell, in his *Religion and Science,* perfectly expresses the difficulties traditional thought would have with both parts of the view of the world mentioned in the preceding section:

Religion in our day has accommodated itself to the doctrine evolution, and has even derived new arguments from it. We are told that "through the ages one increasing purpose runs," and that evolution is the unfolding of an idea which has been in the mind of God throughout. . . . Why the Creator should have preferred to reach His goal by a process, instead of going straight to it, these modern theologians do not tell us. Nor do they say much to allay our doubts as to the gloriousness of the consummation. It is difficult not to feel, as the boy did after being taught the alphabet, that it was not worth going through so much to get so little.[12]

499

That is the difficulty with process as such. In addition, although the evolutionists assumed a progressive evolution ever upwards,

> . . . to the more reflective, another side was apparent. The same laws which produce growth also produce decay. . . . There is no law of cosmic progress, but only an oscillation upward and downward, with a slow trend downward on the balance owing to the diffusion of energy.[13]

This is his basic difficulty: the presence of evil and the presence of process at all, even supposing there were a perfect ending. Both of these he finds incompatible with the idea of religion, of cosmic purpose. And he is quite right that we have not been told by SM either why good should have to be achieved, or why evil should exist out of which to achieve it. Even if there were a glorious progress and everyone was thrilled with happy anticipation of assured success, it would remain unintelligible, on the traditional idea of good purpose, why a cosmic God should have had to postpone the attainment of it in this way. Joad also sees this unintelligibility:

> What, I wondered, could be the motive for creating a temporarily inadequate being, even if he *were* capable of ultimate perfection? . . . The process which was started by the creation of the world and continued by that of man will, therefore, on this assumption end in the achievement of universal perfection. But was not this the condition at the beginning, when there was only a single, all-embracing, perfect God? Assuredly it was. What, then, it may be asked, can be the point of a process which, entailing pain, evil and error by the way and assuming that all goes as well as it can go (which, after all, since there is free will, it may very well not do), has for its end a condition which is identical with its beginning?[14]

Russell ask the question in another way:

> If God really thinks well of the human race — an unplausible hypothesis, as it seems to me — why not proceed as in Genesis, to create man at once? What was the point of the ichthyosaurs, dinosaurs . . . etc. . . . ? The evil which is due

to sin may be explained as the result of our free will, but the problem of evil in the pre-human world remains. . . . An omnipotent Being who created a world containing evil not due to sin must Himself be at least partially evil.[15]

Russell and Joad obviously presuppose the static idea of value, and the assumption that there is a meaning for Good in a state of changeless perfection. Other thinkers such as the pragmatists and personalists, have advanced to being able to accept with real enthusiasm the fact that reality, instead of containing given goods, calls upon us to create them. They are at the stage of gladly welcoming their release from the blank pessimism of pure mechanism; of discovering that the evils in the original states are not total realities in themselves; of accepting the truth that reality is growing, has potentiality, so that good may be created by those who wish to do so.

But they cannot yet feel that this picture might be the intention of a cosmic God.

Dewey labors to eradicate the old Greek habit of hypostatizing the desirable and pretending that it already exists, and asks us frankly to accept the fact that it is not likely to exist until we choose and make it exist. This new thought which the new science supports is exhilarating and inspiring of itself, all questions of cosmic meaning aside.

It is admitted that the objects of religion are ideal in contrast with our present state. What would be lost if it were also admitted that they have authoritative claim upon conduct just because they are ideal? The assumption that these objects of religion exist already in some realm of Being seems to add nothing to their force, while it weakens their claim over us as ideals, in so far as it bases that claim upon matters that are intellectually dubious. . . .[16]

Thus we are relieved of the futile task of trying to explain away evil by trying to find good already somehow existing behind it. We are saved from despair in discovering any present evil, and fills us with the healthy intention and confidence that there is something that can be done about it. Life takes on a certain seriousness when we find ourselves responsible for the appearance of good.

501

The world, then, is found to be a growing process in which goods may be attained by effort. Does Dewey see it as *meaningful,* i.e., as the creation or embodiment of cosmic purpose for good? No he does not make that kind of statement but rests with God as only a selective part of reality that operates to unify ideal ends with given conditions.

That a tendency to slip back into the static idea of good is involved in his failing to consider the possibility of the origin of reality in cosmic value is suggested by his assuming that the idea of a good Creator can only mean that He deposits good in reality not as ideals but as "antecedent existences." But we could mean that the process of achievement is itself the divine good intention; that the cosmic purpose is that ideals are first to be non-existent, then to be achieved, *both ends of which process are equally intrinsic to dynamic good.* That he is sometimes thinking (at least in *A Common Faith*) of good as a state at the end of the process, not containing process-out-of-evil as its very being, is suggested by the phraseology. Goods "exist concretely," they are "there," "good as an end to be striven for."

There are values, goods, actually realized upon a natural basis. . . . The idealizing imagination seizes upon the most precious things found in the climacteric moments of experience and projects them. We need no external criterion and guarantee for their goodness. They are had, they exist as goods, and out of them we form our ideal ends.[17]

Thus, although Dewey may not be simply convicted of using the static idea of good predominantly, nevertheless he has not entertained the possibility here suggested, and his God becomes only a limited factor within process, not the intentional creator of it.

In summary, those who understand both the nature of dynamic reality and the implications of the static idea of good grasp that together they provide no logical basis for belief in cosmic purpose. Some, such as Dewey, James, the Personalists, etc., will work out theories of a "limited God," who finds evil on his hands because He is forced to contend with some foreign element which He himself did not create or intend. This, obviously, is our old friend, the dualistic escape. As Plato states it:

502

Then God, if he be good, is not the author of all things, as the many assert, but he is the cause of a few things only, and not of most things that occur to me. For few are the goods of human life, and many are the evils, and the good is to be attributed to God alone; of the evils the causes are to be sought elsewhere and not in him.[18]

In the Timaeus, God works on a realm of Non-being or Matter already present, and only this realm makes God enter upon unfortunately necessary creative activity in the effort to shape it more closely to the fixed essences. God himself would have been better satisfied in contemplating changeless perfection than to have created anything at all, let alone evil.

The illusionists are also still with us, trying to believe that evil is only an appearance. Christian Science is a prominent example, making evil only a matter of erroneous thinking, able to be overcome by thinking one's way back to reality where no evil exists.

But both these escapes have the usual weaknesses of idealism. They rob the visible, palpable world of reality and significance, and thus fail in our central task of giving meaningfulness to concrete life; and they defy empirical method, making it impossible to solve the science-religion problem in its own terms. The dualist and illusionist escapes actually beg the question, offering as solutions mere words and labels, merely announcing facilely that the problem does not exist.

DM with DR.

Implications of DM: It was clear when we introduced the dynamic idea of good (Chapter III) that, in order to exist, it required disorder, at least, felt as dissatisfaction, at the beginning of processes. Dynamic good requires an "imperfect" world in order to be. To what extent does this already "solve" the problem of evil? We are of course still left asking, does there have to be quite as much evil and pain as there is? Could not good be felt and enjoyed with only a reasonable amount of pain? But before we get to these more difficult degrees of the problem, let us dispose of the easier parts of the problem.

First, let us discuss a little further the "deduction" of disorder from the dynamic idea of value. We find these naturalistic philosophers brushing past the insight but being prevented from

503

using it by their empiricism. They make a kind of statement about which it is difficult to decide whether it is empirical or implicatory in status. Dewey and Whitehead, for instance, seem sometimes to say that order and disorder, good and bad, not only do exist together in this world as a matter of observation; but that we can understand that they *have* to exist together in order for life and satisfaction to be at all, in this or any other world.

> The union of the hazardous and the stable, of the incomplete and the recurrent, is the condition of all experienced satisfaction as truly as for our predicaments and problems. While it is the source of ignorance, error and failure of expectation, it is the source of the delight which fulfillments bring. For if there were nothing in the way, if there were no deviations and resistances, fulfillment would be at once, and in so being would fulfill nothing, but merely be. . . . A purely stable world permits of no illusions, but neither is it clothed with ideals. It just exists. To be good is to be better than; and there can be no better except where there is shock and discord combined with enough assured order to make attainment of harmony possible. . . .[19]

And Whitehead has made such statements as these:

> The essence of life is to be found in the frustrations of established order. The Universe refuses the deadening influence of complete conformity. . . .
> Order is never complete, frustration is never complete. There is transition within the dominant order; and there is transition to new forms of dominant order. Such transition is a frustration of the prevalent dominance. And yet it is the realization of that vibrant novelty which elicits the excitement of life.[20]

True, he does not say that *good* requires frustration so that there can be process. But he has said that excitement requires it.

And to give Fichte, Hegel and their disciples their due, they often explained that the Absolute set up opposition to itself, the world of recalcitrant nature, just because in no other way could experience of various kinds of good exist. In the *Religionsphilosophie*, Hegel, speaking of holiness, shows that in its innermost essence it requires a battle against temptation. The spirit differ-

504

entiates itself into many opposites in order that there may be serious and heroic struggle. However, I do not find him stating that good consists in precisely the transition out of difficulty itself. He still speaks of good as a quality or agent that fights against the evil enemy, just because it turned up to be fought. When the fight is over, the good man will continue to be what he was before. He has only expressed a goodness that was there all the time.

So Dewey and Whitehead, although they say the experience of satisfaction includes as part and parcel of it the experience of preceding dissatisfaction have not gone on to use this insight as an answer to why process exists and frustration, disorder and evil are necessary. Dewey still thinks of evil as having exactly the same status as good — as merely an alternative outcome of the process. He says "to be good is to be better than," but must be thinking of states of being. He should say "to be good is to be becoming better than."

The idea of frustration, however, can be derived directly from the dynamic idea of value itself. We can see that good can consist only in the living movement from worse to better.

A common objection to this claim is made by those thinkers who insist that once an evil has eventuated, it is what it is and cannot be unmade. Ely, for instance, objects to Whitehead's conception that God can envisage new possibilities that might take present evils up into an experience of contrast that would be valuable.

Of course the evil is not really transcended in the world, for what is done is done, and God cannot unmake the past. . . . Would even a full knowledge of how God disposes of my case and the world's case in his mind make my suffering and the world's suffering any less real? It might be argued that even a partial knowledge of the way my evil can contribute to a greater good will at least stimulate me to work toward that good. Yet the very fact that I had to suffer still remains evil to me.[21]

But he has forgotten all Whitehead's good work and is turning concrete processes back into mental states again; thinking of the experience of good as a mere mental contemplation that sets up one static vision of a good complement in contrast to a static evil state; insisting that "what is done is done" and forgetting how present occasions or feelings are *constituted* of past ones. The evil is not just transcended, but it is *involved* in the present good. What is done is not now non-existent but is integral in the present experience of releasing, of escaping. The fact that I had to suffer is not an isolated former state, but enters the present as part of the only kind of existence good can have. Hartshorne makes a clear statement:

> The later event prehends the earlier and so contains it, but the converse is not true; and this one-way relationship remains even when both earlier and later events are in the past. . . . Obviously, it is not because of fading or perishing that earlier is contained in later, though later is not contained in earlier. It is rather *in spite of perishing.* . . . It is reality of the new *as added to that of the old,* rather than the unreality of the old, that constitutes process . . . the fulfillment or disappointment, felt as such, of a purpose or hope includes the memory of the purpose or hope, plus details not foreseen in the anticipatory state . . . as to how things actually "came out."[22]

Dynamic good, then, requires a process out of evil in which to be concretized. Thus to reverse the relationship of the ideas of value and process would take us from a preoccupation with blind busy work inside the process to a contemplation of it from the outside, where we might see its meaning. A two-way direction of thought obtains between the two ideas. Empirically, process is the reason for good in the sense of efficient cause: process produces good existentially. Rationally, we can understand that good is the reason for process in the sense of purpose or final cause: it "requires" process. Observation meets understanding and gives an explanation how. Understanding meets observation and gives a reason why.

Correspondence between DM and DR: Let us now inquire more closely into the implications of this view and the ways in which it can explain the three dilemmas of SM and SMR.

1. Why values are not "rooted in nature." Good, then, cannot be looked for as a *state* at either the beginning or the end of the process. It can only be felt within the transformation. This insight that the very possibility of the existence of good depends upon things not being, to begin with, what they are finally to become, offers the most exact refutation of the reductive opinions in SMR

506

that can be formulated. Whereas SMR, upon discovering crude origins, concludes that they reveal the essence of things, and render later, more refined developments "unnatural," DM implies that origins must be crude, but only for the very purpose of giving scope to processes *out* of them. Aspiration away from those origins becomes the "natural," not "getting back to Nature."

The usual rebuttal of the reductive taunters of religion and morality for not being rooted in nature can only maintain defensively that the roots of religion and values, however primitive they may be, do not determine the present significance of the fruits. This is perfectly true logically. But we can now go on to say that in order for the value to be a value at all, it would have had to spring from primitive roots anyway. No value could be rooted in an anterior fixed form of instinct or in the unalterable given nature of things. Its valuableness lies in its being won out of what it was not.

It is absurd to think that if a value is shown to be a product of human experience, it is therefore an illusion, as though there should be a more solid and palpable foundation for it than this. In insisting that love, for instance, is only a human creation, what else can Krutch suppose it ought to be? What could be more real than the love experience which has survived all other human contrivances in handling the sex drive? How else could love be valuable except in its superiority to other possible sexual behavior?

Thus values cannot be expected to be rooted in nature in the sense of having been placed solidly in their final form into nature at the beginning. But we could understand them to be rooted in nature in the sense that nature is the process which value requires in order to be manifest.

2. Why Evil Is in Man. In regard to the second of utopian disappointments, man's turning out to be imperfect, the dynamic idea of good allows us to answer, "Man can experience good in no other way." We have already answered Russell's and Joad's conviction that the process is uncalled for. What about their belief that its products are unworthy of an omnipotent God? In addition to what has been previously quoted, the following conclusion to Russell's chapter on cosmic purpose expresses his profound contempt for the world and man in this truly shocking way:

I come now to the last question in our discussion of Cosmic Purpose, namely: Is what has happened hitherto evidence of the good intentions of the universe? The alleged ground for believing this . . . is that the universe has produced US. I cannot deny it. But are we really so splendid as to justify so long a prologue? . . . If I were granted omnipotence and millions of years to experiment in, I should not think Man much to boast of as the final result of my efforts.

Man as curious accident in a backwater, is intelligible: his mixture of virtues and vices is such as might be expected to result from a fortuitous origin.[23]

But now we see that man's estate of being a mixture of virtues and vices would be exactly what our idea of cosmic purpose for good calls for. True, the origin may have been fortuitous. But cosmic purpose, if there be such, cannot be expected to have created otherwise. The triumph of God, we can now understand, would have had to be the creation of an unfinished creature, flexible enough to grow and change, stable enough not to fall apart into formless flux. We said in Chapter XII that meditation upon what biology discloses of the tremendous organization of numberless simultaneous functions that underlie this experience of growth and improvement will make us understand why it took millennia to develop it, however "imperfect" it remains. This dogma of Russell's merely convicts him of having a consciousness too narrow to comprehend the actual marvels that are obscured by his one-at-a-time logical propositions.

Religious naturalism is based on the insight that the becoming of something else than what is, is intrinsic not only to existence but to the meaning of good. This interpretation meets a typical objection of modern men to religion more squarely than any other. Religion, in spite of its announced belief in an already good creation, has always exhorted men to deny their immediate selfish impulses, and to try to become better. But many moderns react to this with derision, as though it were sentimental, artificial, goody-goody. On discovering that man is not naturally good, but is born a creature of passion and selfishness, these critics remain profoundly uninterested in any suggestion to remake and transform him. This is because they are convinced that what is just *is* and all efforts for improvement would have no justification in nature, would be to fly in the face of nature, would be only a sign of a softness too timid to face the facts. When men, in the absence of religious effort, relapse into brutes, their reaction is: "See, all your effort was futile. You can't change human nature, and it is merely unnatural or even effeminizing to try." Thus the realists morosely rivet their attention upon the ugliest parts of life, confident that these are the most real. Novelists are afraid of being considered sentimental unless they write only of the most depraved beginning-moments of human nature. The only good they could be interested in would be an automatic, irresistible good which would make it impossible for murder, perversion and disease to exist at all. A good that consists in making man over into what he was not seems fragile at best, at worst a perversion of nature.

But the dynamic view leads us to expect that human nature must always be the same to start with; that aspiration and effort must have scope in order that good may exist. The struggle for goodness and unity out of evil and disunity is neither unnatural nor a futile, obstructing happenstance. Such conflict is part and parcel of the very being of goodness. The beginning-moment of imperfection is not a sign of fortuitous origin, nor of final nature, but is rather a sign that effort is to be made in order that good experience might exist.

C.E.M. Joad reacts to the suggestion that evil (or some of it) is necessary for good by saying:

> Why did not God make us from the first, why does He not remake us now, so that we can recognize good without having to distinguish it from evil?[24]

An assumption that good and evil are foils for each other in only a static, logical sense underlies this protest, obviously. In any case, to charge God to revise the inner necessities of the idea of good so as to conform with what one currently finds himself able to understand, is to refuse capriciously to enter into the search that is the essence of good. If Joad insists on demanding that God's purpose be perfect static happiness, while God knows that a much more significant kind of good can exist in a process of salvation from evil, then Joad merely sentences himself to futile, unteachable complaint. Pringle-Pattison says, "The universe is not perfect in the sense that there is no evil in it; for it is childish to imagine that good can exist for a finite creature except as the conquest of evil."[25]

3. Why External Evil? The third disappointment of the utopians lay in the failure of Utopia to arrive in their lifetime. Suffering and

all the evils of the environment, natural and social, continued and even worsened. They could give no reason why nature produced catastrophes, nor could they tell how they expected to stop nature from so doing.

What can be said on the basis of the dynamic idea of good should now be obvious. Problems are proposed that they may be solved. Man must, as Pringle-Pattison says, "make himself in the stress of circumstance and temptation." For the world to possess a perfectly symmetrical design with everything pre-arranged would simply be a prescription for boredom.

> Nature . . . is an element, savage and dangerous, into which the human being is thrown to show what stuff he is made of . . . the spirit's power to transform the very meaning of the past and to transmute every loss into a gain, "finding even in the worst of tragedies the means of an *otherwise impossible* triumph."[26]

The words which I have italicized (quoted by Pringle-Pattison from Royce) seem squarely to meet Krutch's contention that the transcending of suffering is an illusion based on a fictitious belief in God introduced only to make the suffering bearable. For God, if God there be, would not be in the position of contending against an unlucky accident which He did not intend. We would not be in the position of devoutly hoping that the universe might fortunately contain a power able to retrieve a bad situation that fortuitously appeared. For the suffering and these experiences of transcending it, whether illusory or valid, are exactly the factors that would have to combine if there were a Creator of moral good. Whether there is a God or not, suffering is the sole means to create an "otherwise impossible" good.

But now we are up against the real problem: what about those external (and internal) evils which do not seem to serve the strengthening or deepening of character, but apparently utterly destroy character and all its values? What about all those natural, environmental evils that kill men's bodies or destroy their minds? What about those social evils impinging upon the individual from the sins of other men that ruin their hopes and chances? And what about death?

No doubt, the mere logical unassailability of the dynamic idea of good will not in itself force cynics to consider the possible meaningfulness of evil. Much less will the bare statement of the requirement of disorder inspire them to arduous search for the cosmic purpose and possible divine aid which it makes at least logically thinkable. We will still sound like mere pious sentimentalists until we show that we know of and yet are not dismayed by, the levels of degradation and agony that monopolize their attention, precluding, they say, the existence of a benevolent God.

To begin with, we cannot avoid requiring a serious consideration of the dynamic idea itself, banal though they may consider it at the outset. Schopenhauer and his ilk will refuse this first step, and as long as they do, will be safe from us. It is precisely the dynamic aspect of good experience — its requirement of change, its maddening ephemerality — that sickens the Schopenhauerean mind. They refuse to call such a game good. And much of orthodox Christianity is not too far from them, devoted as it is to dismissing the striving life as mere vanity of vanities, so far from being the center of divine interest as to be the prime proof of God's preference for a static heaven, unpolluted by creative effort.

We can do no more with these minds than children can do with the playmate who cries for the prize without joining the race. They just let him alone and go on with their play. The fact remains that good can be experienced only as resolving process, and he who wishes to keep demanding that it ought to be experienceable as eternal, uninterrupted bliss, must simply miss it.

We pass on, then, to the atheistic existentialists, who are willing to play the game, all while insisting that it is an absurd and nauseating game. They hold this for the same Schopenhauerean reason: the game does not reach the final consummation they still assume to be required by any world to be considered divine. They seem to have accepted much of the dynamic logic, without, however, granting it metaphysical meaningfulness. They are, as a matter of fact, more similar to pragmatists and meliorists than they have admitted, in being ready to undertake the struggle to solve problems, while insisting all the time that the presence of any problems at all rules out the possibility of cosmic purpose or God. They are merely a little more explicit than the pragmatists (who avoided thinking about ultimate meanings at all, in their readiness to be as busy as blank factual reality forced them to be), in positively enunciating that their strenuous activity is meaningless.

What the dynamic idea of good adds to these views is perhaps no more than a certain rearrangement of the sequence of ideas.

They start with the empirically observed processual nature of existence, notice that it sometimes produces a good outcome, sometimes a bad. Retaining the static idea of good as a state or essence existing only at the terminus, the process and struggle now appear to them as a second, arbitrarily introduced and "absurd" principle. Our starting point, "good is the feeling of resolving process," makes the process not an absurd appendage in reality, but integral to the very meaning of value. We can now accept any bit of felt good process as sufficient to its own meaningfulness, whatever may happen in later phases; any bit of felt evil process as a potential requirement in some future good feeling.

Nor is the dynamic idea of good obliged to accept the Myth of Sisyphus as the symbol of life; for it does not follow that, since good requires a process out of disorder and evil, that we therefore must eternally go all the way back down to the bottom of the hill for every good experience we have. We may retain a good part of what we have accomplished, building new experience *upon* that (but, it is true, never permitted to *rest* in it). As for death, when we seem to return to the bottom of the hill, so that all is absurdly undone, I must take this point up last, in the seventh degree of evil below.

If the existentialists, then, demand good as an eternally possessable essence, for meaningfulness (though accepting dynamic reality as a fact), we cannot extricate them from "absurdity." In short, we cannot move the cynics unless they will at least provisionally follow us beyond our starting point.

Now let us get to work on the real objection: that to identify enjoyment with resolving painful disorder is not to come to grips with the problem of evil at all. Cynics might be ready to "accept the universe" if it were true that all pains and evils eventually resolved themselves into release or relief with good feeling. They might even be able to get interested in the dynamic implication that, if good is to continue to be experienced, reality must never be emptied of factors in strain and collision, felt as painful — provided every case of painful disharmony could be counted on to pass eventually into resolution. The problem of evil, however, they will maintain, is constituted precisely by the presence of cases that are doomed never to reach resolution. It is clear that the majority of our writers are preoccupied in seeking out all types of situations where there are unresolvable factors; processes doomed to a disintegrative course, leading to increasing break-down and agony without surcease. The implication which they defend is that any universe that contains such cases cannot possibly be intelligible, cannot possibly be understood to be required as it is by any conceivable notion of value and purpose, no matter how many cases of "successful" process it may also contain.

Now as we try to lead the cynics further in considering what the dynamic idea of value can do with these kinds of evil, we realize that we have to entice them into reconsidering assumptions they made early in the game; and to give up those assumptions will seem to them like throwing in the sponge at the outset. We shall be admitting, for instance, a factor of accident, or at least of unguaranteed experiment in the universe — but shall hold that this is logically entailed in the dynamic idea of good. The critics may immediately balk and refuse to give up their instinctive demand that a universe they will allow to be meaningful or good must not have such loose ends, such accidents.

At this point, the would-be justifier of things can wonder, in his efforts to converse with the pessimist, whether the whole argument is necessarily futile because of the pessimist's possible vested emotional interest in there being no meaning in life, and therefore no demand for a more strenuous attitude against evil. Many of our writers seem so ready to plunge into bitterness at the horrors of life, into railing at the God they have so rushed to repudiate, that we begin to wonder whether they really want an answer. It is at least obvious that if one commits himself early in the game to the thesis that there is no solution and thereupon spends most of his available energy in seeking out negative cases to justify the early repudiation of faith, he is not then liable to be the one who detects positive evidences or discovers solutions. On as difficult and complex a matter, one probably must wish to solve it rather than wish to prove it insoluble, if he is to be able to produce the effort requisite to any possible solution there may be. And if the cynic has in addition a wish to escape from any obligations of effortful behavior that the positive solution may entail, then our argument will be the more ineffectual upon him. If our writers are really mere irresponsibles who would rather get themselves into trouble out of mere negligence so as to complain about it, we may not be able to make much progress.

Be that as it may, we will line up the aspects of the problem of evil in the order of increasing difficulty, and hope they will follow us over each hurdle to the next. Perhaps all these aspects reduce in the end to the problem of death, but we will not get to that until the last.

First, why must there be *any* maladjustment and disorder, felt as painful, to start with? This has been sufficiently explained in the preceding chapters. The real question follows.

Secondly, why must there be as *much* maladjustment and disorder with pain, to start with, as there is? There has been a great ground swell of conviction, during these decades, not only among the bitter repudiators of God, but even among those most ready to defend His existence and His creation of a striving life, that there is really more evil than would be required just to save life from trivial comfort for profound seriousness. Even if they should grant that God must allow problems, they would still ask why He must allow such bad ones. Should there not be a more reasonable amount of suffering, more guaranteed to come out in insight and growth? Thus even the more sophisticated Christian theologians are glad to resort to the traditional "out" of the Fall, in spite of its inveterate threat to the doctrine of God's omnipotence — that is, to hope of understanding all reality as according with divine intention. The humanist assumption of a basic urge toward growth and healing, merely obstructed by untoward infantile traumas, inferiority complexes, fixations, etc., they have concluded, does not account for a definite factor of positive lust for fiendishness that has been revealed in modern returns to persecution, torture, sexual monstrosities and degradation. They feel forced back to the doctrine of the Fall, and the acceptance of the "paradox" and "mystery" that God's creature is now so far from being good as to be repulsive; while God is left at pains to repair the error in His design when and if He will.

But the doctrine of the Fall, we saw, does not silence doubt. I would personally assent to the thesis that its inadequacy is one of the main propellors of the modern mind into its massive unbelief and hopelessness; and can not be expected to assuage this problem which itself has caused. At any rate, I conceive the dynamic idea of value as definitely an alternative to it and I am not intending to restore any "Fall" theory when I say that in dynamic logic, we must understand that any good God must intentionally create man imperfect, nay, with a positive tendency toward destructive experience. For man can experience good feeling only if he first experiences bad feeling, and we have seen that

514

this means experiencing a certain amount of disintegrative process before he experiences integrative.

But even in the dynamic logic, we still have the question whether the amount of evil and pain needs to be as *much* as it is. Why is not there some lower limit to the amount of disintegration that is to be used as a spur to effort, short of some of the worst levels of horrors and disgust?

One familiar answer is that physical evils are a necessary by-product of the uniformity of nature, which itself is a precondition of rational and moral life. It is said that we cannot ask God to be always interrupting the causal sequences of nature to save individuals who happen to be in the way of a tidal wave or out in a blizzard, without making nature too confused for man to work out any orderly understanding of it. This is a significant point, though not very satisfying to those ravaged by disease, drouth and insect.

A second consideration is that certain cases of hopeless destruction are not merely by-products of nature's uniformity, but also demonstrations of the failure that will attend certain kinds of behavior. The only way for the survivors, or the human race in general, to learn certain things, or to be spurred to progress, is to experience to the full the negative failures and catastrophes that follow from mistakes. Men's efforts toward good often require that a problem or a threat become explicit and urgent. It is intrinsic to the idea of process that experience be stirred by a problem. Therefore, some men are sacrificed to hunger or to earthquakes so that other men may perceive tasks to be done. Some men must fail so as to provide unequivocal object-lessons for other men. Some individuals must need help if others are to have opportunity to render Christian service. Strict distributive justice cannot be the bottom principle of moral order and divine government because

. . . it is precisely the inequalities of life which provide the major opportunities for that generous bearing of one another's burdens without which love cannot be manifested.[27]

A third suggestion is derived from the principles of inclusiveness and advance, which I have argued to be implicit in the definition of dynamic good: that the amount of good feeling will be proportional to the amount of progress from disorder and pain toward

515

order. Presumptively, then, we could set no arbitrary lower limit to the amount of disorder and pain, assuming that it remains possible to resolve and organize it. The experience of consummation would only be intensified, proportionally to the terror, agony, misery that has been overcome. Thus our cynics, as they divert themselves with ever more gruesome and disgusting materials, cannot be so certain as they suppose that their lost and depraved characters *might* not be potential to ecstasies beyond compare, if only they were taught to aspire. The insane man might become cured and know a vividness of good feeling he could not have known in solving any lesser problem. The Nazi debacle may lead to a more passionate grasp on wisdom by succeeding men. There is a discernible relationship between the amount of evil an individual has experienced and transcended, and the depth of his insight and comprehension of the goodness of things.

Now, of course, the deeper the problem inherited or thrown up by circumstances, the greater the risk of complete failure and collapse. Yet if such problems are faced and transcended, the person who has won the victory affords the rest of us the deepest plumbings of the meaning and the goodness of creation. The injustice and unhappiness ingredient in the lives of so many saints is no accident that God has neglected to rectify, but quite integral in the project of creating saints.

We still have, however, the problem of those *who* are destroyed by the amount of disorder they find themselves in. But before we get to this question of *failing* processes, we must deal with a lesser, third, degree of difficulty: why is attainment, even at best, only partial, inevitably revealing new facets of problems to solve, new unincorporated materials creating new maladjustments and desires? The answer to this is already present in its essentials. It is clear why we must never arrive at final adjustment, if good feeling is to continue; why problemlessness is tantamount to boredom — the bitterest of truths to the Schopenhauereans. But we do not concede to them that therefore all achievement is really illusory. The experience of partial resolution has been *had;* it may be retained, though only as a foundation for a further episode of creative good. It is not necessary to admit that achievement is entirely undone as we go into the next phase of growth; it may stay done, though it cannot continue to excite good feeling in itself. But even if it *were* undone, I would insist that the good feeling of resolution was had when it was had, and the Schopenhauereans are silly when they argue that it was worthless, merely because it does not persist permanently in time.

However, we are now at the fourth question, why should there ever be any disintegration, after integration, as I have just admitted there may be? (Again the question why there seems to have to be complete disintegration at last, in death, is left to the last point.)

Actually, we have already solved this fourth degree, when we pointed out (p. 497) that evil itself must be defined dynamically, obversely to good: evil is the feeling of disintegrative process, and can be nothing else. This immediately renders the present degree of the problem of evil nothing but the first degree over again, which we have already justified. That is, when we said that maladjustment and disorder, felt as painful, are clearly required at the start of the process, we cannot have meant a *state* of maladjustment, a mere fixed condition of awkwardly juxtaposed factors. We would have to have meant a sort of temporary reversal of restoring process into breaking-down process, where already achieved order was falling away a little, with associated pain. It is the pain and discomfort in this that is the spur to the effort to get the process going back toward greater order again.

Actually, in almost all cases, it would not be so much the mere breaking-down of an organism by itself that is the main source of the pain, but the organisms's colliding with new factors which put it under pressures, requiring it to modify itself to a degree (which will involve some disintegration with pain) in order to incorporate the new materials. Thus it must experience some degree of breakdown and strain before it can get underway toward incorporation and growth again. Of course, it may alternatively experience an insoluble unfittingness in the new factors. In this case they will either be rejected; or, possibly, they may succeed in destroying the organism. This is the case of failure to be considered under the sixth point.

We have these reasons, then, why there must be some disintegration of achieved patterns. The fifth question is: why does there have to be so much disintegration as there is? Here we come to the main body of complaints by the cynics. But the answers to the second and fourth degrees already answer this one. Evil as disintegrative process is necessary, and good is proportional to advance. Therefore we cannot set any arbitrary limit to the amount of disintegration to be permitted in a meaningful, dynamic universe.

It would also seem that high, elaborate creation must approach an upper limit of complexity, where the chances of interference and break-up overtake the tendency toward delicate complexity. The hybrid flower is bred to such a pitch of fragile elaborateness that it becomes more and more impossible to keep one alive in the face of all the disintegrative forces that surround it. The growth process would then be forced over into a disintegrative one which will proceed until a floor of stability is regained from which the native tendency toward experiment and progress may once again take off. This thought points to the necessity of "toppling": of cultures so complicated as to be burdensome; of geniuses so delicate as to be doomed to schizophrenia. But no matter how far the fall, it could not be proven that such disintegrations could not prompt a recovery or a fresh direction of creativity. And the argument under the second point then avails here also: the greater the disintegration, the greater the possible good if it can be reversed into some new creativity.

But we are overlapping the sixth question: the still tougher one, why must there ever be processes that end in total destruction, i.e. failure? Under the fifth point we considered only why there are some of the more dreadful degrees of disintegration, which however are not necessarily final but may precede recoveries and new growths. Here we consider the question of broken men, unsuccessful groups and cultures that endure the permanent loss of their hopes can be argued to end thus, in death, but that comes last. Here we ask, why is success not guaranteed in specific efforts and strivings?

We must first make clear that we do admit the *fact* of failure. The dynamic idea of good must not be taken as holding that, since good can only exist in a resolving process, therefore all processes actually get resolved. The concept is only a statement of requirement, that there must be disorder and pain for good to exist. It does not declare that all disorder and pain actually do succeed in producing good.

But why shouldn't they?, the doubter now asks. Can the dynamic idea offer any reasons why there not only are but should be failing processes in a value-universe? The question can also be stated as whether there is absolute evil, disintegration or failure which can never become an ingredient in some later process of good? The possible instances that trouble our writers most of all are the cases, within one of which they believe we are living now, of cumulative historical and social evil; times of cultural collapse, where evil seems to become so self-multiplying as to run away from the seemingly feeble efforts of good to patch it up. Ignorance and vice begin to multiply from generation to generation. Innocent then suffer and fail with the guilty and, as Whitehead says, evil "has secured a descent toward nothingness."[28]

First let us mention some considerations which cynics are fond of overlooking that might indicate that failure is not so all-pervading as they assume. A long-run factor of self-cancellation of evil may be pointed to. Evil arises essentially out of limitation, cessation or reversal of growth process. It cannot constitute an opening or widening of creativity, for that would be by definition good. Evil is destruction and destruction can go on only as long as there is some organization to destroy. On the biological level, a cancer is a growth, but it is "evil" because it is too limited, too uncoordinated with the whole, so that it ends by killing its host. But it thus eliminates itself as a factor in any further experience. At the social level, the Nazi experiment is analogous. A segment of society sought its own good in a context excluding much of the data that were actually involved in the concrescent occasion (in Whitehead's terms). And at another level, the individuals within that segment adopted principles insufficient to preserve the organization of that fraction of society itself. The group may have succeeded in attaining a limited good, but in the end produced more destruction — which however included its own destruction, both by disintegration of its own constituents (the corrupt individuals) and by pressure from its milieu (other nations) which is pushing toward more inclusive organization. Thus evil, arising from a limitation of good-process, too narrow and restricted for the situation, and thus bringing on disintegration in the end, tends to be self-eliminating in the long run. As soon as its resistance is removed, expansion toward larger good experience proceeds, consisting partly of escaping from this limitation itself. In this sense, evil and failure seem debarred from ever having the last word, at least for the life process at large.

Another rationale for some failure, not to be forgotten just because it is obvious, is the familiar point of moral justice. There are plenty of down-and-outers who may be merely suffering from their own negligence and laziness. And most or all cases of "falling"

519

societies reveal a preceding history of widespread moral lapse and spiritual laziness. If the members of a society have largely given up their search for good, we would hardly argue that they should escape scot-free from the consequences. In fact, many find more reason to believe in God during a period of calamity than during one of prosperity, for thereby it is demonstrated that the universe redresses the moral balance, and greed and corruption are overtaken in the end. This is speaking very much in the large of course, and leaves many cases of individual wickedness seeming to prosper, and of good seeming to suffer unredeemed.

But this is our real problem: *undeserved* failure: failure of individuals for whom social calamity has made conditions too difficult to cope with; failure of individuals for any other reason not their own fault; failure of groups, such as minorities, through undeserved deprivation of the wherewithal of life. If we insist that the fundamental tendency in natural energy fields is toward organization of ingredients, still we must grant that there are cases where the resolving power of the fields — of minds and nervous systems — is not sufficient to overcome the stresses impinging upon them. When the obstacles are above a certain strength, a disintegrative dynamics replaces the integrative, perhaps unto final failure. Modern civilization could well be burdening many minds with too much confusion for them to grapple with.

The strongest point to be made here, perhaps, is the familiar thesis that the higher goods of heroism and character require genuine risk and adventure; and this can only mean *real* possibility of failure. It cannot allow that the universe should waft us along passively upon a process guaranteed to succeed; or that difficulties should be exactly measured to capacities to ensure success. Can we speak of tension where the feeler is sure of its release? Can there be pleasurable relief where there was no real anxiety about the outcome? Can some of the more profound experiences of saintliness and sacrifice be even conceived in a world where there was no chance of failure? It has been recognized through the ages by a few that they could not. Even our cynics can think of this point in their less complaining moments. But they can always forget it to go back to supposing a safe, tepid world of secure and permanent pleasure would really be more to their taste (though they are usually simultaneously complaining about that very kind of life, which is frequently what they have attained through pandering to their readers' desire for reasons not to struggle against evil).

Any evil, then, can be an instigator to, and a potential component of, good experience; and all good experience must have its genesis in evil. But this is not to say that every evil should be foredestined to terminate in good. *Cosmic purpose must create a genuinely open process in order to get the most honestly creative dynamic good.*

But before going to that, let me deal with a question that has been asked: is the dynamic thesis reversible? That is, can we equally well argue that Evil requires a process always striving toward organization, in order that blockings and frustrations of that process might take place, giving rise to disintegrative process, the only possible locus for evil? And therefore, might a Devil be the creator or organizing process as probably as a God?

I am not sure there is any water-tight refutation of this thesis for anyone so perverse as to believe it. And anyone, in those moments when failure and disintegration seem preponderant in his own experience, will be tempted to adopt the notion — not excluding the author himself. A related idea is Freud's: that we have a "Death Instinct" as well as a Life Instinct which can bing us moments of depletion and apathy, or of destructive fury when we do seem positively to long for and aim at suffering.

And yet it seems obvious enough that in a majority of lives, the proportion of time spent in acceptance of life, from stretches of mild contentment to moments of zest and ecstasy, is far greater than that spent in desperation and despair. Even if death ends every life, the time spent in its agonies is only a moment compared to all the hours and days spent in reasonably interested living. Why should this minimum of discontent (whose existence, moreover, has been shown to be required by the dynamic idea of good) be considered a more essential characteristic of existence than the maximum of rewarding life?

To conclude on the question of whether a Devil or a God created the process, then, we must move to our final wrestle on the seventh and last degree of evil: the problem of death. We have sought adequate reasons for the divine permission of failure, and though I realize they may not go very far toward enabling one actually to experience failure with equanimity, they still seem *logically* sufficient. It would seem unfair for the cynic to demand of us that we not only justify failure logically, but also

521

eliminate the anguished feelings themselves. The author, who finds that the dynamic idea of good enables him to pursue the search for God, does not claim that it invariably keeps him from moments of sickness of life.

What then can we say on the basis of the dynamic idea of good about the fact that every creature seems guaranteed to "fail" at last in dying? Before we can advance at all on this problem, we must secure one more acquiescence from the pessimist: he must relinquish the notion that subsequent dissolution somehow undoes formerly existent good feeling.

Most modern thinkers, from the mere primitivist writer of novels of adolescent complaint, to the most complex leader in philosophy, subscribe without a moment's hesitation to Solon's and Aristotle's dictum: that one cannot know whether "good" has won until the moment of death. One cannot know whether one has really *had* good, in any particular episode of process, until he knows how the entire process of processes comes out in the end. Aristotle was satisfied if a man died happy. But moderns can ask whether even in that case "evil" has not had the last word. It is habitual to suppose that the likely eventual end of the solar system, or of earthly life under atom bombs, is sufficient proof that value is not at the root of things. If all empirically known life processes come out in death, is not the presumption that all life, however enjoyable long stretches of it might have been, is really in the end frustrated and all the good undone?

I realize, then, that the cynic will not continue the discussion if he remains adamant on this opinion. Before we can go a step further, it must be accepted that a good feeling experience, when had, is had, and cannot be dismissed as insignificant merely because it is followed (as the dynamic idea shows it must be) by renewed need, desire or frustration; or because, at the terminus comes death.[29]

Now in dynamic logic, we can find reasons why creatures should have to die. If the cynic demands that they should not, he will leave me here. The most important reason is the necessity of finitude, which we have already derived from dynamic value (p. 192). This shows why any particular developing creature must reach an end before it absorbs all reality. The concept of dynamic good cannot allow any process, starting with finite ingredients and increasing in inclusiveness and order, to increase to infinite all-inclusiveness. For if there were no more ingredients to include and no more order to attain, there could be no further organizing, and therefore no further value in existence. Adding the principle of novelty and variety (# 2.7, p. 55) to that of finiteness, we can then see that, if the parts and ingredients must be finite, then novel good feeling could not be derived from them indefinitely for their possibilities or organization must become exhausted within finite time. Thus we have a further reason for the ending of any organism.

Another line of thought indicates that any given creature, solidifying its past experience in its cumulating structure, must progressively limit itself more and more to its own type or habit of functioning. To get new varieties of process new beings must be started. Therefore older beings must be cleared away both because they grow "tired" of their own experience; and also to make room for new beings.

But the cynics are not so scandalized by the clearing away of former beings, provided they *are* old and tired, as they are by the haphazard destruction of beings, whether they are worn-out and fulfilled or not. They may snort, at this point, that the dynamic idea of good has only made room for what they have always accepted anyway, that lives of striving *and achieving* that end in death are justifiable. It is precisely the cases where sufficient process for enjoyment is never granted that constitutes the problem of evil — the permanently unfulfilled suffering of dying children. It is the death of slum denizens, of hopelessly distorted perverts, of war casualties, before they could ever get "straightened out", that preoccupies the pessimists in their hunt for meaningless destruction.

At this point we must claim again that good experience is had when it is had, and is no more undone by an early death than by a late one. A child dying of cancer is seldom totally without some earlier experience of simple consummatory process. Even a still-born child has presumably enjoyed its intra-uterine kickings and stretchings. This reminds us of a large factor that is characteristically ignored by would-be pessimists: that many cases of suffering which so shock their own fully developed sensibilities may not be as vividly sensed by the subject as they suppose. The register of feeling of the dying one may not be as acute as their own. The child dead at birth or at an early age cannot be so anguished at all that is being lost, as the sensitive and exasperated onlooker. The dying child has a less enriched conception of his own potentialities that are being sacrificed than the pitier. And as the destruction of tissues proceeds, his feeling may dim proportionally. This holds for those dying of loathsome diseases and injuries at any age.

I do not mean to say that there is not sufficient horror in writhing children and shrieking adults to supply the writers with as many dark scenes as they wish. But I am sure they often load the dice more than they might if they were as sharply on the lookout for positive modes of interpretation as they are for proofs of their gloomy theses.

The dynamic philosophy also has a kind of answer, which is so pervasive as to be suspect by the pessimist on that very account, for cases of loss of mental or physical powers through injury, illness and old age. Yet this answer has probably produced more decent serenity in the old and handicapped, than the pessimist approach has produced pessimists. This thought is simply that, for life to be so arranged that its latter part is a long decline is a way to guarantee that problems for spiritual adjustment will be continuously supplied. The creature is forced to develop subtler and more refined modes of reaction in place of his earlier more energetic, but cruder, physical modes. And this is to say nothing of a possibility that the pessimist has usually ruled out in advance: that knowledge of the ills flesh is heir to would intrinsically be, in any possible universe, the strongest motivation to seek out, possibly discover, and meditate upon deeper spiritual resources for life and death. Spiritual search could not conceivably be motivated without some such schedule.

This thought avails also for the suffering of those who have been left behind by the deaths of their loved ones. This would comprise only a specially difficult problem for which, however, one might strive for a solution, attaining spiritual depths otherwise incomprehensible in so doing.

In a way, to make one's peace with death is to make one's peace with the entire problem of evil. If one will accept the necessity of death, the question of when and how it comes does not seem fundamentally to add any further problem for the apologist. Thus, if we can find any meaning in individual death, it should not be impossible to understand why there is social death, i.e., the death of cultures, classes, nations, causing, as they all do, mass individual deaths.

We have already seen that large scale social catastrophe is sometimes easier to justify than individual, for the factor of dessert may be easier to discern. The members of the dying entity can be seen not to have been playing the game as we can see they ought. Too many of them have become just the kind of pessimist we are trying to communicate with, who refuses to contribute any energy to the social process. If our writers are only trying to describe to us one of those times when nothing succeeds, and the high achievements of preceding eras are wilting back, they may, of course, be permitted to do so. The only question then would be whether they must do it with so great a lack of perspective. Must they tell of it with such a paranoid self-pity that they refuse to entertain constructive interpretations that might render this time of decay only the more fertile ground for tomorrow's creativity?

The dynamic idea of good can encourage at least those who are not too dehumanized to hope that this dying of an insupportably materialistic civilization (if it is dying) might constitute the opening phase of a most thrilling growth in another direction. If many individuals are destroyed incidentally in innumerable ways all dutifully recorded by the writers, there seems no reason why these same writers might not do a little creative envisioning for us, possibly shortening the time when we must exist within the debacle. All must die and to die resisting evil may be the best way to do it.

Finally, I may remark that other answers to the problem of death devised during the ages are as consonant with this view of good as with any other, especially the thought of immortality. Not assuming its reality to be a foregone conclusion, still one remark is relevant to the dynamic idea of good: The bliss of heaven itself might depend on the evil of this world for the possibility of its being experienced and known. If there were a heaven, we could understand how this kind of world would be necessary as a preliminary for its being appreciated. Those sacrificed here might know the more good there.

The center of what I want to say is that, granting the existence of individual death, of frustration, of the ephemerality of satisfaction, and of times when decay and destruction overbalance growth and creativity, there is none of this that the dynamic idea of good cannot make at least a strong beginning at rationalizing; enough so, that no thinker can ever justify himself in refusing to get into the search for positive or potential meaning in whatever circumstances he finds himself. There have been resources for this suffering in past times of discouragement, and would be again, if our intellectual leadership would spend the time it uses in proving that there can be no sense or succor, in searching for them.

Thus the dynamic idea of good permits us in many ways not merely to try defensively to explain evil away, but positively to accept it as having a significant part to play in any divine plan. If God does not eliminate evil, it may be because of His weakness or limitation of power, but because of the necessities of the nature of good. We can now conceive of an omnipotent Creator, a Cosmic Purpose for Good, without any necessary logical contradiction.

PART V

PHILOSOPHY OF RELIGION
CONCLUSIONS ON MEANINGFULNESS

CHAPTER XIX

CONCLUSIONS ON THE EXISTENCE AND NATURE GOD (COSMIC PURPOSE FOR GOOD)

Of the three essentials of the maximum meaning of meaningfulness which we specified in Chapter II, (1) Cosmic, (2) Purpose for (3) Good, we have dealt with the second and third in the finite, human world which we can study empirically. The corresponding stumbling blocks to belief in their reality — the problems of mechanism and evil, respectively — have proved not entirely intractable for the dynamic interpretation of fact and value. The problem of knowledge, which has a special bearing upon the question of *cosmic* extent of good purpose, has also been discussed, but mainly in connection with finite, earthly knowledge of purpose and value. It remains to summarize the conclusions of the various philosophies as to how far we may extrapolate from our finite knowledge to the cosmos as a whole. In short, can man know a cosmic purpose or God?

If we are right, that man is inherently beset by internal and external weaknesses and evils, but only as the prerequisite for his being able to experience, *provided he finds the energy and inspiration,* the greatest goods of creative overcoming, then we are up against the most crucial of questions: Is there a source of inspiration and energy? And how is man to make contact with it? Where SMR was content to lie down in static self-satisfaction or despair and not even search for inspiration, DR has reawakened our imperious interest in how to find the dynamic for improvement that might be there, since none of the purported proofs of its non-existence has proved to be final.

First, then, in this chapter we will summarize the import of our entire sequence of topics as to the existence of God, Cosmic Purpose for Good. In the last chapter we will conclude with a summary of how the various views may be expected to affect the human spirit. In these chapters our basic framework must be modified a little, since these conclusions arise precisely out of comparing the M and R sides of it. Therefore the subdivisions, "Implications of SM," "Findings of SIR", etc., can be dropped.

For the present chapter we will use the following schedule under each of the positions:

1. Summary of the intellectual contradictions (the problems of mechanism and evil) and statement of what conclusions about the existence of cosmic good purpose are logically permitted for the four different M-R combinations.

2. The problem of knowledge of *cosmic* reality (which still remains, even if the above contradictions are eliminated).

3. The nature of God. On this last topic, the present book is not concerned to present a full discussion, for in some agreement with the Thomistic position, I suspect philosophical reasoning to be able to go no further than clearing away obstacles to believing in the sheer existence of God. Knowing His nature, as DM and DR will imply anyway, would require a more holistic and concrete approach. I will include, then, only the merest hints of some characteristics of God-beliefs that seem to be consonant with the positions.

SM with SIR.

1. Intellectual contradictions. The kind of static purposiveness and the perfection which the static idea of good led men to look for in the real world, as we have seen, always conflicted with experience, whether conceived according to SIR, SMR, or DR. The older views (SIR) wrestled with these contradictions (the presence of change, determinisms of various sorts, and evil) and, primarily by dualist or illusionist devices, achieved some reduction of the conflict, but never a perfect congruence. However much or little change, determinism and evil may be admitted for the world, they are certainly not admitted for the nature of God Himself, as illustrated in the Gods of Aristotle, Plotinus, Brahmanism, orthodox Christianity, et al. The relationship between such a God and the perceived world of change and evil, then, must remain fundamentally unintelligible, and this troubles faith more or less obscurely.

The static approach to belief in cosmic purpose, then, cannot

530

achieve a truly secure intellectual basis in the presence of modern science. Unable to eliminate the contradictions between the implications of static good and experience in any straightforward way, it must to do as best it can by one or the other of its two makeshifts.

2. Problem of Knowledge of God. In this situation, SM-SIR is obliged to fall back upon its authoritarian or intuitional epistemology for grounds to believe. However much "appearances" seem to contradict expectations, one stubbornly maintains faith either in certain mystical insights of one's own, or in the claims of authorities based perhaps on similar mental states. The very absence of clear evidence creates the more urgent demand for miracles or strenuous reiteration as sources of belief.

Rationalistic arguments were also developed to prove God's existence. These are so familiar that we will omit complete presentations. They have resolved themselves into three kinds, in most modern reviews, each, perhaps, revealing a rough affinity for one of our three terms in the definition of God. The Cosmological Argument, that there must have been a purposive first cause or creator of things, bears upon the Purpose term. The Teleological Argument, that the world reveals so much good design as to require to have been designed by a good God, bears upon the Good term. And the Ontological Argument, that man's ability to conceive of something greater or more perfect than himself, or of supreme greatness and perfection, proves that such a greatness or perfection must exist, bears upon the Cosmic term. But our three basic problems, then, invalidate the arguments: The problem of mechanism weakened the faith in a purposive cause, as soon as the possible eternity of mechanistic causation became a conceivable notion. The problem of evil always raises the question why the world is so *inadequately* designed. And the problem of knowledge includes among other difficulties the question whether man does have knowledge of supreme greatness and perfection, and even if he did, whether he could conclude from it to the *existence* of any such reality on a cosmic level.

Thus traditional static belief must fall back once again on sheer stubborn faith, believing in spite of evidence and in the absence of proof, "believing that I may understand." Too often such faith is motivated by reluctance to undergo the effort of revising one's habits of thought, the desire to cling to familiar and comfortable beliefs. Such faith seems difficult to defend to-day, when the refusal to budge from static foundations forces one more and more to avoid or distort evidence in order to preserve easy belief.

3. The Nature of God. The God who is thought to be known through these approaches is generally the static Absolute of Plato, Aristotle, Plotinus, Hinduism and medieval theology. He is sometimes defined by the negations of all the characteristics that are allied to dynamic process — infinitude, immutability, perfection, etc. His radical difference from the developing world forces his banishment from it, so that his *transcendence* is emphasized. We all know of Aristotle's God who could not even be allowed to be aware of his created world, so disturbing of his perfect tranquillity would its imperfections and aspirations be.

Orthodoxy, of course, imported the active God of the Old Testament, and the loving personality of the New into this absolute framework, but generally confessed to the incomprehensibility of the relationship. Jesus Christ and numerous other intermediaries were the result of the effort to bridge the chasm. The personal God who cares, of religion, cannot be successfully fitted to a reality of statically perfect security, though popular religion never gives up trying to have this cake and eat it too.

SM and SIR together, then, reach a Cosmic Purpose for Good by hook or crook, and succeed in deriving from the belief enough dynamic, sometimes, to improve the living of life. But that is the topic of the final chapter.

SM with SMR.

1. Intellectual contradictions: Mechanistic materialism contradicts the idea of purpose in all possible senses. Its denial of the reality of growth and attainment exacerbates the problem of evil, making it intrinsically insoluble. Purposiveness and good for even the finite world thus being cast into doubt, their cosmic extent can hardly be seriously considered. This summary of our book-long analysis of the relations between SM and SMR sufficiently accounts for the atheism that has always accompanied their combination.

Of course, we remember that earlier mechanists, including Newton himself, recoiling from the deserts of meaninglessness they glimpsed beyond, resorted to Deism as a stop-gap — the attempt to preserve God as a machine-maker. There was nothing for this God to do but to create and initiate the movements of the atoms. He should never have to interfere with his machine again once he had started it (if he were the perfect artificer he should be according to the static idea of good). Thus we have already lost a God who can be in any meaningful and living relationship with his creatures, or who can be a continuously creative organizing influence in any other sense. And then eventually it became clear, as we have seen, that God was not even needed to create and start the atoms, since it was just as rational to think of them as eternal and uncreated, as to try to imagine a supposed nothingness prior to their appearance.

While God was thus being deprived of his duties by the further advancement of mechanical science, and men were beginning to wonder whether the self-perpetuating machine thus left stood really in need of any supernatural beginning, Hume's crushing disposal of the ideas of power and causality along another tack were already disturbing the learned world with the suspicion that a First Cause was not as necessary an idea of reason as it had appeared, and Kant was preparing the penetrating analysis which frankly purported to remove God from the realm of knowledge altogether. In short, Newton's cherished theology was rapidly peeled off by all the competant hands that could get at him.[1]

Thus SMR fell back into the atheism which had followed it ever since Democritus and Epicurus. Holbach, La Mettrie and Feuerbach developed the implication and passed it on to Marxism.

2. Problems of Knowledge. We have studied the more atomistic empiricism of SMR, and its inability to reach a satisfactory theory of the knowing and appreciating of qualitative, patterned wholes even within the finite world to say nothing of cosmic wholes. For another expression of such a positivistic approach in summary, we can take one of Russell's attacks on mystical, holistic awareness:

When a man of science tells us the result of an experiment, he also tells us how the experiment was performed; others can repeat it, and if the result is not confirmed it is not accepted as true; but many men might put themselves into the situation in which the mystic's vision occurred without obtaining the same revelation. . . . Science depends upon perception and inference; its credibility is due to the fact that the perceptions are such as any observer can test. . . .[2]

The man of science, when he wishes others to see what he has seen, arranges his microscope or telescope . . . demands of the observer only normal eyesight. The mystic, on the other hand, demands changes in the observer, by fasting, by breathing exercises, and by a careful abstention from external observation. . . . From the scientific point of view, we can make no distinction between the man who eats little and sees heaven and the man who drinks much and sees snakes. Each is in an abnormal physical condition, and therefore has abnormal perceptions.[3]

Underlying these remarks one can see Russell's assumption that knowledge involves only point-to-point correspondences between external factors and sensations, taken more or less one at a time, together with one-way linkings of these points by inferences. This is why he so lightly tosses aside the possibility that, when it is a question of grasping complex patterns of thought in simultaneity, the purification and enhancing of the brain's organic condition might be a most relevant procedure. He is confident that all real knowledge is testable by any observer, because knowledge is never more than a collection of discrete items that can be repeated over again one by one. If you cannot find God by tallying over the pieces separately in the most workaday state of mind, there is no possibility of finding him in an immediately felt design of the pieces, grasped in a white hot moment of fusion.

So, rejecting the faith and authoritarianism of SIR, SMR also excludes holistic modes of knowing, leaving us without any conceivable recourse from the negative arguments above, to any way of knowing that might have taken us "over" them to either human or cosmic purpose and value. Thus all avenues to belief are closed.

3. The Nature of God. There can be no doctrine of God, then, with the combination of SM and SMR. This is the final outcome of our analysis throughout the book for the SM-SMR part of the framework.

The fateful results of this outcome on human affairs has been touched on frequently, and will be summarized in the next chapter. It is, of course, what causes us to turn to DM and DR with anxious hope for an escape from this interdict.

1. Intellectual Contradictions. Taking the problem of purposiveness, first, our question is: how legitimate is it to extrapolate from what DR has found concerning purposiveness in finite beings in this part of the universe, to existence of an overall cosmic purpose?

One of the most popular "proofs" of cosmic purpose which seemed to be allowed by new findings in biology and ecology was a revival of the argument from design. With the problem of mechanism overcome, it seemed that purposive design might be reintroduced. Every so often one will find an article in the popular prints listing the vast number of conditions that had to come together in just the right proportion on earth to enable life to develop. Henderson, perhaps the best known defender of the argument,[4] points out that even before life appeared on the earth an enormous number of conditions had come together: the surface had cooled to exactly the right termperature; carbon, oxygen, hydrogen, etc., were present in the right proportions; water and carbonic acid were sufficient; water's property of expanding upon freezing was just what was necessary to prevent rivers and lakes from freezing solid in winter never to unfreeze; its thermal qualities were just right to moderate summer and winter temperatures, etc. etc. This is only a minute fraction of the conditions that can be listed as concurring in a degree that Henderson argues cannot possibly be taken as merely coincidental. He does not himself claim that this proves there *is* a cosmic designer, but many laymen and religious people happily avail themselves of it as evidence for God's existence.

And yet these findings do not really remove the refutation of the argument from design — when it assumes SM, that is. For the problem of evil remains, prompting the question, "why is the environment so *un*fit for life?" For the world is obviously not the entirely perfect environment static good implies, causing a great deal of pain and destruction of life too. Also the Darwinian theory, we saw, cuts under this argument against coincidence by explaining how life might develop by chance mutations and survival of the fittest out of many kinds of environment. The reason the kind of life we have on earth so beautifully "fits" the environment it lives in could be simply that it is the automatic product of that kind of environment, all forms that didn't fit having died out.

However, we saw in Chapter IX how DM-DR moves to a rather

different notion of purposiveness in the finite realm: from SM's idea of conforming to a pre-existent essence, with means exactly adapted to ends, to the more adventurous picture of creating patterns of resolution out of whatever happens to be offered.

How does this affect our conception of cosmic purpose? Must we think of God as having specifically pre-designed all things?

> Is the world purposive in the sense of being purposed? Has it a design in the sense of being *designed?* If so, we must introduce the notion of *mind,* and think of the world movement as something planned or designed by a mind which can imagine in advance an end or purpose, and in some way *will* it, or create it, or cause it to come into being. The world would exist, then, first as *idea,* and our tendency would be to think of the idea as a kind of efficient cause . . . of the coming of the world into being.[5]

But if we extrapolated from DR's conception of experimental problem solving, the divine purposing mind in this sense might not have to be thought of as an anthropomorphic, external mind, making the world as a watchmaker makes a watch. It could be thought of as immanent in the world, a mind within the world directing the world as the human mind directs its own body. This way of thinking would lessen our need to suppose that some final purposed state has required that preceding existence be set up just so, and that it must succeed in being achieved before we can be sure that mind is really in control of nature. Instead of thinking of the divine mind as specifically blue-printing all events, and having to see whether the final outcome fits the blueprint or not, we need only look at the present situation, its ingredients, its field-tensions, its processes, to see whether wholes or designs that resolve problems are *being* produced, and whether these wholes show the ability to govern or organize their parts toward accomplishment of harmonies. The emphasis is not on whether things look as though they were pre-arranged with some end in view; as on whether we here and now find effortful, creative process going on that finds interesting solutions to problems that turn up. The problems may turn up as arbitrarily as they wish.

If the finite processes reveal these characteristics, we may then pass to the question whether the cosmos or the universe altogether shows any signs of being a single energy field that is creating solutions to problems too. We have seen that, within the bounds of the earth, smaller fields resolving tensions are capable of fusing into larger fields resolving more complex tensions and achieving more complex, inclusive patterns. Is there any reason for setting a boundary to this tendency toward inclusiveness at any particular magnitude? Why would not the presumption be that the including of field patterns continues on up to the all-inclusive field?

We find several thinkers in science and philosophy feeling themselves driven, by purely physical considerations, to the necessity for an overall field that keeps all the sub-fields in some optimum degree of organization. Northrop has a theory of "the macroscopic atom."[6] Reiser[7] speaks of the "Cosmic Lens" or the "Cosmic Imagination" etc. Whitehead[8], approaching the idea of God from the notion of reality as essentially "composition," or an aesthetic process of organizing elements into patterns, work out his famous theory of the Primordial and Consequent natures of God. In a sense this means that the cosmic Being too arises as a process of incorporating ingredients (the Primordial) and working out accomplished patterns (the Consequent) from them. Thus we pass by way of the notion of aesthetic pattern in individual things, to aesthetic pattern in the universe, which is cosmic purpose.

The metaphysical doctrine, here expounded, finds the foundations of the world in aesthetic experience, rather than — as with Kant — in the cognitive and conceptive experience. All order is therefore aesthetic order, and the moral order is merely certain aspects of aesthetic order. The actual world is the outcome of the aesthetic order, and the aesthetic order is derived from the immanence of God.[9]

Thus DR tends to clear the way for the possibility of *purpose* at a cosmic level, a purpose, moreover, that is in very real contact with the individual creatures. For the overall field would "guide" all things just as any smaller field guides its components.

However, as long as the static idea of value is maintained, it remains logically impossible to say that this purpose is both *really* cosmic, in the sense of omnipotent, *and* good or omnibenevolent, at once. The problem of evil, as we have seen, remains to force all thinkers working with this combination (SM and DR) either to limited God doctrines, or to humanism and agnosticism. In Chapter IV, we suggested that most or all of the popular philosophies of our day fall into this class — our positivisms and realisms, pragmatisms, existentialisms, and even personalistic idealism. Our great enterprise has been to see whether we can get farther than these toward meaningfulness.

2. Problems of Knowledge. In Chapter VI, we noted tentative grounds in new theories of holistic field states of the brain for taking intuitional and mystical insights more seriously than Russell, for instance, will do. A possibility is opened up, after you have been reviewing separate strands of thought, in a normal workaday fashion and understanding them well enough, that the grasping of them altogether might constitute a further step in real though different knowing, and one that would require a special exercise of brain stuff. All other organs of the body achieve their highest functions only after special practice and regimen. Most great experiences come as consummations of effortful learning to grasp or control many factors together in some excellent order and skill. Why should we be surprised that divine meanings should be seizable only occasionally when millions of brain cells have achieved a precarious but wonderful crystallization?

Our thought that the knowing process, like possibly every natural process in existence, begins in undifferentiated wholeness, passes through a differentiation accompanied by a certain amount of confusion and loss of wholeness, and then works itself by stages back to a definite, organized wholeness, provides, we have suggested, loci for two moments of holistic intuition. One would be the prior phase of vague awareness, lacking any specific concepts or proofs of anything, yet pregnant with mystery, profundity, conviction of the serious importance and meaning of life. The other would be the final return to wholeness, with a certain, always finite, number of details definitely worked out and incorporated into the design, but still surrounded by the original penumbra of vague meaning and grandeur (cf. p. 137 f.) There is also the moment of creative synthesis at the hypothesis stage, with an intuitional nature. These conceptions, originally suggested in gestalt studies of sensory functioning, in being thus expanded to the whole brain field, or to the entire contents of organic life, remind us that we should hardly have expected knowledge of God to arise out of so limited a part of our awareness as is encompassed by the rationalistic "proofs" of God's existence, confined as they are to some relatively superficial nerve tracts on top of the brain. Discrete propositions must be too limited for such a conviction. The existential thesis that the whole concrete living of life with all of its feeling, despair and recovery from despair is a minimal foundation for awareness of God, must be brought in. And the thesis of the mystics, that we must cultivate a direct awareness of the All, must be added. Nothing less would appear commensurate with the magnitude of what we are aspiring to know.

An important ingredient in the total awareness of any individual must be the contribution of the historical and social experience of the human race. Presumptively the experience of a single finite being, excluding what he receives from many others, would hardly be able to gather and organize enough of the data. And conceivably there might be periods of history when analytic and synthetic awareness stand in more optimal relationship than at other times. These periods might then be expected to contribute especially valuable "data" and suggestions to holistic truth for the religious conclusions of individuals who follow. This approach seems to me the most valid reason to set any special store by the Biblical record in coming to our conclusions as to the existence of God; or any special store by the Greek period, or Italian Renaissance, or any other "great" period, as particularly important for setting any other kind of standards, for that matter. We might argue that the "Revelation" had to be delivered when it was, because truths of personal, social and religious wisdom could only be discovered when human life was not yet too buried under detail for them to be disentangled. The early beliefs may not have been so much false as merely relatively unanalyzed, corresponding thus roughly to our "first" phase of development. The outlines may have been sound enough. To compare a modern "religion," for instance Nazism, concocted from items snatched rather blindly out of the welter of modern biological and social science, with Biblical religion suggests that the less knowledgeable Hebrews had included and balanced the principles of life more adequately than such modern "experts." On this ground, then, we might give considerable weight to the age-old conviction that there is a meaningful purpose behind existence, when it comes to adopting our own supreme beliefs.

This holistic conviction can begin to operate, both in more limited areas of knowledge, and in the area of religious belief, before the detailed reasonings or the intellectual proofs are finished and perfected — which state, in a dynamic view, we do not expect them to reach anyway. Also our thesis that the knowing process begins in a vague awareness of meaningfulness would imply that one might retain such a conviction throughout, however much his confusions among the details in the second stage might temporarily seem to contradict it. The reasons why any man *could* doubt the existence of a God would have to be, from this point of view, what we listed in the first chapter: first, his losing this prior sense of the whole through excessive fragmentation of his mind in analytic experience; and secondly and only *after* this has happened, becoming too focussed on the intellectual contradictions, i.e., the other two problems of mechanism and evil, which arise from the static errors that tend to follow so closely upon men's first efforts to analyze experience. But if we, as people have done throughout history, retained the direct, mystical awareness as superior to any of our formulations, we would not necessarily have to be so unhappy about the negative results of our reasonings. They are persuasive and preëmptive only in the absence of whole, personal awareness, a knowledge that should surpass all of our precise descriptions of it. Anyone who can commune with his deeper awareness would find the ratiocination valuable only as a means of eliminating errors and refining concepts. He would keep the contradictions between inherited dogmas, and new but equally partial "scientific data," in their place, toiling conscientiously to reduce them, but not having necessarily to be without God during the interim (except insofar as to pass through some amount of darkness and despair to "salvation" is required for experiencing God's reality anyway).

The third stage of knowledge, the attaining of a more definite synthesis, should not be conceived as having to wait upon the perfect completion of logical and empirical proofs before it begins to operate. It is a sense of conviction, but not entirely dependent upon intellectual conviction. But, let me hasten to add, lest I be accused of anti-scientism, the distinction is not between ordinary knowing and some kind of clairvoyance; it is only the difference between dealing with one-way sequences between part sensations, causes, ideas, versus contemplating the design of all the parts together infused with an appreciation of arrangement and meaning. This appreciation, then can begin before intellectual proofs are perfected, though it bears some relationship to that kind of mental effort. For the more confident we are in the accuracy of our separate strands of causal knowledge, the happier we are when those strands out of their own nature, so to speak, begin to take their place in a greater and greater interwoven order. Although the emerging pattern may not be what we were taught to expect (i.e., the SM-DR contradiction still troubles us) we nonetheless feel religious wonder welling up around the still unfinished scientific picture.

For me, the best paradigm of this relationship on a smaller scale was again my experience in a biology course (cf. Ch. XII). Passing beyond the myopic absorption in the separate parts of bodies, so prosaic and even repulsive in themselves, and becoming able to comprehend their unitary organization in the dynamic whole, a *mysterium tremendum* began to reverberate in spite of the fact that the course was being taught on a mechanistic basis, and many of the students could not get beyond the conviction that the body had been proven worth no more than an epidemic of ribald jokes.

So our awareness of the whole is restored (only in part, of course), but now it filled out to a degree with definitely known and organized detail. This later Gestalt may not be in any essential contradiction to the earlier, vaguer views. There are many evidences that current discoveries of organismic science are assuming a shape that surely would be more recognizable by the Hebrew prophets, Aristotle or St. Thomas than were the spectres of mechanism, or even idealism.

We have not, however, in this claim that knowledge of the existence of God should be expected to involve a much more total reaction than the mere manipulation of concepts by the intellect, settled the main objection of positivistic critics. They will probably grant the possibility of holistic states of mind which might be quite worth striving for merely for the sake of private enjoyment. But the question always remains, how can these mental states testify to the existence of any objective correlate or God beyond themselves? And there is always the fact that mystics and enthusiasts have testified throughout history to the existence of things that finally turned out to be erroneous. The sheer tremendousness of the experience as such does not seem to qualify as verification of objective actualities.

At this point DR's theory of mystical awareness, in contrast to SM-SIR's belief in intuitive certainty, or quasi-magical direct visions of God, self-authenticating and independent of all ordinary experience, must admit that the mystical experience does stand in need of further steps of verification. We mentioned above, and in Chapter VI that the mystical intuition may also be thought of as occupying the "hypothesis" spot in the general method of knowledge: the most all-inclusive, synthetical "induction" available to man. As such it requiries the training and practice which we have argued, against Russell, to be relevant to its conceiving. Ordinary scientific hypotheses themselves are nowadays reaching such levels of complexity that they require specially elevated states of mind to conceive. How much more then should the hypothesis of God require! Yet these great ideas still need verifying!

The synthetic hypothesis, then, is intimately connected to the analytic thinking and the accumulation of specific knowledge in former cycles of scientific thought. The vision does not flash independently out of the blue, but is partly constituted out of special experiences and thought. The value of the insight is the better, the more adequate the data and organization that have gone into it. And although in conceiving the insight our minds are functioning more deeply and vividly than ordinary, this still does not guarantee its correctness. DR, then, accepts that the God hypothesis should subject itself to verification procedures as much as possible, as any knowledge must, though verification of such a broad belief would presumably require so much experience as never to be completed in this life. Perhaps the most we could be sure of accomplishing was the negative project of removing such parts of the great conviction as were definitely contradicted by evidence. A complete positive verification might only be approached through the total living of life.

Perhaps, though, we can do a little better than that. We saw that the conceptions of the space-time continuum, the quantum, the electron, etc. are no more directly observable that of God. But we understand that these complex theories already possess some verification when they are first conceived. Insofar as they correlate and pull together into coherent, logical systematization many previously verified theories, we "add those verifications unto them." Our mystic conviction of the existence of God, then, might already take up into itself hosts of other experiences and the hypotheses they supported, deriving that much verification from them. The "coherence" test would be much involved at this point.

But scientists usually demand some additional verification: some observables *other* than those we started with should be deducible and testable — Einstein's bent star-light for instance. A religious man at this point might fall back on the testing that William James was ready to admit: the general effects on his subsequent life and spirit of "cosmic confidence." We concluded in Chapter VI, however, that this test should not be permitted except for hypotheses that had first passed the "correspondence" and "coherence" tests.

But here for SM-DR we come back to the intellectual contradictions (#1). The God hypothesis conceived on the basis of SM *does not correspond nor cohere with the objective evidence of DR!* The mystical insights that produced the traditional idea of God are not verified by our findings. The contradiction, in fact, is becoming so evident in modern times that mystical experiences, however possible for man — at least those in terms of static ideas — to-day seem to be broken up before they can even be had tentatively, and we hear reports of very few of them. Or we see, I think, quite a few sad cases of those who thought they had known God, but then lost confidence that they had.

We have, then, to return to our intellectual work in DM, before we can find a God hypothesis which at least presents no definite contradictions to modern evidence, and thus by that much will support our mystical convictions, making it at least possible that we have knowledge of an objective reality.

3. Nature of God. However much conviction of religious reality DR might be able to arrive at through holistic insight, the lack of entire agreement between SM and DR on the nature of purpose, and the problem of evil, would still prevent belief in *cosmic* good purpose. This position, then, issues, at most, in theories of a limited God, as we said above; more often in humanism or agnosticism. William James, Brightman and others defend the first. Other pragmatists and existentialists are usually agnostic and humanist. Marxism is atheistic. The literary world remains mostly apathetic on the whole question.

But the limited God view, as the best that SM-DR can offer, has, I will always maintain, already relinquished the pearl of great price: the sense of wondrous purpose and meaning behind the very substance of reality itself. To concede a pointless "given," unrequired, unintended by any divine understanding, as the basic content of things, always blindly producing its haphazard evils, definitely loses the deepest sense of holy meaningfulness and inspiration. This inadequacy leaves us exposed to that possibility of degeneration in the human spirit which constitutes our most pressing motivation for pushing on to seek a truly cosmic purpose.

DM with DR.

1. Intellectual Contradictions. We saw in Part II, that in the more advanced cycles of scientific method, more and more inclusive and complex hypotheses are conceived which, upon test, become theories which offer a kind of limited answer to the question "why" for all subordinate theories or phenomena which are deducible from the broader theory. That is, we can understand a relationship of logical "requirement" from the inclusive theory to the subordinate theory or the phenomena. However, for theories of the external world we never arrive at any *ultimate* reason or answer to the question why; we are finally left with a blank assertion that things just "are" as they are. For instance, if, as many scientists and philosophers think today, the ultimate generalization or theory of objective science is the concept of "process," and that every existing theory or phenomena of the external world is an instance or exemplification of the concept of process, and that this idea of process explains "why" all subordinate ideas and phenomena are as they are, we are still left with no answer as to "why" everything is process; process remains a mere blank given, something that just *is*, with no further explanation why it is.

I have suggested that any ultimate reason for things, if there is any, would have to be a concept of value, good. What is needed is to be able to show that all reality, as science knows it, is "required" or can be logically deduced from an idea of value. Or, in other words, that the idea of process (the summary of the nature of reality) be able to be deduced from the idea of value.

In the DM sections all through the bock, then, we have been finding how the idea of process itself and thence all other details in DR can be logically deduced from a dynamic idea of value or good. This conception of the nature of good experience is itself an empirical product, arising from a proper study of the directly experienced feelings of human beings. I have taken this conception then as an ultimate metaphysical principle, from which statements of logical requirement can be made. Just as the larger scientific theories enable us to see *why* the more limited theories and data are as they are, so the theory of feeling and enjoyment (coming from the second kind of science, p. 127) provides an ultimate answer "why" for the whole of reality.

The contradictions between our idea of meaningfulness, and our findings about reality are thus eliminated in principle when

544

the two are conceived dynamically. This is to demolish the dis-proofs of cosmic good purpose upon which agnostics and atheists rely: the problem of mechanism by a reinterpretation of the facts in recent science; the problem of evil by a reinterpretation of the nature of value. The existence of a fully cosmic, omnipotent purpose for *(dynamic)* good thus becomes logically *permissible*.

2. The Problem of Knowledge of God. But have we logically and positively proved the existence of such a cosmic purpose? The author does not claim that we have. To be sure, we now have a God hypothesis that "fits" far more coherently with the evidence than the former one. But like all theories forthcoming from this knowledge method, it can not be considered certain. This God idea still shares with the ideas of electron or gravity a lack of direct observability. We draw implications from it as to what *should* be observed, and do find much of that. But it remains a logical non-sequitur to say that, *if* there were a divine purposer of dynamic good, He could be expected to create just such a world as we find, and therefore finding such a world proves that it did come from such a purposer. This is the fallacy of "affirming the consequent," and although all science confesses to committing it when it "believes" in its constructs, scientists and religionists alike must admit the absence of certain proof at this point. Also, we must admit not knowing empirically what the nature of reality is throughout all the reaches of the universe, and therefore whether it is everywhere as it should be to fit DM. And although the dynamic idea of good gives us strong ammunition against the problem of evil, it seems we can never be intellectually certain that the amount of evil which exists *is* just the "right" amount, or the optimum that would testify to the "best" divine designer. In other words, positive proof of God's existence apparently cannot be had from arguing from design, since we cannot say just how much design is the minimum requirement, nor measure amount of design there is, nor be sure that design might not just happen without any cosmic Creator.

We are thrown back, then, upon our claim that the conviction of God's existence should not be expected to be a merely intel-lectual resolution. The dynamic idea of good itself implies that knowledge of God *should not* be attainable by so superficial and soon-finished a method as mere observation and formulation of partial theories about the external environment, to which positivistic scientists confine themselves. Such knowledge *should* be a more living thing than that; it *should* be as much more holistic, experiential, concrete and dynamic as we saw above that DR indicated.

And if awareness of meaning and God must be such a total, simultaneous encompassment of dynamic experience, we should not be surprised to find it ineffable and confined to our highest moments. This is why degrees of effort and special cultivation of faculties are pertinent to discovering and feeling God. That religious awareness should accompany and reward efforts to refresh and clear the mind, then, should not strike Russell as an artificial feature of it. This is only the ultimate application of our new conception of good: aspiration and striving are indispensable for the creation of harmonies. Even Russell ought to be capable of drawing a distinction between abnormal conditions resulting from sharpening and purging the mind of obstructions and distortions; and those resulting from dulling it and throwing it into a chaos. It is amazing that he should fail to see a difference between breathing exercises that increase organic efficiency and alcohol that decreases it. The fluid currents of the organism cannot effect these balances often, nor hold them when they are reached. The mystic is left with a memory of a great insight which he cannot doubt, though he may not be able to reproduce it at will. As for others failing to capture it when they "put themselves into the situation in which the mystic's vision occurred," we can no longer be surprised at this when we understand the vision as a highly practiced skill rather than Rusell's perception of single particular phenomena.

These moments, we might also expect, cannot be conveyed in words or propositions. Words must fall into linear sequence; they tell one thing at a time, whereas this reality is a totality-at-once. No amount of talking around it will recreate it, or prove it. No chapter on knowledge of God can force the conviction into another's mind. Each individual must cultivate the immediate conviction for himself. We are here not merely retreating from Russell's demand for precise proof with our tail between our legs. We are giving a positive reason for the absence of strict proof.

Finally, there is also an implication from DM to the necessity for our relation to God to be on the basis of *faith*, rather than of finished knowledge. But we mean faith in the same way that science itself uses it: faith on the basis of a preponderance of the evidence, faith as readiness to act without certainty just for the purpose of creating a little additional verification through the act itself! We can *expect* God not to show himself fully prior to our act, but only *in* the act, in the process itself.

What our resolution of the contradictions under #1 should be understood as accomplishing, then, is to open the way for ventures in religious faith and experience. We are being told, "Now there is no proof of the absence of God; He might be found to exist if you cared to seek Him. Surely it is now worth your while to start the search by entering into the concrete struggle itself."

When one sees that an omnipotent, omnibenevolent God could not be expected to create a perfect universe, but rather something exceedingly like what we find in reality, does it not begin to seem rather perverse self-deprivation to refuse to make at least a try for the living experience of knowing Him?

3. Nature of God. Confining our remarks under this topic, as we said we would, to mere hints of what views seemed consonant with the dynamic approach, we will begin by claiming that the dynamic God obviously suggested finds considerable support in Biblical literature. The great stipulation that led me to the dynamic idea of value was that God must be defended as the truly *cosmic* Creator of all reality. With the problem of evil resolved as dynamic good allows it to be, the biblical idea of God as the purposing Mind designing all existence, yet who continues to act within it, even changing it, becomes permissible, not to say convincing. But the Greek importation into this biblical picture of a creator of *a priori* perfection, or of a realm of finished Being, must be deported again. The image of a God whose mind is concerned only with abstract, perfect and unchanging essences roots back, of course, in the static idea of value. The dynamic idea of value ultimately issues in giving preëminent reality to the concrete, that is to the intersection of the many in the one, and to its felt development. Thus again it points to the Biblical God who is nothing if not concerned with concrete, specific events. "The most real" for dynamic thinking is the fully concrete rather than the abstract. This would suggest that God Himself must be conceived more concretely than abstractly.

If this approach may seem to point in a pantheistic direction — that God is the concrete universe itself — it also would provide a hospitable framework for belief in a God who might do such a thing as perform special acts of concrete revelation, such as are recorded in the Old and New Testaments. Of course, my approach has been naturalistic, so that I would have to understand God's work in e.g. Jesus Christ as involving all the natural and cultural forces of that age, making use of the notion mentioned above (p. 539) that certain points in history reach optimum conditions for the general creative process, so that it succeeds in producing at that moment something particularly adequate. Since all creative process must in this view be seen as part of divine creation, any doctrine of Christ's special revelation of God's nature would have to be grounded in the special superiority of that portion of creative process. But my view has no difficulty in believing that God would be specially manifest in such a thoroughly concrete phenomenon as a human life.

But no doubt I am subject to the age-old criticism hinted above: that insofar as this approach falls toward pantheism, I am besmirching God with evil, dirt and the rest of the repulsive things in the universe which fastidious idealists have hated to associate with Him. But who can deny that the supreme project of modern thought — to bring the scientific world view under a religiously meaningful belief — demands a large shift from the traditional transcendent God toward an immanent God? We cannot locate God "up there" or "out there," in our present kind of universe, as Bishop Robinson's much-read *Honest to God*[10] seems to have stirred some newly extended tracts of believers to admit, and it is hard to resist associating Him with that creative energy itself of which we are now told that all things consist. And the dynamic idea of good, to my mind, removes the last reason for being reluctant to let God have any contacts with evil. Not that I am not willing to have Him associated more especially with the creative energy's tendency to resolve evils; but, as I will discuss a bit more in the next chapter, I am clear that God was not concerned to make evil impossible within His energy.

Personally, I am unsatisfied at this point with even so "modern" a treatment as Tillich's of God's relationship to the concrete Existence we experience. Concerned as he is, like myself, to bring meaningfulness, holiness, depth back into our lives, Tillich still seems to conceive existence only as a falling away from the realm of essence, and denies any ultimate logical necessity for existence at all, let alone a fallen away one. Even though he exhibits existence as now of integral concern to the divine mind, one still feels a rueful tone in his discussion, the same one that has been present throughout the history of Christian theology, confessing the inability to understand why God ever allowed the existent world to happen, bringing all its frustrations, antinomies, disunities. The static idea of good assuredly lurks behind this characterizing of existence as fundamentally representing destruction, estrangement, pride — especially when we catch the hidden feeling that it all might as well never have been. Man's salvation consists of a return to his essence, and never loses its flavor as a kind of guilty making amends, a pointless and tiresome repairing of an accident that should never have occurred at all.

The dynamic idea of good, on the other hand, makes Existence absolutely necessary, absolutely integral in God's only purpose of having Value be. Man does not distort himself gratuitously into Existence. God intends and creates him in it; and at the bottom, too, so he may rise, not at the top from which he can only fall. This approach imparts to the creation a positive character, for the basic thought is *building*. And I do not at all admit that I am trying to escape from recognizing that existence is full of dark and despair. I claim to know of that as much as any "crisis" theologian; but I see no need to feel rueful and lugubrious about it. In the next chapter I will indicate how this attitude toward our imperfection or sin fits with what psychiatry seems to consider healthier and more conducive to moving forward than the traditional shame.

The process philosophies, on the other side, take process as the original fact rather than a realm of perfect essences. But still wedded to a static idea of value, we have seen them follow in the steps of Plato, if they arrive at a doctrine of God at all, and espouse a limited god struggling with a brute Given, not of matter but of process itself which, left alone, is as apt to produce evil as good. Now it is not man but the energy itself that causes separation from God. Whitehead's Platonic God is a principle of limitation upon formless creativity. God is "in the grip of the ultimate metaphysical ground."[11] Of course since God himself is proceeding from His primordial to his consequent phases, He may be almost all inclusive. Yet these activities of His seem to be performed upon an already existing process or creativity. When the latter produces errors or mishaps, these are outside of God's design, and He is compelled to cope with them as best He can, to wrest good from them.

Laird, defending the view that process is ultimate and need

not be explained, admits that no answer is thus given to "why" it exists.

> I may seem to have paid too little attention . . . to the question *why* and *how* there was the creation of the universe; and similarly regarding its emanation. The reason was that I was trying to show that existence itself, even God's must be held to be in a certain sense a creative process and that such creation or emanation is ultimate.[12]

> Evidently, therefore, there is the greatest possible disparity between the theory that all that there is, including God, is in process just because it is in being, and the usual Christian doctrine that the world of becoming is generated or created by an ingenerable uncreated being who does not himself become or proceed but is "above" process as well as "above" the world. . . .[13]

I again maintain that there is a vast and important difference between saying with Laird that "things are in process because they are in being" and saying that "things are in process because the nature of value requires it." The latter gives a reason why in a sense that the former does not. I for one am aware of a chasm separating the two when I consider my experience of meaning and holiness. It requires that I realize purposive value as ultimate rather than brute fact, and only the dynamic idea of good can accomplish this to-day.

If it be argued that this still permits only a limited God, limited by the given nature of good, I again feel a wide chasm between being limited by brute fact and limited by the nature of value. In seeking a meaningful world, one surely requires a God who *is* limited by the nature of value. To give up that limit is to give up the meaningfulness itself that one had begun by stipulating. We stop short of answering "why" for the nature of good itself only because it is itself the ultimate why we were looking for.

Laird predictably, then, settles for the figure of God the Potter versus God the Creator:

> The potter may be a limited creator in the sense in which a great artist may be a limited creator; but he operates upon

a preëxistent material and is limited by the capacities of such material.[14]

But we can say that God created the clay as well as shaped it. He created the clay shapeless on purpose; it had to be without shape in order for the good experience of becoming shaped to be wrought in it. This is the image of God portrayed by the author of Genesis. The second verse of the Bible tells us the earth was first created "waste and void" and thereafter it was shaped.

> . . . if it is to be a "serious" enterprise [the universe must] start from a condition as remote as possible from its goal, a condition namely in which there is as much incoherence and confusion as there can possibly be.[15]

Other questions about God's nature might be listed with only a sentence or two of rejoinder:

Is God to be conceived as separate from, and prior to, the process, a preëxisting mind? The only thesis I am concerned to defend here is that good purpose is *logically* prior to existence as process, and not just a by-product that it occasionally produces existentially. This does not necessarily imply a dated creation or God's existence prior to the creation in time. The divine Mind may be embodied eternally in the process, His concern for value continuously sustaining it.

Is God coextensive with the process? Does He grow, too, experiencing His good as all creatures do? Or does He contemplate from the beginning, as He does in Aristotle and Hegel, the essences or forms in which the process is to culminate? The conception of an adventurous, experimental process, of emergent evolution, as opposed to Aristotelian return to preëxisting form, seems to favor the belief that God starts (if not at an absolute "beginning" in the above "eternal" process, then perhaps in ever new beginnings) with a bare minimum of conditions for moral development. The dynamic idea of value as inherent in *genuine* creation, i.e., genuine experimental problem-solving, seems to militate against theories of fore-knowledge or omniscience (and I would deny that this subtracts at all from God's cosmic dimension). God, then does not need to be thought of as knowing in detail, ahead of time, all that will happen. Creation would be a career of invention that God is constantly engaged in. It becomes natural to think of Him as deriving his own enjoyment from His success in working out harmonies after disorders, out of the risks and triumphs of an unguaranteed struggle. God may be the absolute Creator of all reality, having imposed upon it its general structure and energy. But He may still have to wait to behold what concrete adventures, beauties and good can be actualized from moment to moment under these conditions (cf. Lawrence p. 342). And it was through no accident or incompetence that He originally wrought it abounding in disorders. This again brings us close to the Biblical picture of a God whose interest is excited by new events and creations in every epoch; and who is at pains from time to time to exert himself to save the whole show by some emergency ingenuity from debacle.

No doubt the Bible implies that God can guarantee that the whole process of processes does not end up in ruin and failure. Men perhaps can not bear this possibility in the nature of their God. What I said in the discussion of evil about the necessity of real risk might seem to bind me to the non-guaranteed status of God's work. But I confess to wishing to believe that God can save what needs to be saved if one universe "wears out"; and that he is never without resource for starting another.

Hartshorne speaks as I have been doing here, using love rather than the dynamic idea of good as his ultimate concept. But I would certainly not object to labelling the dynamic idea of good as "love."

> The theist . . . has the key to facts and the key to values in a single idea, since participation, i.e., love, is traditionally recognized as in some manner the supreme ethical standard. To find the key to facts and values in the same principle is, I submit, an intellectual achievement than which none could be greater.[16]

I recommend Hartshorne's book for a more thorough discussion of the relation of the "neo-classical", i.e., dynamic, cosmology and theology to the older static one than I have space for here. But I might give a hint or two about what might become of static essences in our view. Whitehead expounds his "Eternal Objects" and Santayana his "Essences", both conceived as eternal, unchanging entities contained either in God's primordial nature, or subsisting in some realm of their own. Actual events combine a certain selection of these essences, such as redness, triangularity, weight, and aim at others for their future. For Aristotle and Hegel, essences are the true forms of things, latent in the germ, to be achieved in the unfolding of predirected process. In orthodox Christianity man was created initially in his perfect essence, then fell, and now is seeking to recover his pristine form. The doctrine has been used to explain why anything bothers to strive out of its existing condition at all: it envisages somehow its true form and is attracted toward it. But this is a static and purely ideational concept of desire and striving. The end in view is disconnected from the present dynamic condition of strained feeling.

We have seen that the dynamic view implies God's purposely creating existence as process from the first. Good cannot be imagined as preëxisting, unchanging essence, since its sole and entire being lies in process. Thus, we do not need essences in the original creation; and perhaps we do not need them either as ideals to be selected in the future. What happens seems more like a solving of actual present tensions, frustrations, problems. The aim of processes is closely related to present, dynamically felt discomfort of a very special, concrete sort. It is a very concrete direction implied by these existing forces, rather than an arbitrary election of some ideal fom a floating realm of ready-made essences. What looks like an eternal form appears to be rather a successful solution of a problem, and if it seems to be often repeated, this must mean that the originating conditions are often repeated resulting in many similar solutions of the same sort of problem. When conditions change, a new solution will be evolved, but it will be generated out of the particular conglomeration of factors existence presents, and not out of a realm of essences. Existence precedes essence.

Hartshorne has an amusing characterization of what any doctrine of preëxisting essences, and prior divine omniscience is saying: it is giving us a doctrine of duplication.

> . . . if process is not (in some degree) always creation, what is it? This was Bergson's point, still poorly digested in philosophy. If it is only ignorance of causes which prevents us from mentally seeing the effect in advance, then the entire character of "coming events" is real beforehand. Before events happen, they lack nothing except a totally transparent, featureless something called "actual occurrence." . . . If becoming

does not create new quality and quantity, new determinateness, then, we argue, it creates nothing, and nothing ever really becomes. . . . A causal destiny, no less determinate than what happens, is just the happening twice over, once as already true but not yet real, and then as true and also real.[17]

One form of teleology that we are, I think, well rid of is the notion of a single absolute world-plan, complete in every detail from all eternity, and executed with inexorable power. The objection is not solely that God would be made responsible for the imperfect adaptations and discords in nature. There is the further objection that the world process would be the idle duplicate of something in eternity. A god who eternally knew all that the fulfillment of his purpose would bring could have no need of the fulfillment of that purpose.[18]

Here is an existentialism, then, that sees no conflict between creative responsibility in man, and the presence of cosmic purpose. The evil of the world does not drive it to the despairing negations of atheistic existentialism, nor to the queer hope of inspiring men to heroic sacrifice within an absurd and nauseous reality. The life of struggle and decision is now seen as quite appropriate for the content of the cosmic creator's work; in fact, only such a life would be worthy of divine creation. Religion does not have to mean the inert dependence upon a coddling miracle-worker that post-war sophisticates assume it to be. There can be a God who means tragic situations to exist, but who stands ready to enable us to bring great experiences out of them, as we never shall by merely striking heroic attitudes on the edge of an abyss of meaninglessness. A humble conviction of the holy grandeur of that which contains us will be more efficacious in steeling us against weakness than a pride in our own firmness wedded to a basic despising of the world and life.

CHAPTER XX

EFFECT ON THE HUMAN SPIRIT

Our sequence of topics culminates logically in that fateful practical question with which we began: what can the dynamic resolution do about saving man from the disintegration he sinks into to-day, when the old faiths leave his mind too doubtful and divided, and the materialistic philosophy too despairing, to appropriate very much of the inspiration or power that may await him somewhere in this cosmos?

Three topics, then, remain to review our positions upon:

1. The emotional feeling about life, the inspiration or lack of it, that results from the conclusions under the preceding topic concerning the existence of God and Meaning.

2. The effects on Man's behavior of such beliefs and feelings. Included here will be brief reviews of theories of salvation, if any, under the positions.

3. Beliefs about Man's ultimate destiny, and further effects upon his behavior emanating from them.

If we are right in our suggestion in the preceding chapter that religious knowledge must be approached through steps analogous to those of scientific method, only conceived on the most all-inclusive basis, then the present chapter would occupy the position of Verification, insofar as such beliefs can be verified in finite life. I am taking up the gauntlet which much religion shrinks from accepting: that an adequate religion should show some definite power to produce change for the better in human behavior. I suspect that the rather large failure of much recent religion to do so, which sends many of its believers to psychiatrists for their change and its leadership to doctrines of salvation through the goodness of the saviour rather than through change of the believer, is due in part at least to the unintelligibilities we have analyzed in SM, SIR and SMR.

SM with SIR.

1. Problem of Inspiration. However shaky SIR's foundations for belief may now seem, there was a day when, thanks to the vagueness of men's notions of the facts, the conflicts were not insistent enough to bother their minds. A great structure of belief was erected upon the static foundations, and, at the end of the middle ages, for instance, all things were integrated into a meaningful design. The resulting conviction of divinity and sense of holiness suffusing things is still an ideal that modern man could well "shoot" for. Meaningfulness for us, too, would require our grasping in some degree an intelligible principle of value that requires reality to be as we find it; and our understanding a total design that gives deep significance to each part. Before the conflicts between the static idea of meaning and scientific fact became so obtrusive, Christianity was able to hallow life by explaining why things were as they were. The lower existed for the higher, and all things played an integral role in a great drama of salvation. The creaturely body, daily work, social institutions, art: all thus had mysterious importance, awesome significance.

I hold that such a general feeling about existence is intrinsically productive of a greater energy and conscientiousness in the living of it. And, if one cultivates such conviction, requiring as it does "higher" states of wholeness and focus in the mind, by living prayer, it will be found indispensable for the higher achievements of character. Only, I say, SM with the modern view of the facts cannot produce it.

2. Effects on Behavior (Theory of Salvation). Now the traditional theology, as we saw in Chapter XVIII, had a theory of salvation which was dynamic in itself, although it stood in conflict with other parts of the theology. For an unsatisfactorily explained reason, man had fallen and become a helpless sinner requiring to be restored to what he was in origin. The paradoxes, so loved by theologians, that have swarmed about this conflict have confused thought for millennia. Predestination was defended simultaneously with freedom of will, necessity to sin with responsibility for sinning, a God of wrath with a God of grace and mercy, man as a worm with man as God's image, etc. "Insoluble mystery to be accepted by faith" has been the most usual outcome of argument; or, in recent times, the all-excusing word "paradox." Nevertheless, however confused the theory was, there

556

was never any doubt that men had to seek for all they were worth to get out of the state they were in and into another. The ways and means of changing one's inner state were studied out with the closest attention, and everything from asceticism, monastic living and years of deep meditation to rosaries, believing on Christ and revival meetings were tried and practiced with intensity.

And there is no doubt that transformation was often attained by individuals, and that a smaller or larger number of that kind of Christian which even our cynics cannot debunk was produced. Only the most dogmatic reductivist would deny that there was some elevation of human character during the religious ages. The feelings of rapt wonder and sacred meaningfulness of life, and the various ways of contacting the divine, when practiced with sufficient genuineness, did really produce many instances of that phenomenon our writers refuse to accept as a possibility: transformation for the better. When men felt that, although they were depraved and helpless, yet through their very weakness they were the object of divine concern and grace, they seemed to find more ability to aspire to high things than in other ages when they are assured of their already existing power, but doubt their own significance in the eyes of any divine.

But the static idea of good, underlying all this worship and spiritual attainment, ended by vitiating it. Today those who seek to achieve salvation in these traditional terms must inevitably suffer from a dividedness of mind, a half-heartedness, as their environment of scientific technology, newspaper discussions of human evolution, consultations with psychiatrists, comic book stories of outer galaxies all hint at another world view. Even those who cling to the revival fun in the most obscurantist churches are liable to experience less "salvation" than backsliding, as they return to week-day business that reveals no point of contact with the preacher's parroting of ancient myths. Certainly, these old methods of transformation are so dead for all writers of any stature today, that they almost never mention them, even to ridicule them. They merely pay them the supreme insult: absolute indifference.

But the static formulation is a cause of modern unbelief in a still more direct way: besides not integrally calling for a salvation process in the first place, as we have seen, it also led to unwarranted expectations which prompt unnecessary disappointment on the part of the defectors. It continually led men to expect a much neater and less wasteful world than they presently found; a more spiritual and less bodily human nature than biology revealed; a more precise and less haphazard providence than modern life testifies to. This expectation still lurks behind the glumness of nihilists. As Randall says:

> That we have dropped the search for a purpose is in large part due to the too easy finding of purposes in all things that marked scholasticism.[1]

We have also seen how these expectations were held by the secular utopians with even less qualification than by Christian theorists. They dropped even orthodoxy's creaky theory that man had become a sinner, and began to look for him to be perfect without any transformation at all. This demand for perfection is another way of naming the root cause of the modern sickness.

3. Human Destiny. The tradition's holding out of a promise of eternal life of more or less static bliss was perhaps even more motivational to conscientious living than its belief in God. As far as Christian orthodoxy is concerned, it often looks as though every part of the theology could be doubted with impunity except the story of the resurrection of Jesus, and its supposed relevance to the immortality of other men. At Christianity's height, in the middle ages, this part of religion could monopolize minds to such an extent that everything we materialists to-day find most attractive became unreal compared to the dream of the next world.

Yet in the heyday of that static heaven, many could wonder in their off moments whether the unending and unvarying bliss of Paradise or the dreadful but at least exciting pains of hell were the more unbearable prospect. Perhaps it was the hope of seeing one's departed loved ones again that did most to make Heaven desirable, even more than the hope of escaping death oneself. And perhaps this is still the part of the ancient belief that supplies most of the dynamic it is still capable of. Many still feel that the only way for Reality to be Meaningful would be for it to culminate in immortality for themselves and their loved ones. For life, no matter how grandly complex in its development, to issue in discontinuation seems self-evidently pointless; to make the wonderful creativity, however glorious, meaningless.

But it is precisely the resurrection materials that are easiest for SMR to tear to shreds in every way. And it is life after death that is the most utterly non-empirical of all concepts. Few of those thoroughly conversant with modern knowledge and its method can be present at an Easter service without considerable distress. Can any thing be found in DM or DR to help?

SM with SMR.

1. Problem of Inspiration. It is important to make explicit what must have been becoming obvious as we pursued the findings of SMR: the outcome of the tremendous thinking prowess of Galileo, Newton and the rest of them was, after all, a dull, flat and un-inspiring picture, at least as far as all other sides of human ex-perience than the mathematical was concerned.

But it was of the greatest consequence for succeeding thought that now the great Newton's authority was squarely behind that view of the cosmos which saw in man a puny, irrelevant spectator . . . of the vast mechanical system whose regular motions according to mechanical principles constituted the world of nature. The gloriously romantic universe of Dante and Milton, that set no bounds to the imagination of man as it played over space and time, had now been swept away. Space was identified with the realm of geometry, time with the continuity of number. The world that people had thought themselves living in — a world rich with colour and sound, redolent with fragrance, filled with gladness, love and beauty, speaking everywhere of purposive harmony and creative ideals — was crowded now into minute corners in the brains of scattered organic beings. The really important world outside was a world of mathematically computable motions in me-chanical regularity. The world of Qualities as immediately perceived by man became just a curious and quite minor effect of that infinite machine beyond. . . .[2]

We need add no further expression of the profane feeling than what we had in the first chapter.

2. Effects on Behavior. We have seen in many connections SMR's lack of basis for any doctrine of higher levels of behavior, of inspiration to it, of salvation, of human transformation in any sense. It determines man to be, first and last, the Darwinian, Freudian brute. Men of course could not quickly accept this in-tolerable doctrine. Before our current writers settled into it with-

559

out any reservation whatever, all kinds of escapes were tried, which we might briefly mention.

We are familiar enough now with the dualist and illusionist methods of idealism to recover some kind of foundation for belief in God. They were, even in their ascendancy, relatively pallid and non-influential with the many. But let us remember more especially the humanist and utopian attempts to base hope and verve upon believing static good was fully present in man's instincts, and let us here inquire about the fate of meaningfulness, holy importance and regeneration under these auspices.

It is true that those who could hold this view without doubts preserved much of the sense of glory and grandeur underlying reality. They could be inspired and sacrificial toilers for the future. They were full of rapt reverence and praise for the ideal creature man. Yet even in the heyday of hope, there was a paradoxical attenuation of the sence of serious, profound, sacred purpose in life. For, in this basically perfect world, where only some superficial perversions were to be eliminated, and where men were instinctively noble and good, there was no place for the mystery and urgency of the salvation drama where God came into immediate and living relationship to sinners. There was not much to do with God but to think hazily of Him occasionally. The Unitarians advised man to save *himself* by conscientious effort. The Deists admired God for starting the perfect machine, and for dealing out eventual rewards and punishments with infinite wisdom, but they had little use for Him between times. The purpose of life changed from being an awesome adventure of salvation, to being the more or less idle enjoyment by good men of the blessings of the perfect world. Such men had little need of calling on God for inspiration, for power to improve. The struggle to surpass one's weakness, then, was largely given up, to be replaced by the calculus of pleasure in utilitarianism. Thus, even on the supposition that utopianism did correspond to the facts, its static character would already lose the essence of holy feeling and aspiring.

But, of course, it fails to be an adequate safeguard of holy importance for the must more massive reason that it was not borne out in experience. These are the illusions that the realists so joyfully debunk — all while continuing to hold that they were what *ought to have been true if God existed*. That Russell thinks this way seems clear enough. The utopians held the only think-able conception of purpose, waited for the only kind of evidence that would demonstrate its existence. He is an atheist because that kind of evidence did not come in. All forms of the idea of cosmic purpose, he says "have in common the conception of evolution as having a direction towards something ethically valuable, which in some sense gives the reason for the long process."[3] His con-sequent perplexity (see p. 499) as to why the Creator bothered with the process at all is founded on the idea that the final good end of the process can be an entity in its own right independently of process, and so might as well have been instituted at the begin-ning as not. When he finds that it not only was not instituted at the beginning, but apparently is not even going to arrive in the foreseeable future, then all meaning is gone, since all meaning is in the end alone, and none in the process.

Let us ask this question also: if it should be true that reality *is* a process of aspiration and striving, and that men must seek inspiration and power from their awareness and belief in cosmic purpose to do tasks which require that they surpass themselves, what will happen when they have discontinued such prayer and training? The optimists did largely stop that kind of discipline. Was there a softening of character which proceeded to invite just the troubles and breakdown which their view had declared un-necessary and had left them without resources to meet? Far from bringing on Utopia, their hope of guaranteed goodness admitted extra evil and thence the bitter debunking. Bertrand Russell as-sumes that men are so far from requiring inspiration and power from a source greater than themselves, that they can carry on human economy upon a basis of despair. (See p. 239). We have a generation of practical men who pride themselves on their courage in facing the comfortless facts. They can be vastly ener-getic in working for satisfactions of their desires, though they have no belief in any holy importance of anything they accomplish. And they assume that their desires are adequate just as nature presents them. They never undertake any regeneration of them-selves and so never discover that this is a task which requires inspiration. Besides at the same time that science is removing the possibility of belief in sacred things, it is filling the world with so many intriguing gadgets that men's attention is diverted enjoyably for a while. There is also the sense of freedom from old taboos, freedom to enjoy the pleasurable things of this life, which obscures

561

for a time the loss of the deeper joys of knowing a meaning for life.

But then comes the experience of ennui with this life in a squirrel cage of succeeding desires and attainments. They would almost ask what is the meaning of it, except that their fellows jeer at the question and tell them to get back to their busyness. But this is the profane living from which we began our thinking. My favorite word for the feel of life when we have lost the consequence and hallowedness which belief in divine purpose gave, is "stuffiness." And these gay, free livers know, somehow, that they are engulfed in an earthbound, prosaic stuffiness and that their "glamour" never comes near the glamour that life would have if it were known to be part of the profound drama of creation. Their own personalities are stuffy, because an essential implication of this view is self-satisfaction. It does not recognize man as unfinished, as needing to meditate humbly upon things greater than himself, so as to be changed. And so, naturally, the greater kinds of personalities are not developed, since no one is even trying to do it.

Then, as the logic of selfish pursuit of this world's goods works itself out, the general economy begins to recede, since men must contribute some surplus to his fellows or fall into a chaos of suspicious, grasping individuals incapable of supporting complex civilization. The death and frustration for which this view has no answer force themselves into view. Men only pursue their self-realization with all the more intensity, trying to crowd the thought of tragedy and death out of consciousness. Thus this godless state cannot maintain itself and must come apart. It is only good for those relatively friendly and secure environments which preceding religious ages bequeath upon their successors. By itself it cannot call up that enthusiasm and power which is requisite to keep life from sinking into that very excess of calamity and misfortune for which this philosophy has no solace. It tells of no meaning which would reconcile men to tragedy, and would supply an enthusiasm and power to recover and maintain kindness and goodwill.

So we come to some of the other philosophical straws at which men clutch as substitutes for a real meaningfulness in life. There is the devotion to truth, to scientific research. Many men seem to be inspired to a selfless labor in grubbing out more and more bits of truth. They hope that this may eventually lead man out of his troubles and conceive it to be the best that can be asked of them. But this does not *create* character nor nourish joyous goodwill, the more necessary and efficacious means to human betterment. If the truth-seekers do possess such traits they are likely to have received them as habits trained into them by Christian parents, certainly not as a result of their cold analysis. Nor does their science help much to replenish the supply of serenity for themselves or to instill it into the third generation.

Then there are those seeking consolation in art and beauty. Art for its own sake is made the ultimate concern of man. But we have seen that art becomes a pallid experience, largely celebrating sterile abstraction and chaos, when not informed by a sense of meaningfulness. And there is the Nietzschean answer: to take nature, with its ruthless survival of the fit, as our model, and to derive enjoyment from the fight itself. In fact Nietzsche goes deep enough to find some meaning for tragedy.

Life for the pessimist is meaningless, the sooner over the better; for the optimist, whose ideal is guaranteed, it is also without essential significance. For Nietzsche, it is hard, it is cruel, it is tragic; but in its very tragedy he found supreme joy. To fight, to lose, perhaps, against great odds, to win for our children; that is the lesson of Nature and Nature's processes.[4]

But even Nietzsche finds no ultimate meaning in the process. He wades into the fight because it is there, and he finds that tragedy gives a depth to life that the shallow utopian expectation does not. But he lacks the power to overcome tragedy, and in the end the fight merely tires him out and leaves him in despair and insanity. He dreamed wistfully of a superman to save us — a strange throwback to the romantic idea of a perfect man. But it was Chaplinesque Hitler and the Nazis that emerged as the supermen.

This reminds us of the glaring contemporary question: how do the communists and fascists seem to do so well on this problem of motivation and inspiration? It now seems clear that in strict logic, dialectical materialism or communism offer nothing but a choice between the prosy meaninglessness of materialism; or the unrealistic dreams of Utopianism; and we have argued that both of these are sentenced to an inexorable downward spiral by their neglect of the problem of regenerating and strengthening individuals.

How then, is it that they seem to succeed so well in inspiring individuals to enthusiastic and sacrificial efforts for the system? Well, certainly part of it is simply the above-mentioned Utopian enthusiasm — the hope for final consummation in the near future, that lasts as long as such static faith can be kept alive; but which is doomed to attenuation by the passage of time with indefinite postponement of the perfectionistic outcome. Another part of their dynamic is dependent upon avoiding recognition of communism's imperfection and failure by blaming the other side for all shortcomings. Still another basis for the enthusiasm is their quasi-cosmic doctrine that the evolutionary process of nature guarantees communism's final success: this provides them with a and hysterical self-immolation, they have not shown the ability people.

All of these sources of sacrificial enthusiasm, however, are subject to collapse whenever signs of imperfection or failure become too glaring to be obscured any longer by these faiths themselves. It seems very likely that if communism ever did wipe out all opposition, leaving itself with no scapegoat to blame its weaknesses on, its dynamic would rather suddenly evaporate. People would then soon discover their need of more genuine foundations at the level of cosmic meaningfulness.

But it is not necessary to wait until then to find signs of such need. Men insist on having a dimension of holy importance after all, and if a "scientific" society refuses to supply it in a valid form, then they will find benighted and confused substitutes for it — primarily by turning the system and its leaders themselves into abortive cosmic substitutes. Our secular age propels peoples into frantic clutchings after cosmic meaningfulness. We have witnessed during these recent humanistic decades, how supposedly irreligious masses will flock to narrow nationalistic religions, worshiping the entombed bodies of former premier-Gods (like the ancient Egyptians) or joining mystic processions across the Red Square. Denied the worship of a Cosmic Creator, men worshiped a Führer. Denied ultimate beliefs, they erected a weak human instrumentality — the state — into an ultimate. Consigned to drab secular lives, they flocked to pagan Nuremberg Festivals. But while these noncosmic religions have inspired man to plunder band-wagon psychology that is always helpful for motivating

564

to inspire him to a steady reverence for all human souls, to simple brotherly love and kindness to all creatures known to be important, if erring, seekers of divine salvation. Nor do they answer the individual's need when close to death. The non-disappearance of the church in Russia is revealing.

Some humanists, noting the fanaticism of these narrow religions continue to advise the suppression of all religious belief. They continue to preach a general humanitarianism, a pragmatic affirmation of men's worth, ungrounded however, in cosmic reality. But these are the *issue* of inspiration and power, not the *source* of it. The supposedly innocuous transfer of faith from cosmic purpose to human objectives is a transfer from the supply of power to what consumes power; from the source of sacramental enthusiasm to pointless toil. Our writers seem to feel this, unconsciously perhaps, but enough to render them entirely apathetic to the humanistic challenge.

The cosmic dimension of awareness cannot be thus lightly tossed aside. Today's disappointments in the utopian quest may reawaken this need. Just because poor religions lead to mischief is no reason for enlightened policies to refrain from undergirding themselves with cosmic inspiration. Humanistic liberalism not only did not reach Utopia but bids fair to be unable to hold humanity at the level it had achieved.

Can we, on the basis of dynamic thinking, open the way to a more genuine source of power? Can we find, for our side in the struggle, a dynamic that does not depend upon unrealistic, static dreams; nor upon traditional myths and hoary theologies whose terms and concepts lack vitality because they split our minds into compartments? The harmony between DM and DR should give us a more secure ground for faith than traditional absolutism, and less subject to disillusionment than Utopian communism.

3. Human Destiny. The concept of immortality of the individual soul, and SIR's grounds for believing in it are, of course for SMR, misconceived in every way. Leaving aside the material impossibility of the concept itself, the authoritarian grounds for believing it have been criticized endlessly for three centuries, Hume's criticisms of testimony as a proof of the occurrence of resurrection or any lesser miracle being perhaps the most classic. The orthodox Christian basis of belief — in the resurrection stories of the New Testament — is precisely the supreme example of untrustworthy testimony, from this point of view. Of all reports,

it is the most subject to the charge of wishful concoction. But as if this was not weakening enough to its evidential force, the resurrection material must needs also be fatally self-contradictory and unintelligible in itself, no two accounts bearing any great deal of resemblance to each other.

Quite apart from its dubious status as accurate testimony is its entire uselessness for proving what it is supposed to prove. In the space age, the story of Jesus' body ascending upward from the surface of the earth is hopelessly irrelevant to the question of immortality for us. To the extent that traditional belief has inclined to emphasize the uniqueness of Jesus, either as the one and only perfect man, or as the God-man, *his* immortality carries no logical implication whatsoever to any other man's immortality. And if bodies rising from graves and ascending through the air were the mode of immortality, we would seem to have complete proof that no one else can hope to be immortal, knowing what we know about the fate of their bodies in the grave.

As for any other empirical evidence of individual immortality (and incidentally, scripture accepts its obligation to produce empirical evidence), i.e. spiritualistic evidence, SMR has run down all alleged cases for centuries and none have been verified definitely enough to promote spiritualism to more than an invisibly minute sect, largely despised by the orthodox themselves.

Thus, one way or another, SMR arrives preponderantly at the opinion of Epicurus, when he held that the individual disperses into his blind atoms at death and nothing whatever survives of him. Also, being bravely empirical, SMR boldly faces the fact death produces terrible crescendo of repulsiveness, indignity and horror. Looked at without idealistic or mythological spectacles, it seems to provide the final proof of the fiendishness of life. Reality seems not satisfied to be merely emptily meaningless, but takes it upon itself to be actively, outrageously, insistently meaningless. All this adds to the non-inspiration of SMR an acute misery; to its debilitating anxiety a great jolt of gratuitous agony. Without any recourses, men are further than ever from being inspired to higher lives.

I fear that SMR's negatives are stubbornly obstructive enough to ruin the power of SIR's solaces for death, for anyone who honestly takes account of what is valid in its criticisms of SIR's arguments. Those not entirely paralyzed by the awful scene will admit to hoping more desperately than ever for a meaning to replace what has been shaken. It seems impossible to turn back to the traditional grounds. Have DM and DR any resources for this last and most awful of problems?

SM with DR.

1. Problem of Inspiration. The reverence one can feel on the basis of humanistic or limited God views is certainly increased over what was possible in mechanistic materialism. And the increased knowledge of relations of "requirement" brings with it an increase of the sense of wonder and admiration for existence. Whether the deepest experiences of holiness is possible with this view is debatable; the author, at least, is definitely conscious that it is lacking for him. There is an earth-boundedness in humanism that does not reach those heights of raptness and adoration possible in true religion. Prayer, for one thing, is unthinkable; nor is one instigated to practice toward the supreme mystical experiences. The limited God belief falls short of making us feel that every part of reality has a reason. They leave us with too much sense of being surrounded with dead, accidental matter and an oblivious universe.

And after all, the more usual reaction to the SM-DR combination is, as we said at the beginning, the existentialist absurdity or the Schopenhauerean weariness. Whether an invitation to prayerful exaltation is offered or not, these minds are not usually inclined to accept it. They simply work away at the problems with such interest and energy as they can find, fatigue and age inexorably sapping that interest and energy.

2. Effects on Behavior: Theory of Salvation. Aside from the above tendency to miss the highest states of exaltation, all views in SM-DR are broken-backed for instigating regeneration because of the continuing failure of SM to provide any real reason or significance for such process. Although DR reveals the need of salvation in some sense, and the factual possibility of it, minds based on this combination cannot fully invest themselves in the task because of the ever nagging and vitiating question, "why should this tiresome problem have to exist at all?"

The views under this head might be roughly divided into the liberal-humanist type which still strives to find that SM's implications are somehow, in spite of appearances, factually true: i.e., that man is really fundamentally good and saved already; and exis-

567

tentialist types, theistic or non-theistic, which admit, with DR, that man is in an evil "predicament" and needs transformation, but still, with SM, see no real reason why. These views also tend to remain infected with some of SMR's doubt that the process of transformation is factually possible, at least in this life. Even the theistic, neo-orthodox, forms lack hope of any real progress toward goodness, and are curiously unconcerned with practical ways and means of building good character.

The attempt of existentialist theology to rehabilitate the orthodox theory of Fall and Salvation seems to me to have been clearly abortive since it has made no progress whatever in explaining what we saw was the inveterate anomaly of the traditional view: why omnipotent, perfect (in the static sense) God would have created a creature with an inclination to use its free will evilly. In returning to the traditional feeling that man, out of sheer, unnecessary mischief, was the sole cause of all evil, the neo-orthodox view also tends to restore what many psychologists to-day are convinced is a mentally unhealthy kind of guilt feeling, the practical reflection, I am convinced, of a faulty metaphysics.

This theology correctly recognizes that man is helpless not to "sin"; or in more modern terminology, that man starts out caught in various bad habits, weaknesses, perversions. Modern theories of heredity and environment strongly suggest that the individual man cannot be blamed for all of these imperfections; that the Old Testament was strictly factual in declaring that the sins of the fathers are visited upon the sons. It seems obvious that human beings necessarily begin their lives in a total self-centeredness, as far as possible from Christian agape. They then get caught in various fixations, as they grow up, which hold them back from mature responsibility and love, keeping them more or less perverted. But the fear, ignorance and bad environment which we find invariably associated with these failures, strongly press us to admit that some of the evil, at least, is beyond the individual's control, not his own fault, but given in his endowment, that is, by the Creator.

This supposition, of course, has always been so repugnant to static theology, that it has preferred to hold to the ways of circumventing the attribution of evil to God which we have reviewed, however much "a mystery beyond human comprehension" they must confess them to be. Brunner, for instance, asks us to believe both sides of the contradiction that man necessarily must sin yet is responsible for it.

> The biblical revelation, however, shows us both in one. . . . It recognizes the fatal sense of the inevitable, the sense of Fate in evil; it calls us "slaves of sin" who have no free choice not to commit sin, or not to be sinners; but it also recognizes man's absolute responsibility and does not attempt to ascribe it to some impersonal force. . . . This paradox cannot be grasped by thought. . . .[5]

And Tillich strives to find a meaning for original perfection and for the Fall as man's self-chosen entrance into sin and evil. But his effort to find some kind of locus for the original perfection, in the absence of any historical or psychological data to support it, leads to much obscure manipulation of metaphysical abstractions. He ends by suggesting that creation and fall constitute one and the same act, but that creation is dependent upon the divine life, and the fall on creaturely freedom. This is surely a bad case of moving word counters about without much attention to observable experience.

As Hartshorne says:

> Tillich denies that contingency and novelty can apply literally to God. Yet he rightly holds that God must be all-inclusive. If then the creatures are literally contingent, there must be divine constituents which are literally contingent. But in truth Tillich never reaches a clear notion of the root of contingency in creativity; he speaks sometimes quite like an Augustinian determinist. He never clearly envisages the issue between classical and neoclassical views, whether of God or of the creatures. And the idea of a God who responds lovingly to the world is lost in the indifferent absolute-ness of "unconditioned" being. I think Whitehead's God is closer to Christianity than this.[6]

The original sin itself, creditably, is usually interpreted by these theologies as an existential event in present life. The older location of the freely-willed fall in Adam, so that all his descendants inherit a substantial fatedness to sin along with full responsibility for it, is presumably out of the question for modern minds. The notions of corporate responsibility and God's justice as forensic are not revived. The original sin, or Fall, then, tends to be described as each individual's own self-will, rebellion and separation from the Father, finite desires, one-sidedness, pride, etc. But, due to the static presuppositions which can only honor original essences and perfections, these characteristics of existence tend to be condemned as having no essential part to play but to import unneeded trouble into the creation.

The resulting state of mind, recommended to sinners, is a kind rueful ashamedness, a self-hatred for one's ridiculous and meaningless imperfection. This is that guilt-as-shame, mentioned above, which many psychiatrists do not feel is at all conducive to growth, aspiration, recovery. Throughout Christian history, I am convinced, orthodox conceptions of sin have tended to produce this self-denigration which the accompanying doctrine of forgivenness has not always succeeded in converting into an energetic readiness for reform. And to-day I think we can find signs — in Barth for instance — that this feeling toward sin causes him to place regenerative salvation as far outside of this life within some future state as any medieval mind ever did. Motivation for change in this life is undermined by our two sources of doubt: lingering strains of SMR's mechanistic and deterministic denial of the possibility of change; and SM's implication that such change, even if possible, would not be called for by any static divine plan anyway.

It is interesting to observe how one outside of this theological tradition reacts to its apparent near-exultation in the rediscovery of man's despicability. Van Wyck Brooks cannot bring himself to admire the supposed profundity of the writers, critics and theologians who have so enthusiastically embraced the doctrine of human depravity, with the claim of its being so much "deeper" than the old liberal optimism. I agree that they make a rather unsavory spectacle as they mock at such partial gains as men of good will had succeeded in making in the hey-day of Enlightenment, scientific advance, and democracy. Barth, Berdyaev, Eliot and Hulme are cited as rejecting all human accomplishments as worthless just because they have not been, as SM would demand, finally and ultimately perfect.

History for Barth is a "never ending process that never gets to its goal" and forces "the cry for another world" out of the

570

heart, while all that happens on this earth is an illusion or a maze, — a "cheat and a disappointment," as T. S. Eliot puts it. But more influential even than Barth in the literary world has been T. E. Hulme, who . . . lashed out at Goethe's "stupidity" for denying that the human mind, which seemed to repeat itself endlessly, was travelling in a circle, saying, "No, it is not a circle, it is a spiral," because, as a child of the Renaissance, Goethe exulted in the world and men and believed that in a sense they were tending both forward and upward. But was Goethe "stupider" than Hulme, who gloried in being "inhuman" as much as he gloried in being "pessimistic?"[7]

And Berdyaev rejects one period after another of human history because none of them arrived at a final end of human problems. "The Renaissance came to nothing; the Reformation came to nothing; the Enlightenment came to nothing; so did the Revolution inspired by the Enlightenment." Thus they all refuse to accept a world of continuous transformation as conceivably worthy of the intention of God. They correctly reject the assumption of perfection by man in this life, but wrongly consider this as tantamount to denying any creative accomplishment whatever as real. If each age of human history achieves its own unique quality of experience, its invariably giving onto a complementary set of problems whose solving can produce the next unique quality would seem to be no reason for rejecting its own achievements.

Having neatly proved that nothing of value can be achieved in this life, these schools of writers go on then, as I said above and as Brooks finds, to lose their interest in "salvation" as a real possibility for which many practical ways and means might be sought. He describes them as preoccupied rather with the more aesthetic and quaint aspects of religious tradition. They are happy to mouth creeds devoid of experiential meaning, simply because the creeds are old and atmospheric. They do not care to undergo the difficult internal struggles of *living* religion, but only play at a "game of religion" because it happens to be "more amusing" than secular pessimism.

So there are twenty who find it amusing to think of man as

"fallen" to one who *believes* man has fallen, and believes it with regret, while for others "evil" and "sin" are words which they use for aesthetic effect and even for decorative purposes.[8]

Must we not, then, accuse the SM-DR philosophers and theologians of blocking salvation for modern man in their refusal to allow the dynamization of value and the meaningfulness of imperfect reality? I have become convinced that, the august thunderings of the much-worshipped Barth, the supreme Niebuhr, the all-conquering Tillich notwithstanding, their hopelessness for rationality, their paradoxes, their separated God and their scripture worship have taken us on a great detour and left us with a vast amount of cobwebbing to sweep out of the way of the transforming of man.

Still following Van Wyck Brooks, it is again interesting to see that his own suggestions for escaping the impasse only illustrate the other possibility under SM-DR: that man is somehow already good, and that motivating him to grapple with his difficulties depends upon convincing him of his "natural" nobility. He cannot put his finger on the real weakness of the pessimist because he shares that weakness: the supposition that to demonstrate the possibility of human goodness, you must demonstrate it is fully established in the original essence. The pessimists admit that it is not so established, and so lose their interest in any possibility of partial achievement of it. But since they are correct in denying its prior establishment, they rightly remain unimpressed, as Brooks regretfully admits, with his appeal to return to a pious belief that it somehow, after all, is already there. His criticism of the pessimists misses their actual error to concentrate upon a point where they are unassailable; his solution is exactly the one which they have properly exploded.

His humanistic faith leads him to suppose that the pessimists have begun by denying man's goodness and accepting his depravity quite arbitrarily; and that *thereupon* men, thus needlessly discouraged and robbed of confidence, proceed into the decay and destruction or sin. To get back to constructiveness, we supposedly have only to declare once again that man is basically good, and men will return to behaving so.

. . . this recent return to the medieval notion, — that men are more radically evil than potentially good, — is it not this notion which has spread through the world in the last three decades that has caused the movement of reaction?[9]

But the modern mind will very probably continue apathetic to this declaration of human goodness, for the realists and pessimists were not wrong on this point, nor was the Middle Ages. The dark evidence exists, and if there is any positive answer, it must incorporate these facts of human evil. The false claim of optimistic humanists of man's given goodness, in fact, can only operate to keep the writers bitter, as long as it leads them to suppose that it *ought* to have been true. As long as they accept that there can be no other kind of basis for human worth but instinctive endowment, then the discovery of the perversity of instincts will constitute sufficient grounds for giving up all efforts toward goodness; for, in fact, positively seeking out perversity as the final and permanent goal of man. For this is the note that has been appearing in literature since the second world war.[10]

Now the humanist, if pressed, may deny that he means "natural goodness" in Rousseau's sense of an original deposit in primitive men and infants of a compassion that would automatically flood the world with perfection if it were not for certain accidental blocks. He will probably shift his ground to claiming only that human nature is "potentially" good; is neutral, perhaps, at the start, and only needs reasonable stimulation toward decent humanity. He may hold only that the human organism has a natural tendency toward growth and resolution of maladjustments, but that such tendency, then, constitutes goodness. He could then accuse the naturalistic pessimist of not being as realistic as he pretends, when he sedulously ignores these facts of human aspiration to concentrate on certain exceptional states of "stuck" fixation as though they were universally typical.

It seems hard to deny that the pessimists *are* unfactual to this extent. They do offer us an incredibly distorted portrait of man, fatally mistaken in its implication that we not only must but should accept our fragmentary and destructive passions; in fact some of them almost approve such "daring" to follow anarchic impulses in rebellion against the self's own, and society's call for more balanced patterns of behavior. But growth of human personalities toward organized control and successful management of

573

life is a phenomenon that factually occurs, and to ignore the data on ways and means to accomplish it seems infinitely senseless.

And yet we cannot feel that the liberal optimist will become an effective voice without knowing more intimately than he does those phenomena of failure and horror that so paralyze the pessimist. The pessimist's reaction of inert disgust, or else of stupid fascination, with such fiendish states of personality is wrong-headed enough; but not more so than the optimists' facile exhortation to the monsters, "Come now, only believe you can do better than this." The pessimist gives up all too soon the attempt to understand the depths in terms of comprehensible causes and conceivable therapies, settling too soon into a doctrine of innate, incorrigible devilishness. But the optimist, in not allowing himself to know these depths familiarly enough, also fails to find cures. He always brings too little medicine too late.

The fact is that, if a tendency toward growth is native to human nature, it still has its limits; and cases are exceedingly possible where obstacles are too difficult, turning the integrative process back on itself toward dreadful decomposition. These are the situations about which the optimists fail to convince the pessimists that they know whereof they speak, or that they possess a sufficiently powerful antidote to treat them. And so, neither optimist nor pessimist in SM-DR are motivated to seek deeply enough for adequate resources: the pessimist because he gives up the possibility of cure, the optimist because he will not admit the seriousness of the case. Both inadequacies root back in the failure of the static idea of good to suggest that problems of any depth should have been expected.

Neither side, then, develops an intimate knowledge of the ways and means of acquiring the readiness and strength to undertake the task, which might include ways and means of contacting an increment of energy from divine sources. To avoid appearing to appeal too naively to magical help from external Gods, let us put it this way: the humanists do not consider seriously enough the possible need of encouragement to human aspiration that comes from a faith in meaningfulness in this book's sense of the word—metaphysical and cosmic meaningfulness. They have assumed that their naturally good and able human nature will always find the power in itself to grapple manfully with problems no matter how overwhelming they may be, without benefit of any explicit "confidence in the universe." This false promise, then, is the main source of the pessimists' discouragement, when they find the bootstrap operation failing.

Brooks, then, although he disclaims Rousseau's noble savage, and speaks rather of man's needing to "strive" for goodness, yet falls back again to citing Schweitzer, Melville, Ellis, etc., for opinions that savages are normally peaceful and loving.

> . . . although man is prone to err, still, through obscurest aspiration, he has "an instinct of the one true way." To say the least are not men ambivalent? Their nature is not unalterable; there is no scientific evidence to support the assumption that the psyche comes into the world with an original stain . . . faith in human goodness has meant so much for the advance of man that I cannot abandon it lightly or in the fashion of the moment.[11]

Here we see recognition of the need of "alteration" of human nature, but it is immediately lost in the thought of essential, preëxistent goodness. And this keeps Brooks and the liberal humanists from thinking clearly and solidly enough about practical methods of regenerating, and what it takes to inspire men to them in the face of fear, weakness and failure. The psyche comes into the world with a tendency to inertia at least, and to selfishness and cruelty too, we had better admit. It takes something more than itself to activate it to striving.

The main literary tradition, in America anyway, pursues its cynical way with little attention to either of these bases for human salvation. It does not ask whether man did or did not have a fall, and certainly gives us no reason to undertake a rise nor any method of doing it. Mostly it stays with SMR, describing man as he is, and implying that he should continue to be what he finds himself to be, however evil and perverted.

> The novelists . . . were unable to see active goodness in developed human beings, or, rather, they were scarcely able to see developed types at all, or anything but "irresponsible criminals" as Edith Wharton put it. Auden has said, "Heroes without honour" whose only virtue was "a stoic endurance of pain and disaster," "irresponsible victims" who were never "responsible agents."[12]

575

There is, then, no whole-hearted search for salvation emanating from the various views based on the SM-DR combination. Even those who have retreated to some form of orthodoxy today have found it so little capable of producing inner transformation, as to end by softpedaling the whole salvation side of it in their embarassment. Personal regeneration is handed over to the psychiatrists if to anybody. We may summarize: to the pessimist, neo-orthodox, etc., the prior state of imperfection is real but uncalled for, the process of regeneration is dubiously real but also uncalled for, the final good is questionable, but the only state that is called for; to the optimist, the prior imperfection is not real and not called for, the process is real but not called for, the final state is already real somehow, because the only state that is called for.

3. Human Destiny. The massive acquaintance with death combined with the utmost apparent meaninglessness and injustice, characteristic of the world wars, together with SMR's further uglifying of the subject provide sufficient explanation of the scurrying back to resurrection theology which we have seen in recent times. Even so, I doubt that the orthodox proof of immortality by means of biblical testimonies, whose confusion and irrelevance was so fatally criticized by SMR, can affect many who are capable of understanding the criticism. It must be largely those who had the belief drilled into them before the Jesuitical age of seven who can make it real to themselves, for it becomes almost like direct experience itself for them, not dependent upon hazy reports from another age with a different world-view.

Even those who can contrive to believe the traditional account of immortality cannot, I find, believe it deeply and undividedly enough to derive much security or additional confidence in the living of this life — a boon which orthodoxy has never hesitated to promise as a main reason for seeking the belief. Also, even the most faithful, living in the midst of DR's world to-day must confess difficulty in shifting from a life where serious problems are creatively solved through dynamic processes and structured bodies, to trying to feel any importance in SM's static heaven of idle bliss. There is a pervasive attenuation of interest in a Dantean Paradise. Only a heaven of continued processes in bodies really concerns any one, and perhaps even then they are not sure they want it to confine itself to the easier and more comfortable processes. A favorite plot of one-act plays and fantasies concerns the bored inmates of heaven longing for a little hell-like spice.

Perhaps, then, a completely dynamized foundation can give us a more consistent and unifying attitude on this fateful topic. We have seen that it can give us a more solid reason why there must be death (Chapter XVIII). What may it be able to do in bringing meaning to man's final destiny?

DM with DR.

1. Problem of Inspiration. Having robbed the basic arguments against belief in Cosmic Purpose for Good of cogency; and permitting us to pay serious attention to certain moments of supreme mystical consciousness, DM and DR together invite us to approach the divine. And even though we do not claim to have here a positive proof that all reality emanates from a Divine Purposer, does it not begin to seem a little captious to refuse to entertain the possibility, when we find the dynamic idea of value giving "requiredness" to almost every finding of ordinary experience and science? A sacramental consciousness rises within one's awareness however much positivistic empiricism demands that one maintain a non-committal matter-of-factness. This is not quite the medieval belief in God's specific planning of every detail for a specific purpose, giving one a half fearful awe for every trivial event around him. Such a picture of pre-set design has already assumed the static idea of good. Dynamic good points rather to a looser universe, with a place for adventure and novel creativity. It requires that an omnipotent, omnibenevolent God should leave things to be worked out somewhat independently of His fiats. Yet one has a sense of knowing a general "why" of things that makes all the difference between a secular, profane attitude and a sacred one.

2. Effects on Behavior. The dynamic approach offers a way of incorporating most of the valid parts of the traditional idea of salvation without recourse at every turn to "insoluble paradoxes" and "mysteries we cannot understand." We have seen how it solves the traditional dilemma as to why God created anything at all (Chapter XIII). We no longer ask why God, being "perfect," should initiate any change. A salvation process, which orthodoxy never could intelligibly found upon the static Greek basis, now becomes intrinsic to the existence of good. Redemption is not an emergency operation by which God seeks to restore his original plan, but the only conceivable content of a good creation. It is

577

not a question of making the best of a bad situation, but exactly what God must have intended.

Next, we can eliminate the orthodox "paradox" (p. 569) of having to recognize that individual men are helplessly enslaved to sin, yet feeling obliged to place the entire blame of it on them in order to excuse God from it. We can now start by dropping the orthodox assumption of an original perfection, either in Nature or in man. The realm of Existence, with all of its finiteness, imperfection and struggle, rather than a realm of perfect essences, we posit, with the existentialists, as prior. That is, God Himself posits it so, since good itself cannot have meaning or existence without such a beginning. Since the "sin" and self-will of this prior state have a vital part to play in the psychological process of good experience, they cannot be considered as mere unfortunate lapses, as in orthodoxy. To do so, as we suggested above, produces the wrong sort of psychological attitude in the self — that rueful guilt feeling which psychiatry has shown not to conduce to growth but to a more inert discouragement, anxiety, false humility, self-abnegation. A certain foundation of self-esteem, not identical with pride, is known to be necessary before the ability to love others can develop at all. Our sin does not consist in pursuing finite desires, in willing the development of ourselves (always called "rebellion" by the neo-orthodox) as such. These tendencies are entirely necessary, placed in man by God on purpose, to ensure that processes will take place.

Not even those perversions and exaggerations of self-will with which we find ourselves burdened at the age of responsibility, inherited from hereditary or environmental misfortunes, can be called our own responsible sin. The fear, self-centeredness, disunity, errors of self-assertion are not conditions which God would have preferred to avoid if it had not been for human mischief. They are quite necessary at the beginning, if man is ever to be able to feel the good of being extricated from them. What pleases us about the way of love, when we come to it eventually, is its wonderful efficacy in contrast to our frustration in bald self-demand.

God then must have endowed man with both self-will and the tendency toward its exaggeration as the only conceivable means of bringing good into existence. This is the "necessary" part of sin. But we can drop the paradox of necessity and responsibility, and not consider man responsible for this part of sin at all. God may not be as insistent upon our remaining in a state of permanent puzzlement with "paradoxes" as Kierkegaard and his progeny have declared. For, in dynamic terms, we can find another locus for the sin that is man's own responsibility.

Brunner, as a matter of fact, has pointed to it, but failed to realize its import because of his lack of a genuinely dynamic foundation. He states that man's only freedom is to turn to God, to answer God's call and to allow himself to be saved. His only responsibility, then, is to turn to God for help out of the state of imperfection he finds himself created in. Now, of course, in refusing to turn to God, he commits his real sin. *Thereafter,* all the given evil, which was not his fault to begin with, starts to become his own sin through his choice to remain in it. He is not responsible for the original presence of the evil in him, for that really is necessary in an even deeper sense than has been traditionally meant. But he *becomes* responsible for it if he refuses to enter the process out of it.

If the evil now worsens, as it is likely to do if no effort is made against it, God need not be held responsible for that. But if man aspires and seeks God or other resources, we have much evidence for believing that he will find. Good can now come into existence, consisting equally of that original unhappiness and the feeling of overcoming it.

Another way of putting it is to say that the evil which we inherit is at first a propulsion both toward effort and salvation — an inducement to search — and also a necessary potential component of any possible good we can know. It is both a future component itself, and the instigation of the process that is also a necessary future component. Responsibility starts with our ability to choose to search. But if we choose not to search, that original given evil begins to turn into our own sin in so far as we rest in static self-satisfaction and pride. Unhappiness and evil now begin to take on the other aspect of punishment as well as of inducement. From this point on, determinism tightens its grip, and the excesses of misery that ensue are not God's doing. At any time, however, we can presumably turn back to God and aspiration and recover lost ground. It is significant that some of those saved from an especially deep and prolonged evil report the more vivid sense of the mercies of God, the more enthusiasm for life as transforming salvation.

A better description of sin, or fall, would put the emphasis not on self-will as such, which is a general source of process, but upon such self-will as negates process, so to speak — that pride and self-satisfaction which renounce further search and improvement. Our sin would be the refusal to undertake the task God is proposing by having our present inadequacies and selfishness produce unpleasant experiences. Our sin would not be the initial act of self-will that proved an error, but our persistence thereafter in the same course. Sin as refusal to change would certainly describe that of the Pharisee; like the paranoid, he is convinced that he has attained perfection and that others can have no reason to question his behavior. His is the reverse of the virtue most often commended by Jesus: humility, which is best defined as readiness to admit imperfection and to undertake rectification. Thus Jesus' most frequent characterization of sin fits most exactly with the implications of dynamic good. Sin is clinging to the original state when the fundamental requirement of God's plan is change from the condition He starts us in.

Dynamic good, then, offers no black and white answer whether God or man has the whole responsibility for evil. We must endeavor to penetrate more subtly into the dynamic requirements to find which part each plays.

Having an understanding of why imperfection and sin meaningfully exist, then, we come to the practical problem of ways and means of attaining the will and energy to change, of making contact with the divine aid that might be available if we bothered to seek it. But first the dynamic idea of good suggests a reason why any such a resource *should* require a little seeking. Here we come upon a complaint of modern men against the universe which is only now, at long last, becoming fully conscious, and is, I suspect at the root of those most modern terms, "absurdity" and "nausea," by which the writers characterize reality. It is the question, "why does God hide Himself, if He exists, and is omnipotent? How could, and why should, the existence of such a being ever be in doubt?" Static presuppositions have finally induced men to ask why they should have to seek their salvation, why God should play a game of hide and seek. Joad cannot see why God does not show His face in the sky as plainly as the sun:

> . . . if so to read the appearance of things is to misread them, why are the appearances deceptive? If, to see this

world as the handiwork of a "brute and blackguard" is to belie God's character, why did He choose to disguise Himself? Why in fact couldn't he make Himself plain?[13]

But the beatitude of knowing God, we can now see, resembles any other good: it can exist only as a discovery, as a resolving of need through process. The delight of the mystics in finding God, and of any man in achieving salvation, must consist in the escape from ignorance and deliverance from despair, and must include the memory of the previous state of want. Men must first see God through a glass darkly, since knowing Him can consist only in the increasing of light by moral struggle and divining of symbols. The finding of God and salvation, then, is integral to reality; redemption is not, as in traditional views, rectification of an inadvertent mistake. The only way for God to get Himself felt by His creatures is for them to start from a condition of lostness so that they can feel themselves drawn out of it by Him.

The sense of holiness, too, requires mystery and darkness. Our sense of the grandeur of God requires His transcendence. He must be beyond our complete understanding and must be partly hidden; otherwise God would be only as trivial and thin as our conceptions. Partial finding is the most we can expect, the most we even want. God must remain partly invisible and partly revealed — but only to those who aspire and work toward Him.

The religious view of life is thus bound up with the belief that man must seek what is beyond his present state. The ordinary expressions of religion are forms to enliven and spur on this aspiration. But for SMR's naturalists, who have no theory of any growth that might need inspiration, such forms must naturally appear pointless. They cannot tolerate prayer or any other religious practice, for they know nothing of infusing these forms with inner purpose. Of course they remain dead for those who deny the possibility of levels beyond what "is."

But the dynamic approach suggests a reason why higher levels of divine knowledge and experience should first be hidden, then partly revealed to seekers; that perplexity and doubt of God's existence should hold at first, itself constituting a necessary part of the ultimate experience of finding. To realize this might serve to interest a few of the doubters in what may stretch ahead for them to seek. If the process of finding is the essence of the matter, then there must be a stage of not having found.

As to how man actually makes contact with the God whose saving action is thus made a completely expectable part of our world-view, there are the experiences of God-finders to seek out, read, and study for ways and means. The anomalies of SM with DR, we have said, have kept all schools of thought within that combination, from a serious and meticulous investigation of methods of regeneration. The pessimists hypostatized the beginning of the process, the optimists the end of it, and thus both were equally unconcerned with the transition from the one to the other. Now if it is true that any dynamic God must purposely have arranged for life to require transformation, and possibly that His dynamic aid must also be sought in order to succeed in the task, then obviously human affairs are not going to get on at their best if all search for it is cut off by negative metaphysics. If life has been made so that we either keep a current of inspiration coming in, or else we decay and sink to rottenness, then the optimistic humanist promise that we have sufficient power already within us would be a dangerous beguilement away from the fatefully necessary search and practice of recharging and directing. On the other hand, the pessimist hopelessness would also cut the nerve of aspiration. The neo-orthodox escape to a supine dependence on God is too close to this latter attitude to discover many really effective methods for actual living change. It would have been better to resurrect from the Middle Ages, not their neurotic condemnation and belittling of man, their disdain of this life, their obscure mythology and petrified forms; but rather some of the things the Middle Ages knew about ardent aspiration, meditation and communion with God.

Of course, if older formulations and terminologies alienate the modern mind, then new ones presumably can be found that will be effective. The "old-time" religion that works for the simpleminded is not what we are thinking about for the modern educated man. And if cynics assure us that there is nothing to take the place of the old time religion, we can justifiably suspect that they have allowed the contradictions of static thinking to keep them from looking very hard for anything else. Many seem not even to have begun on such elementary and obvious directions as to study likely models — those personalities of history or the present who have expressed hope and enthusiasm for life; or to read likely books—the great time-tested ones rather than what they find on the nearest magazine rack. One might conceivably spend an hour of meditation on the Bible, even, for every hour he spends reading comics. Thomas Wolfe observed with indignation the sophisticates for whom "life is too short" for Tolstoy, Goethe, Whitman; they must save their time for Piggy Logan and his obscene doll show.[14]

But why should we trouble ourselves at all over the negative opinions of those who have never even tried meditation and prayer? Is it such a wild idea that man, who has a brain three times the size of any other animal's, might have been "meant" to use, say a quarter of his waking time in restorative and synthesizing meditation, instead of ninety-five percent of it in thoughtless and fragmentary activity of which any chimpanzee is capable? If the admittedly greatest human beings—the Schweitzers, Gandhis, Whiteheads, St. Francises, the prophets, and the saviors—all who have said "yea" to life—confess their dependence on these things, why are we surprised that those who do not seek thus inform us that they have not found?

Characters have indubitably been regenerated in human history. Let us seek out and study these phenomena and tell about them. Until the cynics have gone through the years and years of persistent effort and training all such characters report doing, their complaints should not influence us over much.

Lastly, let us suggest a connection between the holistic, unified awareness which we have earlier suggested as the result of these practices, and increased energy and power in the individual. This unity of awareness implies that the organism must have reached a unity of its energies, an elimination of conflict and self-cancellation. We know that great energy has often come with the mystic awareness of God. Strength and stamina have appeared enabling men to surpass their former selves. The fear and fatigue of mundane life no longer blunt their aims and a serene confidence in the cosmic, sustaining purpose frees them for exploits of good will. If enough men sought and appropriated that divine increment, then we might expect positive forces to outweigh negative ones in the affairs of men. The sacrifices of immediate pleasures and selfish wants, requisite to stay the tides of destruction would be forthcoming. Calamity and bestiality would recede, and men could move forward again less hectically and fragmentedly. Thus religious awareness of the holy and divine is not only a means to deepen and fulfill every individual life, but is the most practical necessity for repairing the social catastrophes of our times.

3. Human Destiny. At the end, the dynamic logic saves me from having to paint a finished picture of Heaven, complete with golden streets and banquets of mead. It legislates that I must end with the invitation to search, with the implication that a search which has found so much may yet find more. The conviction of immortality, no less than that of God, could be expected to come, if at all, only as the culminating reward of the most arduous seeking; we could not expect it to be transmittible by any easy formula of words. Faith in a God who has created things *meaningfully*, if one practices to get it, may bring him also to serenity about death. Perhaps, whether one ends confident of his personal survival or not, he will at least be ready to say "whatever Thou wilt, so be it." The ultimate destiny of our self or soul, we would be sure, would be whatever is most meaningful. The attempt to specify its details through resurrection stories or anything else smacks dangerously of impiety, from this viewpoint. If anything is strongly suggested, it is that we are not to have any simple empirical evidence on this matter. It is implied that we were to strive to live the creative process to the best of our ability without certainty about rewards or punishments beyond it. Otherworldliness, the mind thoroughly imbued with the dynamic mood begins to feel, is almost the arch-sin — an improper lust for a release from our duties here, a temptation away from making this life's process better, a diverting of attention and effort from the only reality that should concern us. Must not the great wish of the devils and the villains of this world be that their victims should fall to dreaming of another life, rather than to rise in criticism of what *this* life has been reduced to?

If the world were ever to grow more beautiful, if men were ever to grapple seriously with the supreme problems of the age — war, population, despoilment of the earth — if a life of greater quality ever rose from the quantitative rubble men content themselves with to-day, then we would know that static Eternity had been relinquished as the central idea of religion, and real organizing process undergirding dynamic good had been adopted in its place as the foundation of thought and life.

584

NOTES TO CHAPTER I

1. Rudolf Otto, *The Idea of the Holy*. Oxford: University Press, 2nd. Ed. (1950), p. 82.

NOTES TO CHAPTER II

1. Some positivists refuse to give this ultimate synthetic function to philosophy and include it under science. They assign to philosophy only ultimate metaphysical statements concerning, e.g. whether all things are material or spiritual, etc., but then deny that such statements have any meaning or sense. Our project of deducing all reality from an idea of value does not commit this error, if it is an error.
2. Randall and Buchler, *Philosophy: An Introduction*. New York: Barnes and Noble, 1942, pp. 28 and 30.

NOTES TO CHAPTER III

1. Plato, *Philebus* 60. Jowett transl.
2. A. E. Taylor, *Plato, the Man and His Work*. London: Methuen Co., 1926, 6th Ed., 1949, p. 413.
3. A. E. Taylor, *Op. Cit.*, p. 182.
4. Plato, *Republic,* 583. Jowett transl.
5. Plato *Ibid.,* 584.
6. Taylor, *Op. Cit.,* pp. 427-428.
7. Philebus, 31-32. Cf. Taylor, *Op. Cit.,* p. 418 ff.
8. Taylor, *Op. Cit.,* p. 424. *Philebus 45.*
9. *Philebus,* 51.
10. *Philebus,* 32-33.
11. *Philebus* 43.
12. *Philebus* 54.
13. Taylor, *Op. Cit.,* p. 429.
14. See my *Science and Cosmic Purpose.* New York: Harpers, 1949, p. 93 ff.
15. I have considered starting with no more than "satisfying feeling" as my minimum essential definition of value, and then deriving "organizing process" as a necessary implicate from it. The concept of

"satisfying" might be argued to contain within it already the notion of organizing process. However, rather than argue that, I have decided to make my opening concept express both the feeling and the content aspects simultaneously.

NOTES TO CHAPTER IV

1. See my *Science and Cosmic Purpose.* New York: Harper & Bros., 1949.

NOTES TO CHAPTER V

1. Descartes, *Rules for the Direction of the Mind,* 3rd Rule.
2. G. T. W. Patrick, *Introduction to Philosophy,* Rev. Ed. Boston: Houghton, Mifflin Company, 1935, p. 55.
3. Descartes, *Op. Cit.,* 3rd Rule.
4. Hume, *A Treatise of Human Nature,* Bk. I, Pt. 4, Sec. 6.
5. Dampier, W. C., *A History of Science,* 4th Ed. Cambridge: University Press, 1949, p. 125.
6. Dampier, *Ibid.,* p. 129.
7. John Dewey, *Reconstruction in Philosophy.* New York: Henry Holt, 1920, p. 86 ff.
8. A. N. Whitehead, *Modes of Thought.* New York: MacMillan, 1938, p. 43 f.
9. *Ibid.,* p. 159.
10. A good illustration of this point can be found in F. S. C. Northrop's *Science and First Principles,* Ch. 1. New York: The MacMillan Co., 1931.
11. Philip Wheelwright, *The Way of Philosophy.* New York: The Odyssey Press, 1954 edition, p. 41.
12. A. N. Whitehead, *Modes of Thought,* Ch. III.
13. *Ibid.,* Ch. 1.
14. Cf. Northrop, *The Logic of the Sciences and Humanities.* New York: MacMillan, 1947, Ch. II.
15. I. M. Copi, *Introduction to Logic.* New York: The MacMillan Co., 1954, p. 402.
16. Henry, Margenau, *The Nature of Physical Reality.* New York: McGraw-Hill Book Company, 1950, p. 28. Used by permission.
17. Cf. Copi, *Op. Cit.,* p. 425 ff.
18. Margenau, *The Nature of Physical Reality,* Ch. V.
19. Randall and Buchler, *Op. Cit.,* p. 69 f.

NOTES TO CHAPTER VI

1. Patrick, *Op. Cit.*, p. 327.
2. John Dewey, *Reconstruction in Philosophy*. New York: Henry Holt, 1920, p. 158.
3. A. N. Whitehead, *Process and Reality*. New York: MacMillan, 1929, pp. 7, 8.
4. Randall and Buchler, *Op. Cit.*, p. 223 ff.
5. John Dewey, *Essays in Experimental Logic*, pp. 239-240. Chicago: Univ. of Chicago Press, 1917.
6. A. N. Whitehead, *Adventures of Ideas*, Mentor Book Edition, p. 216. (Original Edition, New York: MacMillan Co., 1933.)
7. Cf. Margenau's "requirements on constructs," supra p. 104.
8. Margenau, *Op. Cit.*, p. 287.
9. A. N. Whitehead, *Modes of Thought*, p. 208.
10. Margenau, *Op. Cit.*, pp. 169-70.
11. *Ibid.*, p. 356.
12. Patrick, *Op. Cit.*, p. 60.
13. Rudolf Carnap, *Philosophy and Logical Syntax*, Chapter I. London: Routledge and Kegan Paul, 1935.
14. Wheelwright, *Op. Cit.*, p. 41 ff.
15. J. A. Leighton, *The Field of Philosophy*. New York: D. Appleton and Co., 1923, p. 360. (Permission of Appleton-Century-Crofts, 4th Ed. 1930.)
16. Randall and Buchler, *Op. Cit.*, p. 240.

NOTES TO CHAPTER VII

1. John Dewey, *Reconstruction in Philosophy*. New York: Henry Holt and Co., 1920. Mentor Edition, p. 97.
2. *Ibid.*, p. 96.
3. Cf. James Jeans, *Physics and Philosophy*. New York: MacMillan, 1943, p. 9 ff.
4. A. N. Whitehead, *Process and Reality*, p. 43.
5. A. N. Whitehead, *Science and the Modern World*, Mentor Edition, p. 18. (Original Edition, New York: The MacMillan Co., 1925.)
6. Hermann Weyl, *Philosophy of Mathematics and Natural Science*. Princeton: Princeton Univ. Press, 1949, p. 169.
7: Einstein and Infeld, *The Evolution of Physics*. New York: Simon and Schuster, 1938, p. 129.
8. Einstein and Infield, *Op. Cit.*, pp. 157-8.
9. Patrick, *Op. Cit.*, p. 193.
10. Werner Heisenberg, *Physics and Philosophy*. New York: Harper and

Bros., 1958, pp. 59-63.
11. Whitehead, *Science and the Modern World*, p. 104.
12. Einstein and Infield, *Op. Cit.*, p. 148.
13. *Ibid.*, p. 259.
14. Cf. Margenau, *Op. Cit.*, Chapter 10.
15. Whitehead, *Modes of Thought*, p. 131.
16. Whitehead, *Process and Reality*, p. 10.
17. *Ibid.*, p. 31.
18. *Ibid.*, p. 46.
19. *Modes of Thought*, p. 280.
20. *Ibid.*, p. 281.
21. *Process and Reality*, p. 135.
22. W. E. Hocking, "Whitehead on Mind and Nature" in Schlipp, Ed., *The Philosophy of Alfred North Whitehead*. Evanston & Chicago: Northwestern Univ. Press, 1941, p. 383.
23. *Process and Reality*, p. 43.

NOTES TO CHAPTER VIII

1. Archie Bahm, *Philosophy, An Introduction*. New York: John Wiley, 1953, p. 206.
2. *Ibid.*, p. 205.
3. See Northrop, *Science and First Principles*. New York: the MacMillan Co., 1932, p. 8.
4. J. Donald Butler, *Four Philosophies and their Practice in Education and Religion*. New York: Harper and Bros., 1951, p. 170.
5. F. S. C. Northrop, *Science and First Principles*. New York: The MacMillan Co., 1932, p. 11 ff.
6. Newton, *Principles*, II, 161.
7. Weyl, *Op. Cit.*, p. 169.
8. Margenau, *Op. Cit.*, p. 309.
9. *Ibid.* p. 326.
10. Northrop, *Op. Cit.*, pp. 136-9.
11. Jeans, *Physics and Philosophy*, p. 178.
12. Oliver L. Reiser, *The Integration of Human Knowledge*. Boston: Porter Sargent, 1958, p. 306.
13. *Ibid.*, p. 342.
14. Weyl, *Op. Cit.*, p. 171.
15. Einstein and Infeld, *Op. Cit.*, p. 270.
16. Whitehead, *Science and the Modern World*, Mentor Ed., p. 105.
17. Harold T. Davis, *Philosophy and Modern Science*. Evanston: The Principia Press, 1953, p. 17.
18. *Ibid.*, p. 18.
19. Margenau, *Op. Cit.*, p. 443.

588

20. *Ibid.,* pp. 442-445.
21. Whitehead, *Process and Reality,* p. 32.
22. Whitehead, *Science and the Modern World,* p. 79.
23. Whitehead, "Mathematics and the Good," in Schilpp, *Op. Cit.,* p. 674.
24. Whitehead, *Modes of Thought,* p. 133.
25. Whitehead, *Science and the Modern World,* p. 178.
26. Whitehead, *Process and Reality,* p. 31.

NOTES TO CHAPTER IX

1. A. E. Taylor, *Plato, The Man and His Work,* London, Methuen & Co., p. 441.
2. Edwin A. Burtt, *The Metaphysical Foundations of Modern Science,* Anchor Edition, New York, Doubleday, 1954, [orig. ed., 1924], p. 99.
3. Jeans, *Physics and Philosophy,* p. 13 ff.
4. Isaac Newton, 3rd Letter to Bentley, *Opera* IV, 438, quoted by Burtt, *Op. Cit.,* p. 266.
5. Jeans, *Physics and Philosophy,* p. 109.
6. Einstein and Infeld, *The Evolution of Physics,* p. 57.
7. Whitehead, *Science and the Modern World,* p. 78.
8. Thomas Hobbes, *Elements of Philosophy,* Bk. II, Ch. 9, Par. 7.
9. Burtt, *Op. Cit.,* p. 134.
10. Wheelwright, *The Way of Philosophy,* p. 145.
11. Whitehead, *Science and the Modern World,* p. 76 f.
12. W. E. Hocking in *Preface to Philosophy: Textbook.* New York: The MacMillan Co., 1947, p. 433.
13. Whitehead, *Modes of Thought,* p. 162.
14. Reiser, *Op. Cit.,* pp. 312-3.
15. Reiser, *Ibid.,* p. 275.
16. R. B. Perry, *Realms of Value,* p. 25, footnote. Cambridge: Harvard Univ. Press, 1954.
17. Bosanquet, *The Principle of Individuality and Value,* p. 149.
18. Patrick, *Op. Cit.,* p. 177.
19. Reiser, *Op. Cit.,* p. 436.
20. Randall and Buchler, *Op. Cit.,* p. 231 f.
21. Whitehead, *Process and Reality,* p. 143.
22. Whitehead, *Science and the Modern World.* Mentor Edition, pp. 71-74.
23. Reiser, *Op. Cit.*
24. Wilhelm Windelband, *An Introduction to Philosophy,* p. 144 ff. New York: Henry Holt and Co.
25. C. Hartshorne, *The Logic of Perfection.* La Salle, Ill.: Open Court Publishing Co., 1962. pp. 184-5. For a more thorough discussion

of this point see Hartshorne, and M. Capek, *Philosophical Impact of Contemporary Physics*. New York, Van Nostrand, 1961.

26. Northrop, *The Logic of the Science and the Humanities*. New York: The MacMillan Co., 1947, pp. 156-7.
27. See Whitehead, *Science and the Modern World*, p. 113.
28. Reiser, *Op. Cit.*, p. 225.

FOOTNOTES TO CHAPTER X

1. Weyl, *Op. Cit.*, p. 167.
2. Jeans, *Op. Cit.*, p. 20 f.
3. Bertrand Russell, *Mysticism and Logic*. New York: Longmans, Green and Co., 1918, pp. 47-57.
4. J. S. Mill, *A System of Logic*, Book III, Ch. V.
5. J. A. Thomson, *Introduction to Science*. New York: Henry Holt & Co., 1911, p. 133.
6. Margenau, *Op. Cit.*, p. 405.
7. Einstein and Infeld, *Op. Cit.*, p. 300.
8. W. Heisenberg, *Physics and Philosophy, The Revolution in Modern Science*. New York: Harper and Bros., 1958.
9. *Ibid.*, p. 40.
10. William James, *Some Problems of Philosophy*. New York: Longmans, Green & Co., 1911, pp. 139-141.
11. Wolfgang Köhler, *The Place of Value in a World of Facts*. New York: Liveright Publishing Corp. 1938.
12. Hartshorne, *Op. Cit.*, Chapter Six, "Freedom Requires Indeterminism and Universal Causality," esp. p. 185.

NOTES TO CHAPTER XI

1. Harold Titus, *Living Issues in Philosophy*. 2nd Ed. New York: American Book Co., p. 92. (4th Ed. 1964).
2. Jacques Loeb, *The Mechanistic Conception of Life*. Chicago: The University of Chicago Press, 1912.
3. C. Judson Herrick, *The Thinking Machine*. Chicago: The University of Chicago Press, 1932. Also other writings.
4. Patrick, *Op. Cit.*, pp. 110-1.
5. Whitehead, *Science and the Modern World*, Mentor Edition, pp. 78-80. See also Hartshorne's discussion of the levels of organisms, *Op. Cit.*, ch. 7, "A World of Organisms."
6. Warren S. McCulloch, "Mysterium Iniquitatis of Sinful Man Aspiring unto the Place of God," *Scientific Monthly*, Jan. 1955.

7. *Ibid.*
8. Whitehead, *Modes of Thought,* pp. 204-206.
9. Wolfgang Köhler, *Gestalt Psychology,* Ch. 4. New York: Liveright Publ. Corp. Rev. Ed. 1947. "Direction of Processes in Living Systems," *Scientific Monthly,* Jan. 1955. For further discussion, see my *Science and Cosmic Purpose,* p. 151 f.
10. *Genesis,* 1: 3, 9, 24.
11. Patrick. *Op. Cit.,* p. 121.
12. Whitehead, *Science and the Modern World,* Mentor Edition, pp. 109-10.
13. Reiser, *Op. Cit.,* p. 225.
14. Hartshorne, *Op. Cit.,* p. 206.
15. Darwin, *The Origin of Species,* Chapter 3.
16. Whitehead, *Science and the Modern World,* pp. 206-7.
17. B. J. Loewenberg, *Darwinism, Reaction or Reform?* New York: Rinehart & Co., Source Problems in World Civilization, 1959.

    Gail Kennedy, Ed., *Evolution and Religion, The Conflict Between Science and Theology in Modern America.* Boston: D. C. Heath & Co., Problems in American Civilization, 1957.

    Sheldon Grebstein, *Monkey Trial.* Boston: Houghton Mifflin, Research Series # 4, 1958.
18. C. E. M. Joad, *God and Evil.* New York, Harper & Brothers, 1943, p. 41.

NOTES TO CHAPTER XII

1. Hobbes, *Leviathan,* Chapter 1.
2. Hume, *A Treatise of Human Nature,* Bk. I, Pt. 4, Sec. 6.
3. Bertrand Russell, *Religion and Science,* p. 126. New York: Oxford University Press, 1935.
4. *Ibid.,* p. 205.
5. *Ibid.,* p. 202.
6. John Dewey, *The Quest for Certainty,* p. 227. New York: G. P. Putnam's Sons, 1929.
7. Titus, *Op. Cit.,* (2nd Edition), p. 147.
8. Wolfgang Köhler, *Gestalt Psychology,* Ch. 4.
9. *Idem.*
10. Charles M. Harsh and H. G. Schrickel, *Personality Development and Assessment.* New York: Ronald Press Co., 1950.
11. The dynamic idea of value of course would question this distinction, and doubt whether there are any "end pleasures," at least if that means pleasure after all activity or process is finished.
12. Joseph Wood Krutch, *The Modern Temper.* New York: Harcourt, Brace and Co., 1929, p. 15 f.

13. *Ibid.*, p. 96 f.
14. Cf. D. S. Savage, "Aldous Huxley and the Dissociation of Personality," *Sewanee Review*, Autumn, 1947.
15. Whitehead, *Modes of Thought*, Lecture II, "Expression."
16. Whitehead, *Religion in the Making*, p. 112 f. New York: The MacMillan Co., 1920.
17. Hartshorne, *Op. Cit.*, pp. 124-5.
18. Köhler, *The Place of Value in a World of Fact.*

NOTES TO CHAPTER XIII

1. Quoted by J. H. Randall from J. J. Fahie's *Galileo*, in *The Making of the Modern Mind*, p. 233. Rev. Ed. Boston: Houghton, Mifflin Co., 1940.
2. Galileo, *Dialogue on the Two Chief Systems of the World*, quoted by Randall, *Op. Cit.*, p. 233.
3. Bertrand Russell, *Religion and Science*, p. 211.

NOTES TO CHAPTER XIV

1. Sir David Ross, *The Right and the Good.* Oxford: The Clarendon Press, 1930, Chapter II.
2. *Ibid.*, p. 90.
3. Cf. Havelock Ellis's *The Dance of Life;* Whitehead's *Modes of Thought.*
4. Perry, *Op. Cit.*, p. 164.
5. G. C. Field, "The Place of Definition in Ethics"; *Studies in Philosophy*, University of Bristol Studies # 3, 1935.
6. G. C. Field, *Moral Theory.* London: Methuen and Co., Ltd., 1921, p. 48.
7. J. L. Mothershead, *Ethics.* New York: Henry Holt and Co., 1955, p. 236.
8. W. L. Reese, *The Ascent from Below.* Boston: Houghton-Mifflin Co., 1959, p. 242.
9. Perry, *Op. Cit.*, p. 47.
10. Perry, *Op. Cit.*, p. 42.
11. Perry, *Op. Cit.*, pp. 27-28.
12. Bertram Morris, "The Art Process and the Aesthetic Fact in Whitehead's Philosophy" in Schilpp (ed.) *The Philosophy of Alfred North Whitehead.* Evanston: Northwestern University Press, 1941, p. 464.
13. A. N. Whitehead, *Science and the Modern World*, Mentor Book Edition, p. 202.

14. A. N. Whitehead, *Adventures of Ideas*, p. 328.
15. J. B. Pratt, *Reason in the Art of Living*. New York: The MacMillan Co., 1958, p. 114.
16. *Ibid.*, p. 119.
17. Moritz Schlick, *Problems of Ethics*. New York: Prentice-Hall, Inc., 1939.

NOTES TO CHAPTER XV

1. Cf. W. D. Ross, *The Right and the Good*, p. 75.
2. A. J. Ayer, *Language, Truth and Logic*, Ch. VI. Oxford: University Press, 1936.
3. Cf. C. D. Broad, *Five Types of Ethical Theory*, p. 46. New York: Harcourt, Brace and Co., 1930.
4. Cf. C. D. Broad, "Some Reflections on Moral-Sense Theories in Ethics." *Proceedings of the Aristotelian Society*, 45, 1944-5. Especially the theory analogous to naive realism.
5. Pratt, *Op. Cit.*, pp. 157-8.
6. C. D. Broad, *Five Types of Ethical Theory*, p. 115.
7. W. D. Ross, *The Right and the Good*, Chapter 2.
8. *Ibid.*
9. G. E. Moore, *Principia Ethica*, Chapter I # 6, 7, 9, 10, 11. Cambridge: The University Press, 1903.
10. A. C. Ewing, "Subjectivism and Naturalism in Ethics", *Mind* 53, 1944.
11. W. D. Ross, *Op. Cit.*, p. 75.
12. *Ibid.*
13. *Ibid.*
14. *Ibid.*
15. Ross, *Op. Cit.*, Ch. I.
16. C. D. Broad, *Op. Cit.*, pp. 93-97.
17. Ross, *Op. Cit.*
18. B. Russell, "The Elements of Ethics," in *Philosophical Essays*, George Allen & Unwin, Ltd., 1910, # 5, 6, 8.
19. C. A. Campbell, "Moral and Non-Moral Values: A Study in the First Principles of Axiology." *Mind*, 44, 1935.
20. H. D. Aiken, "Evaluation and Obligation: Two Functions of Judgments in the Language of Conduct." *The Journal of Philosophy*, 47, 1950.
21. John Dewey, "Theory of Valuation." From *International Encyclopedia of Unified Science*, v. 2, 1939.
22. Ross, *Op. Cit.*
23. G. C. Field, "The Place of Definition in Ethics," in *Studies in Philosophy*, J. W. Arrowsmith, Ltd., 1935.

24. W. K. Frankena, "The Naturalistic Fallacy." *Mind,* 48, 1939.
25. In a footnote accompanying the reprinting of his essay in Sellars and Hospers, *Reading in Ethical Theory.* New York: Appleton-Century-Crofts, Inc., 1952, p. 1.
26. George Santayana, "Hypostatic Ethics" in *Winds of Doctrine.* London: J. M. Dent & Sons, 1940. New York: Charles Scribner's Sons, 1913, pp. 138-154.
27. *Ibid.*
28. John Dewey, *The Quest for Certainty.* New York: G. P. Putnam's Sons, 1929.
29. C. A. Campbell, *Op. Cit.*
30. Pratt, *Op. Cit.,* p. 170.
31. C. J. Ducasse, *Art, the Critics, and You.* New York, Oskar Piest, 1944.
32. DeWitt H. Parker, *Human Values,* New York, Harper & Bros., 1931.
33. Aiken, *Op. Cit.*
34. *Ibid.*
35. *Ibid.*
36. Parker, *Op. Cit.*
37. *Ibid.*
38. *Ibid.*

NOTES TO CHAPTER XVI

1. Cf. Ogden and Richards, *The Meaning of Meaning,* 4th Ed., p. 125.
   A. J. Ayer, *Language, Truth and Logic,* Ch. VI.
   Rudolf Carnap, *Philosophy and Logical Syntax,* Ch. I.
2. Herbert Feigl, "Meanings in Ethical Discourse," from *Twentieth Century Philosophy,* D. D. Runes, Ed. New York: Philosophical Library, 1947.
3. Ayer, *Op. Cit.*
4. Lewis Mumford, *In the Name of Sanity,* p. 151. New York: Harcourt, Brace, 1954.
5. Mumford, *Ibid.,* p. 128.
6. A. N. Whitehead, *Science and the Modern World.* Mentor Edition, p. 195.
7. Pratt, *Op. Cit.,* p. 77 f.
8. Mothershead, *Op. Cit.,* p. 63.
9. Pratt, *Op. Cit.,* pp. 15-19.
10. L. Mumford, *In the Name of Sanity,* p. 119.
11. Ross, *The Right and the Good,* Chapter II.
12. Moritz Schlick, *Problems of Ethics.* New York: Prentice-Hall, Inc., 1939.
13. Bertrand Russell, *Religion and Science,* p. 126.

14. R. B. Perry, *Realms of Value*, pp. 90-93.
15. H. Feigl, "Validation and Vindication, An Analysis of the Nature and the Limits of Ethical Arguments," in Sellars and Hospers, *Readings in Ethical Theory*, New York: Appleton-Century-Crofts, Inc., 1952, p. 675.
16. *Ibid.*, p. 677.
17. *Ibid.*, p. 679.
18. C. D. Broad, *Op. Cit.*, p. 185 f.
19. G. E. Moore, *Ethics*, Ch. II.
20. Henry Margenau, *Op. Cit.*, Chapter 5.
21. Pratt, *Op. Cit.*, p. 185.
22. John Dewey, *Reconstruction in Philosophy*, Ch. 7.
23. A. N. Whitehead, *Adventures of Ideas*, p. 375.
24. DeWitt Parker, *Op. Cit.*

NOTES TO CHAPTER XVII

1. Ayer, *Op. Cit.*
2. Ross, *The Right and the Good*, Ch. I.
3. Pratt, *Op. Cit.*, p. 33.
4. H. A. Prichard, "Does Moral Philosophy Rest on a Mistake?" *Mind*, 21, 1912.
5. R. B. Perry, *Realms of Value*, pp. 106-8.
6. Parker, "The Analysis of Value," in *Human Values*. (*Op. Cit.*)
7. Pratt, *Op. Cit.*
8. C. D. Broad, "Some Reflections on Moral-Sense Theories in Ethics." *Proceedings of the Aristotelian Society*, 45, 1944-45.
9. R. B. Perry, *Realms of Value*, p. 110.
10. Reese, *Op. Cit.*, p. 237.
11. H. D. Aiken, *Op. Cit.*
12. Aiken, *Ibid.*
13. Wilfrid Sellars, "Obligation and Motivation," *Philosophical Studies*, 2, 1951.
14. Pratt, *Op. Cit.*, p. 291.
15. Pratt, *Op. Cit.*, p. 265.

NOTES TO CHAPTER XVIII

1. C. E. M. Joad, *God and Evil*. New York: Harper & Co., 1943, p. 35.
2. John Dewey, *Experience and Nature*. Chicago: Open Court Publ. Co., 1926, p. 54.
3. J. H. Randall, *The Making of the Modern Mind*, Rev. Ed. Boston: Houghton Mifflin, 1940, p. 402.

4. Quoted by Randall, *Ibid.,* p. 445.
5. Joseph Krutch, *The Modern Temper.* New York: Harcourt, Brace & Co., 1929, p. 84.
6. *Ibid.,* p. 88.
7. *Ibid.,* p. 13.
8. C. E. M. Joad, *Op. Cit.,* p. 20.
9. Krutch, *Op. Cit.,* p. 128.
10. Dewey, *Experience and Nature,* p. 47.
11. Whitehead, *Modes of Thought,* p. 69.
12. Bertrand Russell, *Religion and Science.* New York: Oxford University Press, 1935, p. 79.
13. *Ibid.,* p. 81.
14. Joad, *Op. Cit.,* p. 42.
15. Russell, *Op. Cit.,* p. 194.
16. Dewey, *A Common Faith.* New Haven: Yale Univ. Press, 1934, p. 41.
17. Dewey, *Ibid.,* p. 48.
18. Plato, *Republic,* 379.
19. Dewey, *Experience and Nature,* p. 62 f.
20. Whitehead, *Modes of Thought,* p. 119.
21. Stephen Lee Ely, *The Religious Availability of Whitehead's God.* Madison: University of Wisconsin Press, 1942, pp. 37, 44.
22. Charles Hartshorne, "Whitehead's Idea of God," in Schilpp, *Op. Cit.,* p. 542 f.
23. B. Russell, *Religion and Science,* p. 231 f.
24. Joad, *God and Evil,* p. 84.
25. A. Seth Pringle-Pattison, *The Idea of God in the Light of Recent Philosophy.* London: Oxford University Press, 1917.
26. Pringle-Pattison, *Op. Cit.,* p. 407. (My italics.)
27. H. H. Farmer, *The World and God.* New York: Harpers, 1935, p. 244.
28. Whitehead, *Religion in the Making.* New York: The MacMillan Co., 1926, p. 96.
29. Cf. Hartshorne, *The Logic of Perfection,* p. 239 f.:
    ". . . each moment of life is an end in itself, and not just a means to some future goal. Not only is the evil of the day sufficient thereof, but so is the good." Compare the discussion following.

NOTES TO CHAPTER XIX

1. E. A. Burtt, *Metaphysical Foundations of Modern Science,* p. 299.
2. B. Russell, *Religion and Science,* p. 178.
3. *Ibid.,* p. 187.

4. L. J. Henderson, *The Fitness of the Environment*. New York: The MacMillan Co. *The Order of Nature*. Cambridge: Harvard University Press.
5. Patrick, *Op. Cit.*, p. 171.
6. Northrop, *Science and First Principles*.
7. Reiser, *Op. Cit.*
8. Whitehead, *Process and Reality*.
9. Whitehead, *Religion in the Making*, p. 104 ff.
10. John T. Robinson, *Honest to God*. Philadelphia: Westminster Press, 1963.
11. Whitehead, *Process and Reality*, p. 529.
12. Laird, *Theism and Cosmology*, p. 142. New York: Philosophical Library, 1942.
13. *Ibid.*, p. 137.
14. *Ibid.*, p. 117.
15. Dorohy Emmet, *Whitehead's Philosophy of Organism*, p. 259. London: The MacMillan Co., 1932.
16. Hartshorne, *The Logic of Perfection*, p. 129.
17. *Ibid.*, p. 165.
18. *Ibid.*, p. 205.

NOTES TO CHAPTER XX

1. J. H. Randall, *The Making of the Modern Mind*, p. 99.
2. E. A. Burtt, *Op. Cit.*, pp. 238-9.
3. Russell, *Religion and Science*, p. 79.
4. Randall, *The Making of the Modern Mind*, p. 609.
5. Emil Brunner, *Man in Revolt*, p. 116. New York: Charles Scribner's Sons, 1939.
6. Hartshorne, *Op. Cit.*, p. 144.
7. Van Wyck Brooks, *The Writer in America*, p. 136. New York: Dutton and Co., 1953.
8. *Ibid.*, p. 170.
9. *Ibid.*, p. 111.
10. Cf. Edmund Fuller's *"Man in Modern Fiction."*
11. Van Wyck Brooks, *Op. Cit.*, p. 174 ff.
12. *Ibid.*, p. 165.
13. C. E. M. Joad, *God and Evil*, p. 56.
14. Thomas Wolfe, *You Can't Go Home Again*, p. 223.

INDEX

Buddhism, 49, 373
Burtt, E. A., 200, 204, 533

C

Campbell, C. A., 399 f., 412
Carnap, Rudolf, 135 f., 141, 404
Cassirer, Ernst, 227
first cause, 531, 533
Causality, 123, 450 f.
atomistic, 200 f., 359
creative, dynamic causation, 215 f., 223 f.
and determinism, 241 f.
and feeling, 211
first cause, 531, 533
Hume on, 241 f.
ingredients, 248, 253, 312, 469
partial cause, 243
plurality of causes, total cause, 201, 209 f., 295
and purposiveness, Ch. IX
Chance, 224, 248
Christ, 455, 532, 557, 566, 580
Christian, 557,
Christian Science, 64, 150, 312, 503
Christianity, 34, 472
and body, 304
and creation, 340, 553
and ends, 220
and evil 487 f., 511
on Fall and Sin, 235, 553
on God, 151, 461, 530 f.
on immortality, 558, 565
and Inspiration, 472, 484, 556
and knowledge, 108
Orthodox, 65
and purpose, 196
Christology, 10, 548, 558
Clerk-Maxwell, James, 158 f., 164, 181, 188, 202
Classicism, 369, 421
Closure, 212, 250 f., 294, 469
Cognition, Part II
integration in, 370
motivation in, 360
and satisfaction, 376 f.
Cognitive value, 352, 421, 426
evaluation of 449 f.
Coherence theory of truth, 110 f., 112, 128, 354, 376 f., 401, 437 f., 542 f.
Communism, 6, 7, 13, 17, 35, 67 f., 207, 241, 290, 563 f.
Complexity, 55, 274, 280, 347, 363, 416, 444, 450

Composition, 98 f., 138, 210 f., 214, 359, 466
Comte, Auguste, 113
Consequences and Value, Ch. XV, Item 5 throughout. 392, 398, 434
Consummation, 58, 299, 300, 311, 373 f.
Contemplation, 373
Contrast, 55 f. (#2.7), 446
Cooperation, 279
Copernicus, 129, 333
Copi, Irving, 101
Correspondance Theory of Truth, 112, 376 f.
dynamic pragmatic form, 121, 123
in value theory, 437 f.
in God theory, 542 f.
Cosmic, 151, 487 f., 531, 537, 547
Cosmic Purpose for Good, 22, 33 f., 59
for static good, 47 f., 507 f., 526
conclusions on, Ch. XIX, Item 2 throughout
Creation, 340 f., 550
of Body, 364
of Life, Ch. XI, Part 2
Special Creation, 269
of World, 325 f.
Creativity, 56, 165 f., 193, 222, 265
Curies, the, 181
Cybernetics, 262 f.

D

Dante, 331, 338, 559, 576
Darwin, 5, 62, 99, 156 f., 216, 268, 269 f., 275, 277, 281 f., 326, 491, 535, 559
Death, 522 f., 562, 566
de Broglie, 183, 186 f.
Deduction, 88, 104, 110
Definiteness, 54 (#2.32)
Definition, Canons of, 381 f., Ch. XV, Item 3 throughout
Degeneration, 1 ff., 473, f., 483, 562
Deism, 341, 532 f., 560
Democritus, 62, 98, 153, 177, 224, 258, 347, 533
Descartes, 66, 177, 180, 238, 337
dualism, 154, 203, 207, 287, 304, 318 f.
epistemology, 80, 82, 83, 88
Descriptive knowledge, 132, 134; of value, 441

600

601

and body, 305
dynamic idea of, 497
and life, Ch. XI, part 4
and man, 283 f.
natural evil, 325, 327 f.
worse degrees of 512 f., 566
Evolution, 156 f., Ch. XI, parts 2
and 3
emergent, creative theory of, 272
f., 275
and ethics, 423
mechanistic theory of 157 f., 268
f., 326
Ewing, A. C., 394, 403, 406
Existence, God and, 549, 553, 578
Existentialism, 14, 67, 69 f., 170,
239, 312, 511, 538, 554, 568 f.
Explanatory knowledge, 132, 134;
of value, 441
External world, 127, 139

F
Facts, 25
of value experience, Ch. XIV,
part II
and value, 388, 420, Ch. XVIII,
item 1 throughout
Failure, 214, 516, 518 f.
Faith, 79, 531, 534, 546 f.
Fallacy of affirming consequent, 545
of misplaced concreteness, 131
of simple location, 179
reductive, see reductive fallacy
Fall of man, 65, 486, 514, 576 f.,
571, 580
Faraday, Michael, 158
Farmer, H. H., 515
Fascism, 98, 563 See Nazism
Fatalism, 234, 237
Feeling, 31, 49, 167, 474
and causation, 211
and cognition, 376 f.
deduction of, 169 f., 378
feeler, 53 (#1.1), 143, 169, 298,
310, 314
and good, 49 f., 53, 376, 435 f.,
437
knowledge of, 125 f., 136 f., 140,
424 f.
and mechanism, 265
and motivation 358 f.
Feigl, Herbert, 424 f., 435, 436, 439
f.
Fermat, 188

Feuerbach, Ludwig, 533
Fichte, J. G., 92, 240, 504
Field, G. C., 358, 360, 403 f., 445
Field theory, 63, 158 f., 163 f., 186
field strains, 211, 224, 229, 250 f.,
298 f., 536 And see Strains
in epistemology, 95
and freedom, 246 f.
and obligation, 467 f.
in psychology, 296 f.
self-field, 213
universal field, 537
in motivation, 359 f., 364
Final causation, 215 f., 225 f.
Finiteness, 193, 313, 316, 523
Form, 156 f., 228 f.
Formal cause, 198 f.
Framework of discussion, after table
of contents, 72, 529 f.
Frankena, W. W., 404
Freedom, Ch. X.
and obligation, 467 f.
Freud, Sigmund, 5, 290, f., 367, 371
f., 429, 461, 492, 521, 559

G
Galileo, 88 f., 99 f., 112, 121, 132,
153, 200, 203, 332 f., 559
Generation, 156
Genesis, 266, 269, 276 f., 325, 486,
550
Gestalt, 21, 95 f., 131, 188, 212, 292
f., 538, 540
and right and obligation 250 f.,
359, 467 f.
the "three phases," 96 f., 538
Good, 39, Ch. III, 354 And see
Static and Dynamic Ideas of,
and Life, Ch. XI, part 4
Nature and Definition of, Ch. XV
and Truth, Beauty, 346
God, 14, 25, 28 f., 34 f., 59, Ch.
XIX
and creation of body, 304; of
world, 325 f., 549 f., 561, 577
as a construct, hypothesis, 115,
135, 542, 545
and evil, Ch. XVIII, Ch. XIX,
item 1 throughout. 548
in Hegel, 240
in Hinduism, 174 f.
and inspiration, 474
knowledge of, 117, 127, 135 f.,
Ch. XIX, item 2 throughout

nature of, Ch. XIX, item 3
throughout
in Naturalism, 68
in Plotinus, 174
and process, 551
and providence, 325 f., 329 f.,
552
seeking God, 580 f.
and Space-Time, 339
as statically perfect, 174 f., 196
and universe, 331 f.
Goethe, 571

H

Habit, 300, 378 f.
Haldane, J. S. 259, 291
Hamilton, W. R., 188 f.
Happiness, see Pleasure, Satisfaction,
Consummation
Hartman, Edouard von, 318, 389,
506
Hartshorne, Charles, 227 f., 252,
275, 321, 552, 553 f., 569
Hedonism, 358, 360, 375, 429 f.,
439, 442, 454 f., 462, 474
Heisenberg, Werner, 125, 184 f.,
243 f.
Hegel, G. W. F., 92, 147, 154, 176,
180, 240, 328, 504, 551, 553
Hemingway, Ernest, 11, 302, 368
Henderson, Lawrence, 535
Heraclitus, 63, 98, 152, 163
Hinduism, 64, 148, 150, 174 f., 196,
230, 530, 532
Hippocrates, 156
Hobbes, Thomas, 83, 203 f., 207,
258, 287 f., 291, 320, 347
Holbach, 258, 533
Holiness, 8 f., 32 f., 35, 111, 304,
487, 540 f., 548, 550, 554, 556
f., 560, 564, 581
Hulme, T. E., 570 f.
Humanism, 8, 10 f., 35, 67, 345, 494,
514, 560, 565, 567, 572 f.
Hume, David, 83, 88, 91
on cause, 123, 242
on epistemology, 114, 119, 121
on ethics, 391, 396 f., 476
on mind-self, 86, 288 f., 320
on miracles, 565
Huxley, Aldous, 302 f.
Huxley, Thomas, 320
Huyghens, Christian, 181, 201
Hypostatization, 131, 405, 501

Hypothesis, 103 f.; increasing complexity of, 128 f., 541 f.

I

Idealism, 61 f., 63 f., 66, 70, 116 f.,
176, 207, 240, 431, 560
Illusionism, 64, 70, 150, 175, 207,
235, 287, 488, 503, 560
Immortality, 474, 525, Ch. XX, item
3 throughout
Incitation, Ch. XVII, Part II
Inclusiveness, 55 (#2.6), 274, 280,
437, 444, 446, 458
Indeterminism, 234 f., 247 f., 253
Indeterminacy, 241 and see Uncertainty
Induction, 88, 102 f. Problem of,
114
Inspiration, 33, 240, Ch. XVII, Part
II; Ch. XX, item 1 throughout.
529
Instincts in mechanistic value theory,
348, 358 f., 366 f., 379, 423,
462
Instrumental value, Ch. XV, items
2 and 5 throughout
Integration, Ch. IX, Part II, item 1
throughout. 299, 300, 310, 315,
365 f., 436
Intensity, 56 (#2.8), 58, 426, 443,
446, 458
Interest, 214, 365, 369, 398, 414 f.,
436
Intrinsic value, Ch. XV, item 2
throughout. 414
Intuition, 79
as a priori knowledge, 79
Descartes' view, 80
in dynamic knowledge theory, 98,
137 f.
of God, 531, 538 f.
in hypothesizing, 103
in value theory, 348, 358, 386,
392 f., 401, 419 f., 421 f., 430
f., 444 f., 470, 481 f.
Isomorphism, argument from, 140,
167, 211, 251, 322

J

James, William, 68, 480
on God, 502, 543
on indeterminism, 247, 253
on knowing, 93, 121 f., 542 f.

603

on mind, 293 f.
on will to believe, 141
Jeans, Sir James, 152, 189, 237, 246
Joad, C. E.M., 282, 495, 500 f., 507, 509, 580 f.
Job, 345
Judaism, 421 and see Bible
Jung, C. G., 296

K

Kant, Immanuel, 66, 181, 207, 292
on duty, 360, 362, 462, 464 f., 470
epistemology, 91 f., 95
on God, 533, 537
on noumena, 118
on organism, 226
on value knowledge, 430, 432 f., 474, 476
Kelvin, Lord, 267
Kepler, 132, 333
Kierkegaard, S., 579
Knowledge, Problem of, 18, Part II
Normative Knowledge, Ch. XVI, item 2 throughout
of God, Ch. XIX, item 2 throughout
Köhler, Wolfgang, 211, 250 f., 265, 293 f., 322
Krutch, Joseph W., 301 f., 304 f., 493, 495, 507, 510

L

Laird, John, 212, 321, 389, 549 f.
Lamarck, 270, 274, 276
Language, Ordinary meaning, 381.
Use of, Ch. XV, item 1 throughout
Laplace, 242
Lawrence, D. H., 342, 552
Learning, 213 f., 379
Least Action, 188; in evaluation, 446 f.
Leibniz, G. W., 176, 180, 207, 238, 319
Leucippus, 153, 177
Lewin, Kurt, 296
Liberal theology, 12 f., 570
Life, nature of, Ch. XI, Part I
origin of, Ch. XI, Part 2
on other worlds, 333, 335
Light, 160 f.
Limited God, 14, 36, 67, 502, 537, 543, 549 f., 567
Locke, John, 83, 88, 420

Loeb, Jacques, 258
Logic, 355, 383 f.; and see Truth, Cognition, Epistemology
Logical Empiricism, 15, 66, 424 f.
Lotze, 318
Love, 65, 196, 308, 493, 568
LSD, 312
Lucretius, 267, 347

M

Man, Ch. XII
effect on human spirit, Ch. XX
goodness and evil of, 282 f., Ch. XVIII, item 2 throughout, 570 f.
origin, evolution of, Ch. XI, part 5
significance of, 282 f., 507 f., 560
Margenau, Henry:
on causation, 243, 247
on constructs, 103 f., 128, 133, 450
on correlational science, 102
on exclusion principle, 189 f.
on non-mechanistic science, 182 f.
Marxism, 6, 20, 67 f., 98, 207, 240, 492, 533, 543
Materialism, 12, 20, 62, 151 f., 155, 525
and motivation, 473 f.
refutation of, 190 f., 262
Matter, 152 f., 156 f., 163 f.
aggregates of, 324
denial of, 148
meaning of, 172, 228, 229, 379 f.
Maupertuis, 188
McCulloch, Warren, 262 f.
Meaningfulness, 7 f.
conclusions on, Part V.
dynamic idea of, 61 f., 169 f., 577
And DM throughout
and process, 169 f., 544 f.
knowledge of, 27 f., 111, 127
"maximum," 35
requirements of, 15 f., Ch. II, 58 f.
static idea of, 61, f., 487, 556 And SM throughout
Means, Ch. IX, Part II, Item 2 throughout
Earthly environment as Means, Ch. XIII, Part 1. 325, 402
Measurement, 124; of Value, 442 f.

Mechanism (mechanistic materialism), 20, 22, 62, 65 f., 151 f.,
155
and art, 427 f.
and body, 305 f., 312
and causation, 200 f.
and determinism, 236 f., 241 f.,
461 f.
and environment, 326 f.
and evil, 491 f., 496
and evolution, 269
knowledge theory, Part II, SMR.
Knowledge of value, 423 f.
and life, 257 f., 262 f., 267 f.
and mind, 287 f., 320
and motivation, 290 f., 294
non-creative motion in, 221, 223
and personality, 297
problem of, Part III. 345. Ch.
XIX, Item 1 throughout. 531 f.
refutation of, 190 f., 262
summary, 238 f.
and value, 347 f., 366 f., 387 f.,
422 f.
Meliorism, 69, 511
Memory, 213 f., 299 f., 378 f.
Mendel, Gregor, 268, 270, 271
Mentalism, 147 f., 318
Mental substance, 148
Michelson-Morley experiment, 129,
160
Mill, John Stuart, 243, 390
Mind, Ch XII, part I, throughout
aspects of, 298 f.
functional theory of, 292 f.
mechanistic theory of, 262 f., 287
f.
mind-body relationship, 317 f.
and value, Ch. XV, item 6
throughout
Minimal principles, 188, 446 f.
Miracles, 107 f., 326 f., 531
Monism (Appearance-Reality), 21,
62, 64, 149 f., 318, 488
Moore, G. E., 389 f., 393 f., 356,
404 f., 433, 443 f., 463
Most and least, 130, 446 f.
Mothershead, J. L., 363, 429 f.
Motion, 154
Motivation, 290 f., 298, 300, 357 f.
Problem of elevating, Ch. XVII,
Part II
Motive, 130, Ch. IX, item 5 through-
out, 209, 212 f., 407, 414

M-S-I-R-C-P sequence, 300, 310,
357, 359
Multiplicity, see Pluralism
Mumford, Lewis, 427 f., 432
Murray, Henry A., 296 f.
Music, see Art
Mutations, 216, 273, 275, 327
Mystical experience, 81, 531, 533 f.,
538 f., 546, 577, 582 f.

N

Naturalism, 62, 68; Dynamic, 66 f.
Naturalistic definitions of value, 382,
423 f., 462, 466, Ch. XV, Item
3
Naturalistic Fallacy, 390, 393, 404,
438 f.
Nature, meaning of, Ch. XIII, part
I, 563
and evil, Ch. XVIII, Item 1
throughout
and quality, 347 f.
Nazism, 6, 306, 492, 516, 519, 539,
563 f.
Needs, Drives, Ch. IX Item 3
throughout, 211, 213, 298 f.,
310, 314, 357 f., 364, 414 f.
plurality of, 358, 364 f.
specific needs, 314 f.
sublimation of, 371 f.
Neo-orthodoxy, 13, 548 f., 568 f.,
576, 582
Neurosis, see Sin
Newton, Isaac, 62, 129, 132, 142,
153 f., 158, 181, 208, 236, 243,
245 f., 287 f.
on astronomy, 333
on atoms, 177 f., 183, 193, 201,
268
on causation, 201 f., 224, 242
on God, 532, 559
on Space and Time, 338, 341
New Wave, 14
Niebuhr, Reinhold, 572
Nietzsche, Friedrich, 278, 348, 563
Non-Aristotelian thought, 14, 435
Nominalism, 111
Normative Knowledge, See Knowledge
Northrop, F.S.C., 99, 101, 103 f.,
137, 177, 537
Novelty, 55 f. (#2.7), 225, 274, 450,
523

605

O

Object, 53 (#2.22), 143, Ch. IX, Item 4 throughout, 299, 357 f., 415
Objective World, 139, 329
Objective Value, 40 f., 383, 413, 440 f., 448, Ch. XV, Item 6 throughout
Obligation, 235-237, 250 f., 348 f., 386, 400, 441, Ch. XVII, Part I
and good, 392 f.
and motivation, 359 f.
One and Many, 174, 176, 193
Ontological Argument, 531
Ontology, Part III
Operationalism, 69
Order, 54 (#2.4), 193, 504
Organicism, Organismic Philosophy, 69, 71, 188, 262
and motivation, 358 f.
Organisms as units, 187; Hierarchy of, 324
vs. machines, 262 f., 265, 272
Organization, 188, 225, 399
Organizing Process, 53 (#2.0)
Otto, Rudolf, 8, 487

P

Pain and value, 43 f., 51, 371, Ch. XVIII
Pan-Psychism, 168, 259 f., 321
Pantheism, 547 f.
Parker, DeWitt, 413, 415 f., 438, 467 f.
Parmenides, 64, 147, 150, 175, 193, 383
Parsimony, 129, 450
Parts, 53 (#2.2), 159, Ch. VIII, 185 f., 313
and changelessness, 174 f.
and field, 213, 246
part-whole relationship 180 f., and see Whole
Pascal, Blaise, 336
Pasteur, Louis, 267
Patrick, G. T. W., 108, 215, 536
Paul, Saint, 304, 314, 340, 460 f., 472 f.
Pauli, 189
Pavlov, 290
Peirce, Charles, 68, 93, 121, 275
Perfection, 48, 149, 175, 385, 485 f.
Permanence, 229, 259, 379 f., 450

Perry, R. B., 213, 349, 353 f., 365, 369, 397, 414, 436 f., 441, 445 f., 447, 466 f., 470, 476
Personalism, 71, 502, 538
Personality, 276 f., 299
Phaedo, 42, 174
Philebus, 44 f., 46, 48, 405
Philosophy, 26
analytic, 26, 30
and inspiration, 478 f.
of Religion, Part V
and Science, 26
synthetic, 26, 31
types, Ch. IV, 63 f.
as value, 353
Planck, Max, 181
Plato, 14, 17, 34, 56, 57, 98, 315, 332, 383
on body, 148, 286 f., 303 f.
on cause and purpose, 198 f.
dualism, 64
on ends, 220
on essences, 108
on God, 151, 196, 502 f., 532, 549
on good, 40-48, 49, 51, 346, 373, 405, 461, 484 f.
on ideas, 176
on knowledge, 77, 79, 108, 111; of value, 420
on mind, 287, 292
on soul, 174
on substance, 147, 150
on will, 235, 472
Pleasure, 43 f., 48, 297, 348, 358 f., 374 f., 393 f., 396 f., 404, 415 f., 443
Plotinus, 149, 174-176, 530, 532
Pluralism, 69, 172
of causes, 201, 209 f., 295
of needs and drives, 359, 369, 437
of value qualities, 350 f.
Positivism, 15, 113 f., 115
and ethical knowledge, 424 f., 437, 462, 474
and religious knowledge, 134 f., 538, 545
Practical value, 352, 354, 451
Pragmatism, 14, 67, 68, 312, 511, 538
as dynamic correspondence theory, 121 f.
and appreciation, 138
and value theory, 406 f.

Pratt, J. B., 374 f., 389, 413, 429 f.,
433 f., 454, 464, 468, 480
Prayer, 326, 327, 473, 567, 581
Predestination, 234, 237, 255, 556,
569
Prehension, 224, 506
Prichard, H. A. 464 f., 470, 477
Pringle-Pattison, Seth, 509 f.
Probability, 124 f., 184, 244 f.
Process, Ch. VII, 165 f.
and causation-purpose, Ch. IX,
Item 1 throughout
and evaluation, 447
and evil, 498 f.
and good, 48 f., 53, 169 f., 365 f.,
406 f., 415 f., 544, 550
and obligation, 466
and parts, 175
phases of purposive process, Ch.
IX, 357, 374, 444
and Space-Time, 339 f.
and structure, 148 f.
three phases of, 96 f., 538
ultimate concept of science, 136,
544, 550
and value quality, 350 f.
and wholes, 192 f.
Process philosophy, 14, 549
and value, 169 f.
Psychoanalysis, see Freud
Psychological egoism and hedonism,
347, 423, 429 f., 443
Psychology of value experience,
357 f.
Ptolemaic astronomy, 129, 331 f.
Puritanism, 301, 304, 308
Purpose, 36 f., 213, 531
and causation, Ch. IX, Items 1 and
5 throughout, 359 f.
cosmic, 38, Ch. XIX
dynamic idea of, 214 f., 217 f.,
226 f., 535 f.
knowledge of, 117, 130
Pythagoras, 332

Q

Quality, 52
absence of in mechanism, 347
in Nature, 350 f.
knowledge of, 114 f., 125 f., 136
primary and secondary, 153, 559
qualitative feeling, 167, 288, 320
varieties of, Ch. XIV, Part I

Quantitative approach to evaluation,
426, 443 f.
emphasis of materialism, 347, 559
knowledge, 114, 124
Quantum theory, 103, 156, 180 f.,
184, 189, 194, 244, 247, 542

R

Radiation, 181 f.
Randall, J. H., 332 f., 489 f., 558,
563
Rationalism, 82, 110
and incitation, 474 f., 481 f.
relation to impulse in motivation,
358 f., 375
and obligation, 460 f., 462 f., 470
in value theory, 358 f., 384, 391
f., 408, 419 f., 430 f.
Realism, 66, 70, 491
in literature, Ch. I, 479, 494, 509,
513 f., 570 f., 575
medieval, 111, 138 f.
Reality (as required by value), 24 f.,
544
Reductive fallacy, 20, 115, 131, 179,
221, 222, 231, 292, 493
in value theory, 367, 369 f.
Reese, Sheldon, 364, 474 f.
Reiser, Otto, 187, 211 f., 216, 225,
274, 537
Relational (dynamic) value, 52, 383,
Ch. XV, Item 4 throughout
Relativism, 366, 390 f., 422 f., 466
Relativity, 156, 160 f., 171, 188
Religion, Part V
and evil, 508 f.
and ethical action, Ch. XX, Item
2 throughout
knowledge of, 134 f.
and motivation, 364, 472, 478 f.
and philosophy, 27 f., 33, 36, Part
V
as value, 353
Republic (Plato), 41 f.
Requiredness, 7, 128, 132 f., 171,
250 f., 322, 544, 567, 577
Resolving, 54 (#2.5), 224
Response, 299, 300, 315
Responsibility, 253 f., 569, 578 f.
Revelation, 539
Right, 250, Ch. XVII, Part I
and good, 384 f., 391 f., 394
Robinson, John T. (*Honest to God*),
548

607

Romanticism, 308, 369, 379, 431 f.,
474
Ross, Sir David, 348, 391 f., 394 f.,
397 f., 403 f., 406 f., 412, 430 f.,
433, 463, 477
Rousseau, J. J., 68, 277, 362, 488 f.,
491 f., 573 f.
Russell, Bertrand, 224, 239 f., 258,
291 f., 295, 336 f., 398 f., 404
f., 436, 499 f., 507 f., 533 f.,
538, 542, 546, 560 f.

S

Sacredness, see Holiness
Salvation, 484, 487 f., 549, Ch. XX,
Item 2 throughout, 568 f., 577
f., 581
Santayana, George, 217, 404 f., 552
Satisfaction, 53, 214, 299, 358, Ch.
IX, Part II, Item 3 throughout,
373 f., 403, 408, 414 f., 437,
475 f.
Scheduling, 297, 299, 436 f.
Schlick, Moritz, 376, 436
Schopenhauer, Arthur, 58, 92, 171,
241, 511, 516, 567
Schrödinger, 185, 316, 330, 336
Schweitzer, Albert, 283, 575, 583
Science, 25, 26 f., Part II
revolution in, 154 f.
Scientific Method, 16, Part II, 87,
99 f.
and religious knowledge, 533 f.
Second Law of Thermodynamics,
222 f., 230, 233, 341, 446
Self, 86, Ch. XII, Part 1 throughout,
298, 303
Self-determinism, 246 f., 254
Selfishness, 361 f., 364
Sellars, R. W., 477
Sensory Experience, 81, 422 f.
Sensory value, 352
Sex, 308, 311, 316, 368, 371 f., 483,
507 (incl. reproduction)
Sin, 368, 468, 483, 484, 494, 508 f.,
578 f.
Sisyphus, Myth of, 512
Skepticism, 119, 142
Social Value, 352, 361, 451
Socializing drives, 371
Socrates, 405, 460 f., 472 f., 477
Solipsism, 117 f.
Soul (Spirit), 154, 174 f., 286 f., 298,
302 f.

and body, 310, 314, 318
and drugs, 312
Space, 162, 337 f.
Space-Time Continuum, 162, 189,
191, 339 f.
Specialization and Fragmentation,
18, 97
Spencer, Herbert, 241, 271, 491
Spinoza, Baruch, 66, 172, 180, 207,
238, 319, 388, 498
Spirit (see Soul)
Spiritual motivation, 364, 474, Ch.
XX
Standard, 493, Ch. XVI, item 1
throughout
place of absolute standard in dynamic theory, 57, 457
Static Idealistic Theory of Reality,
61 f., 63 f., and SIR throughout
Static Idea of Value (Good), 14,
40-48
conflict with static and dynamic
ideas of reality, 346
and cosmic purpose 47, Ch. XIX
and evil, Ch. XVIII, 499 f.
nature and definition of, Ch. XV
and value development, 363 f.,
373 f.
Static Idea of Meaningfulness, SM
throughout. Ch. IV
Static Mechanistic Theory of Reality,
62 and SMR throughout
Steinbeck, John, 11
Stimulation, 299, 300, 310, 315 f.
Strain, 165, 168, 210 f., 216, 314
and see Field strains
Structure, 304
deduction of from value, 171 f.
and process, 148 f., 309 f.
Sub-atomic particles, 181
Subject, 53 (#1.1), 195, Ch. IX,
item 2 throughout, 298, 357 f.
Subjective (static) value, 43 f., 413
Subjectivism in epistomology, 116 f.,
138 f.
in value theory, 383, Ch. XV, item
6 throughout, 423
Substance, Ch. VII
Synthetic, see Whole-part relation-
ship
Synthetic definitions, 382
Systematizing in science, 98 f., 103,
128 f., 133 f., 136 f.

608